MEN OF
WRATH

ICON

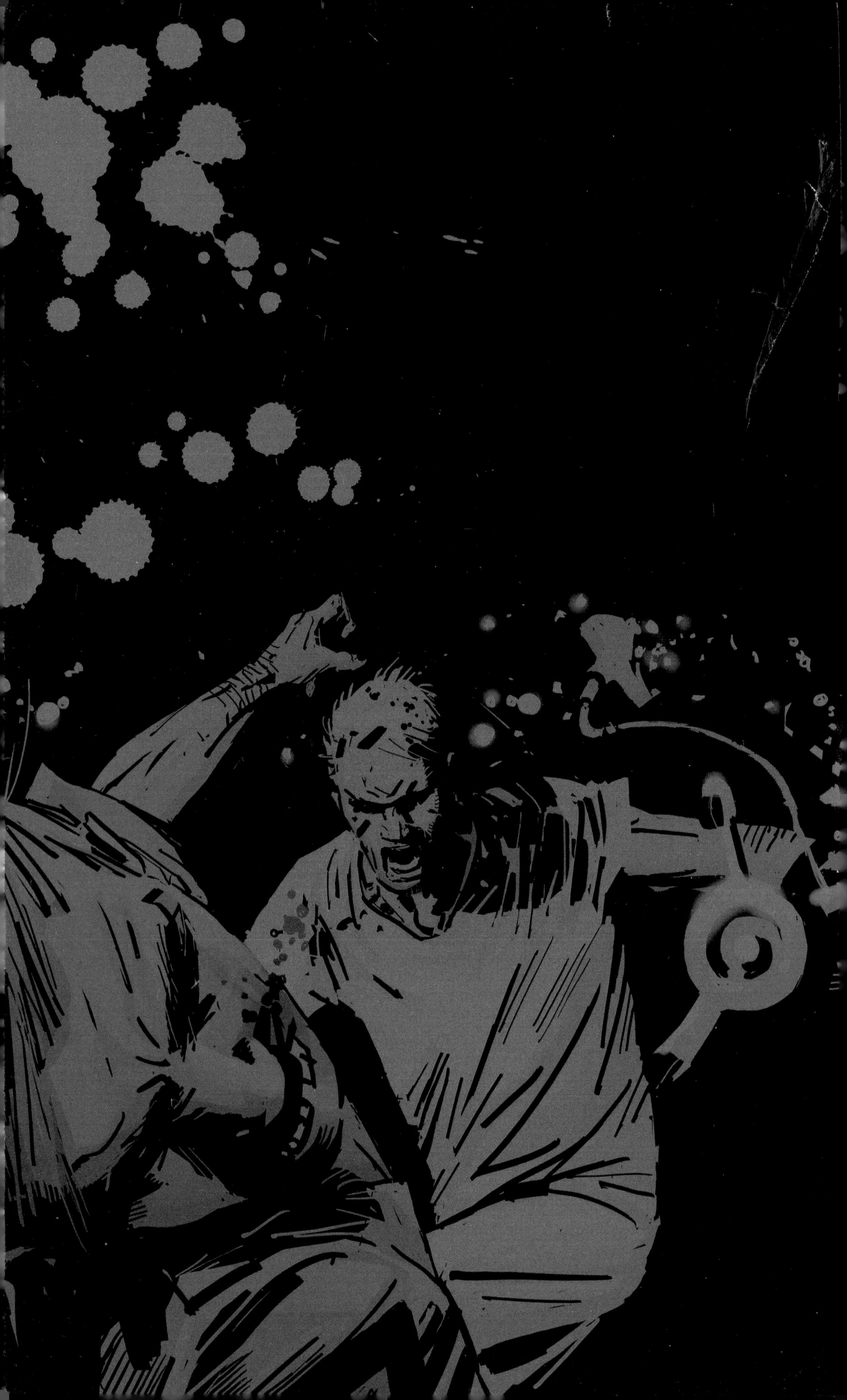

MEN OF WRATH

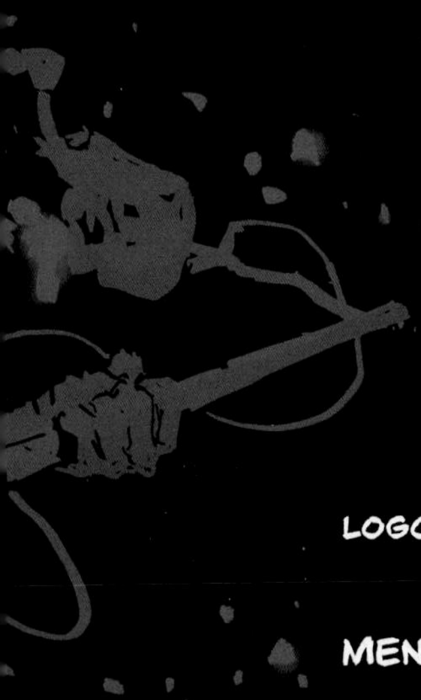

JASON AARON WRITER
RON GARNEY ARTIST

MATT MILLA COLORS
JARED K. FLETCHER LETTERS
SEBASTIAN GIRNER EDITOR

LOGO AND BOOK DESIGN BY JARED K. FLETCHER

MEN OF WRATH CREATED BY AARON & GARNEY

MEN OF WRATH. CONTAINS MATERIAL ORIGINALLY PUBLISHED IN MAG-
AZINE FORM AS MEN OF WRATH #1-5. FIRST PRINTING 2015. ISBN#
978-0-7851-9168-1. PUBLISHED BY MARVEL WORLDWIDE, INC., A
SUBSIDIARY OF MARVEL ENTERTAINMENT, LLC. OFFICE OF PUBLICA-
TION: 135 WEST 50TH STREET, NEW YORK, NY 10020. COPYRIGHT ©
2014 AND 2015 GOLGONOOZA, INC. AND RON GARNEY. ALL RIGHTS RE-
SERVED. MEN OF WRATH, THE MEN OF WRATH LOGO, AND ALL CHAR-
ACTERS AND CONTENT HEREIN AND THE LIKENESSES THEREOF ARE
TRADEMARKS OF GOLGONOOZA, INC. AND RON GARNEY, UNLESS OTH-
ERWISE EXPRESSLY NOTED. ICON AND THE ICON LOGO ARE TRADE-
MARKS OF MARVEL CHARACTERS, INC. NO SIMILARITY BETWEEN ANY
OF THE NAMES, CHARACTERS, PERSONS, AND/OR INSTITUTIONS IN
THIS MAGAZINE WITH THOSE OF ANY LIVING OR DEAD PERSON OR IN-
STITUTION IS INTENDED, AND ANY SUCH SIMILARITY THAT MAY EXIST
IS PURELY COINCIDENTAL. THIS WORK MAY NOT BE REPRODUCED, EX-
CEPT IN SMALL AMOUNTS FOR JOURNALISTIC OR REVIEW PURPOSES,
WITHOUT PERMISSION OF THE AUTHORS. PRINTED IN CANADA. ALAN
FINE, EVP - OFFICE OF THE PRESIDENT, MARVEL WORLDWIDE, INC. AND
EVP & CMO MARVEL CHARACTERS B.V.; DAN BUCKLEY, PUBLISHER &
PRESIDENT - PRINT, ANIMATION & DIGITAL DIVISIONS; JOE QUESADA,
CHIEF CREATIVE OFFICER; TOM BREVOORT, SVP OF PUBLISHING; DAVID
BOGART, SVP OF OPERATIONS & PROCUREMENT, PUBLISHING; C.B. CE-
BULSKI, SVP OF CREATOR & CONTENT DEVELOPMENT; DAVID GABRIEL,
SVP PRINT, SALES & MARKETING; JIM O'KEEFE, VP OF OPERATIONS &
LOGISTICS; DAN CARR, EXECUTIVE DIRECTOR OF PUBLISHING TECH-
NOLOGY; SUSAN CRESPI, EDITORIAL OPERATIONS MANAGER; ALEX
MORALES, PUBLISHING OPERATIONS MANAGER; STAN LEE, CHAIRMAN
EMERITUS. FOR INFORMATION REGARDING ADVERTISING IN MARVEL
COMICS OR ON MARVEL.COM, PLEASE CONTACT NIZA DISLA, DIRECTOR
OF MARVEL PARTNERSHIPS, AT NDISLA@MARVEL.COM. FOR MARVEL
SUBSCRIPTION INQUIRIES, PLEASE CALL 800-217-9158. MANUFAC-
TURED BETWEEN 2/25/2015 AND 3/30/2015 BY SOLISCO PRINTERS,
SCOTT, QC, CANADA.

10 9 8 7 6 5 4 3 2 1

SOMETIME AROUND 1900, MY GREAT GREAT GRANDFATHER, IRA AARON, STABBED A MAN TO DEATH IN AN ARGUMENT OVER SOME SHEEP.

HIS YOUNG SON, SAMMIE, WAS THERE AND WITNESSED THE KILLING. IT WAS HIS KNIFE THAT WAS USED IN THE STABBING.

YEARS LATER, IN 1924, SAMMIE AARON, MY GREAT GRANDFATHER, WOULD MEET HIS OWN STRANGE DEMISE.

HE'D DIE OF RABIES, AFTER BEING BITTEN BY A RABID DOG.

FROM THIS DARK LITTLE BIT OF MY OWN FAMILY HISTORY WAS BORN MEN OF WRATH.

IRA AND RUBEN RATH ARE THE CULMINATION OF A LONG, BLOODY CYCLE OF SOUTHERN VIOLENCE, ONE THAT'S BEEN PASSED DOWN FROM FATHER TO SON OVER THE COURSE OF A CENTURY. AND WHAT STARTED WITH SOME SHEEP WILL ONLY END WHEN EVERYONE DIES.

THIS MAY BE THE DARKEST, MEANEST THING I'VE EVER WRITTEN. AND IF YOU'VE READ SOME OF MY WORK ON *WOLVERINE* OR *SCALPED* OR *SOUTHERN BASTARDS*, YOU KNOW I'M NO STRANGER TO THINGS DARK AND MEAN. BUT THERE'S SOMETHING PERSONAL ABOUT ALL THIS AS WELL.

WHATEVER WAS PASSED DOWN TO ME FROM IRA AARON, DOWN THROUGH HIS DOOMED SON SAMMIE, DOWN THROUGH GENERATIONS OF ALABAMA FARMERS AND COAL MINERS AND REBELS AND PREACHERS AND THE OCCASIONAL MURDERER, I'M NOW PASSING ON TO YOU.

THANKS FOR READING *MEN OF WRATH*. THANKS FOR JOINING THE FAMILY.

I SUPPOSE I SHOULD INTRODUCE YOU TO YOUR NEW RELATIVES.

THIS ISN'T THE FIRST TIME THAT RON GARNEY AND I HAVE KILLED A BUNCH OF PEOPLE TOGETHER. NOT EVEN CLOSE. OUR FIRST COLLABORATION CAME BACK IN 2008, IN THE PAGES OF *WOLVERINE*, FOR A STORY CALLED "GET MYSTIQUE." AFTER THAT, THERE WAS *WOLVERINE: WEAPON X* AND *ULTIMATE CAPTAIN AMERICA* AND MOST RECENTLY, *THOR: GOD OF THUNDER.*

THROUGHOUT MUCH OF THAT, WE TALKED ABOUT THE IDEA OF DOING SOMETHING LIKE THIS. SOMETHING THAT WAS OURS. SOMETHING THAT WAS REAL. SOMETHING THAT WAS MEAN. SOMETHING THAT RON COULD CUT LOOSE ON IN A WAY HE NEVER HAD BEFORE.

RON'S A GUY WHO'S DONE IT ALL AT THIS POINT, IN TERMS OF MAINSTREAM SUPERHERO COMICS. HE'S HAD LEGENDARY RUNS FOR BOTH MARVEL AND DC. HE'S DRAWN THE MOST POPULAR CHARACTERS IN THE WORLD. HE'S BODY-SLAMMED PEOPLE IN BARS. BUT HE'S NEVER DONE SOMETHING LIKE THIS. THIS IS RON'S FIRST CREATOR-OWNED SERIES. HIS FIRST TRUE CRIME STORY. HIS FIRST CHANCE TO SHOW YOU JUST HOW DARK AND MEAN HE CAN BE.

JOINING RON AND I ON OUR MURDEROUS QUEST ARE A MOTLEY CREW OF CRACK CRAFTSMEN AND SALTY ROGUES, INCLUDING COLORIST EXTRAORDINAIRE MATT MILLA, LETTERING GURU AND STEVEN SEAGAL-AFICIONADO JARED FLETCHER AND EDITOR/PART-TIME GERMAN NINJA SEBASTIAN GIRNER.

THAT'S QUITE THE LINE-UP. THE MEN OF *MEN OF WRATH*. FEAR AND RESPECT THEM ALL.

WHO KNOWS, WE MIGHT JUST GET THIS BAND BACK TOGETHER SOMEDAY AND DO THIS ALL AGAIN. THERE ARE DEFINITELY SOME MORE STORIES I'D LIKE TO TELL WITH THESE MEN OF WRATH.

MORE STORIES ABOUT SHEEP AND DOGS AND HORSES. OH, THOSE POOR POOR HORSES. MORE STORIES ABOUT FATHERS AND SONS. ABOUT DEBTS NO HONEST MAN COULD PAY. ABOUT DEEPLY-FLAWED MEN WHO FIND IT EASIER TO KILL THAN TO LIVE. ABOUT WHAT IT MEANS TO BE A RATH.

UNTIL THEN...I GUESS I'LL SEE YA AT THE FAMILY REUNIONS. BRING LOTS OF BEER. AND A

CHAPTER ONE

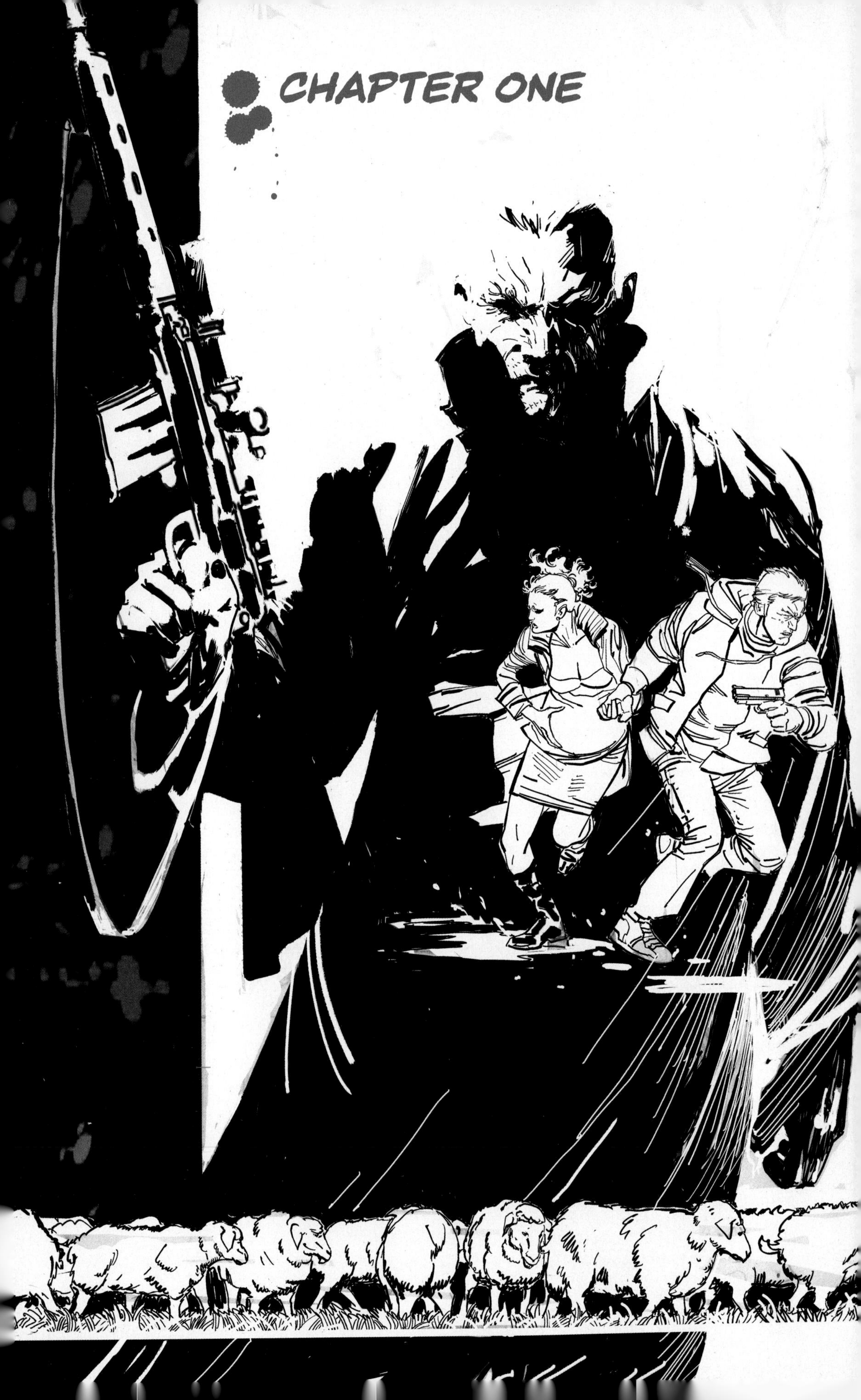

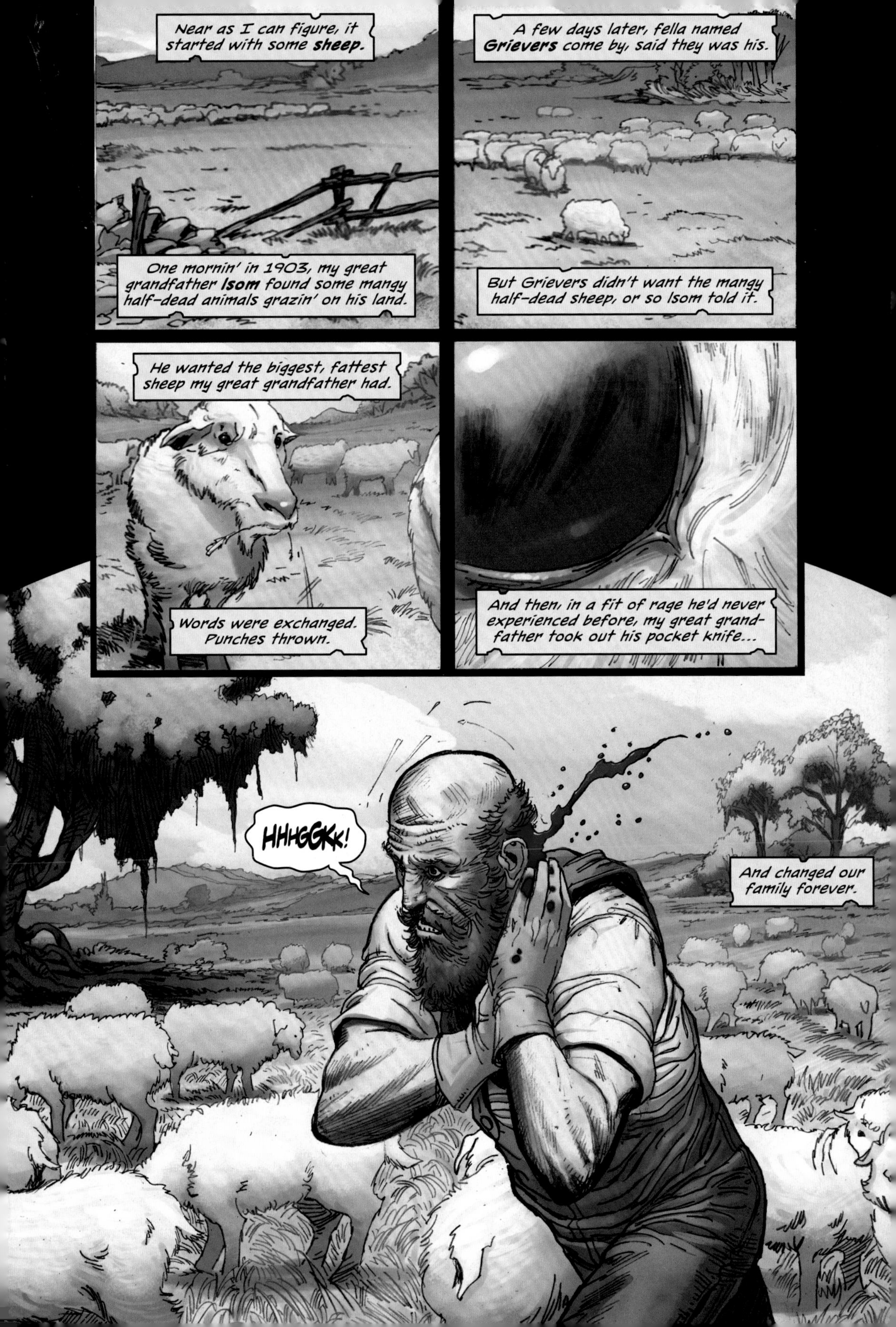
Near as I can figure, it started with some sheep.
One mornin' in 1903, my great grandfather Isom found some mangy half-dead animals grazin' on his land.
A few days later, fella named Grievers come by, said they was his.
But Grievers didn't want the mangy half-dead sheep, or so Isom told it.
He wanted the biggest, fattest sheep my great grandfather had.
Words were exchanged. Punches thrown.
And then, in a fit of rage he'd never experienced before, my great grand-father took out his pocket knife...
HHHGGKK!
And changed our family forever.

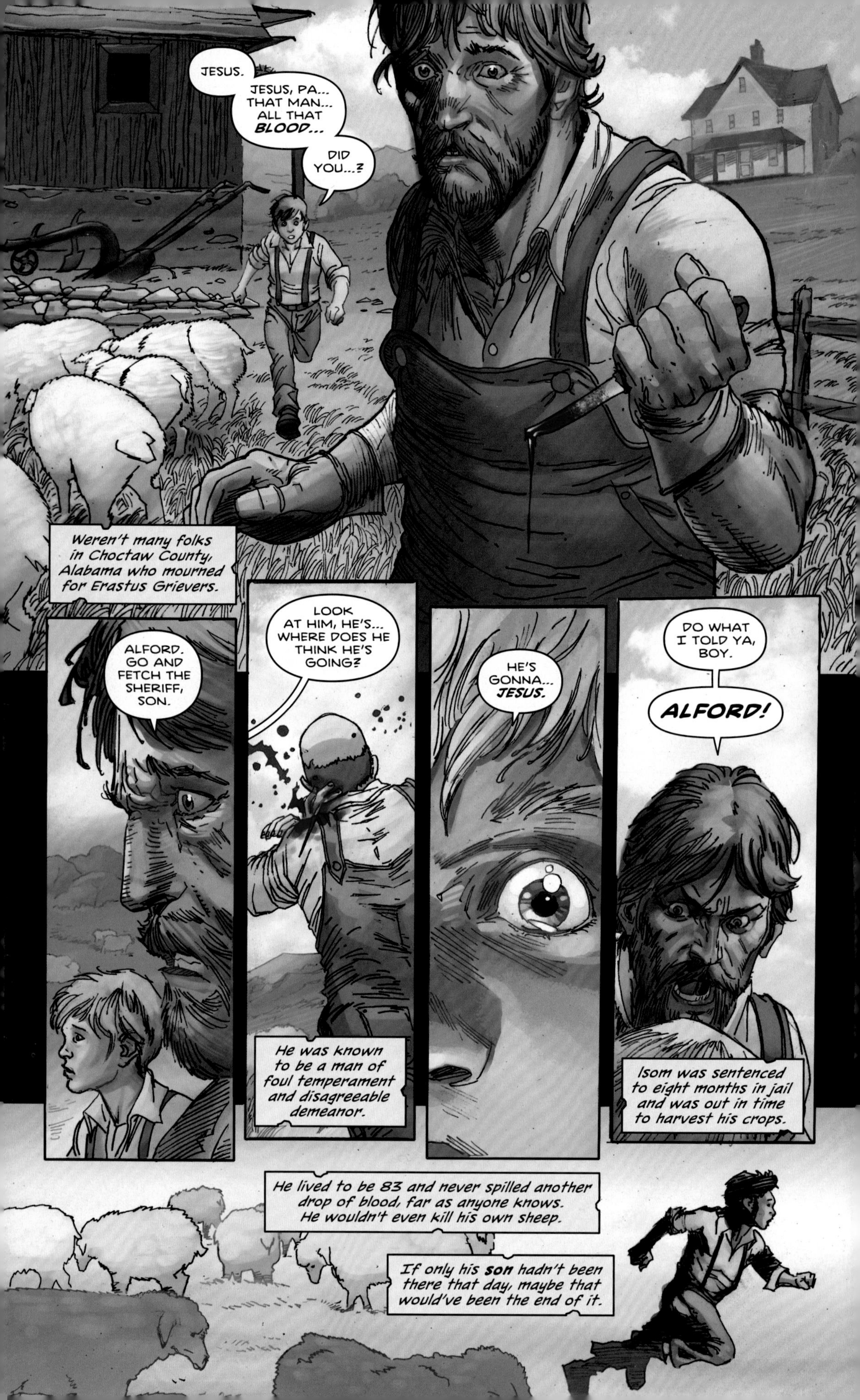

JESUS.
JESUS, PA... THAT MAN... ALL THAT BLOOD...
DID YOU...?
Weren't many folks in Choctaw County, Alabama who mourned for Erastus Grievers.
ALFORD. GO AND FETCH THE SHERIFF, SON.
LOOK AT HIM, HE'S... WHERE DOES HE THINK HE'S GOING?
He was known to be a man of foul temperament and disagreeable demeanor.
HE'S GONNA... JESUS.
DO WHAT I TOLD YA, BOY.
ALFORD!
Isom was sentenced to eight months in jail and was out in time to harvest his crops.
He lived to be 83 and never spilled another drop of blood, far as anyone knows. He wouldn't even kill his own sheep.
If only his son hadn't been there that day, maybe that would've been the end of it.

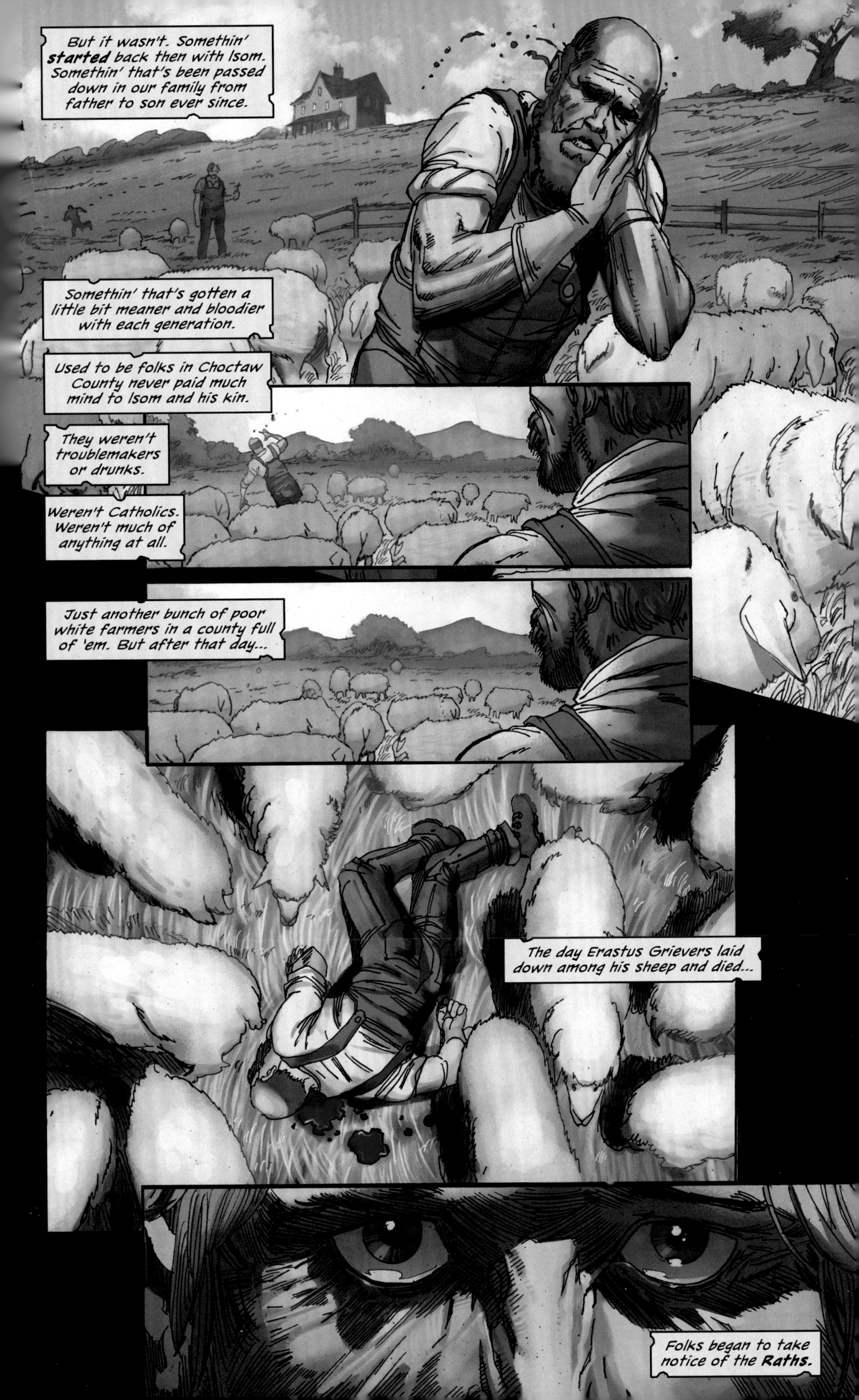
But it wasn't. Somethin' **started** back then with Isom. Somethin' that's been passed down in our family from father to son ever since.
Somethin' that's gotten a little bit meaner and bloodier with each generation.
Used to be folks in Choctaw County never paid much mind to Isom and his kin.
They weren't troublemakers or drunks.
Weren't Catholics. Weren't much of anything at all.
Just another bunch of poor white farmers in a county full of 'em. But after that day...
The day Erastus Grievers laid down among his sheep and died...
Folks began to take notice of the **Raths.**

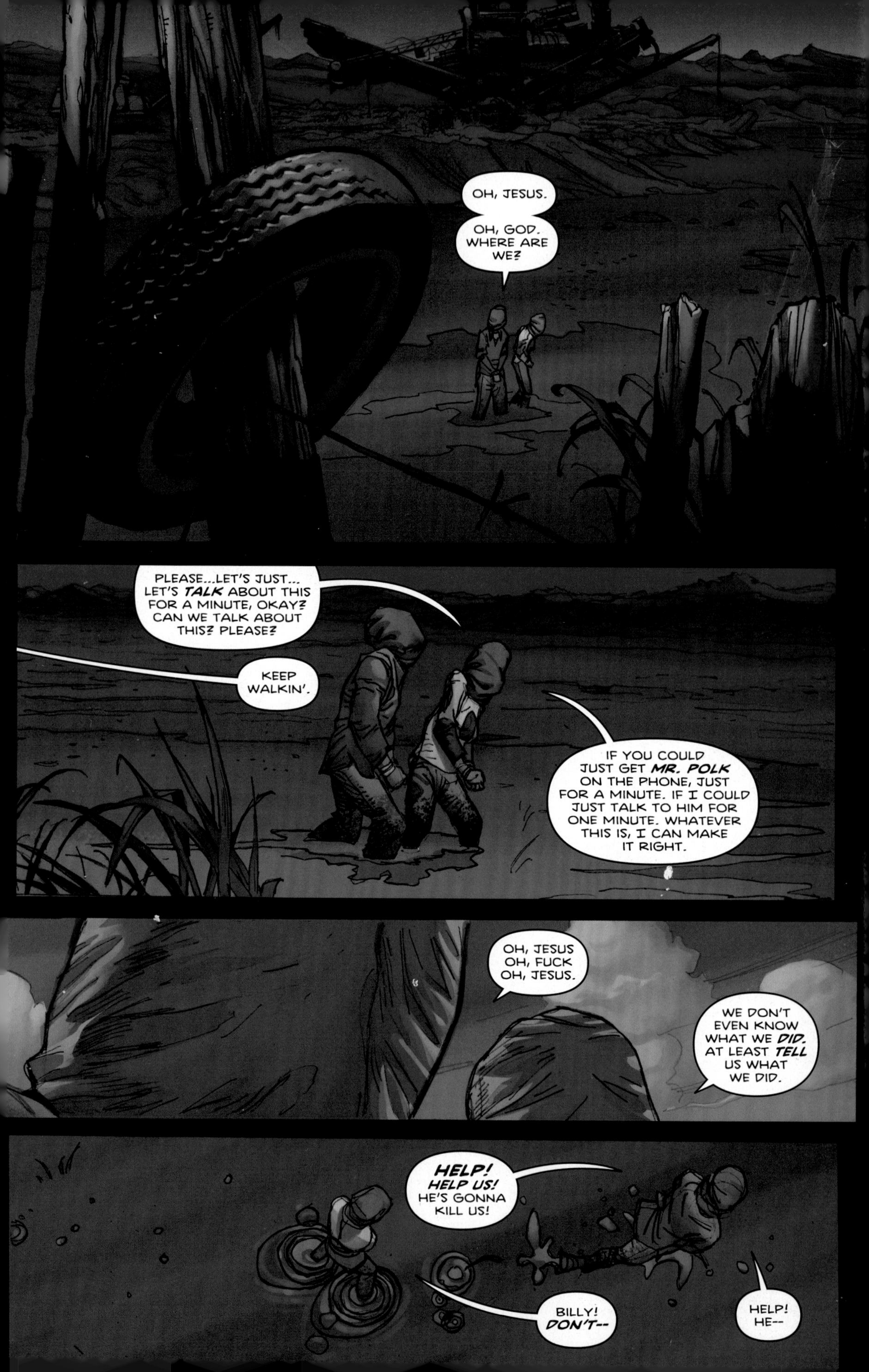
OH, JESUS.
OH, GOD. WHERE ARE WE?
PLEASE...LET'S JUST... LET'S TALK ABOUT THIS FOR A MINUTE, OKAY? CAN WE TALK ABOUT THIS? PLEASE?
KEEP WALKIN'.
IF YOU COULD JUST GET MR. POLK ON THE PHONE, JUST FOR A MINUTE. IF I COULD JUST TALK TO HIM FOR ONE MINUTE. WHATEVER THIS IS, I CAN MAKE IT RIGHT.
OH, JESUS OH, FUCK OH, JESUS.
WE DON'T EVEN KNOW WHAT WE DID. AT LEAST TELL US WHAT WE DID.
HELP! HELP US! HE'S GONNA KILL US!
BILLY! DON'T--
HELP! HE--

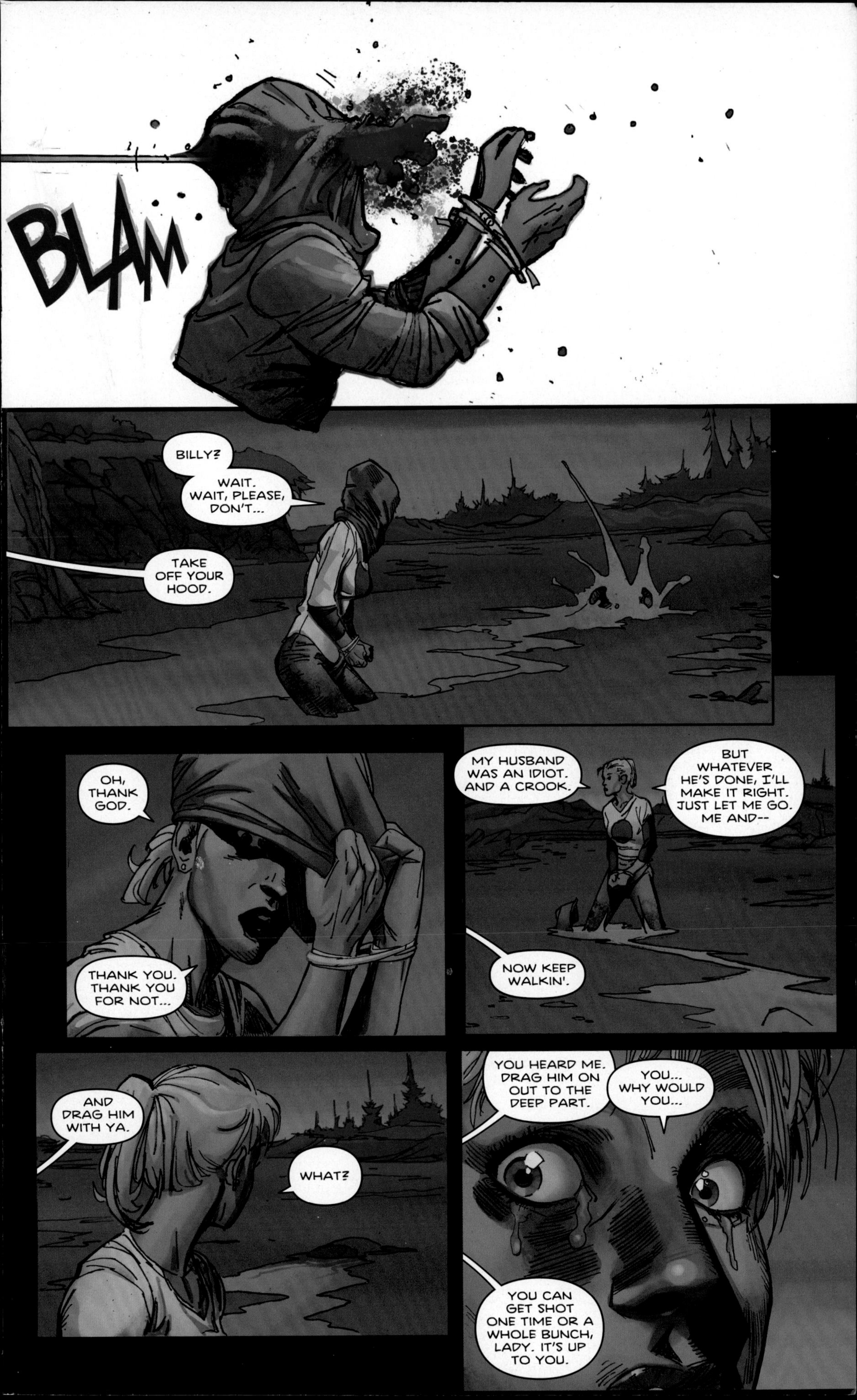
BLAM
BILLY?
WAIT. WAIT, PLEASE, DON'T...
TAKE OFF YOUR HOOD.
OH, THANK GOD.
THANK YOU. THANK YOU FOR NOT...
MY HUSBAND WAS AN IDIOT. AND A CROOK.
BUT WHATEVER HE'S DONE, I'LL MAKE IT RIGHT. JUST LET ME GO. ME AND--
NOW KEEP WALKIN'.
AND DRAG HIM WITH YA.
WHAT?
YOU HEARD ME. DRAG HIM ON OUT TO THE DEEP PART.
YOU... WHY WOULD YOU...
YOU CAN GET SHOT ONE TIME OR A WHOLE BUNCH, LADY. IT'S UP TO YOU.

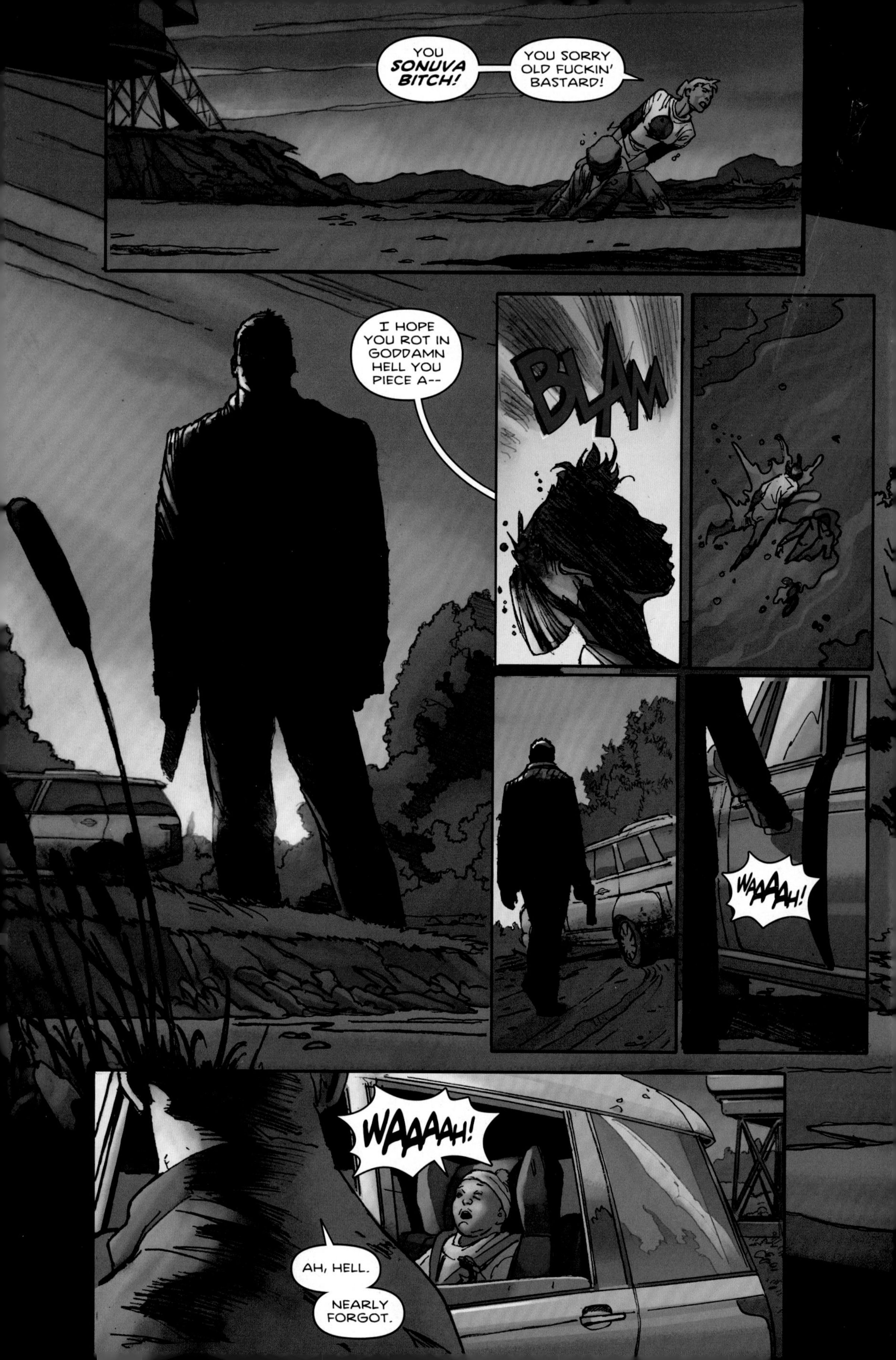
YOU *SONUVA BITCH!*
YOU SORRY OLD FUCKIN' BASTARD!
I HOPE YOU ROT IN GODDAMN HELL YOU PIECE A--
BLAM
WAAAAH!
WAAAAH!
AH, HELL.
NEARLY FORGOT.

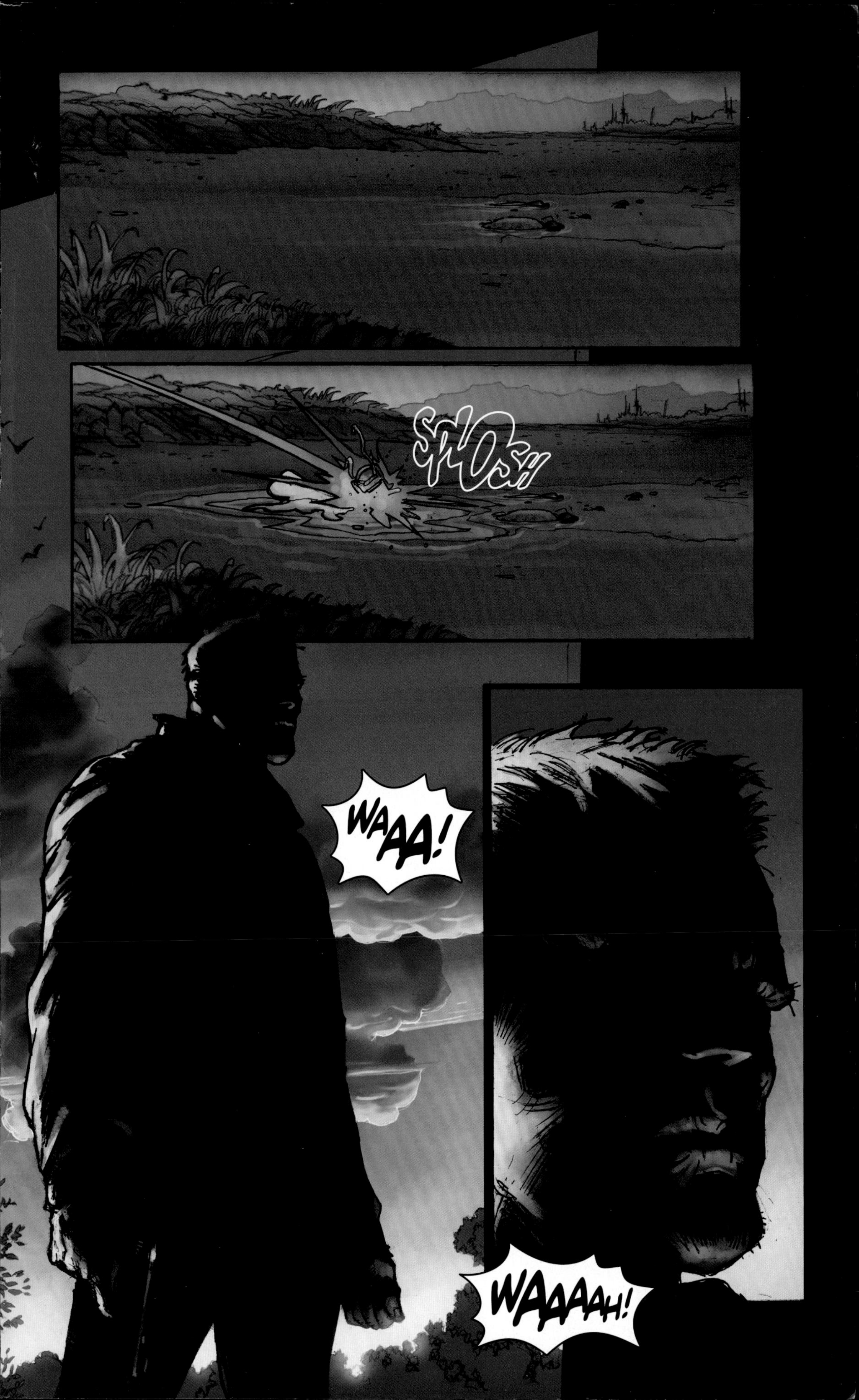
SPLOOSH
WAAA!
WAAAAH!

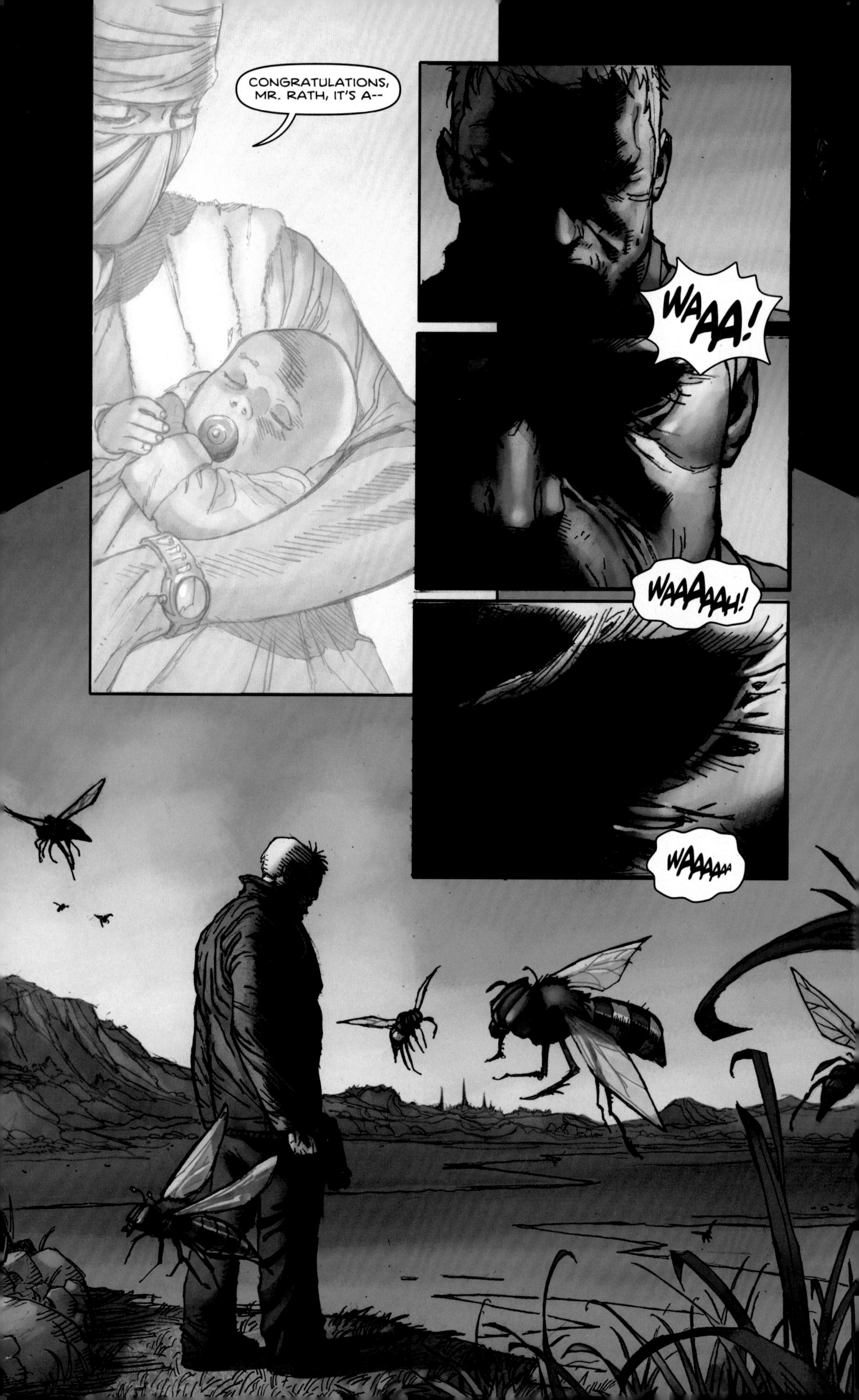
CONGRATULATIONS, MR. RATH, IT'S A--
WAAA!
WAAAAAH!
WAAAAAA

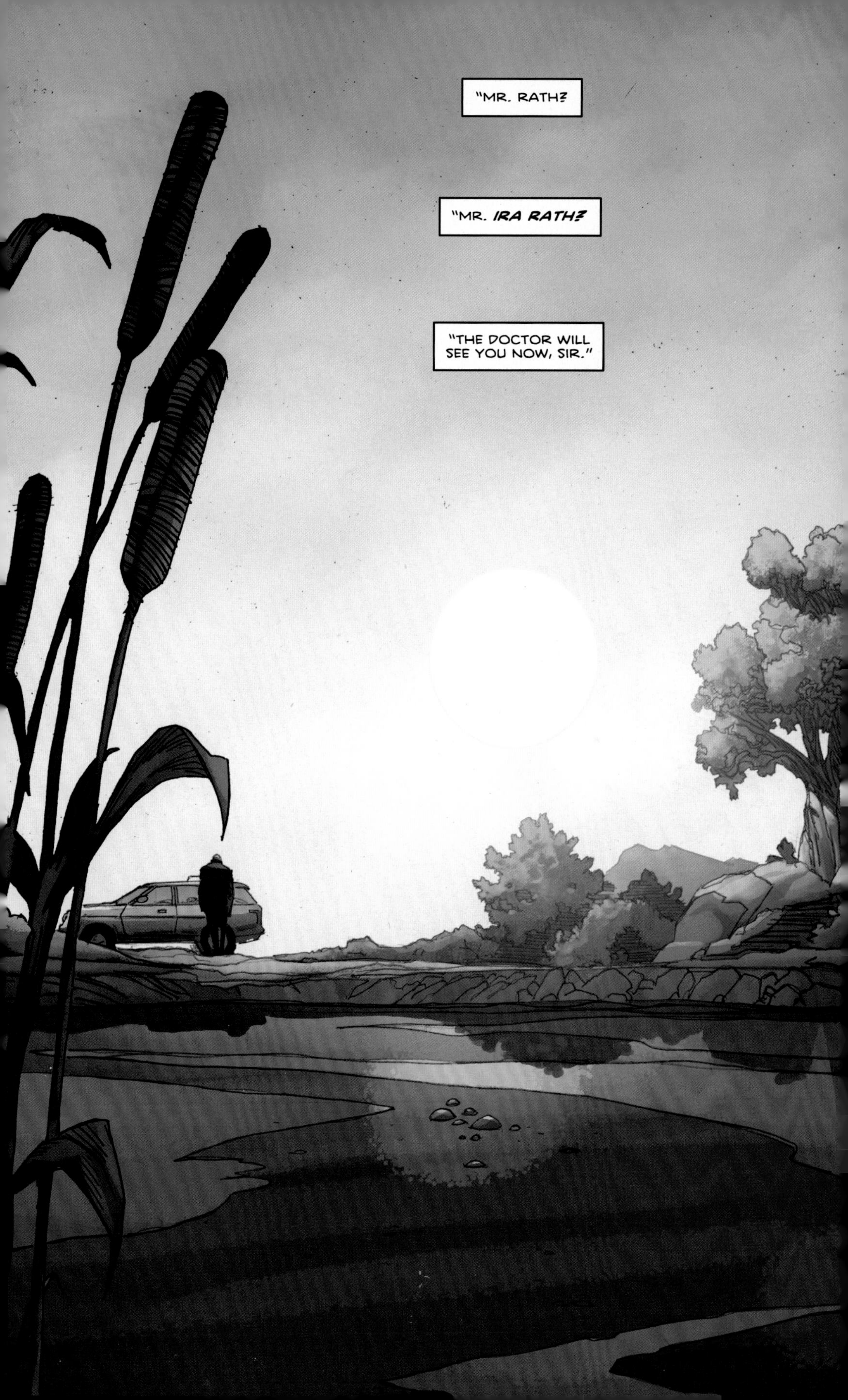
"MR. RATH?
"MR. *IRA RATH?*
"THE DOCTOR WILL SEE YOU NOW, SIR."

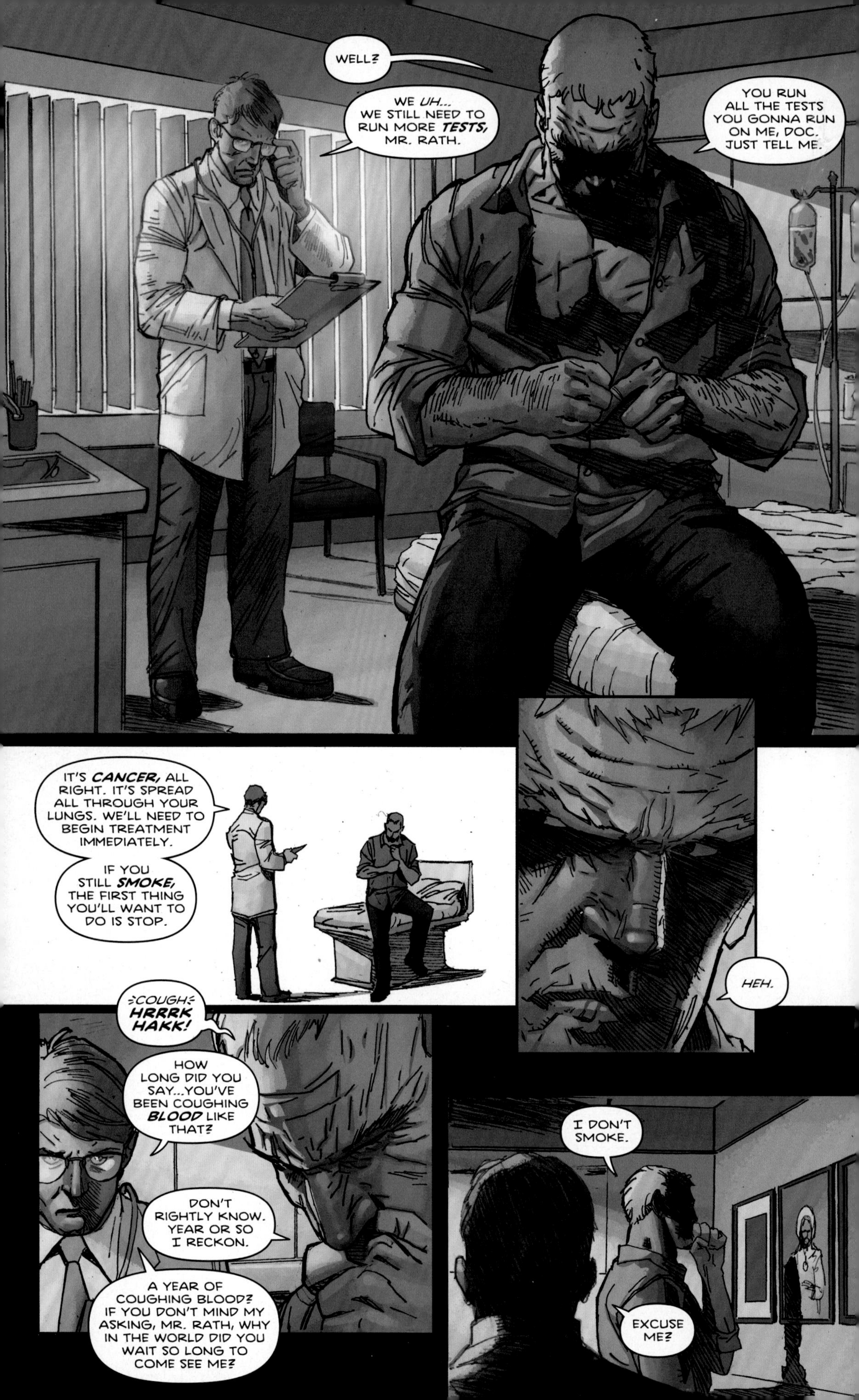
WELL?
WE UH... WE STILL NEED TO RUN MORE TESTS, MR. RATH.
YOU RUN ALL THE TESTS YOU GONNA RUN ON ME, DOC. JUST TELL ME.
IT'S CANCER, ALL RIGHT. IT'S SPREAD ALL THROUGH YOUR LUNGS. WE'LL NEED TO BEGIN TREATMENT IMMEDIATELY.
IF YOU STILL SMOKE, THE FIRST THING YOU'LL WANT TO DO IS STOP.
HEH.
COUGH HRRRK HAKK!
HOW LONG DID YOU SAY...YOU'VE BEEN COUGHING BLOOD LIKE THAT?
DON'T RIGHTLY KNOW. YEAR OR SO I RECKON.
A YEAR OF COUGHING BLOOD? IF YOU DON'T MIND MY ASKING, MR. RATH, WHY IN THE WORLD DID YOU WAIT SO LONG TO COME SEE ME?
I DON'T SMOKE.
EXCUSE ME?

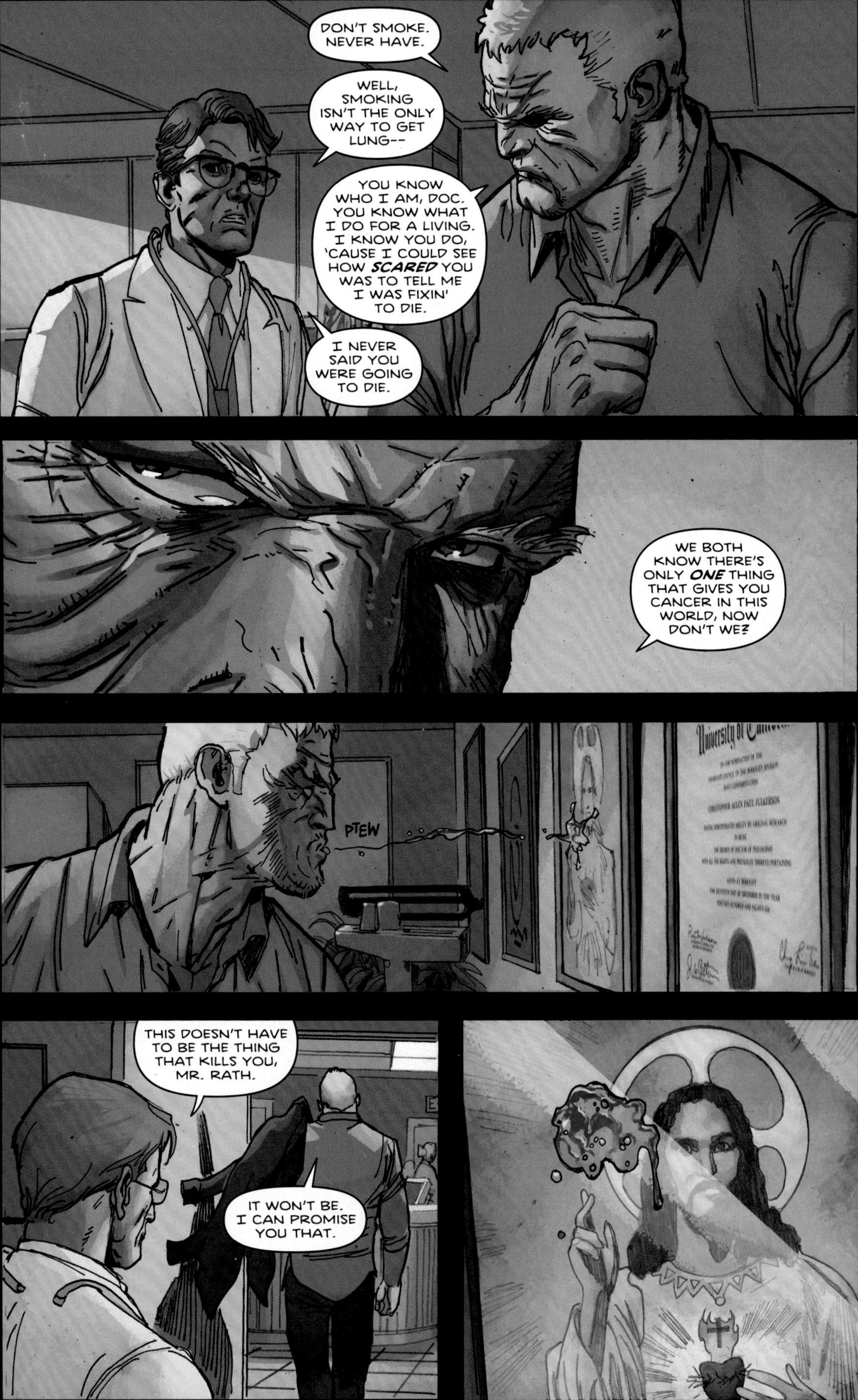
DON'T SMOKE. NEVER HAVE.
WELL, SMOKING ISN'T THE ONLY WAY TO GET LUNG--
YOU KNOW WHO I AM, DOC. YOU KNOW WHAT I DO FOR A LIVING. I KNOW YOU DO, 'CAUSE I COULD SEE HOW SCARED YOU WAS TO TELL ME I WAS FIXIN' TO DIE.
I NEVER SAID YOU WERE GOING TO DIE.
WE BOTH KNOW THERE'S ONLY ONE THING THAT GIVES YOU CANCER IN THIS WORLD, NOW DON'T WE?
PTEW
THIS DOESN'T HAVE TO BE THE THING THAT KILLS YOU, MR. RATH.
IT WON'T BE. I CAN PROMISE YOU THAT.

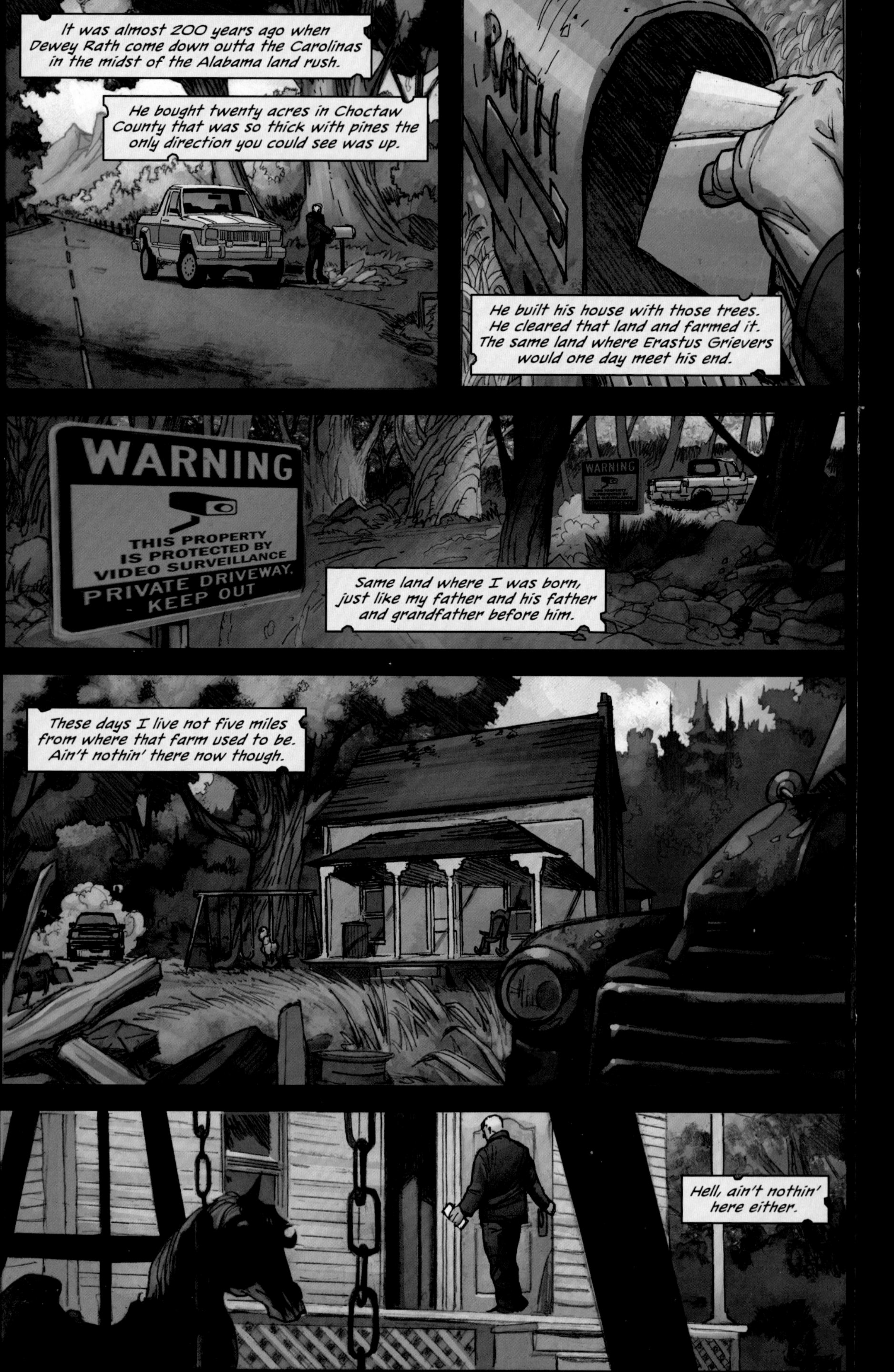
It was almost 200 years ago when Dewey Rath come down outta the Carolinas in the midst of the Alabama land rush.
He bought twenty acres in Choctaw County that was so thick with pines the only direction you could see was up.
RATH
He built his house with those trees. He cleared that land and farmed it. The same land where Erastus Grievers would one day meet his end.
WARNING
THIS PROPERTY IS PROTECTED BY VIDEO SURVEILLANCE
PRIVATE DRIVEWAY, KEEP OUT
WARNING
Same land where I was born, just like my father and his father and grandfather before him.
These days I live not five miles from where that farm used to be. Ain't nothin' there now though.
Hell, ain't nothin' here either.

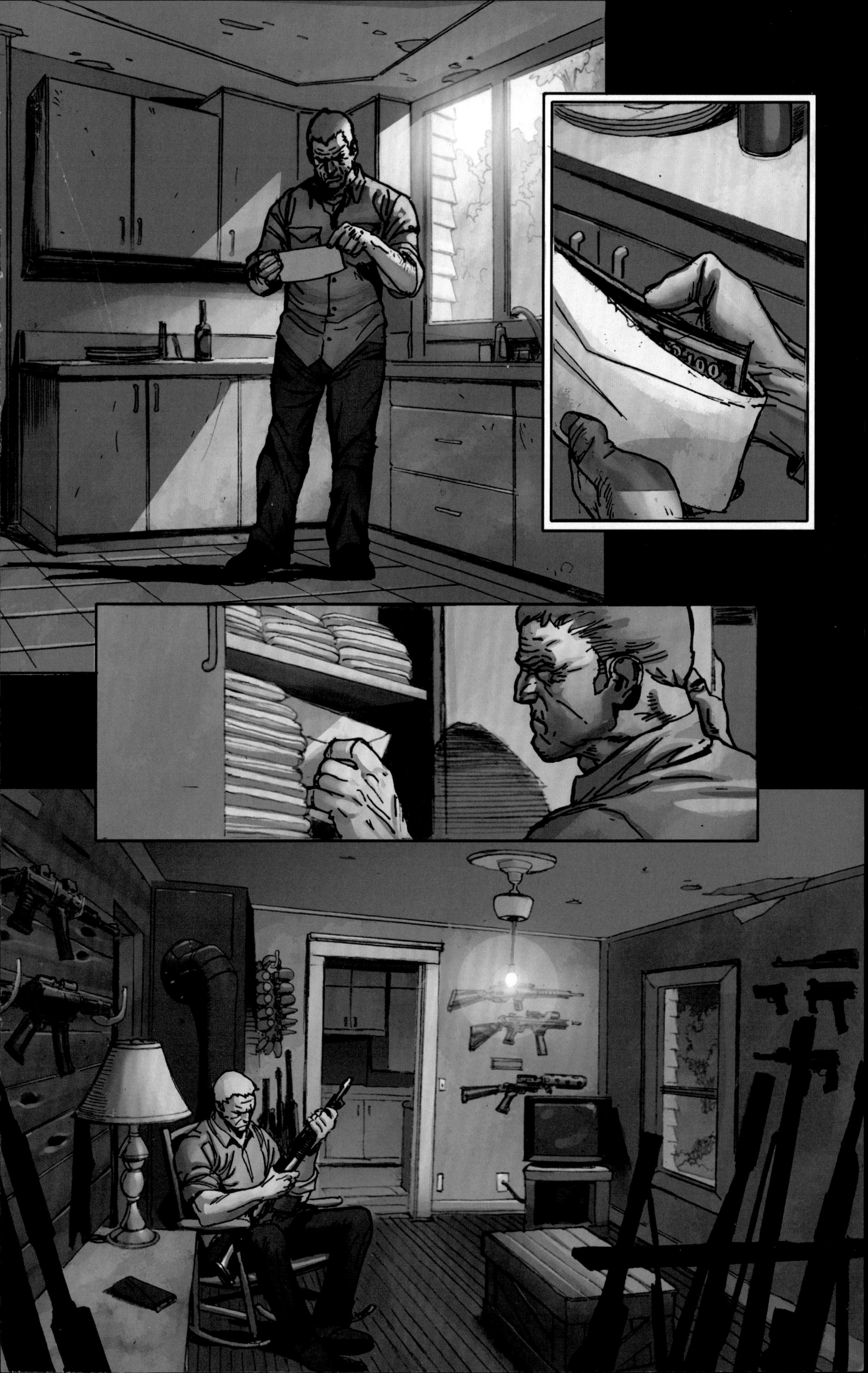

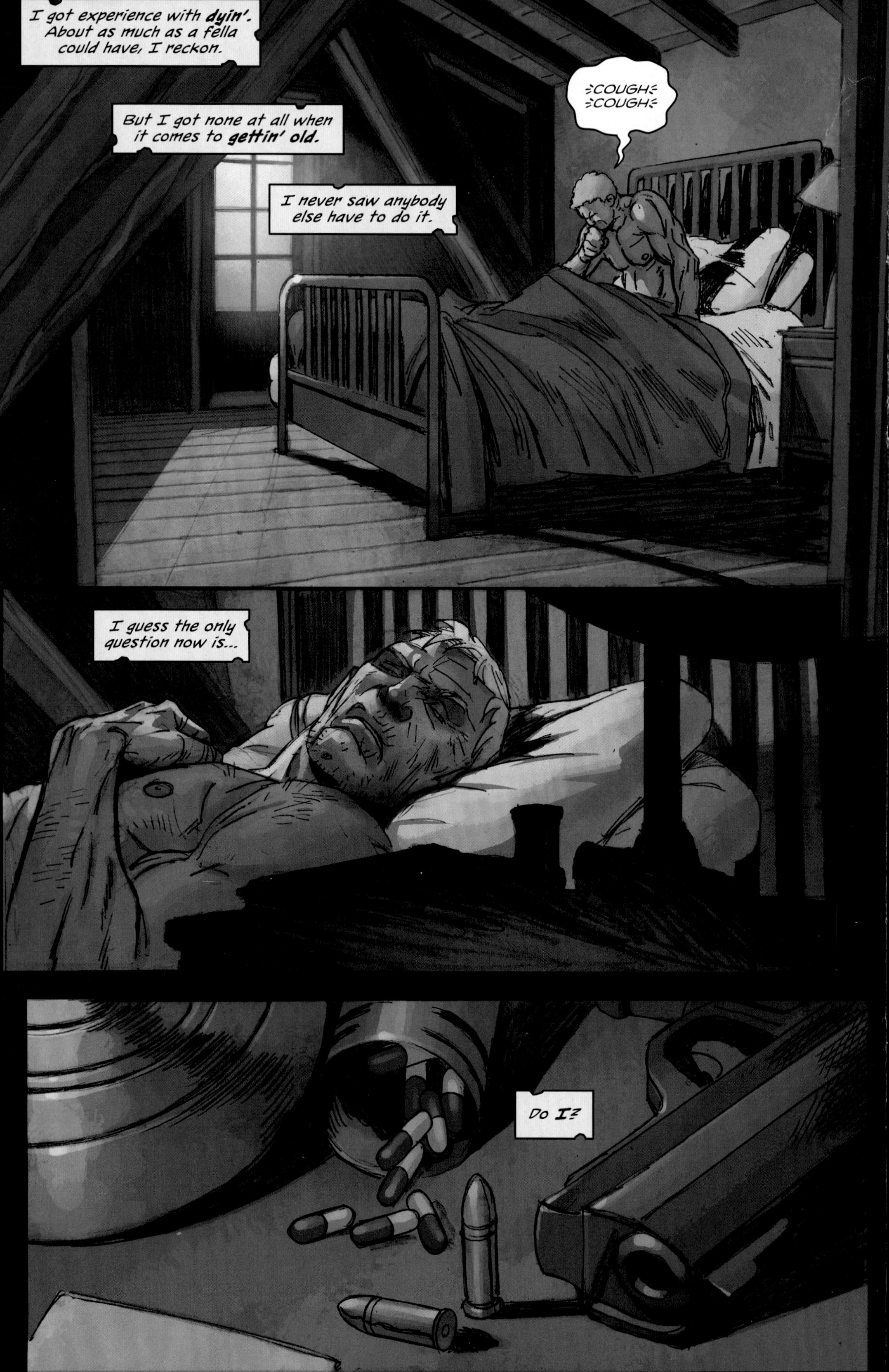
I got experience with **dyin'**. About as much as a fella could have, I reckon.
But I got none at all when it comes to **gettin' old.**
I never saw anybody else have to do it.
COUGH COUGH
I guess the only question now is...
Do **I**?

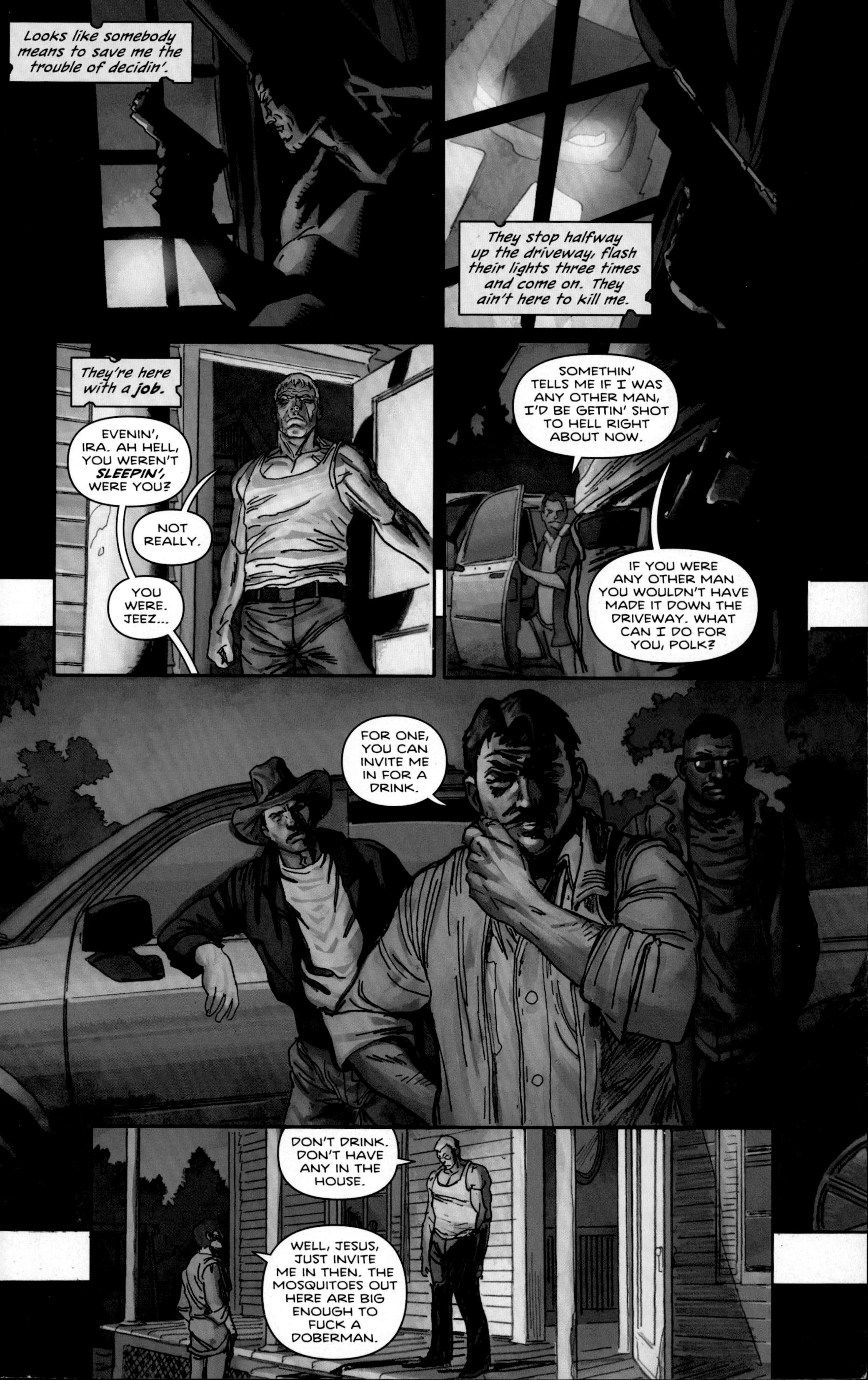
Looks like somebody means to save me the trouble of decidin'.
They stop halfway up the driveway, flash their lights three times and come on. They ain't here to kill me.
They're here with a job.
EVENIN', IRA. AH HELL, YOU WEREN'T SLEEPIN', WERE YOU?
NOT REALLY.
YOU WERE. JEEZ...
SOMETHIN' TELLS ME IF I WAS ANY OTHER MAN, I'D BE GETTIN' SHOT TO HELL RIGHT ABOUT NOW.
IF YOU WERE ANY OTHER MAN YOU WOULDN'T HAVE MADE IT DOWN THE DRIVEWAY. WHAT CAN I DO FOR YOU, POLK?
FOR ONE, YOU CAN INVITE ME IN FOR A DRINK.
DON'T DRINK. DON'T HAVE ANY IN THE HOUSE.
WELL, JESUS, JUST INVITE ME IN THEN. THE MOSQUITOES OUT HERE ARE BIG ENOUGH TO FUCK A DOBERMAN.

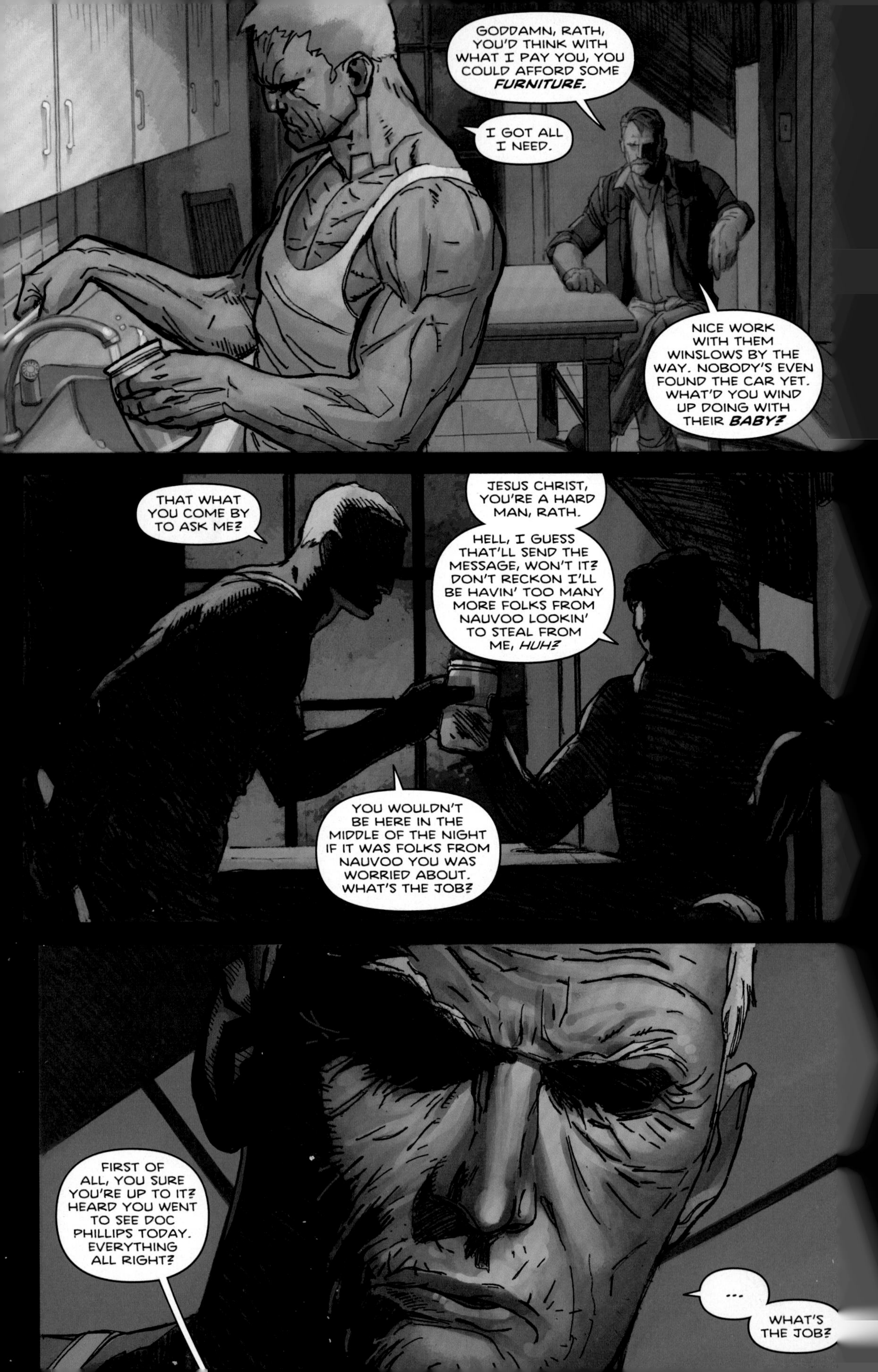
GODDAMN, RATH, YOU'D THINK WITH WHAT I PAY YOU, YOU COULD AFFORD SOME FURNITURE.
I GOT ALL I NEED.
NICE WORK WITH THEM WINSLOWS BY THE WAY. NOBODY'S EVEN FOUND THE CAR YET. WHAT'D YOU WIND UP DOING WITH THEIR BABY?
THAT WHAT YOU COME BY TO ASK ME?
JESUS CHRIST, YOU'RE A HARD MAN, RATH.
HELL, I GUESS THAT'LL SEND THE MESSAGE, WON'T IT? DON'T RECKON I'LL BE HAVIN' TOO MANY MORE FOLKS FROM NAUVOO LOOKIN' TO STEAL FROM ME, HUH?
YOU WOULDN'T BE HERE IN THE MIDDLE OF THE NIGHT IF IT WAS FOLKS FROM NAUVOO YOU WAS WORRIED ABOUT. WHAT'S THE JOB?
FIRST OF ALL, YOU SURE YOU'RE UP TO IT? HEARD YOU WENT TO SEE DOC PHILLIPS TODAY. EVERYTHING ALL RIGHT?
...
WHAT'S THE JOB?

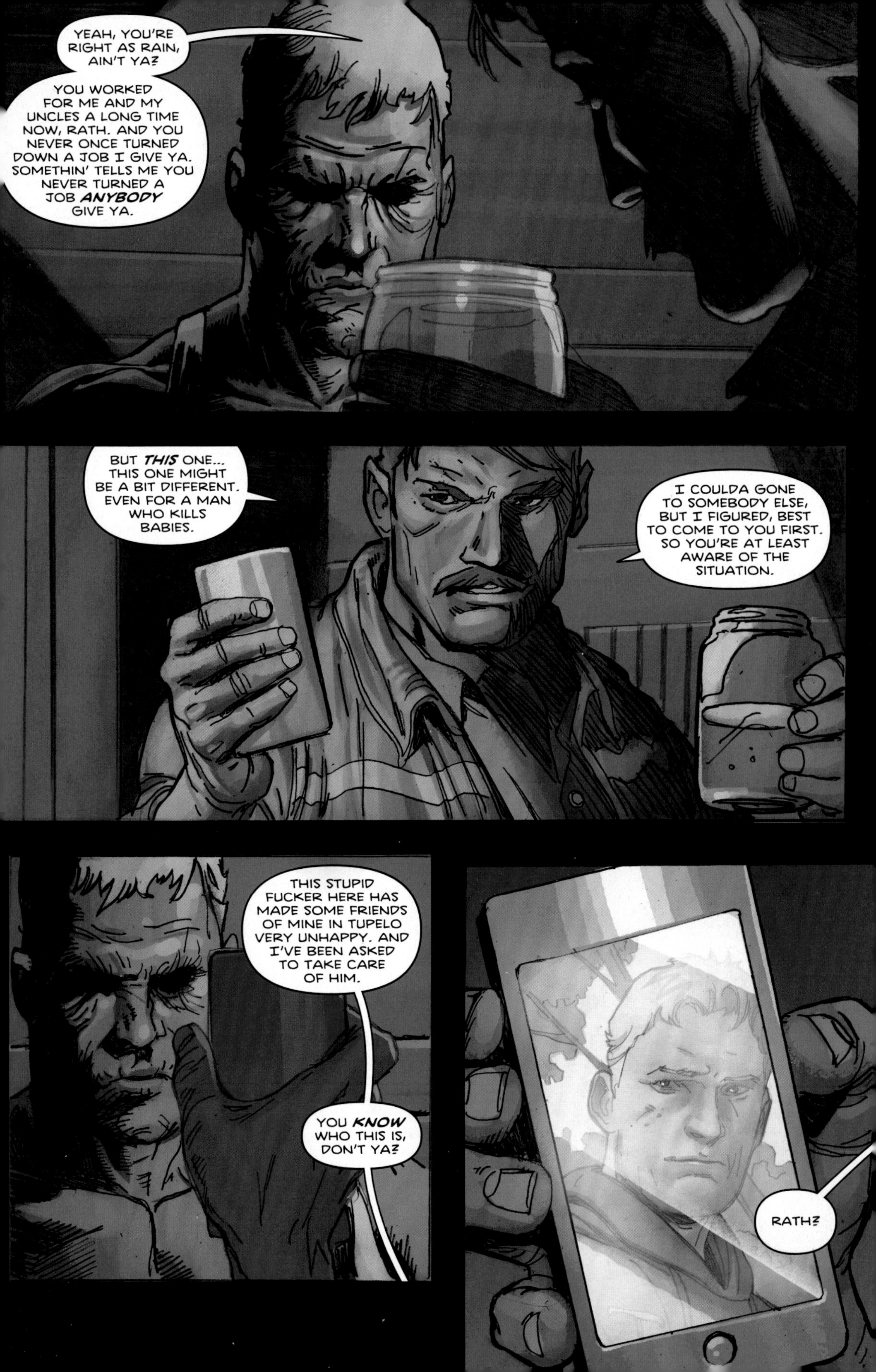
YEAH, YOU'RE RIGHT AS RAIN, AIN'T YA?
YOU WORKED FOR ME AND MY UNCLES A LONG TIME NOW, RATH. AND YOU NEVER ONCE TURNED DOWN A JOB I GIVE YA. SOMETHIN' TELLS ME YOU NEVER TURNED A JOB ANYBODY GIVE YA.
BUT THIS ONE... THIS ONE MIGHT BE A BIT DIFFERENT. EVEN FOR A MAN WHO KILLS BABIES.
I COULDA GONE TO SOMEBODY ELSE, BUT I FIGURED, BEST TO COME TO YOU FIRST. SO YOU'RE AT LEAST AWARE OF THE SITUATION.
THIS STUPID FUCKER HERE HAS MADE SOME FRIENDS OF MINE IN TUPELO VERY UNHAPPY. AND I'VE BEEN ASKED TO TAKE CARE OF HIM.
YOU KNOW WHO THIS IS, DON'T YA?
RATH?

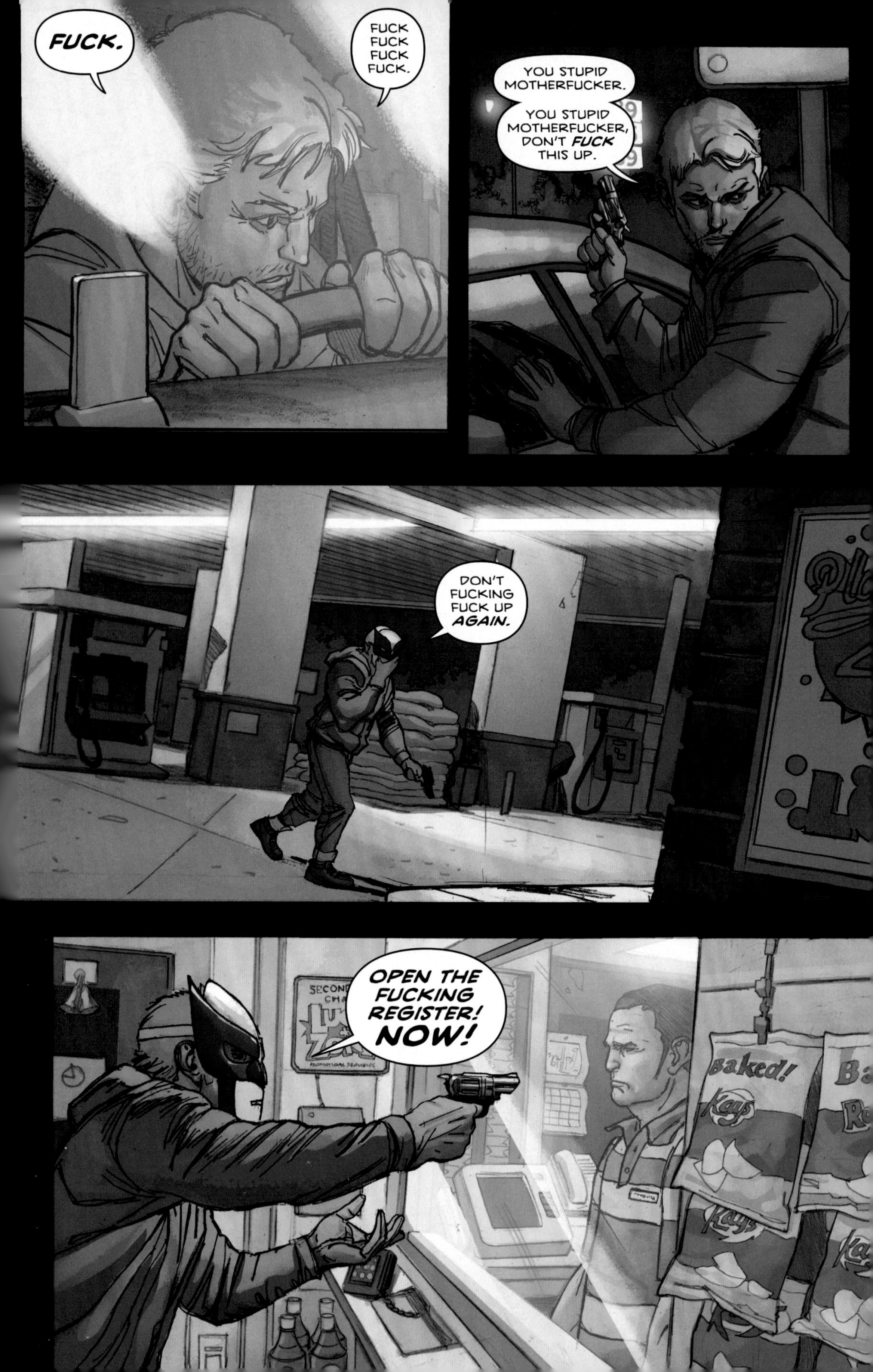
FUCK.
FUCK FUCK FUCK FUCK.
YOU STUPID MOTHERFUCKER.
YOU STUPID MOTHERFUCKER, DON'T FUCK THIS UP.
DON'T FUCKING FUCK UP AGAIN.
OPEN THE FUCKING REGISTER! NOW!
Baked!
Kays

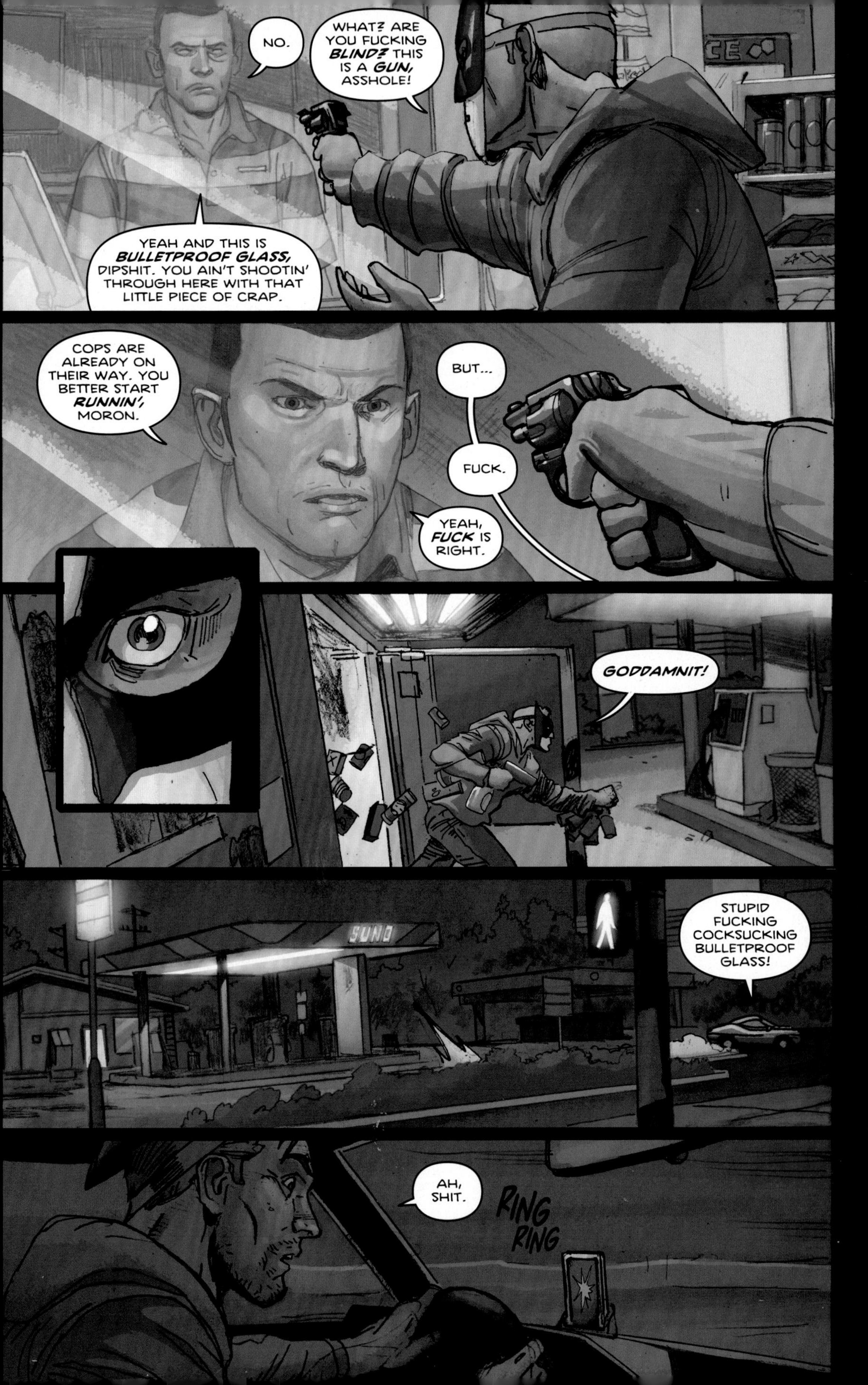
NO.
WHAT? ARE YOU FUCKING BLIND? THIS IS A GUN, ASSHOLE!
YEAH AND THIS IS BULLETPROOF GLASS, DIPSHIT. YOU AIN'T SHOOTIN' THROUGH HERE WITH THAT LITTLE PIECE OF CRAP.
COPS ARE ALREADY ON THEIR WAY. YOU BETTER START RUNNIN', MORON.
BUT...
FUCK.
YEAH, FUCK IS RIGHT.
GODDAMNIT!
SUNO
STUPID FUCKING COCKSUCKING BULLETPROOF GLASS!
AH, SHIT.
RING RING

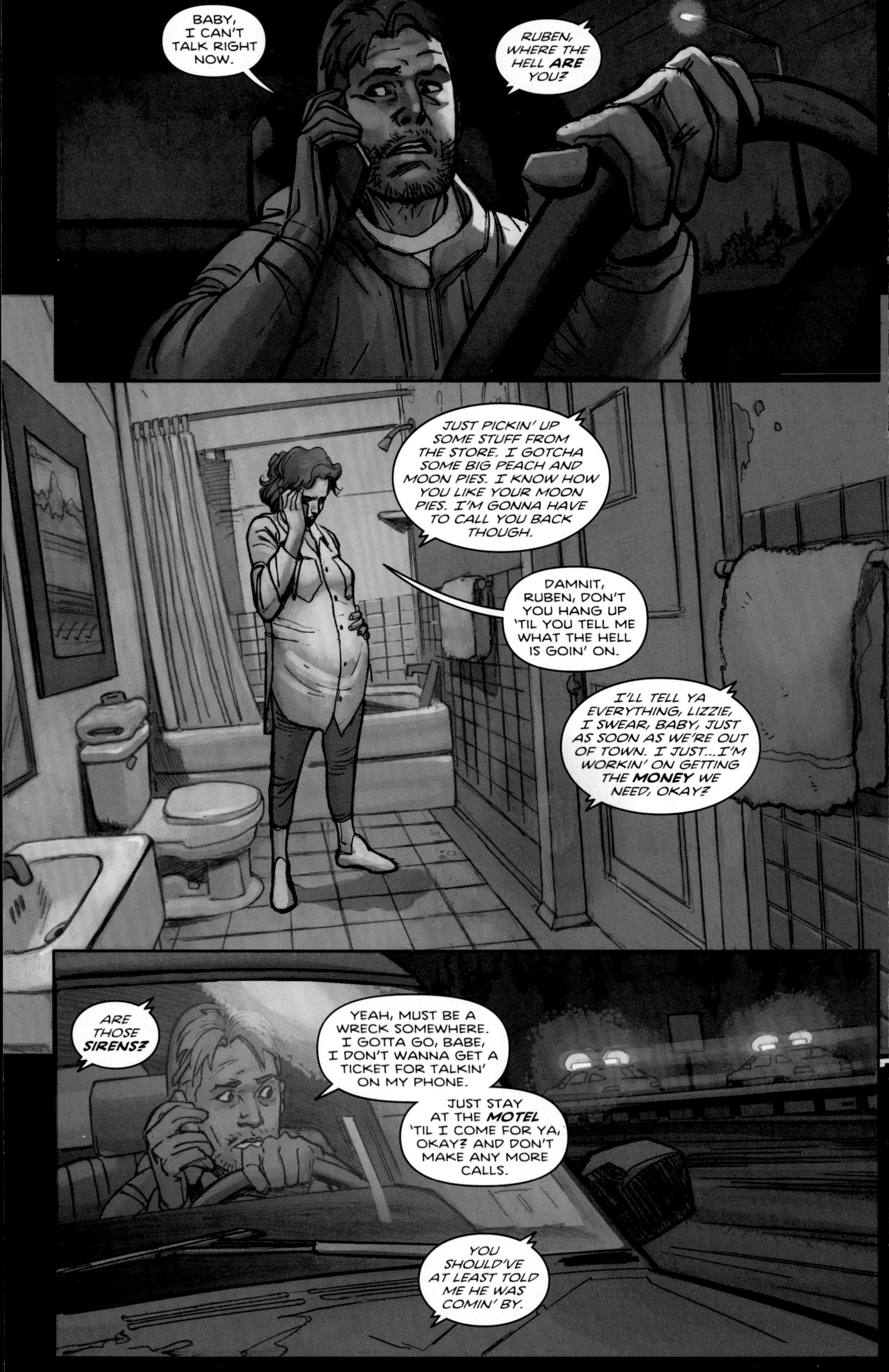

BABY, I CAN'T TALK RIGHT NOW.
RUBEN, WHERE THE HELL ARE YOU?
JUST PICKIN' UP SOME STUFF FROM THE STORE. I GOTCHA SOME BIG PEACH AND MOON PIES. I KNOW HOW YOU LIKE YOUR MOON PIES. I'M GONNA HAVE TO CALL YOU BACK THOUGH.
DAMNIT, RUBEN, DON'T YOU HANG UP 'TIL YOU TELL ME WHAT THE HELL IS GOIN' ON.
I'LL TELL YA EVERYTHING, LIZZIE, I SWEAR, BABY, JUST AS SOON AS WE'RE OUT OF TOWN. I JUST...I'M WORKIN' ON GETTING THE MONEY WE NEED, OKAY?
ARE THOSE SIRENS?
YEAH, MUST BE A WRECK SOMEWHERE. I GOTTA GO, BABE, I DON'T WANNA GET A TICKET FOR TALKIN' ON MY PHONE.
JUST STAY AT THE MOTEL 'TIL I COME FOR YA, OKAY? AND DON'T MAKE ANY MORE CALLS.
YOU SHOULD'VE AT LEAST TOLD ME HE WAS COMIN' BY.

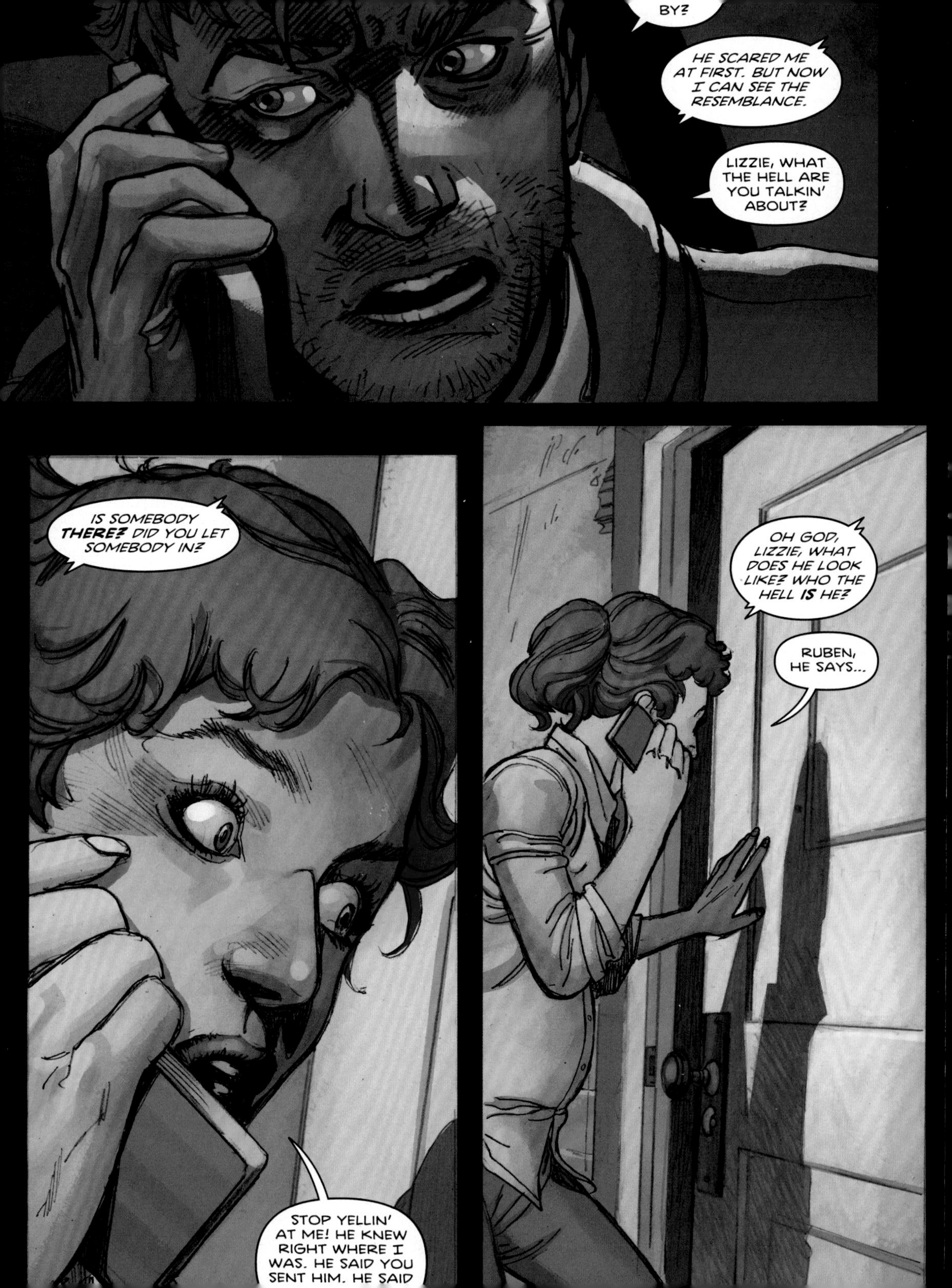
BY?
HE SCARED ME AT FIRST. BUT NOW I CAN SEE THE RESEMBLANCE.
LIZZIE, WHAT THE HELL ARE YOU TALKIN' ABOUT?
IS SOMEBODY THERE? DID YOU LET SOMEBODY IN?
OH GOD, LIZZIE, WHAT DOES HE LOOK LIKE? WHO THE HELL IS HE?
RUBEN, HE SAYS...
STOP YELLIN' AT ME! HE KNEW RIGHT WHERE I WAS. HE SAID YOU SENT HIM. HE SAID

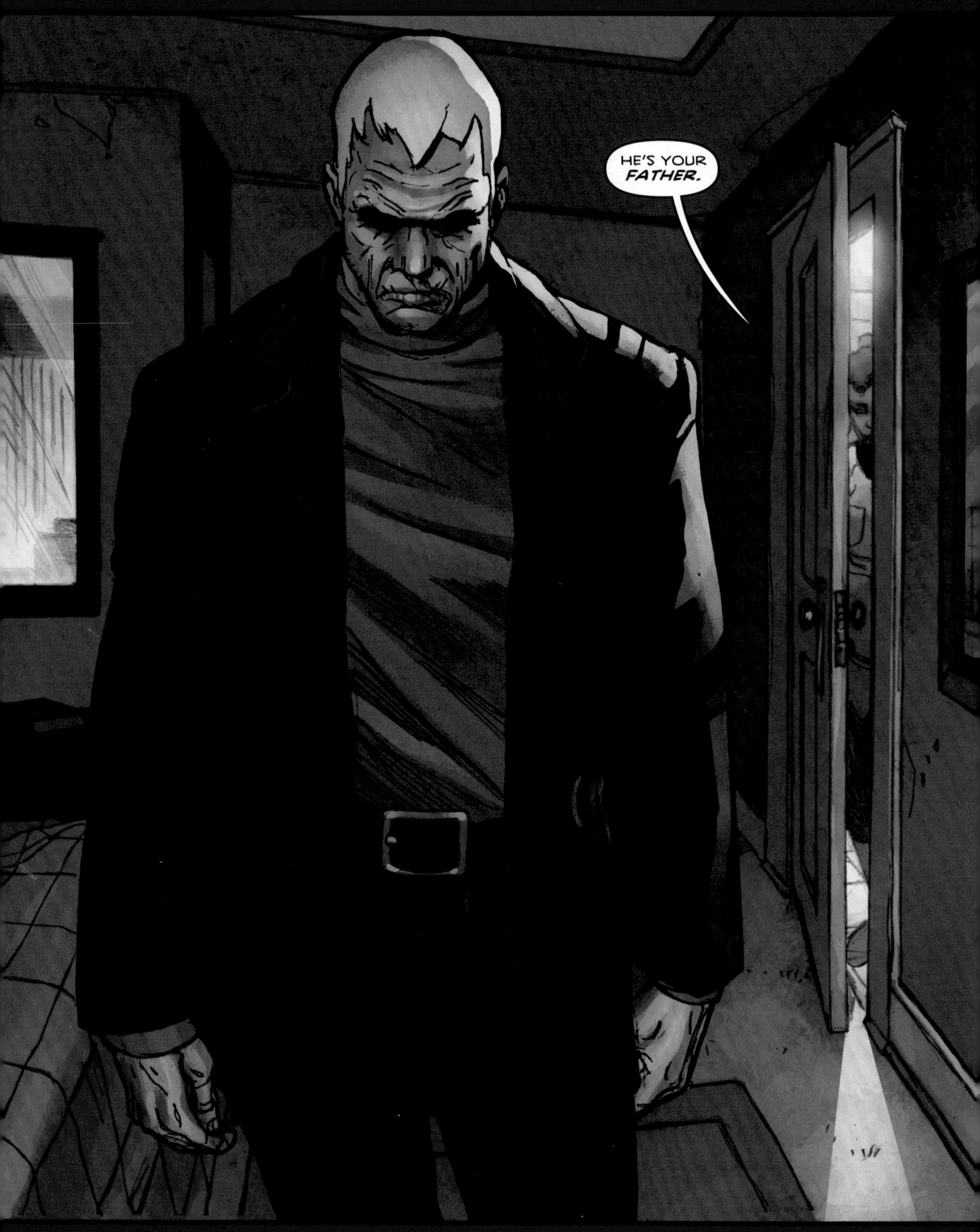
HE'S YOUR FATHER.

CHAPTER TWO

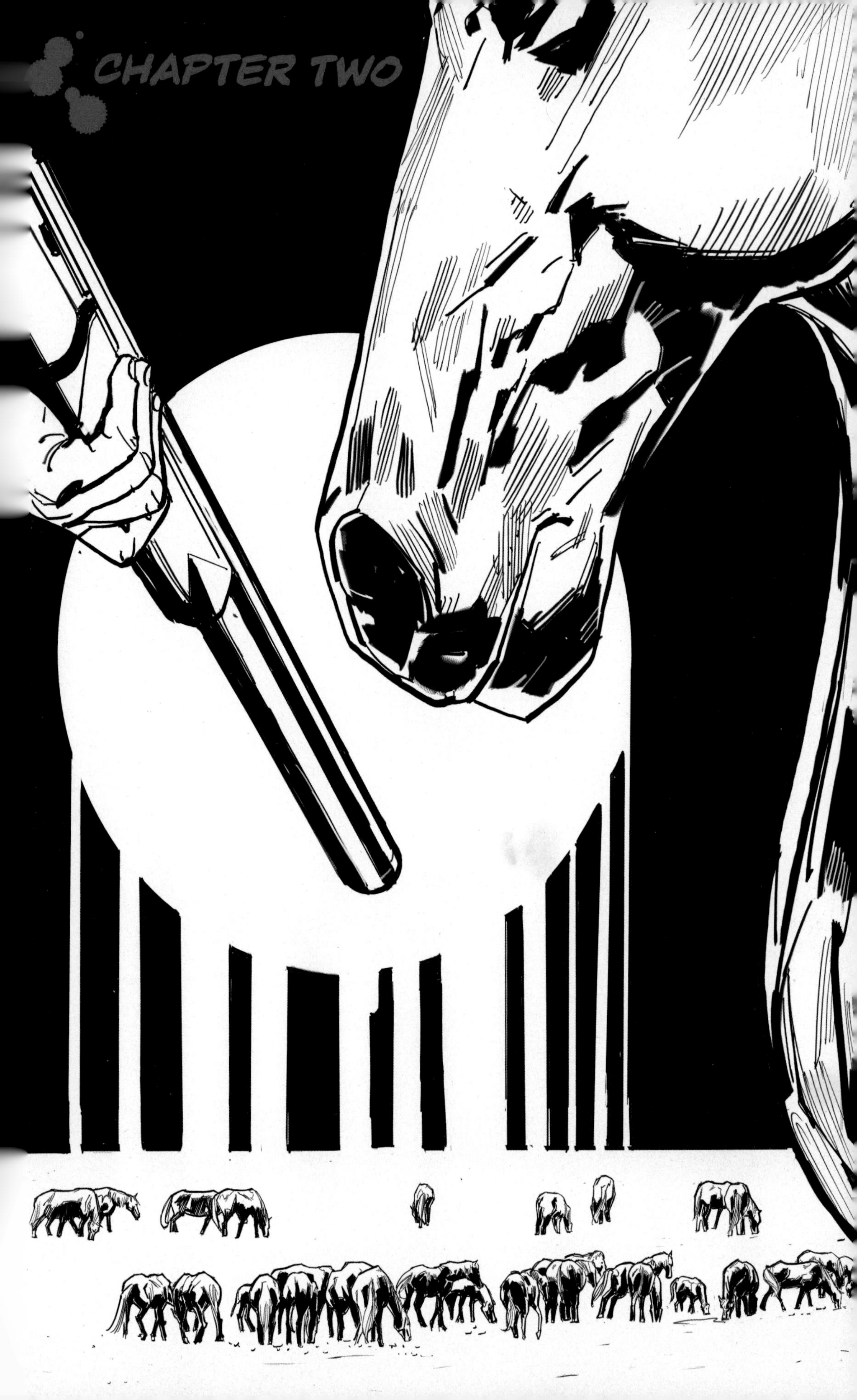

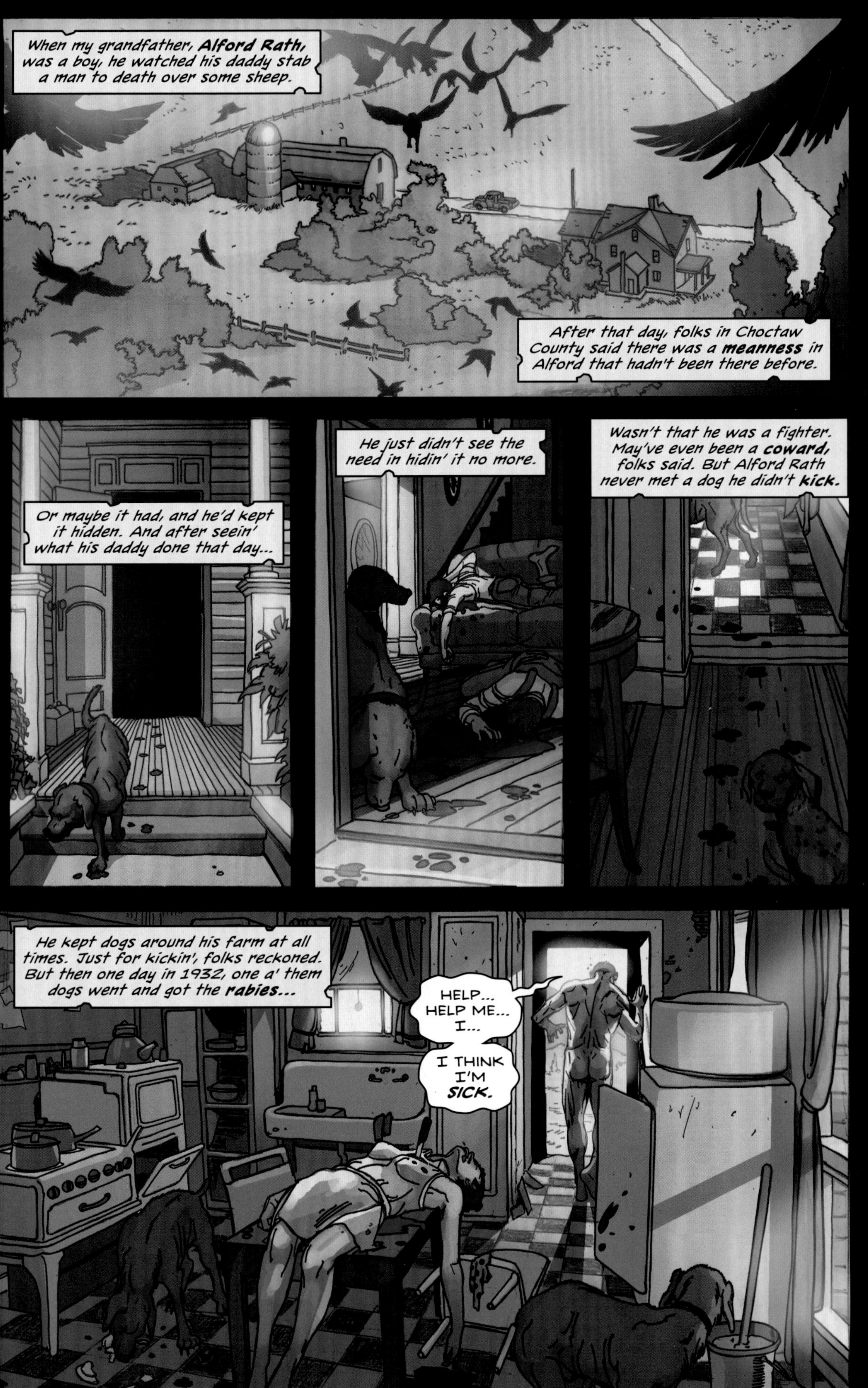
When my grandfather, **Alford Rath**, was a boy, he watched his daddy stab a man to death over some sheep.
After that day, folks in Choctaw County said there was a **meanness** in Alford that hadn't been there before.
Or maybe it had, and he'd kept it hidden. And after seein' what his daddy done that day...
He just didn't see the need in hidin' it no more.
Wasn't that he was a fighter. May've even been a **coward**, folks said. But Alford Rath never met a dog he didn't **kick**.
He kept dogs around his farm at all times. Just for kickin', folks reckoned. But then one day in 1932, one a' them dogs went and got the **rabies...**
HELP... HELP ME... I...
I THINK I'M ***SICK.***

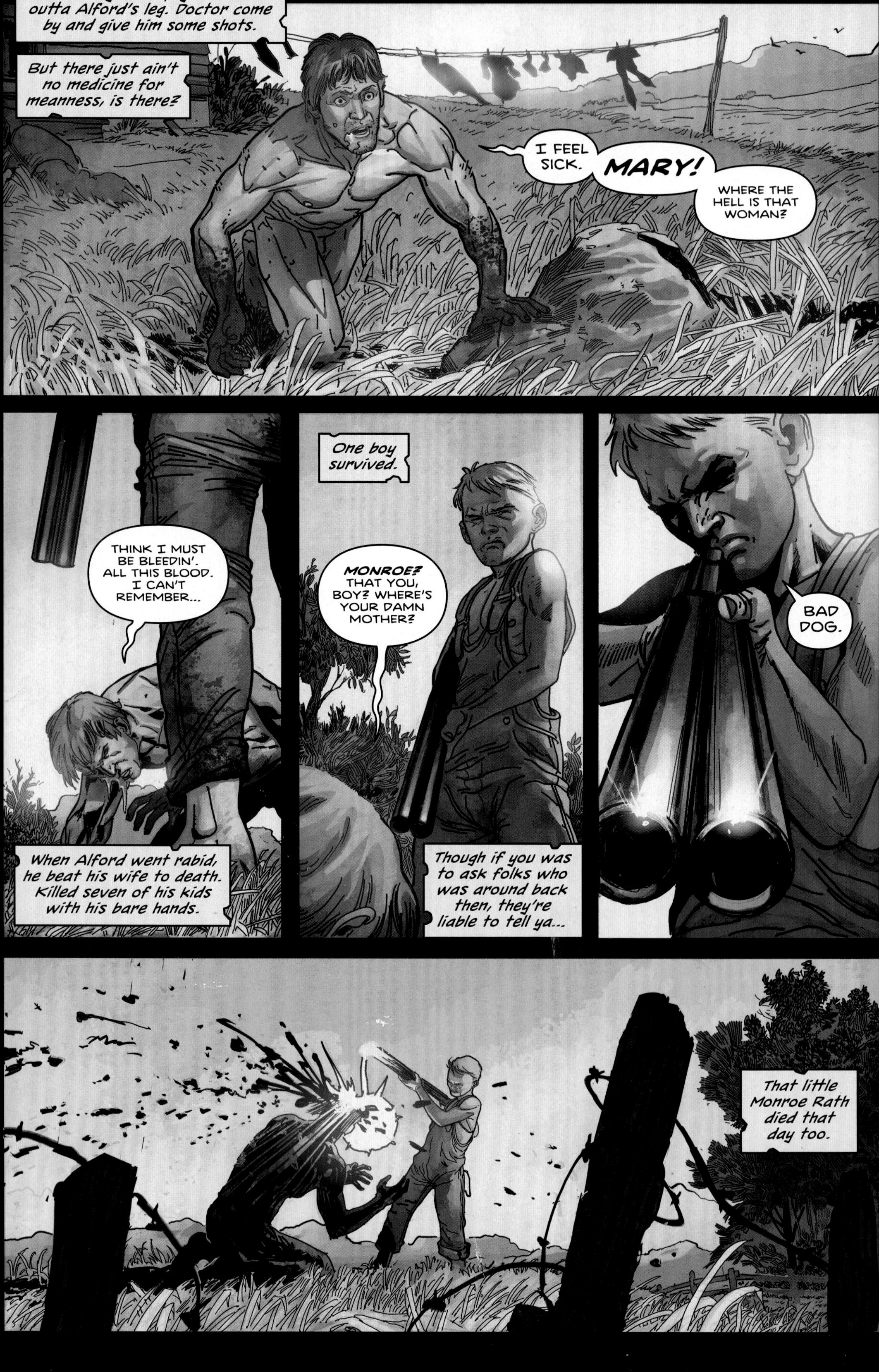
They had to break the dog's neck 'fore they could pry its teeth outta Alford's leg. Doctor come by and give him some shots.
But there just ain't no medicine for meanness, is there?
I FEEL SICK.
MARY!
WHERE THE HELL IS THAT WOMAN?
THINK I MUST BE BLEEDIN'. ALL THIS BLOOD. I CAN'T REMEMBER...
When Alford went rabid, he beat his wife to death. Killed seven of his kids with his bare hands.
One boy survived.
MONROE? THAT YOU, BOY? WHERE'S YOUR DAMN MOTHER?
Though if you was to ask folks who was around back then, they're liable to tell ya...
BAD DOG.
That little Monroe Rath died that day too.

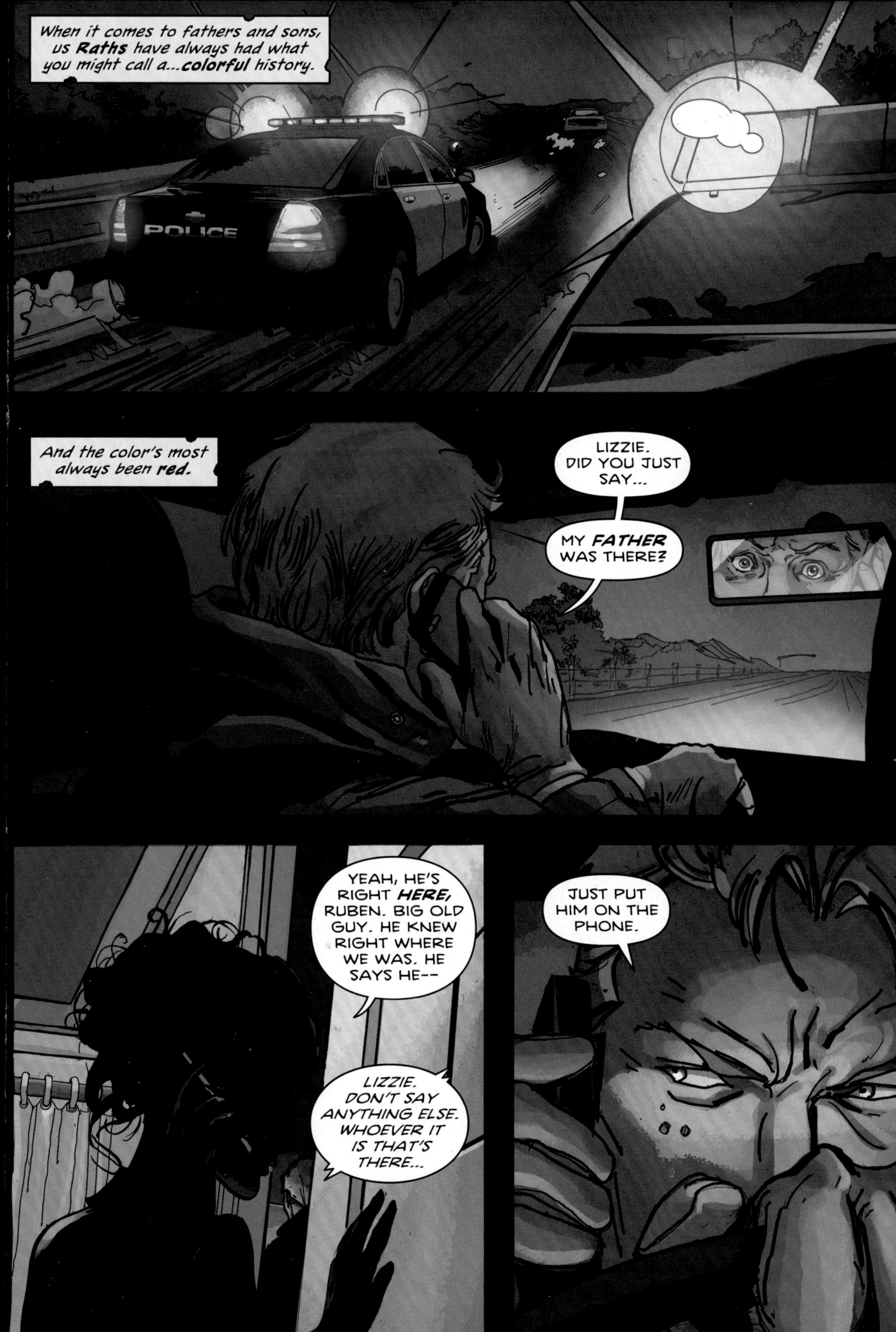
When it comes to fathers and sons, us Raths have always had what you might call a...colorful history.
POLICE
And the color's most always been red.
LIZZIE. DID YOU JUST SAY...
MY FATHER WAS THERE?
YEAH, HE'S RIGHT HERE, RUBEN. BIG OLD GUY. HE KNEW RIGHT WHERE WE WAS. HE SAYS HE--
JUST PUT HIM ON THE PHONE.
LIZZIE. DON'T SAY ANYTHING ELSE. WHOEVER IT IS THAT'S THERE...

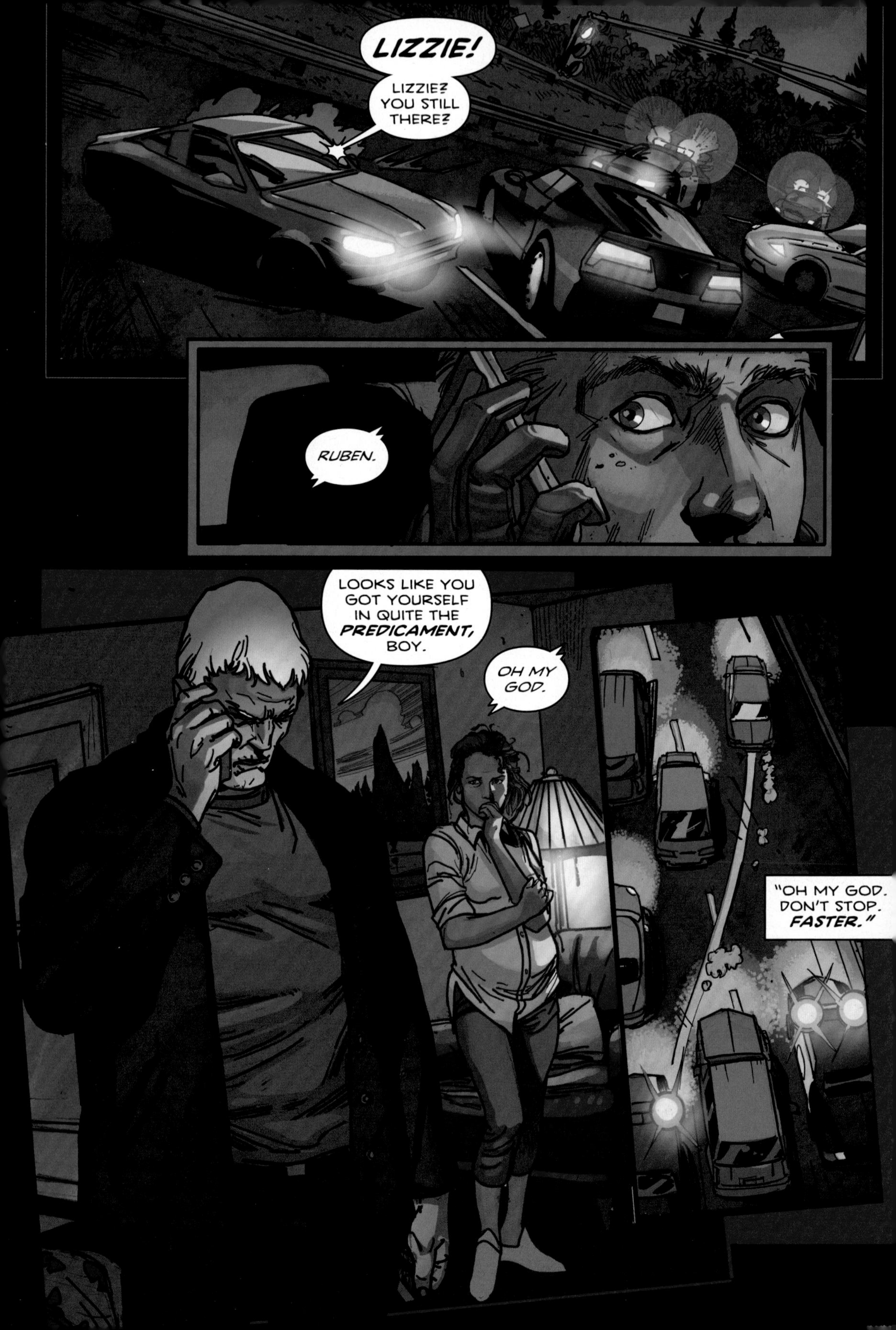
LIZZIE!
LIZZIE? YOU STILL THERE?
RUBEN.
LOOKS LIKE YOU GOT YOURSELF IN QUITE THE PREDICAMENT, BOY.
OH MY GOD.
"OH MY GOD. DON'T STOP. FASTER."

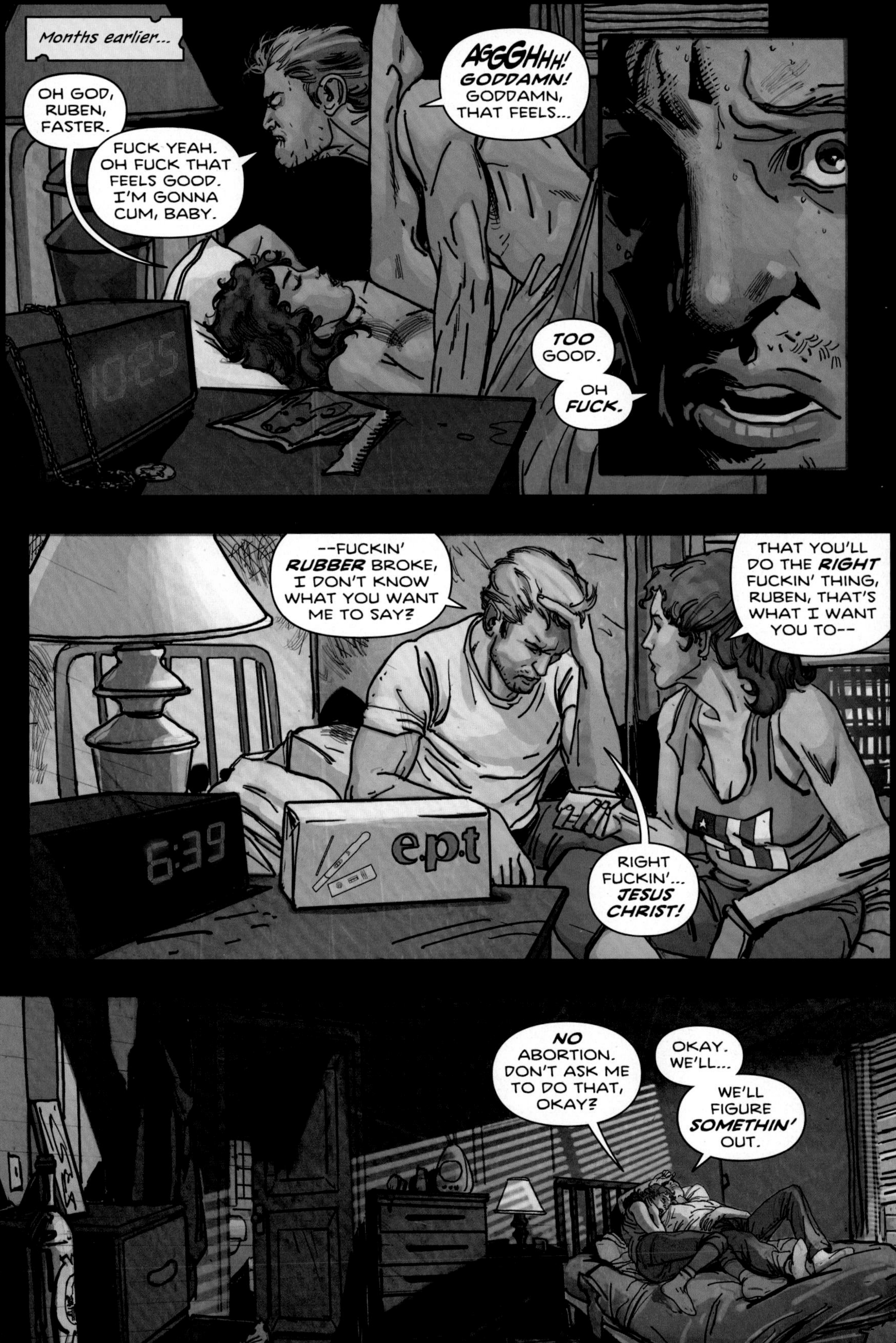
Months earlier...
OH GOD, RUBEN, FASTER.
FUCK YEAH. OH FUCK THAT FEELS GOOD. I'M GONNA CUM, BABY.
AGGGHHH! GODDAMN! GODDAMN, THAT FEELS...
TOO GOOD.
OH FUCK.
--FUCKIN' RUBBER BROKE, I DON'T KNOW WHAT YOU WANT ME TO SAY?
THAT YOU'LL DO THE RIGHT FUCKIN' THING, RUBEN, THAT'S WHAT I WANT YOU TO--
RIGHT FUCKIN'... JESUS CHRIST!
6:39
e.p.t
NO ABORTION. DON'T ASK ME TO DO THAT, OKAY?
OKAY. WE'LL...
WE'LL FIGURE SOMETHIN' OUT.

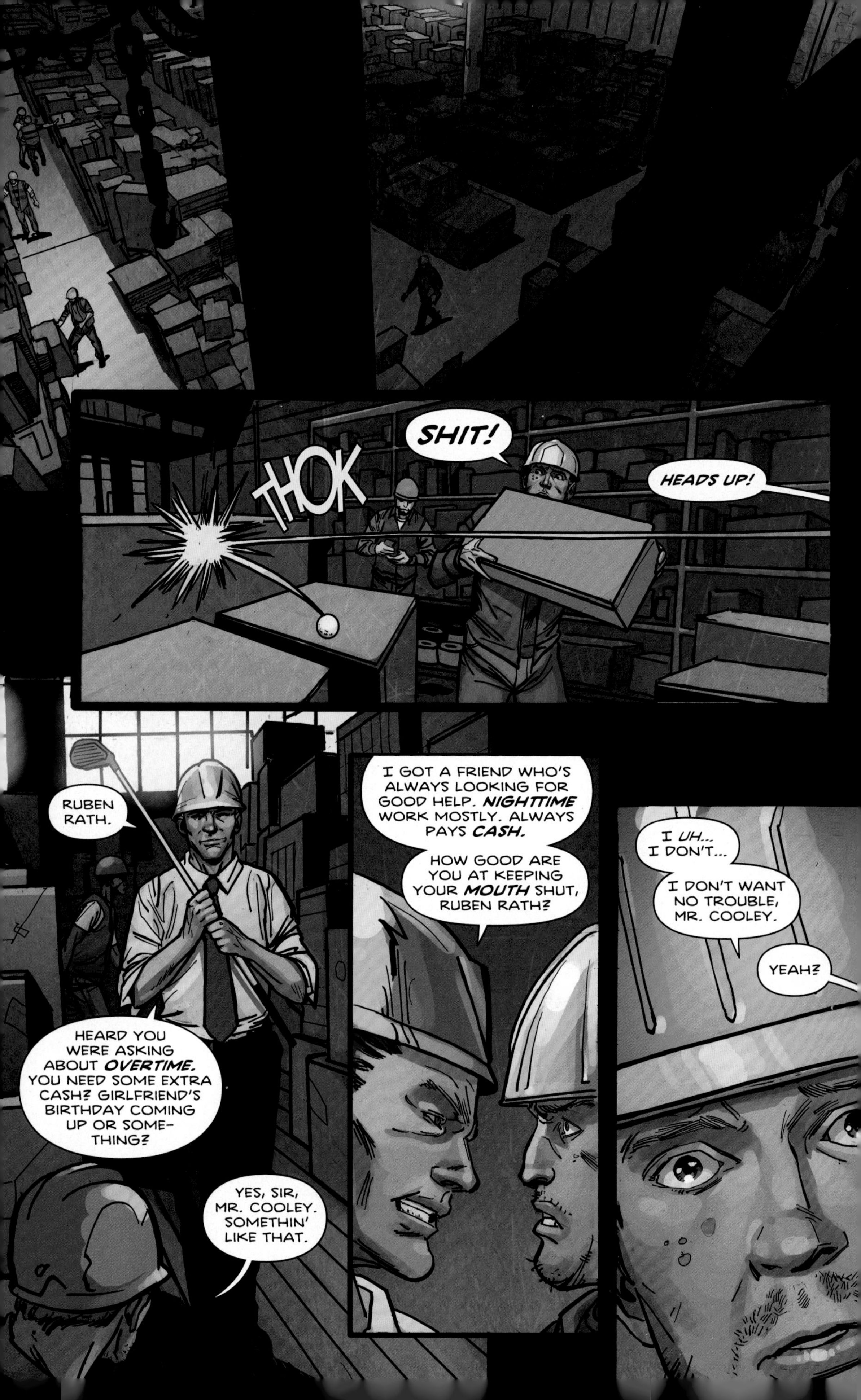
SHIT!
THOK
HEADS UP!
RUBEN RATH.
HEARD YOU WERE ASKING ABOUT OVERTIME. YOU NEED SOME EXTRA CASH? GIRLFRIEND'S BIRTHDAY COMING UP OR SOME-THING?
YES, SIR, MR. COOLEY. SOMETHIN' LIKE THAT.
I GOT A FRIEND WHO'S ALWAYS LOOKING FOR GOOD HELP. NIGHTTIME WORK MOSTLY. ALWAYS PAYS CASH.
HOW GOOD ARE YOU AT KEEPING YOUR MOUTH SHUT, RUBEN RATH?
I UH... I DON'T...
I DON'T WANT NO TROUBLE, MR. COOLEY.
YEAH?

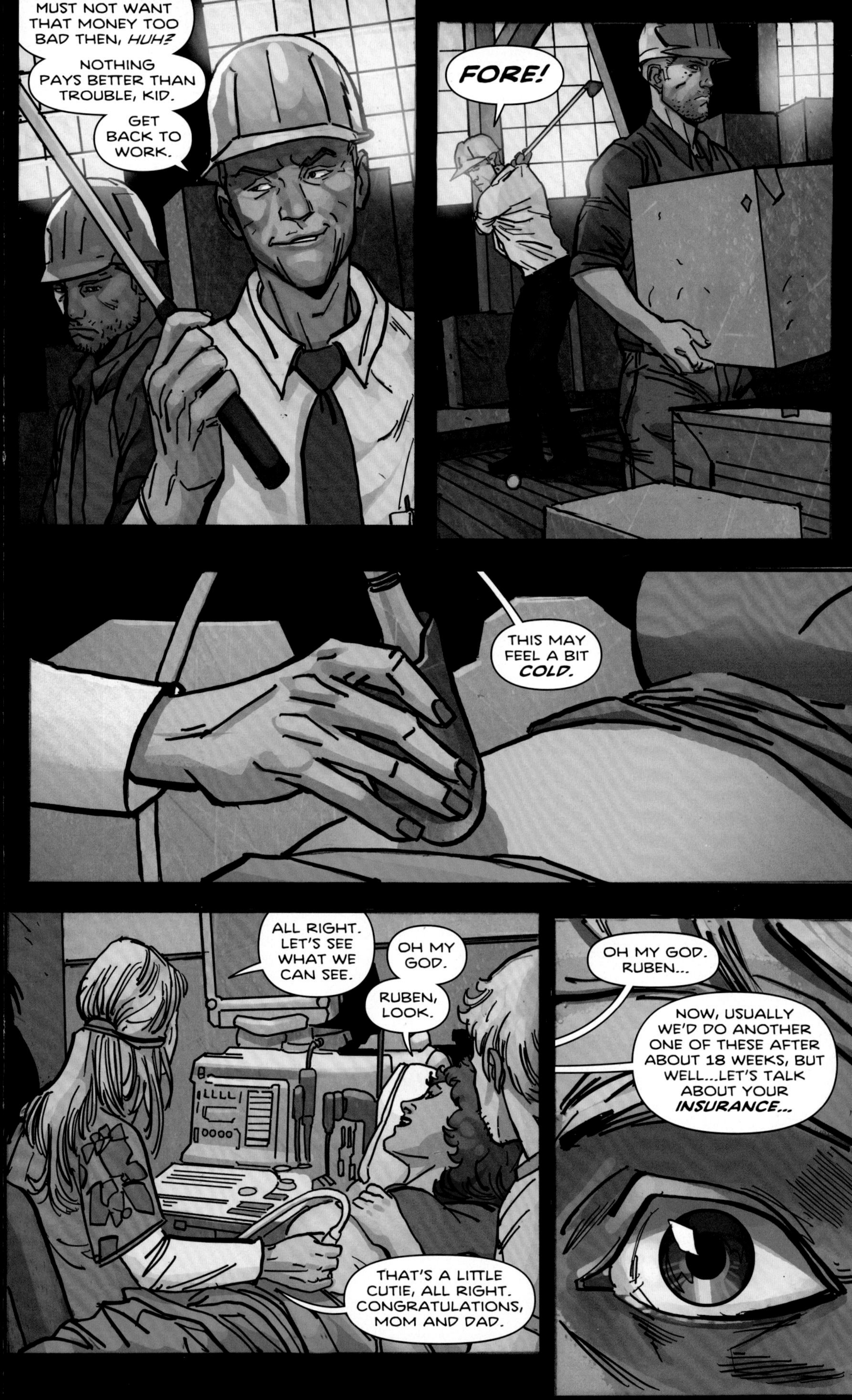
MUST NOT WANT THAT MONEY TOO BAD THEN, HUH?
NOTHING PAYS BETTER THAN TROUBLE, KID.
GET BACK TO WORK.
FORE!
THIS MAY FEEL A BIT COLD.
ALL RIGHT. LET'S SEE WHAT WE CAN SEE.
OH MY GOD.
RUBEN, LOOK.
THAT'S A LITTLE CUTIE, ALL RIGHT. CONGRATULATIONS, MOM AND DAD.
OH MY GOD. RUBEN...
NOW, USUALLY WE'D DO ANOTHER ONE OF THESE AFTER ABOUT 18 WEEKS, BUT WELL...LET'S TALK ABOUT YOUR INSURANCE...

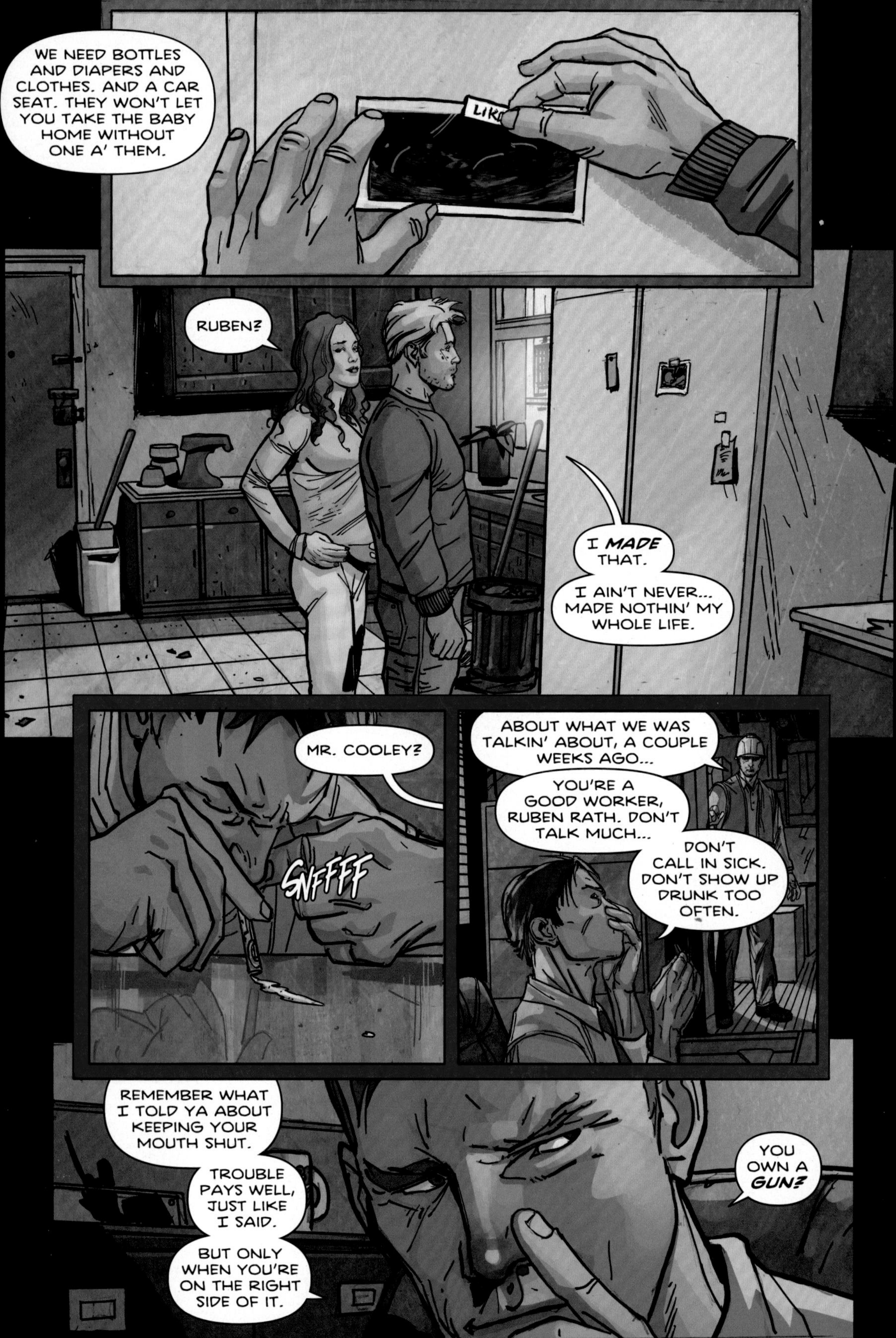

WE NEED BOTTLES AND DIAPERS AND CLOTHES. AND A CAR SEAT. THEY WON'T LET YOU TAKE THE BABY HOME WITHOUT ONE A' THEM.
RUBEN?
I *MADE* THAT.
I AIN'T NEVER... MADE NOTHIN' MY WHOLE LIFE.
MR. COOLEY?
SNFFFF
ABOUT WHAT WE WAS TALKIN' ABOUT, A COUPLE WEEKS AGO...
YOU'RE A GOOD WORKER, RUBEN RATH. DON'T TALK MUCH...
DON'T CALL IN SICK. DON'T SHOW UP DRUNK TOO OFTEN.
REMEMBER WHAT I TOLD YA ABOUT KEEPING YOUR MOUTH SHUT.
TROUBLE PAYS WELL, JUST LIKE I SAID.
BUT ONLY WHEN YOU'RE ON THE RIGHT SIDE OF IT.
YOU OWN A *GUN?*

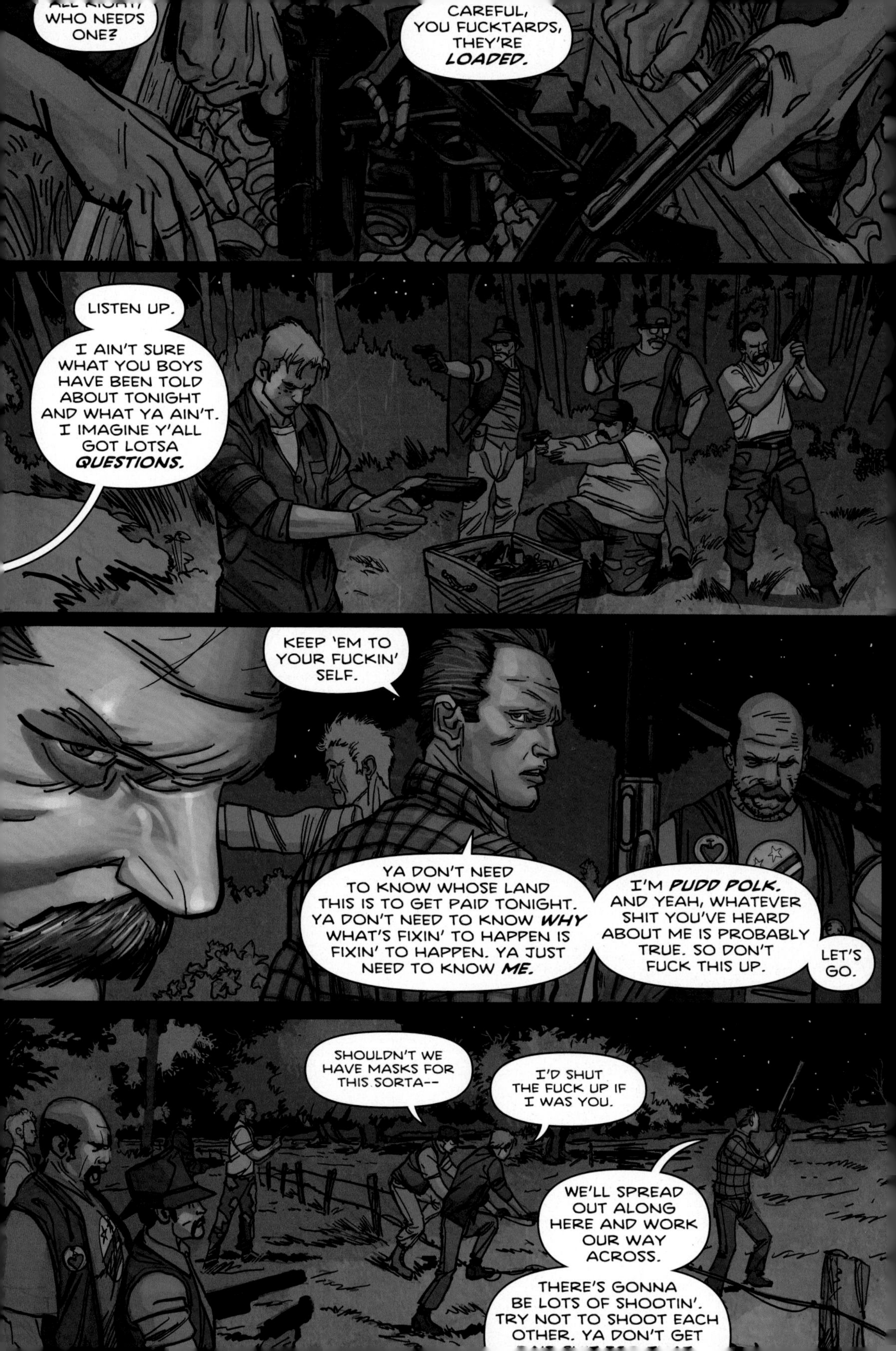
WHO NEEDS ONE?
CAREFUL, YOU FUCKTARDS, THEY'RE *LOADED.*
LISTEN UP.
I AIN'T SURE WHAT YOU BOYS HAVE BEEN TOLD ABOUT TONIGHT AND WHAT YA AIN'T. I IMAGINE Y'ALL GOT LOTSA *QUESTIONS.*
KEEP 'EM TO YOUR FUCKIN' SELF.
YA DON'T NEED TO KNOW WHOSE LAND THIS IS TO GET PAID TONIGHT. YA DON'T NEED TO KNOW *WHY* WHAT'S FIXIN' TO HAPPEN IS FIXIN' TO HAPPEN. YA JUST NEED TO KNOW *ME.*
I'M *PUDD POLK.* AND YEAH, WHATEVER SHIT YOU'VE HEARD ABOUT ME IS PROBABLY TRUE. SO DON'T FUCK THIS UP.
LET'S GO.
SHOULDN'T WE HAVE MASKS FOR THIS SORTA--
I'D SHUT THE FUCK UP IF I WAS YOU.
WE'LL SPREAD OUT ALONG HERE AND WORK OUR WAY ACROSS.
THERE'S GONNA BE LOTS OF SHOOTIN'. TRY NOT TO SHOOT EACH OTHER. YA DON'T GET

YOU GET PAID...FOR SHOOTIN' *THEM.*

FIFTY DOLLARS CASH FOR EVERY HORSE YA KILL.

AND NO ARGUIN' OVER WHO KILLED WHAT. WE'LL CHECK THE FUCKIN' SLUGS IF WE GOT TO.

READY?

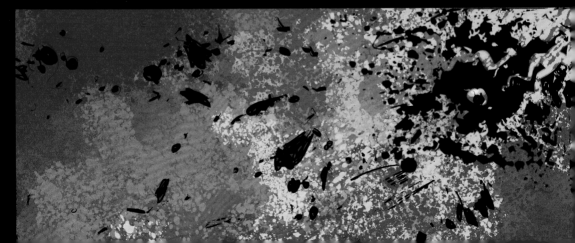

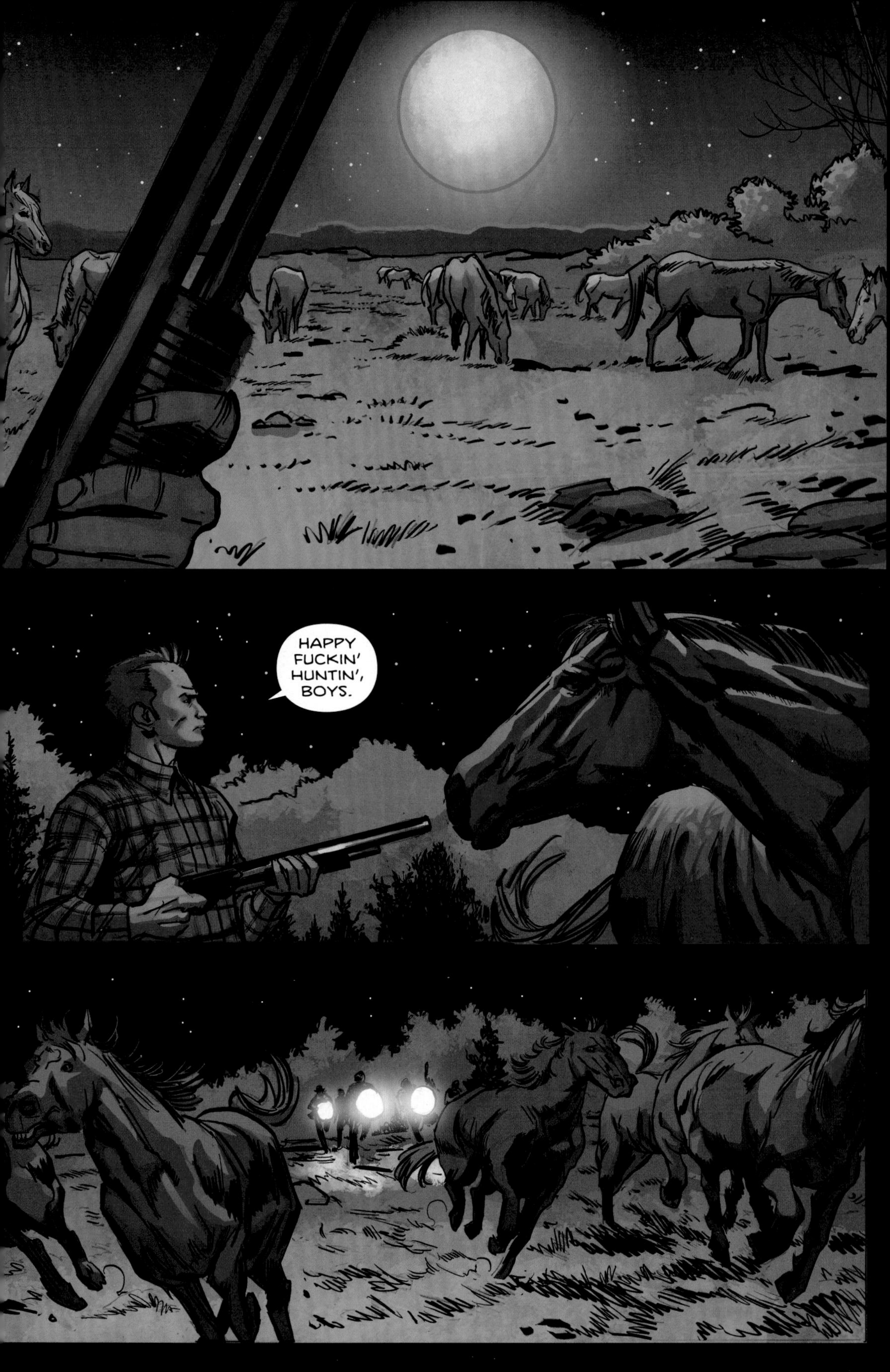
HAPPY FUCKIN' HUNTIN', BOYS.

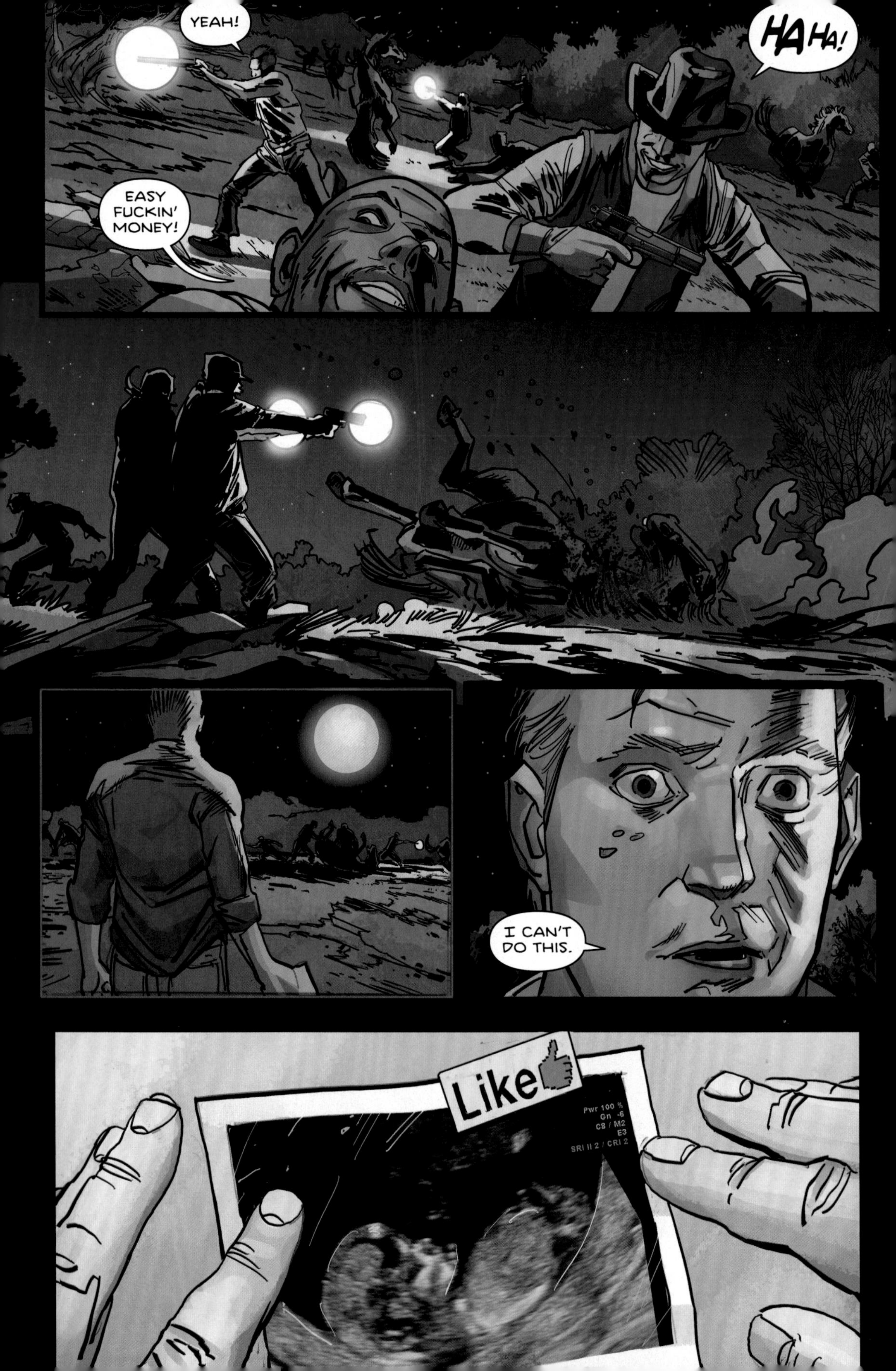
YEAH!
HA HA!
EASY FUCKIN' MONEY!
I CAN'T DO THIS.
Like
Pwr 100 %
Gn -6
C8 / M2
E3
SRI II 2 / CRI 2

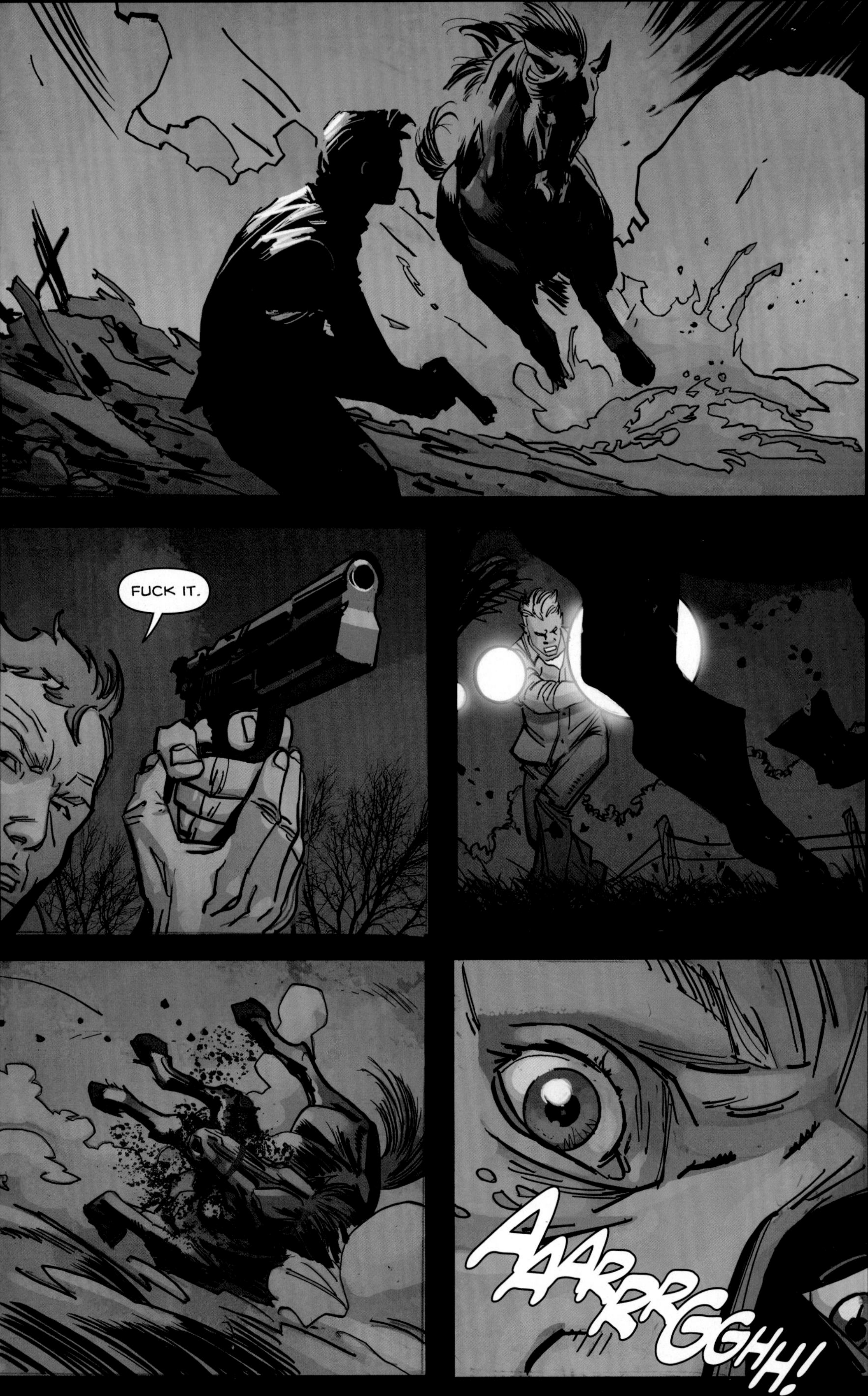
FUCK IT.
AAARRRGGHH!

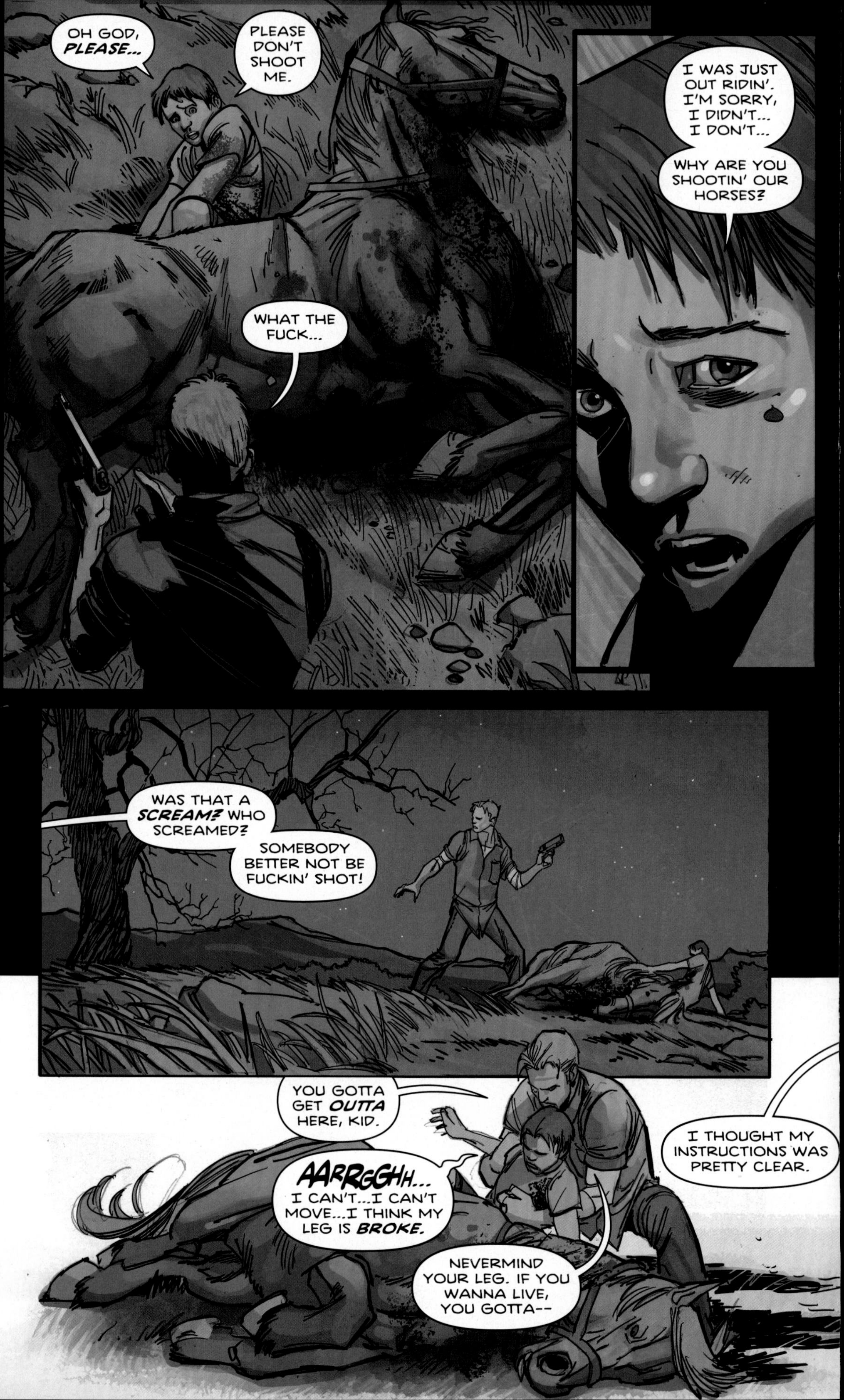
OH GOD, PLEASE...
PLEASE DON'T SHOOT ME.
WHAT THE FUCK...
I WAS JUST OUT RIDIN'. I'M SORRY, I DIDN'T... I DON'T...
WHY ARE YOU SHOOTIN' OUR HORSES?
WAS THAT A SCREAM? WHO SCREAMED?
SOMEBODY BETTER NOT BE FUCKIN' SHOT!
YOU GOTTA GET OUTTA HERE, KID.
AARRGGHH... I CAN'T...I CAN'T MOVE...I THINK MY LEG IS BROKE.
NEVERMIND YOUR LEG. IF YOU WANNA LIVE, YOU GOTTA--
I THOUGHT MY INSTRUCTIONS WAS PRETTY CLEAR.

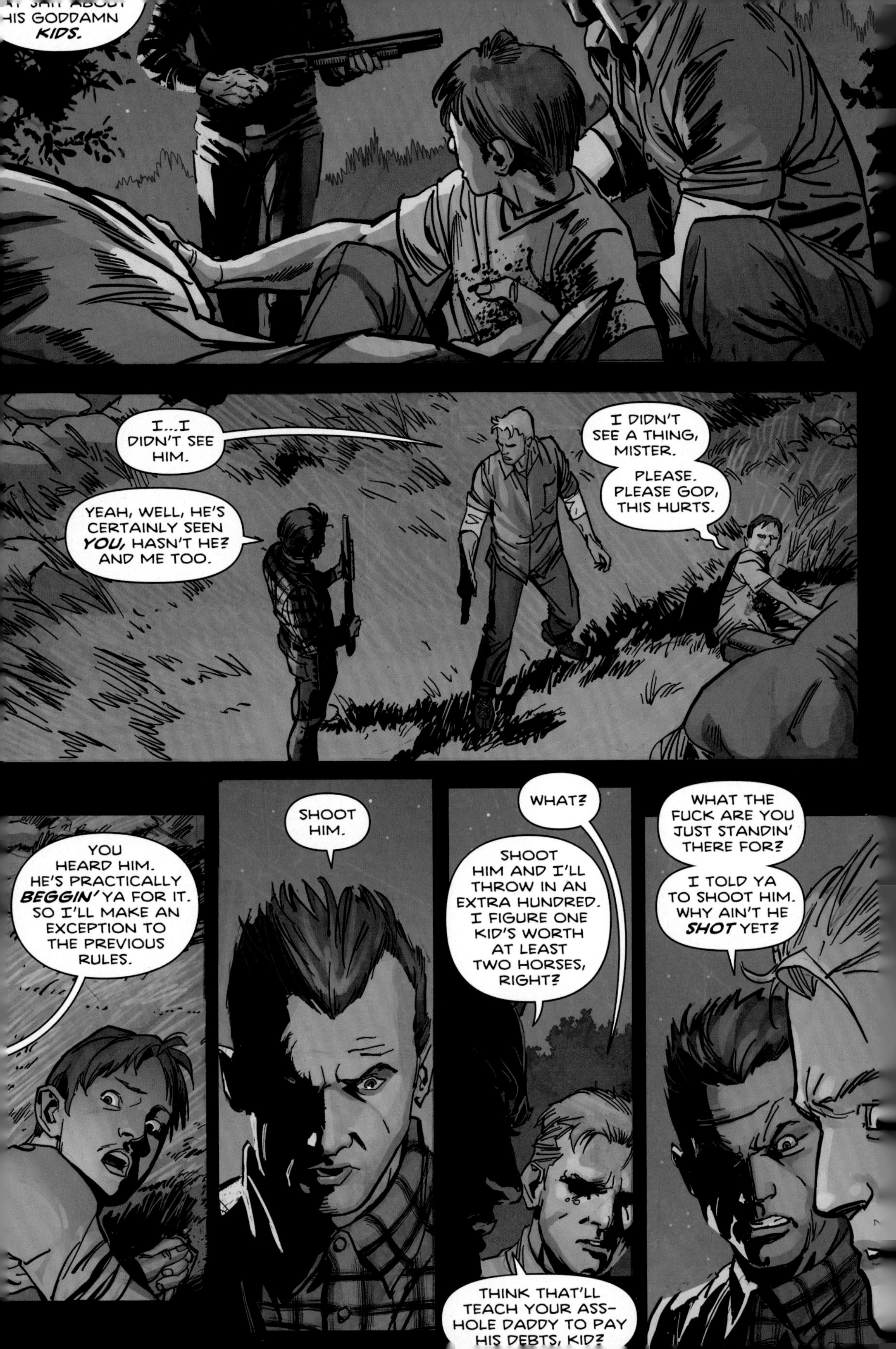
HIS GODDAMN KIDS.
I...I DIDN'T SEE HIM.
YEAH, WELL, HE'S CERTAINLY SEEN YOU, HASN'T HE? AND ME TOO.
I DIDN'T SEE A THING, MISTER.
PLEASE. PLEASE GOD, THIS HURTS.
YOU HEARD HIM. HE'S PRACTICALLY BEGGIN' YA FOR IT. SO I'LL MAKE AN EXCEPTION TO THE PREVIOUS RULES.
SHOOT HIM.
WHAT?
SHOOT HIM AND I'LL THROW IN AN EXTRA HUNDRED. I FIGURE ONE KID'S WORTH AT LEAST TWO HORSES, RIGHT?
THINK THAT'LL TEACH YOUR ASS-HOLE DADDY TO PAY HIS DEBTS, KID?
WHAT THE FUCK ARE YOU JUST STANDIN' THERE FOR?
I TOLD YA TO SHOOT HIM. WHY AIN'T HE SHOT YET?

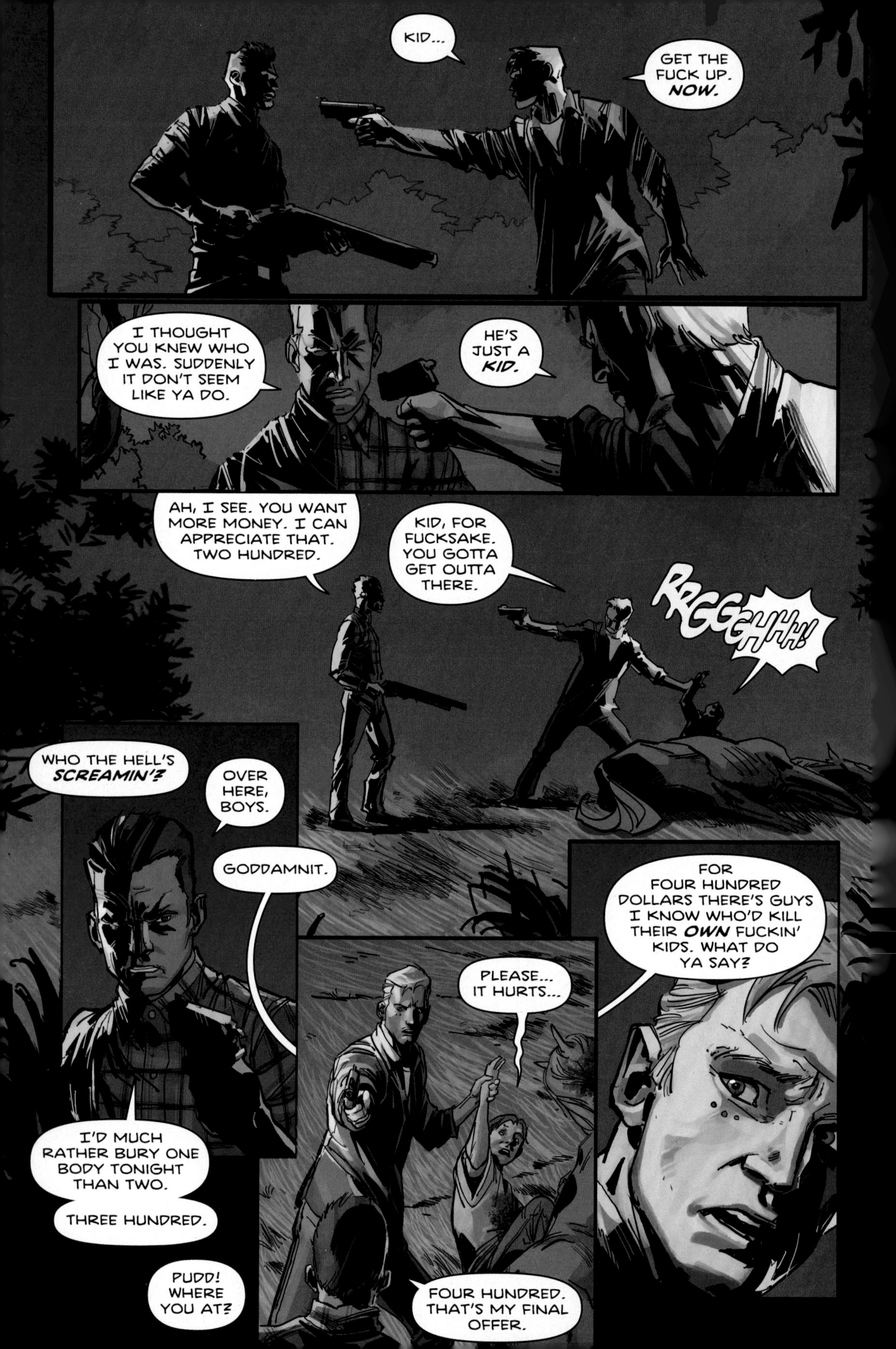
KID...
GET THE FUCK UP. NOW.
I THOUGHT YOU KNEW WHO I WAS. SUDDENLY IT DON'T SEEM LIKE YA DO.
HE'S JUST A KID.
AH, I SEE. YOU WANT MORE MONEY. I CAN APPRECIATE THAT. TWO HUNDRED.
KID, FOR FUCKSAKE. YOU GOTTA GET OUTTA THERE.
RRGGGHHH!
WHO THE HELL'S SCREAMIN'?
OVER HERE, BOYS.
GODDAMNIT.
I'D MUCH RATHER BURY ONE BODY TONIGHT THAN TWO.
THREE HUNDRED.
PUDD! WHERE YOU AT?
PLEASE... IT HURTS...
FOUR HUNDRED. THAT'S MY FINAL OFFER.
FOR FOUR HUNDRED DOLLARS THERE'S GUYS I KNOW WHO'D KILL THEIR OWN FUCKIN' KIDS. WHAT DO YA SAY?

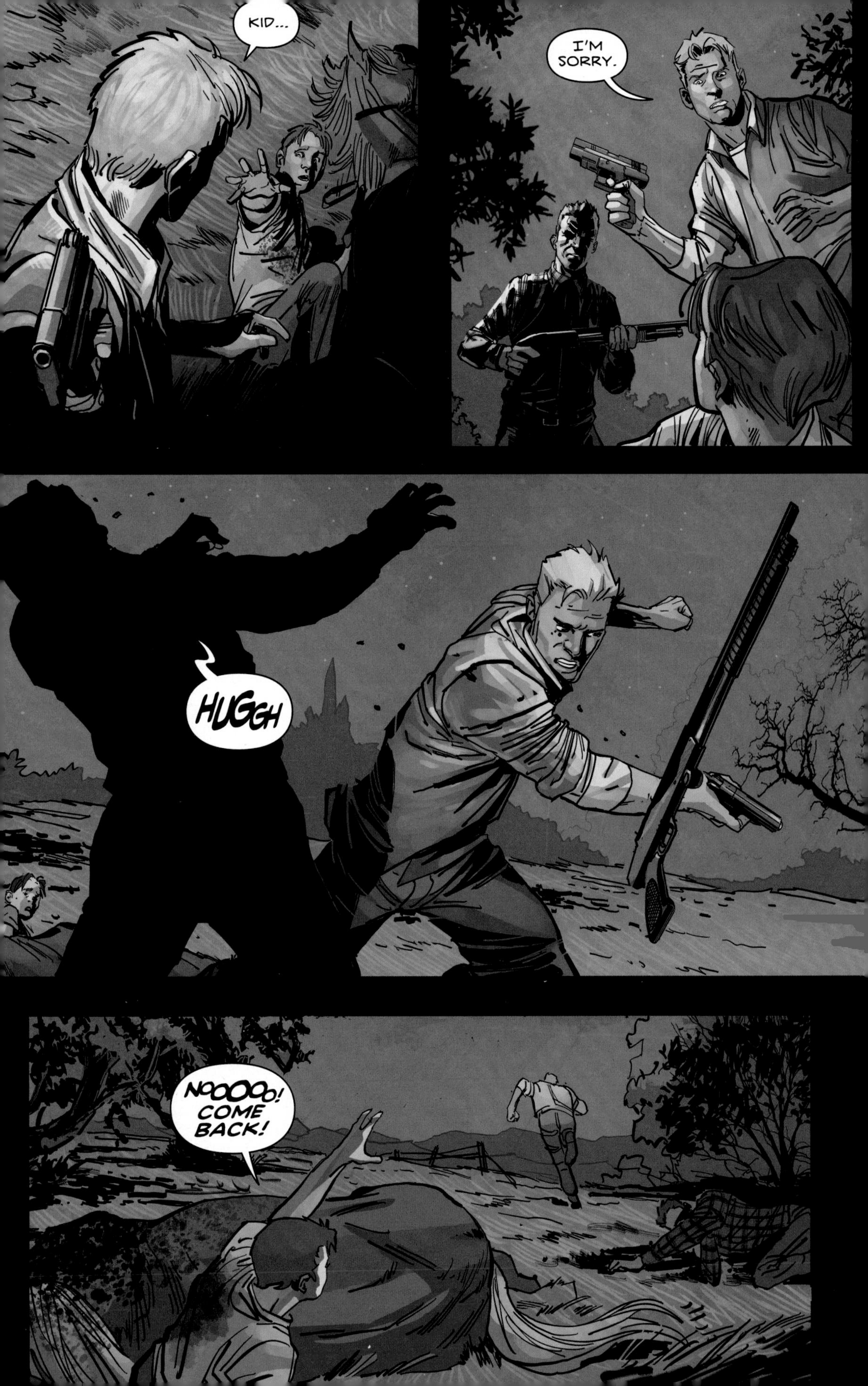
KID...
I'M SORRY.
HUGGH
NOOOOO! COME BACK!

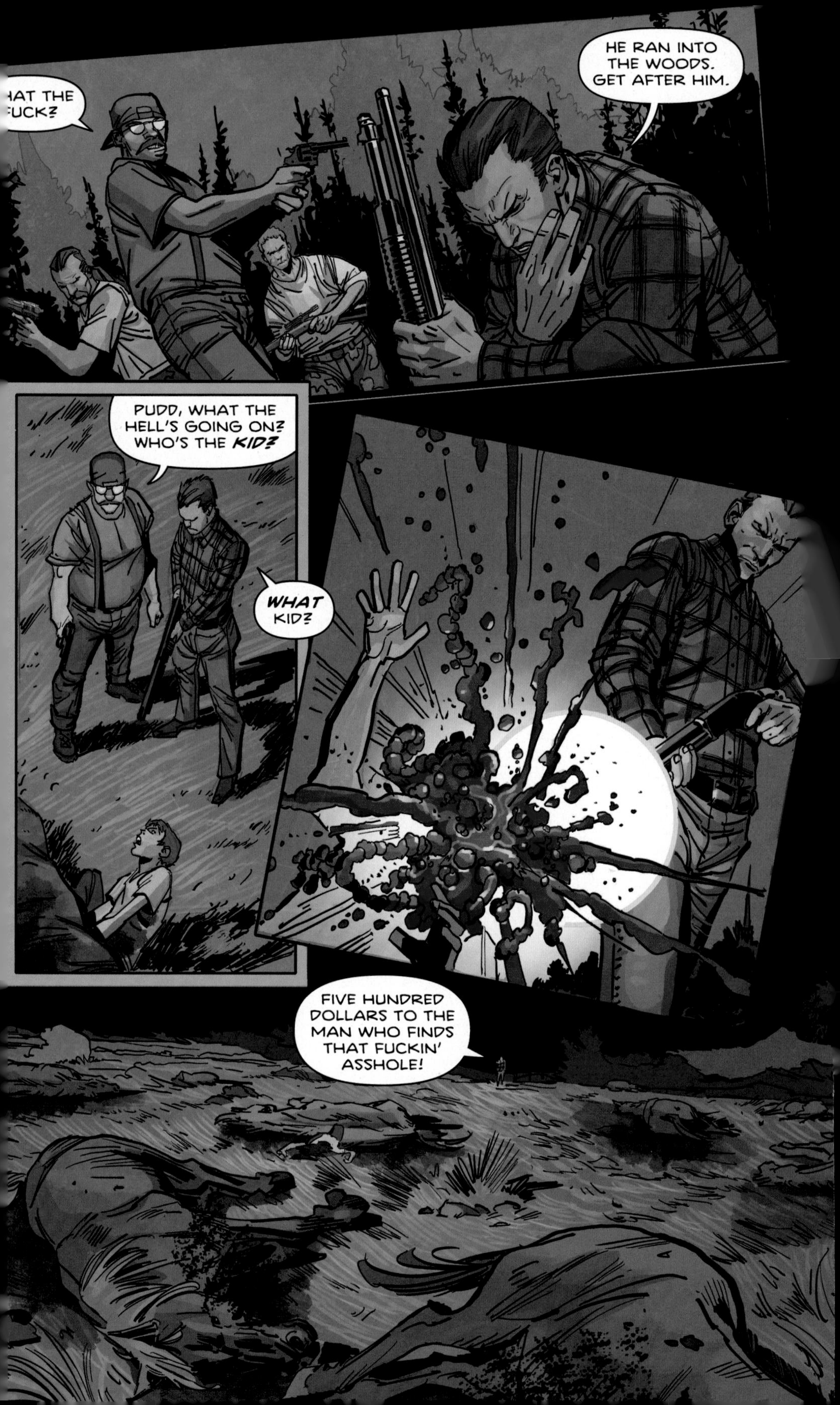
HAT THE FUCK?
HE RAN INTO THE WOODS. GET AFTER HIM.
PUDD, WHAT THE HELL'S GOING ON? WHO'S THE KID?
WHAT KID?
FIVE HUNDRED DOLLARS TO THE MAN WHO FINDS THAT FUCKIN' ASSHOLE!

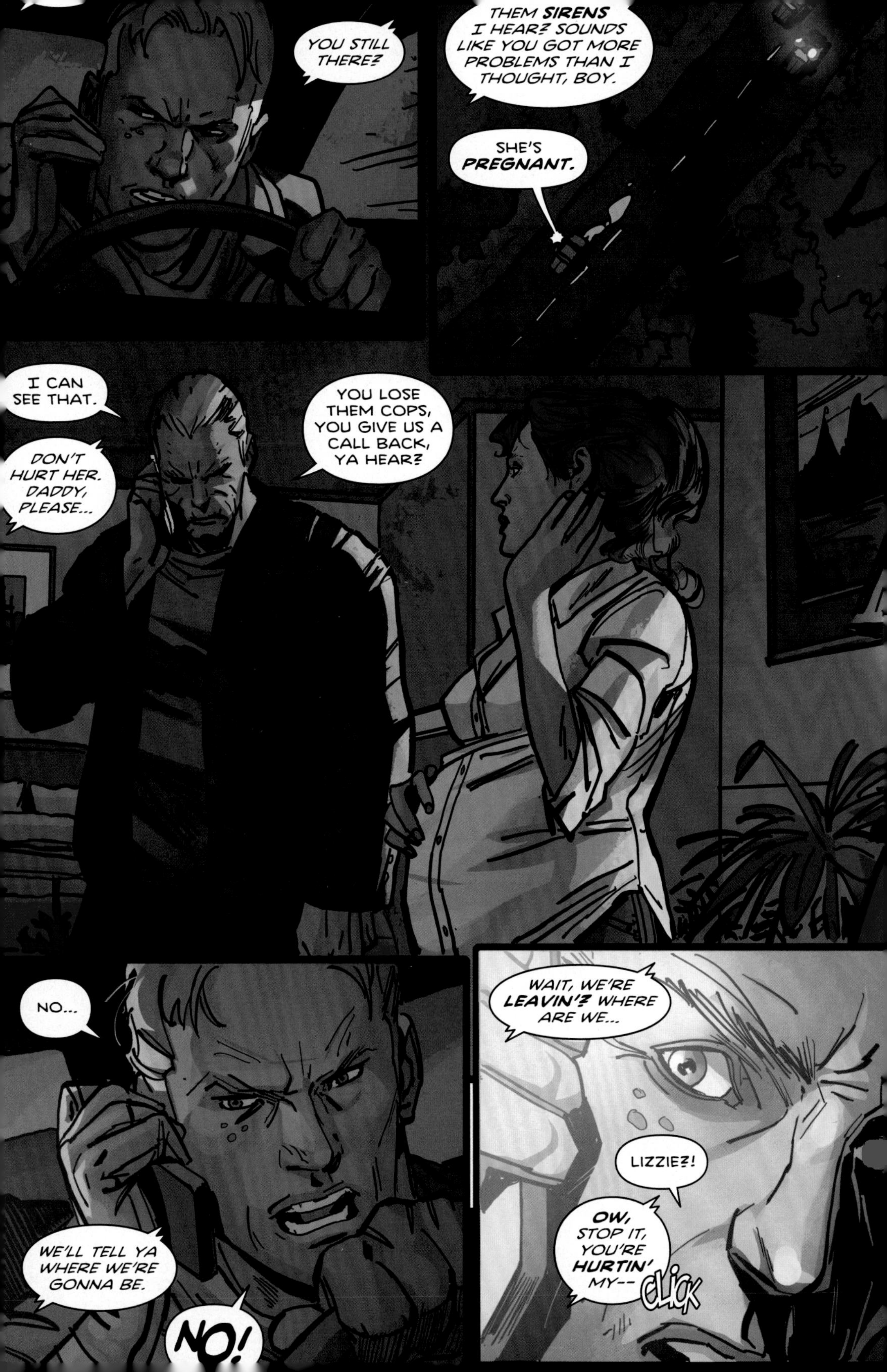
YOU STILL THERE?
THEM SIRENS I HEAR? SOUNDS LIKE YOU GOT MORE PROBLEMS THAN I THOUGHT, BOY.
SHE'S PREGNANT.
I CAN SEE THAT.
DON'T HURT HER. DADDY, PLEASE...
YOU LOSE THEM COPS, YOU GIVE US A CALL BACK, YA HEAR?
NO...
WE'LL TELL YA WHERE WE'RE GONNA BE.
NO!
WAIT, WE'RE LEAVIN'? WHERE ARE WE...
LIZZIE?!
OW, STOP IT, YOU'RE HURTIN' MY--
CLICK

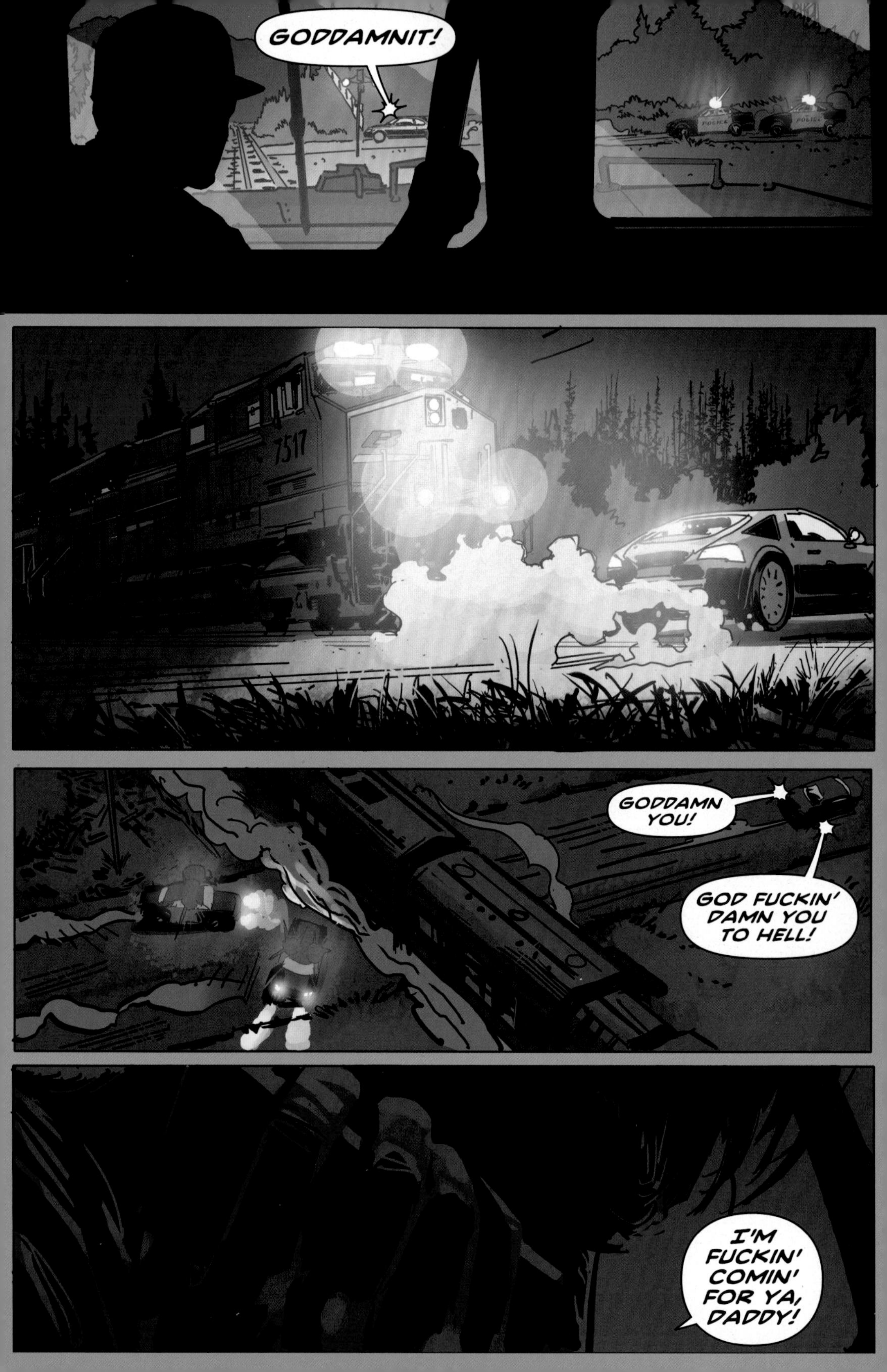
GODDAMNIT!
POLICE
POLICE
7517
GODDAMN YOU!
GOD FUCKIN' DAMN YOU TO HELL!
I'M FUCKIN' COMIN' FOR YA, DADDY!

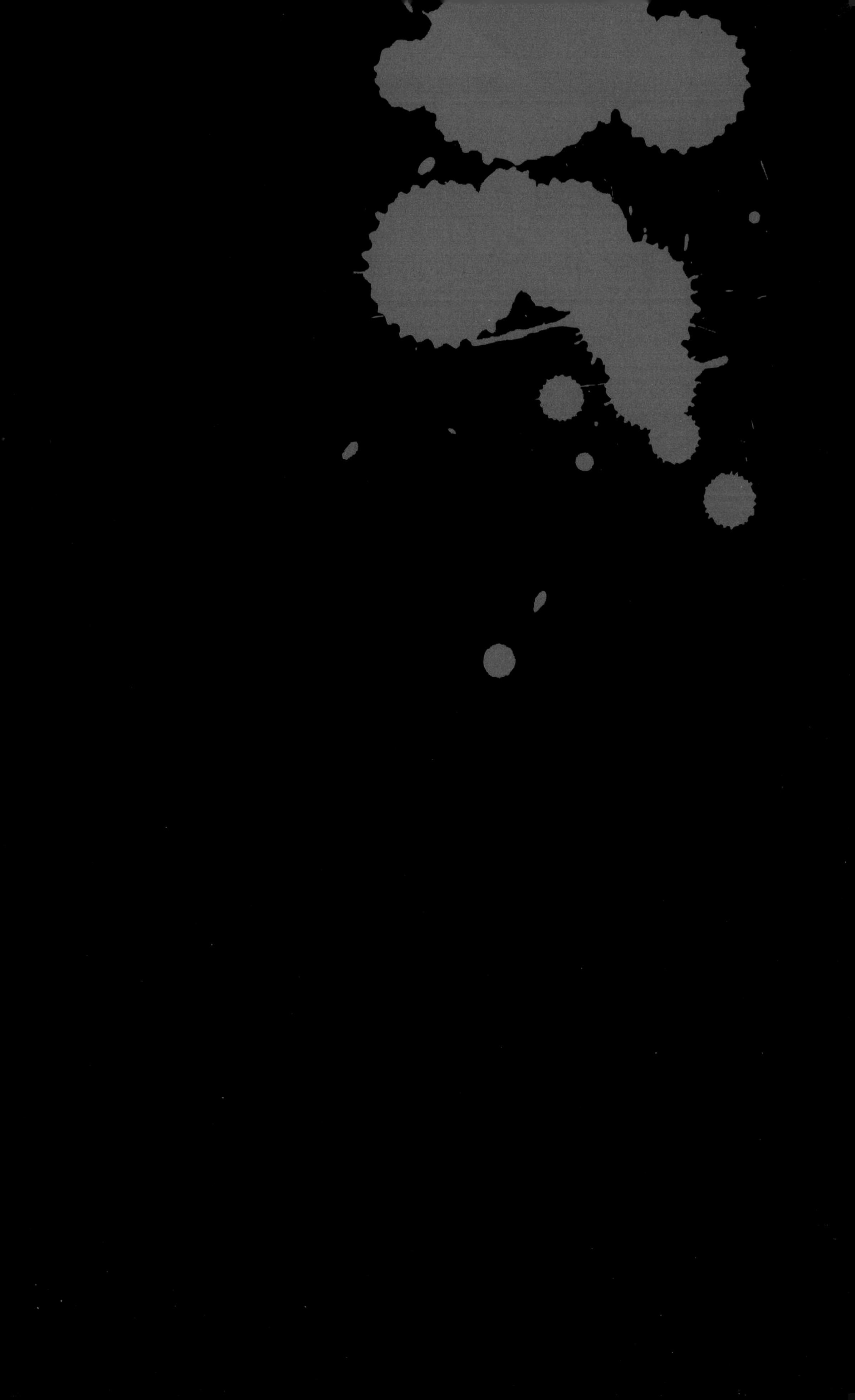

CHAPTER THREE

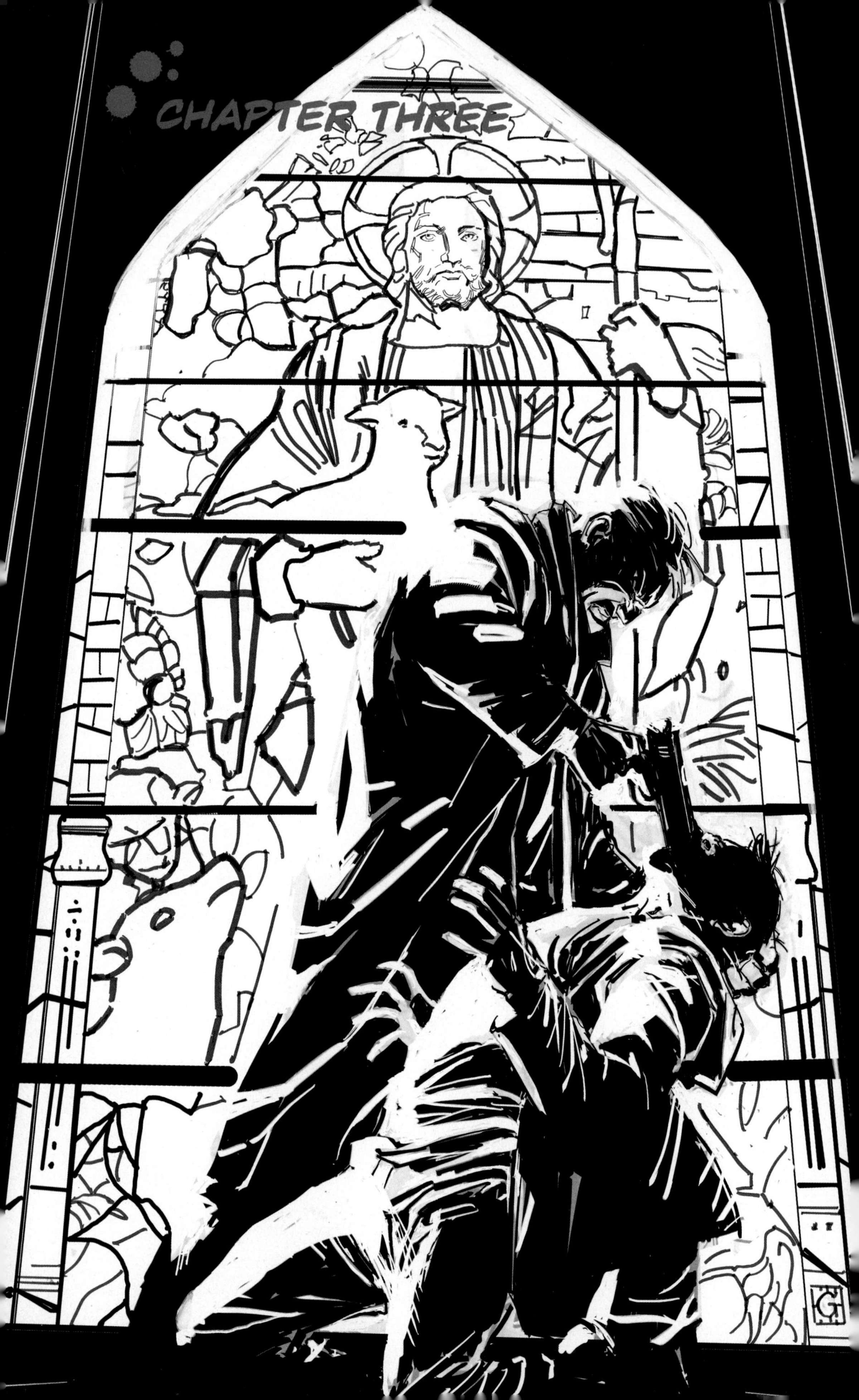

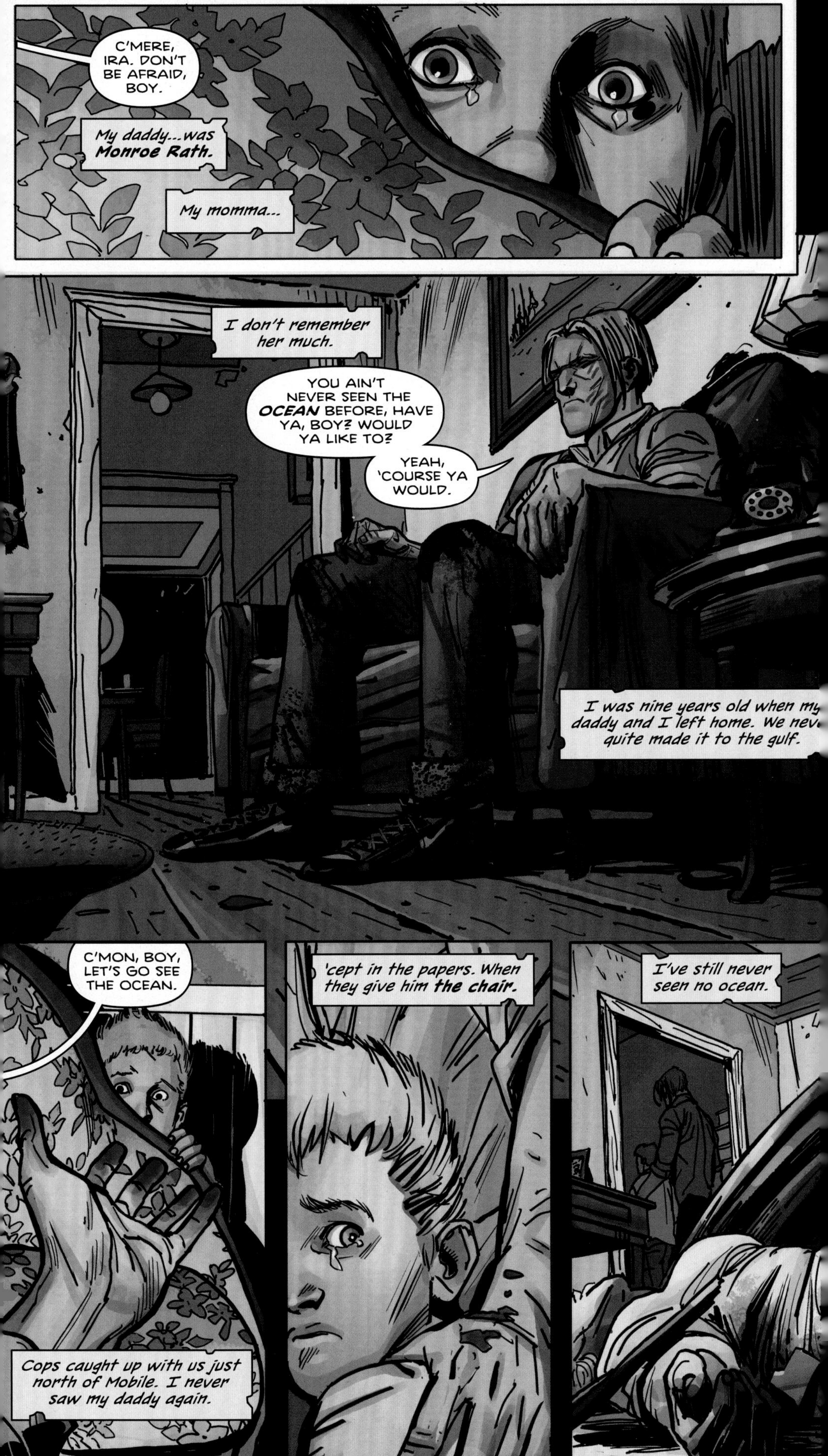
C'MERE, IRA. DON'T BE AFRAID, BOY.
My daddy...was Monroe Rath.
My momma...
I don't remember her much.
YOU AIN'T NEVER SEEN THE OCEAN BEFORE, HAVE YA, BOY? WOULD YA LIKE TO?
YEAH, 'COURSE YA WOULD.
I was nine years old when my daddy and I left home. We neve quite made it to the gulf.
C'MON, BOY, LET'S GO SEE THE OCEAN.
Cops caught up with us just north of Mobile. I never saw my daddy again.
'cept in the papers. When they give him the chair.
I've still never seen no ocean.

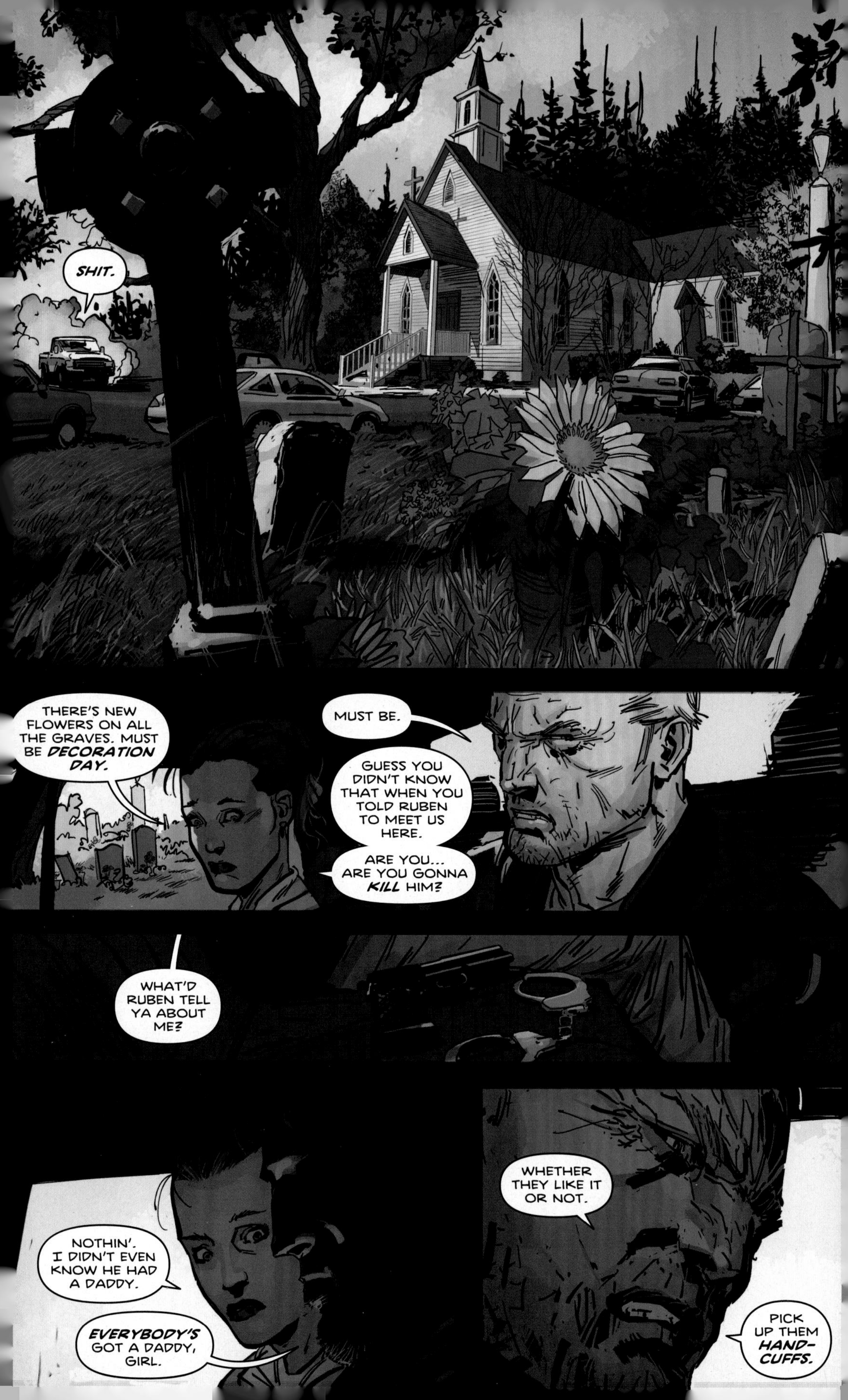
SHIT.
THERE'S NEW FLOWERS ON ALL THE GRAVES. MUST BE *DECORATION DAY.*
MUST BE.
GUESS YOU DIDN'T KNOW THAT WHEN YOU TOLD RUBEN TO MEET US HERE.
ARE YOU... ARE YOU GONNA *KILL* HIM?
WHAT'D RUBEN TELL YA ABOUT ME?
NOTHIN'. I DIDN'T EVEN KNOW HE HAD A DADDY.
EVERYBODY'S GOT A DADDY, GIRL.
WHETHER THEY LIKE IT OR NOT.
PICK UP THEM *HAND-CUFFS.*

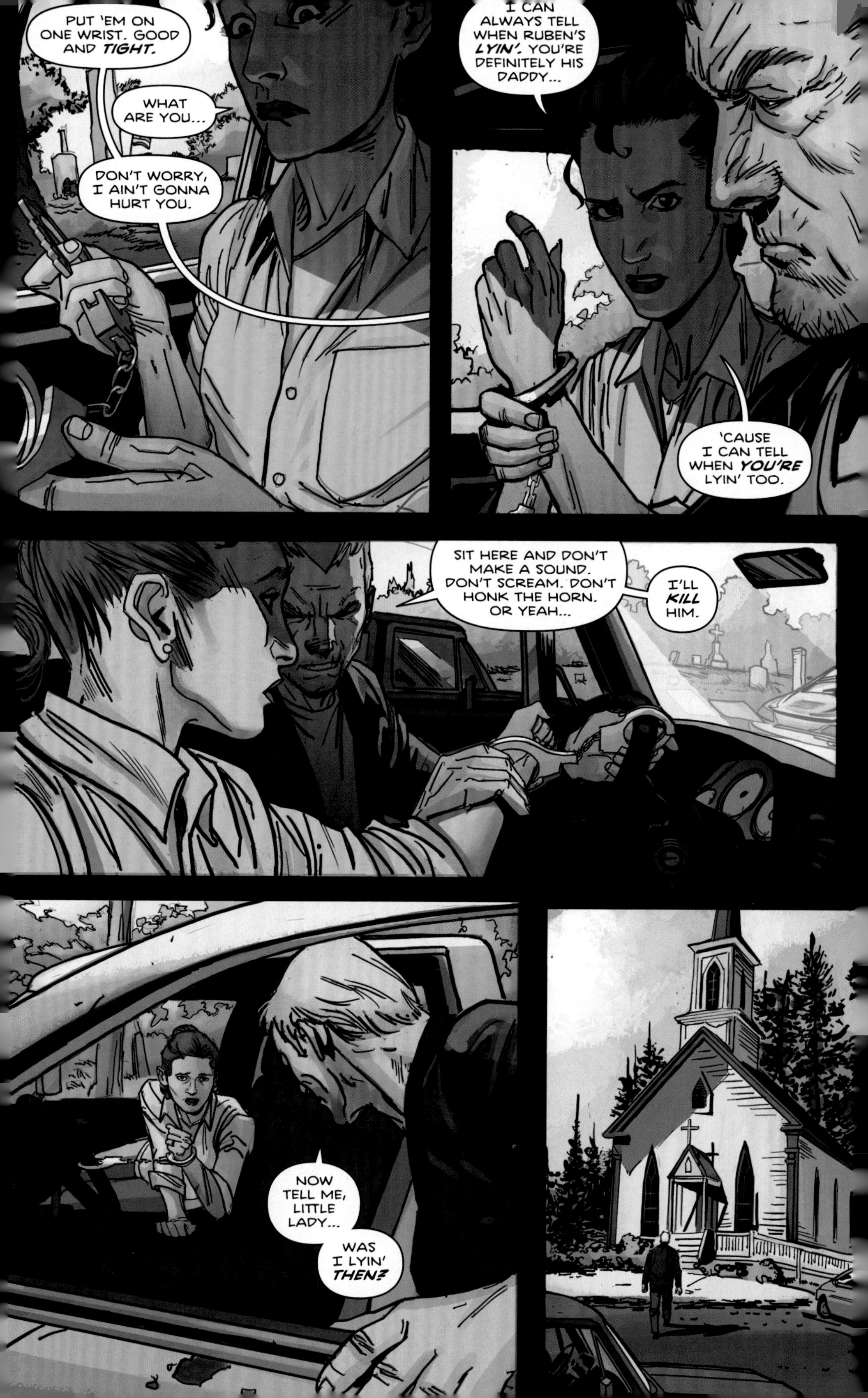
PUT 'EM ON ONE WRIST. GOOD AND TIGHT.
WHAT ARE YOU...
DON'T WORRY, I AIN'T GONNA HURT YOU.
I CAN ALWAYS TELL WHEN RUBEN'S LYIN'. YOU'RE DEFINITELY HIS DADDY...
'CAUSE I CAN TELL WHEN YOU'RE LYIN' TOO.
SIT HERE AND DON'T MAKE A SOUND. DON'T SCREAM. DON'T HONK THE HORN. OR YEAH...
I'LL KILL HIM.
NOW TELL ME, LITTLE LADY...
WAS I LYIN' THEN?

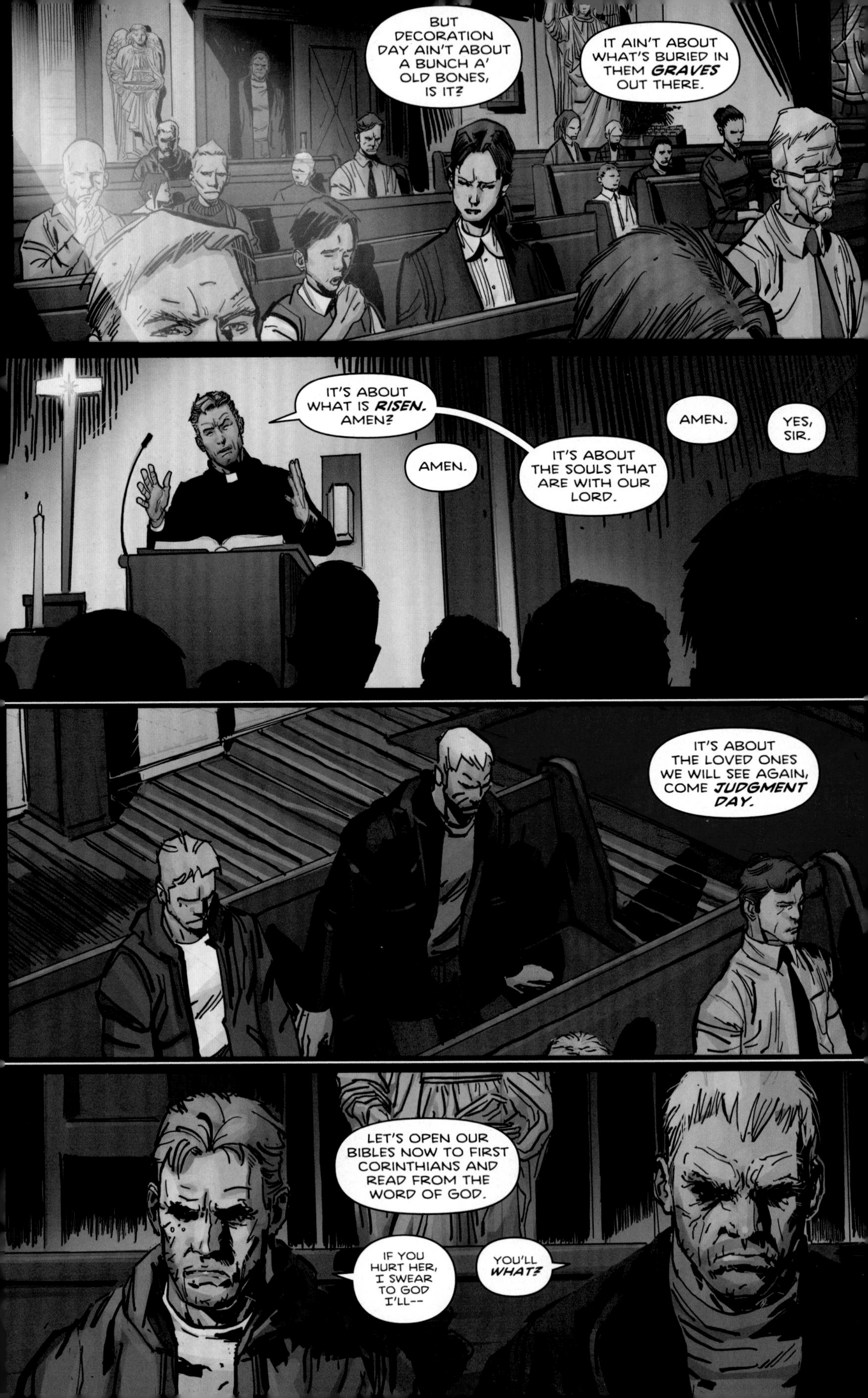
BUT DECORATION DAY AIN'T ABOUT A BUNCH A' OLD BONES, IS IT?
IT AIN'T ABOUT WHAT'S BURIED IN THEM GRAVES OUT THERE.
IT'S ABOUT WHAT IS RISEN. AMEN?
AMEN.
IT'S ABOUT THE SOULS THAT ARE WITH OUR LORD.
AMEN.
YES, SIR.
IT'S ABOUT THE LOVED ONES WE WILL SEE AGAIN, COME JUDGMENT DAY.
LET'S OPEN OUR BIBLES NOW TO FIRST CORINTHIANS AND READ FROM THE WORD OF GOD.
IF YOU HURT HER, I SWEAR TO GOD I'LL--
YOU'LL WHAT?

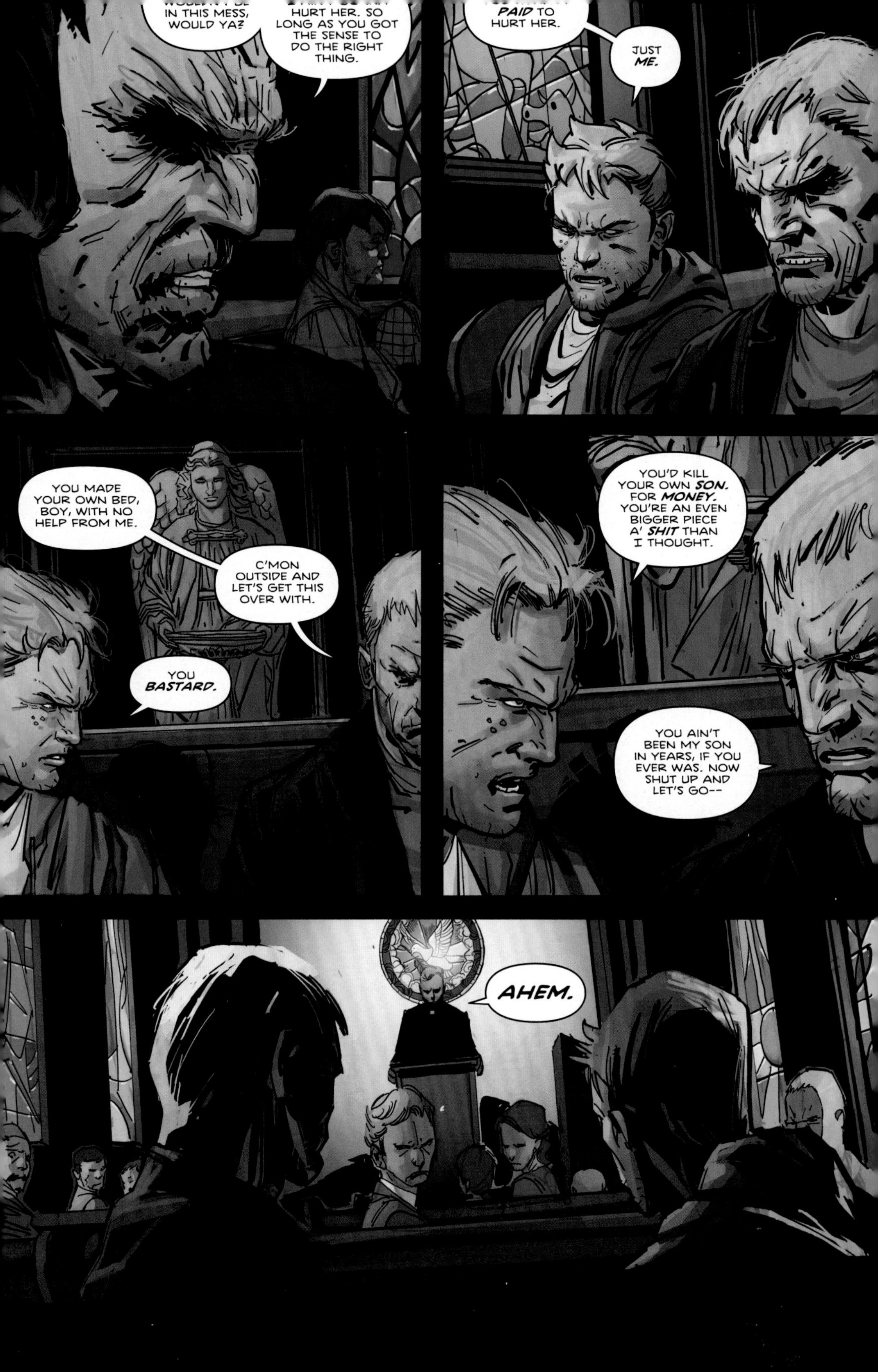
IN THIS MESS, WOULD YA?
HURT HER. SO LONG AS YOU GOT THE SENSE TO DO THE RIGHT THING.
PAID TO HURT HER.
JUST ME.
YOU MADE YOUR OWN BED, BOY, WITH NO HELP FROM ME.
C'MON OUTSIDE AND LET'S GET THIS OVER WITH.
YOU BASTARD.
YOU'D KILL YOUR OWN SON. FOR MONEY. YOU'RE AN EVEN BIGGER PIECE A' SHIT THAN I THOUGHT.
YOU AIN'T BEEN MY SON IN YEARS, IF YOU EVER WAS. NOW SHUT UP AND LET'S GO--
AHEM.

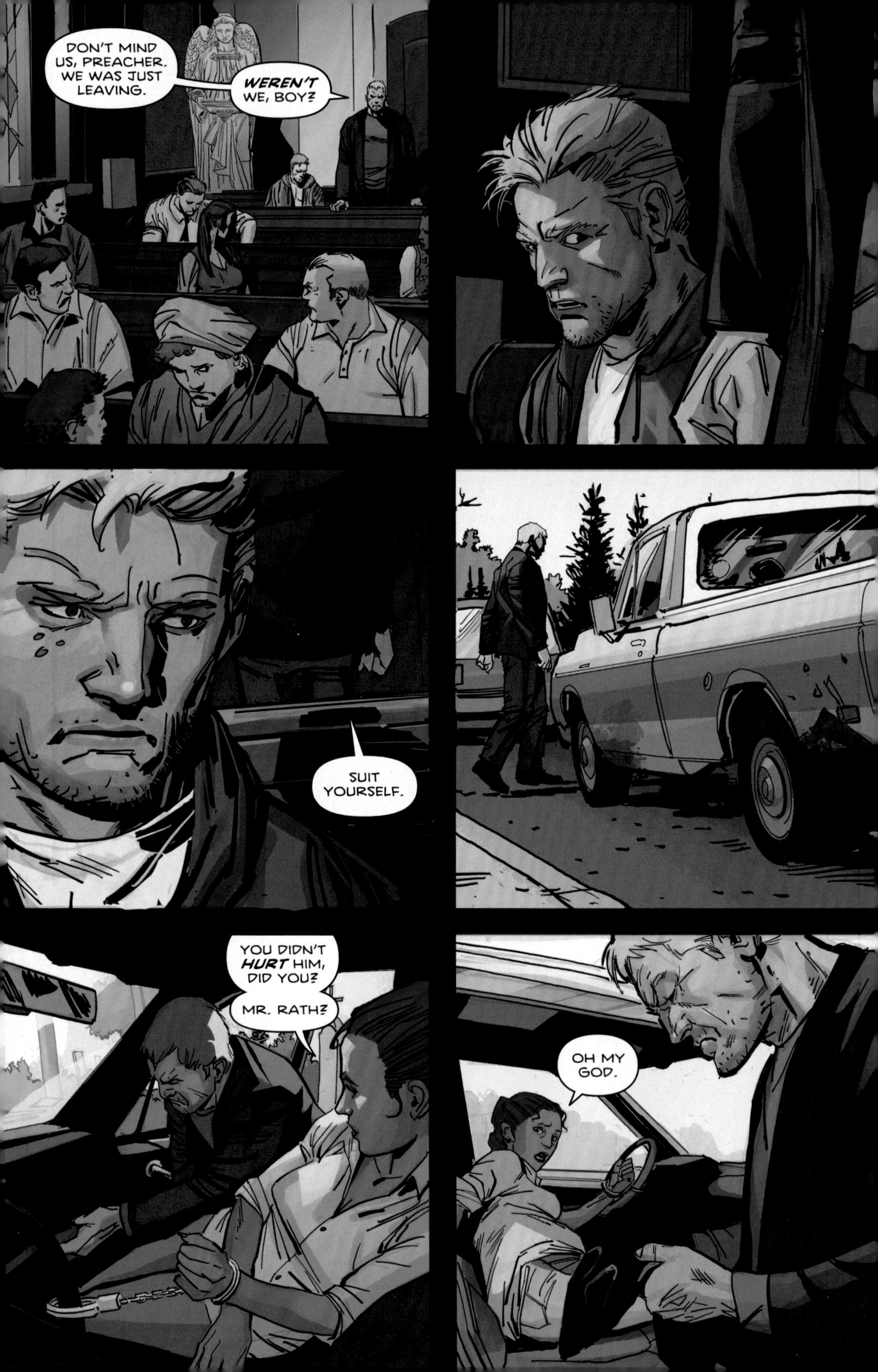
DON'T MIND US, PREACHER. WE WAS JUST LEAVING.
WEREN'T WE, BOY?
SUIT YOURSELF.
YOU DIDN'T HURT HIM, DID YOU?
MR. RATH?
OH MY GOD.

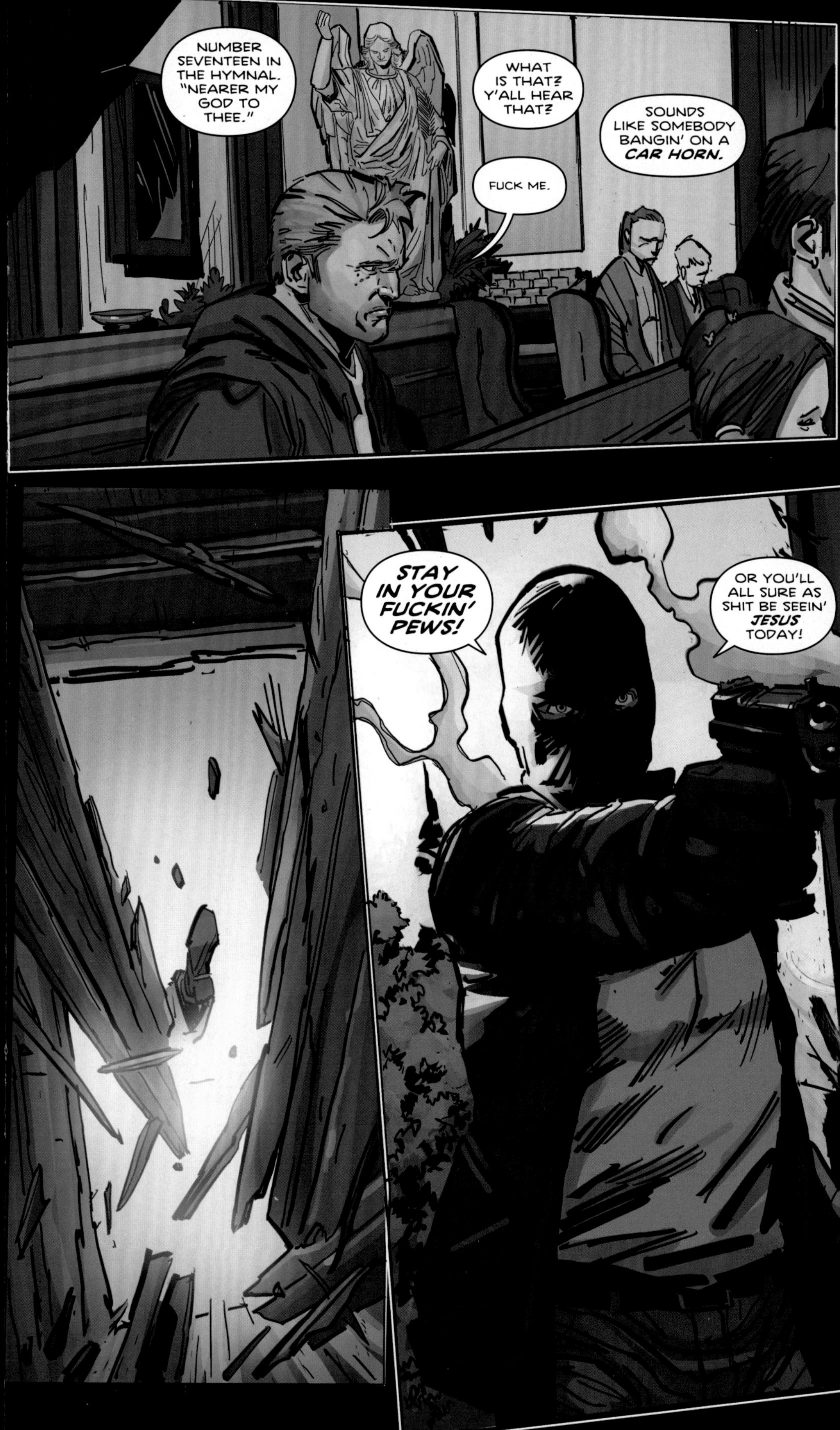
NUMBER SEVENTEEN IN THE HYMNAL. "NEARER MY GOD TO THEE."
WHAT IS THAT? Y'ALL HEAR THAT?
SOUNDS LIKE SOMEBODY BANGIN' ON A CAR HORN.
FUCK ME.
STAY IN YOUR FUCKIN' PEWS!
OR YOU'LL ALL SURE AS SHIT BE SEEIN' JESUS TODAY!

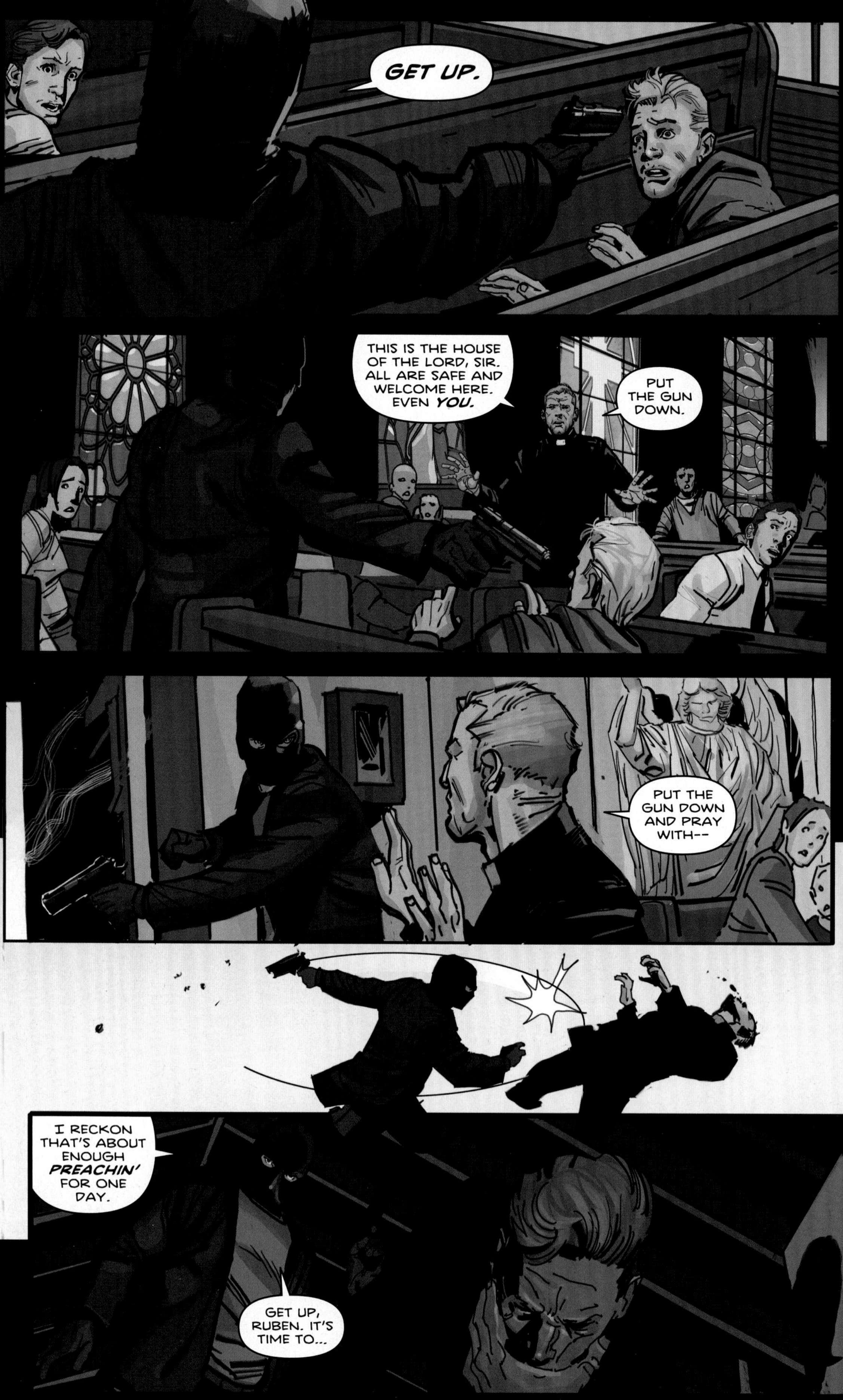
GET UP.
THIS IS THE HOUSE OF THE LORD, SIR. ALL ARE SAFE AND WELCOME HERE. EVEN YOU.
PUT THE GUN DOWN.
PUT THE GUN DOWN AND PRAY WITH--
I RECKON THAT'S ABOUT ENOUGH PREACHIN' FOR ONE DAY.
GET UP, RUBEN. IT'S TIME TO...

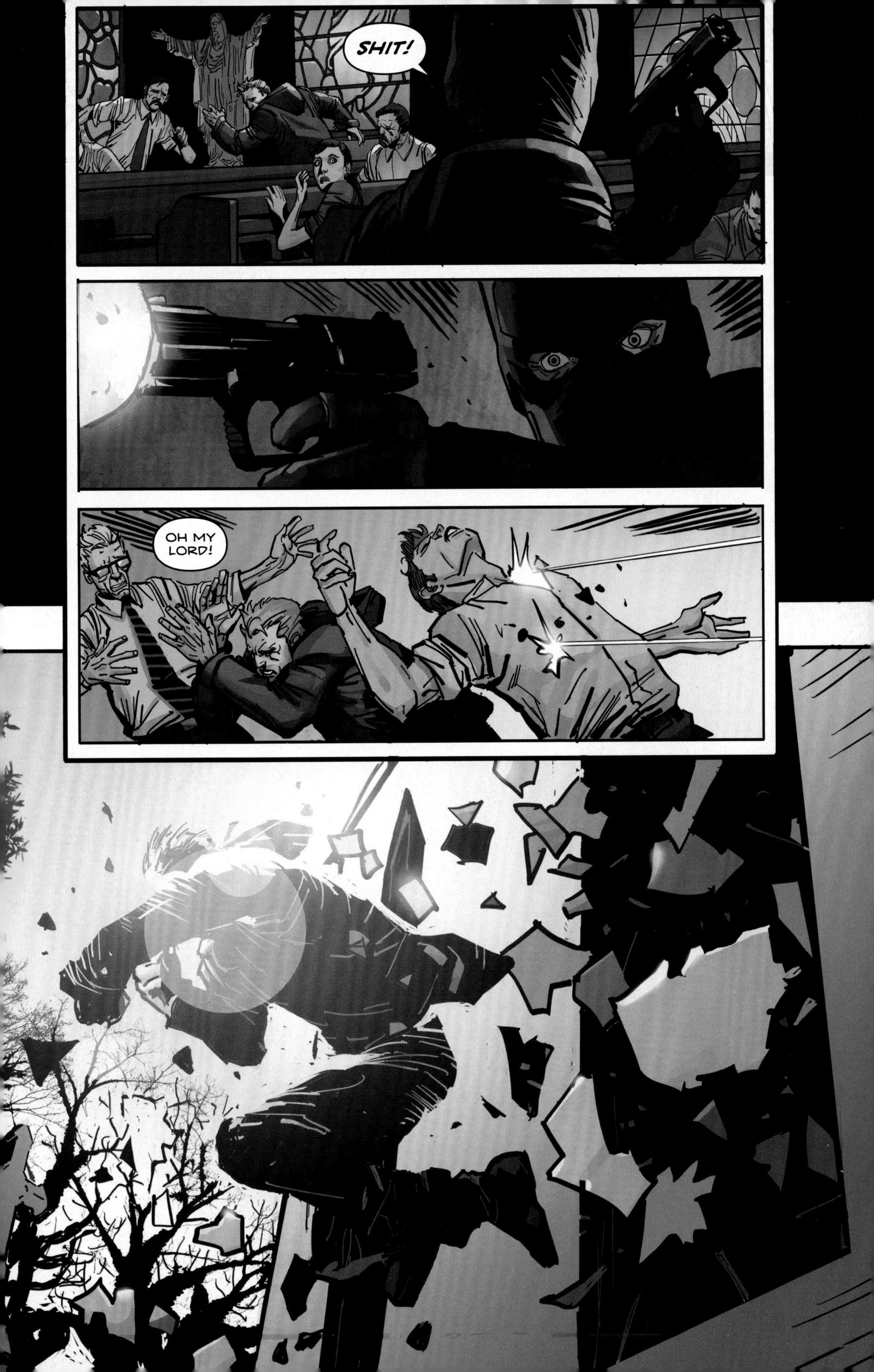
SHIT!
OH MY LORD!

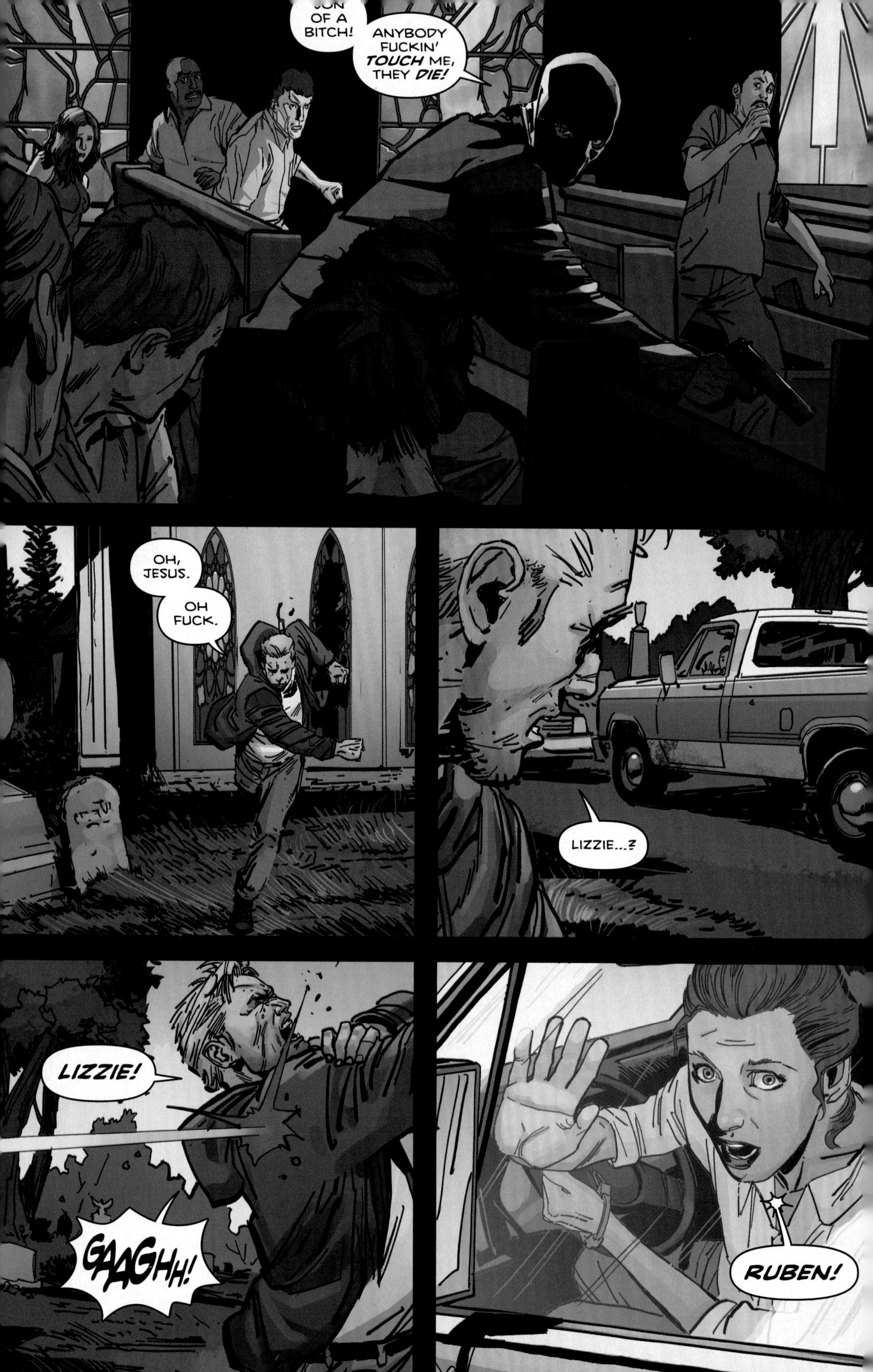

OF A BITCH!
ANYBODY FUCKIN' *TOUCH* ME, THEY *DIE!*
OH, JESUS.
OH FUCK.
LIZZIE...?
LIZZIE!
GAAGHH!
RUBEN!

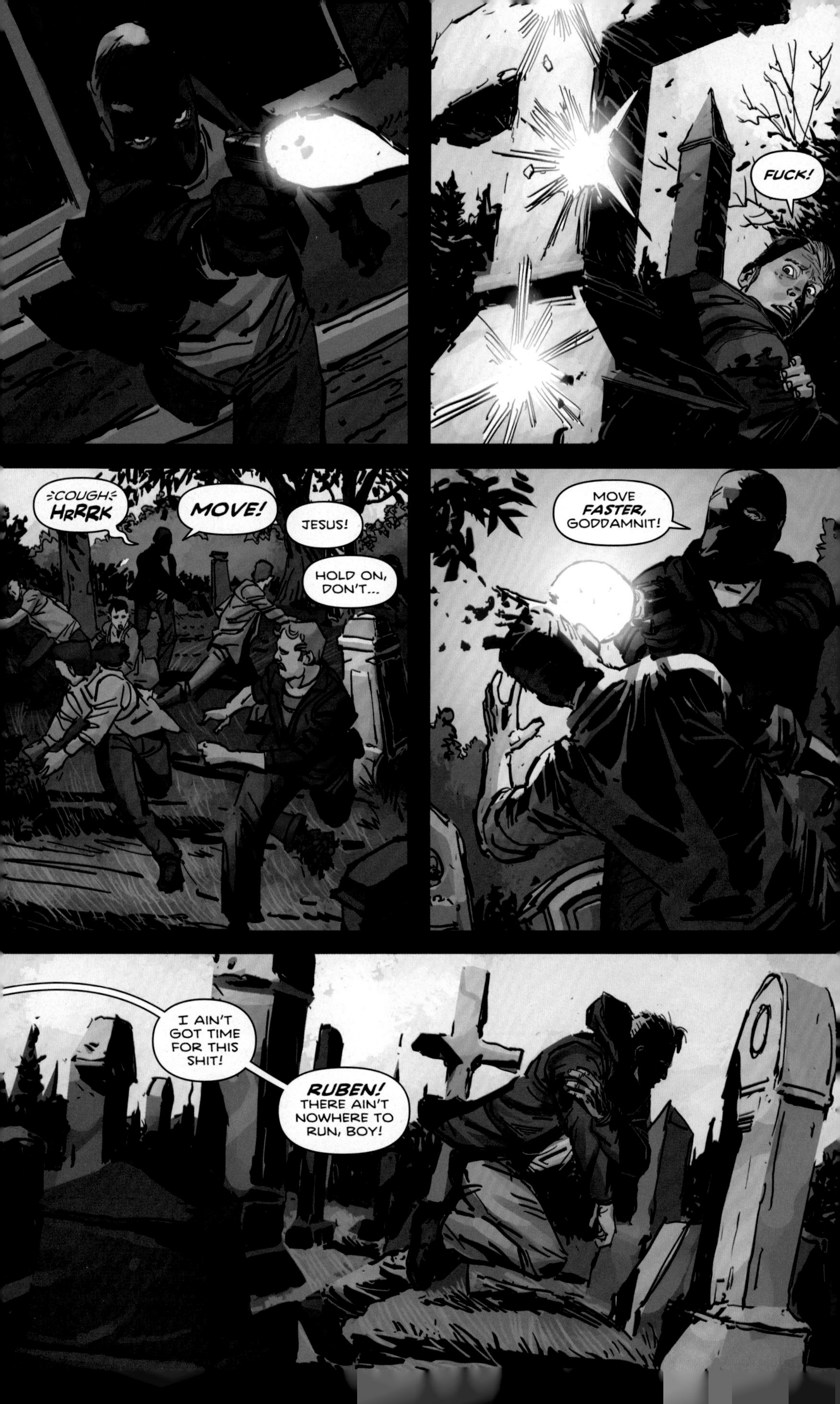
FUCK!
COUGH
HRRRK
MOVE!
JESUS!
HOLD ON, DON'T...
MOVE FASTER, GODDAMNIT!
I AIN'T GOT TIME FOR THIS SHIT!
RUBEN! THERE AIN'T NOWHERE TO RUN, BOY!

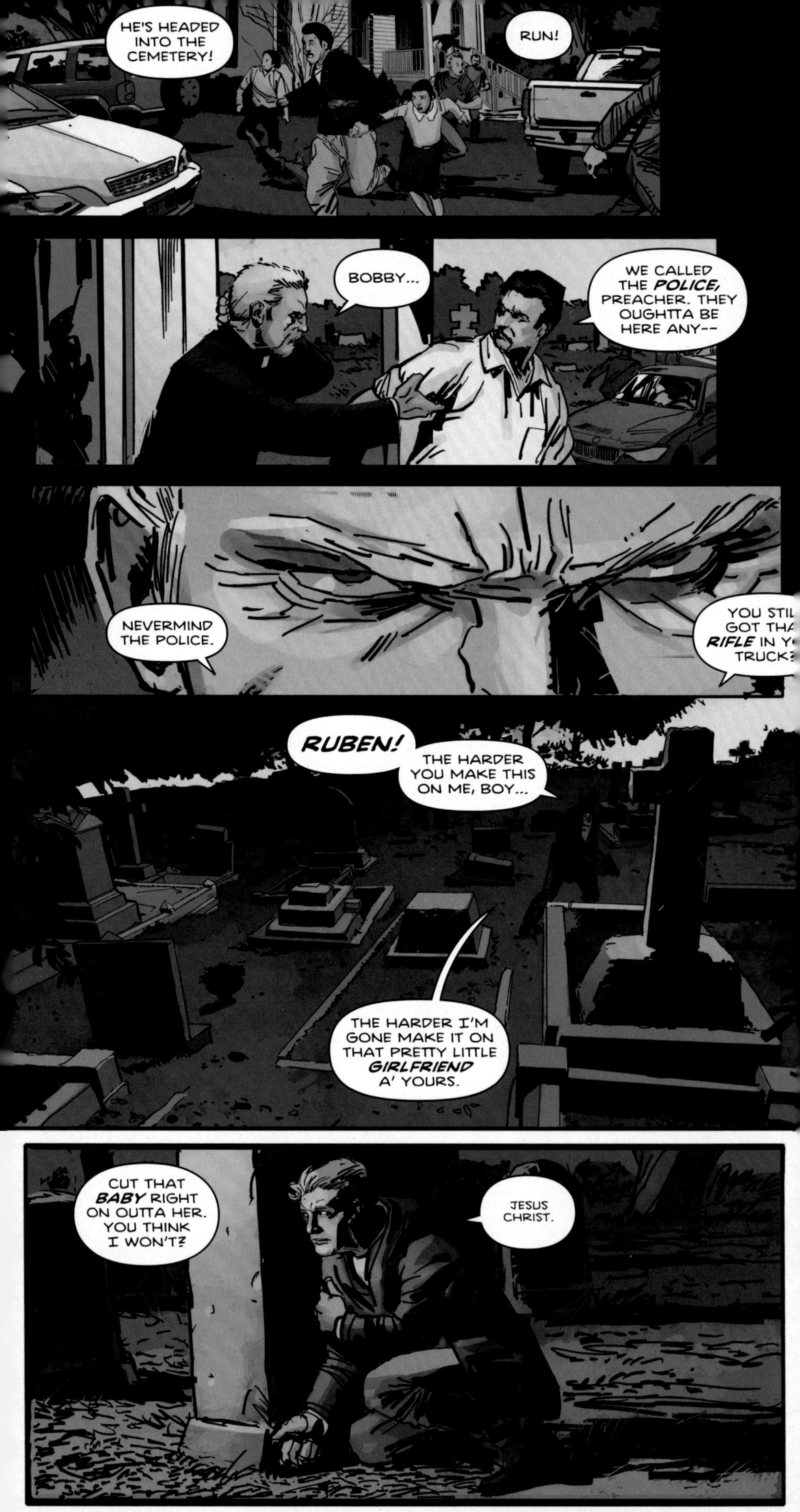
HE'S HEADED INTO THE CEMETERY!
RUN!
BOBBY...
WE CALLED THE *POLICE,* PREACHER. THEY OUGHTTA BE HERE ANY--
NEVERMIND THE POLICE.
YOU STIL GOT THA *RIFLE* IN Y TRUCK?
RUBEN!
THE HARDER YOU MAKE THIS ON ME, BOY...
THE HARDER I'M GONE MAKE IT ON THAT PRETTY LITTLE *GIRLFRIEND* A' YOURS.
CUT THAT *BABY* RIGHT ON OUTTA HER. YOU THINK I WON'T?
JESUS CHRIST.

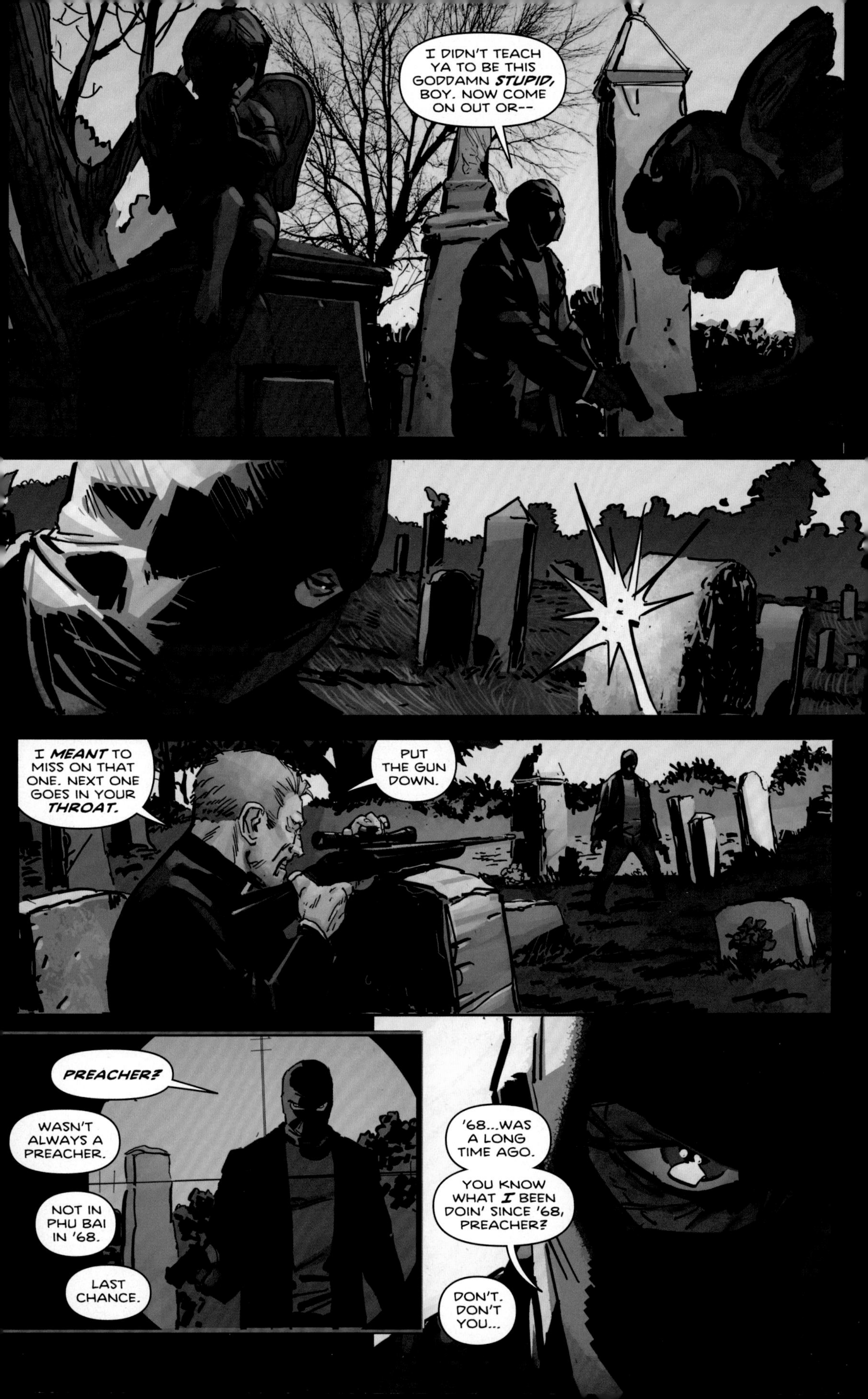
I DIDN'T TEACH YA TO BE THIS GODDAMN STUPID, BOY. NOW COME ON OUT OR--
I MEANT TO MISS ON THAT ONE. NEXT ONE GOES IN YOUR THROAT.
PUT THE GUN DOWN.
PREACHER?
WASN'T ALWAYS A PREACHER.
NOT IN PHU BAI IN '68.
LAST CHANCE.
'68...WAS A LONG TIME AGO.
YOU KNOW WHAT I BEEN DOIN' SINCE '68, PREACHER?
DON'T. DON'T YOU...

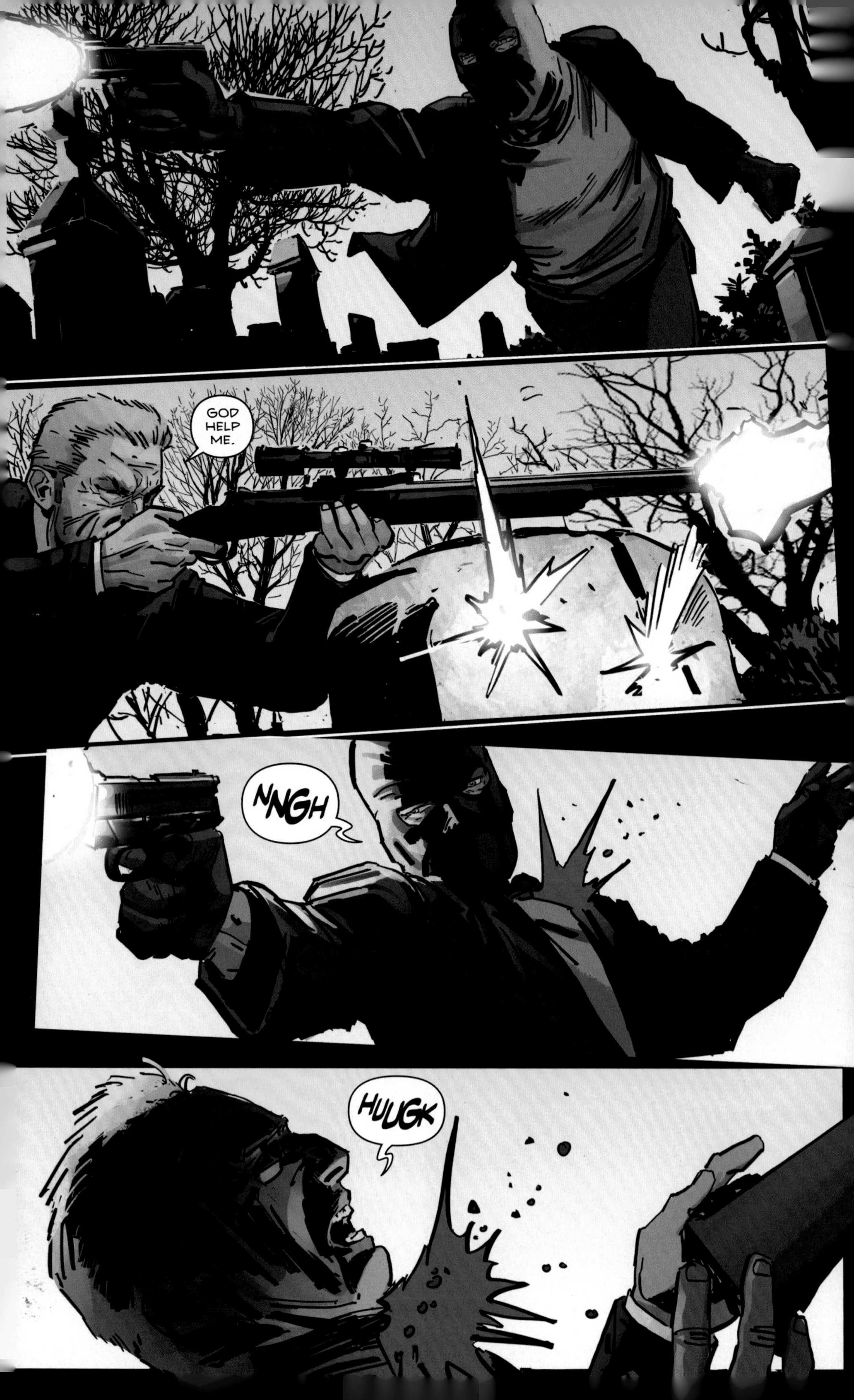
GOD HELP ME.
NNGH
HUUGK

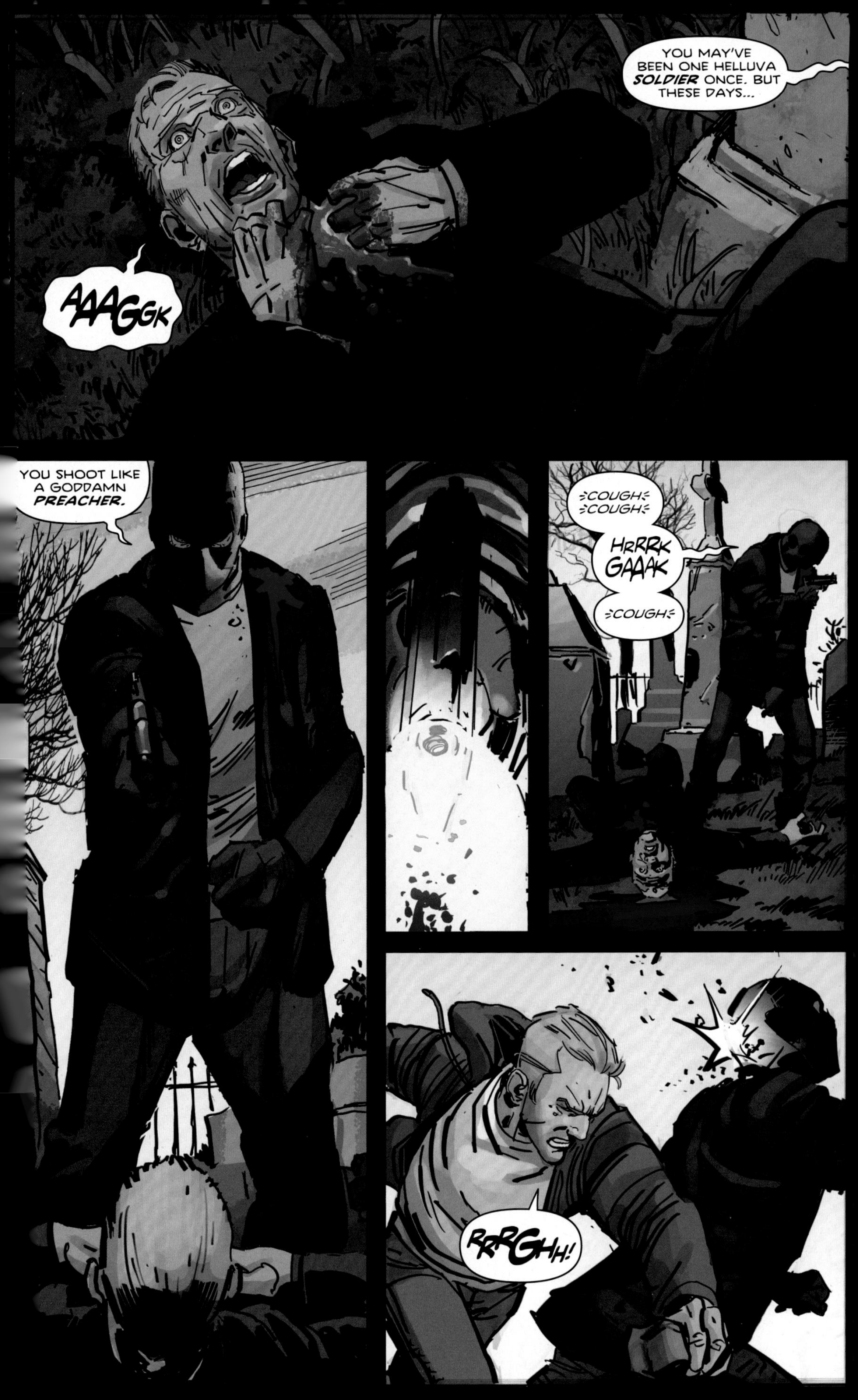
YOU MAY'VE BEEN ONE HELLUVA SOLDIER ONCE. BUT THESE DAYS...
AAAGGK
YOU SHOOT LIKE A GODDAMN PREACHER.
COUGH COUGH
HRRRK GAAAK
COUGH
RRRGHH!

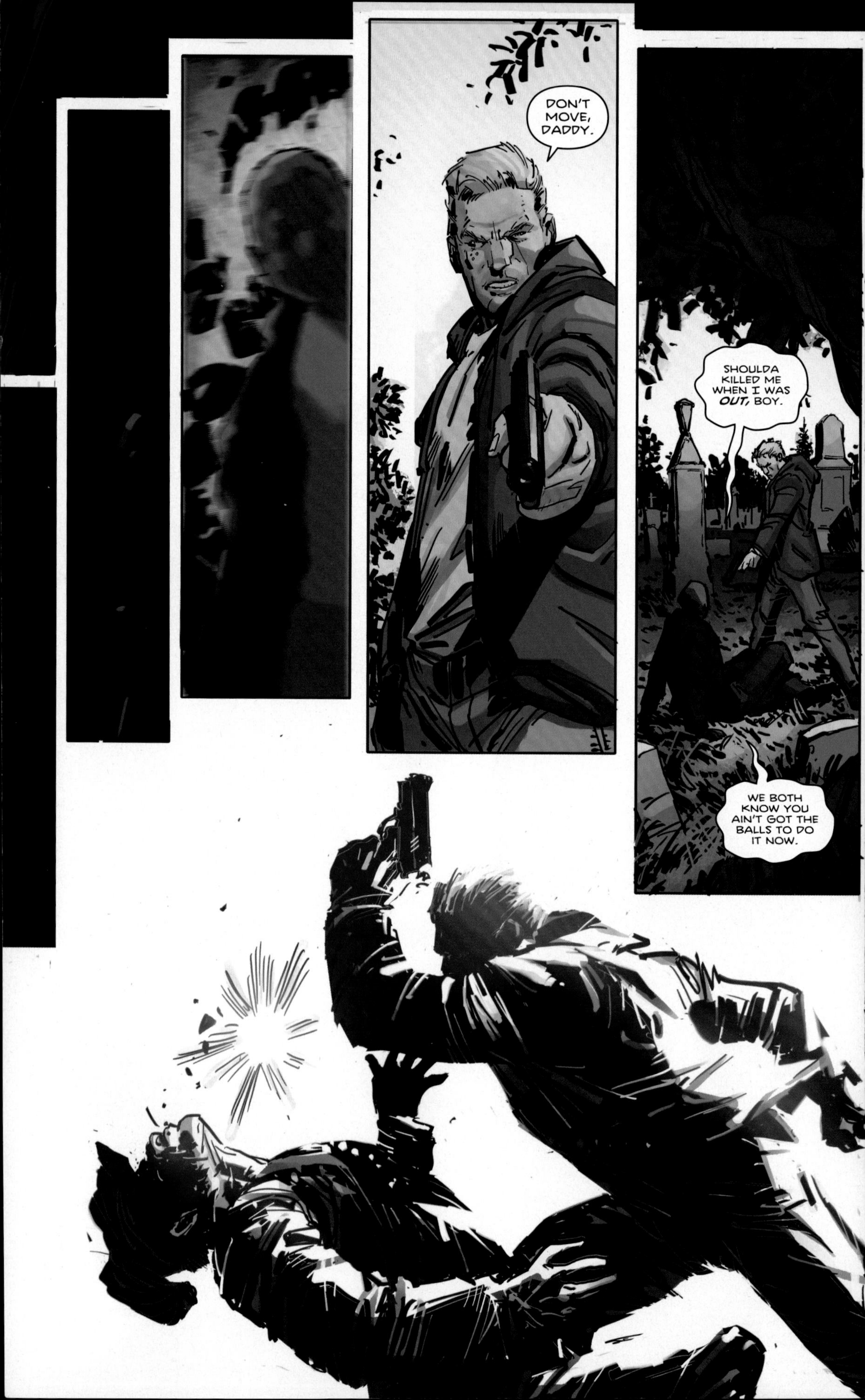
DON'T MOVE, DADDY.
SHOULDA KILLED ME WHEN I WAS *OUT,* BOY.
WE BOTH KNOW YOU AIN'T GOT THE BALLS TO DO IT NOW.

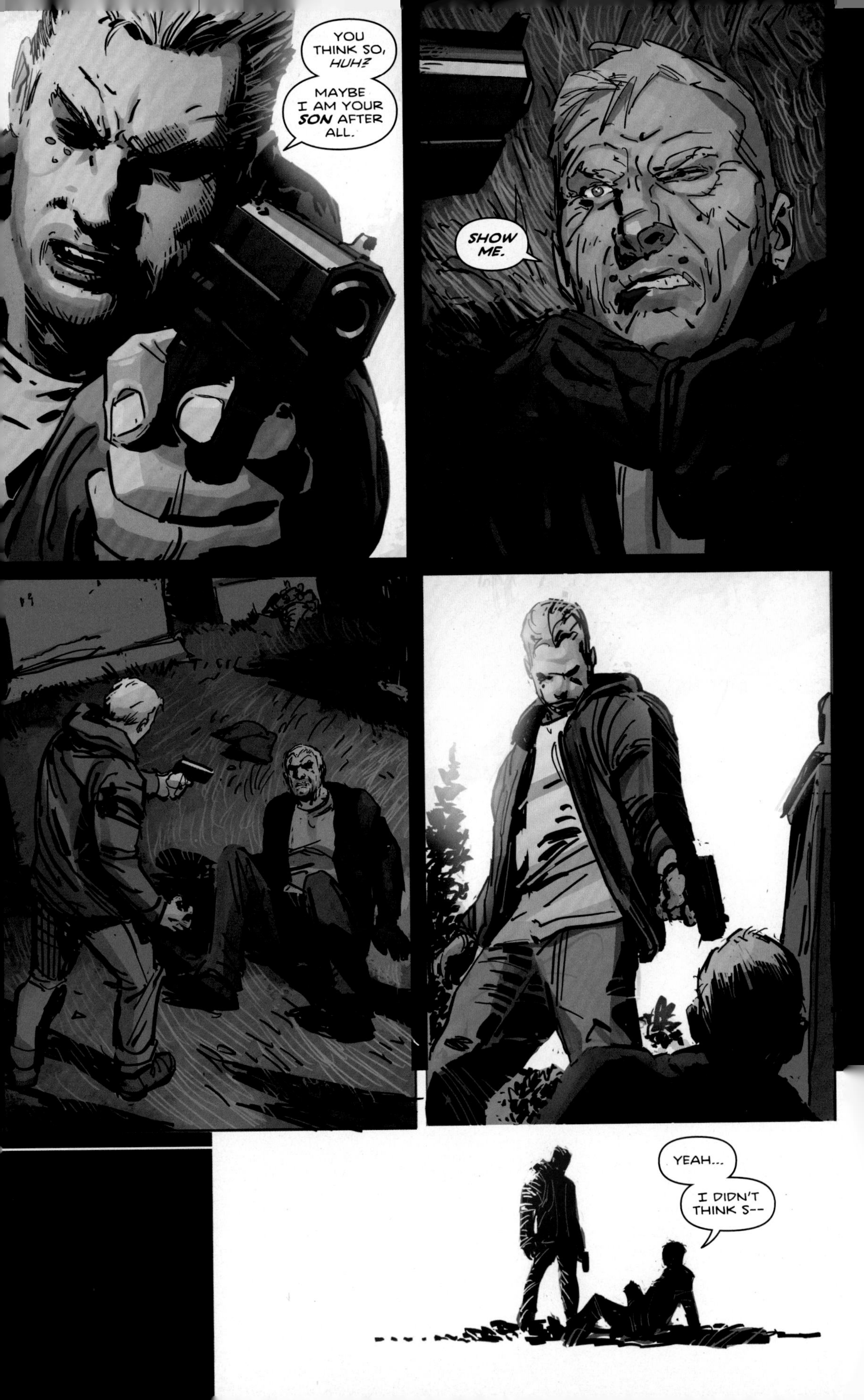
YOU THINK SO, HUH?
MAYBE I AM YOUR SON AFTER ALL.
SHOW ME.
YEAH...
I DIDN'T THINK S--

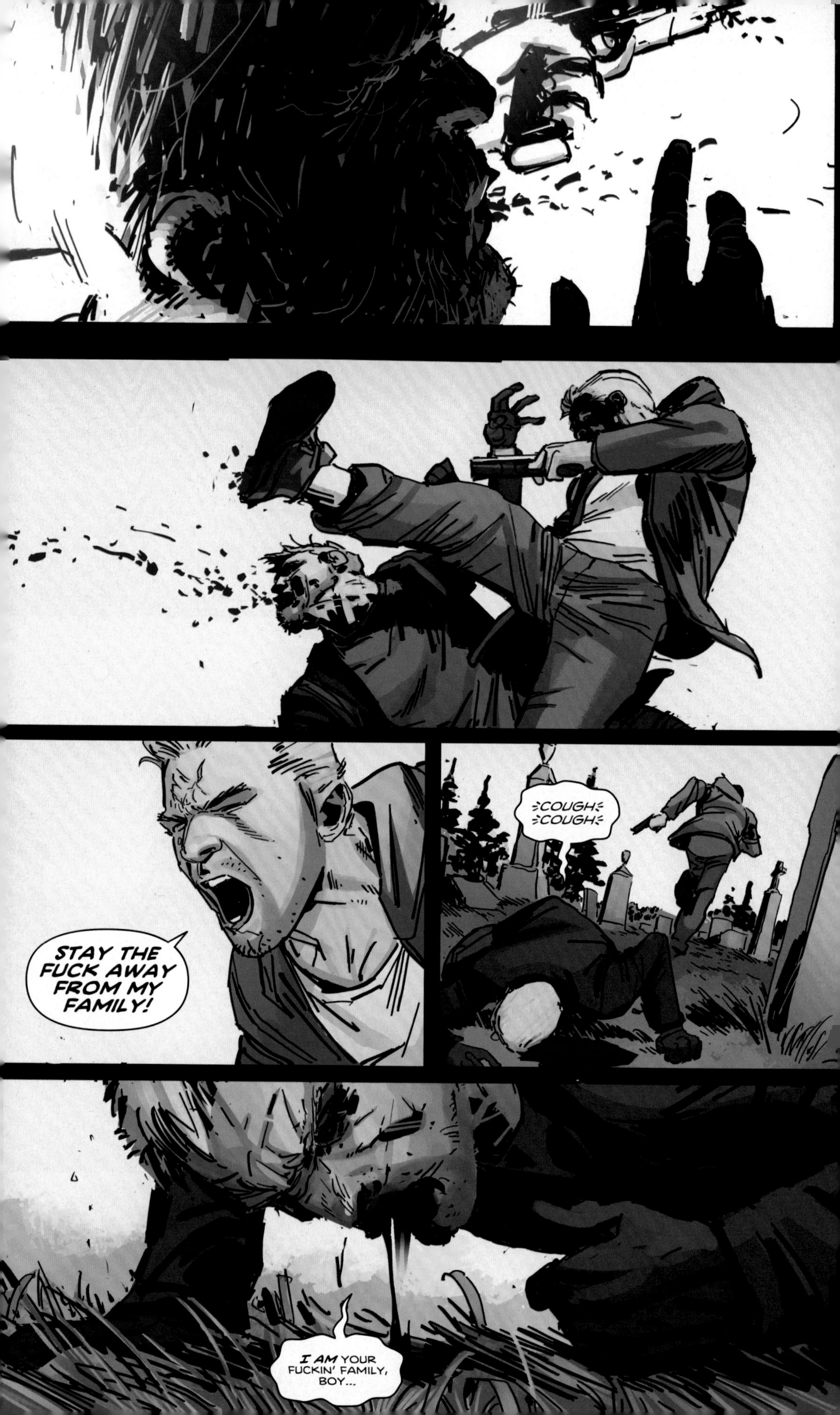
STAY THE FUCK AWAY FROM MY FAMILY!
COUGH COUGH
I AM YOUR FUCKIN' FAMILY, BOY...

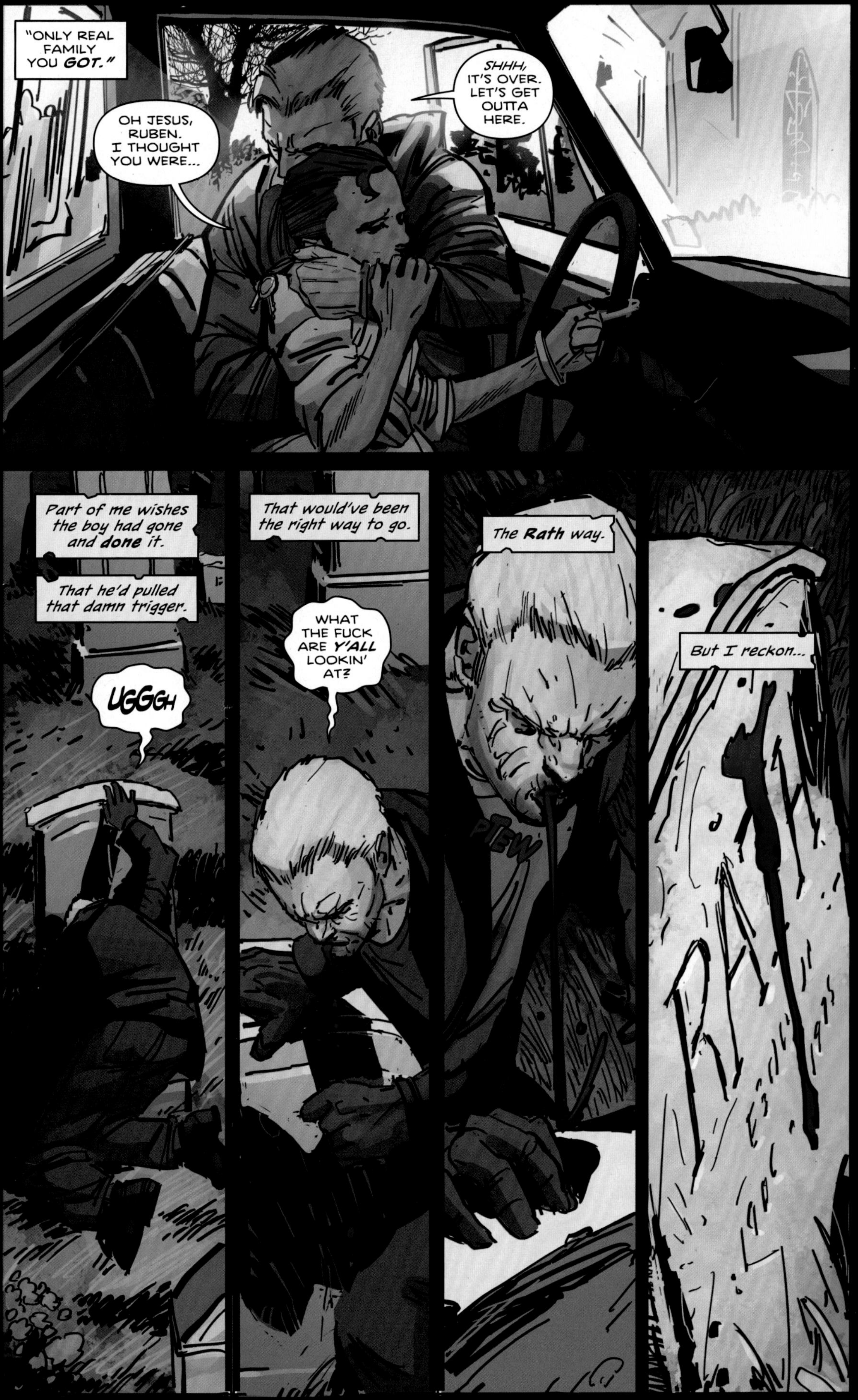
"ONLY REAL FAMILY YOU **GOT.**"
OH JESUS, RUBEN. I THOUGHT YOU WERE...
SHHH, IT'S OVER. LET'S GET OUTTA HERE.
*Part of me wishes the boy had gone and **done** it.*
That he'd pulled that damn trigger.
UGGGH
That would've been the right way to go.
WHAT THE FUCK ARE ***Y'ALL*** LOOKIN' AT?
*The **Rath** way.*
PTEW
But I reckon...

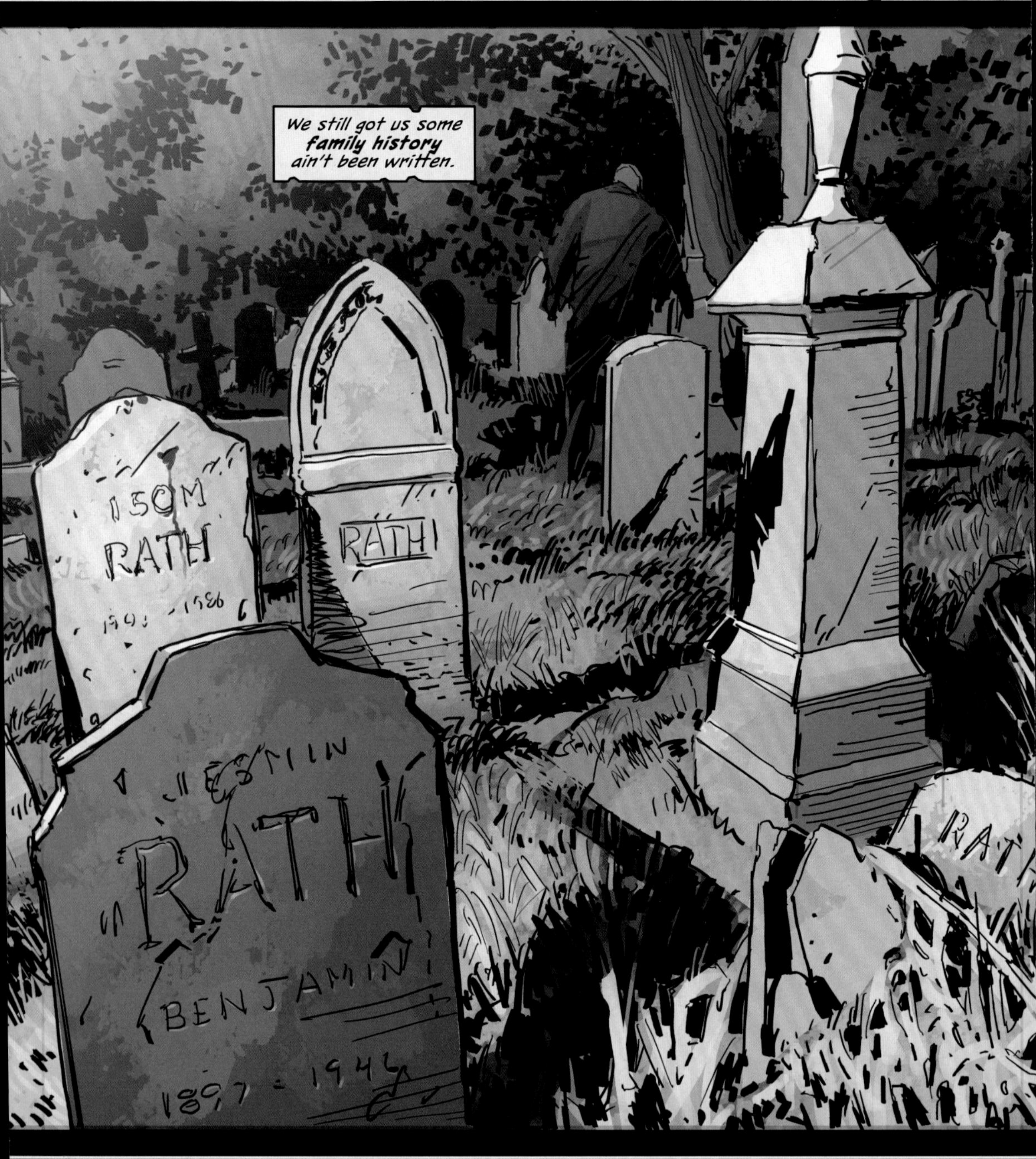
We still got us some **family history** ain't been written.
ISOM
RATH
RATH
RATH
BENJAMIN
1897 - 1946

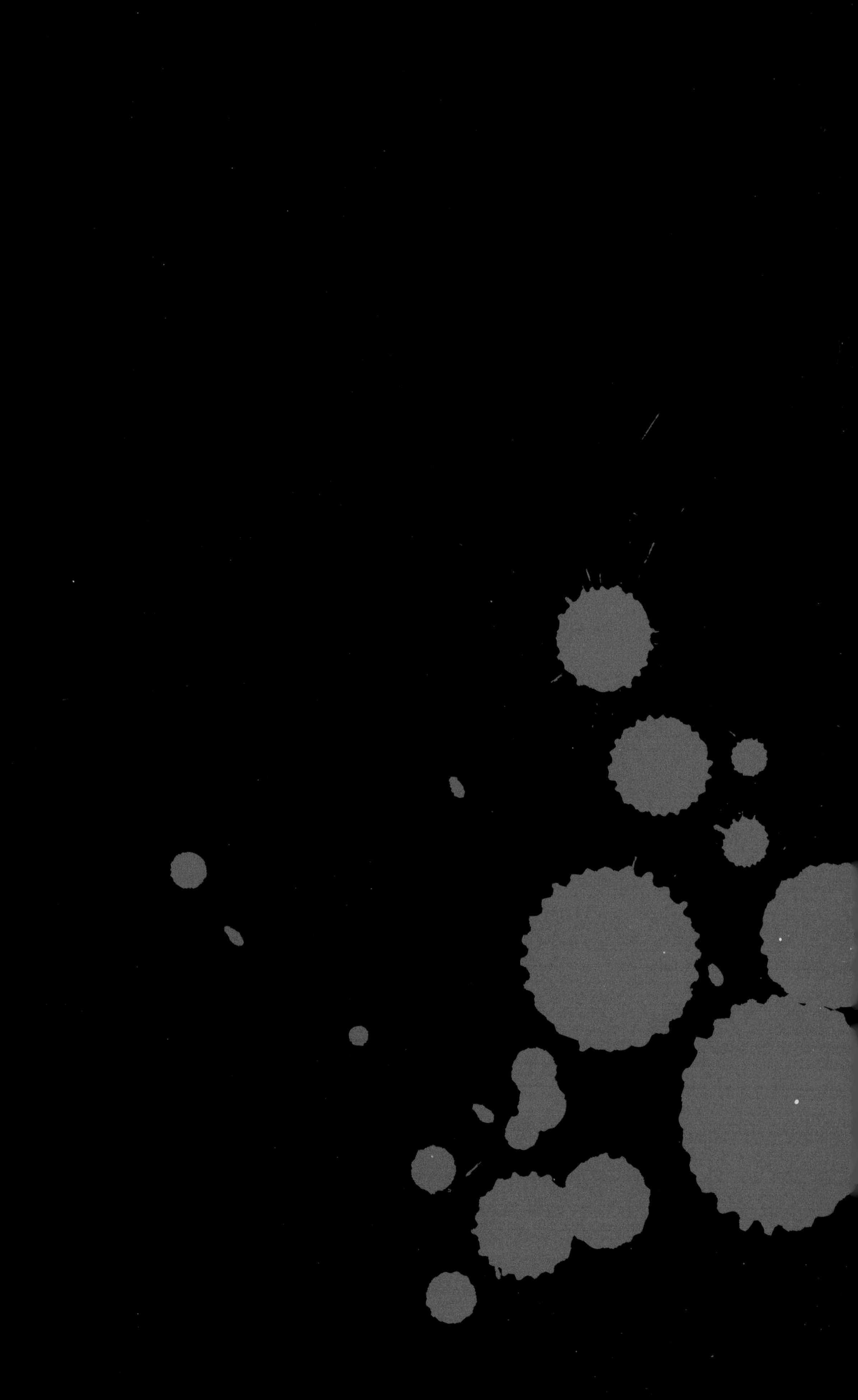

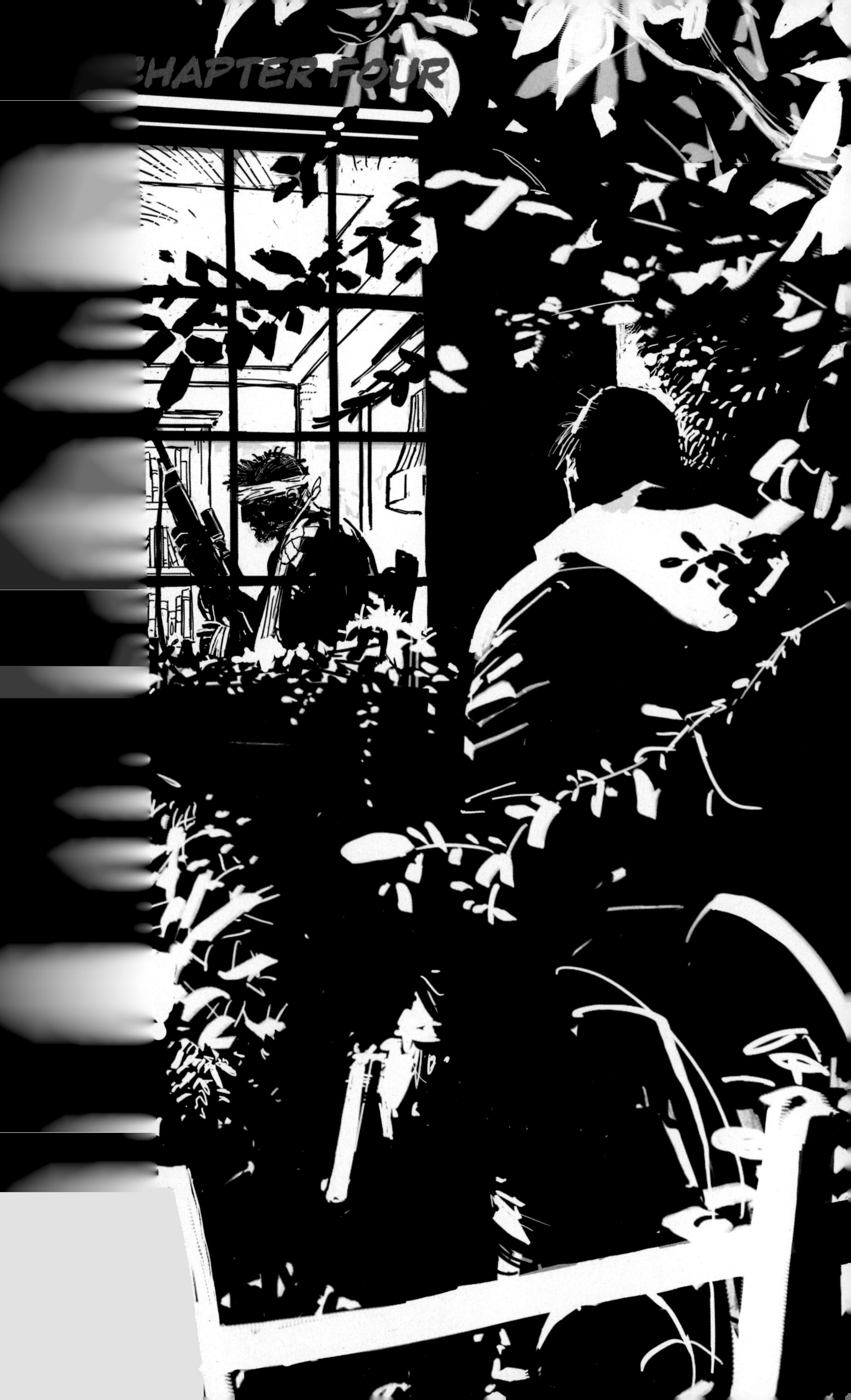
CHAPTER FOUR

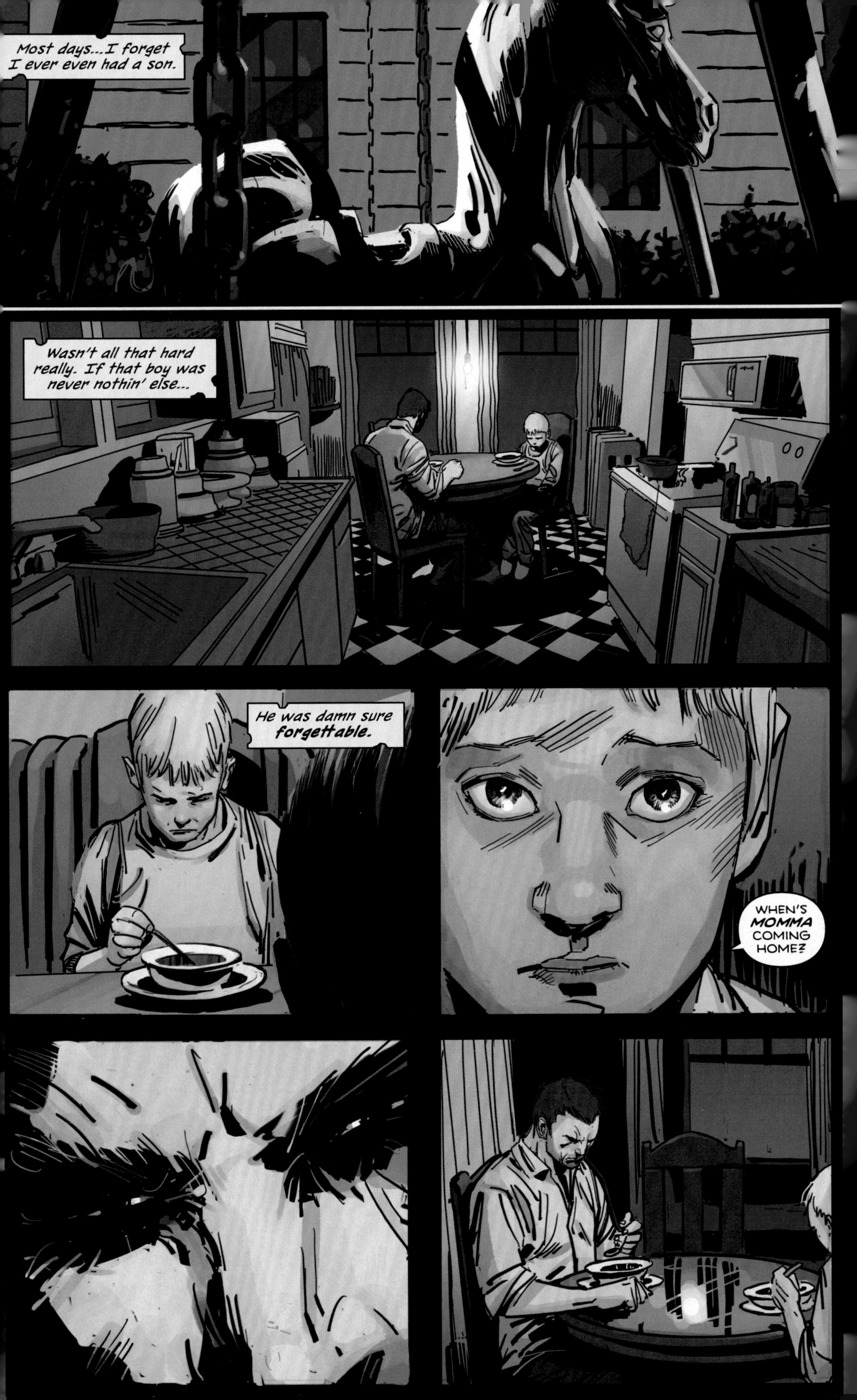
Most days...I forget I ever even had a son.
Wasn't all that hard really. If that boy was never nothin' else...
He was damn sure forgettable.
WHEN'S MOMMA COMING HOME?

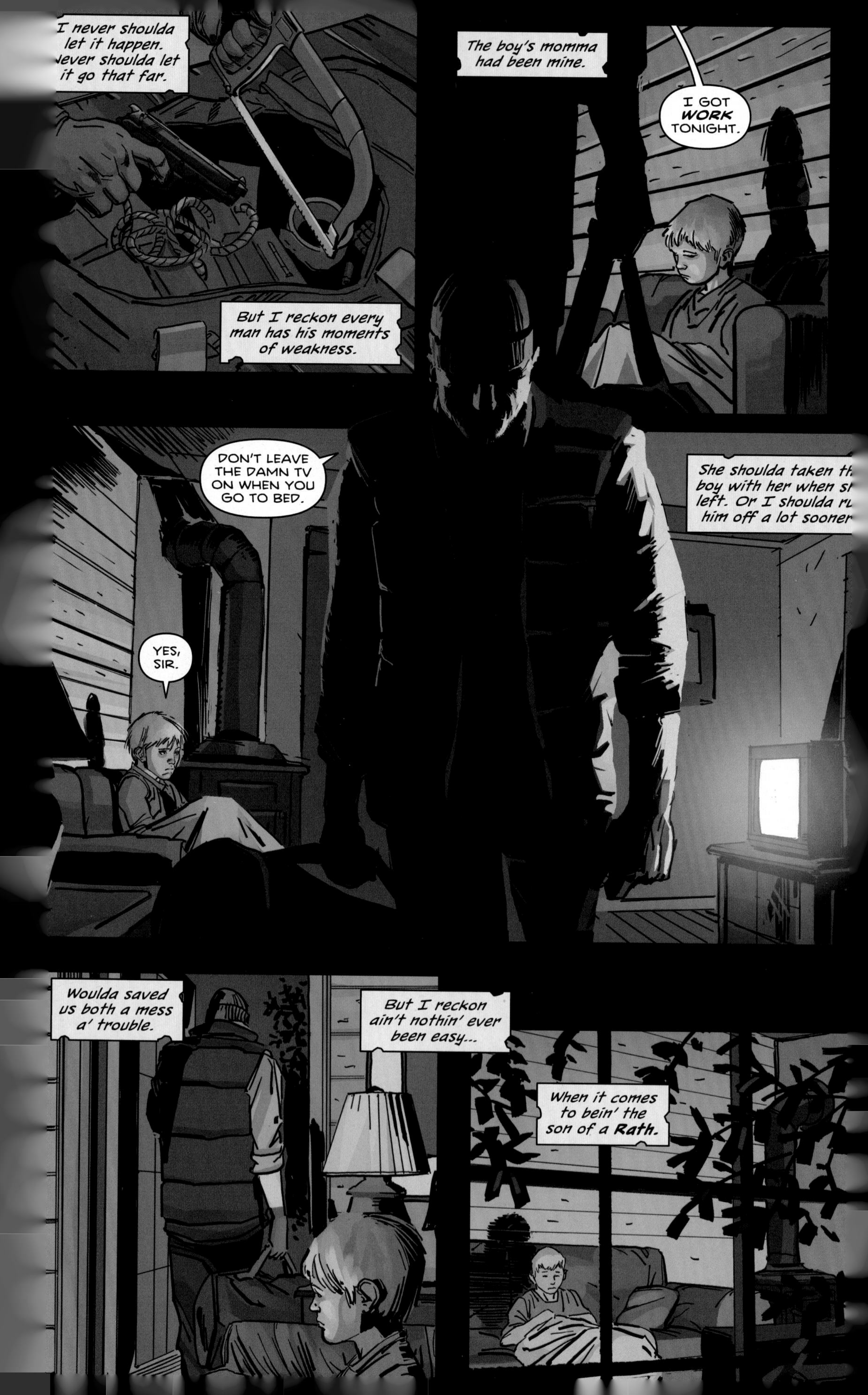
I never shoulda let it happen. Never shoulda let it go that far.
But I reckon every man has his moments of weakness.
The boy's momma had been mine.
I GOT WORK TONIGHT.
DON'T LEAVE THE DAMN TV ON WHEN YOU GO TO BED.
YES, SIR.
She shoulda taken the boy with her when she left. Or I shoulda run him off a lot sooner.
Woulda saved us both a mess a' trouble.
But I reckon ain't nothin' ever been easy...
When it comes to bein' the son of a Rath.

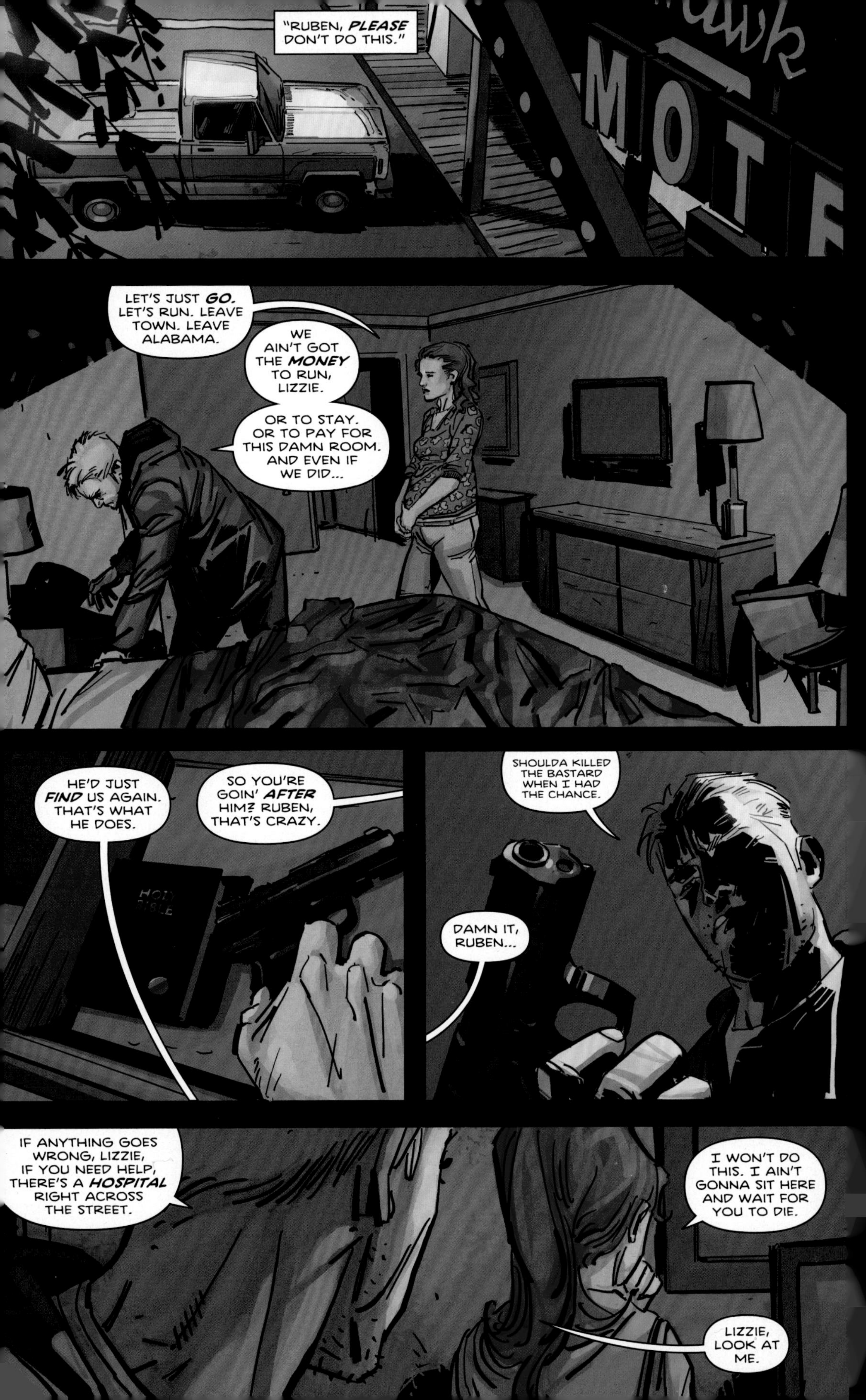
"RUBEN, PLEASE DON'T DO THIS."
MOTE
LET'S JUST GO. LET'S RUN. LEAVE TOWN. LEAVE ALABAMA.
WE AIN'T GOT THE MONEY TO RUN, LIZZIE.
OR TO STAY. OR TO PAY FOR THIS DAMN ROOM. AND EVEN IF WE DID...
HE'D JUST FIND US AGAIN. THAT'S WHAT HE DOES.
SO YOU'RE GOIN' AFTER HIM? RUBEN, THAT'S CRAZY.
SHOULDA KILLED THE BASTARD WHEN I HAD THE CHANCE.
DAMN IT, RUBEN...
IF ANYTHING GOES WRONG, LIZZIE, IF YOU NEED HELP, THERE'S A HOSPITAL RIGHT ACROSS THE STREET.
I WON'T DO THIS. I AIN'T GONNA SIT HERE AND WAIT FOR YOU TO DIE.
LIZZIE, LOOK AT ME.

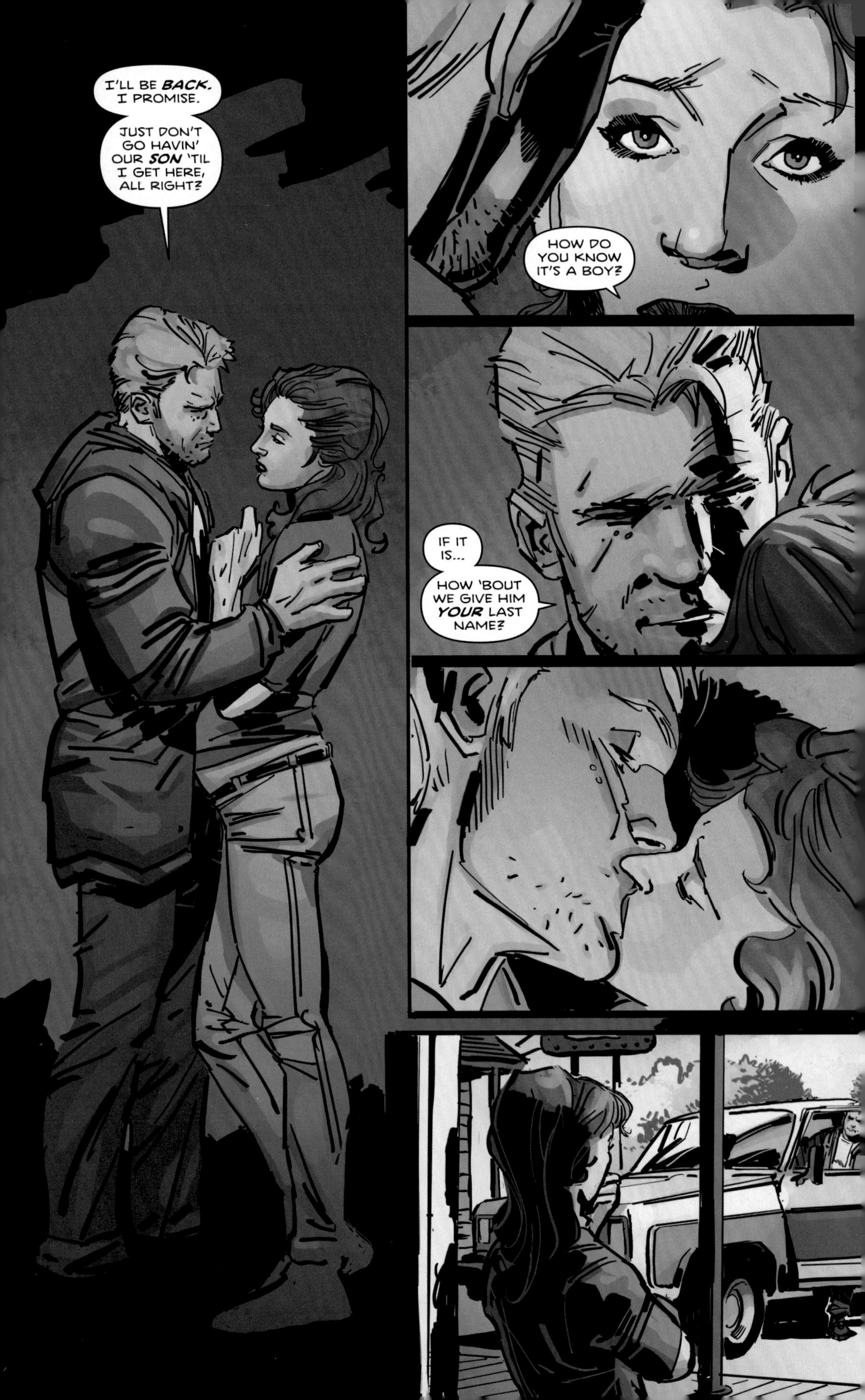

I'LL BE *BACK.* I PROMISE.
JUST DON'T GO HAVIN' OUR *SON* 'TIL I GET HERE, ALL RIGHT?
HOW DO YOU KNOW IT'S A BOY?
IF IT IS...
HOW 'BOUT WE GIVE HIM *YOUR* LAST NAME?

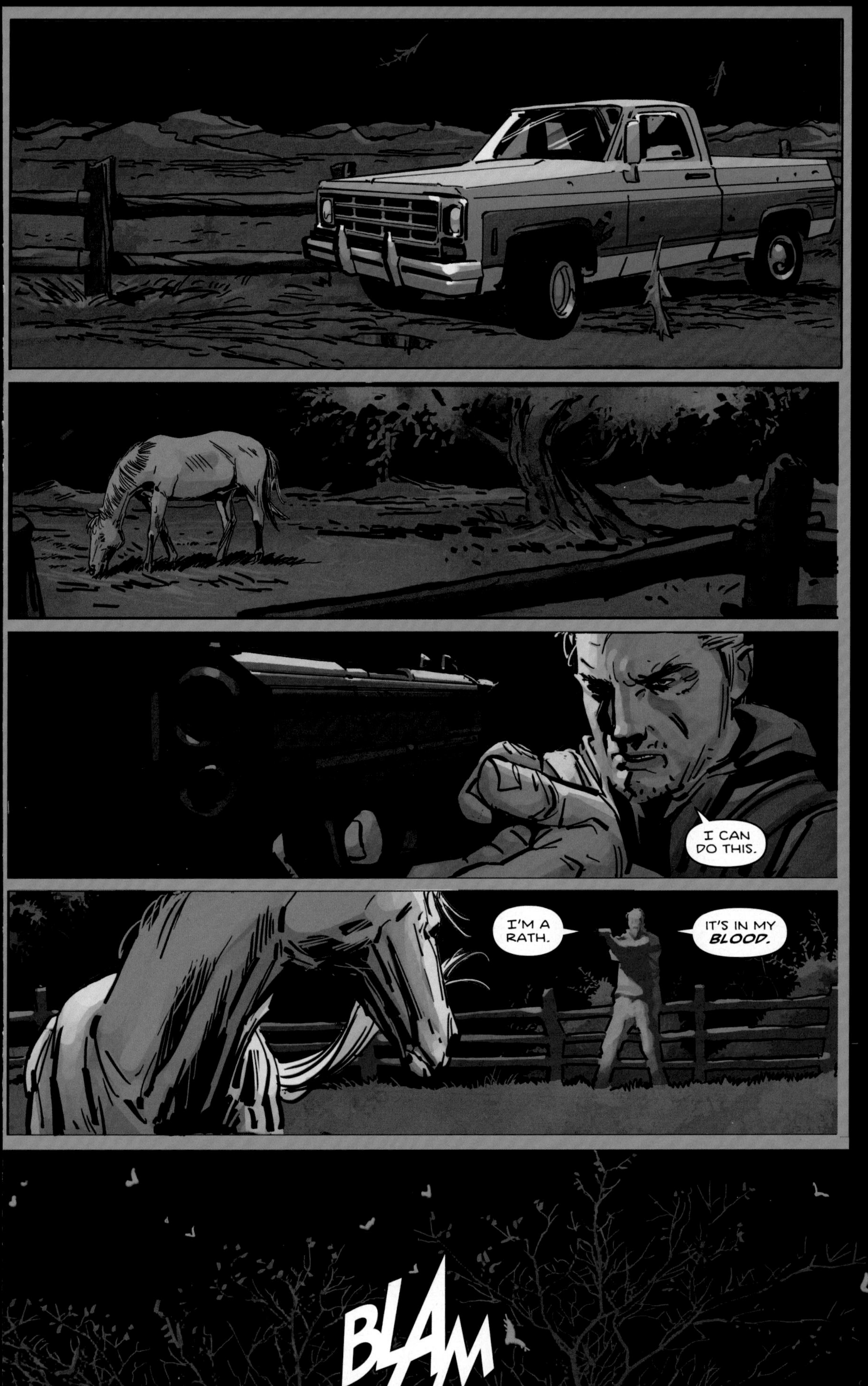
I CAN DO THIS.
I'M A RATH.
IT'S IN MY *BLOOD.*
BLAM

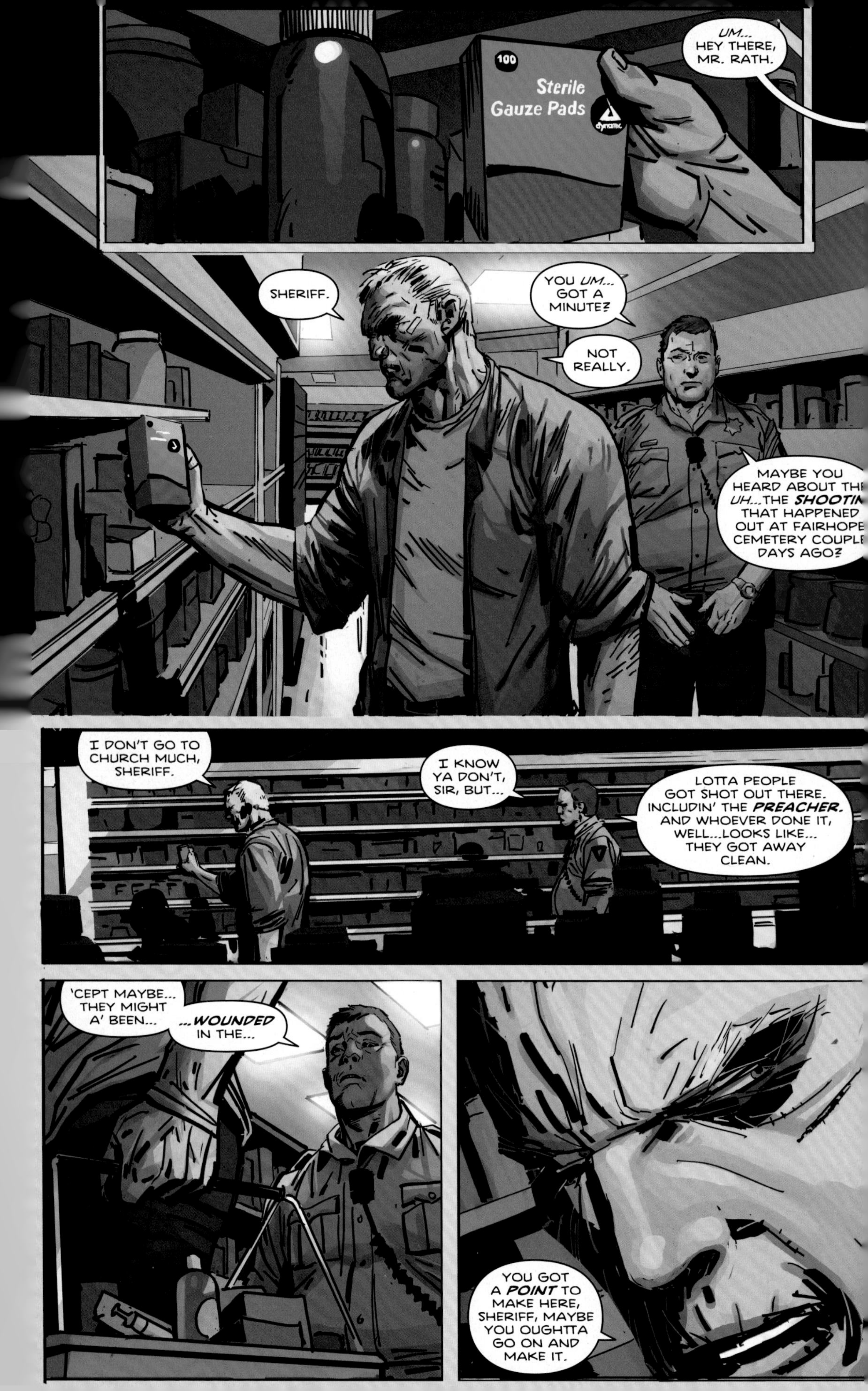
100
Sterile Gauze Pads
dynamic
UM... HEY THERE, MR. RATH.
SHERIFF.
YOU UM... GOT A MINUTE?
NOT REALLY.
MAYBE YOU HEARD ABOUT TH UH...THE SHOOTIN THAT HAPPENED OUT AT FAIRHOPE CEMETERY COUPL DAYS AGO?
I DON'T GO TO CHURCH MUCH, SHERIFF.
I KNOW YA DON'T, SIR, BUT...
LOTTA PEOPLE GOT SHOT OUT THERE. INCLUDIN' THE PREACHER. AND WHOEVER DONE IT, WELL...LOOKS LIKE... THEY GOT AWAY CLEAN.
'CEPT MAYBE... THEY MIGHT A' BEEN...
...WOUNDED IN THE...
YOU GOT A POINT TO MAKE HERE, SHERIFF, MAYBE YOU OUGHTTA GO ON AND MAKE IT.

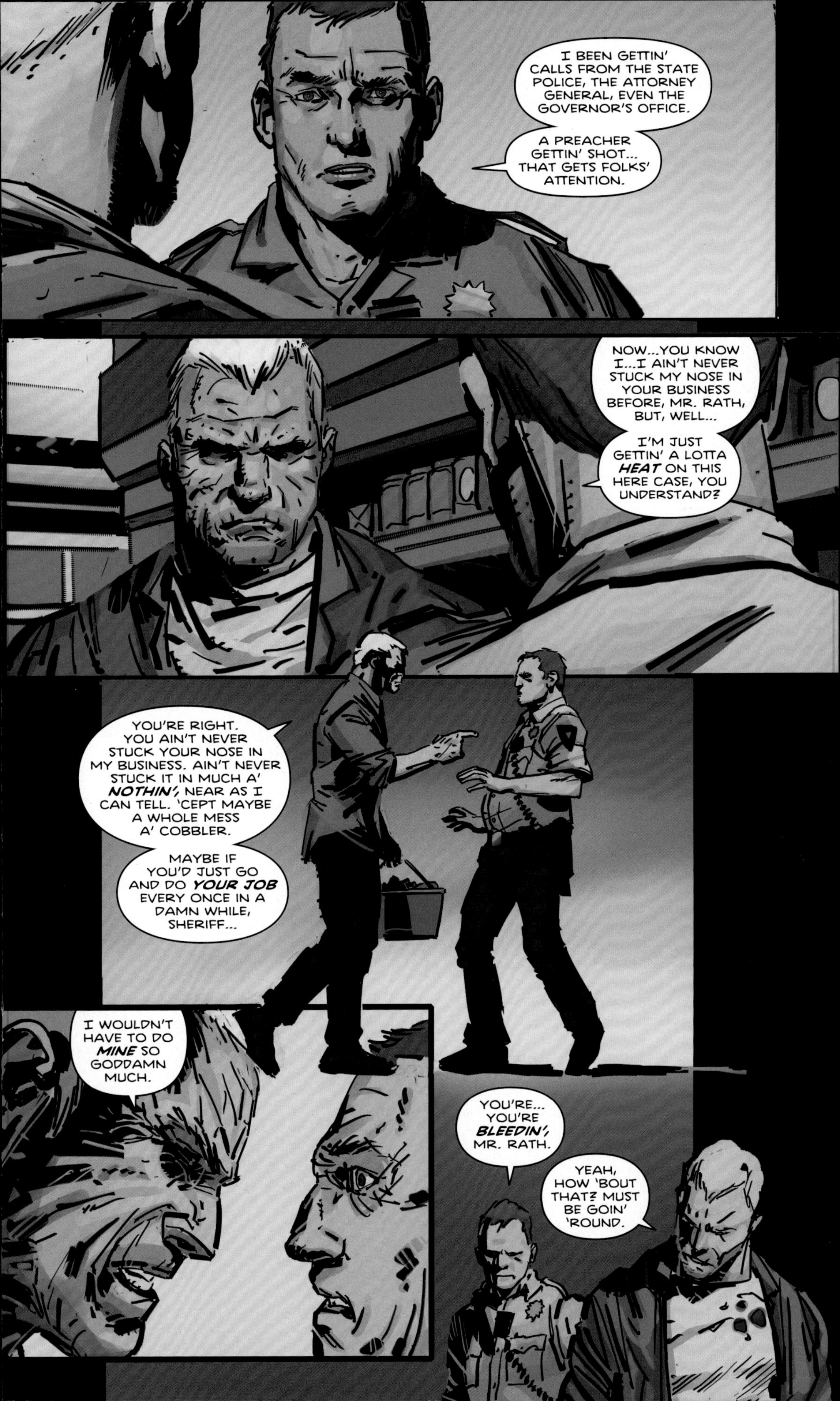
I BEEN GETTIN' CALLS FROM THE STATE POLICE, THE ATTORNEY GENERAL, EVEN THE GOVERNOR'S OFFICE.
A PREACHER GETTIN' SHOT... THAT GETS FOLKS' ATTENTION.
NOW...YOU KNOW I...I AIN'T NEVER STUCK MY NOSE IN YOUR BUSINESS BEFORE, MR. RATH, BUT, WELL...
I'M JUST GETTIN' A LOTTA HEAT ON THIS HERE CASE, YOU UNDERSTAND?
YOU'RE RIGHT. YOU AIN'T NEVER STUCK YOUR NOSE IN MY BUSINESS. AIN'T NEVER STUCK IT IN MUCH A' NOTHIN', NEAR AS I CAN TELL. 'CEPT MAYBE A WHOLE MESS A' COBBLER.
MAYBE IF YOU'D JUST GO AND DO YOUR JOB EVERY ONCE IN A DAMN WHILE, SHERIFF...
I WOULDN'T HAVE TO DO MINE SO GODDAMN MUCH.
YOU'RE... YOU'RE BLEEDIN', MR. RATH.
YEAH, HOW 'BOUT THAT? MUST BE GOIN' 'ROUND.

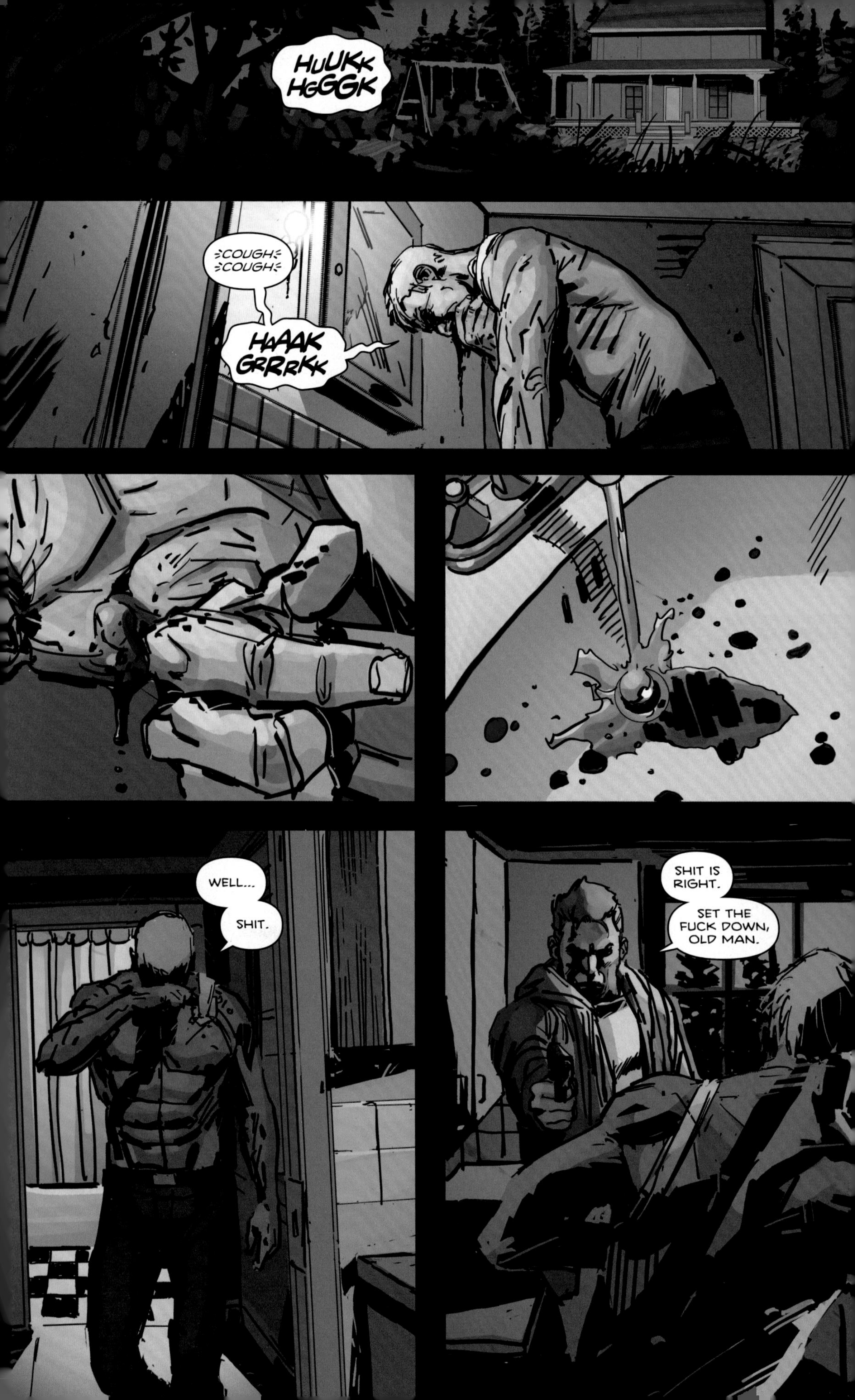
HUUKK HGGGK
COUGH COUGH
HAAAK GRRRKK
WELL...
SHIT.
SHIT IS RIGHT.
SET THE FUCK DOWN, OLD MAN.

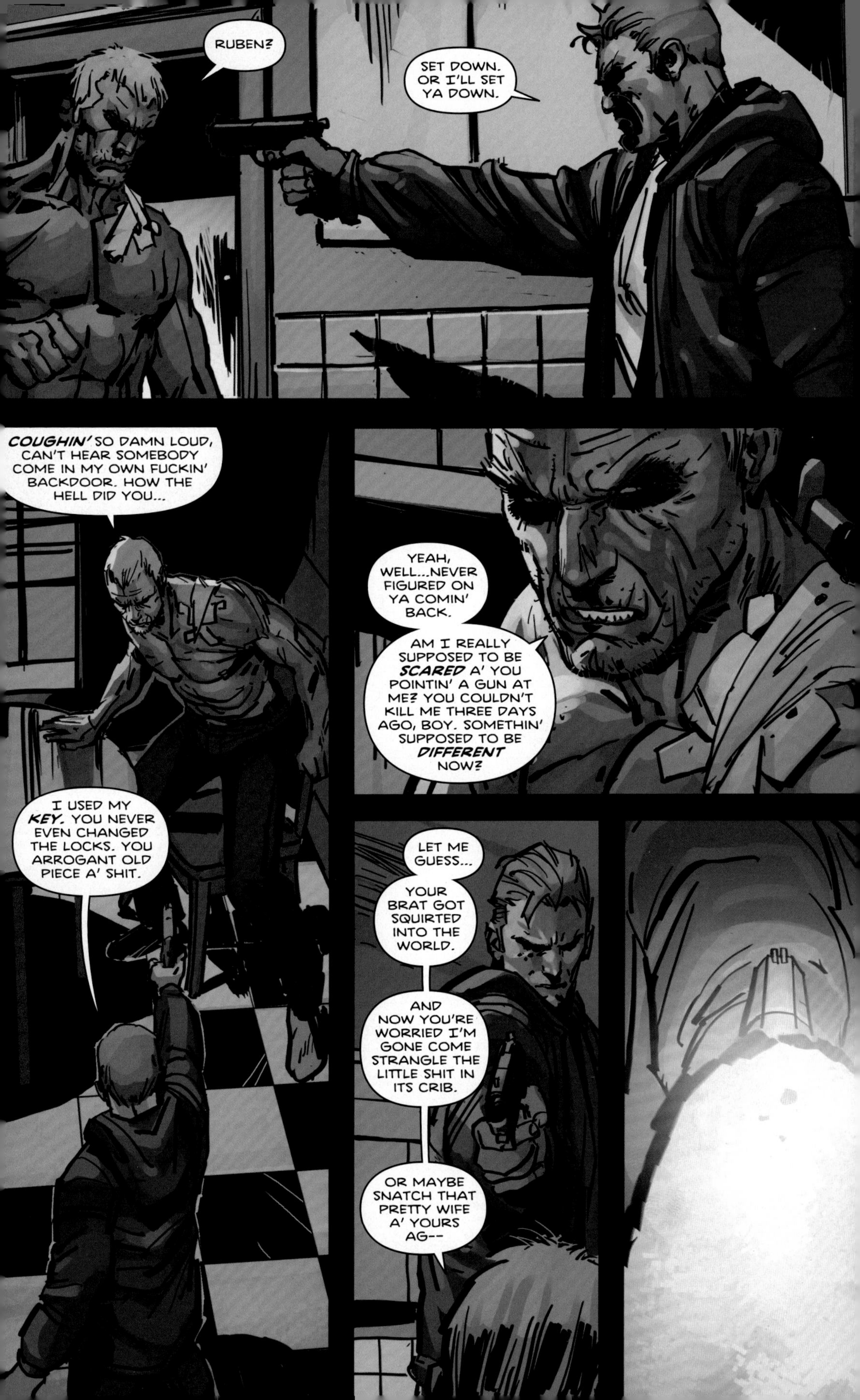
RUBEN?
SET DOWN. OR I'LL SET YA DOWN.
COUGHIN' SO DAMN LOUD, CAN'T HEAR SOMEBODY COME IN MY OWN FUCKIN' BACKDOOR. HOW THE HELL DID YOU...
I USED MY KEY. YOU NEVER EVEN CHANGED THE LOCKS. YOU ARROGANT OLD PIECE A' SHIT.
YEAH, WELL...NEVER FIGURED ON YA COMIN' BACK.
AM I REALLY SUPPOSED TO BE SCARED A' YOU POINTIN' A GUN AT ME? YOU COULDN'T KILL ME THREE DAYS AGO, BOY. SOMETHIN' SUPPOSED TO BE DIFFERENT NOW?
LET ME GUESS...
YOUR BRAT GOT SQUIRTED INTO THE WORLD.
AND NOW YOU'RE WORRIED I'M GONE COME STRANGLE THE LITTLE SHIT IN ITS CRIB.
OR MAYBE SNATCH THAT PRETTY WIFE A' YOURS AG--

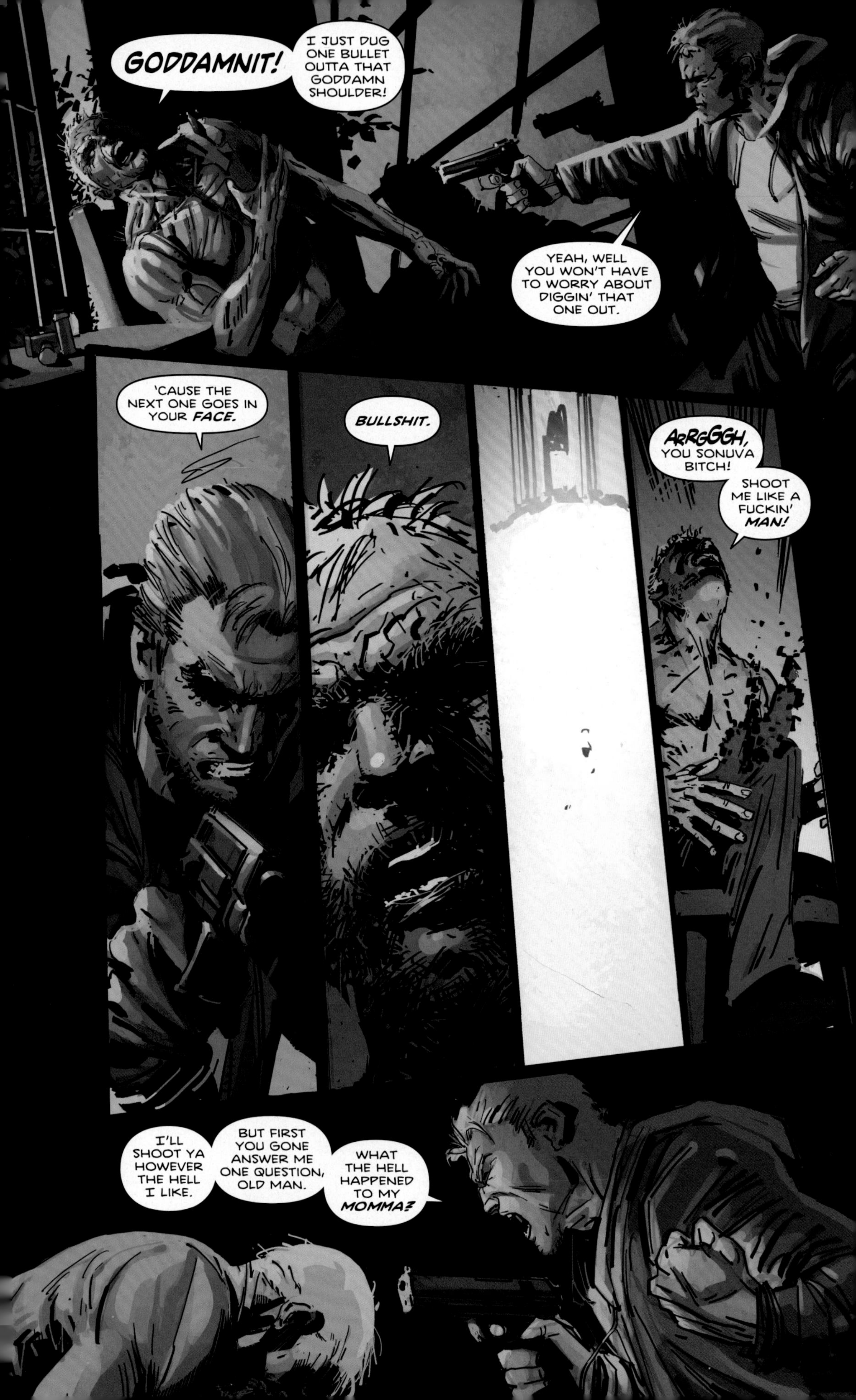
GODDAMNIT!
I JUST DUG ONE BULLET OUTTA THAT GODDAMN SHOULDER!
YEAH, WELL YOU WON'T HAVE TO WORRY ABOUT DIGGIN' THAT ONE OUT.
'CAUSE THE NEXT ONE GOES IN YOUR *FACE.*
BULLSHIT.
ARRGGGH, YOU SONUVA BITCH!
SHOOT ME LIKE A FUCKIN' *MAN!*
I'LL SHOOT YA HOWEVER THE HELL I LIKE.
BUT FIRST YOU GONE ANSWER ME ONE QUESTION, OLD MAN.
WHAT THE HELL HAPPENED TO MY *MOMMA?*

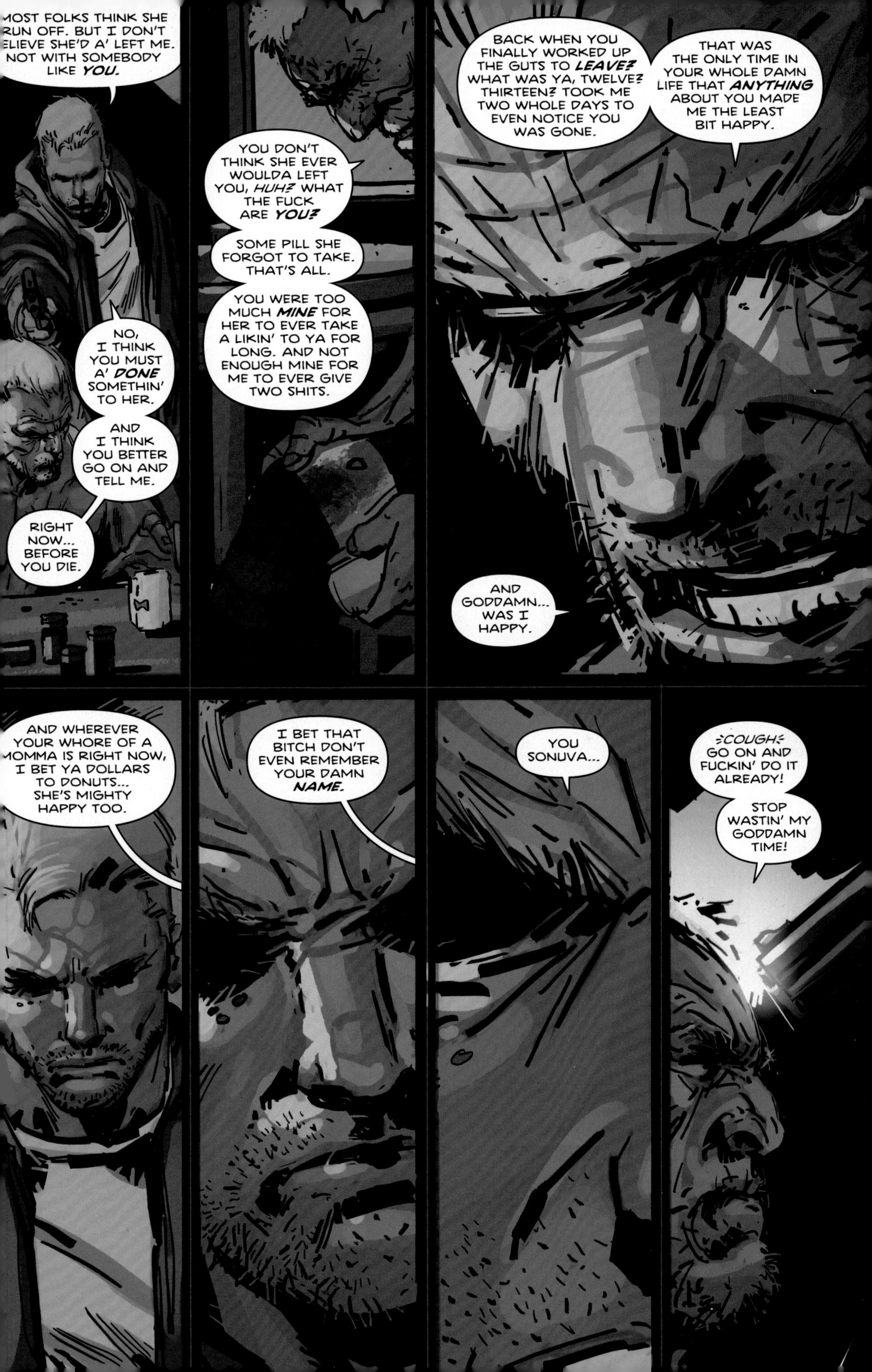
MOST FOLKS THINK SHE RUN OFF. BUT I DON'T BELIEVE SHE'D A' LEFT ME. NOT WITH SOMEBODY LIKE YOU.
YOU DON'T THINK SHE EVER WOULDA LEFT YOU, HUH? WHAT THE FUCK ARE YOU?
SOME PILL SHE FORGOT TO TAKE. THAT'S ALL.
YOU WERE TOO MUCH MINE FOR HER TO EVER TAKE A LIKIN' TO YA FOR LONG. AND NOT ENOUGH MINE FOR ME TO EVER GIVE TWO SHITS.
NO, I THINK YOU MUST A' DONE SOMETHIN' TO HER.
AND I THINK YOU BETTER GO ON AND TELL ME.
RIGHT NOW... BEFORE YOU DIE.
BACK WHEN YOU FINALLY WORKED UP THE GUTS TO LEAVE? WHAT WAS YA, TWELVE? THIRTEEN? TOOK ME TWO WHOLE DAYS TO EVEN NOTICE YOU WAS GONE.
THAT WAS THE ONLY TIME IN YOUR WHOLE DAMN LIFE THAT ANYTHING ABOUT YOU MADE ME THE LEAST BIT HAPPY.
AND GODDAMN... WAS I HAPPY.
AND WHEREVER YOUR WHORE OF A MOMMA IS RIGHT NOW, I BET YA DOLLARS TO DONUTS... SHE'S MIGHTY HAPPY TOO.
I BET THAT BITCH DON'T EVEN REMEMBER YOUR DAMN NAME.
YOU SONUVA...
COUGH GO ON AND FUCKIN' DO IT ALREADY!
STOP WASTIN' MY GODDAMN TIME!

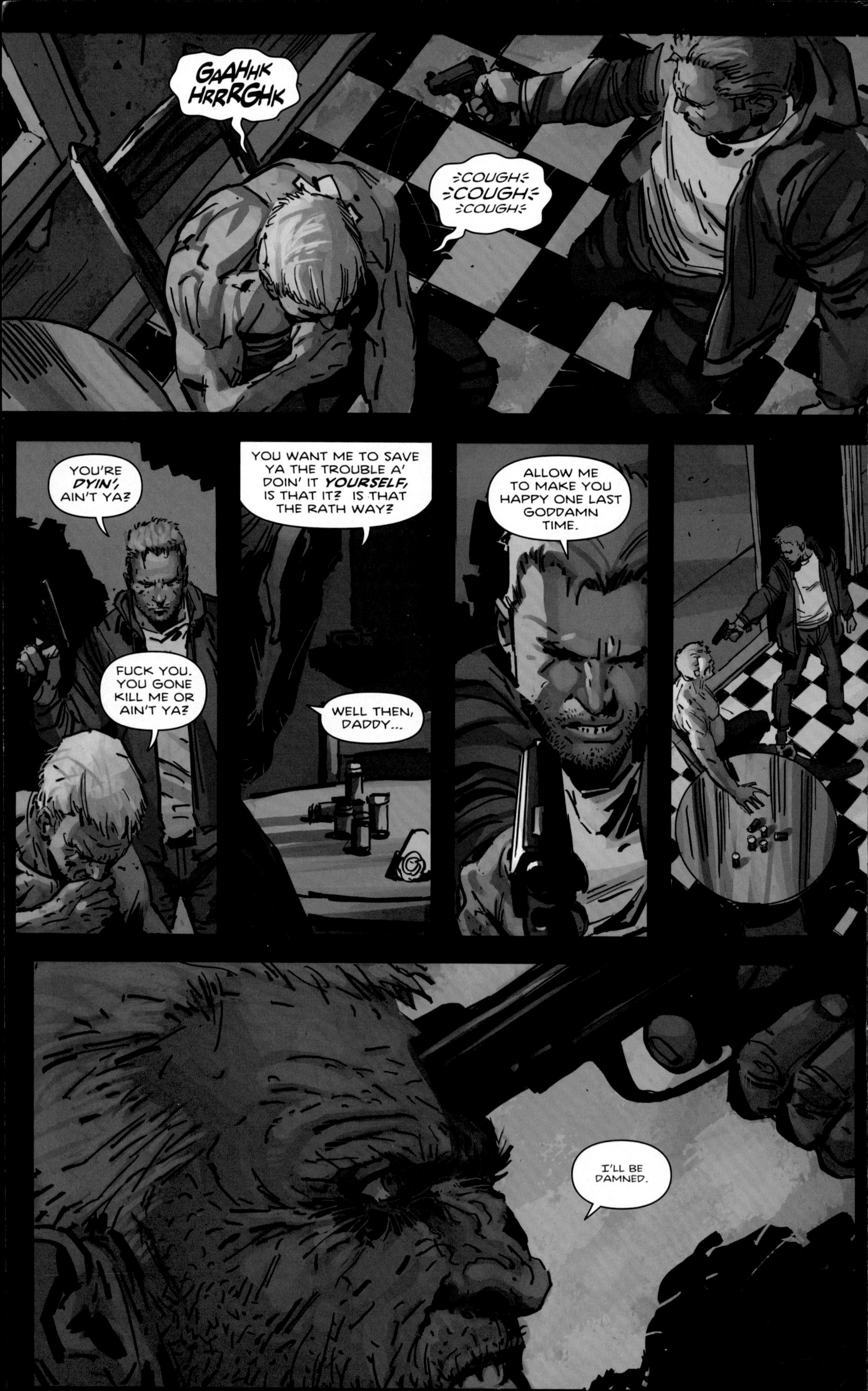
GAAHHK HRRRGHK
COUGH COUGH COUGH
YOU'RE DYIN', AIN'T YA?
FUCK YOU. YOU GONE KILL ME OR AIN'T YA?
YOU WANT ME TO SAVE YA THE TROUBLE A' DOIN' IT YOURSELF, IS THAT IT? IS THAT THE RATH WAY?
WELL THEN, DADDY...
ALLOW ME TO MAKE YOU HAPPY ONE LAST GODDAMN TIME.
I'LL BE DAMNED.

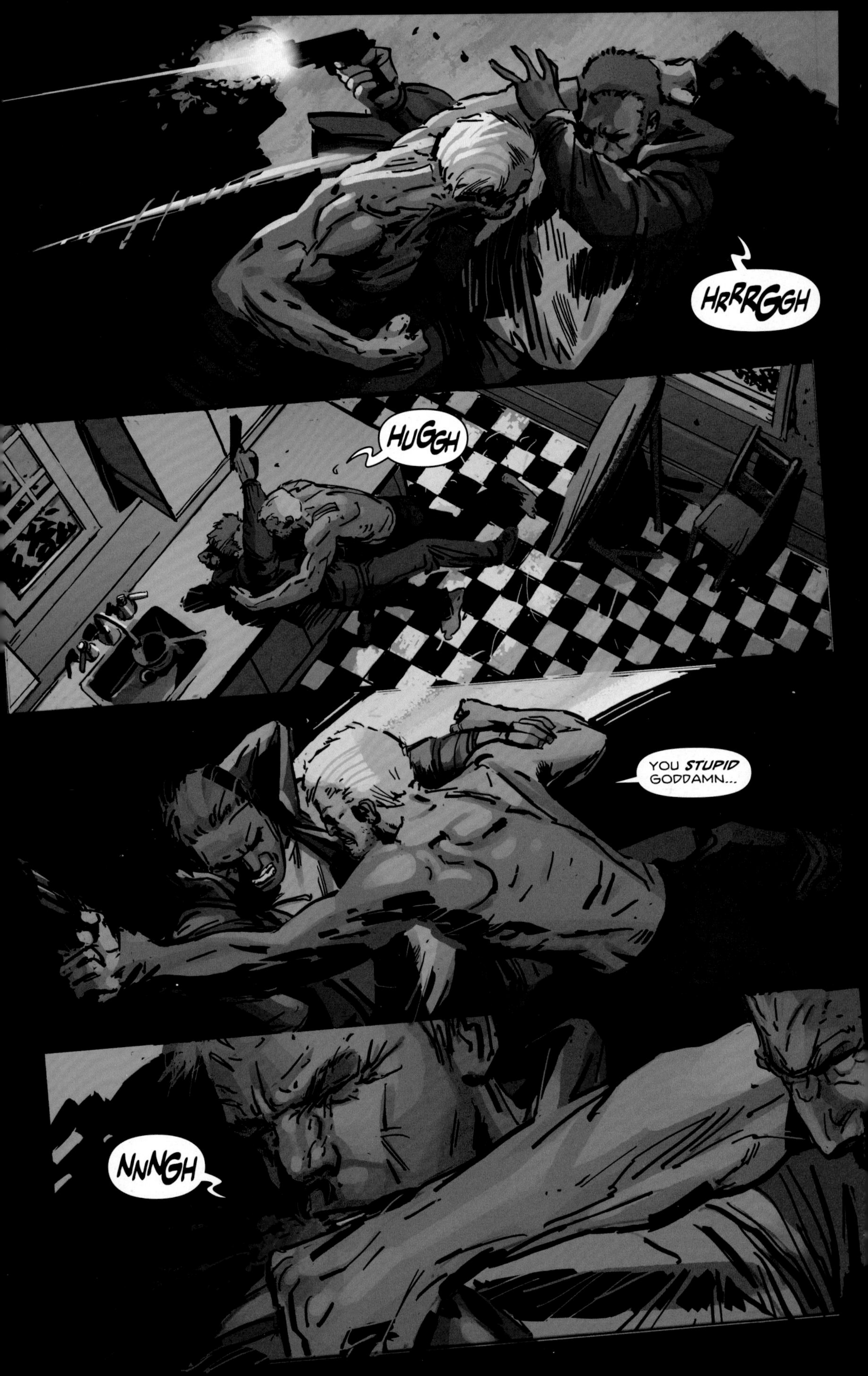
HRRRGGH
HUGGH
YOU STUPID GODDAMN...
NNNGH

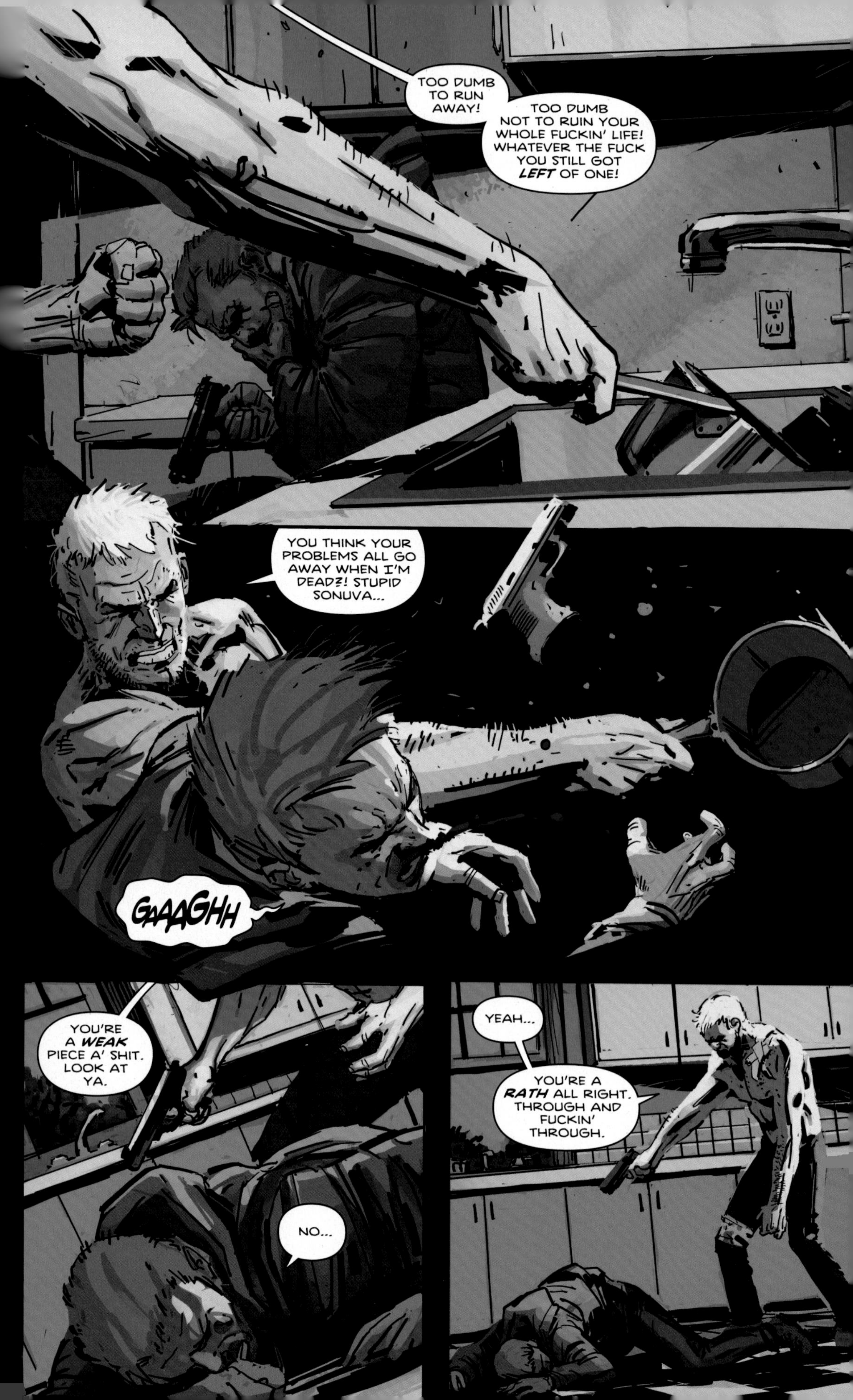
TOO DUMB TO RUN AWAY!
TOO DUMB NOT TO RUIN YOUR WHOLE FUCKIN' LIFE! WHATEVER THE FUCK YOU STILL GOT LEFT OF ONE!
YOU THINK YOUR PROBLEMS ALL GO AWAY WHEN I'M DEAD?! STUPID SONUVA...
GAAAGHH
YOU'RE A WEAK PIECE A' SHIT. LOOK AT YA.
NO...
YEAH...
YOU'RE A RATH ALL RIGHT. THROUGH AND FUCKIN' THROUGH.

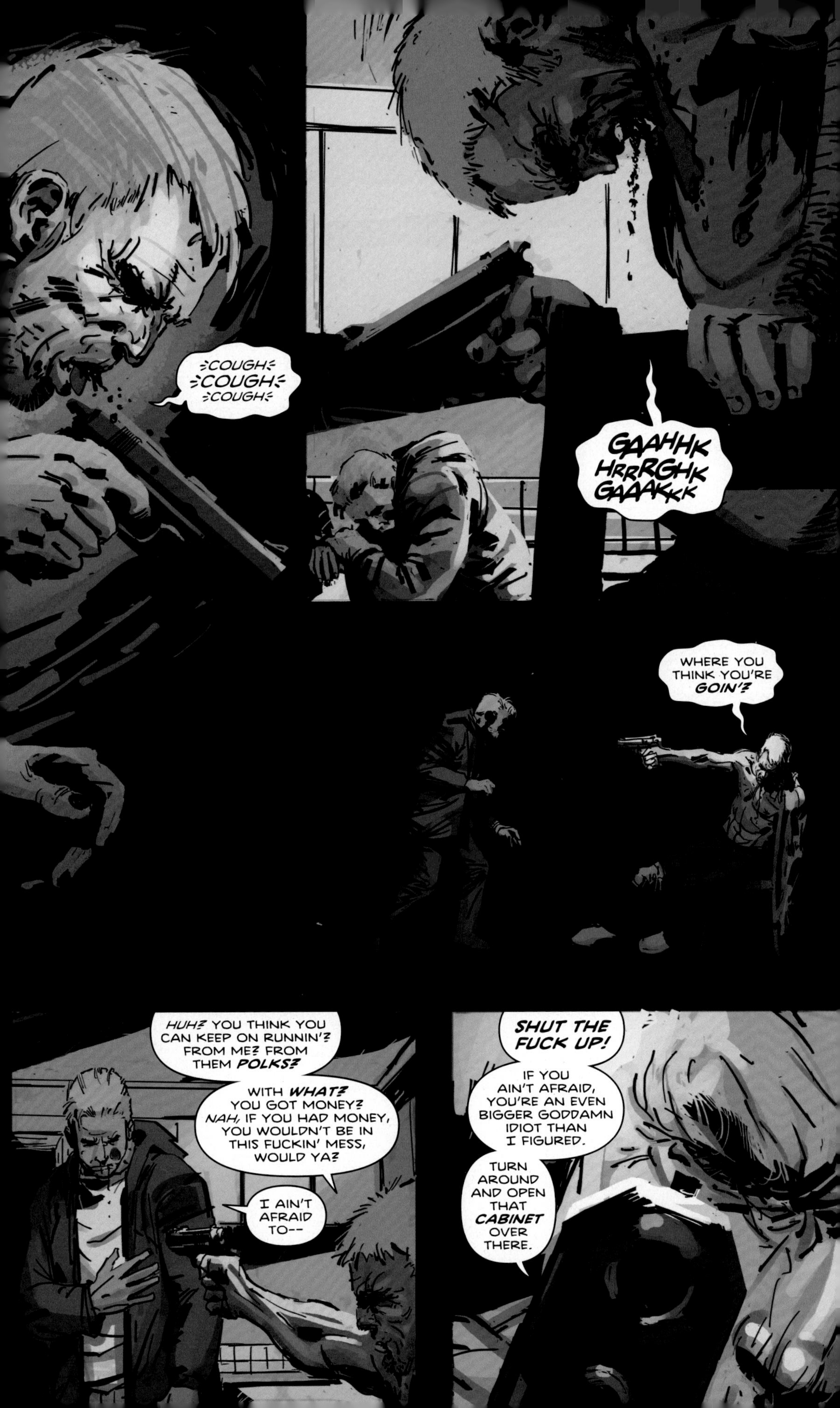
COUGH COUGH COUGH
GAAHHK HRRRGHK GAAAKKK
WHERE YOU THINK YOU'RE GOIN'?
HUH? YOU THINK YOU CAN KEEP ON RUNNIN'? FROM ME? FROM THEM POLKS?
WITH WHAT? YOU GOT MONEY? NAH, IF YOU HAD MONEY, YOU WOULDN'T BE IN THIS FUCKIN' MESS, WOULD YA?
I AIN'T AFRAID TO--
SHUT THE FUCK UP!
IF YOU AIN'T AFRAID, YOU'RE AN EVEN BIGGER GODDAMN IDIOT THAN I FIGURED.
TURN AROUND AND OPEN THAT CABINET OVER THERE.

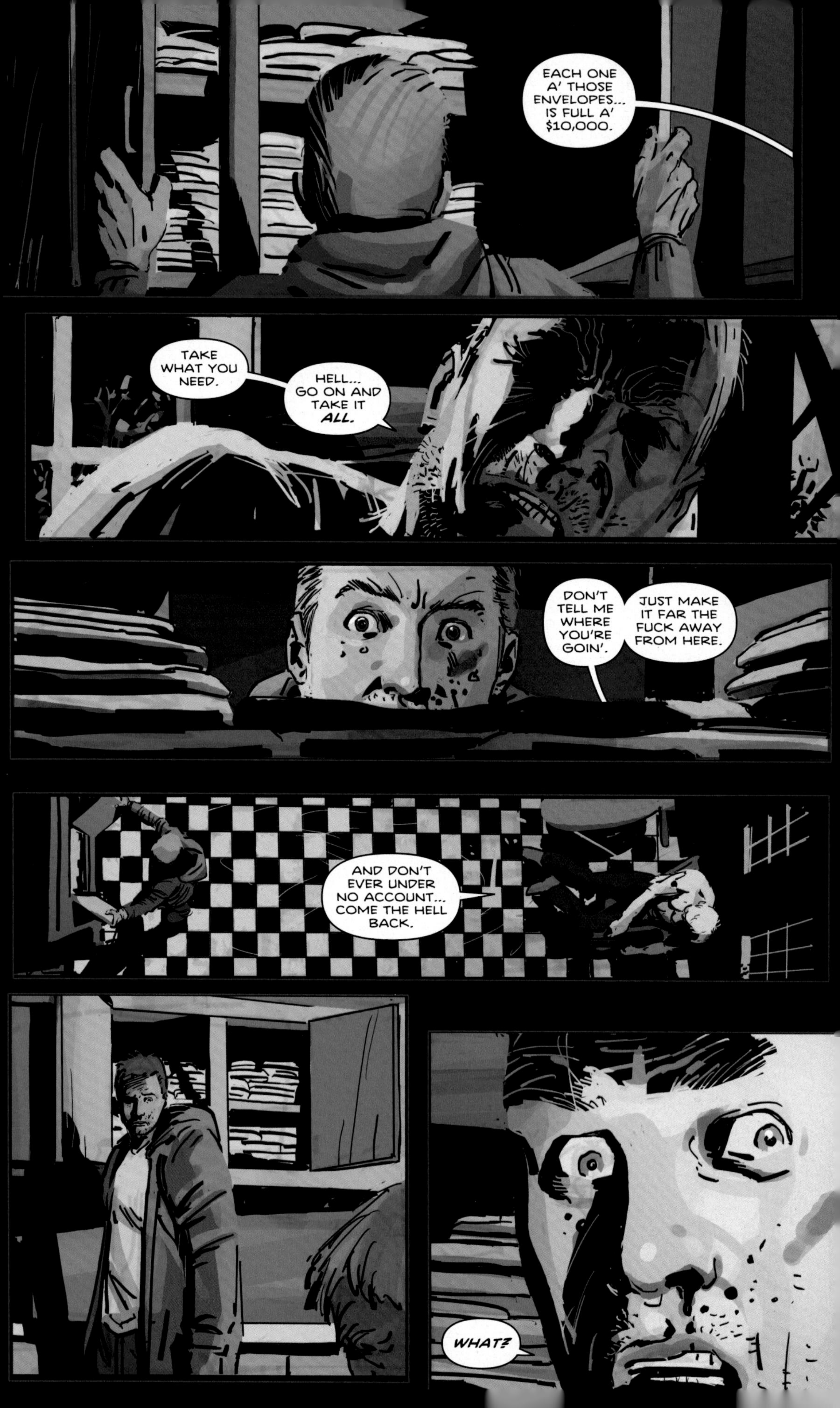

EACH ONE A' THOSE ENVELOPES... IS FULL A' $10,000.
TAKE WHAT YOU NEED.
HELL... GO ON AND TAKE IT ALL.
DON'T TELL ME WHERE YOU'RE GOIN'.
JUST MAKE IT FAR THE FUCK AWAY FROM HERE.
AND DON'T EVER UNDER NO ACCOUNT... COME THE HELL BACK.
WHAT?

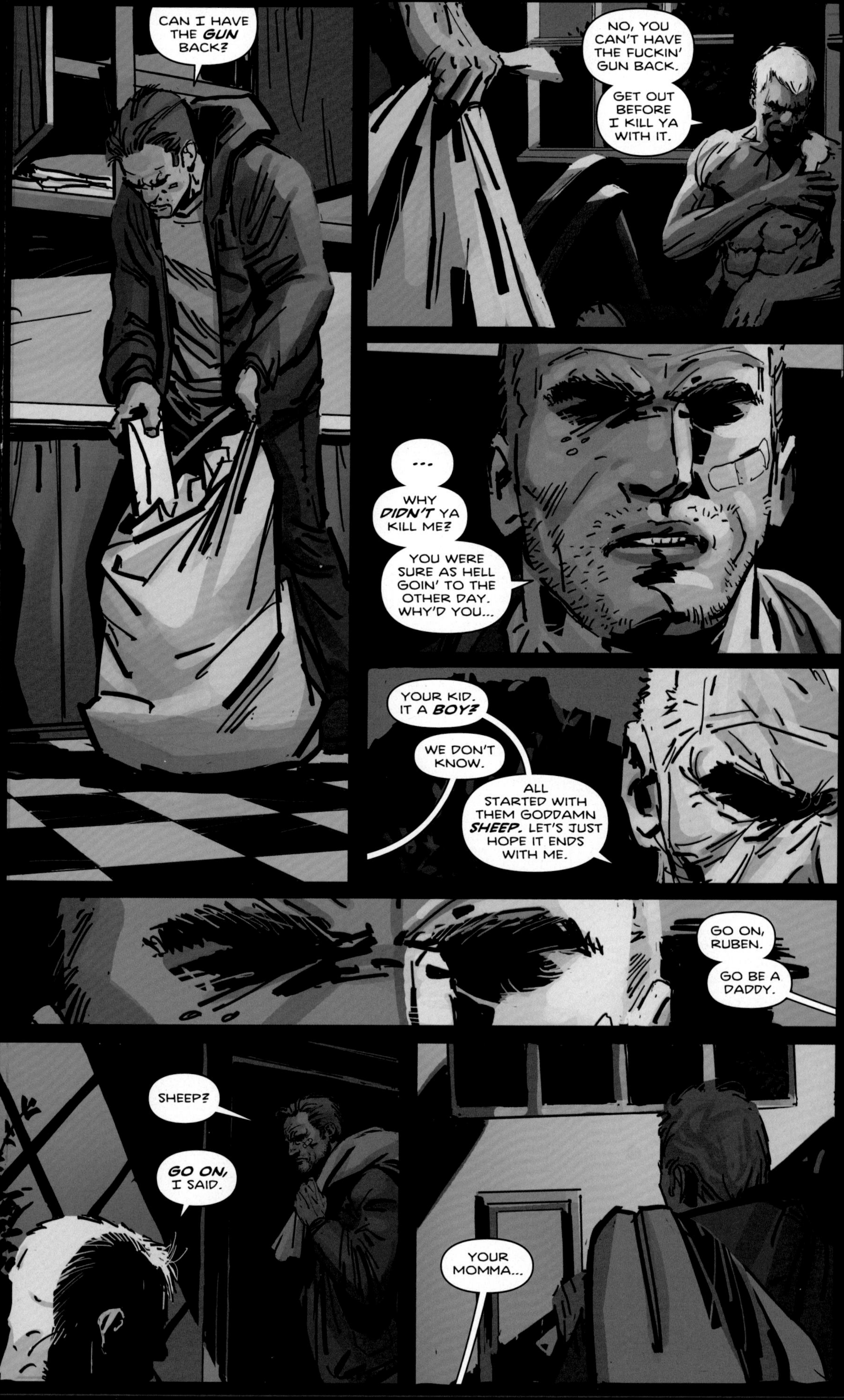
CAN I HAVE THE GUN BACK?
NO, YOU CAN'T HAVE THE FUCKIN' GUN BACK.
GET OUT BEFORE I KILL YA WITH IT.
...
WHY DIDN'T YA KILL ME?
YOU WERE SURE AS HELL GOIN' TO THE OTHER DAY. WHY'D YOU...
YOUR KID. IT A BOY?
WE DON'T KNOW.
ALL STARTED WITH THEM GODDAMN SHEEP. LET'S JUST HOPE IT ENDS WITH ME.
GO ON, RUBEN.
GO BE A DADDY.
SHEEP?
GO ON, I SAID.
YOUR MOMMA...

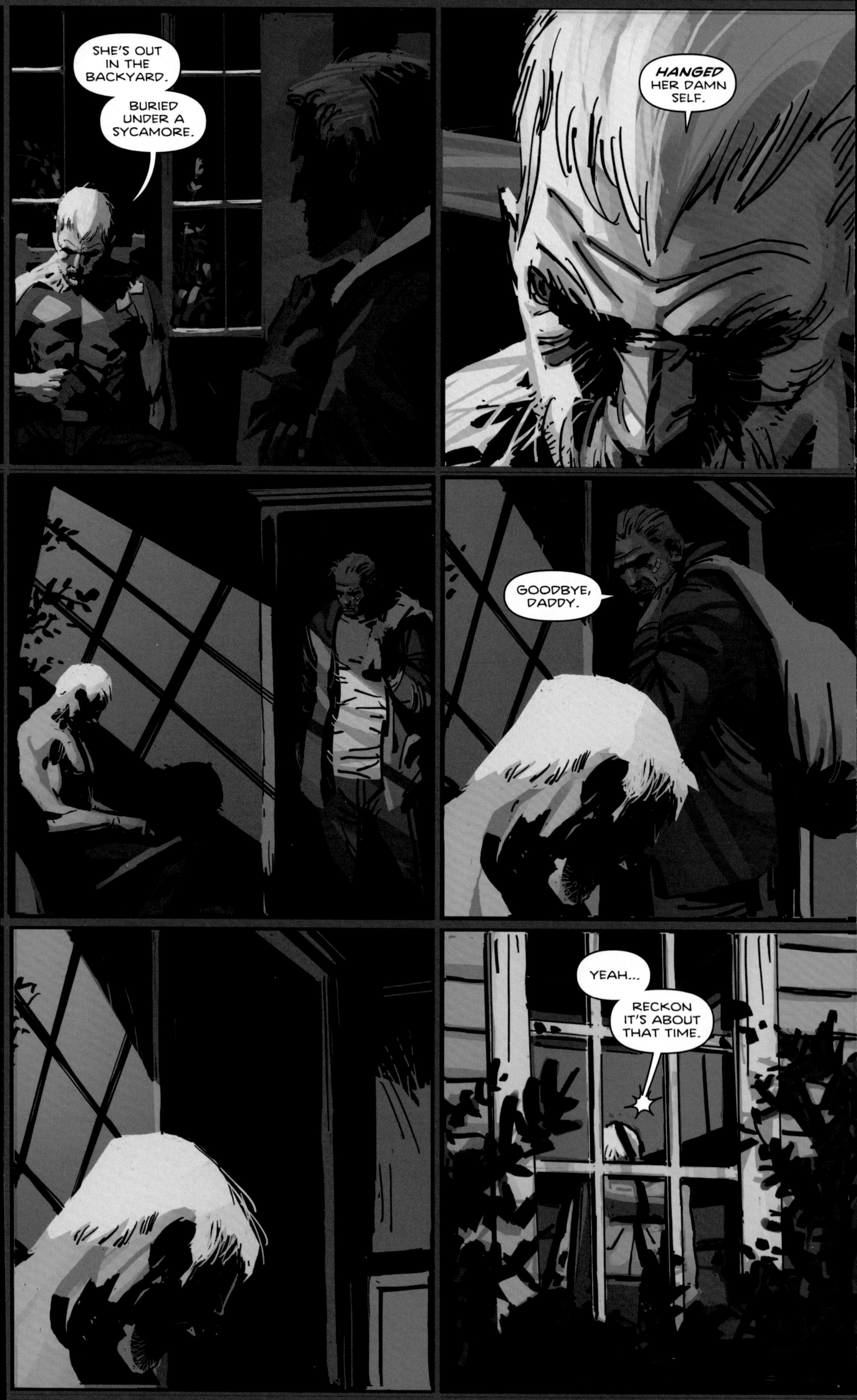
SHE'S OUT IN THE BACKYARD.
BURIED UNDER A SYCAMORE.
HANGED HER DAMN SELF.
GOODBYE, DADDY.
YEAH...
RECKON IT'S ABOUT THAT TIME.

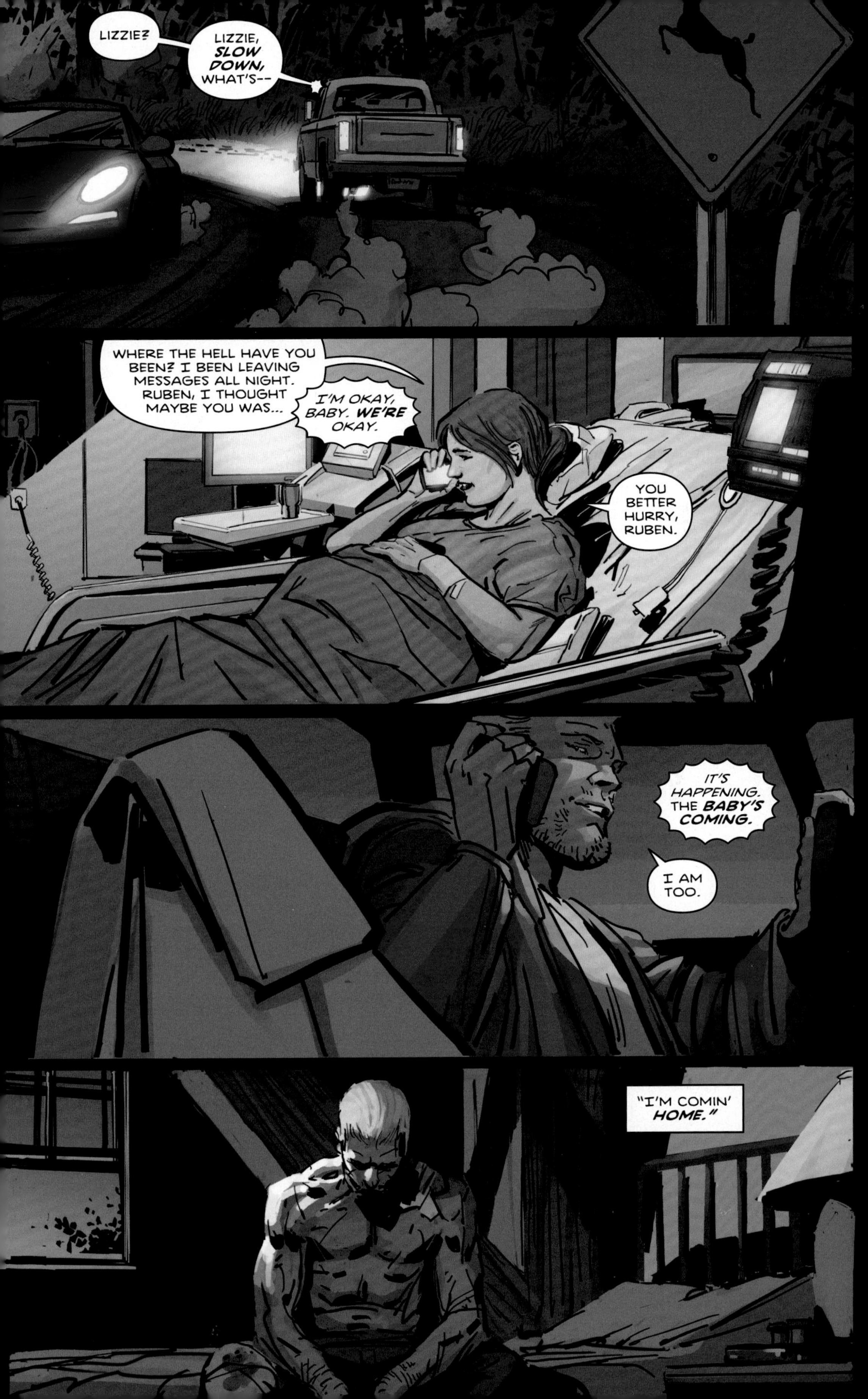
LIZZIE?
LIZZIE, SLOW DOWN, WHAT'S--
WHERE THE HELL HAVE YOU BEEN? I BEEN LEAVING MESSAGES ALL NIGHT. RUBEN, I THOUGHT MAYBE YOU WAS...
I'M OKAY, BABY. WE'RE OKAY.
YOU BETTER HURRY, RUBEN.
IT'S HAPPENING. THE BABY'S COMING.
I AM TOO.
"I'M COMIN' HOME."

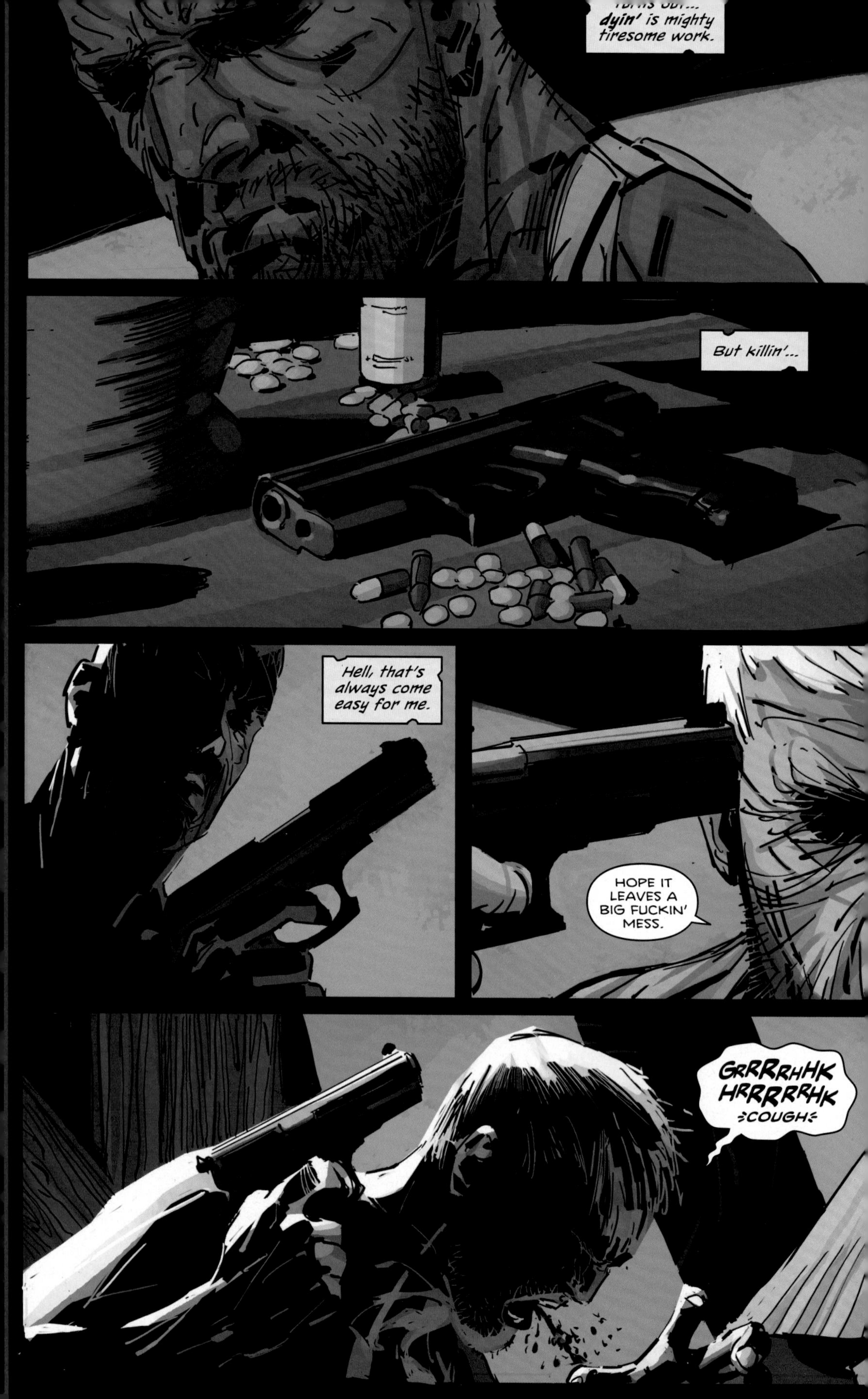
dyin' is mighty tiresome work.
But killin'...
Hell, that's always come easy for me.
HOPE IT LEAVES A BIG FUCKIN' MESS.
GRRRRHHK HRRRRRHK
COUGH

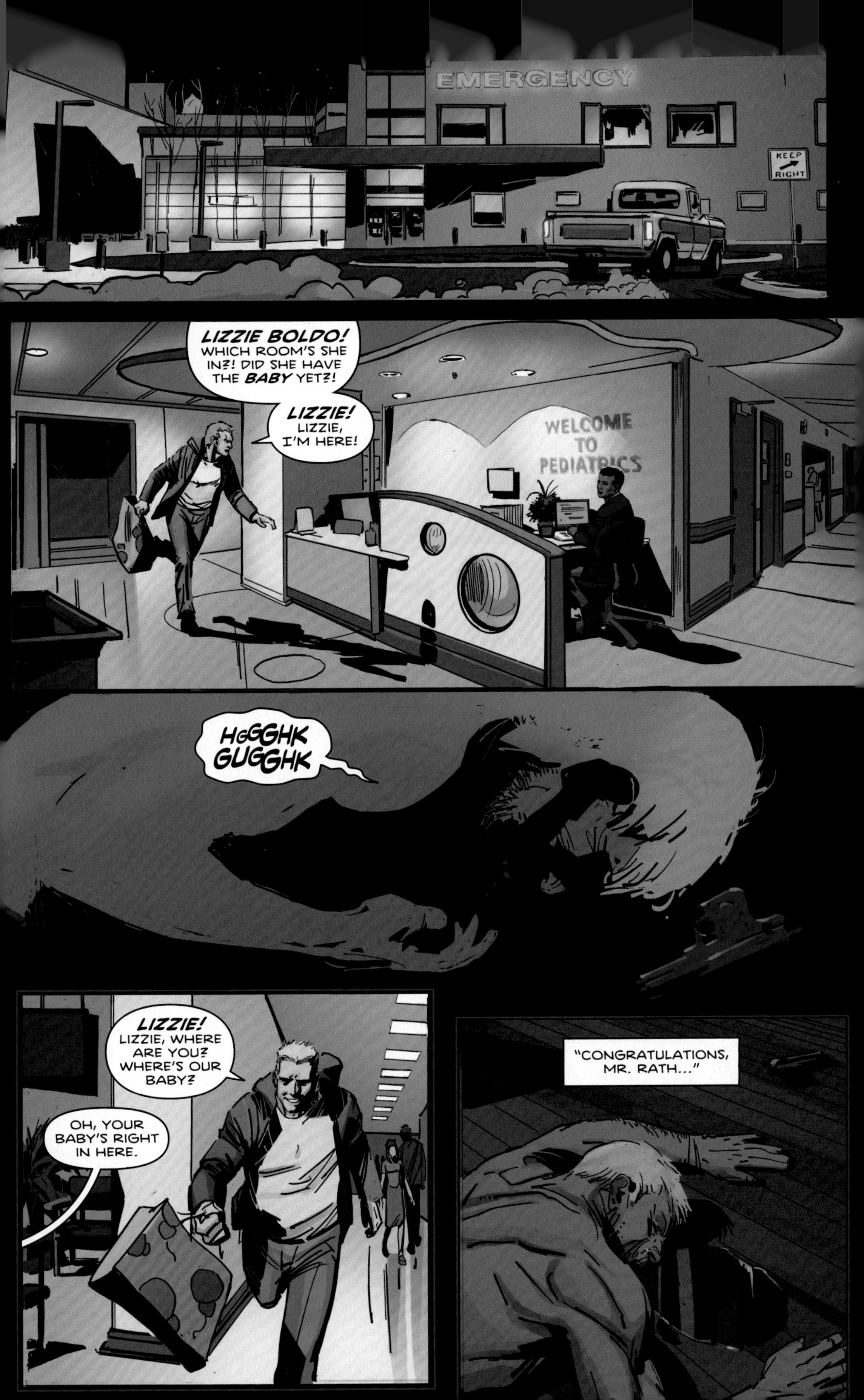
EMERGENCY
KEEP RIGHT
LIZZIE BOLDO! WHICH ROOM'S SHE IN?! DID SHE HAVE THE BABY YET?!
LIZZIE! LIZZIE, I'M HERE!
WELCOME TO PEDIATRICS
HGGGHK GUGGHK
LIZZIE! LIZZIE, WHERE ARE YOU? WHERE'S OUR BABY?
OH, YOUR BABY'S RIGHT IN HERE.
"CONGRATULATIONS, MR. RATH..."

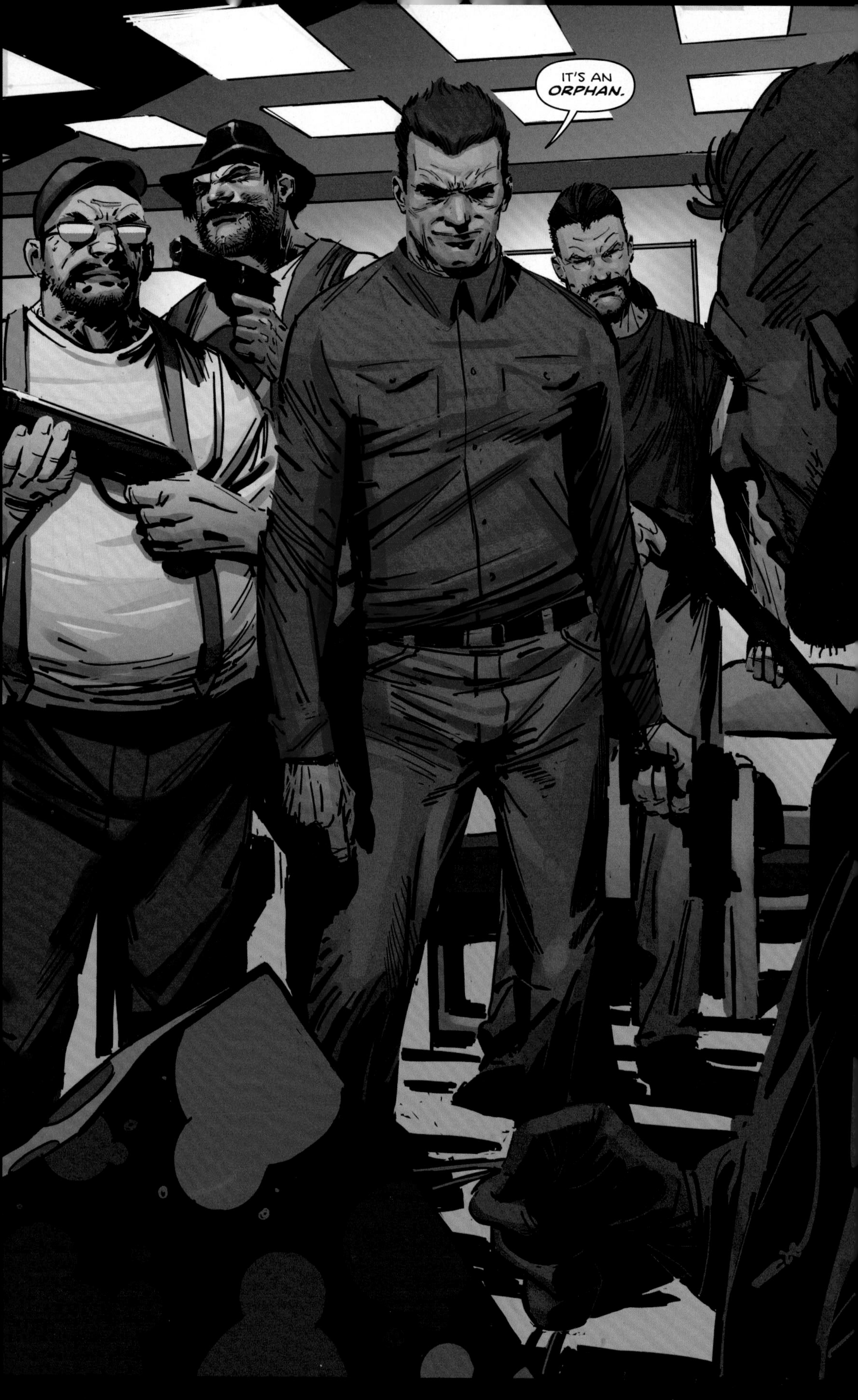
IT'S AN ORPHAN.

CHAPTER FIVE

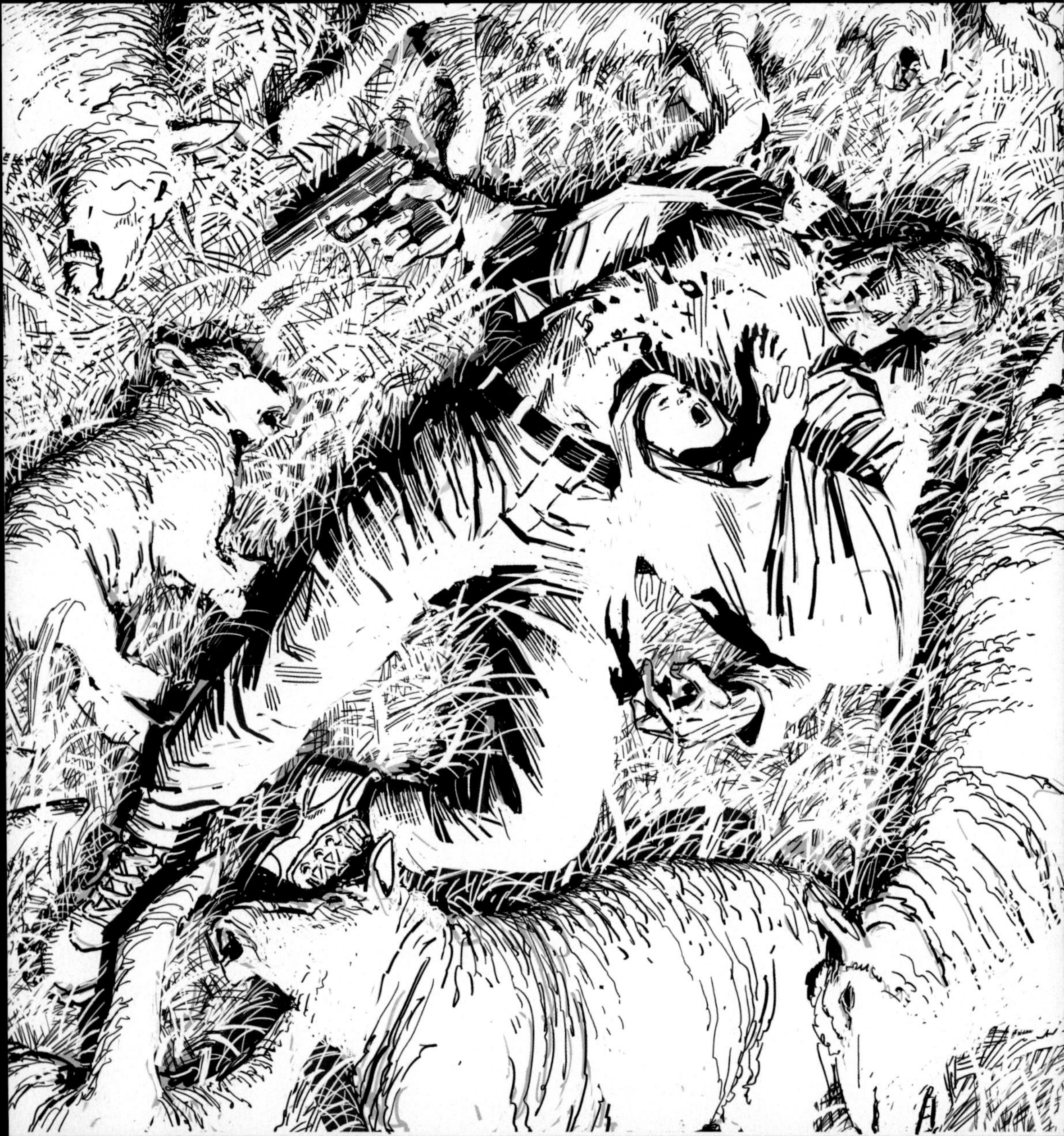

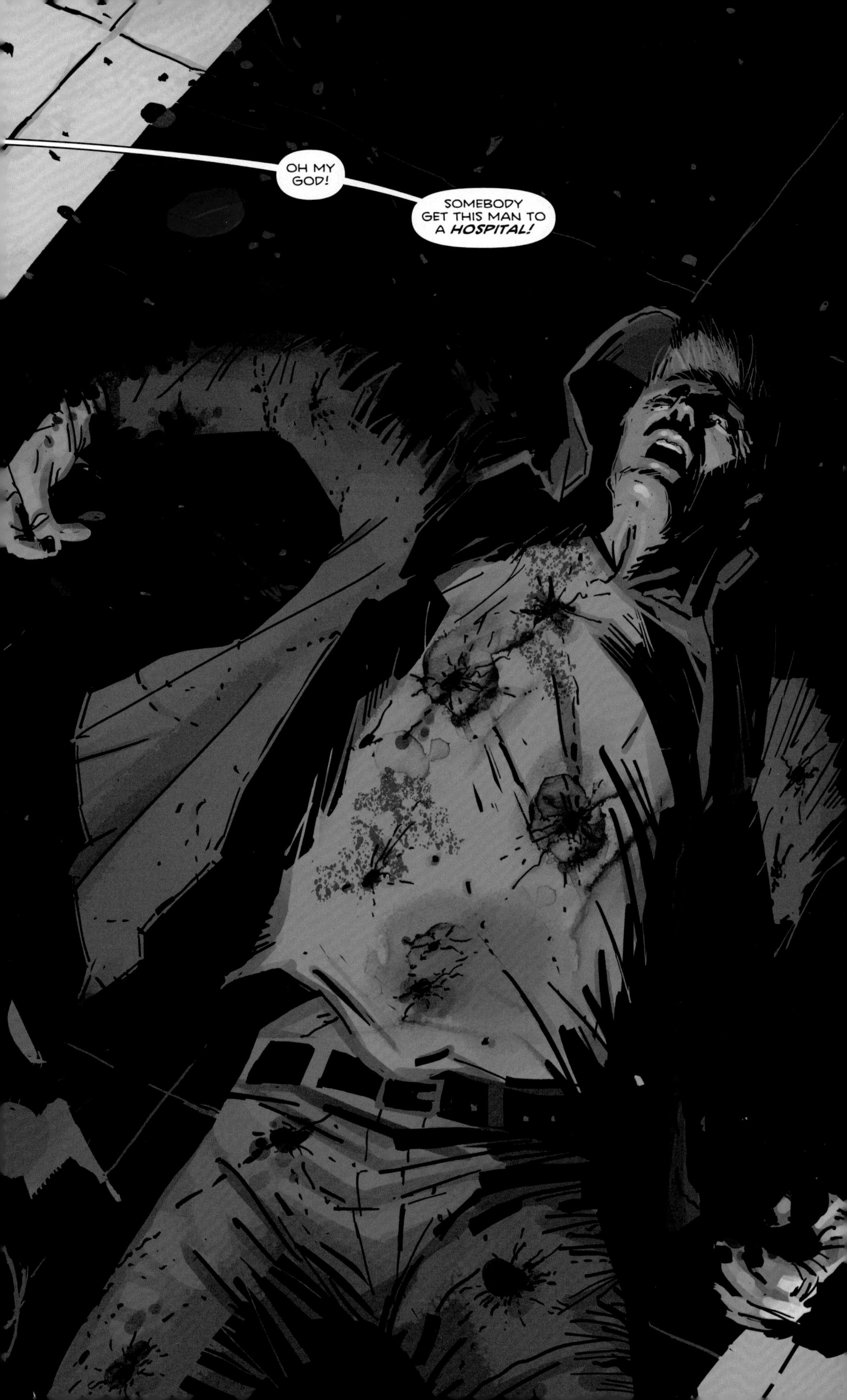
OH MY GOD!
SOMEBODY GET THIS MAN TO A HOSPITAL!

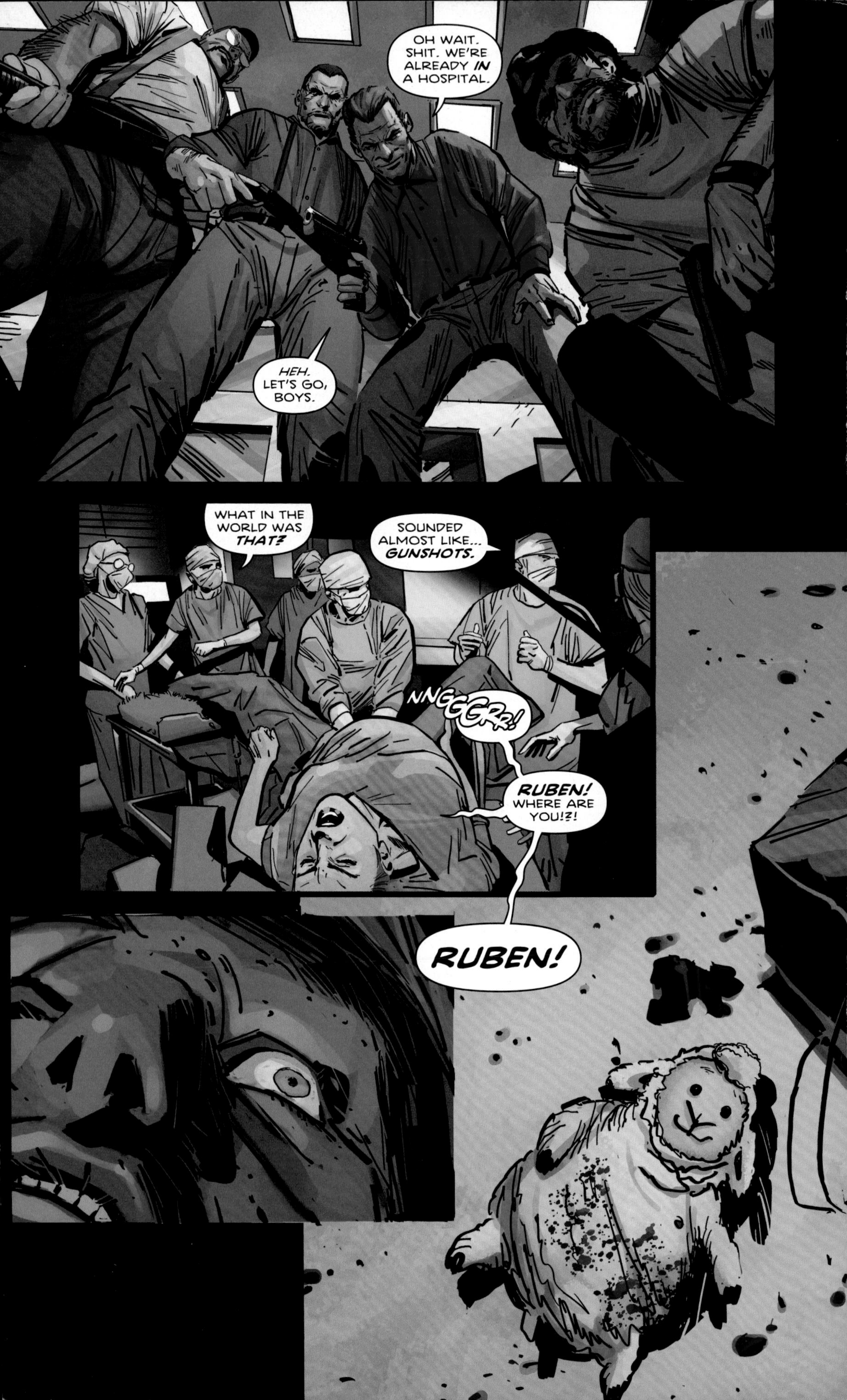
OH WAIT. SHIT. WE'RE ALREADY *IN* A HOSPITAL.
HEH. LET'S GO, BOYS.
WHAT IN THE WORLD WAS *THAT?*
SOUNDED ALMOST LIKE... *GUNSHOTS.*
NNGGGRR!
RUBEN! WHERE ARE YOU!?!
RUBEN!

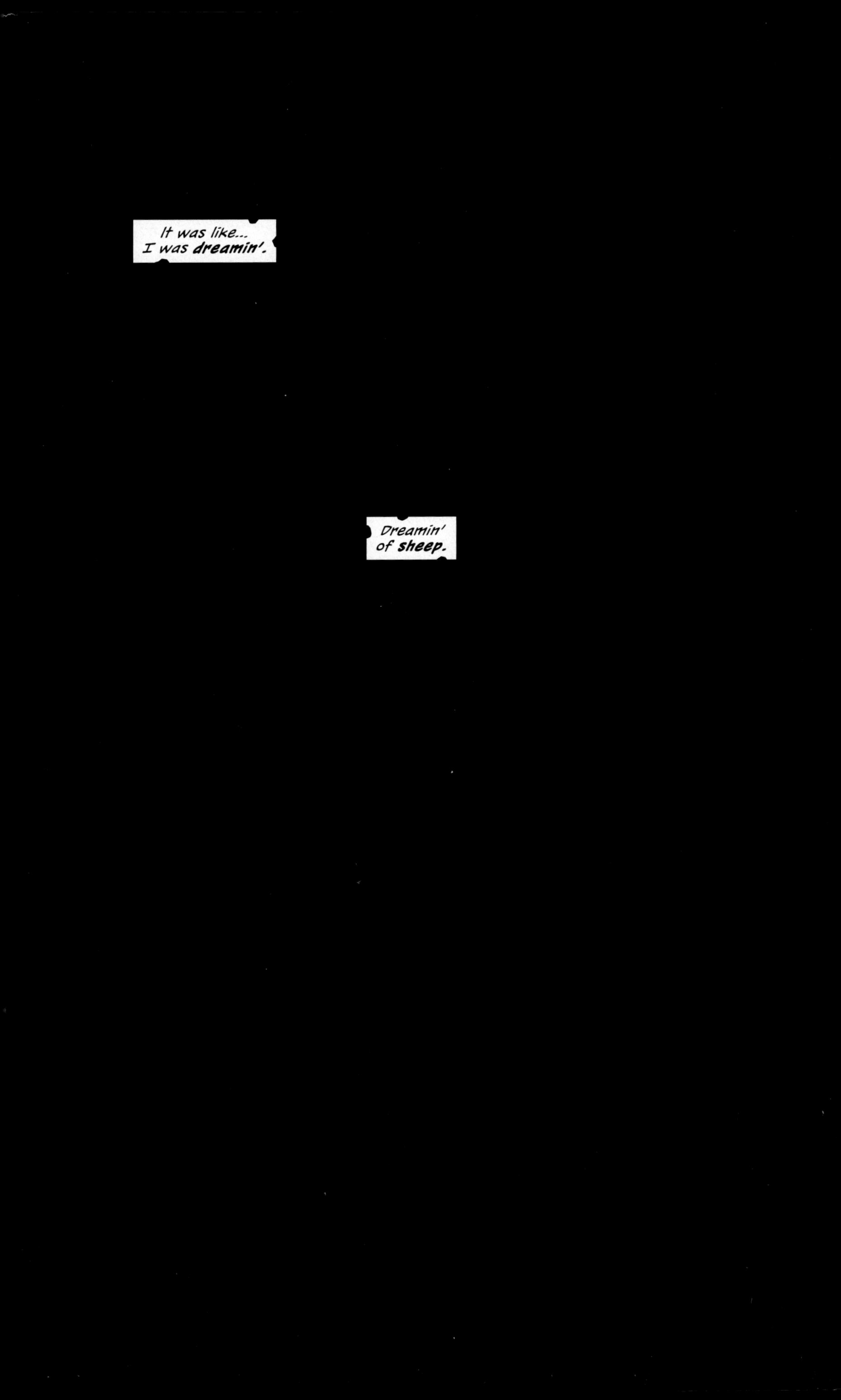
It was like... I was **dreamin'.**
Dreamin' of **sheep.**

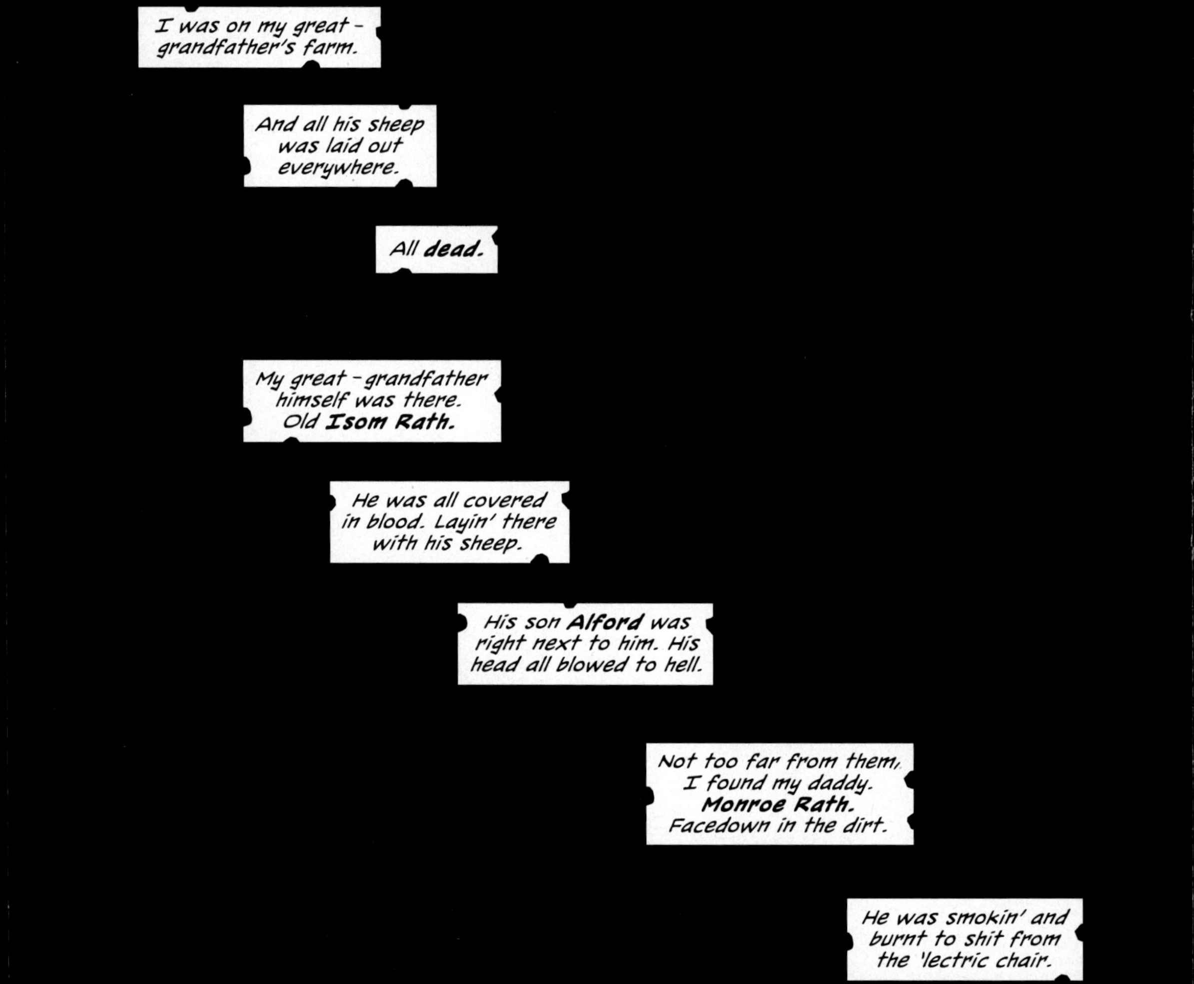
I was on my great-grandfather's farm.
And all his sheep was laid out everywhere.
All **dead.**
My great-grandfather himself was there. Old **Isom Rath.**
He was all covered in blood. Layin' there with his sheep.
His son **Alford** was right next to him. His head all blowed to hell.
Not too far from them, I found my daddy. **Monroe Rath.** Facedown in the dirt.
He was smokin' and burnt to shit from the 'lectric chair.

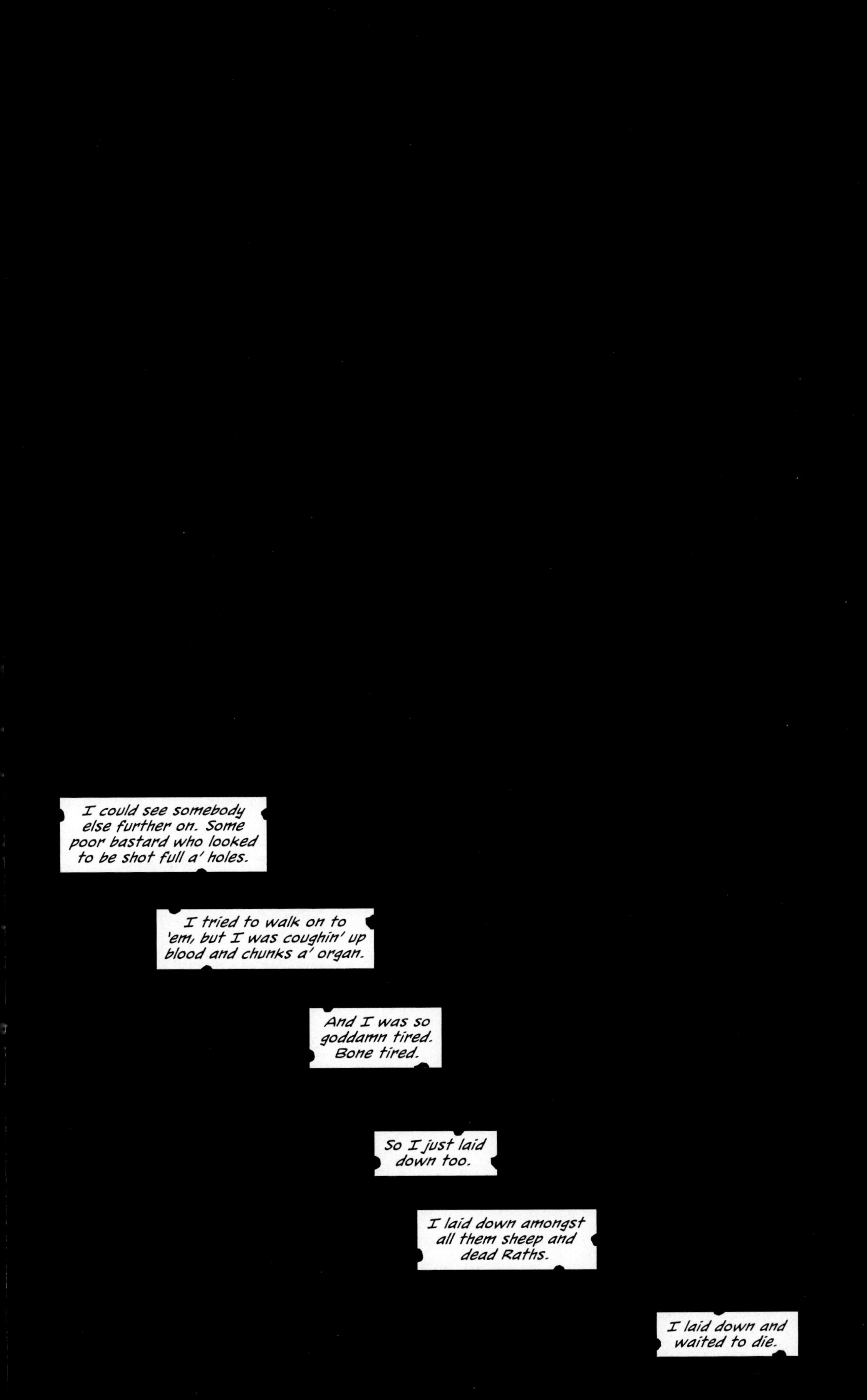
I could see somebody else further on. Some poor bastard who looked to be shot full a' holes.
I tried to walk on to 'em, but I was coughin' up blood and chunks a' organ.
And I was so goddamn tired. Bone tired.
So I just laid down too.
I laid down amongst all them sheep and dead Raths.
I laid down and waited to die.

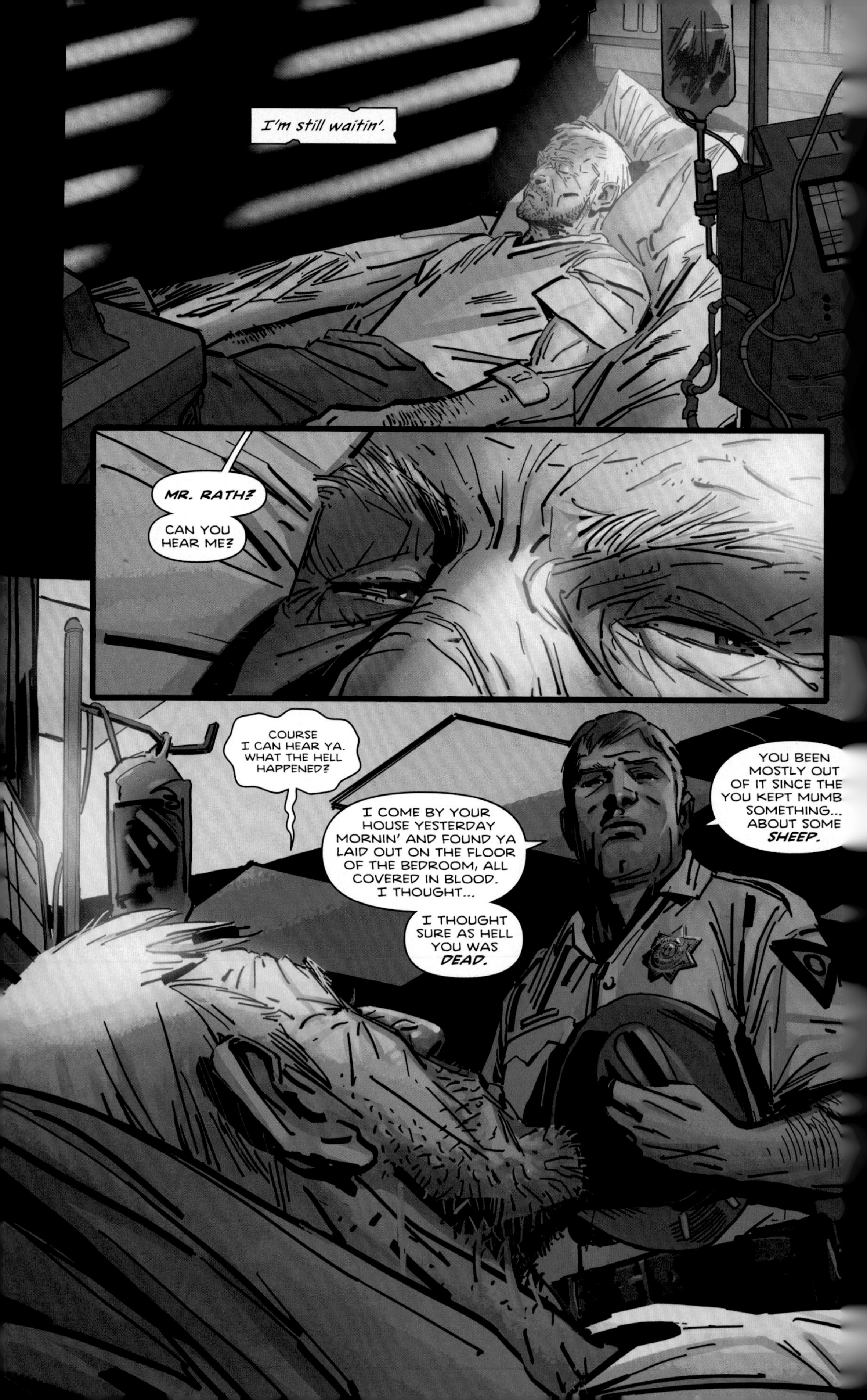

I'm still waitin'.
MR. RATH?
CAN YOU HEAR ME?
COURSE I CAN HEAR YA. WHAT THE HELL HAPPENED?
I COME BY YOUR HOUSE YESTERDAY MORNIN' AND FOUND YA LAID OUT ON THE FLOOR OF THE BEDROOM, ALL COVERED IN BLOOD. I THOUGHT...
I THOUGHT SURE AS HELL YOU WAS DEAD.
YOU BEEN MOSTLY OUT OF IT SINCE THE YOU KEPT MUMB SOMETHING... ABOUT SOME SHEEP.

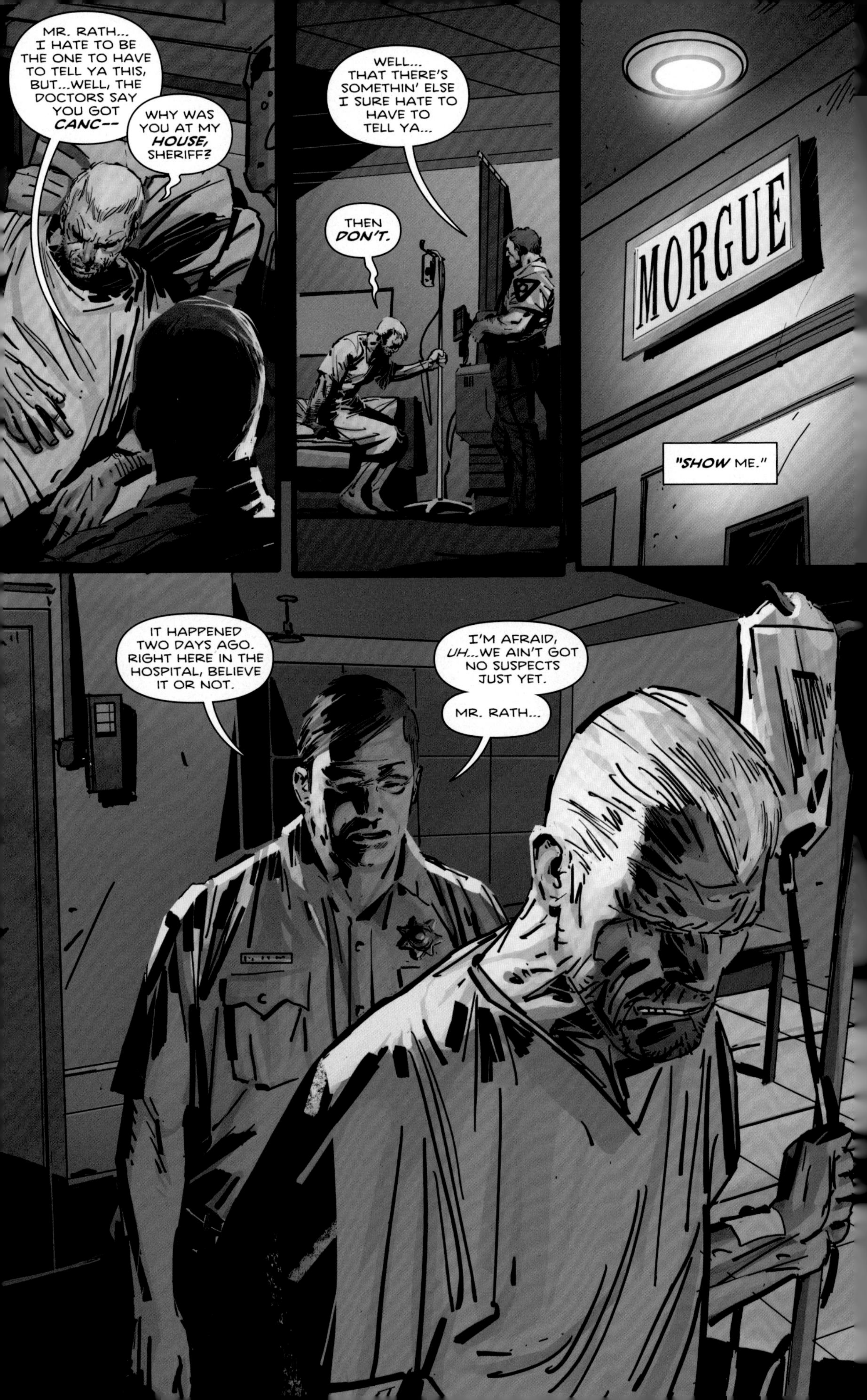
MR. RATH... I HATE TO BE THE ONE TO HAVE TO TELL YA THIS, BUT...WELL, THE DOCTORS SAY YOU GOT CANC--
WHY WAS YOU AT MY HOUSE, SHERIFF?
WELL... THAT THERE'S SOMETHIN' ELSE I SURE HATE TO HAVE TO TELL YA...
THEN DON'T.
MORGUE
"SHOW ME."
IT HAPPENED TWO DAYS AGO. RIGHT HERE IN THE HOSPITAL, BELIEVE IT OR NOT.
I'M AFRAID, UH...WE AIN'T GOT NO SUSPECTS JUST YET.
MR. RATH...

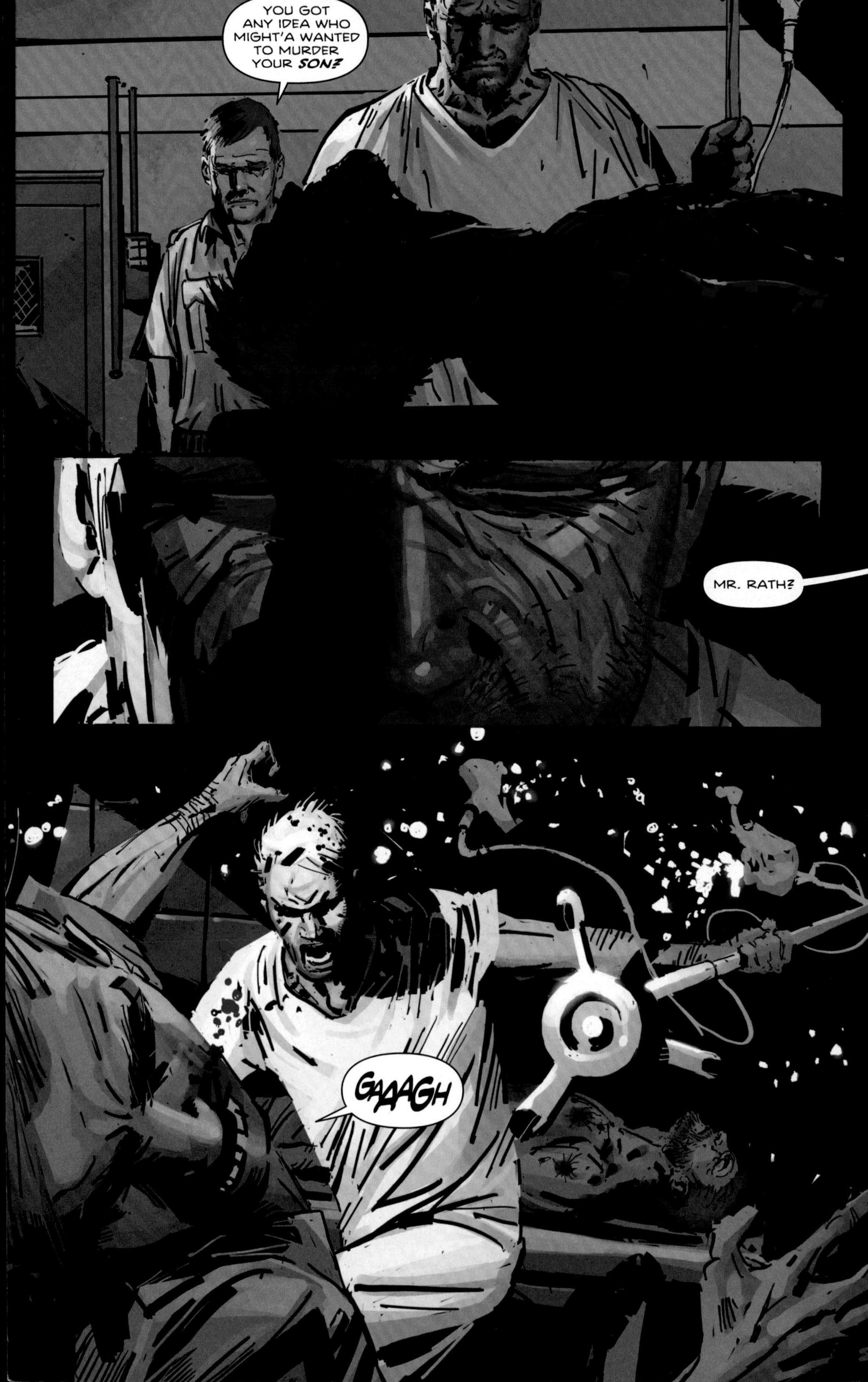
YOU GOT ANY IDEA WHO MIGHT'A WANTED TO MURDER YOUR SON?
MR. RATH?
GAAAGH

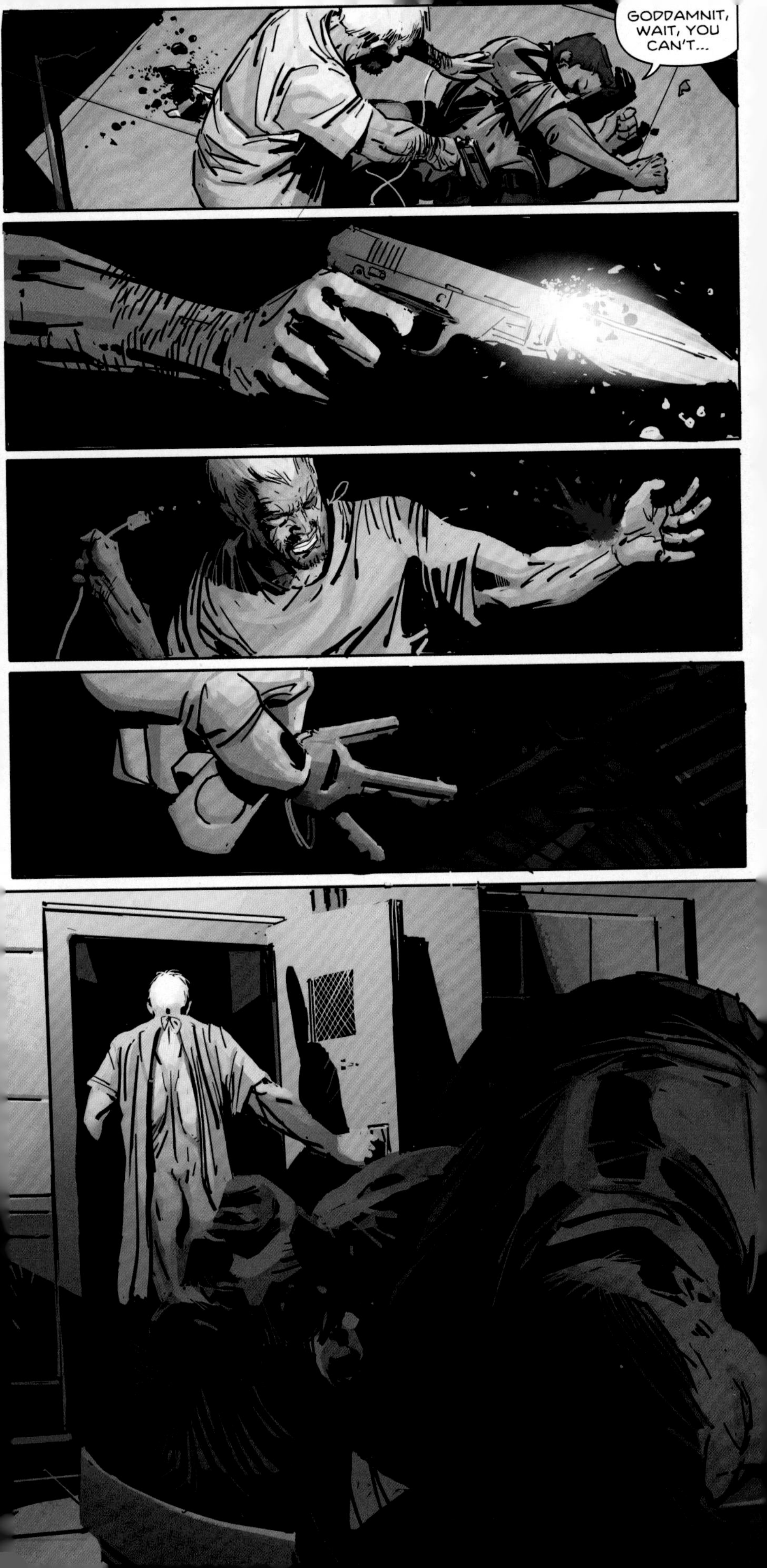
GODDAMNIT, WAIT, YOU CAN'T...

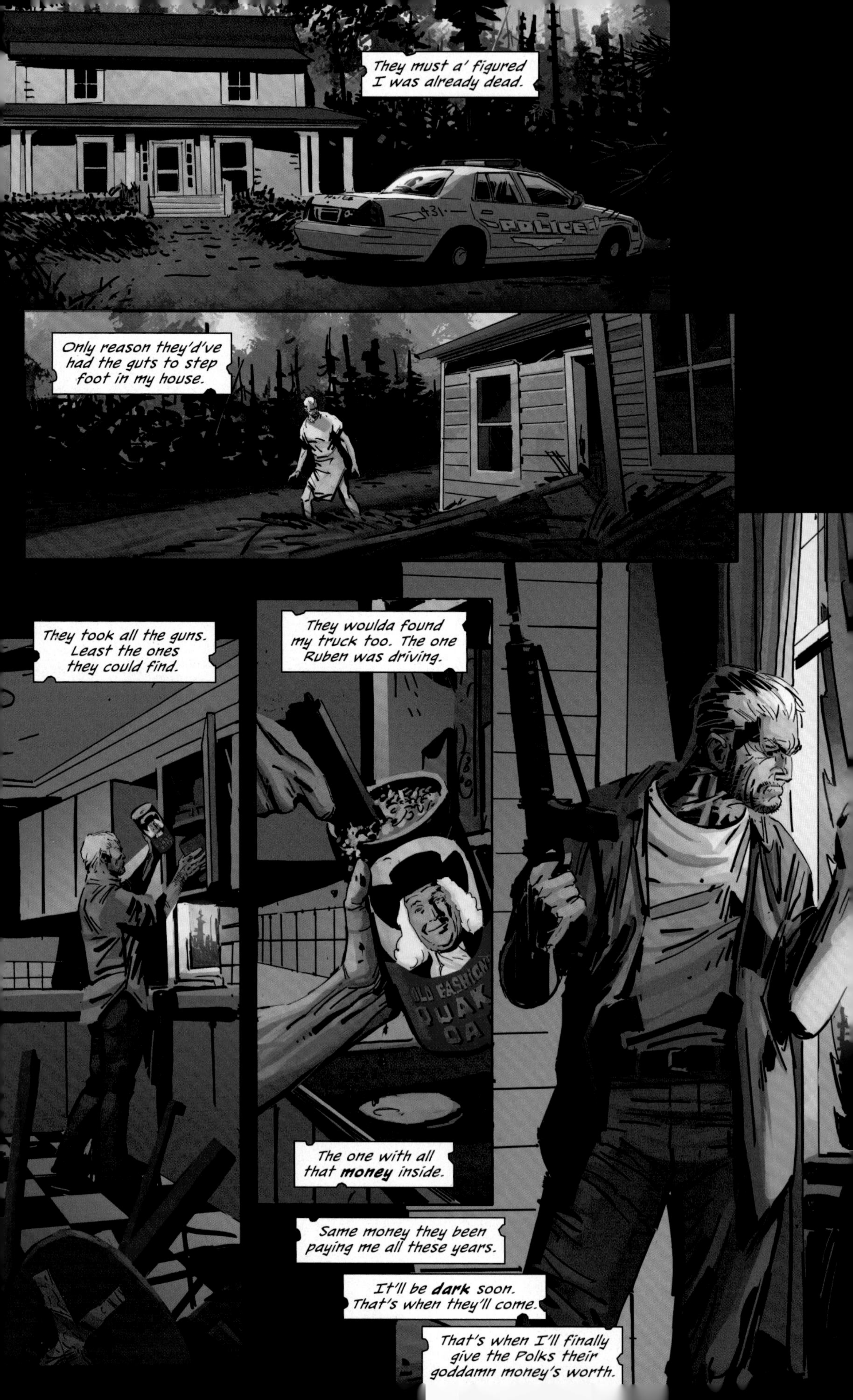
They must a' figured I was already dead.
Only reason they'd've had the guts to step foot in my house.
They took all the guns. Least the ones they could find.
They woulda found my truck too. The one Ruben was driving.
The one with all that **money** inside.
Same money they been paying me all these years.
It'll be **dark** soon. That's when they'll come.
That's when I'll finally give the Polks their goddamn money's worth.

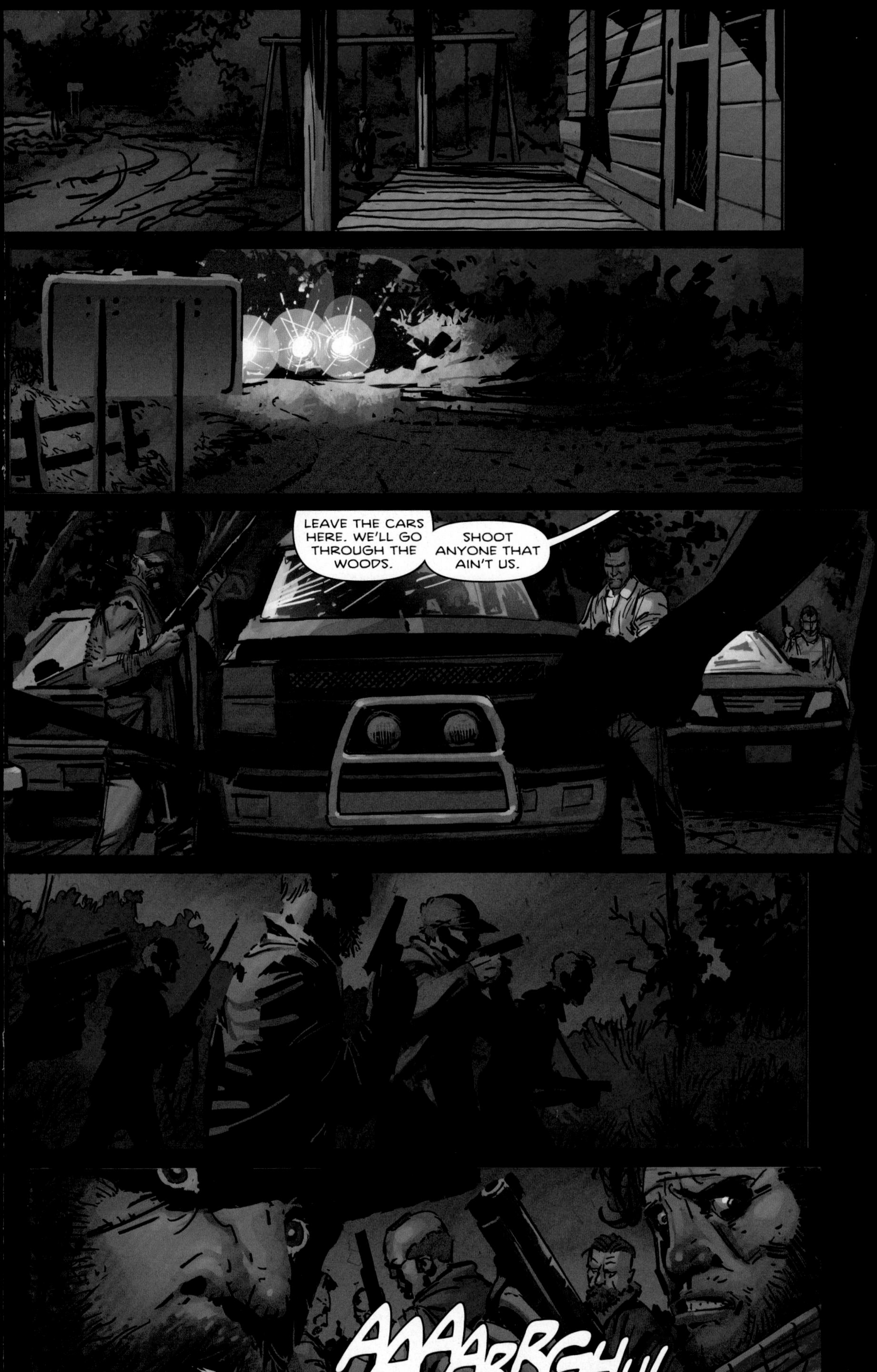
LEAVE THE CARS HERE. WE'LL GO THROUGH THE WOODS.
SHOOT ANYONE THAT AIN'T US.
AAAAARRGH!!

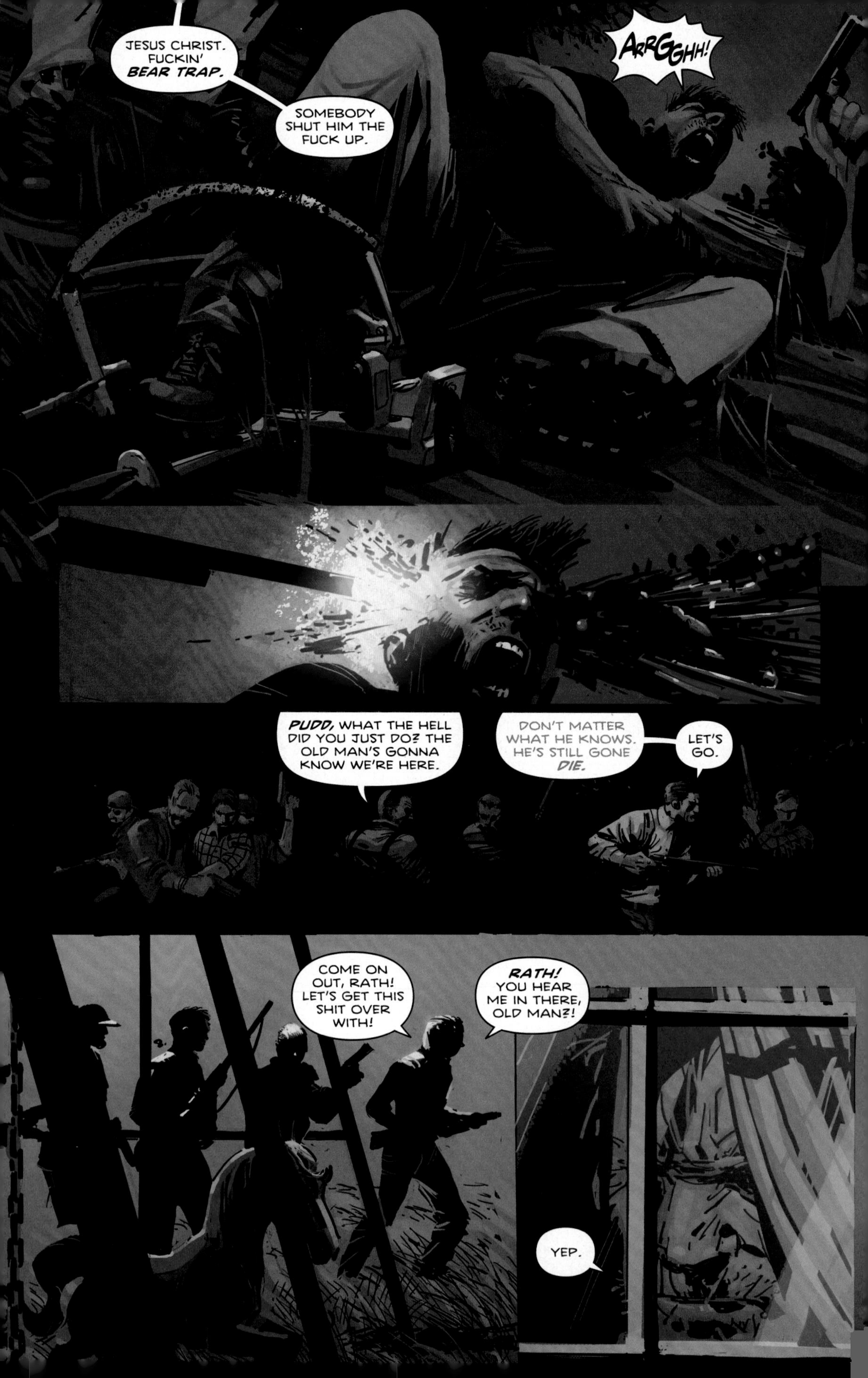

JESUS CHRIST. FUCKIN' BEAR TRAP.
ARRGGHH!
SOMEBODY SHUT HIM THE FUCK UP.
PUDD, WHAT THE HELL DID YOU JUST DO? THE OLD MAN'S GONNA KNOW WE'RE HERE.
DON'T MATTER WHAT HE KNOWS. HE'S STILL GONE DIE.
LET'S GO.
COME ON OUT, RATH! LET'S GET THIS SHIT OVER WITH!
RATH! YOU HEAR ME IN THERE, OLD MAN?!
YEP.

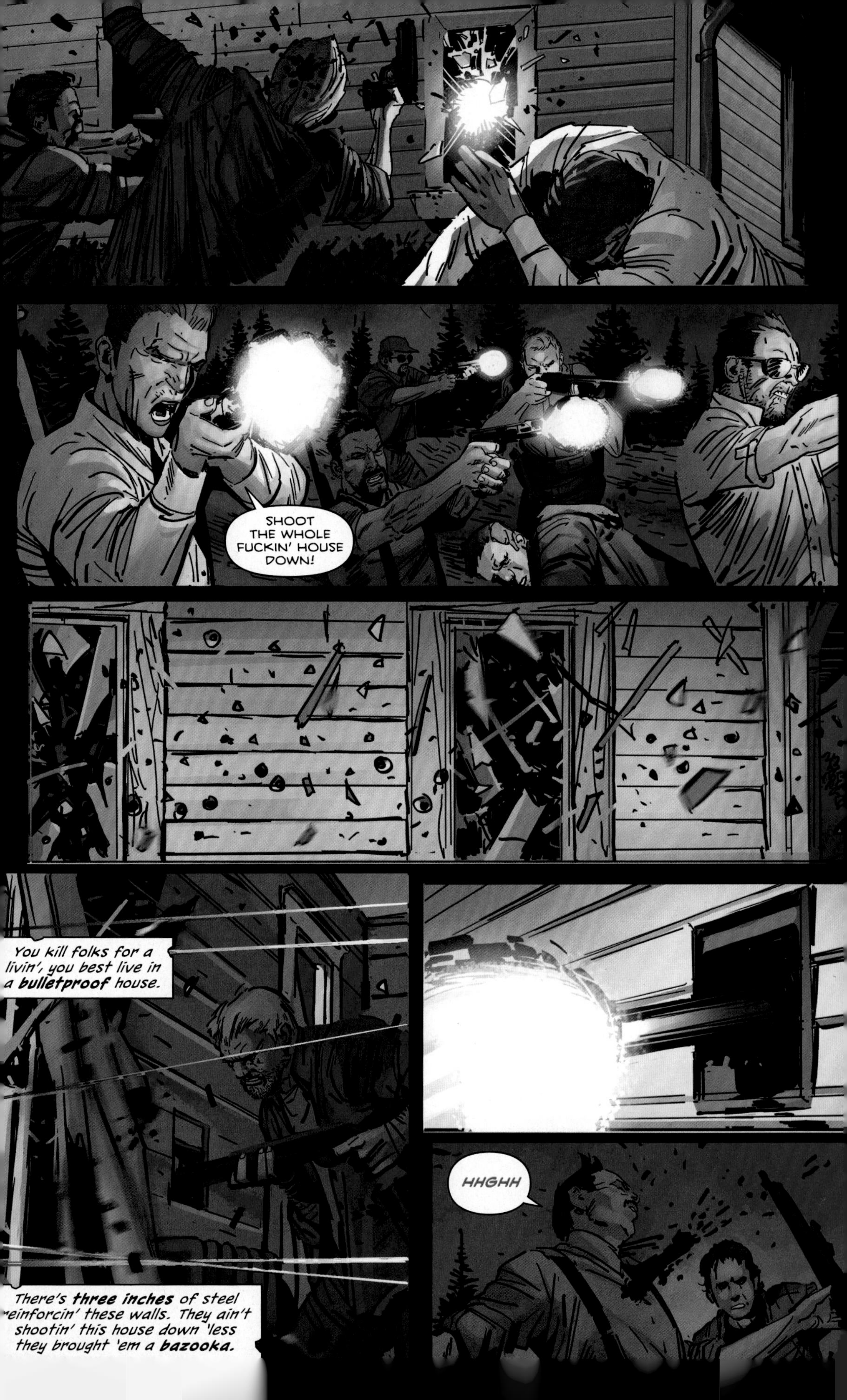
SHOOT THE WHOLE FUCKIN' HOUSE DOWN!
You kill folks for a livin', you best live in a **bulletproof** house.
There's **three inches** of steel reinforcin' these walls. They ain't shootin' this house down 'less they brought 'em a **bazooka.**
HHGHH

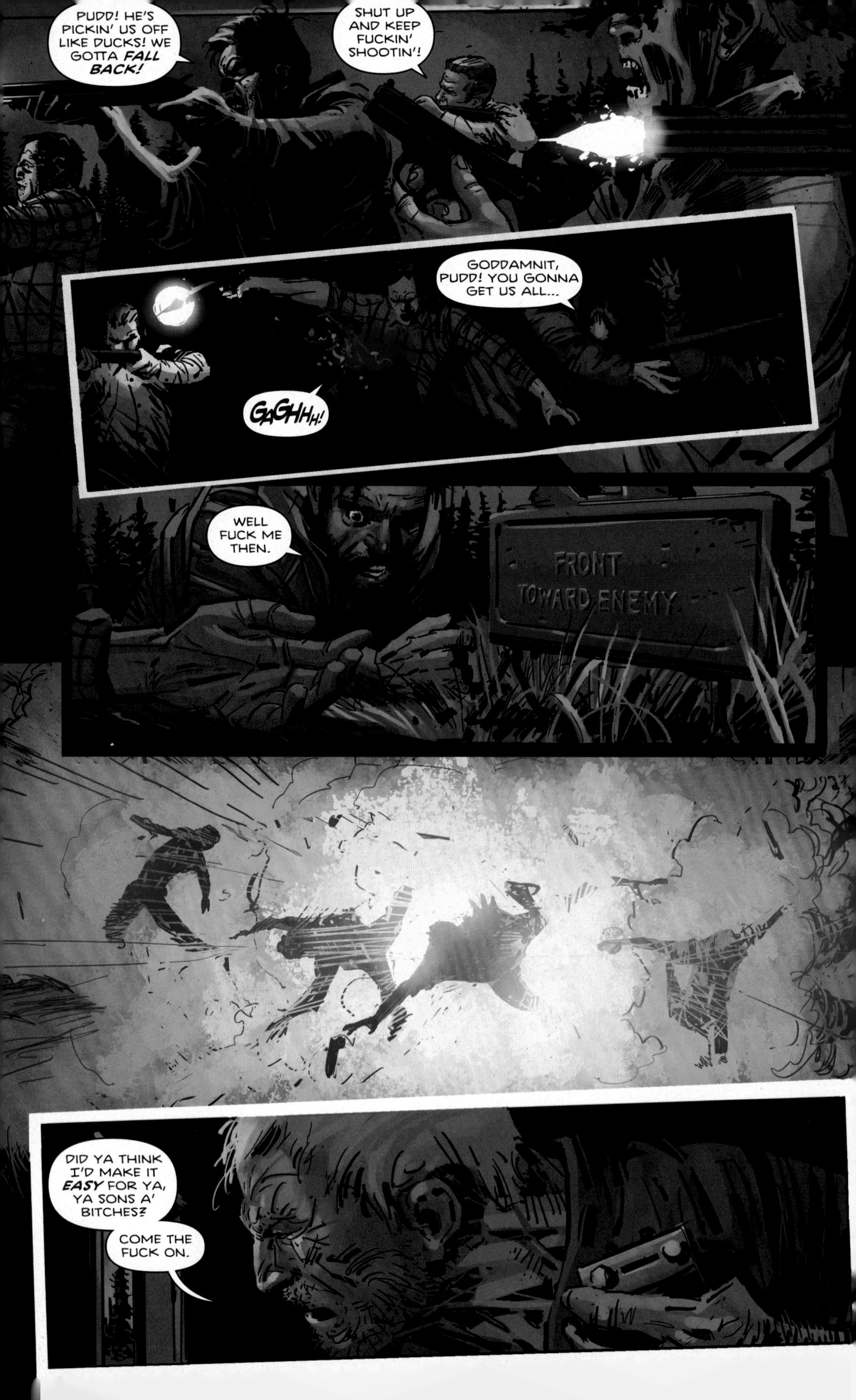
PUDD! HE'S PICKIN' US OFF LIKE DUCKS! WE GOTTA *FALL BACK!*
SHUT UP AND KEEP FUCKIN' SHOOTIN'!
GODDAMNIT, PUDD! YOU GONNA GET US ALL...
GAGHHH!
WELL FUCK ME THEN.
FRONT TOWARD ENEMY
DID YA THINK I'D MAKE IT *EASY* FOR YA, YA SONS A' BITCHES?
COME THE FUCK ON.

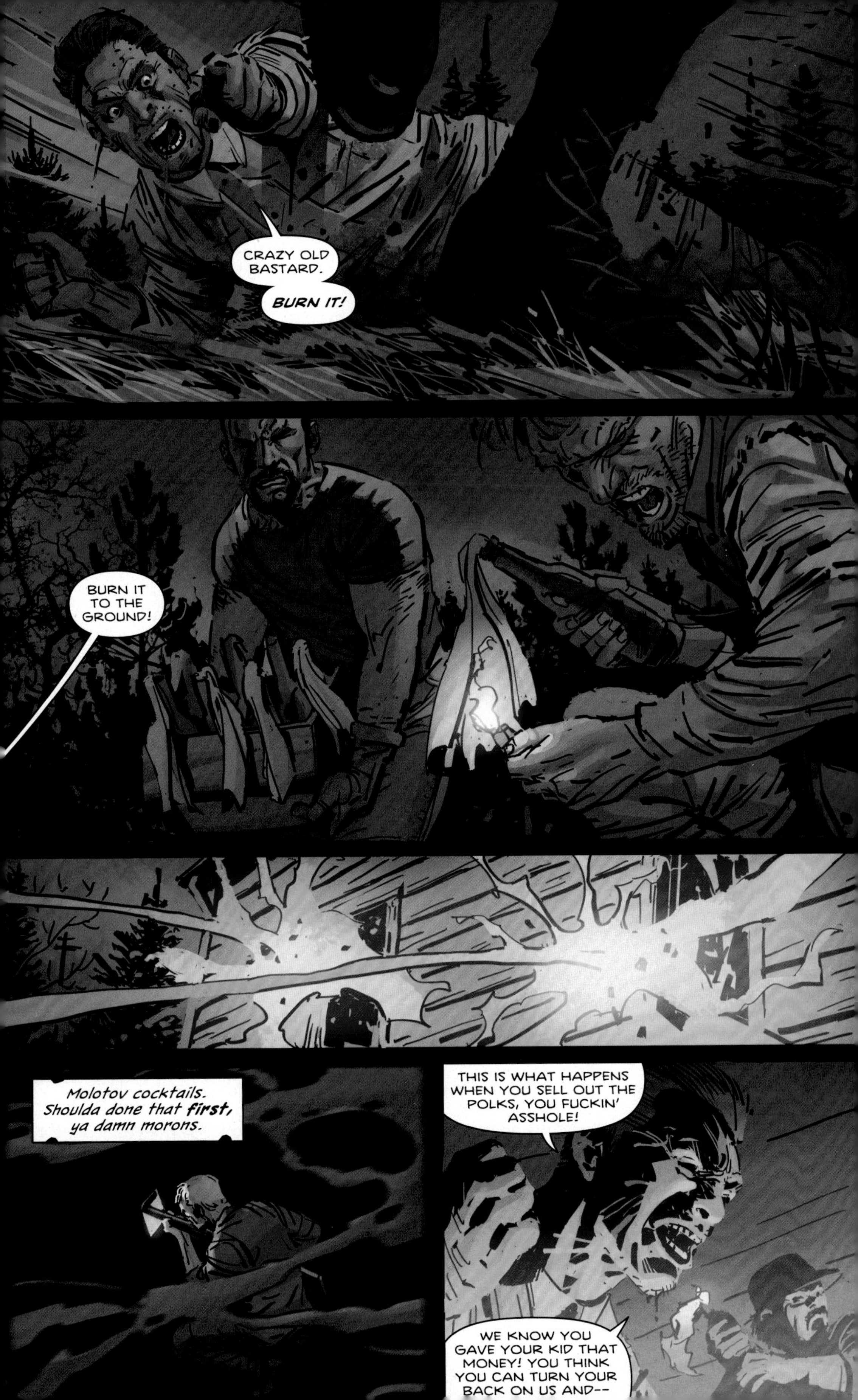
CRAZY OLD BASTARD.
BURN IT!
BURN IT TO THE GROUND!
Molotov cocktails. Shoulda done that first, ya damn morons.
THIS IS WHAT HAPPENS WHEN YOU SELL OUT THE POLKS, YOU FUCKIN' ASSHOLE!
WE KNOW YOU GAVE YOUR KID THAT MONEY! YOU THINK YOU CAN TURN YOUR BACK ON US AND--

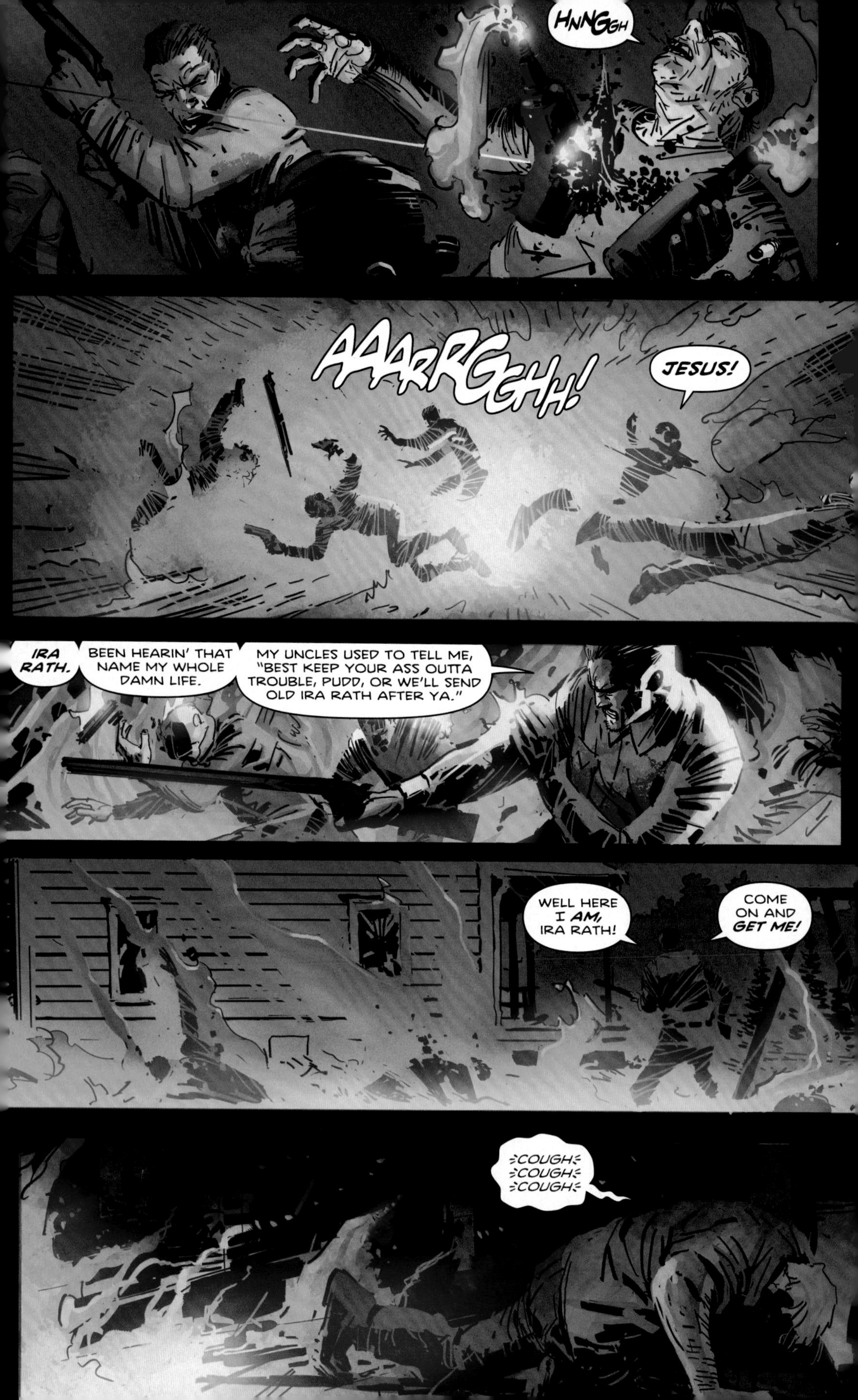
HNNGGH
AAARRGGHH!
JESUS!
IRA RATH.
BEEN HEARIN' THAT NAME MY WHOLE DAMN LIFE.
MY UNCLES USED TO TELL ME, "BEST KEEP YOUR ASS OUTTA TROUBLE, PUDD, OR WE'LL SEND OLD IRA RATH AFTER YA."
WELL HERE I AM, IRA RATH!
COME ON AND GET ME!
COUGH COUGH COUGH

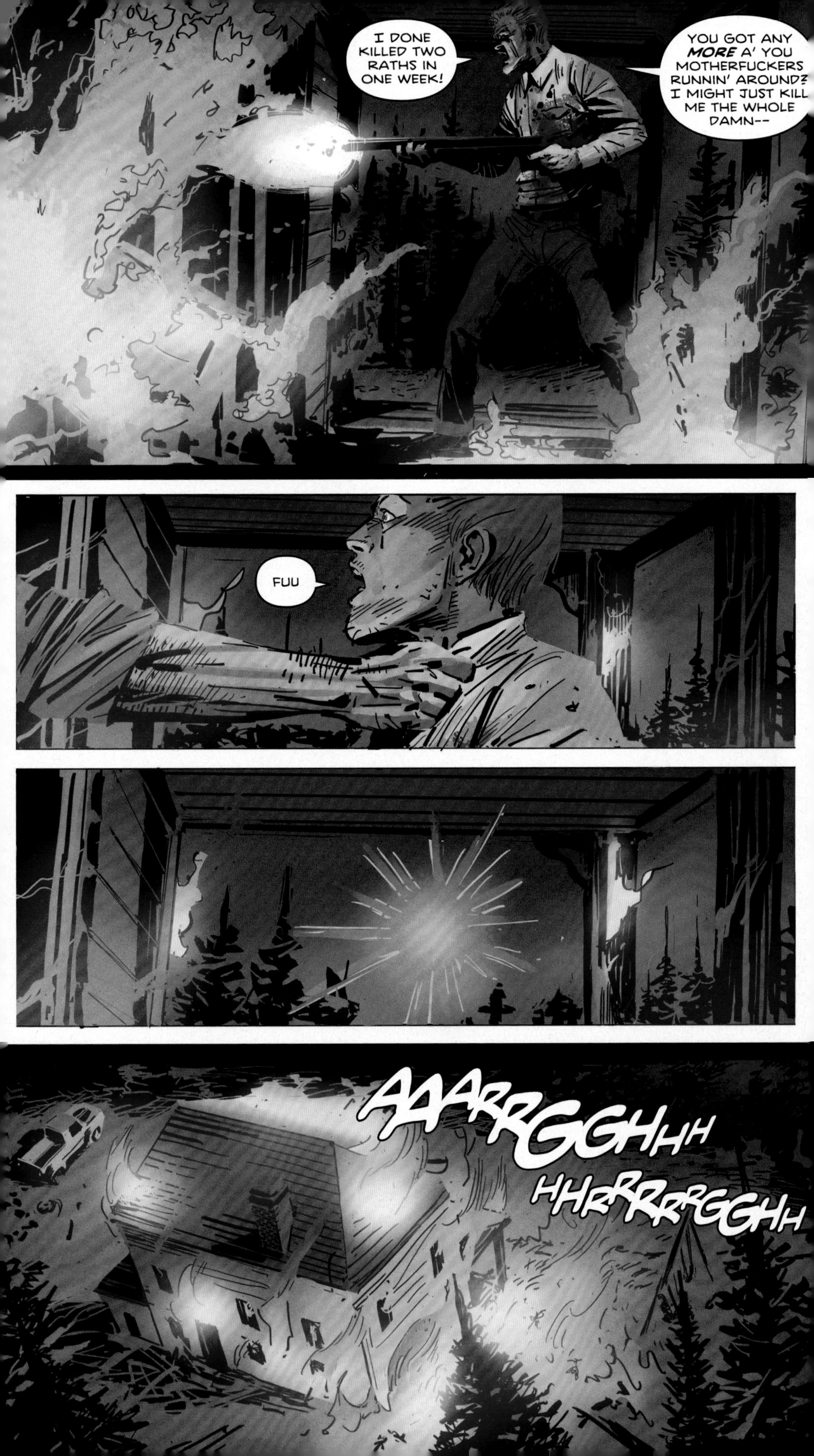
I DONE KILLED TWO RATHS IN ONE WEEK!
YOU GOT ANY MORE A' YOU MOTHERFUCKERS RUNNIN' AROUND? I MIGHT JUST KILL ME THE WHOLE DAMN--
FUU
AAARRGGHHH
HHRRRRRGGHH

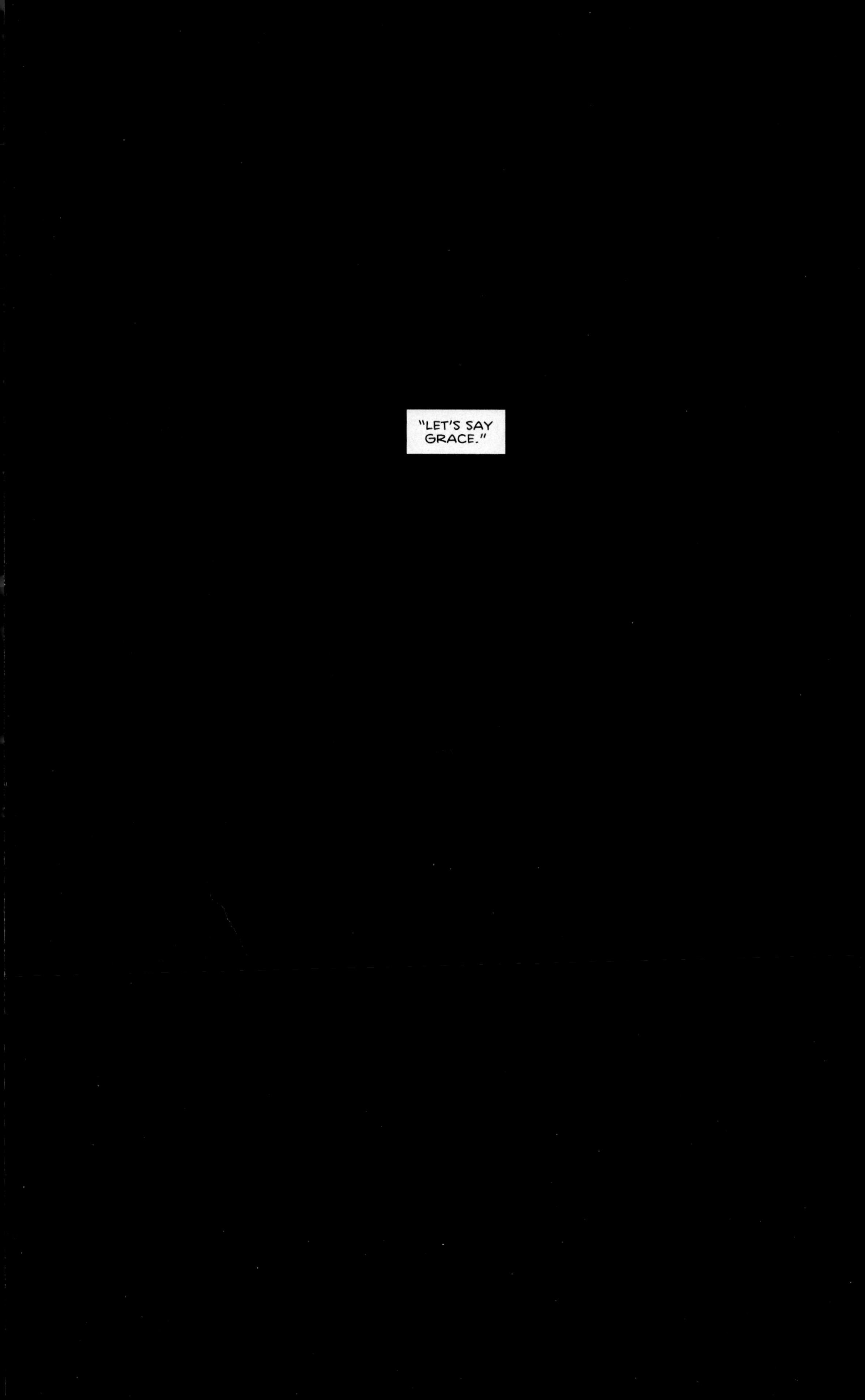
"LET'S SAY GRACE."

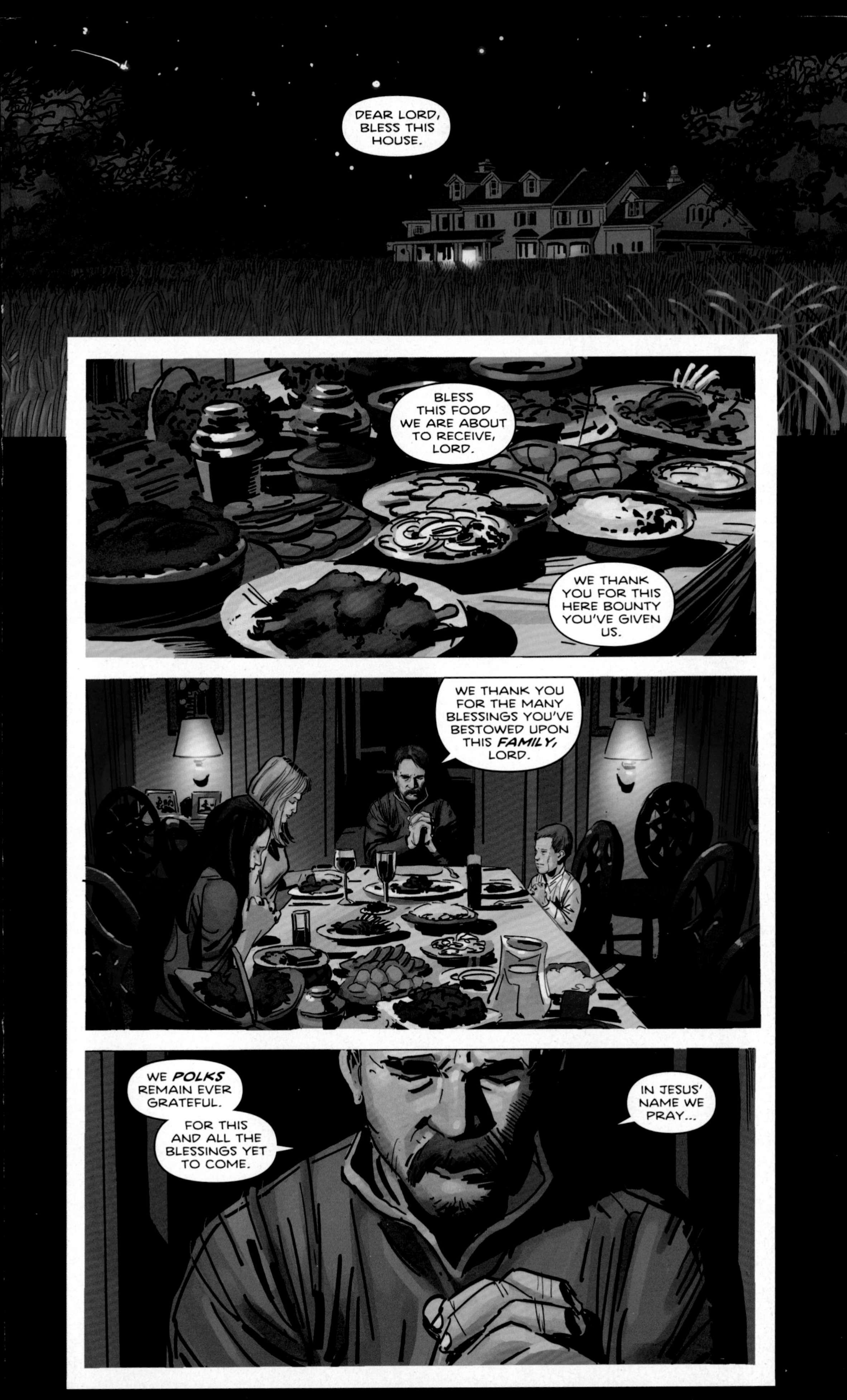
DEAR LORD, BLESS THIS HOUSE.
BLESS THIS FOOD WE ARE ABOUT TO RECEIVE, LORD.
WE THANK YOU FOR THIS HERE BOUNTY YOU'VE GIVEN US.
WE THANK YOU FOR THE MANY BLESSINGS YOU'VE BESTOWED UPON THIS FAMILY, LORD.
WE POLKS REMAIN EVER GRATEFUL.
FOR THIS AND ALL THE BLESSINGS YET TO COME.
IN JESUS' NAME WE PRAY...

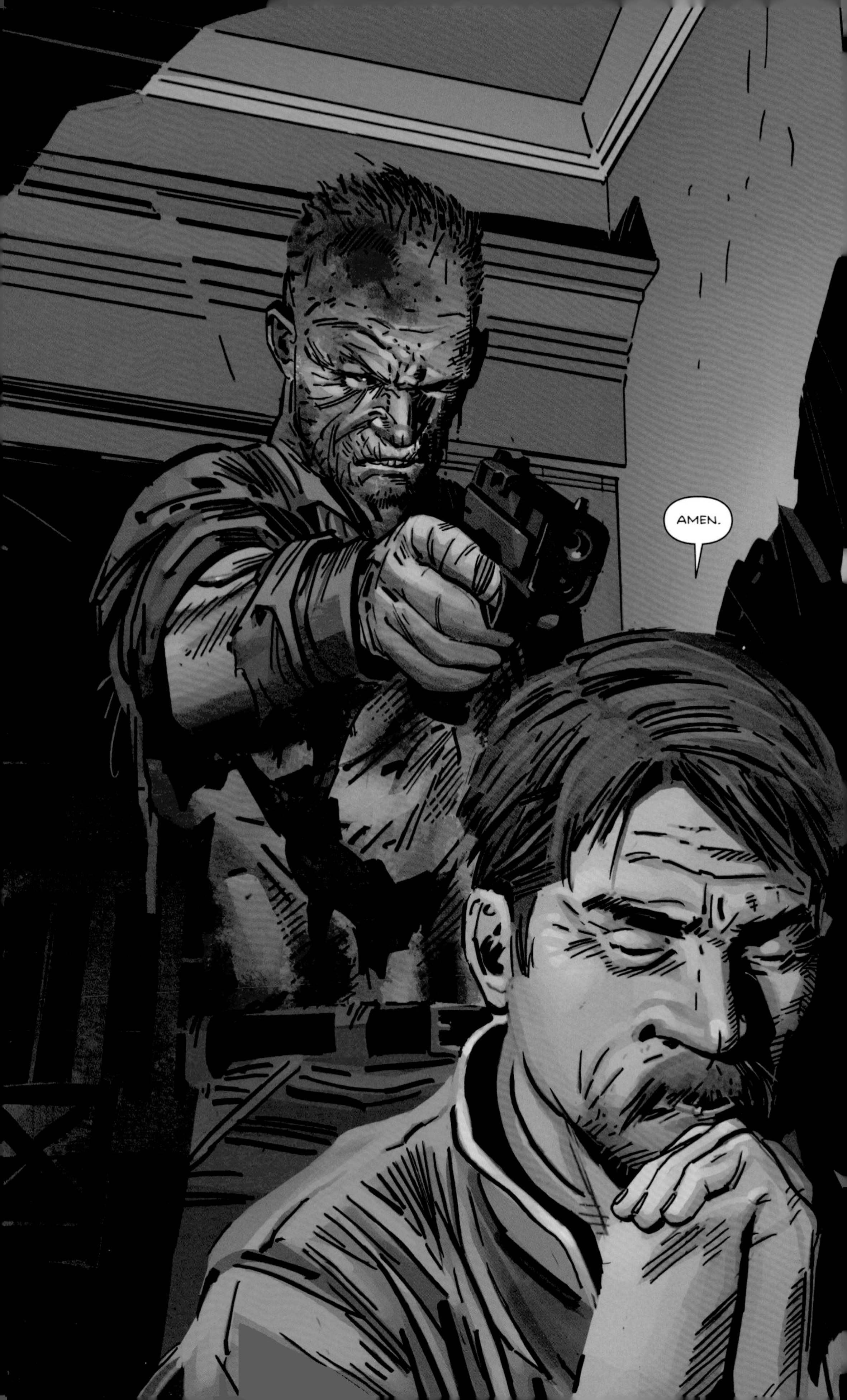
AMEN.

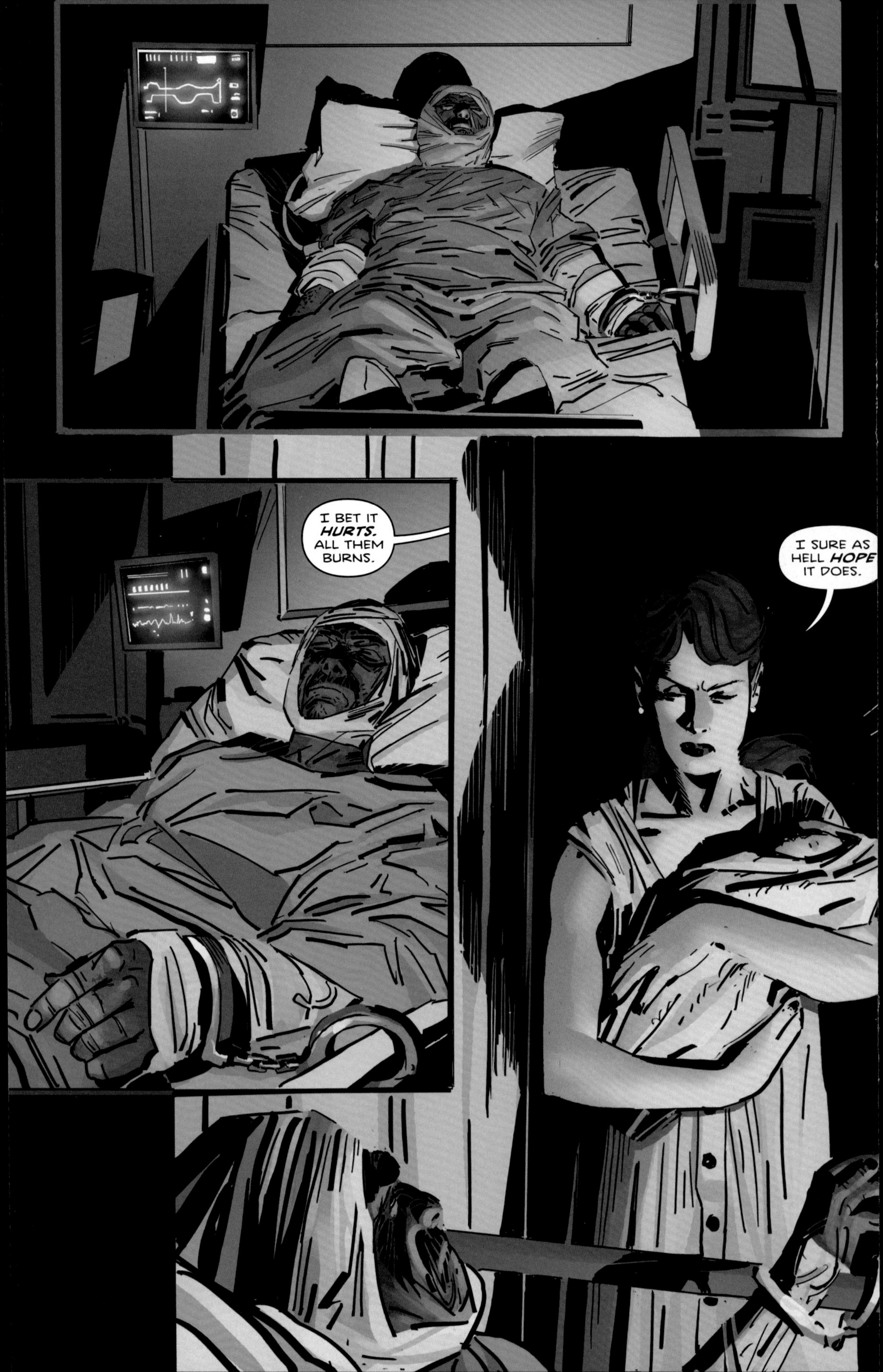
I BET IT ***HURTS.*** ALL THEM BURNS.
I SURE AS HELL ***HOPE*** IT DOES.

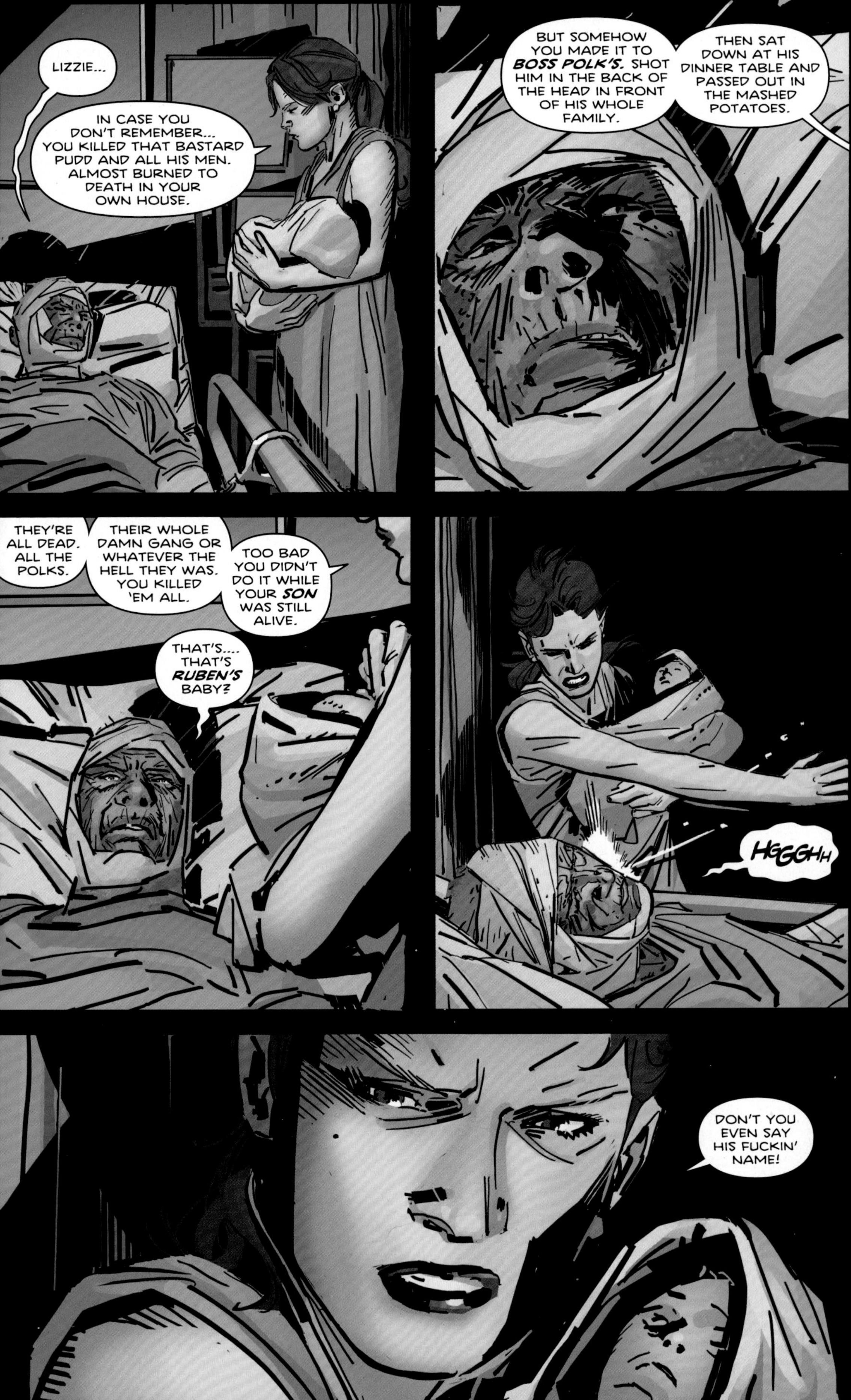
LIZZIE...
IN CASE YOU DON'T REMEMBER... YOU KILLED THAT BASTARD PUDD AND ALL HIS MEN. ALMOST BURNED TO DEATH IN YOUR OWN HOUSE.
BUT SOMEHOW YOU MADE IT TO BOSS POLK'S. SHOT HIM IN THE BACK OF THE HEAD IN FRONT OF HIS WHOLE FAMILY.
THEN SAT DOWN AT HIS DINNER TABLE AND PASSED OUT IN THE MASHED POTATOES.
THEY'RE ALL DEAD. ALL THE POLKS.
THEIR WHOLE DAMN GANG OR WHATEVER THE HELL THEY WAS. YOU KILLED 'EM ALL.
TOO BAD YOU DIDN'T DO IT WHILE YOUR SON WAS STILL ALIVE.
THAT'S.... THAT'S RUBEN'S BABY?
HGGGHH
DON'T YOU EVEN SAY HIS FUCKIN' NAME!

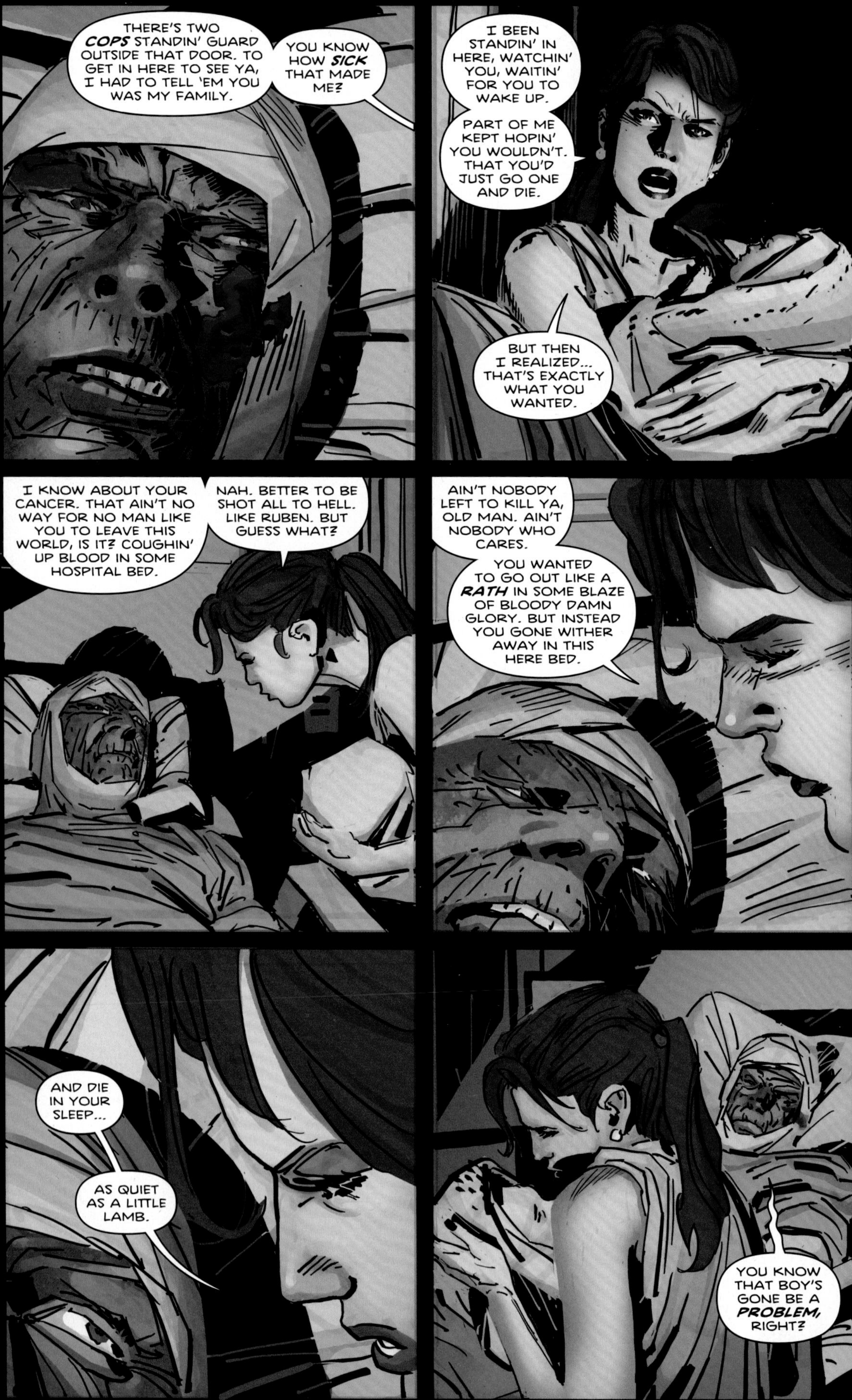

THERE'S TWO COPS STANDIN' GUARD OUTSIDE THAT DOOR. TO GET IN HERE TO SEE YA, I HAD TO TELL 'EM YOU WAS MY FAMILY.
YOU KNOW HOW SICK THAT MADE ME?
I BEEN STANDIN' IN HERE, WATCHIN' YOU, WAITIN' FOR YOU TO WAKE UP.
PART OF ME KEPT HOPIN' YOU WOULDN'T. THAT YOU'D JUST GO ONE AND DIE.
BUT THEN I REALIZED... THAT'S EXACTLY WHAT YOU WANTED.
I KNOW ABOUT YOUR CANCER. THAT AIN'T NO WAY FOR NO MAN LIKE YOU TO LEAVE THIS WORLD, IS IT? COUGHIN' UP BLOOD IN SOME HOSPITAL BED.
NAH. BETTER TO BE SHOT ALL TO HELL. LIKE RUBEN. BUT GUESS WHAT?
AIN'T NOBODY LEFT TO KILL YA, OLD MAN. AIN'T NOBODY WHO CARES.
YOU WANTED TO GO OUT LIKE A RATH IN SOME BLAZE OF BLOODY DAMN GLORY. BUT INSTEAD YOU GONE WITHER AWAY IN THIS HERE BED.
AND DIE IN YOUR SLEEP...
AS QUIET AS A LITTLE LAMB.
YOU KNOW THAT BOY'S GONE BE A PROBLEM, RIGHT?

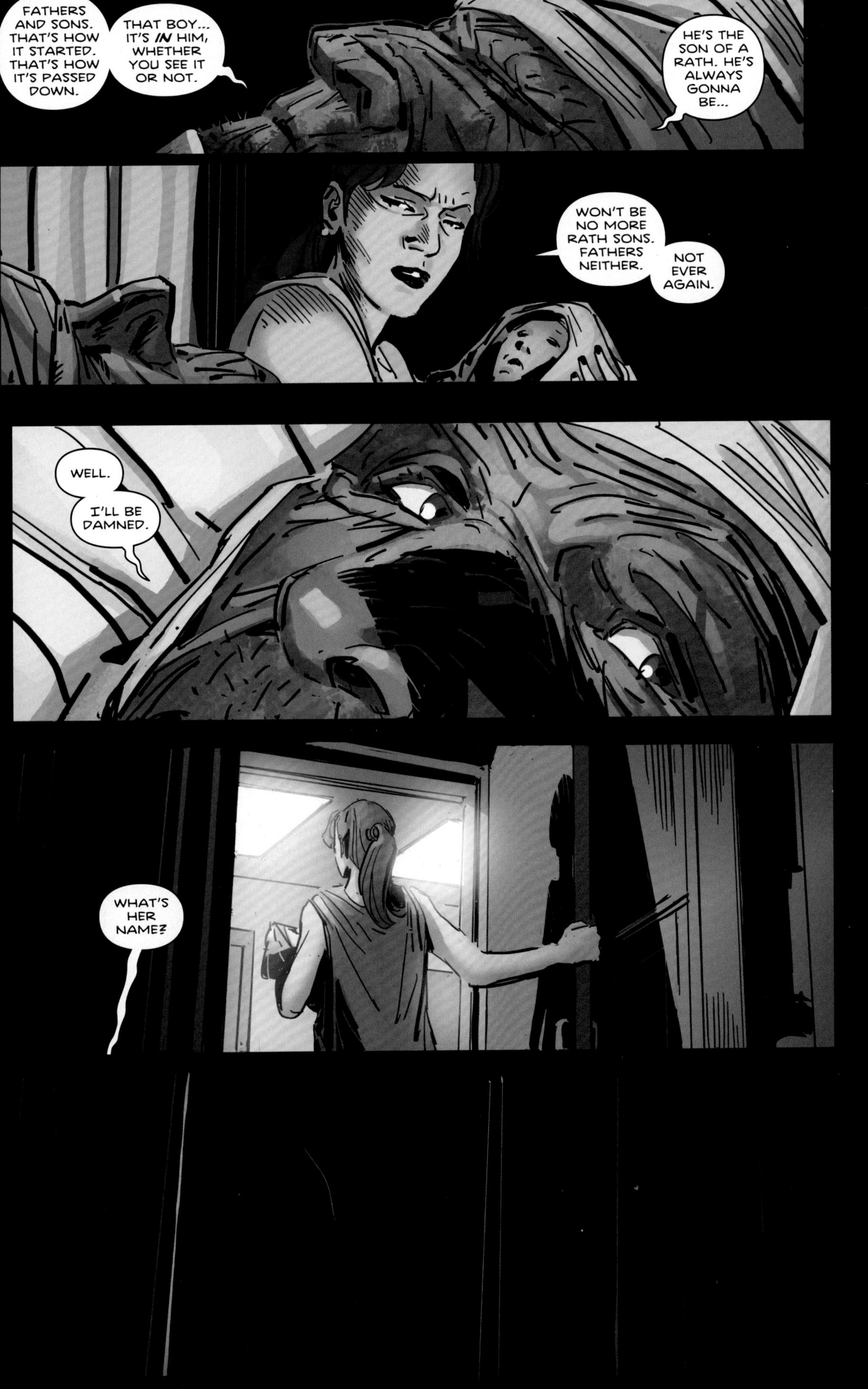
FATHERS AND SONS. THAT'S HOW IT STARTED. THAT'S HOW IT'S PASSED DOWN.
THAT BOY... IT'S *IN* HIM, WHETHER YOU SEE IT OR NOT.
HE'S THE SON OF A RATH. HE'S ALWAYS GONNA BE...
WON'T BE NO MORE RATH SONS. FATHERS NEITHER.
NOT EVER AGAIN.
WELL.
I'LL BE DAMNED.
WHAT'S HER NAME?

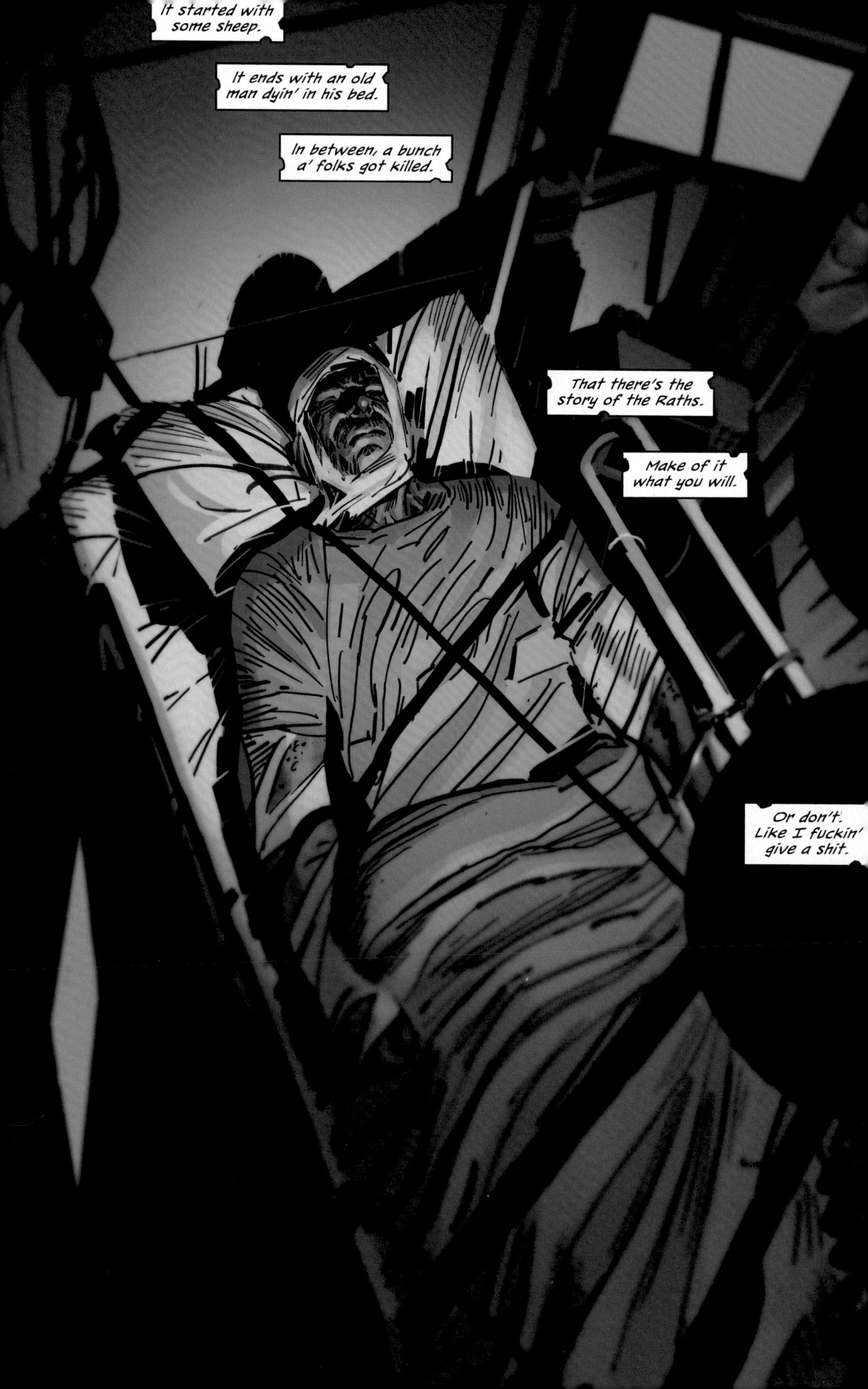
It started with some sheep.
It ends with an old man dyin' in his bed.
In between, a bunch a' folks got killed.
That there's the story of the Raths.
Make of it what you will.
Or don't. Like I fuckin' give a shit.

VARIANT COVER
GALLERY

ISSUE ONE **STEVE DILLON**
WITH **MATT HOLLINGSWORTH**
ISSUE TWO **RM GUERRA**
ISSUE THREE **TONY HARRIS**
ISSUE FOUR **DAVID LAPHAM**
WITH **LEE LOUGHRIDGE**
ISSUE FIVE **ALEX ROSS**

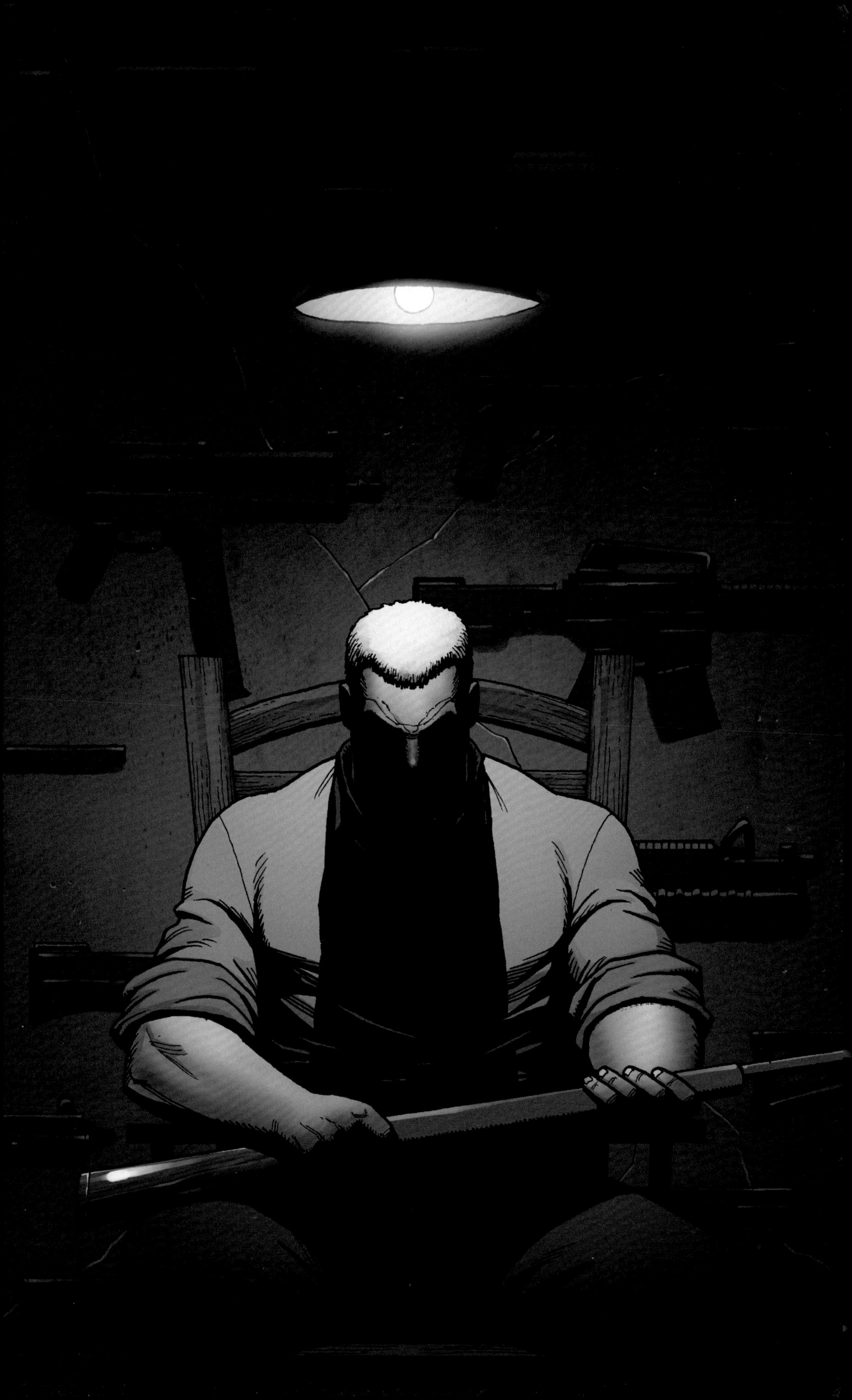

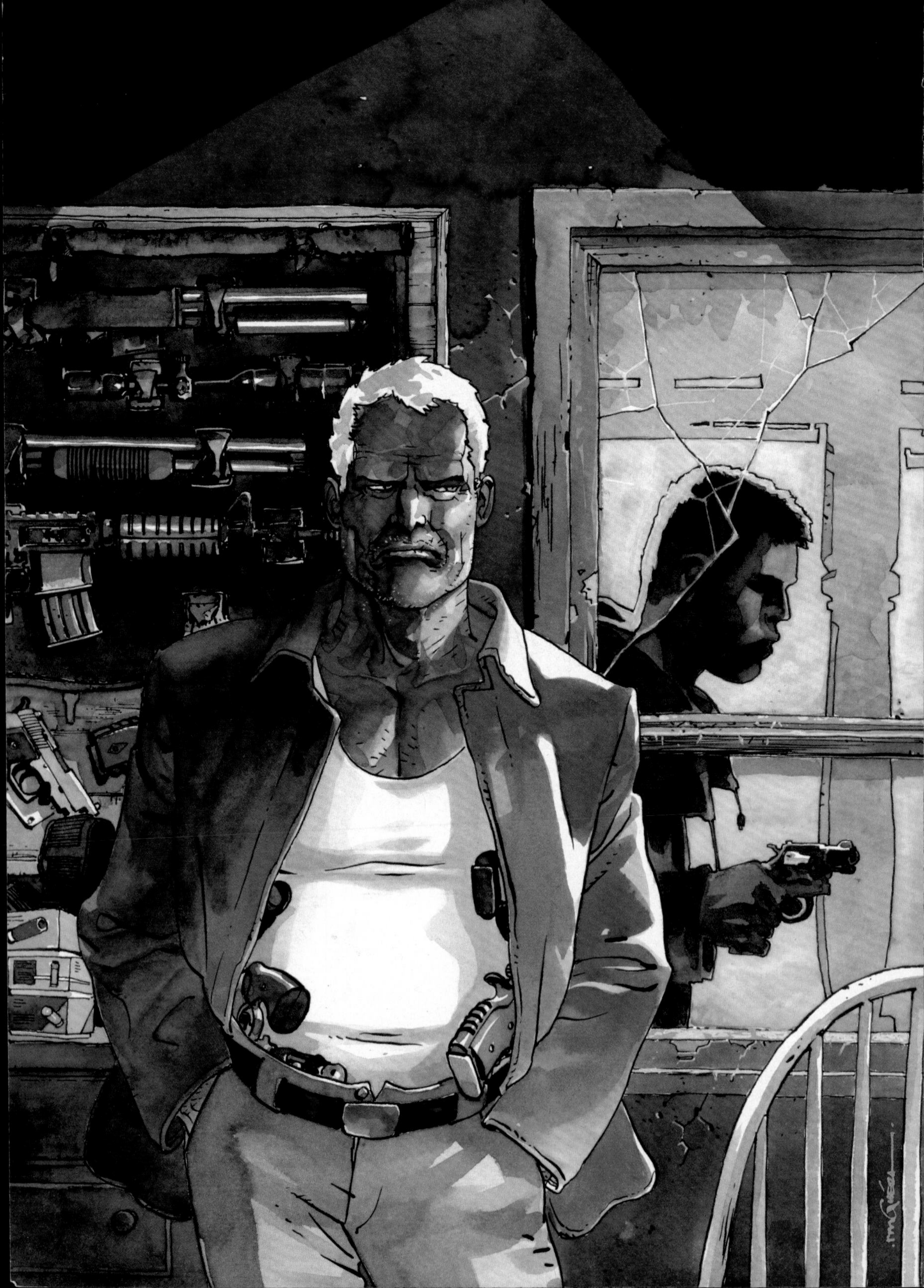

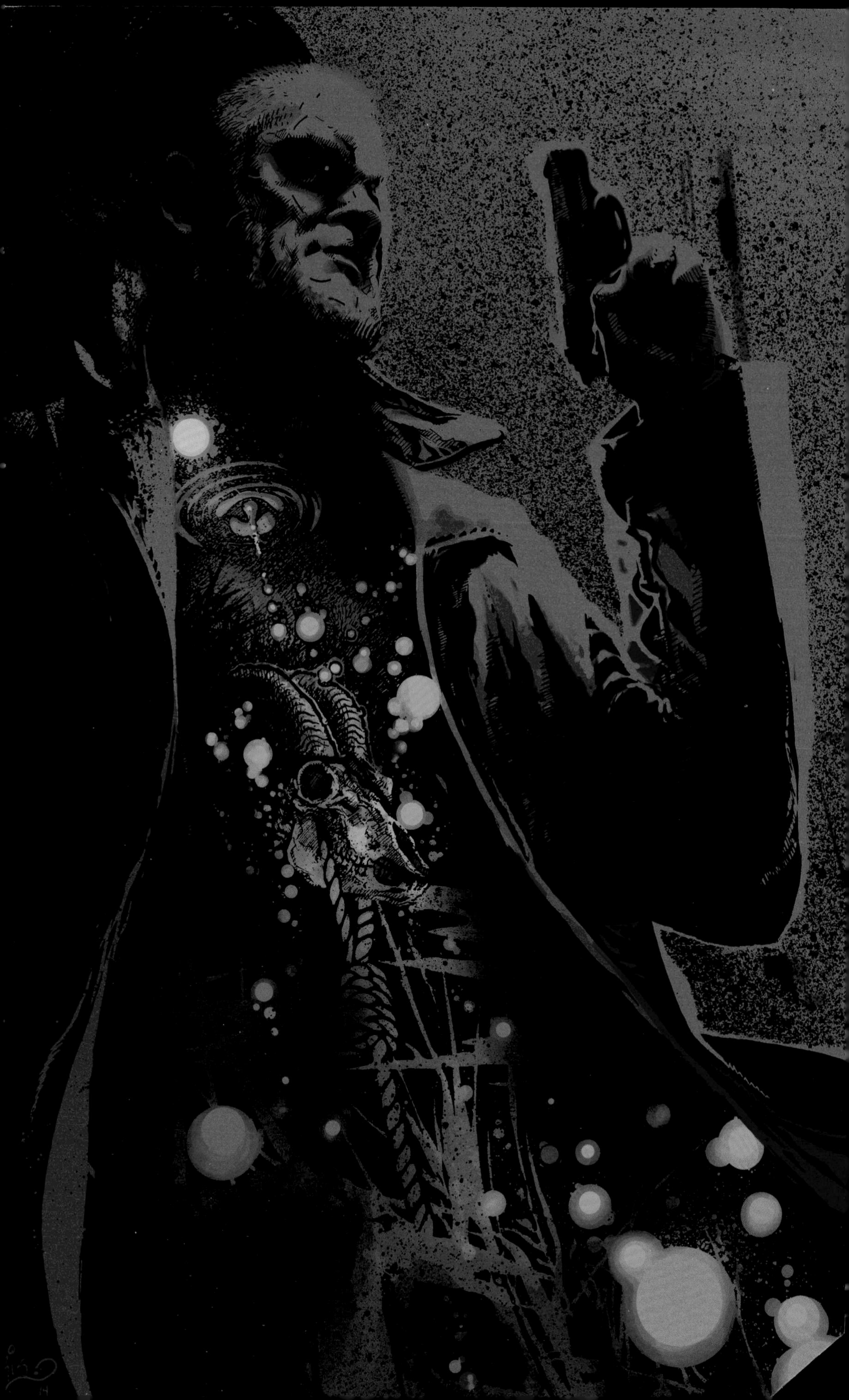

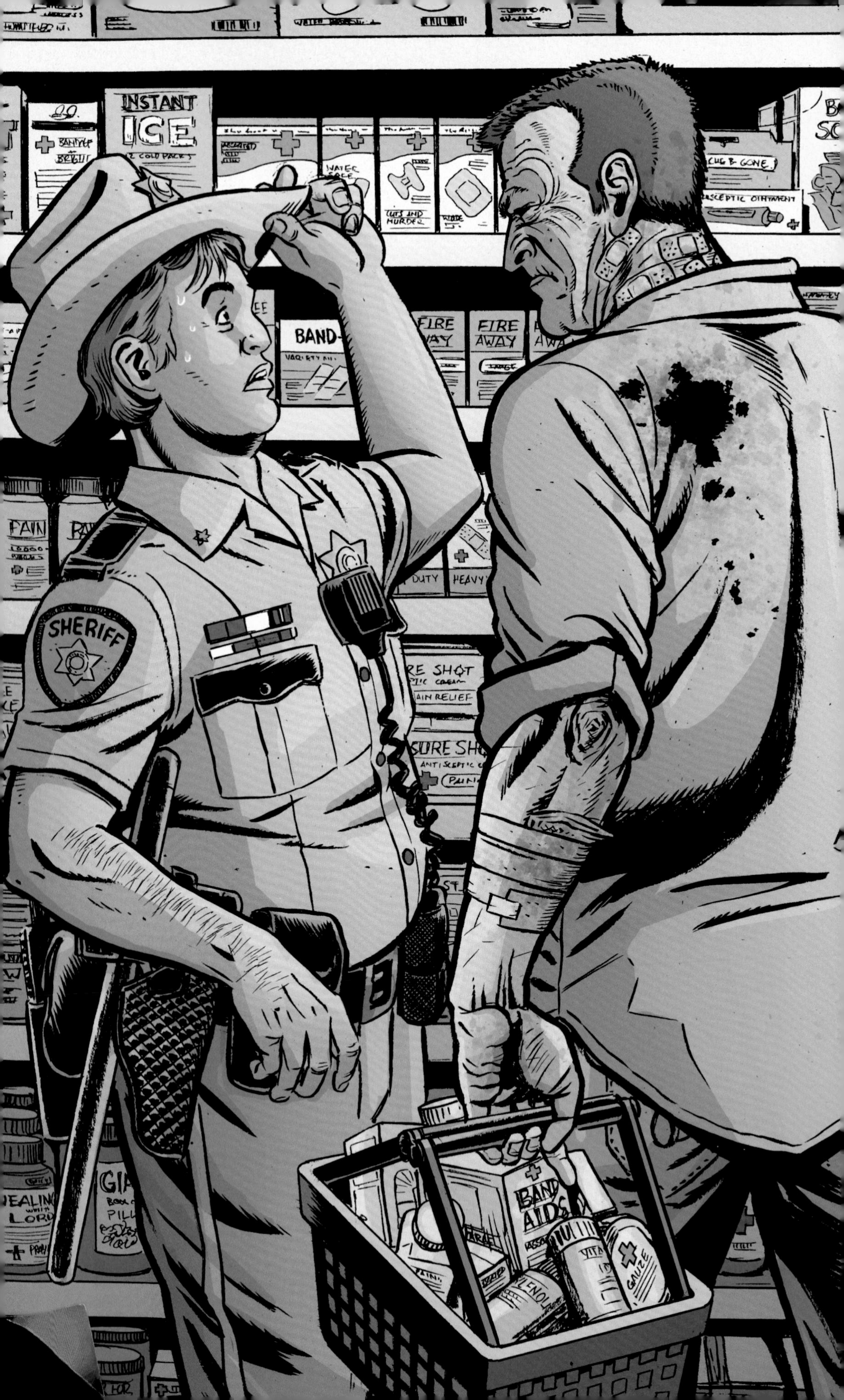

INSTANT ICE
CUTS AND MURDER
BAND-
FIRE AWAY
FIRE AWAY
SHERIFF
DUTY
HEAVY
SURE SHOT
PAIN RELIEF
SURE SHOT
BAND AIDS
GAUZE

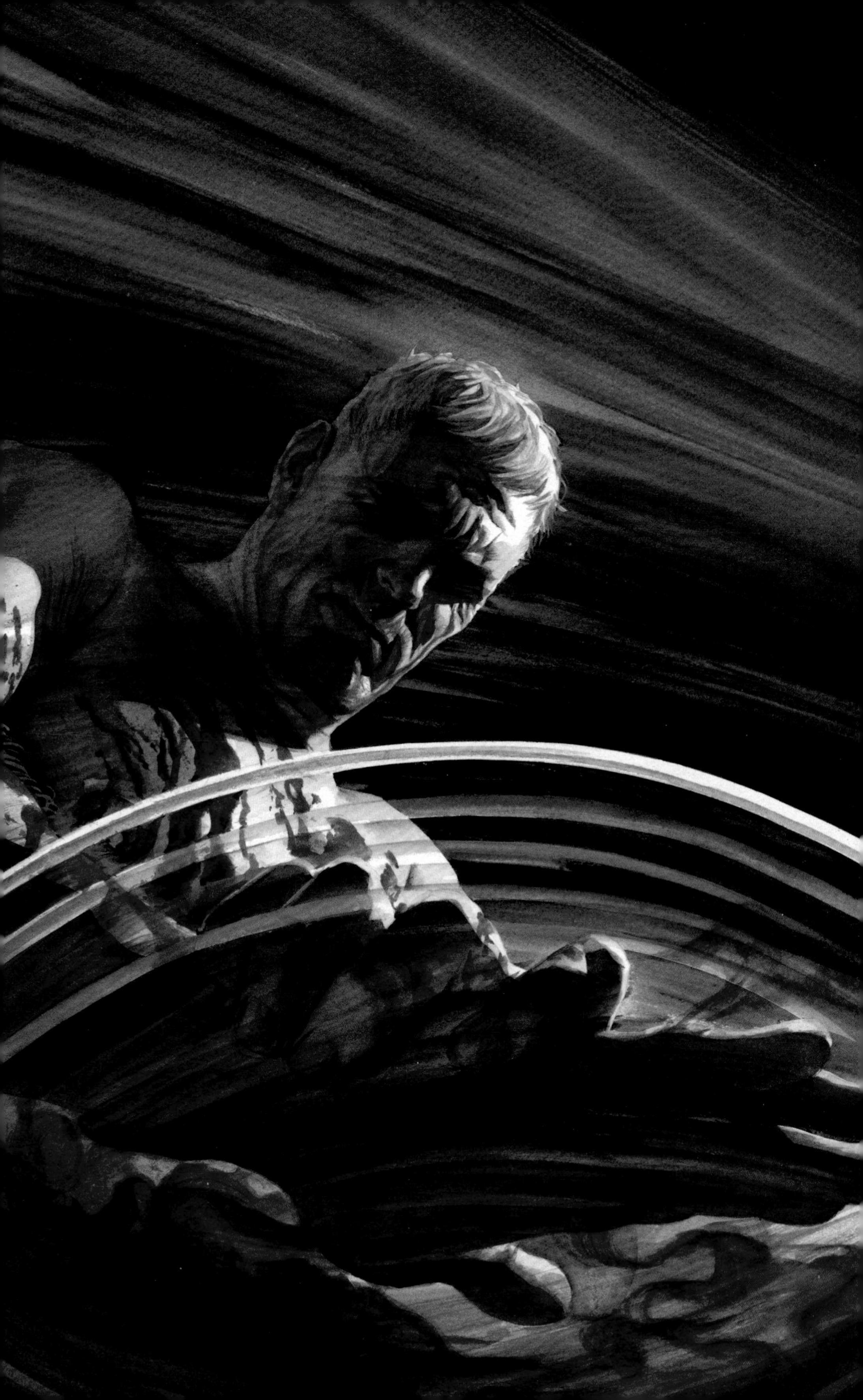

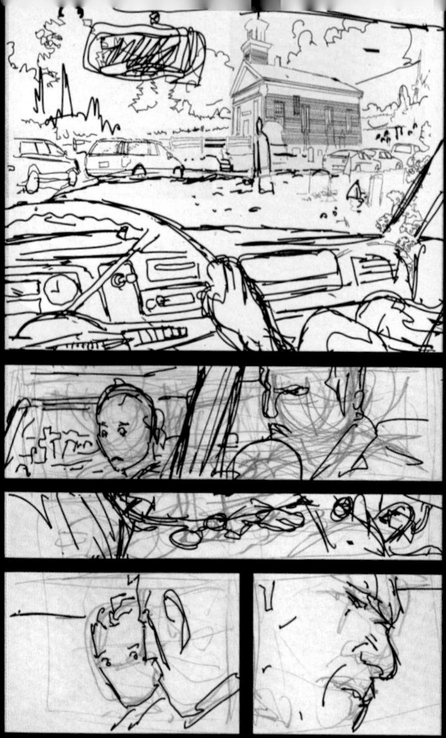

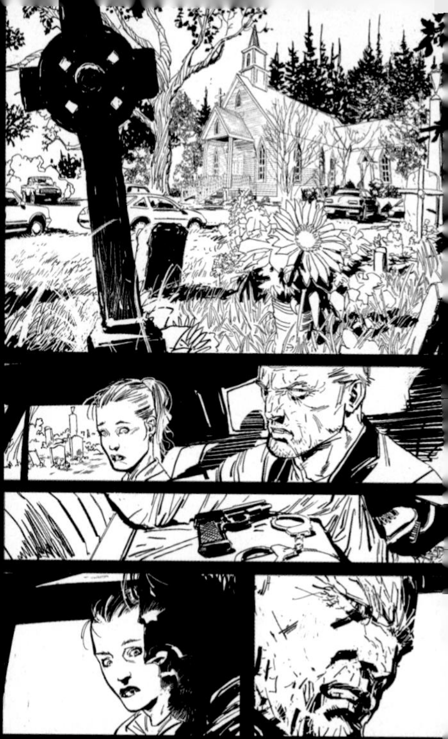

PROCESS

CHAPTER 3 PAGE 12

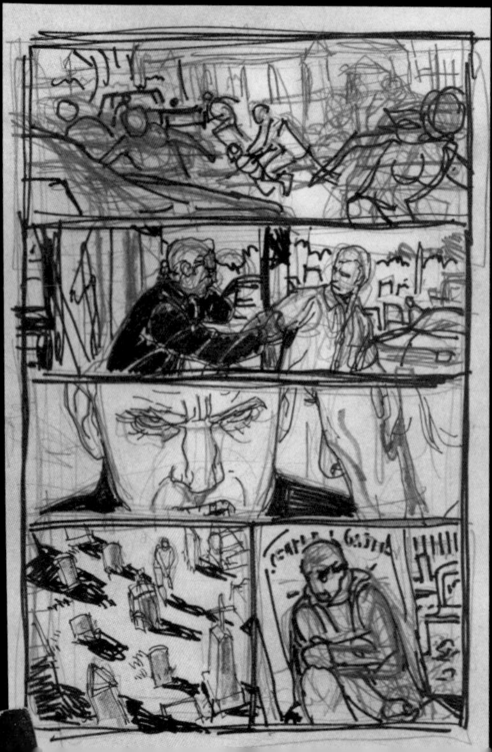

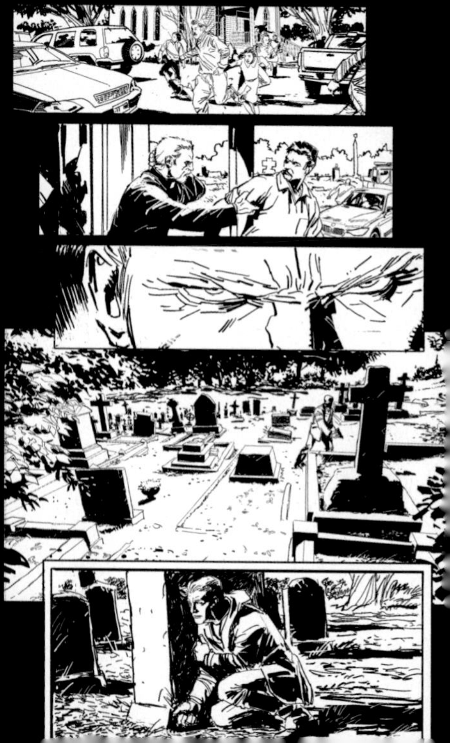

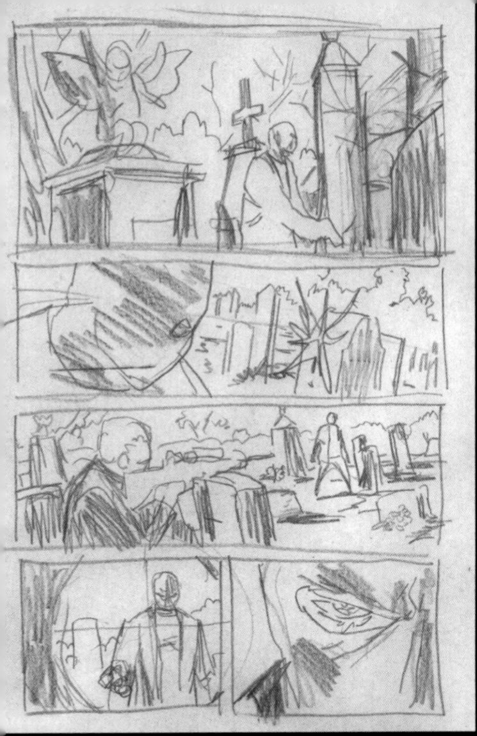

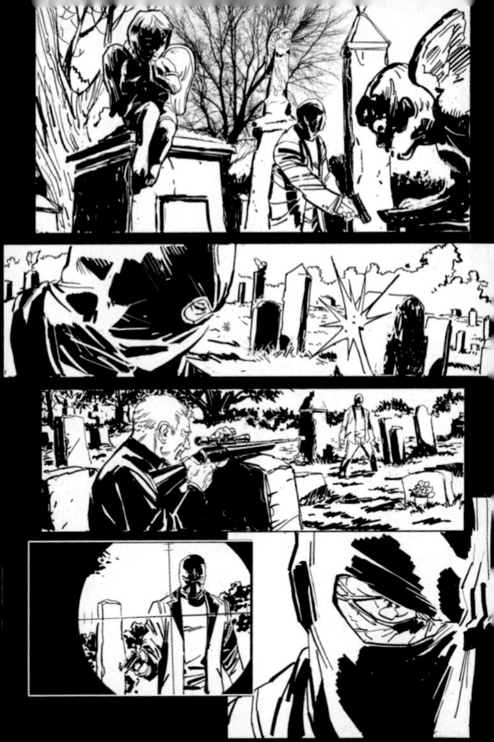

PROCESS

CHAPTER 3 PAGE 16

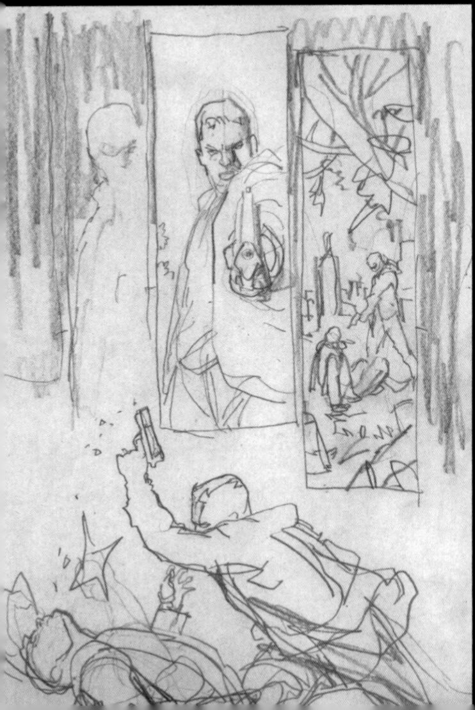

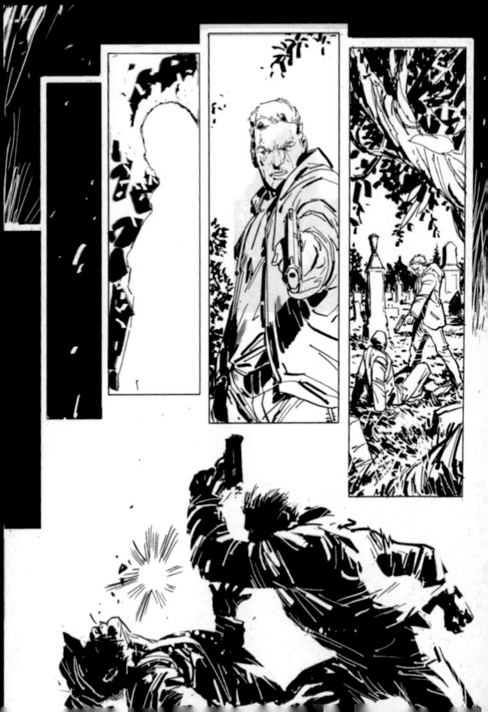

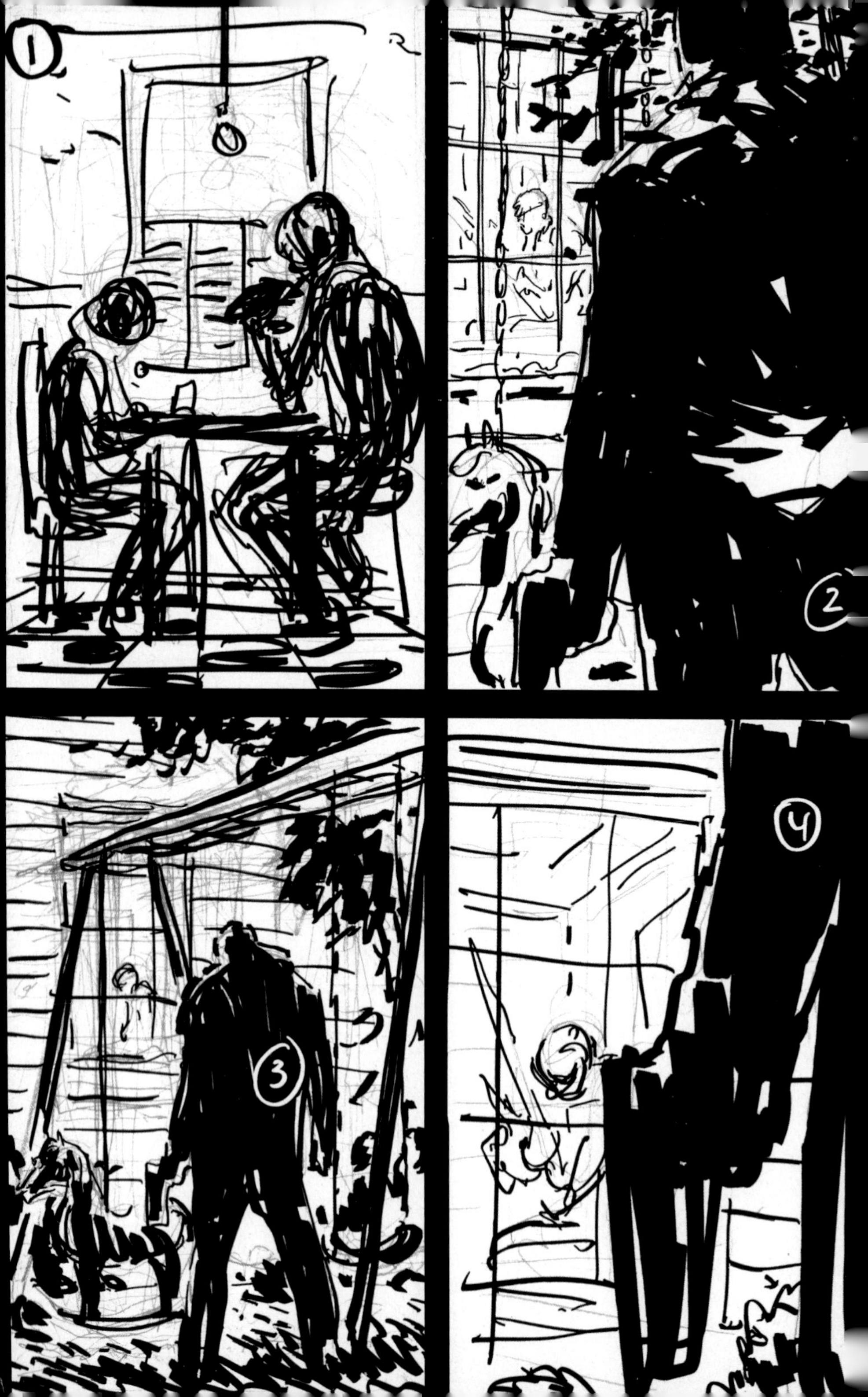
1
2
3
4

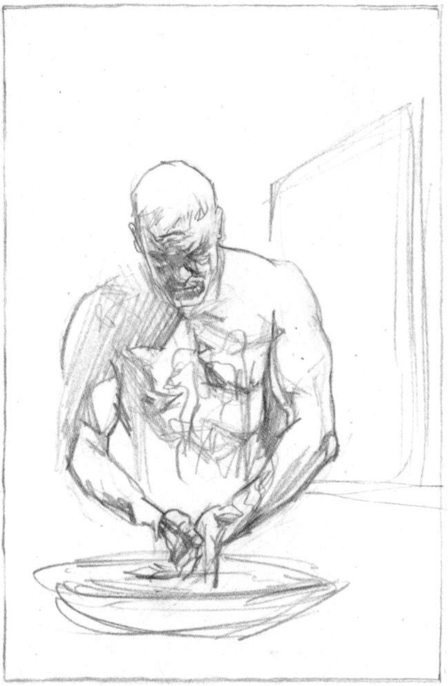

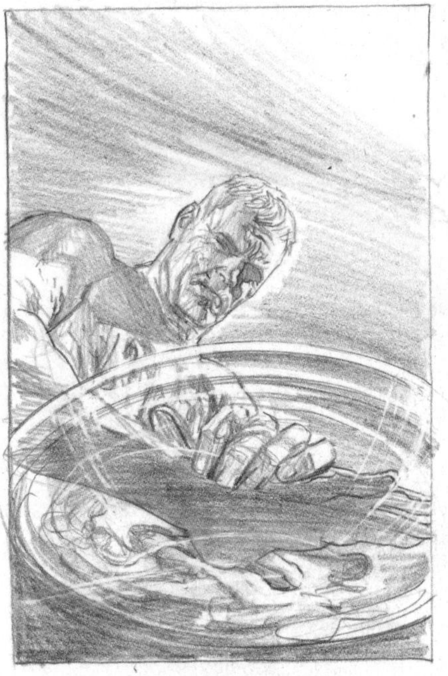

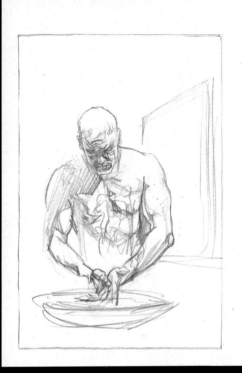

MEN OF WRATH

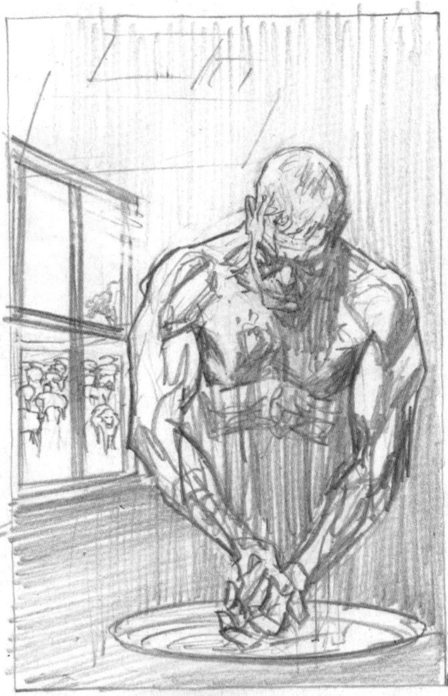

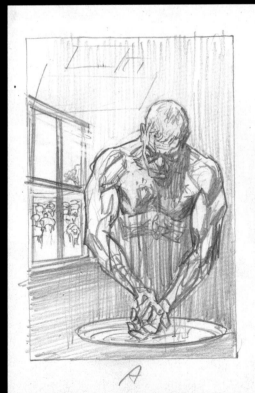

A

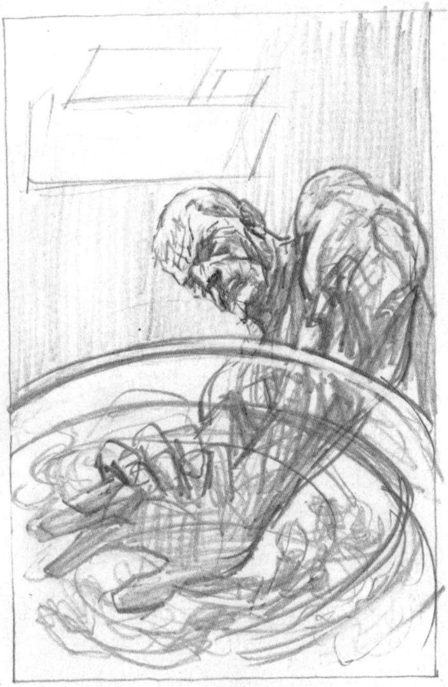

B

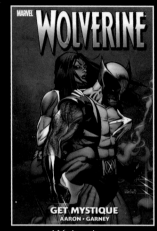

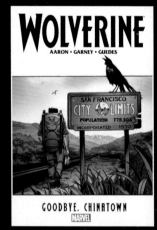

BAKER'S DOZEN

THEY DOT THE LANDSCAPE like beacons of sanctuary, each one an oasis of safety and a little slice of home. It's the place where everybody does know your name, 'cause sometimes that's your arch-foe sitting at the end of the counter. It's the place where heroes and villains can't have a sense-shattering slugfest, but they can toss back a cup o' joe and a few crullers, and shoot the breeze. So check your weapons and attitude at the door, and come in.

Welcome to Common Grounds. May we take you order?

Common Grounds is written by: **Troy Hickman**

For this edition——————————————
Book Design and Layout by:
Robin Spehar and Dreamer Design

Cover Art by: **Rodolfo Migliari,**
The Pride of Argentina

ISBN#:1-58240-436-4

Published by Image Comics®
Common Grounds: Baker's Dozen December 2004. FIRST PRINTING. Office of Publication: 1071
North Batavia Street Suite A. Orange, California 92867. Originally published: Common Grounds Issue
#1-6. Common Grounds™, its logos, all related characters and likenesses are ™ Top Cow Productions,
Inc. All rights reserved. Any similarities to persons living or dead is purely coincidental. All artwork and
the entire contents of this book are © 2004 Top Cow Productions, Inc. With the exception of artwork
used for review purposes, none of the contents of this book may be reprinted in any form without the
express written consent of Top Cow Productions Inc.
PRINTED IN CANADA

To order by telephone call **1-888-TOPCOW1**
(1-888-867-2691) or go to a comics shop near you.

To find the comics shop nearest you call:
1-888-COMICBOOK (1-888-266-4226)

What did you think of this book? We love to hear from
our readers. Please e-mail us at: **fanmail@topcow.com**
Or write us at:
Common Grounds c/o Top Cow Productions Inc.
10350 Santa Monica Blvd., Suite #100
Los Angeles, CA 90025

FOR
image COMICS
Erik Larsen
publisher *image*®
TOP COW®

Marc Silvestri—chief executive officer
Matt Hawkins—president /chief operating officer
Jim McLauchlin—editor-in-chief
Renae Geerlings—vp of publishing / managing editor
Scott Tucker—editor
Chaz Riggs—production manager
Phil Smith—associate editor
Cami Dyson—production assistant
Rob Levin and Peter Lam—editorial interns

visit us on the web at:
www.topcow.com

TABLE OF CONTENTS

"Beyond the Speed of Life": **Dan Jurgens, Al Vey and Guy Major**— Pg. 5

"Head Games": **Michael Avon Oeming and Peter Pantazis**— Pg. 14

"Roles": **Ethan Van Sciver, Jon Holdredge, Roland Paris, Norm Rapmund and Brian Buccellato**— Pg. 27

"Elsewhere": **Dan Jurgens, Al Vey and Guy Major**— Pg. 37

"Sanctuary": **Chris Bachalo, Aaron Sowd, Tom Bar-Or and Brian Buccellato with Sonia Oback**— Pg. 45

"Heir of Truth": **Dan Jurgens, Al Vey and Guy Major**— Pg. 54

"Time of Their Lives": **Carlos Pacheco, Jesus Merino and Guy Major**— Pg. 67

"Fat Chance": **Dan Jurgens, Al Vey and Guy Major**— Pg. 76

"Glory Days": **George Pérez, Mike Perkins and Tom Smith**— Pg. 85

"Where Monsters Dine": **Angel Medina, Jon Holdredge and John Starr with Beth Sotelo**— Pg. 91

"Lovelife": **Dan Jurgens, Al Vey and Guy Major**— Pg. 104

"This'll be the Day": **Sam Kieth and Guy Major**— Pg. 113

"Loose Ends": **Dan Jurgens, Al Vey and Guy Major**— Pg. 121

Cover and Pinup Gallery— Pg. 131

Common Grounds Timeline— Pg. 140

Holey Crullers Bonus Material— Pg. 142

Liberty Balance Pinup by **George Pérez, Mike Perkins and Tom Smith**— Pg. 144

THERE ARE NO LITTLE STORIES. Every great romance starts with a single gesture of love. Every tale of war has its roots in some small, seemingly insignificant insult or slight. The world may change in epic ways, but not without an infinite mosaic that makes up that grand scheme. *Common Grounds* is about those often-overlooked and always underestimated moments, the moments of the mundane in the midst of the cosmic, the events and emotions that make up the human side of the superhuman.

This book is dedicated to Lea, and Gabriel, and my friend Jim, who have helped make this the best chapter so far in the story of my life...

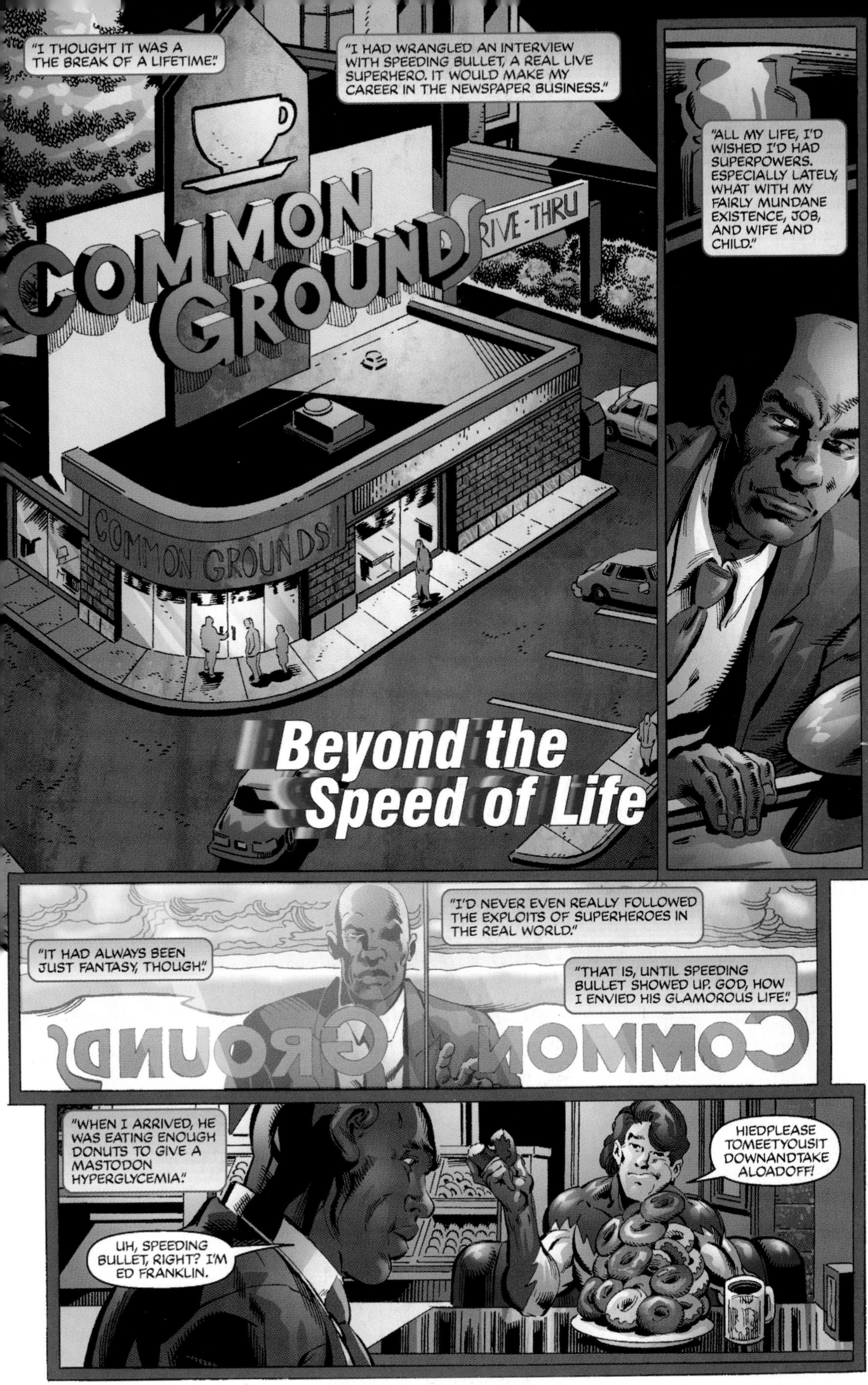
"I THOUGHT IT WAS A THE BREAK OF A LIFETIME."
"I HAD WRANGLED AN INTERVIEW WITH SPEEDING BULLET, A REAL LIVE SUPERHERO. IT WOULD MAKE MY CAREER IN THE NEWSPAPER BUSINESS."
COMMON GROUNDS
RIVE-THRU
COMMON GROUNDS
"ALL MY LIFE, I'D WISHED I'D HAD SUPERPOWERS. ESPECIALLY LATELY, WHAT WITH MY FAIRLY MUNDANE EXISTENCE, JOB, AND WIFE AND CHILD."
Beyond the Speed of Life
"IT HAD ALWAYS BEEN JUST FANTASY, THOUGH."
"I'D NEVER EVEN REALLY FOLLOWED THE EXPLOITS OF SUPERHEROES IN THE REAL WORLD."
"THAT IS, UNTIL SPEEDING BULLET SHOWED UP. GOD, HOW I ENVIED HIS GLAMOROUS LIFE!"
"WHEN I ARRIVED, HE WAS EATING ENOUGH DONUTS TO GIVE A MASTODON HYPERGLYCEMIA."
HIEDPLEASE TOMEETYOUSIT DOWNANDTAKE ALOADOFF!
UH, SPEEDING BULLET, RIGHT? I'M ED FRANKLIN.

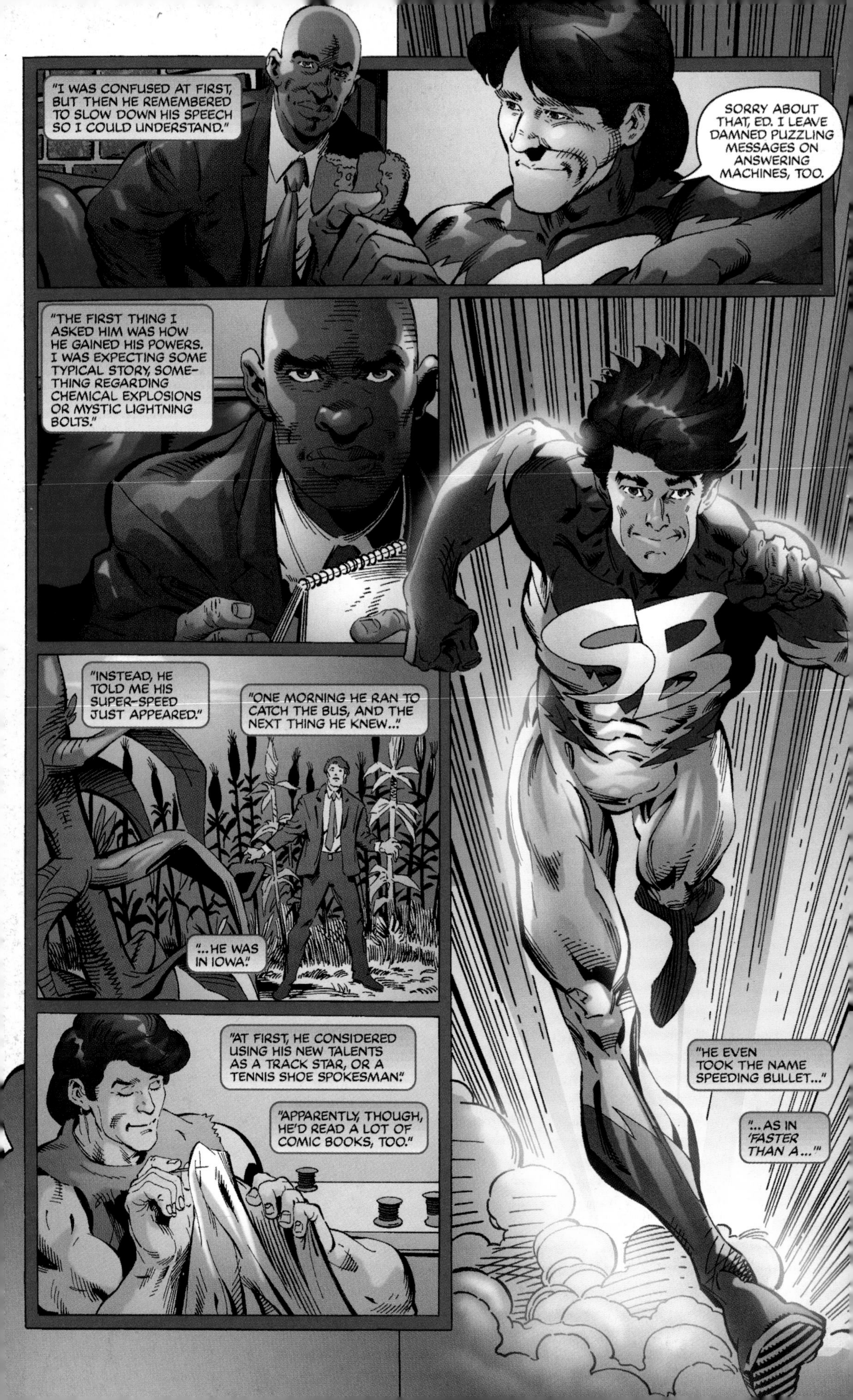
"I WAS CONFUSED AT FIRST, BUT THEN HE REMEMBERED TO SLOW DOWN HIS SPEECH SO I COULD UNDERSTAND."
SORRY ABOUT THAT, ED. I LEAVE DAMNED PUZZLING MESSAGES ON ANSWERING MACHINES, TOO.
"THE FIRST THING I ASKED HIM WAS HOW HE GAINED HIS POWERS. I WAS EXPECTING SOME TYPICAL STORY, SOMETHING REGARDING CHEMICAL EXPLOSIONS OR MYSTIC LIGHTNING BOLTS."
"INSTEAD, HE TOLD ME HIS SUPER-SPEED JUST APPEARED."
"ONE MORNING HE RAN TO CATCH THE BUS, AND THE NEXT THING HE KNEW..."
"...HE WAS IN IOWA."
"AT FIRST, HE CONSIDERED USING HIS NEW TALENTS AS A TRACK STAR, OR A TENNIS SHOE SPOKESMAN."
"APPARENTLY, THOUGH, HE'D READ A LOT OF COMIC BOOKS, TOO."
"HE EVEN TOOK THE NAME SPEEDING BULLET..."
"...AS IN 'FASTER THAN A...'"

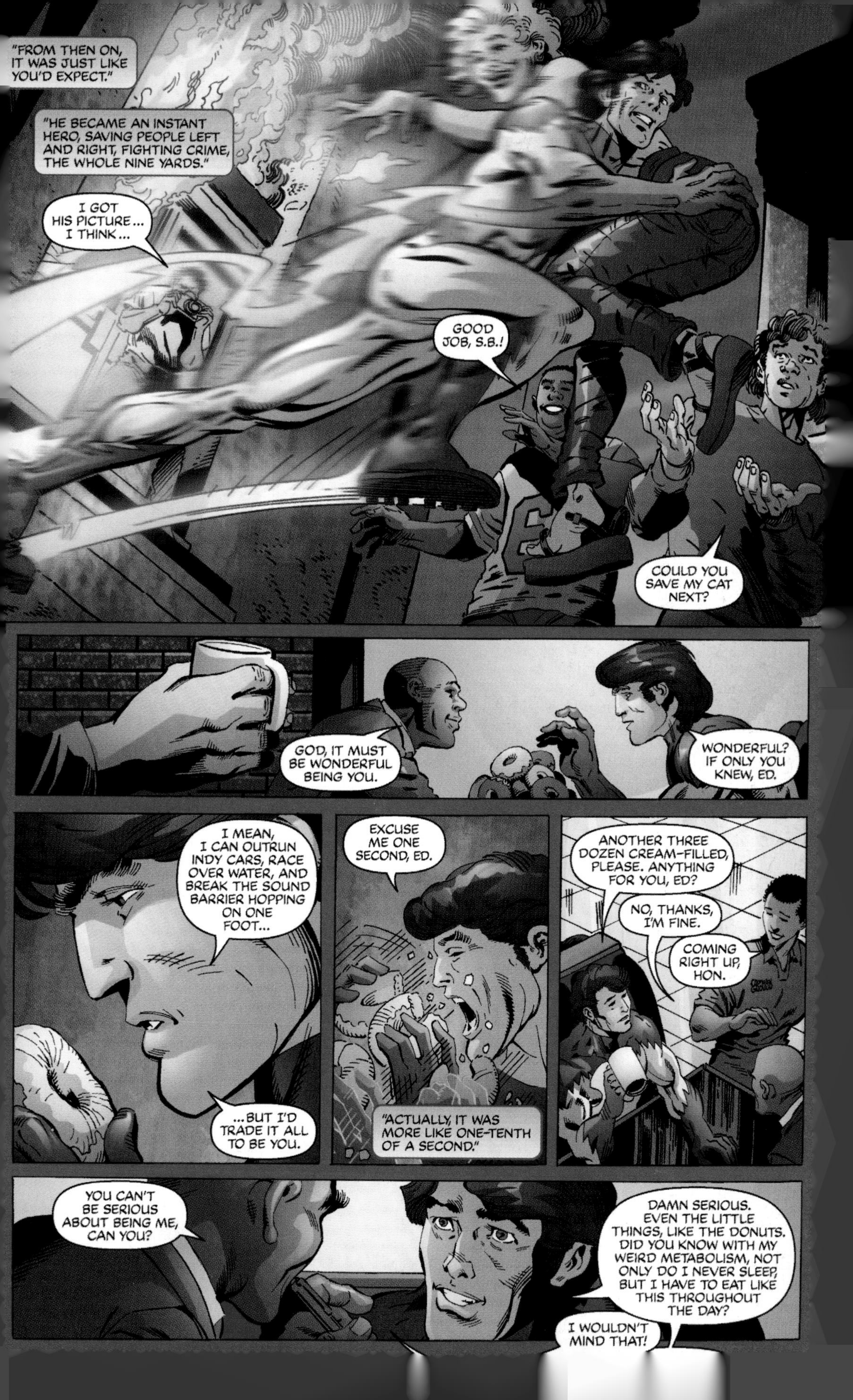
"FROM THEN ON, IT WAS JUST LIKE YOU'D EXPECT."
"HE BECAME AN INSTANT HERO, SAVING PEOPLE LEFT AND RIGHT, FIGHTING CRIME, THE WHOLE NINE YARDS."
I GOT HIS PICTURE... I THINK...
GOOD JOB, S.B.!
COULD YOU SAVE MY CAT NEXT?
GOD, IT MUST BE WONDERFUL BEING YOU.
WONDERFUL? IF ONLY YOU KNEW, ED.
I MEAN, I CAN OUTRUN INDY CARS, RACE OVER WATER, AND BREAK THE SOUND BARRIER HOPPING ON ONE FOOT...
...BUT I'D TRADE IT ALL TO BE YOU.
EXCUSE ME ONE SECOND, ED.
"ACTUALLY, IT WAS MORE LIKE ONE-TENTH OF A SECOND."
ANOTHER THREE DOZEN CREAM-FILLED, PLEASE. ANYTHING FOR YOU, ED?
NO, THANKS, I'M FINE.
COMING RIGHT UP, HON.
YOU CAN'T BE SERIOUS ABOUT BEING ME, CAN YOU?
DAMN SERIOUS. EVEN THE LITTLE THINGS, LIKE THE DONUTS. DID YOU KNOW WITH MY WEIRD METABOLISM, NOT ONLY DO I NEVER SLEEP, BUT I HAVE TO EAT LIKE THIS THROUGHOUT THE DAY?
I WOULDN'T MIND THAT!

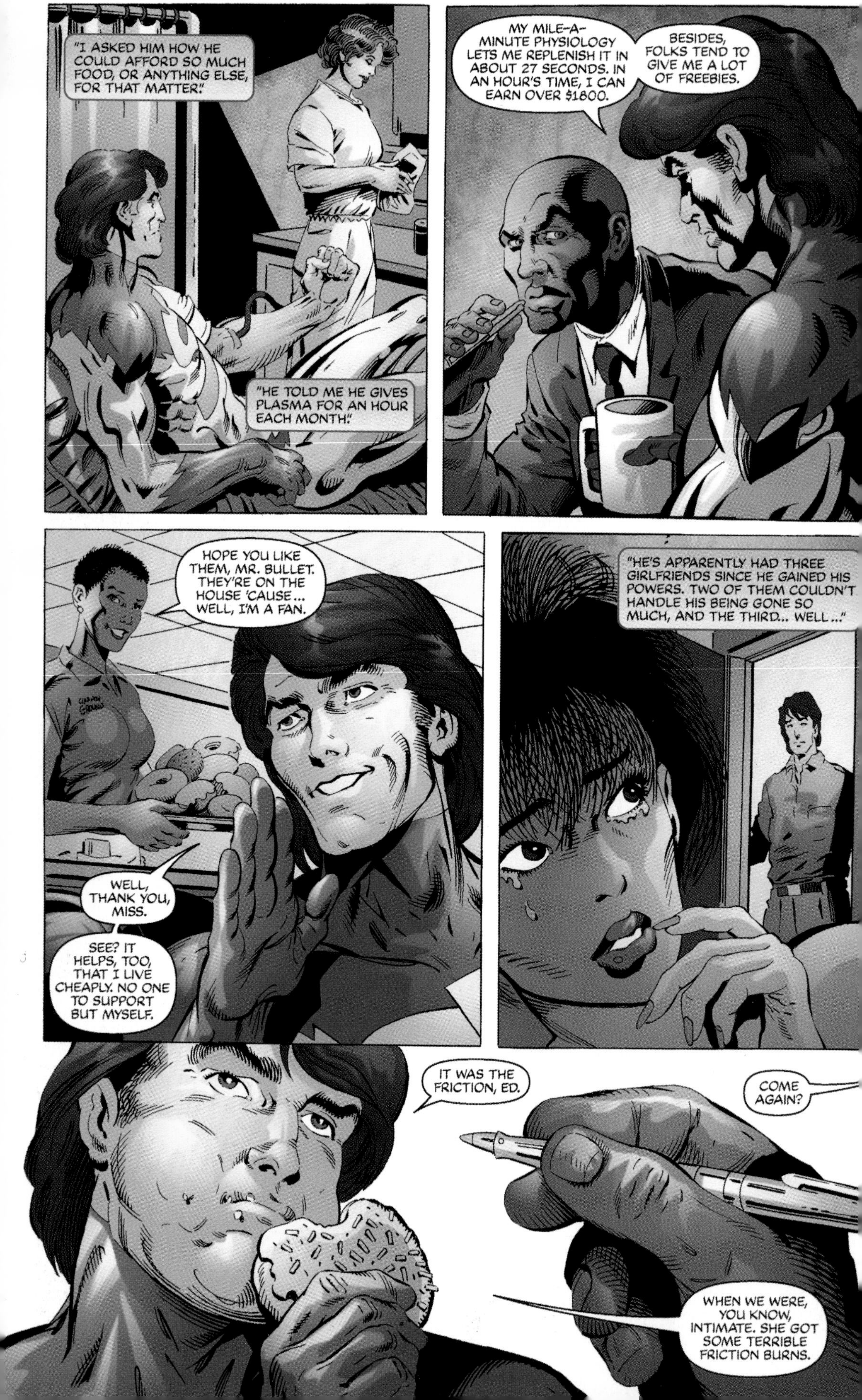
"I ASKED HIM HOW HE COULD AFFORD SO MUCH FOOD, OR ANYTHING ELSE, FOR THAT MATTER."
"HE TOLD ME HE GIVES PLASMA FOR AN HOUR EACH MONTH."
MY MILE-A-MINUTE PHYSIOLOGY LETS ME REPLENISH IT IN ABOUT 27 SECONDS. IN AN HOUR'S TIME, I CAN EARN OVER $1800.
BESIDES, FOLKS TEND TO GIVE ME A LOT OF FREEBIES.
HOPE YOU LIKE THEM, MR. BULLET. THEY'RE ON THE HOUSE 'CAUSE... WELL, I'M A FAN.
WELL, THANK YOU, MISS.
SEE? IT HELPS, TOO, THAT I LIVE CHEAPLY. NO ONE TO SUPPORT BUT MYSELF.
"HE'S APPARENTLY HAD THREE GIRLFRIENDS SINCE HE GAINED HIS POWERS. TWO OF THEM COULDN'T HANDLE HIS BEING GONE SO MUCH, AND THE THIRD... WELL..."
IT WAS THE FRICTION, ED.
COME AGAIN?
WHEN WE WERE, YOU KNOW, INTIMATE. SHE GOT SOME TERRIBLE FRICTION BURNS.

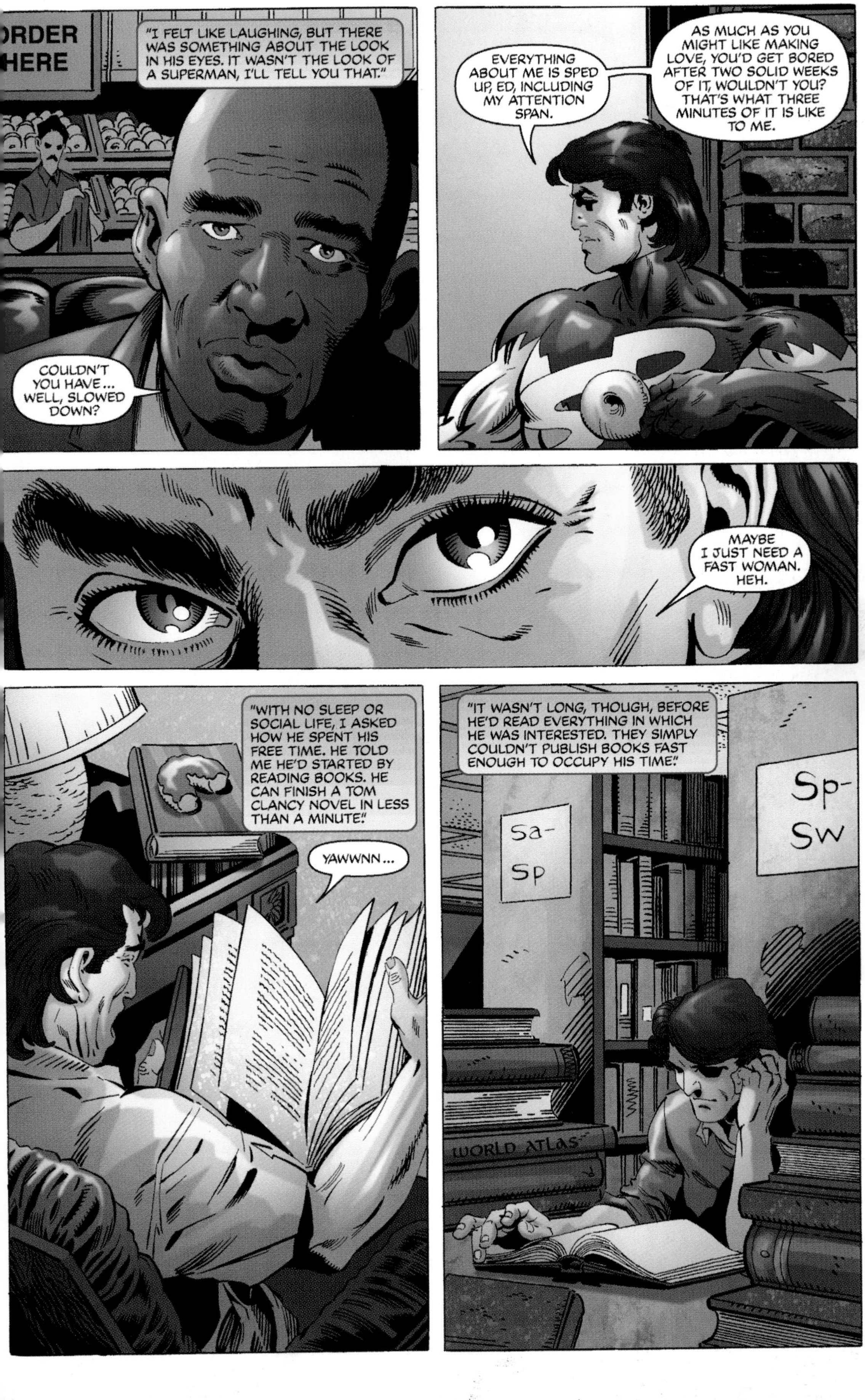
ORDER HERE
"I FELT LIKE LAUGHING, BUT THERE WAS SOMETHING ABOUT THE LOOK IN HIS EYES. IT WASN'T THE LOOK OF A SUPERMAN, I'LL TELL YOU THAT."
COULDN'T YOU HAVE... WELL, SLOWED DOWN?
EVERYTHING ABOUT ME IS SPED UP, ED, INCLUDING MY ATTENTION SPAN.
AS MUCH AS YOU MIGHT LIKE MAKING LOVE, YOU'D GET BORED AFTER TWO SOLID WEEKS OF IT, WOULDN'T YOU? THAT'S WHAT THREE MINUTES OF IT IS LIKE TO ME.
MAYBE I JUST NEED A FAST WOMAN. HEH.
"WITH NO SLEEP OR SOCIAL LIFE, I ASKED HOW HE SPENT HIS FREE TIME. HE TOLD ME HE'D STARTED BY READING BOOKS. HE CAN FINISH A TOM CLANCY NOVEL IN LESS THAN A MINUTE."
YAWWNN...
"IT WASN'T LONG, THOUGH, BEFORE HE'D READ EVERYTHING IN WHICH HE WAS INTERESTED. THEY SIMPLY COULDN'T PUBLISH BOOKS FAST ENOUGH TO OCCUPY HIS TIME."
Sa- Sp
Sp- Sw
WORLD ATLAS

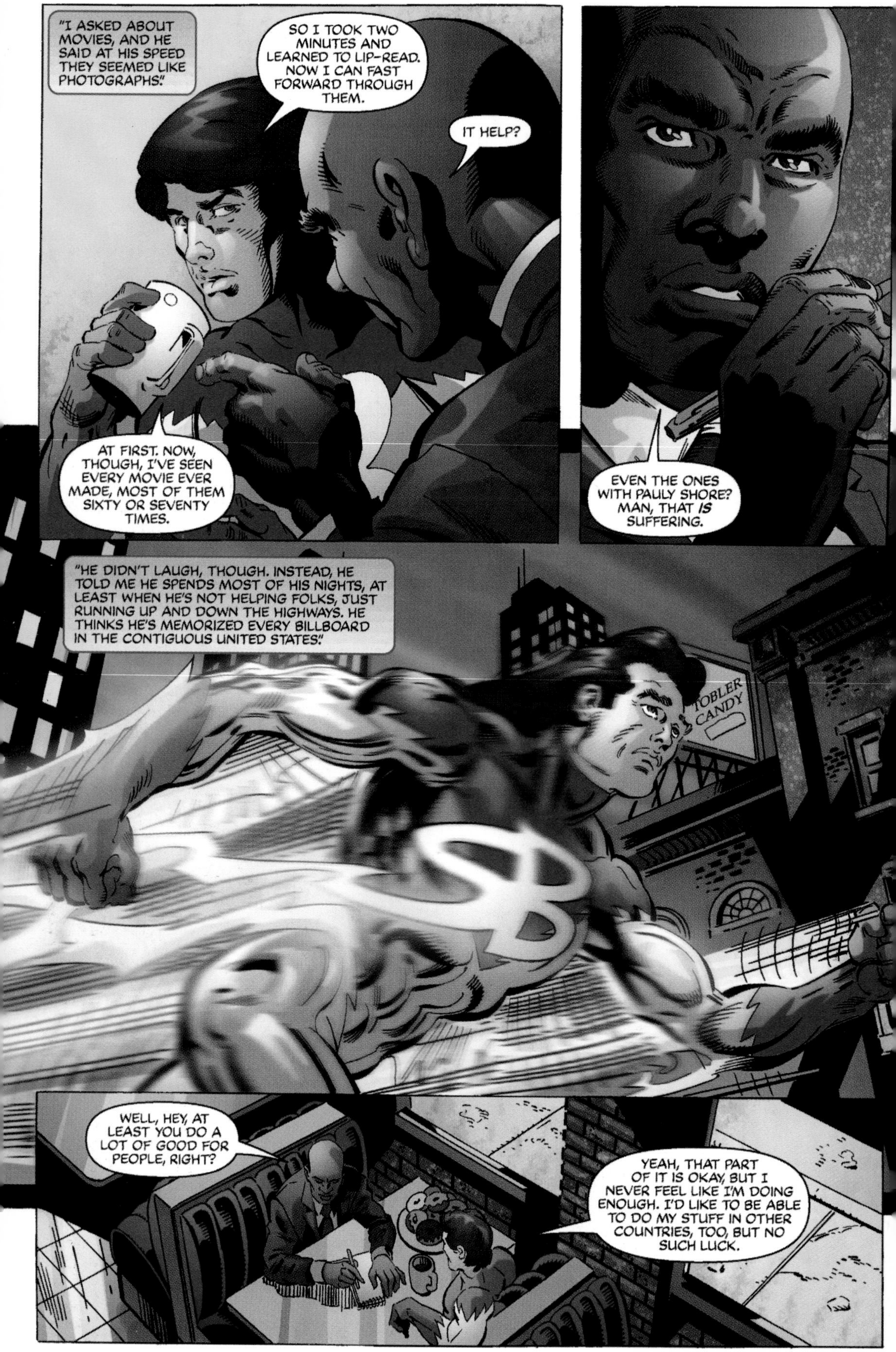

"I ASKED ABOUT MOVIES, AND HE SAID AT HIS SPEED THEY SEEMED LIKE PHOTOGRAPHS."
SO I TOOK TWO MINUTES AND LEARNED TO LIP-READ. NOW I CAN FAST FORWARD THROUGH THEM.
IT HELP?
AT FIRST. NOW, THOUGH, I'VE SEEN EVERY MOVIE EVER MADE, MOST OF THEM SIXTY OR SEVENTY TIMES.
EVEN THE ONES WITH PAULY SHORE? MAN, THAT *IS* SUFFERING.
"HE DIDN'T LAUGH, THOUGH. INSTEAD, HE TOLD ME HE SPENDS MOST OF HIS NIGHTS, AT LEAST WHEN HE'S NOT HELPING FOLKS, JUST RUNNING UP AND DOWN THE HIGHWAYS. HE THINKS HE'S MEMORIZED EVERY BILLBOARD IN THE CONTIGUOUS UNITED STATES."
TOBLER CANDY
WELL, HEY, AT LEAST YOU DO A LOT OF GOOD FOR PEOPLE, RIGHT?
YEAH, THAT PART OF IT IS OKAY, BUT I NEVER FEEL LIKE I'M DOING ENOUGH. I'D LIKE TO BE ABLE TO DO MY STUFF IN OTHER COUNTRIES, TOO, BUT NO SUCH LUCK.

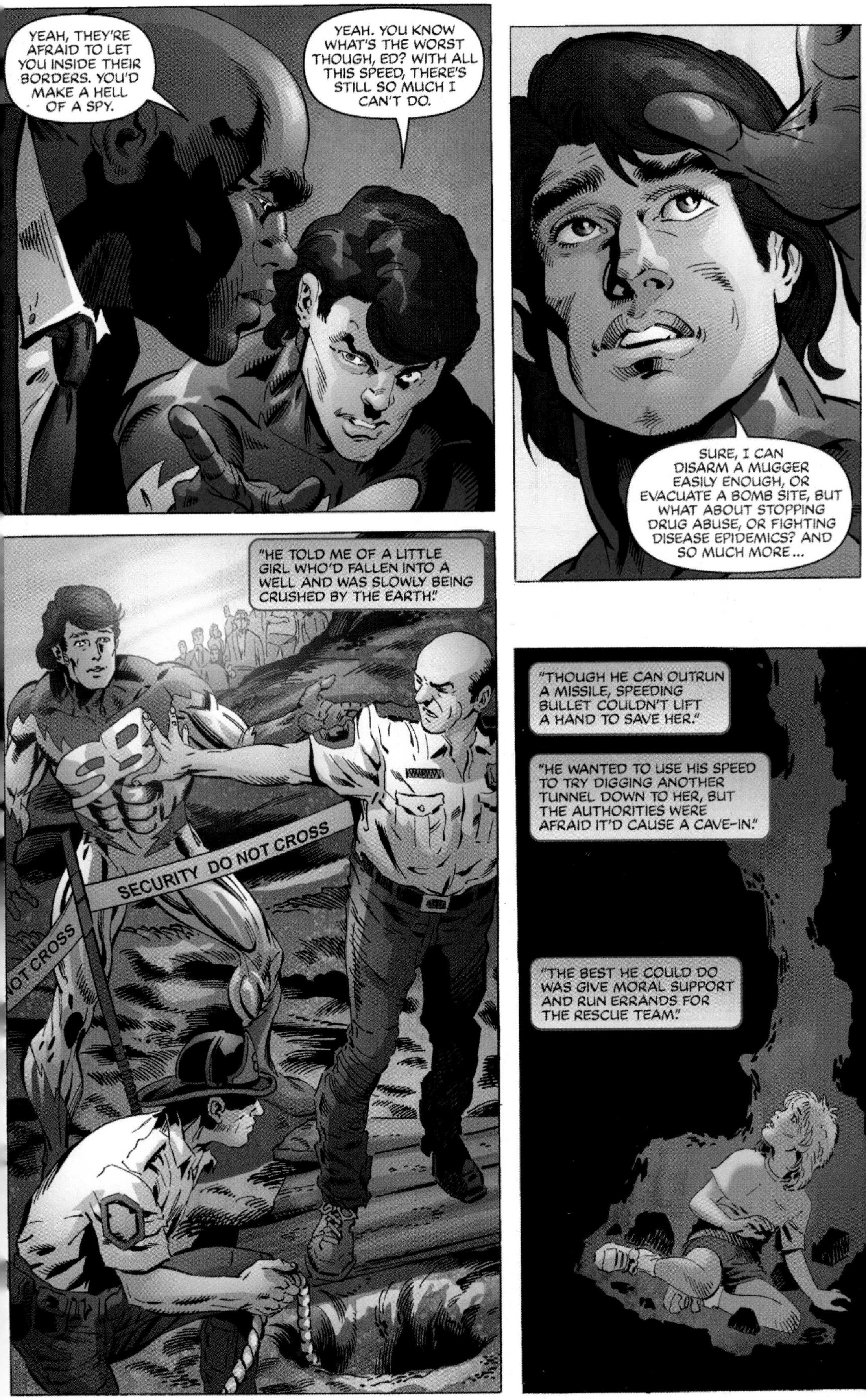
YEAH, THEY'RE AFRAID TO LET YOU INSIDE THEIR BORDERS. YOU'D MAKE A HELL OF A SPY.
YEAH. YOU KNOW WHAT'S THE WORST THOUGH, ED? WITH ALL THIS SPEED, THERE'S STILL SO MUCH I CAN'T DO.
SURE, I CAN DISARM A MUGGER EASILY ENOUGH, OR EVACUATE A BOMB SITE, BUT WHAT ABOUT STOPPING DRUG ABUSE, OR FIGHTING DISEASE EPIDEMICS? AND SO MUCH MORE...
"HE TOLD ME OF A LITTLE GIRL WHO'D FALLEN INTO A WELL AND WAS SLOWLY BEING CRUSHED BY THE EARTH."
SECURITY DO NOT CROSS
NOT CROSS
"THOUGH HE CAN OUTRUN A MISSILE, SPEEDING BULLET COULDN'T LIFT A HAND TO SAVE HER."
"HE WANTED TO USE HIS SPEED TO TRY DIGGING ANOTHER TUNNEL DOWN TO HER, BUT THE AUTHORITIES WERE AFRAID IT'D CAUSE A CAVE-IN."
"THE BEST HE COULD DO WAS GIVE MORAL SUPPORT AND RUN ERRANDS FOR THE RESCUE TEAM."

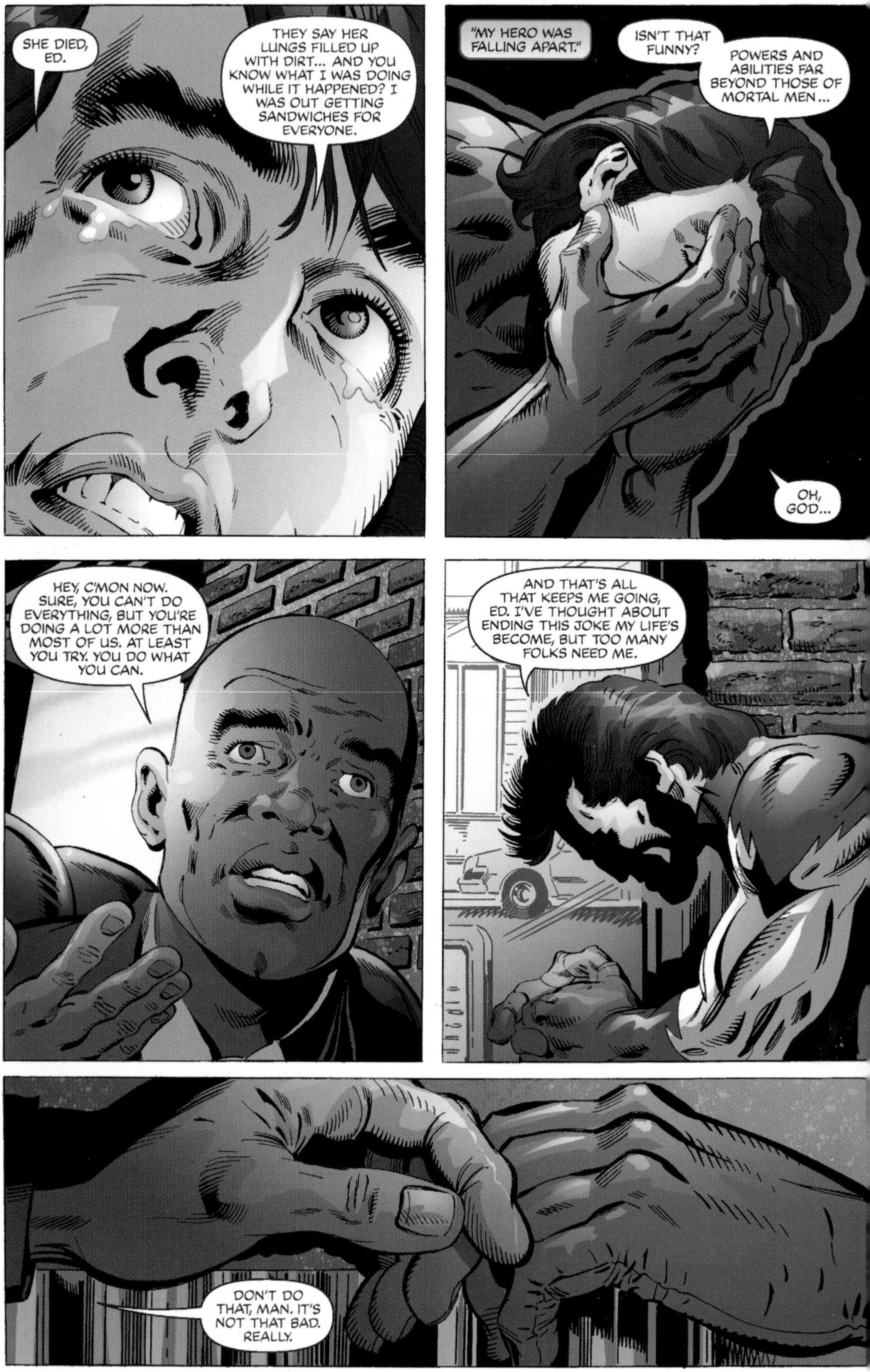
SHE DIED, ED.
THEY SAY HER LUNGS FILLED UP WITH DIRT... AND YOU KNOW WHAT I WAS DOING WHILE IT HAPPENED? I WAS OUT GETTING SANDWICHES FOR EVERYONE.
"MY HERO WAS FALLING APART."
ISN'T THAT FUNNY?
POWERS AND ABILITIES FAR BEYOND THOSE OF MORTAL MEN...
OH, GOD...
HEY, C'MON NOW. SURE, YOU CAN'T DO EVERYTHING, BUT YOU'RE DOING A LOT MORE THAN MOST OF US. AT LEAST YOU TRY. YOU DO WHAT YOU CAN.
AND THAT'S ALL THAT KEEPS ME GOING, ED. I'VE THOUGHT ABOUT ENDING THIS JOKE MY LIFE'S BECOME, BUT TOO MANY FOLKS NEED ME.
DON'T DO THAT, MAN. IT'S NOT THAT BAD. REALLY.

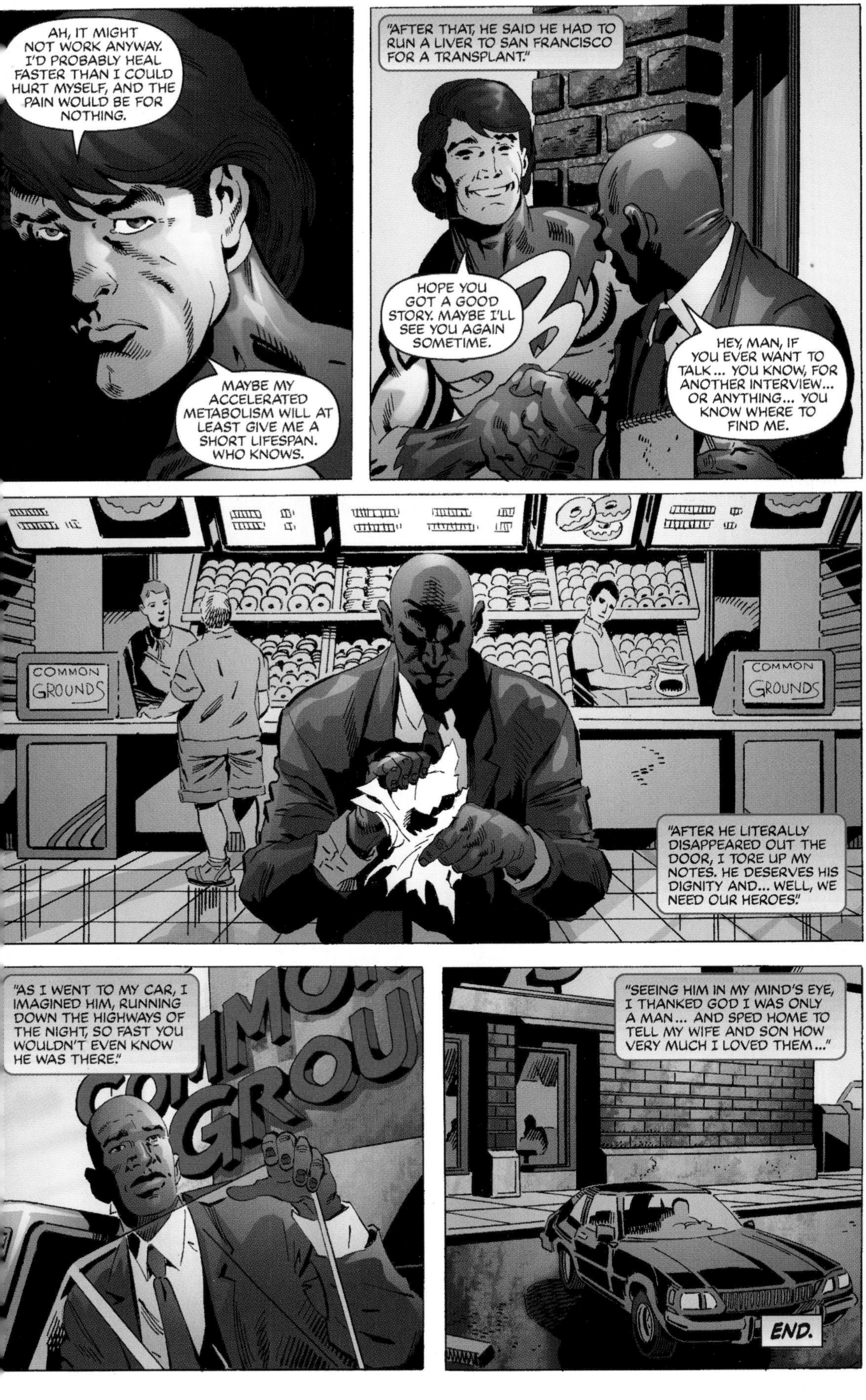
AH, IT MIGHT NOT WORK ANYWAY. I'D PROBABLY HEAL FASTER THAN I COULD HURT MYSELF, AND THE PAIN WOULD BE FOR NOTHING.
MAYBE MY ACCELERATED METABOLISM WILL AT LEAST GIVE ME A SHORT LIFESPAN. WHO KNOWS.
"AFTER THAT, HE SAID HE HAD TO RUN A LIVER TO SAN FRANCISCO FOR A TRANSPLANT."
HOPE YOU GOT A GOOD STORY. MAYBE I'LL SEE YOU AGAIN SOMETIME.
HEY, MAN, IF YOU EVER WANT TO TALK... YOU KNOW, FOR ANOTHER INTERVIEW... OR ANYTHING... YOU KNOW WHERE TO FIND ME.
COMMON GROUNDS
COMMON GROUNDS
"AFTER HE LITERALLY DISAPPEARED OUT THE DOOR, I TORE UP MY NOTES. HE DESERVES HIS DIGNITY AND... WELL, WE NEED OUR HEROES."
"AS I WENT TO MY CAR, I IMAGINED HIM, RUNNING DOWN THE HIGHWAYS OF THE NIGHT, SO FAST YOU WOULDN'T EVEN KNOW HE WAS THERE."
"SEEING HIM IN MY MIND'S EYE, I THANKED GOD I WAS ONLY A MAN... AND SPED HOME TO TELL MY WIFE AND SON HOW VERY MUCH I LOVED THEM..."
END.

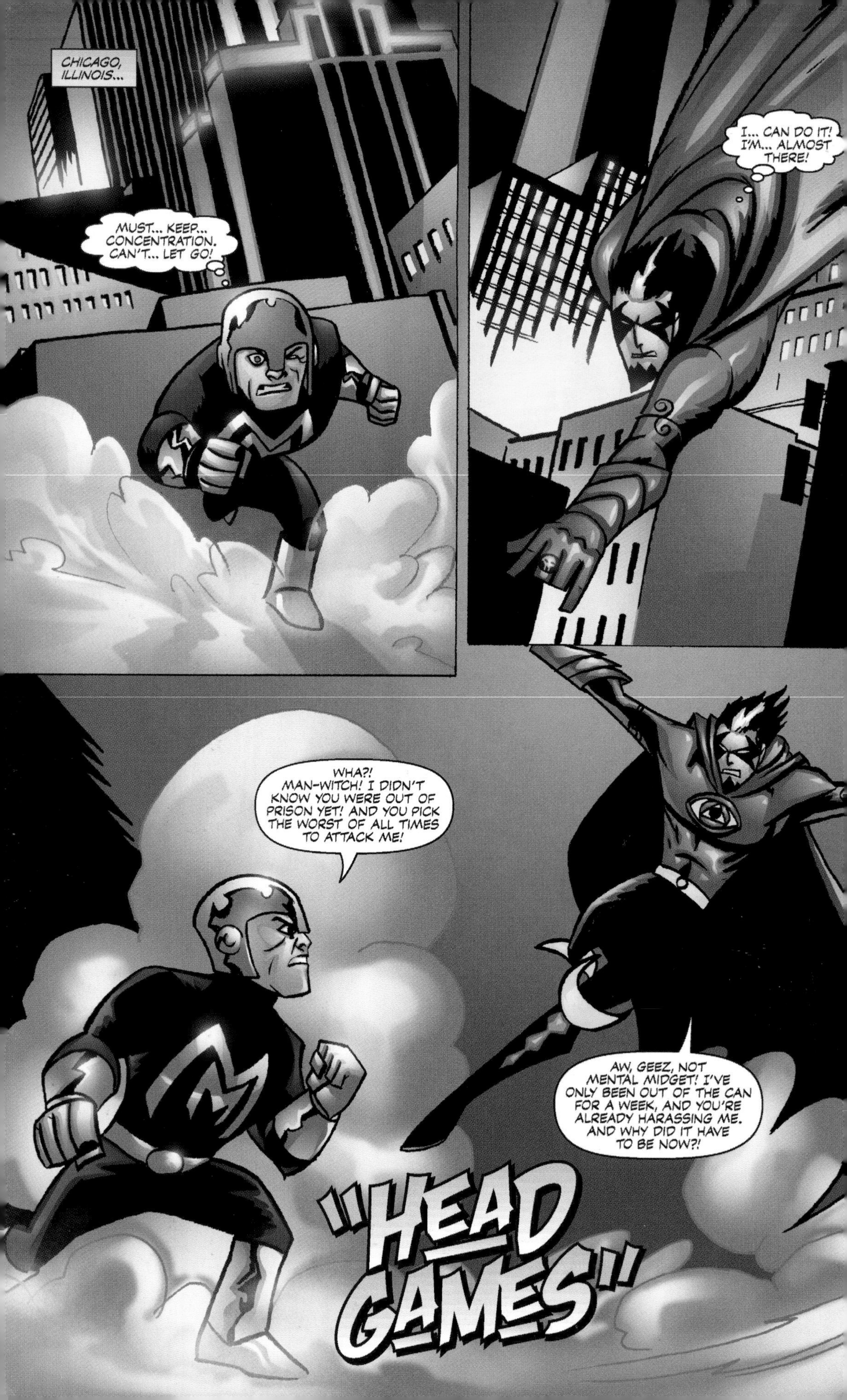
CHICAGO, ILLINOIS...
MUST... KEEP... CONCENTRATION. CAN'T... LET GO!
I... CAN DO IT! I'M... ALMOST THERE!
WHA?! MAN-WITCH! I DIDN'T KNOW YOU WERE OUT OF PRISON YET! AND YOU PICK THE WORST OF ALL TIMES TO ATTACK ME!
AW, GEEZ, NOT MENTAL MIDGET! I'VE ONLY BEEN OUT OF THE CAN FOR A WEEK, AND YOU'RE ALREADY HARASSING ME. AND WHY DID IT HAVE TO BE NOW?!
"HEAD GAMES"

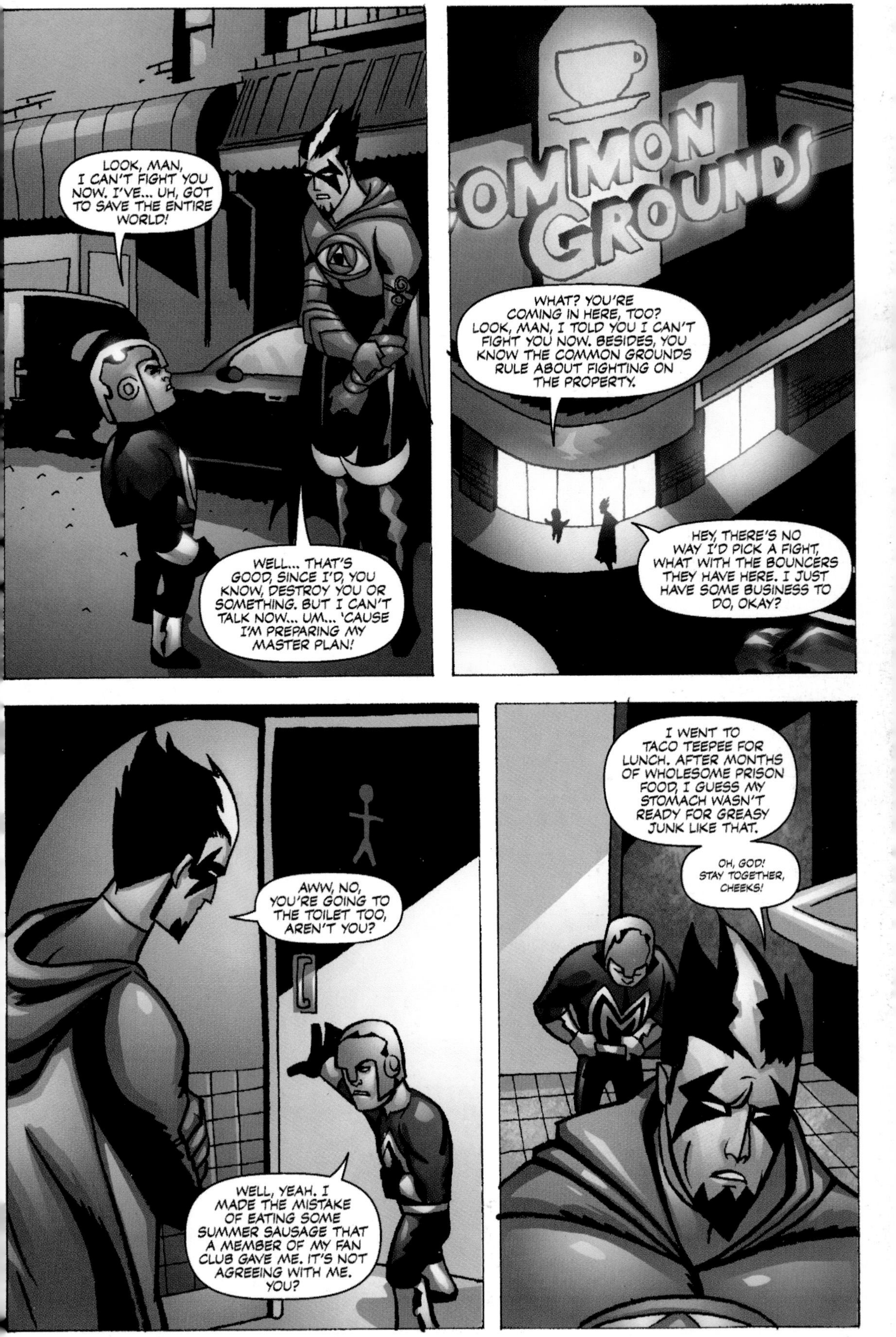
LOOK, MAN, I CAN'T FIGHT YOU NOW. I'VE... UH, GOT TO SAVE THE ENTIRE WORLD!
WELL... THAT'S GOOD, SINCE I'D, YOU KNOW, DESTROY YOU OR SOMETHING. BUT I CAN'T TALK NOW... UM... 'CAUSE I'M PREPARING MY MASTER PLAN!
COMMON GROUNDS
WHAT? YOU'RE COMING IN HERE, TOO? LOOK, MAN, I TOLD YOU I CAN'T FIGHT YOU NOW. BESIDES, YOU KNOW THE COMMON GROUNDS RULE ABOUT FIGHTING ON THE PROPERTY.
HEY, THERE'S NO WAY I'D PICK A FIGHT, WHAT WITH THE BOUNCERS THEY HAVE HERE. I JUST HAVE SOME BUSINESS TO DO, OKAY?
AWW, NO, YOU'RE GOING TO THE TOILET TOO, AREN'T YOU?
WELL, YEAH. I MADE THE MISTAKE OF EATING SOME SUMMER SAUSAGE THAT A MEMBER OF MY FAN CLUB GAVE ME. IT'S NOT AGREEING WITH ME. YOU?
I WENT TO TACO TEEPEE FOR LUNCH. AFTER MONTHS OF WHOLESOME PRISON FOOD, I GUESS MY STOMACH WASN'T READY FOR GREASY JUNK LIKE THAT.
OH, GOD! STAY TOGETHER, CHEEKS!

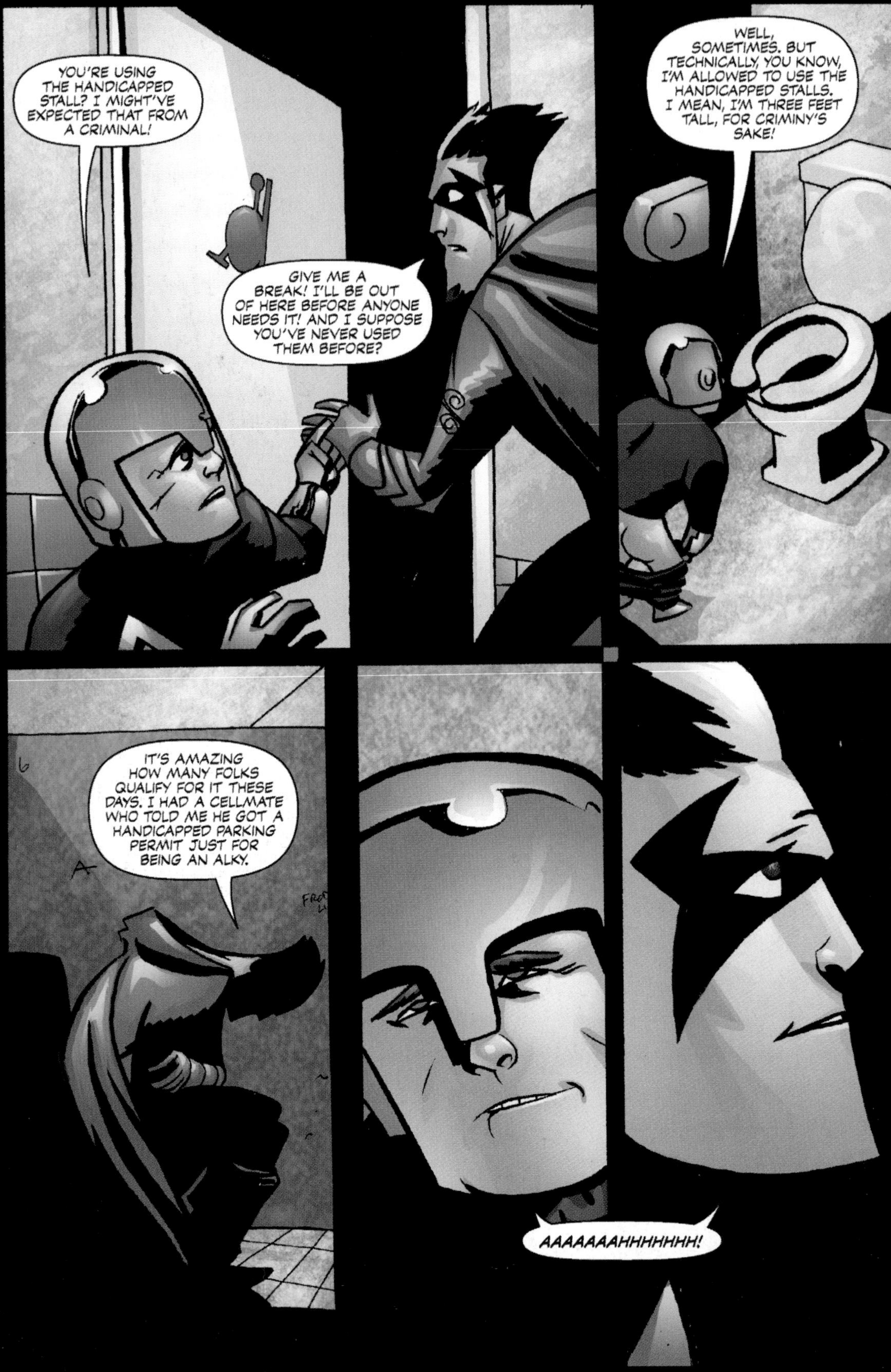
YOU'RE USING THE HANDICAPPED STALL? I MIGHT'VE EXPECTED THAT FROM A CRIMINAL!
GIVE ME A BREAK! I'LL BE OUT OF HERE BEFORE ANYONE NEEDS IT! AND I SUPPOSE YOU'VE NEVER USED THEM BEFORE?
WELL, SOMETIMES. BUT TECHNICALLY, YOU KNOW, I'M ALLOWED TO USE THE HANDICAPPED STALLS. I MEAN, I'M THREE FEET TALL, FOR CRIMINY'S SAKE!
IT'S AMAZING HOW MANY FOLKS QUALIFY FOR IT THESE DAYS. I HAD A CELLMATE WHO TOLD ME HE GOT A HANDICAPPED PARKING PERMIT JUST FOR BEING AN ALKY.
AAAAAAAHHHHHHH!

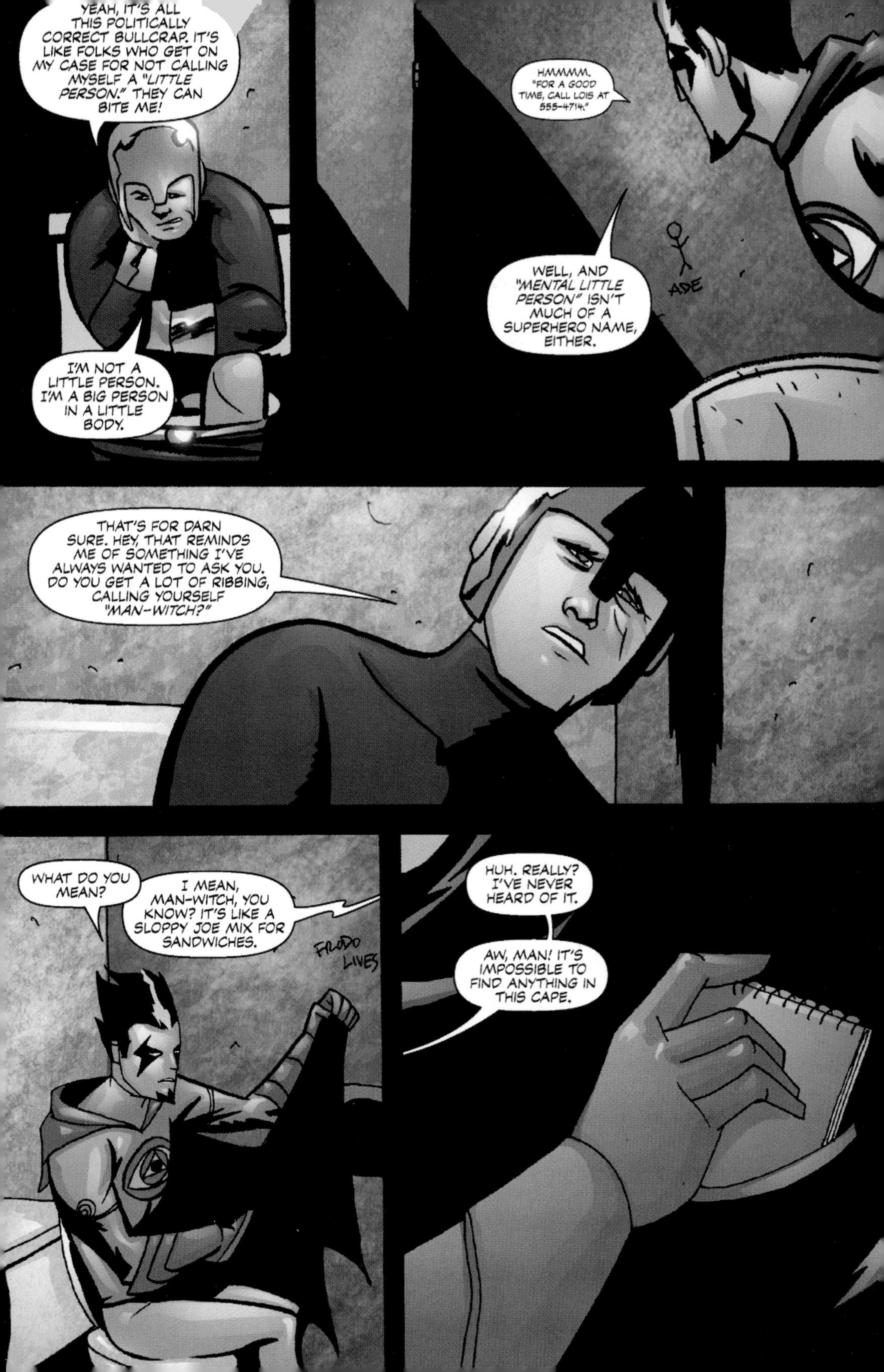
YEAH, IT'S ALL THIS POLITICALLY CORRECT BULLCRAP. IT'S LIKE FOLKS WHO GET ON MY CASE FOR NOT CALLING MYSELF A "LITTLE PERSON." THEY CAN BITE ME!
I'M NOT A LITTLE PERSON. I'M A BIG PERSON IN A LITTLE BODY.
HMMMM. "FOR A GOOD TIME, CALL LOIS AT 555-4714."
WELL, AND "MENTAL LITTLE PERSON" ISN'T MUCH OF A SUPERHERO NAME, EITHER.
ADE
THAT'S FOR DARN SURE. HEY, THAT REMINDS ME OF SOMETHING I'VE ALWAYS WANTED TO ASK YOU. DO YOU GET A LOT OF RIBBING, CALLING YOURSELF "MAN-WITCH?"
WHAT DO YOU MEAN?
I MEAN, MAN-WITCH, YOU KNOW? IT'S LIKE A SLOPPY JOE MIX FOR SANDWICHES.
FRODO LIVES
HUH. REALLY? I'VE NEVER HEARD OF IT.
AW, MAN! IT'S IMPOSSIBLE TO FIND ANYTHING IN THIS CAPE.

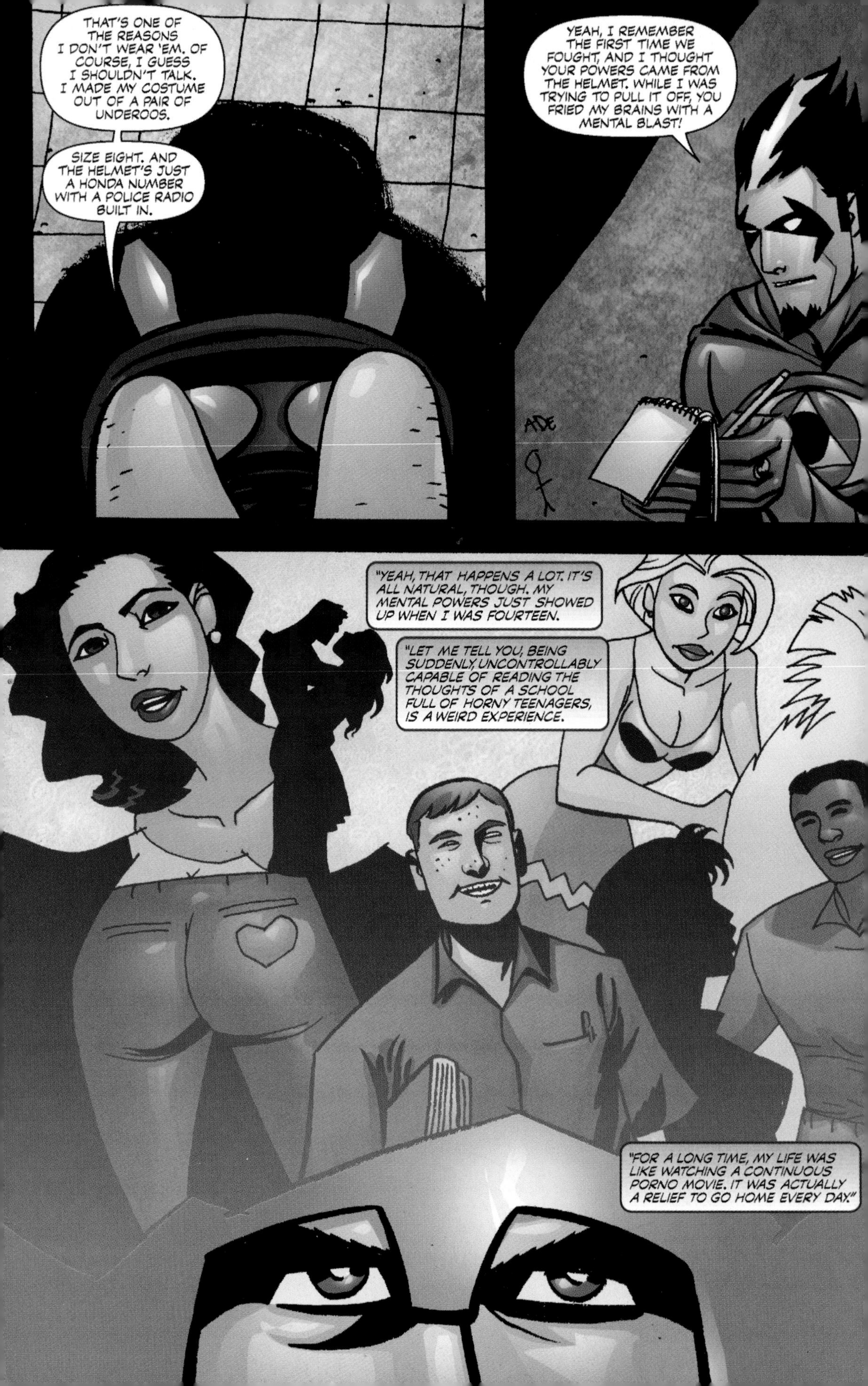
THAT'S ONE OF THE REASONS I DON'T WEAR 'EM. OF COURSE, I GUESS I SHOULDN'T TALK. I MADE MY COSTUME OUT OF A PAIR OF UNDEROOS.
SIZE EIGHT. AND THE HELMET'S JUST A HONDA NUMBER WITH A POLICE RADIO BUILT IN.
YEAH, I REMEMBER THE FIRST TIME WE FOUGHT, AND I THOUGHT YOUR POWERS CAME FROM THE HELMET. WHILE I WAS TRYING TO PULL IT OFF, YOU FRIED MY BRAINS WITH A MENTAL BLAST!
ADE
"YEAH, THAT HAPPENS A LOT. IT'S ALL NATURAL, THOUGH. MY MENTAL POWERS JUST SHOWED UP WHEN I WAS FOURTEEN.
"LET ME TELL YOU, BEING SUDDENLY, UNCONTROLLABLY CAPABLE OF READING THE THOUGHTS OF A SCHOOL FULL OF HORNY TEENAGERS, IS A WEIRD EXPERIENCE.
"FOR A LONG TIME, MY LIFE WAS LIKE WATCHING A CONTINUOUS PORNO MOVIE. IT WAS ACTUALLY A RELIEF TO GO HOME EVERY DAY."

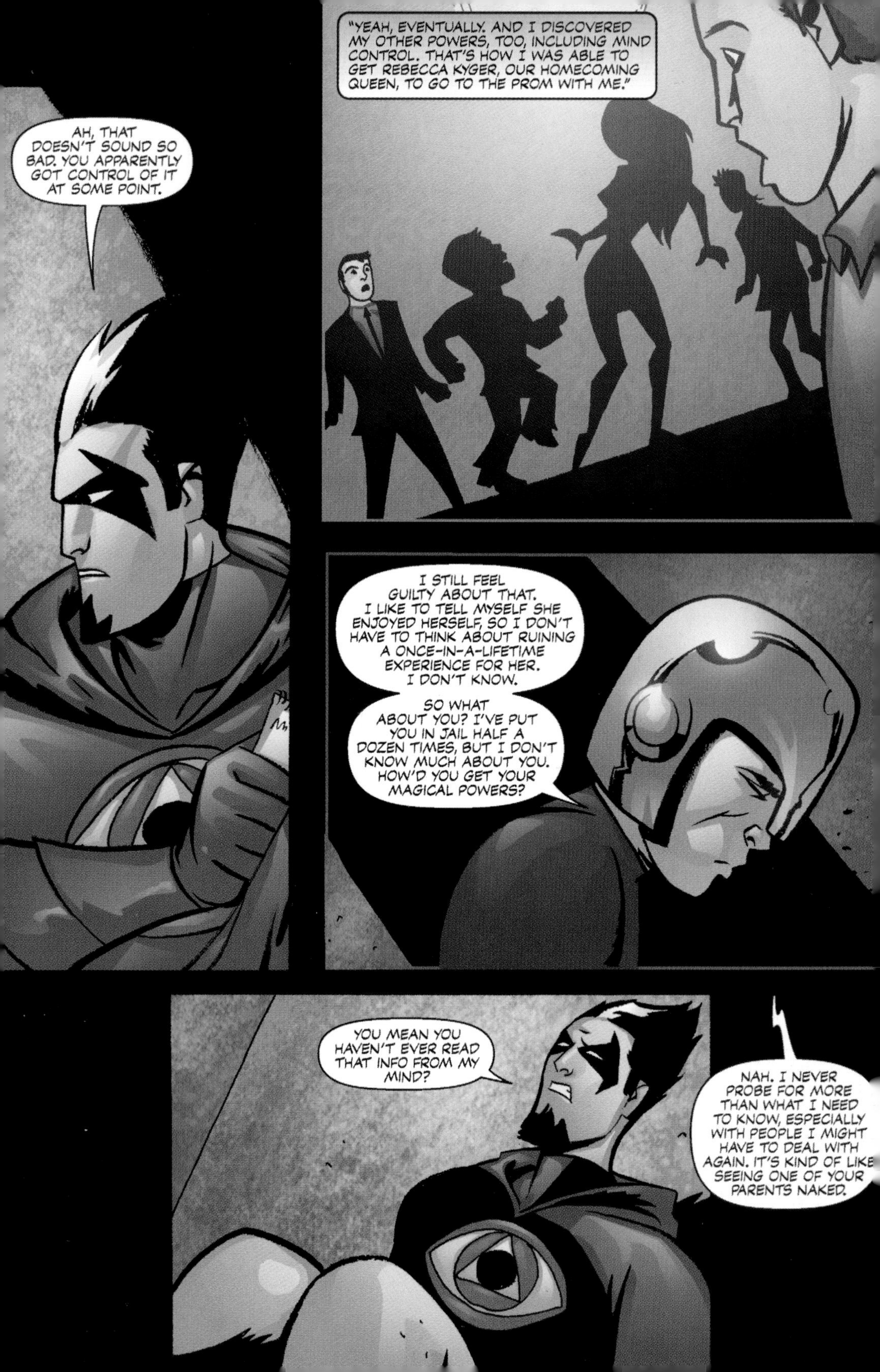
"YEAH, EVENTUALLY. AND I DISCOVERED MY OTHER POWERS, TOO, INCLUDING MIND CONTROL. THAT'S HOW I WAS ABLE TO GET REBECCA KYGER, OUR HOMECOMING QUEEN, TO GO TO THE PROM WITH ME."
AH, THAT DOESN'T SOUND SO BAD. YOU APPARENTLY GOT CONTROL OF IT AT SOME POINT.
I STILL FEEL GUILTY ABOUT THAT. I LIKE TO TELL MYSELF SHE ENJOYED HERSELF, SO I DON'T HAVE TO THINK ABOUT RUINING A ONCE-IN-A-LIFETIME EXPERIENCE FOR HER. I DON'T KNOW.
SO WHAT ABOUT YOU? I'VE PUT YOU IN JAIL HALF A DOZEN TIMES, BUT I DON'T KNOW MUCH ABOUT YOU. HOW'D YOU GET YOUR MAGICAL POWERS?
YOU MEAN YOU HAVEN'T EVER READ THAT INFO FROM MY MIND?
NAH. I NEVER PROBE FOR MORE THAN WHAT I NEED TO KNOW, ESPECIALLY WITH PEOPLE I MIGHT HAVE TO DEAL WITH AGAIN. IT'S KIND OF LIKE SEEING ONE OF YOUR PARENTS NAKED.

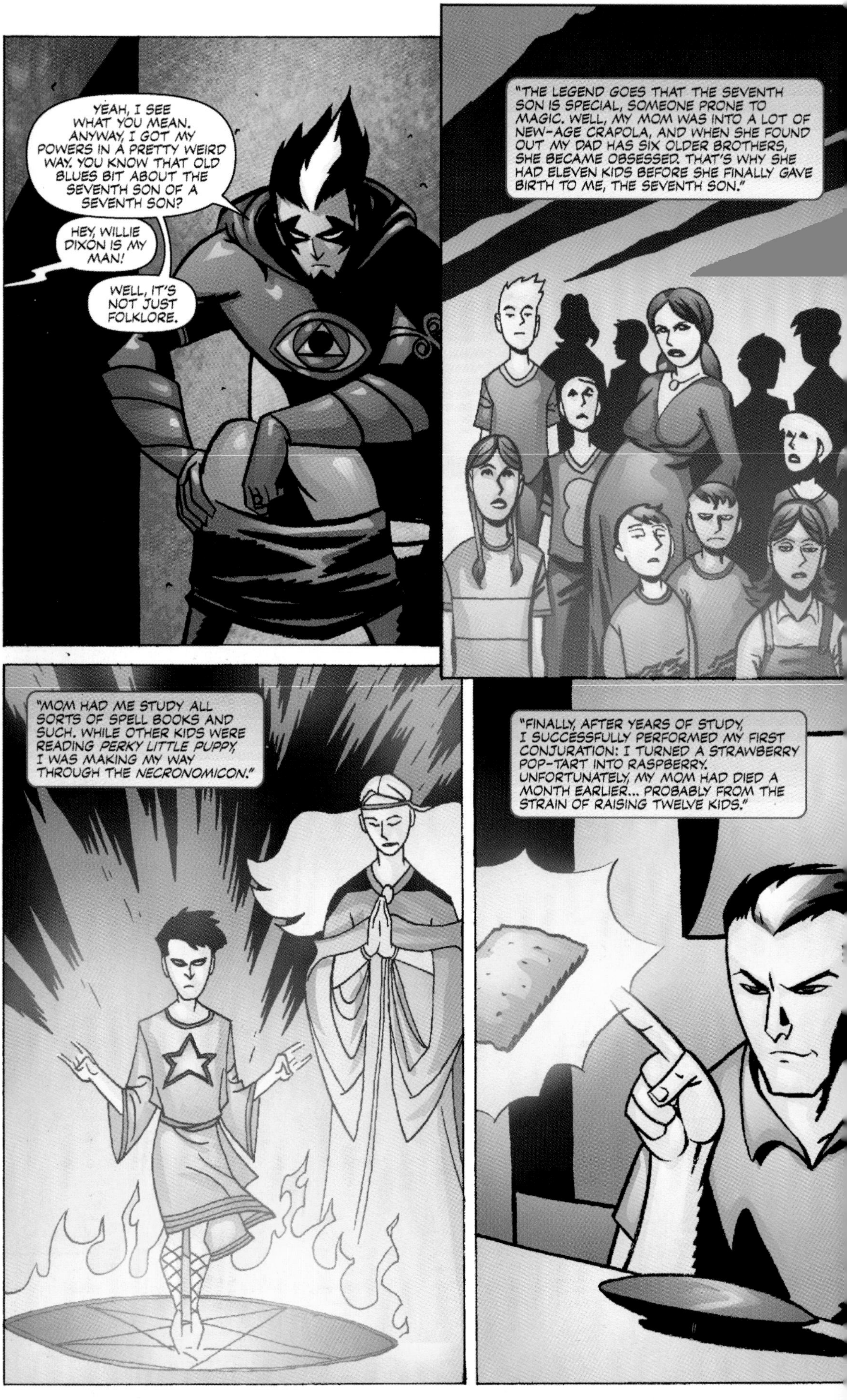
YEAH, I SEE WHAT YOU MEAN. ANYWAY, I GOT MY POWERS IN A PRETTY WEIRD WAY. YOU KNOW THAT OLD BLUES BIT ABOUT THE SEVENTH SON OF A SEVENTH SON?
HEY, WILLIE DIXON IS MY MAN!
WELL, IT'S NOT JUST FOLKLORE.
"THE LEGEND GOES THAT THE SEVENTH SON IS SPECIAL, SOMEONE PRONE TO MAGIC. WELL, MY MOM WAS INTO A LOT OF NEW-AGE CRAPOLA, AND WHEN SHE FOUND OUT MY DAD HAS SIX OLDER BROTHERS, SHE BECAME OBSESSED. THAT'S WHY SHE HAD ELEVEN KIDS BEFORE SHE FINALLY GAVE BIRTH TO ME, THE SEVENTH SON."
"MOM HAD ME STUDY ALL SORTS OF SPELL BOOKS AND SUCH. WHILE OTHER KIDS WERE READING *PERKY LITTLE PUPPY*, I WAS MAKING MY WAY THROUGH THE *NECRONOMICON*."
"FINALLY, AFTER YEARS OF STUDY, I SUCCESSFULLY PERFORMED MY FIRST CONJURATION: I TURNED A STRAWBERRY POP-TART INTO RASPBERRY. UNFORTUNATELY, MY MOM HAD DIED A MONTH EARLIER... PROBABLY FROM THE STRAIN OF RAISING TWELVE KIDS."

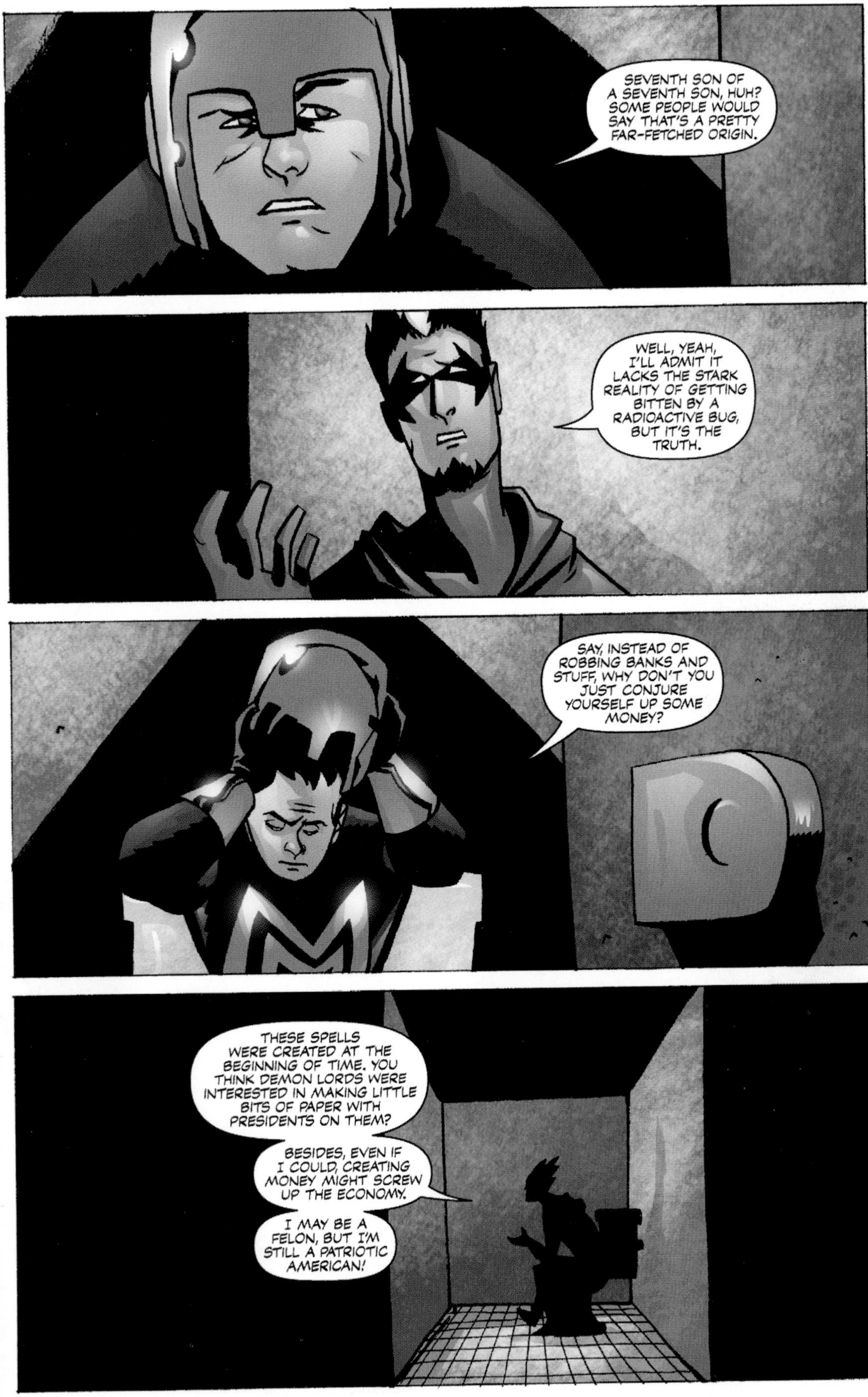
SEVENTH SON OF A SEVENTH SON, HUH? SOME PEOPLE WOULD SAY THAT'S A PRETTY FAR-FETCHED ORIGIN.
WELL, YEAH, I'LL ADMIT IT LACKS THE STARK REALITY OF GETTING BITTEN BY A RADIOACTIVE BUG, BUT IT'S THE TRUTH.
SAY, INSTEAD OF ROBBING BANKS AND STUFF, WHY DON'T YOU JUST CONJURE YOURSELF UP SOME MONEY?
THESE SPELLS WERE CREATED AT THE BEGINNING OF TIME. YOU THINK DEMON LORDS WERE INTERESTED IN MAKING LITTLE BITS OF PAPER WITH PRESIDENTS ON THEM?
BESIDES, EVEN IF I COULD, CREATING MONEY MIGHT SCREW UP THE ECONOMY.
I MAY BE A FELON, BUT I'M STILL A PATRIOTIC AMERICAN!

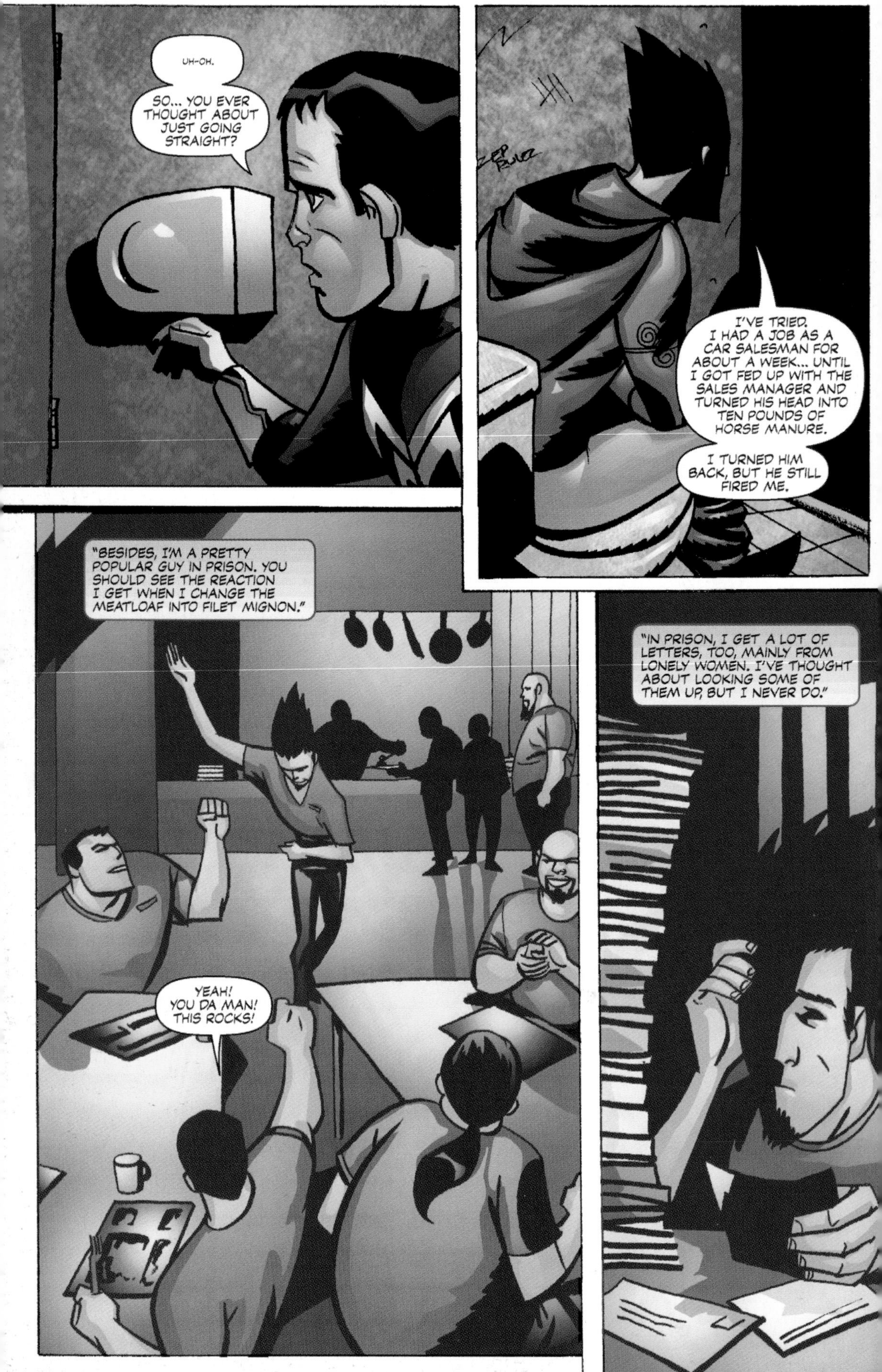
UH-OH.
SO... YOU EVER THOUGHT ABOUT JUST GOING STRAIGHT?
I'VE TRIED. I HAD A JOB AS A CAR SALESMAN FOR ABOUT A WEEK... UNTIL I GOT FED UP WITH THE SALES MANAGER AND TURNED HIS HEAD INTO TEN POUNDS OF HORSE MANURE.
I TURNED HIM BACK, BUT HE STILL FIRED ME.
"BESIDES, I'M A PRETTY POPULAR GUY IN PRISON. YOU SHOULD SEE THE REACTION I GET WHEN I CHANGE THE MEATLOAF INTO FILET MIGNON."
YEAH! YOU DA MAN! THIS ROCKS!
"IN PRISON, I GET A LOT OF LETTERS, TOO, MAINLY FROM LONELY WOMEN. I'VE THOUGHT ABOUT LOOKING SOME OF THEM UP, BUT I NEVER DO."

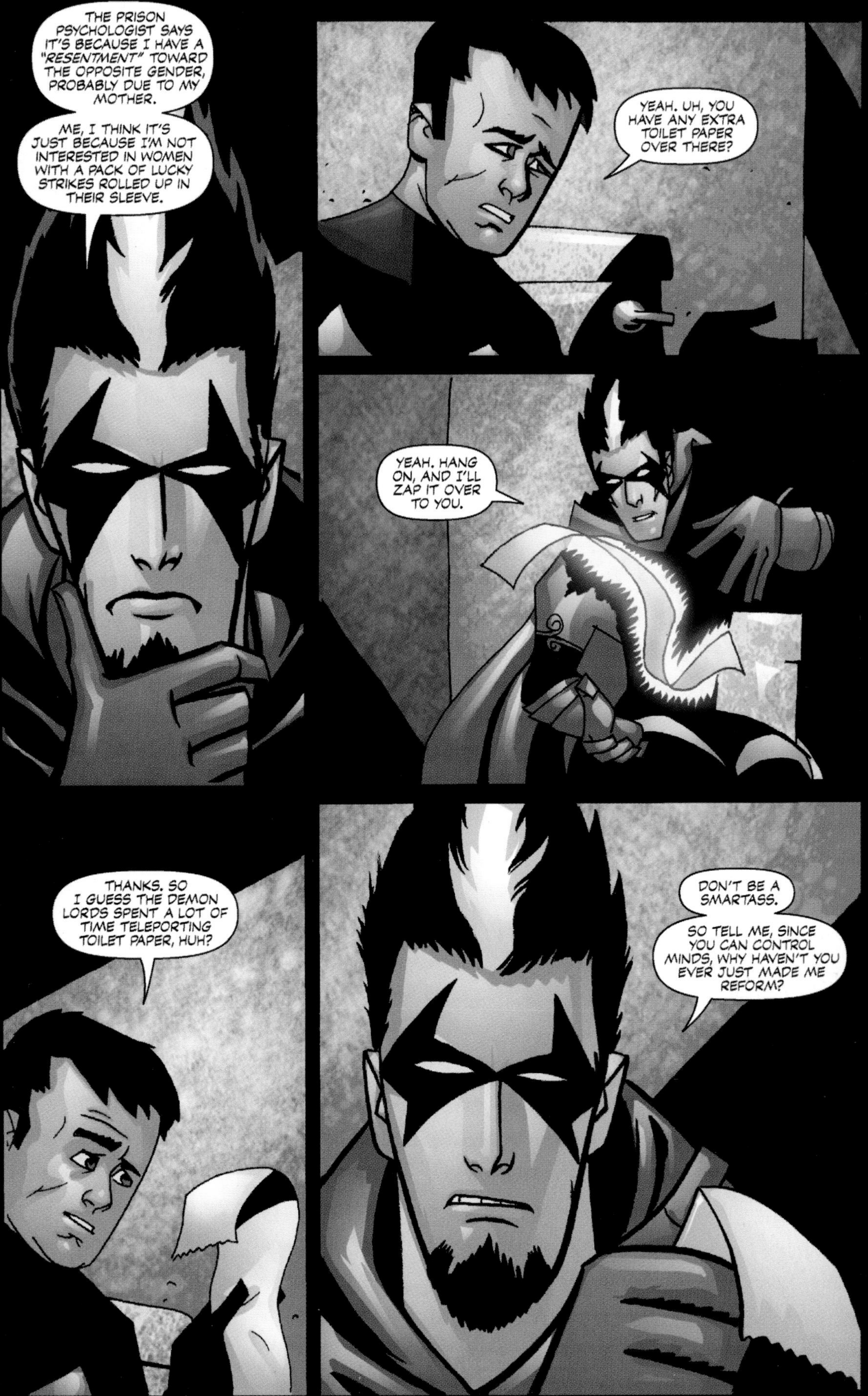
THE PRISON PSYCHOLOGIST SAYS IT'S BECAUSE I HAVE A "RESENTMENT" TOWARD THE OPPOSITE GENDER, PROBABLY DUE TO MY MOTHER.
ME, I THINK IT'S JUST BECAUSE I'M NOT INTERESTED IN WOMEN WITH A PACK OF LUCKY STRIKES ROLLED UP IN THEIR SLEEVE.
YEAH. UH, YOU HAVE ANY EXTRA TOILET PAPER OVER THERE?
YEAH. HANG ON, AND I'LL ZAP IT OVER TO YOU.
THANKS. SO I GUESS THE DEMON LORDS SPENT A LOT OF TIME TELEPORTING TOILET PAPER, HUH?
DON'T BE A SMARTASS.
SO TELL ME, SINCE YOU CAN CONTROL MINDS, WHY HAVEN'T YOU EVER JUST MADE ME REFORM?

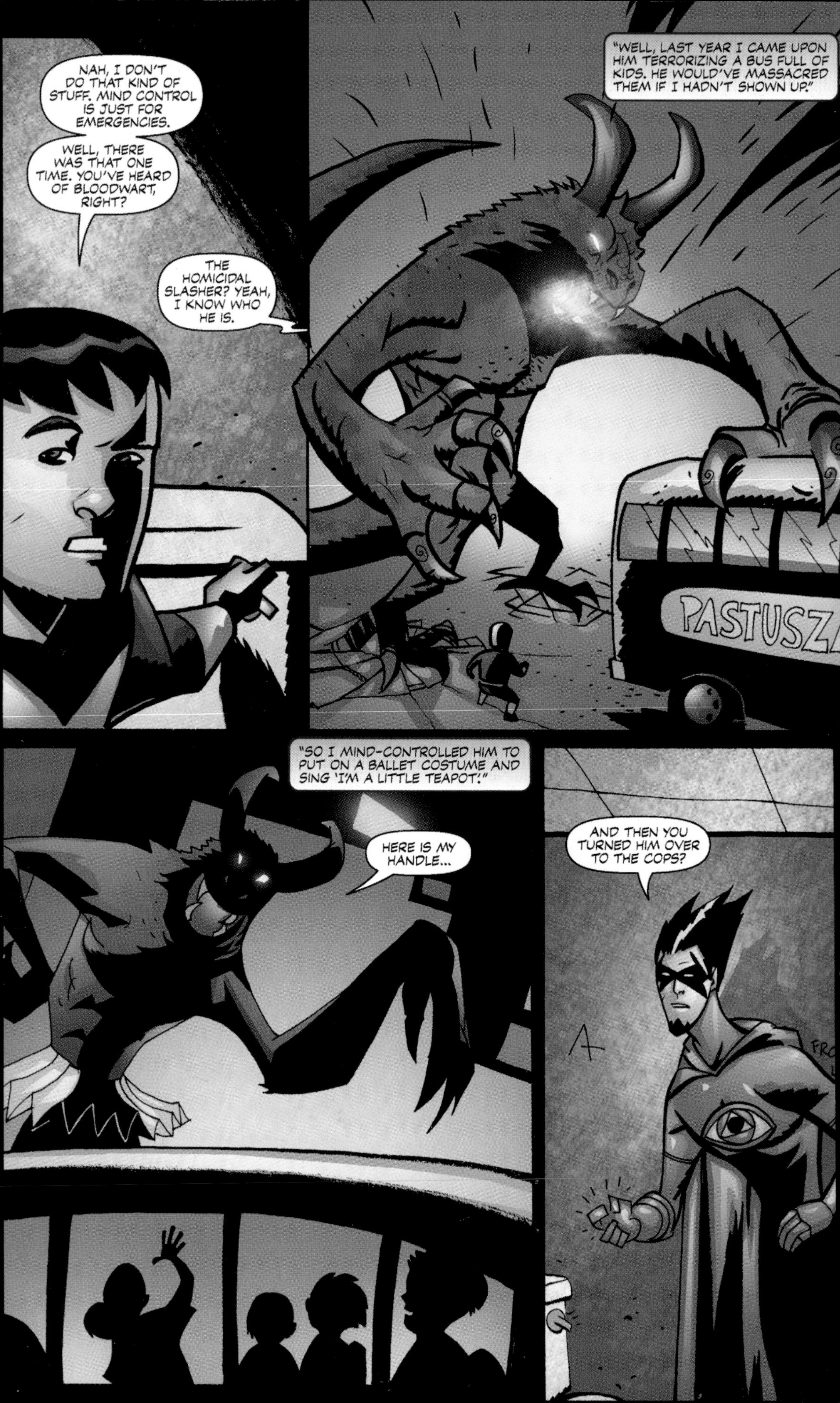
NAH, I DON'T DO THAT KIND OF STUFF. MIND CONTROL IS JUST FOR EMERGENCIES.
WELL, THERE WAS THAT ONE TIME. YOU'VE HEARD OF BLOODWART, RIGHT?
THE HOMICIDAL SLASHER? YEAH, I KNOW WHO HE IS.
"WELL, LAST YEAR I CAME UPON HIM TERRORIZING A BUS FULL OF KIDS. HE WOULD'VE MASSACRED THEM IF I HADN'T SHOWN UP."
PASTUSZ
"SO I MIND-CONTROLLED HIM TO PUT ON A BALLET COSTUME AND SING 'I'M A LITTLE TEAPOT.'"
HERE IS MY HANDLE...
AND THEN YOU TURNED HIM OVER TO THE COPS?

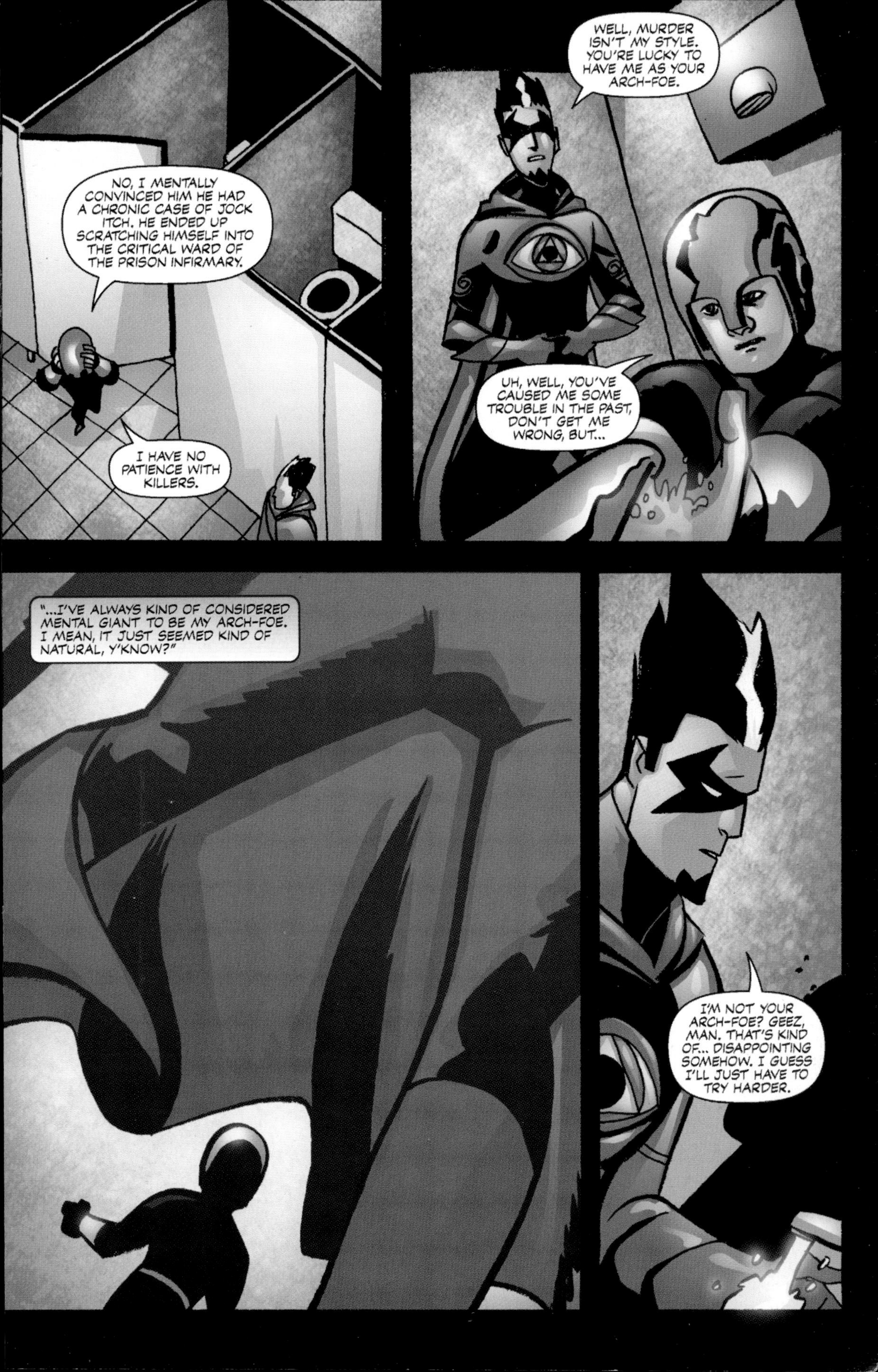
NO, I MENTALLY CONVINCED HIM HE HAD A CHRONIC CASE OF JOCK ITCH. HE ENDED UP SCRATCHING HIMSELF INTO THE CRITICAL WARD OF THE PRISON INFIRMARY.
I HAVE NO PATIENCE WITH KILLERS.
WELL, MURDER ISN'T MY STYLE. YOU'RE LUCKY TO HAVE ME AS YOUR ARCH-FOE.
UH, WELL, YOU'VE CAUSED ME SOME TROUBLE IN THE PAST, DON'T GET ME WRONG, BUT...
"...I'VE ALWAYS KIND OF CONSIDERED MENTAL GIANT TO BE MY ARCH-FOE. I MEAN, IT JUST SEEMED KIND OF NATURAL, Y'KNOW?"
I'M NOT YOUR ARCH-FOE? GEEZ, MAN. THAT'S KIND OF... DISAPPOINTING SOMEHOW. I GUESS I'LL JUST HAVE TO TRY HARDER.

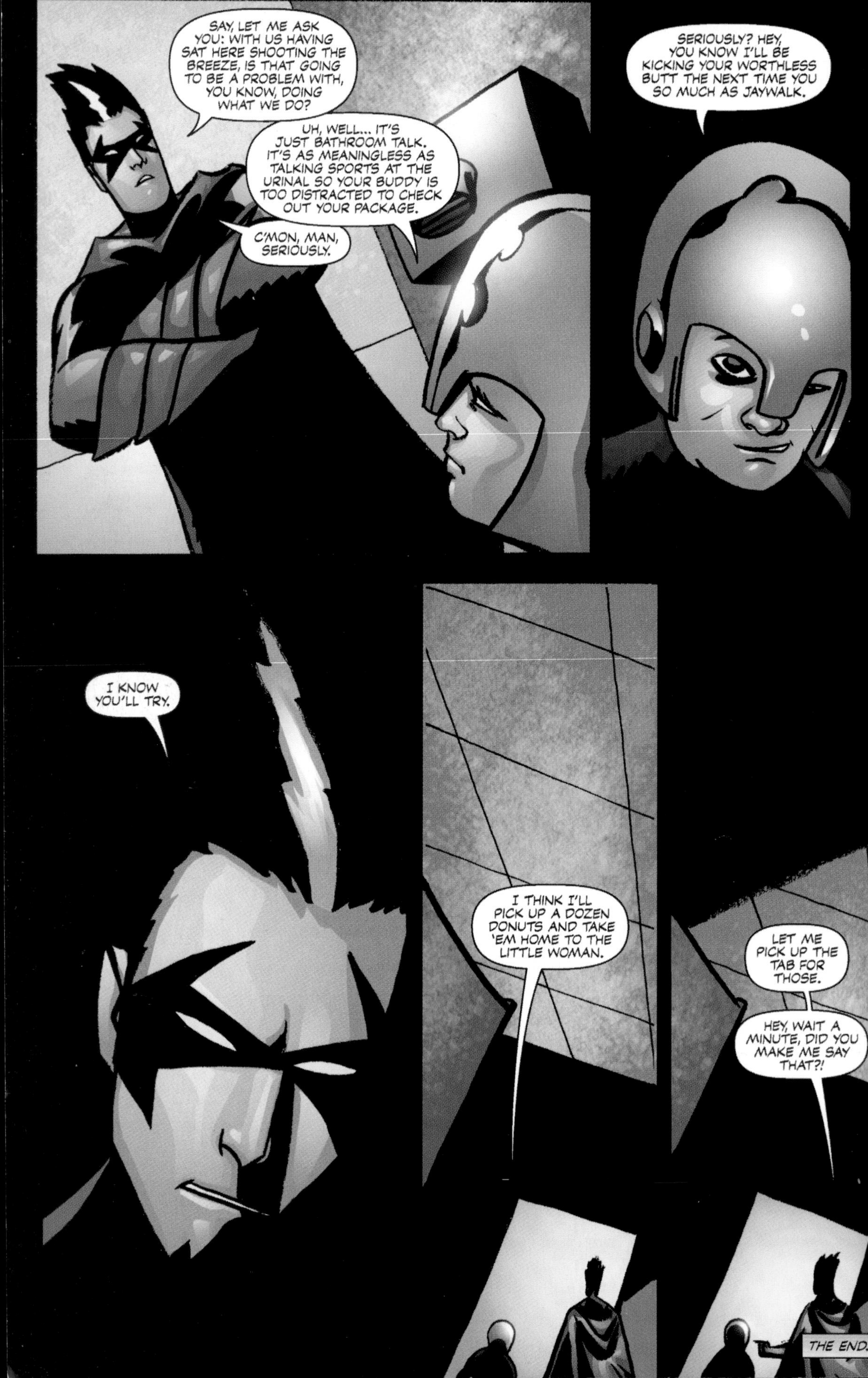
SAY, LET ME ASK YOU: WITH US HAVING SAT HERE SHOOTING THE BREEZE, IS THAT GOING TO BE A PROBLEM WITH, YOU KNOW, DOING WHAT WE DO?
UH, WELL... IT'S JUST BATHROOM TALK. IT'S AS MEANINGLESS AS TALKING SPORTS AT THE URINAL SO YOUR BUDDY IS TOO DISTRACTED TO CHECK OUT YOUR PACKAGE.
C'MON, MAN, SERIOUSLY.
SERIOUSLY? HEY, YOU KNOW I'LL BE KICKING YOUR WORTHLESS BUTT THE NEXT TIME YOU SO MUCH AS JAYWALK.
I KNOW YOU'LL TRY.
I THINK I'LL PICK UP A DOZEN DONUTS AND TAKE 'EM HOME TO THE LITTLE WOMAN.
LET ME PICK UP THE TAB FOR THOSE.
HEY, WAIT A MINUTE, DID YOU MAKE ME SAY THAT?!
THE END.

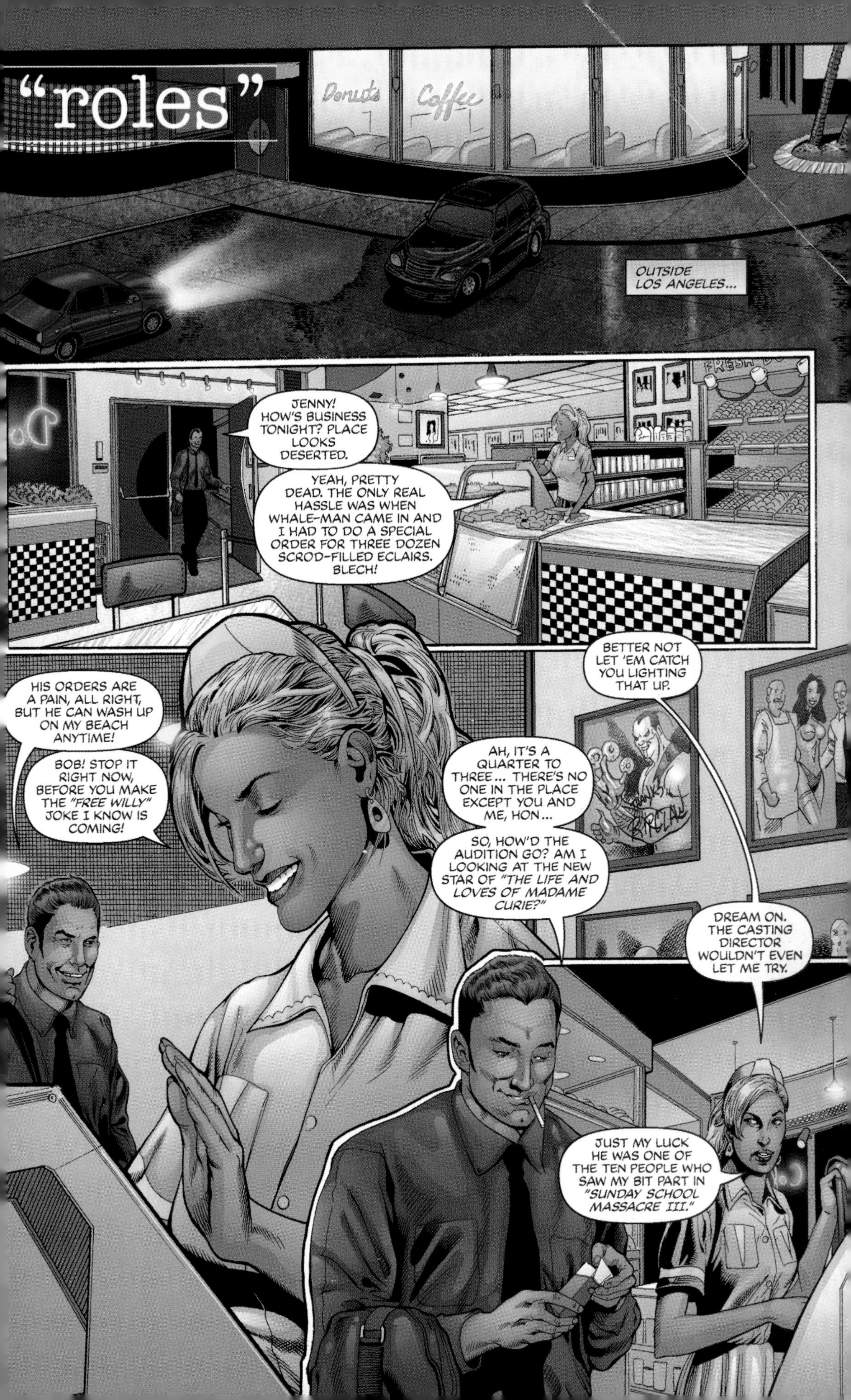
"roles"
Donuts
Coffee
OUTSIDE LOS ANGELES...
JENNY! HOW'S BUSINESS TONIGHT? PLACE LOOKS DESERTED.
YEAH, PRETTY DEAD. THE ONLY REAL HASSLE WAS WHEN WHALE-MAN CAME IN AND I HAD TO DO A SPECIAL ORDER FOR THREE DOZEN SCROD-FILLED ECLAIRS. BLECH!
HIS ORDERS ARE A PAIN, ALL RIGHT, BUT HE CAN WASH UP ON MY BEACH ANYTIME!
BOB! STOP IT RIGHT NOW, BEFORE YOU MAKE THE "FREE WILLY" JOKE I KNOW IS COMING!
AH, IT'S A QUARTER TO THREE... THERE'S NO ONE IN THE PLACE EXCEPT YOU AND ME, HON...
SO, HOW'D THE AUDITION GO? AM I LOOKING AT THE NEW STAR OF "THE LIFE AND LOVES OF MADAME CURIE?"
BETTER NOT LET 'EM CATCH YOU LIGHTING THAT UP.
DREAM ON. THE CASTING DIRECTOR WOULDN'T EVEN LET ME TRY.
JUST MY LUCK HE WAS ONE OF THE TEN PEOPLE WHO SAW MY BIT PART IN "SUNDAY SCHOOL MASSACRE III."

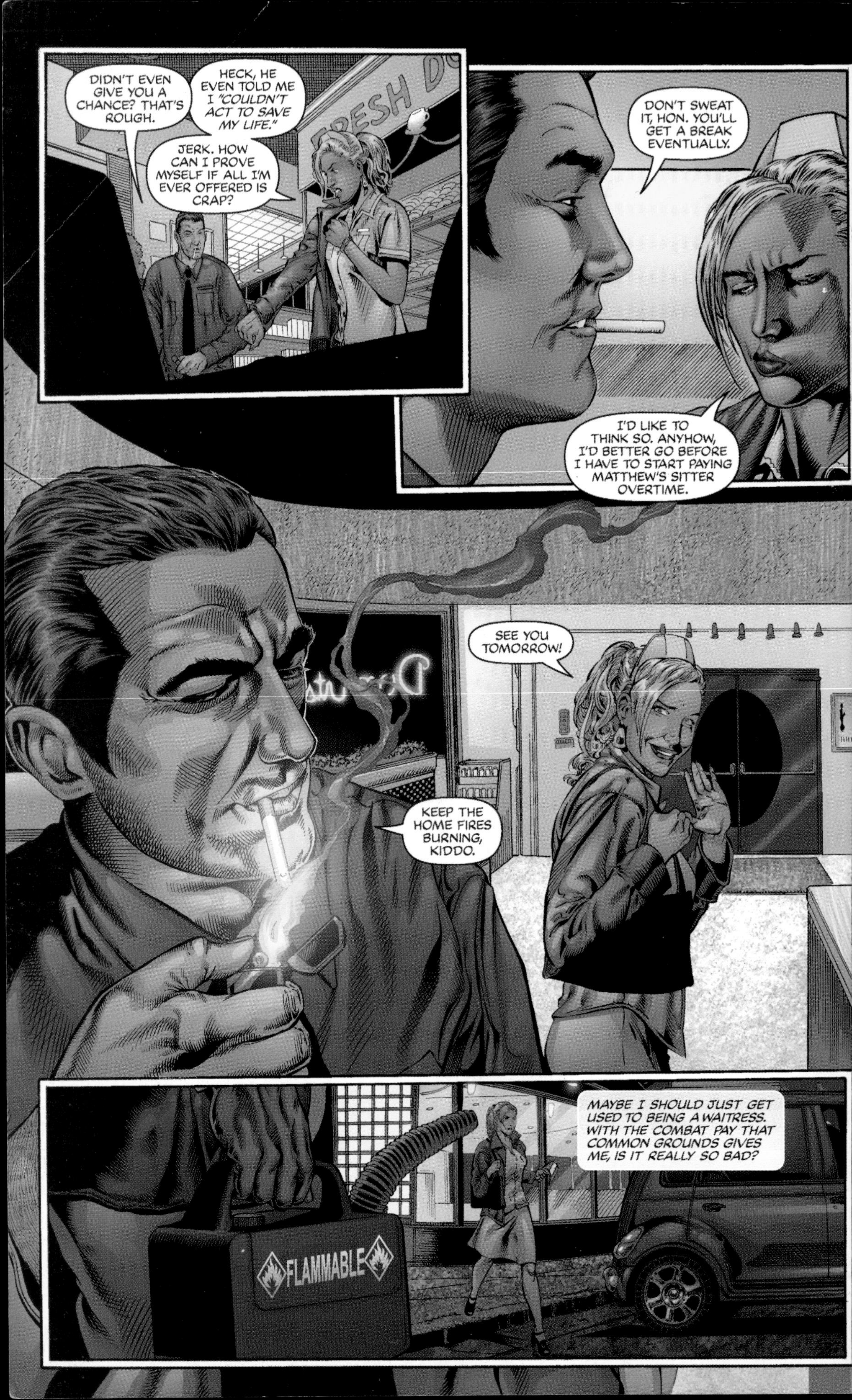
DIDN'T EVEN GIVE YOU A CHANCE? THAT'S ROUGH.
HECK, HE EVEN TOLD ME I "COULDN'T ACT TO SAVE MY LIFE."
JERK. HOW CAN I PROVE MYSELF IF ALL I'M EVER OFFERED IS CRAP?
FRESH DO
DON'T SWEAT IT, HON. YOU'LL GET A BREAK EVENTUALLY.
I'D LIKE TO THINK SO. ANYHOW, I'D BETTER GO BEFORE I HAVE TO START PAYING MATTHEW'S SITTER OVERTIME.
SEE YOU TOMORROW!
KEEP THE HOME FIRES BURNING, KIDDO.
MAYBE I SHOULD JUST GET USED TO BEING A WAITRESS. WITH THE COMBAT PAY THAT COMMON GROUNDS GIVES ME, IS IT REALLY SO BAD?
FLAMMABLE

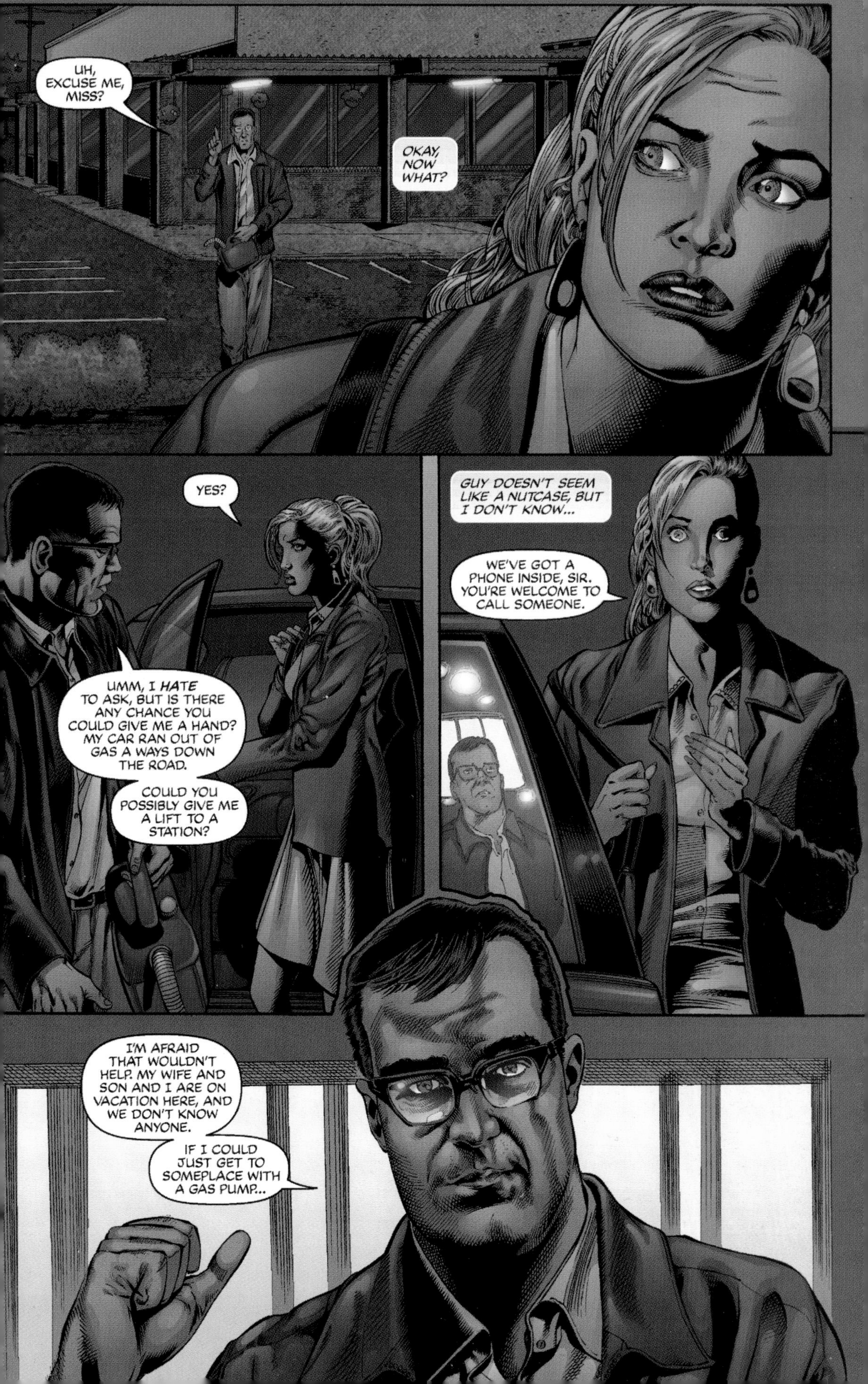
UH, EXCUSE ME, MISS?
OKAY, NOW WHAT?
YES?
UMM, I *HATE* TO ASK, BUT IS THERE ANY CHANCE YOU COULD GIVE ME A HAND? MY CAR RAN OUT OF GAS A WAYS DOWN THE ROAD.
COULD YOU POSSIBLY GIVE ME A LIFT TO A STATION?
GUY DOESN'T SEEM LIKE A NUTCASE, BUT I DON'T KNOW...
WE'VE GOT A PHONE INSIDE, SIR. YOU'RE WELCOME TO CALL SOMEONE.
I'M AFRAID THAT WOULDN'T HELP. MY WIFE AND SON AND I ARE ON VACATION HERE, AND WE DON'T KNOW ANYONE.
IF I COULD JUST GET TO SOMEPLACE WITH A GAS PUMP...

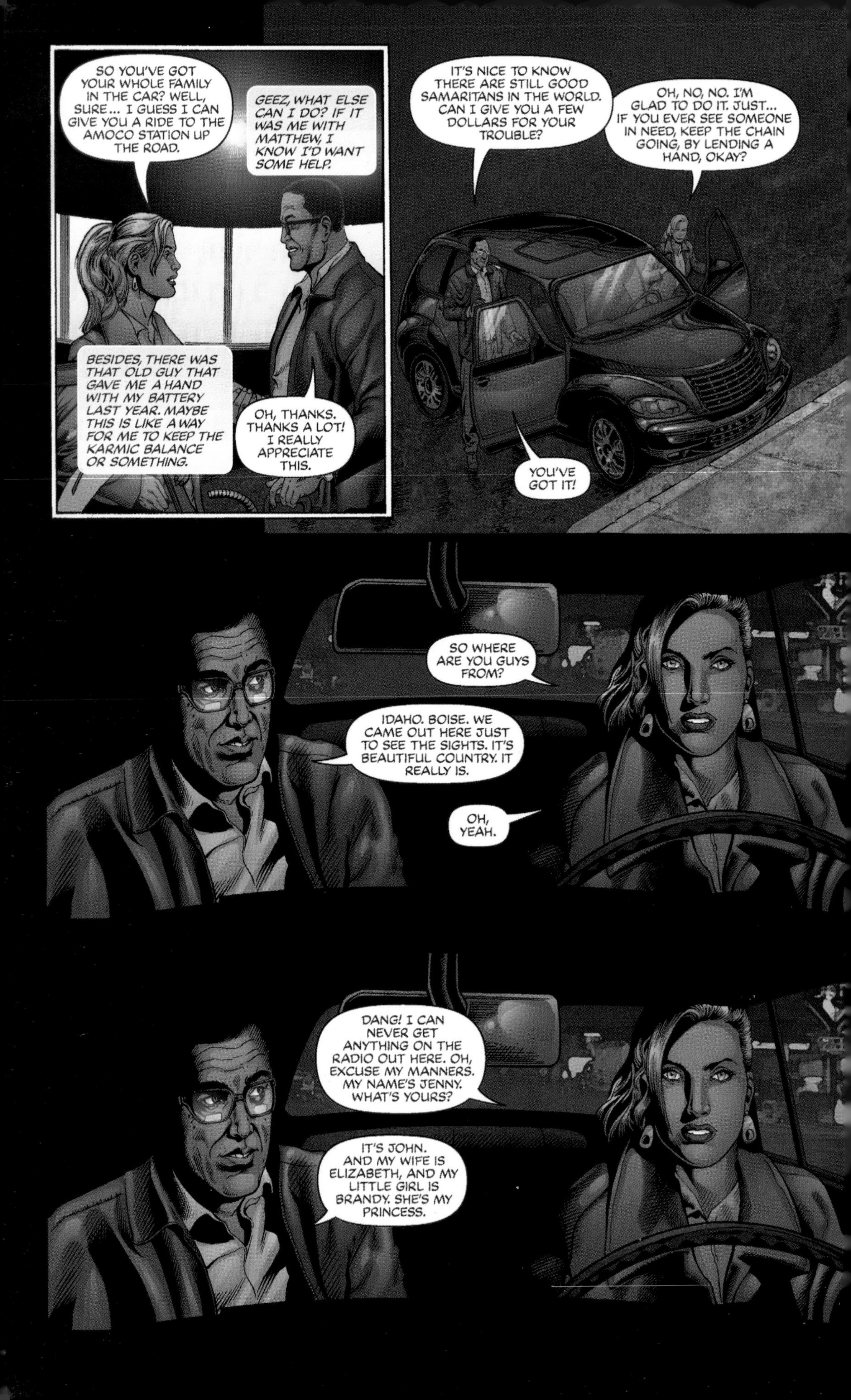
SO YOU'VE GOT YOUR WHOLE FAMILY IN THE CAR? WELL, SURE... I GUESS I CAN GIVE YOU A RIDE TO THE AMOCO STATION UP THE ROAD.
GEEZ, WHAT ELSE CAN I DO? IF IT WAS ME WITH MATTHEW, I KNOW I'D WANT SOME HELP.
BESIDES, THERE WAS THAT OLD GUY THAT GAVE ME A HAND WITH MY BATTERY LAST YEAR. MAYBE THIS IS LIKE A WAY FOR ME TO KEEP THE KARMIC BALANCE OR SOMETHING.
OH, THANKS. THANKS A LOT! I REALLY APPRECIATE THIS.
IT'S NICE TO KNOW THERE ARE STILL GOOD SAMARITANS IN THE WORLD. CAN I GIVE YOU A FEW DOLLARS FOR YOUR TROUBLE?
OH, NO, NO. I'M GLAD TO DO IT. JUST... IF YOU EVER SEE SOMEONE IN NEED, KEEP THE CHAIN GOING, BY LENDING A HAND, OKAY?
YOU'VE GOT IT!
SO WHERE ARE YOU GUYS FROM?
IDAHO. BOISE. WE CAME OUT HERE JUST TO SEE THE SIGHTS. IT'S BEAUTIFUL COUNTRY. IT REALLY IS.
OH, YEAH.
DANG! I CAN NEVER GET ANYTHING ON THE RADIO OUT HERE. OH, EXCUSE MY MANNERS. MY NAME'S JENNY. WHAT'S YOURS?
IT'S JOHN. AND MY WIFE IS ELIZABETH, AND MY LITTLE GIRL IS BRANDY. SHE'S MY PRINCESS.

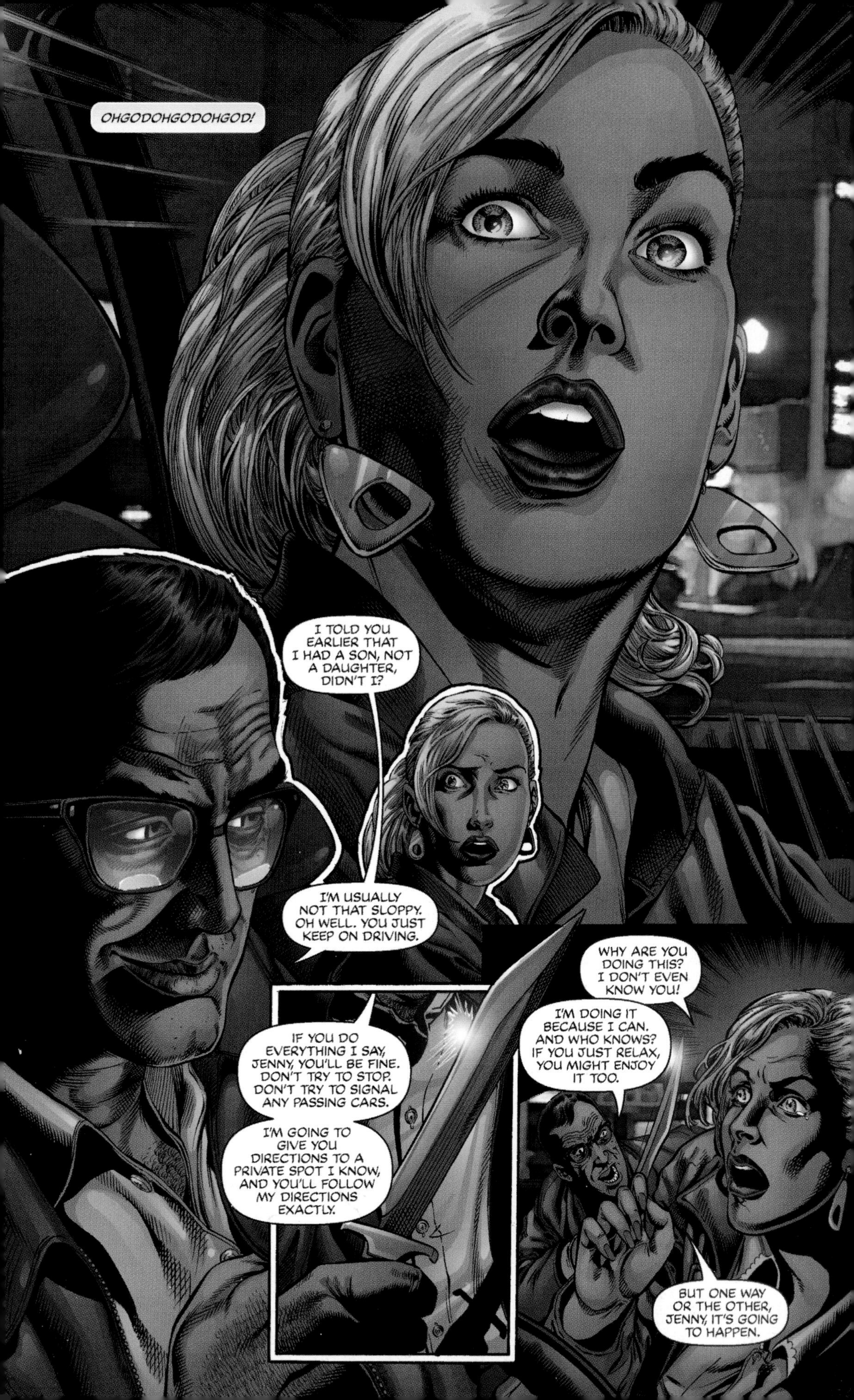
OHGODOHGODOHGOD!
I TOLD YOU EARLIER THAT I HAD A SON, NOT A DAUGHTER, DIDN'T I?
I'M USUALLY NOT THAT SLOPPY. OH WELL. YOU JUST KEEP ON DRIVING.
IF YOU DO EVERYTHING I SAY, JENNY, YOU'LL BE FINE. DON'T TRY TO STOP. DON'T TRY TO SIGNAL ANY PASSING CARS.
I'M GOING TO GIVE YOU DIRECTIONS TO A PRIVATE SPOT I KNOW, AND YOU'LL FOLLOW MY DIRECTIONS EXACTLY.
WHY ARE YOU DOING THIS? I DON'T EVEN KNOW YOU!
I'M DOING IT BECAUSE I CAN. AND WHO KNOWS? IF YOU JUST RELAX, YOU MIGHT ENJOY IT TOO.
BUT ONE WAY OR THE OTHER, JENNY, IT'S GOING TO HAPPEN.

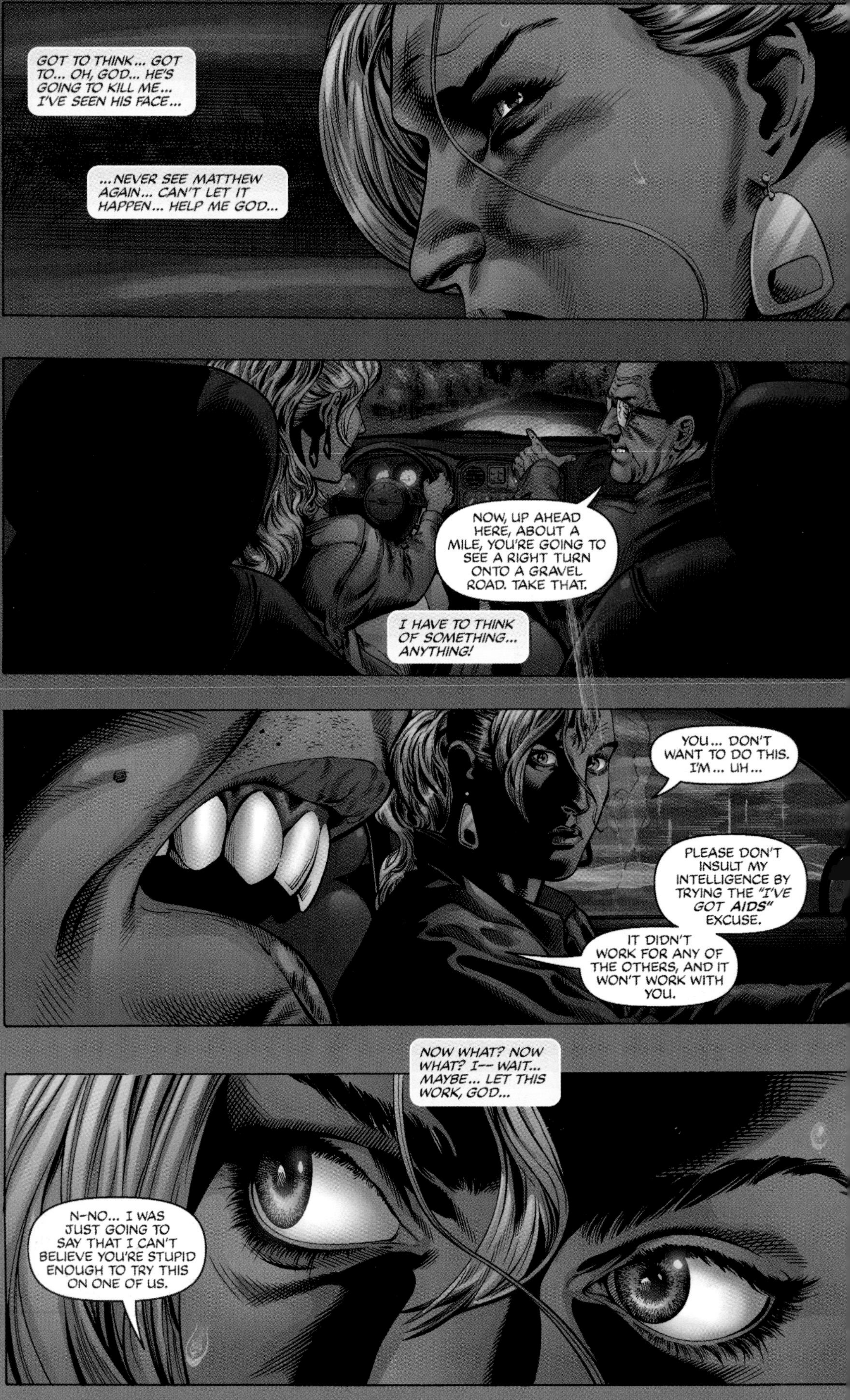
GOT TO THINK... GOT TO... OH, GOD... HE'S GOING TO KILL ME... I'VE SEEN HIS FACE...
...NEVER SEE MATTHEW AGAIN... CAN'T LET IT HAPPEN... HELP ME GOD...
NOW, UP AHEAD HERE, ABOUT A MILE, YOU'RE GOING TO SEE A RIGHT TURN ONTO A GRAVEL ROAD. TAKE THAT.
I HAVE TO THINK OF SOMETHING... ANYTHING!
YOU... DON'T WANT TO DO THIS. I'M... UH...
PLEASE DON'T INSULT MY INTELLIGENCE BY TRYING THE "I'VE GOT AIDS" EXCUSE.
IT DIDN'T WORK FOR ANY OF THE OTHERS, AND IT WON'T WORK WITH YOU.
NOW WHAT? NOW WHAT? I-- WAIT... MAYBE... LET THIS WORK, GOD...
N-NO... I WAS JUST GOING TO SAY THAT I CAN'T BELIEVE YOU'RE STUPID ENOUGH TO TRY THIS ON ONE OF US.

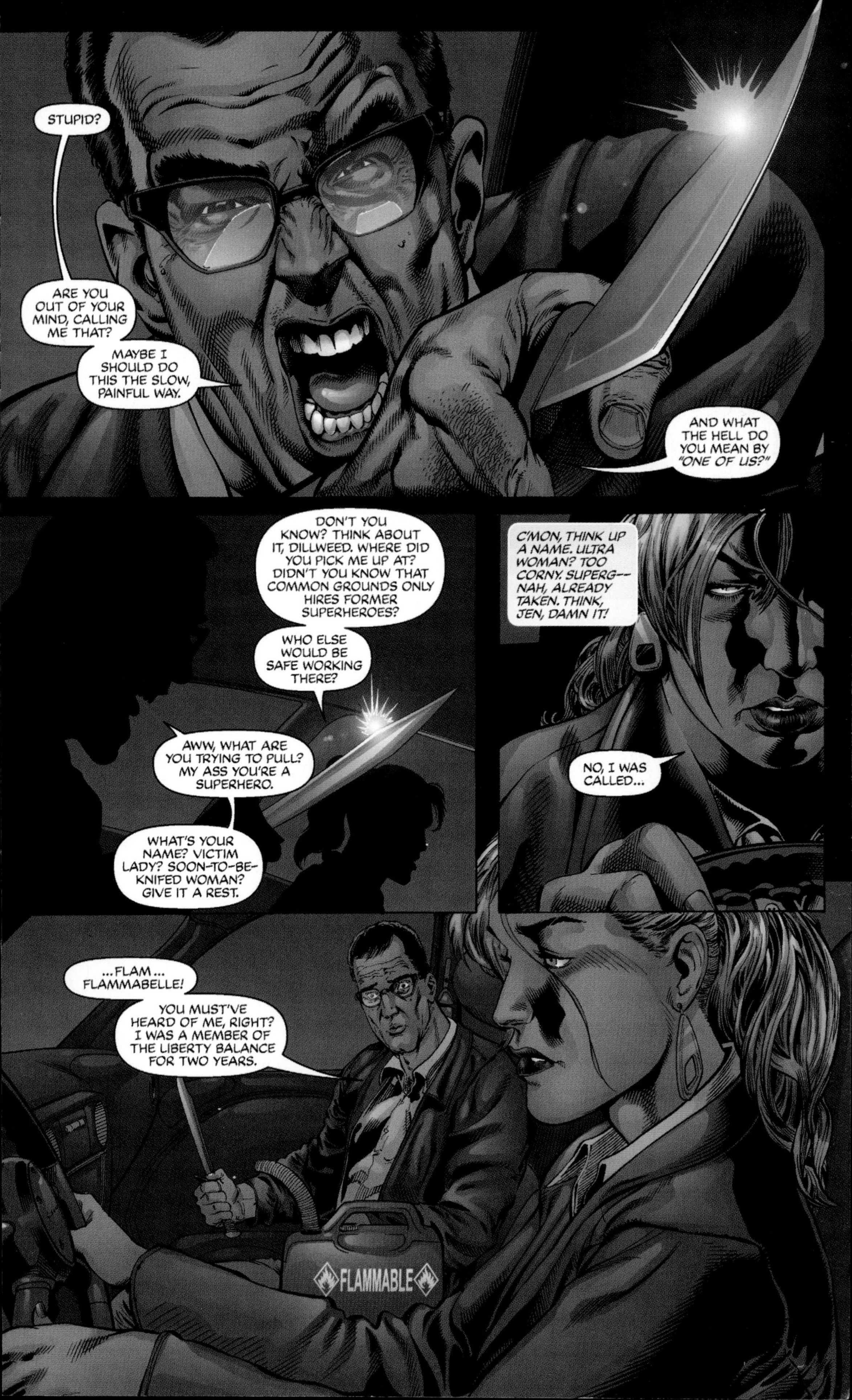
STUPID?
ARE YOU OUT OF YOUR MIND, CALLING ME THAT?
MAYBE I SHOULD DO THIS THE SLOW, PAINFUL WAY.
AND WHAT THE HELL DO YOU MEAN BY "ONE OF US?"
DON'T YOU KNOW? THINK ABOUT IT, DILLWEED. WHERE DID YOU PICK ME UP AT? DIDN'T YOU KNOW THAT COMMON GROUNDS ONLY HIRES FORMER SUPERHEROES?
WHO ELSE WOULD BE SAFE WORKING THERE?
AWW, WHAT ARE YOU TRYING TO PULL? MY ASS YOU'RE A SUPERHERO.
WHAT'S YOUR NAME? VICTIM LADY? SOON-TO-BE-KNIFED WOMAN? GIVE IT A REST.
C'MON, THINK UP A NAME. ULTRA WOMAN? TOO CORNY. SUPERG-- NAH, ALREADY TAKEN. THINK, JEN, DAMN IT!
NO, I WAS CALLED...
...FLAM... FLAMMABELLE!
YOU MUST'VE HEARD OF ME, RIGHT? I WAS A MEMBER OF THE LIBERTY BALANCE FOR TWO YEARS.
FLAMMABLE

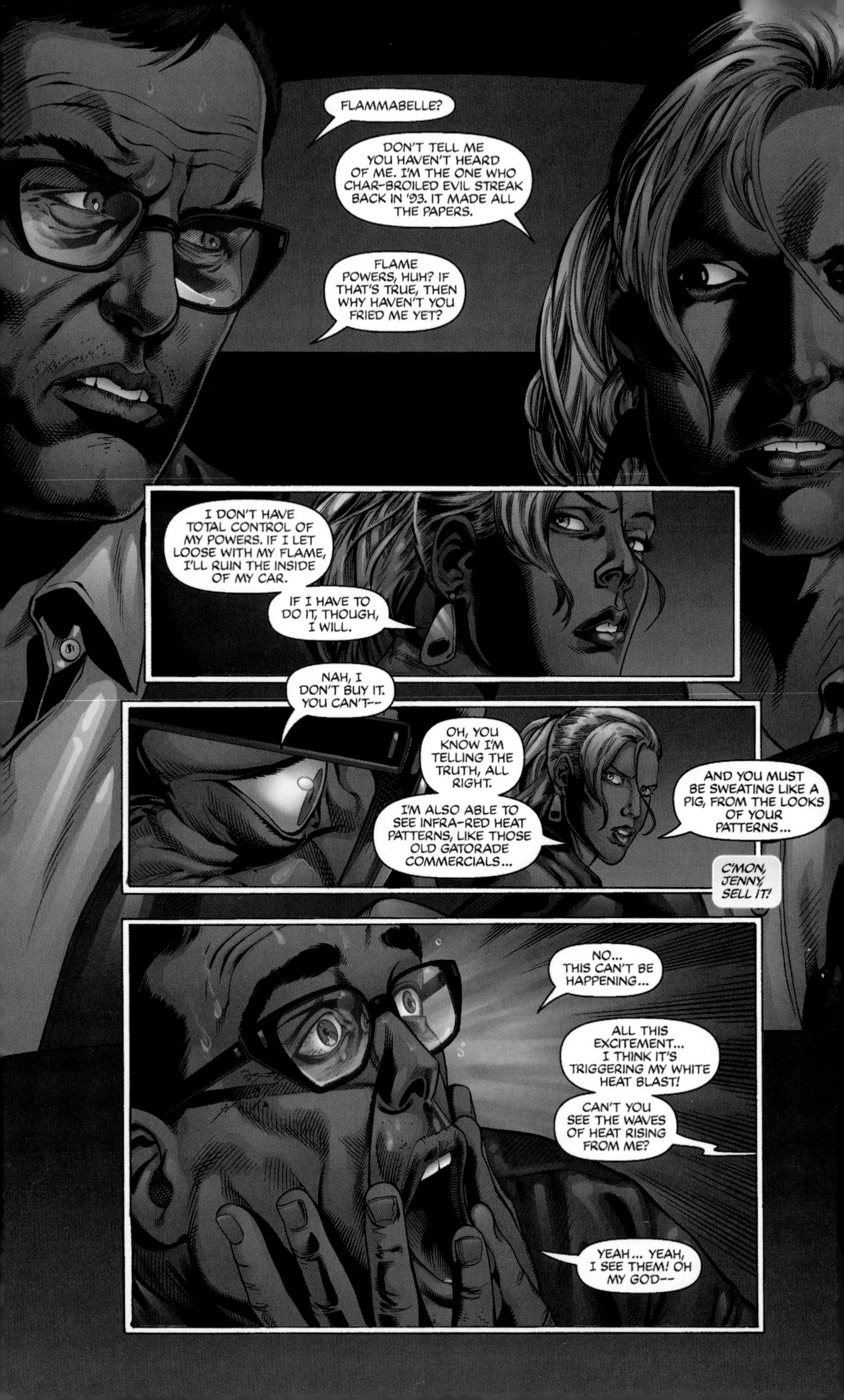
FLAMMABELLE?
DON'T TELL ME YOU HAVEN'T HEARD OF ME. I'M THE ONE WHO CHAR-BROILED EVIL STREAK BACK IN '93. IT MADE ALL THE PAPERS.
FLAME POWERS, HUH? IF THAT'S TRUE, THEN WHY HAVEN'T YOU FRIED ME YET?
I DON'T HAVE TOTAL CONTROL OF MY POWERS. IF I LET LOOSE WITH MY FLAME, I'LL RUIN THE INSIDE OF MY CAR.
IF I HAVE TO DO IT, THOUGH, I WILL.
NAH, I DON'T BUY IT. YOU CAN'T--
OH, YOU KNOW I'M TELLING THE TRUTH, ALL RIGHT.
I'M ALSO ABLE TO SEE INFRA-RED HEAT PATTERNS, LIKE THOSE OLD GATORADE COMMERCIALS...
AND YOU MUST BE SWEATING LIKE A PIG, FROM THE LOOKS OF YOUR PATTERNS...
C'MON, JENNY, SELL IT!
NO... THIS CAN'T BE HAPPENING...
ALL THIS EXCITEMENT... I THINK IT'S TRIGGERING MY WHITE HEAT BLAST!
CAN'T YOU SEE THE WAVES OF HEAT RISING FROM ME?
YEAH... YEAH, I SEE THEM! OH MY GOD--

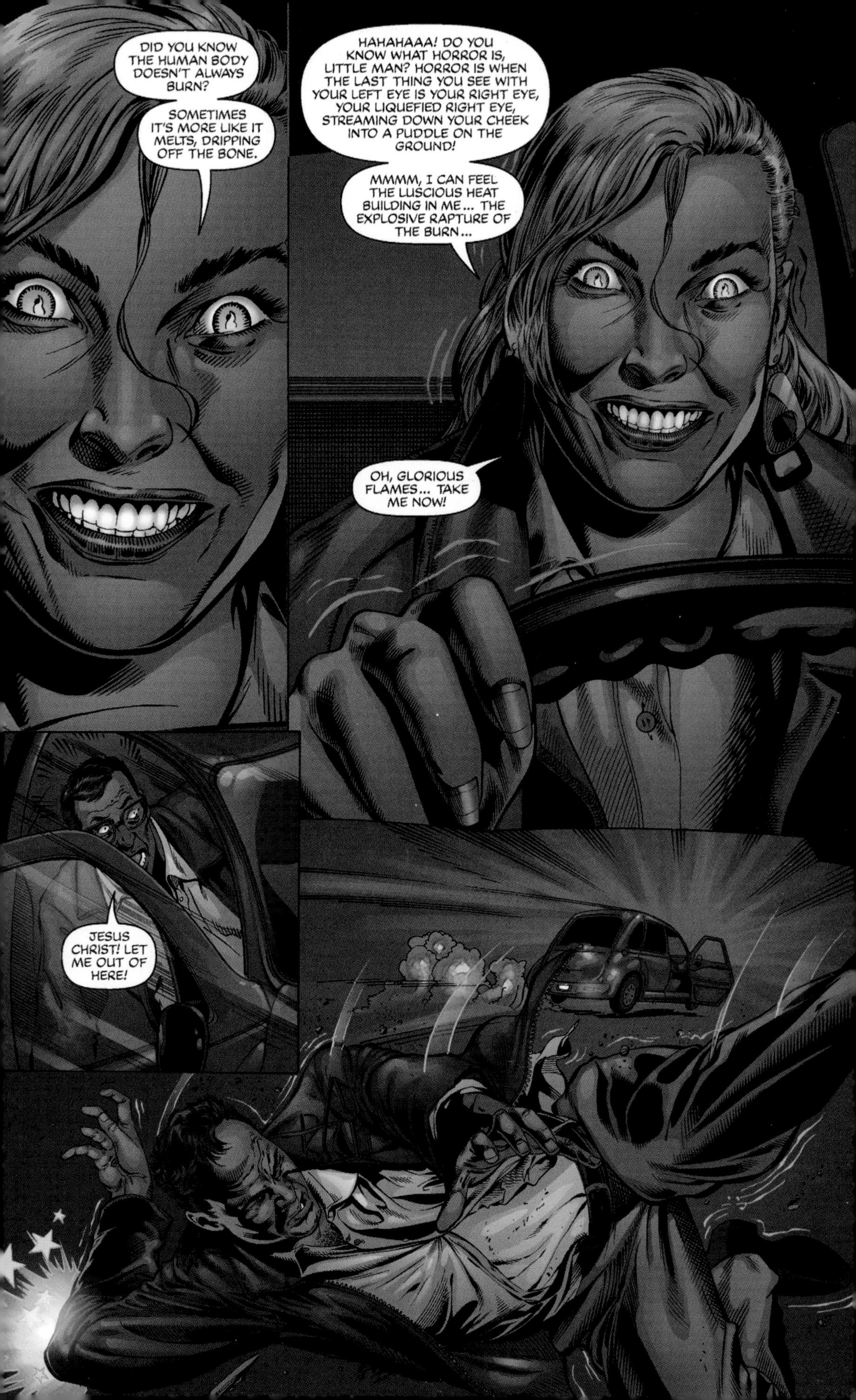
DID YOU KNOW THE HUMAN BODY DOESN'T ALWAYS BURN?
SOMETIMES IT'S MORE LIKE IT MELTS, DRIPPING OFF THE BONE.
HAHAHAAA! DO YOU KNOW WHAT HORROR IS, LITTLE MAN? HORROR IS WHEN THE LAST THING YOU SEE WITH YOUR LEFT EYE IS YOUR RIGHT EYE, YOUR LIQUEFIED RIGHT EYE, STREAMING DOWN YOUR CHEEK INTO A PUDDLE ON THE GROUND!
MMMM, I CAN FEEL THE LUSCIOUS HEAT BUILDING IN ME... THE EXPLOSIVE RAPTURE OF THE BURN...
OH, GLORIOUS FLAMES... TAKE ME NOW!
JESUS CHRIST! LET ME OUT OF HERE!

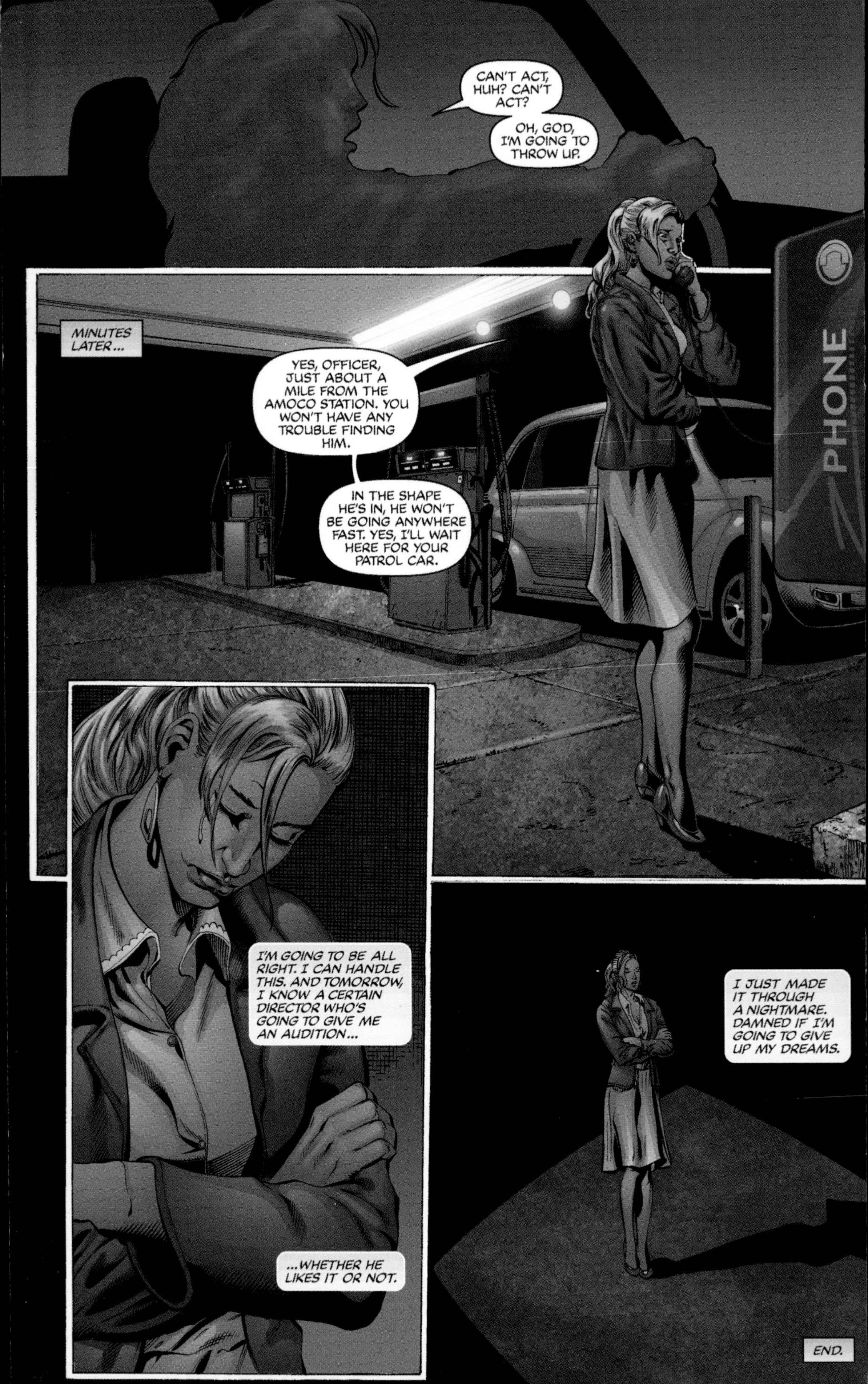
CAN'T ACT, HUH? CAN'T ACT?
OH, GOD, I'M GOING TO THROW UP.
MINUTES LATER...
YES, OFFICER, JUST ABOUT A MILE FROM THE AMOCO STATION. YOU WON'T HAVE ANY TROUBLE FINDING HIM.
IN THE SHAPE HE'S IN, HE WON'T BE GOING ANYWHERE FAST. YES, I'LL WAIT HERE FOR YOUR PATROL CAR.
PHONE
I'M GOING TO BE ALL RIGHT. I CAN HANDLE THIS. AND TOMORROW, I KNOW A CERTAIN DIRECTOR WHO'S GOING TO GIVE ME AN AUDITION...
...WHETHER HE LIKES IT OR NOT.
I JUST MADE IT THROUGH A NIGHTMARE. DAMNED IF I'M GOING TO GIVE UP MY DREAMS.
END.

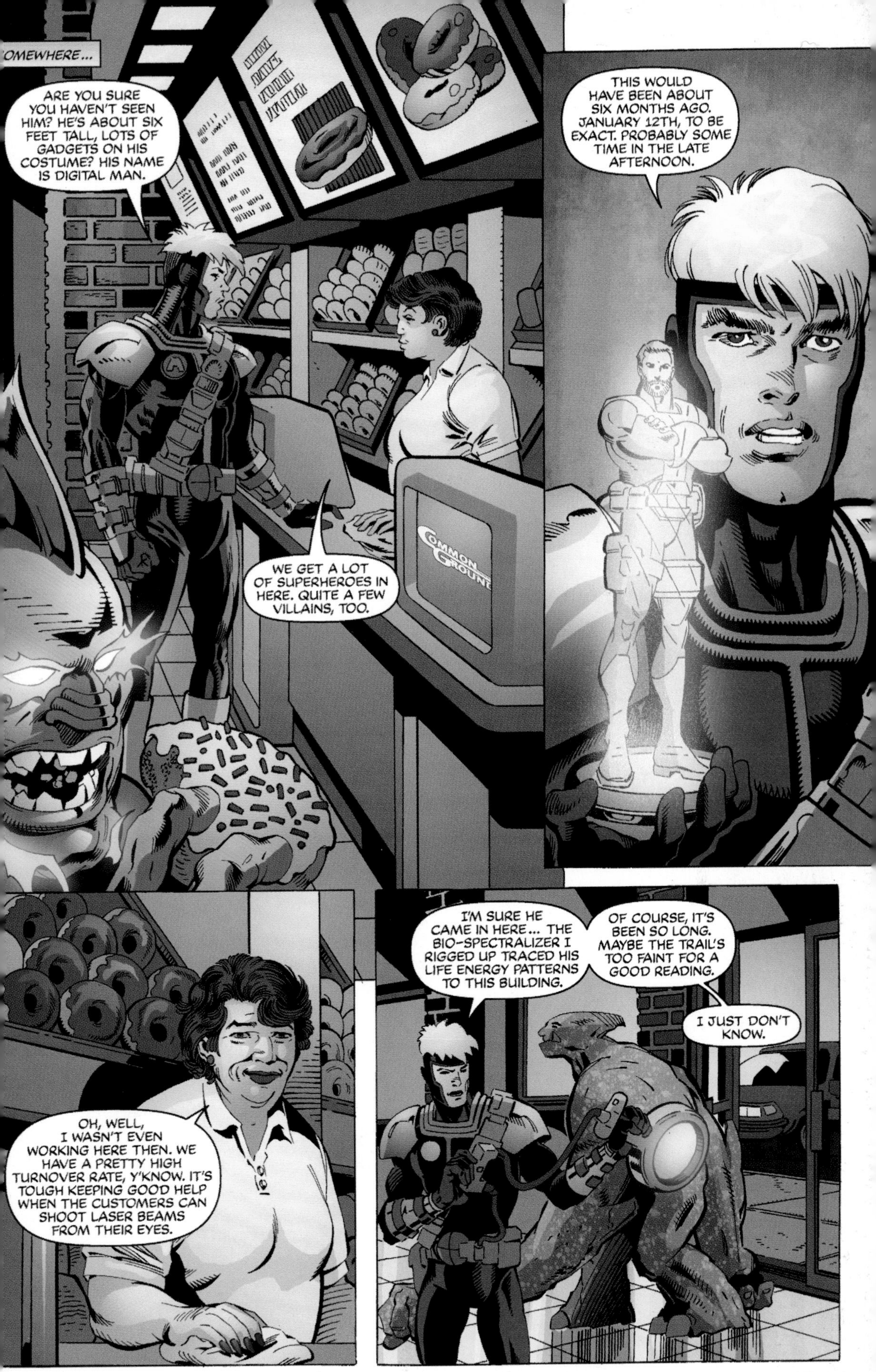
OMEWHERE...
ARE YOU SURE YOU HAVEN'T SEEN HIM? HE'S ABOUT SIX FEET TALL, LOTS OF GADGETS ON HIS COSTUME? HIS NAME IS DIGITAL MAN.
WE GET A LOT OF SUPERHEROES IN HERE. QUITE A FEW VILLAINS, TOO.
COMMON GROUND
THIS WOULD HAVE BEEN ABOUT SIX MONTHS AGO. JANUARY 12TH, TO BE EXACT. PROBABLY SOME TIME IN THE LATE AFTERNOON.
OH, WELL, I WASN'T EVEN WORKING HERE THEN. WE HAVE A PRETTY HIGH TURNOVER RATE, Y'KNOW. IT'S TOUGH KEEPING GOOD HELP WHEN THE CUSTOMERS CAN SHOOT LASER BEAMS FROM THEIR EYES.
I'M SURE HE CAME IN HERE... THE BIO-SPECTRALIZER I RIGGED UP TRACED HIS LIFE ENERGY PATTERNS TO THIS BUILDING.
OF COURSE, IT'S BEEN SO LONG. MAYBE THE TRAIL'S TOO FAINT FOR A GOOD READING.
I JUST DON'T KNOW.

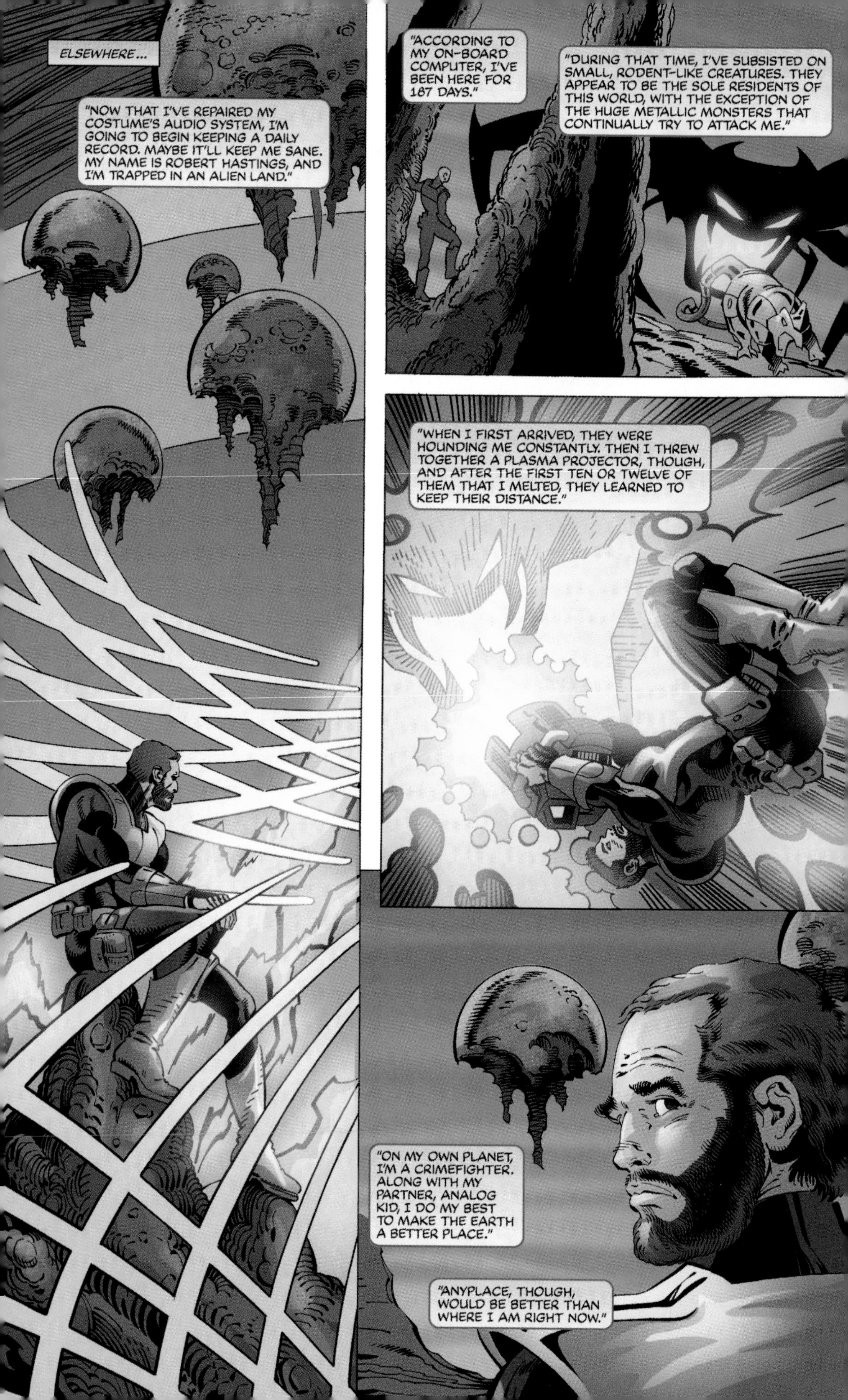
ELSEWHERE...
"NOW THAT I'VE REPAIRED MY COSTUME'S AUDIO SYSTEM, I'M GOING TO BEGIN KEEPING A DAILY RECORD. MAYBE IT'LL KEEP ME SANE. MY NAME IS ROBERT HASTINGS, AND I'M TRAPPED IN AN ALIEN LAND."
"ACCORDING TO MY ON-BOARD COMPUTER, I'VE BEEN HERE FOR 187 DAYS."
"DURING THAT TIME, I'VE SUBSISTED ON SMALL, RODENT-LIKE CREATURES. THEY APPEAR TO BE THE SOLE RESIDENTS OF THIS WORLD, WITH THE EXCEPTION OF THE HUGE METALLIC MONSTERS THAT CONTINUALLY TRY TO ATTACK ME."
"WHEN I FIRST ARRIVED, THEY WERE HOUNDING ME CONSTANTLY. THEN I THREW TOGETHER A PLASMA PROJECTOR, THOUGH, AND AFTER THE FIRST TEN OR TWELVE OF THEM THAT I MELTED, THEY LEARNED TO KEEP THEIR DISTANCE."
"ON MY OWN PLANET, I'M A CRIMEFIGHTER. ALONG WITH MY PARTNER, ANALOG KID, I DO MY BEST TO MAKE THE EARTH A BETTER PLACE."
"ANYPLACE, THOUGH, WOULD BE BETTER THAN WHERE I AM RIGHT NOW."

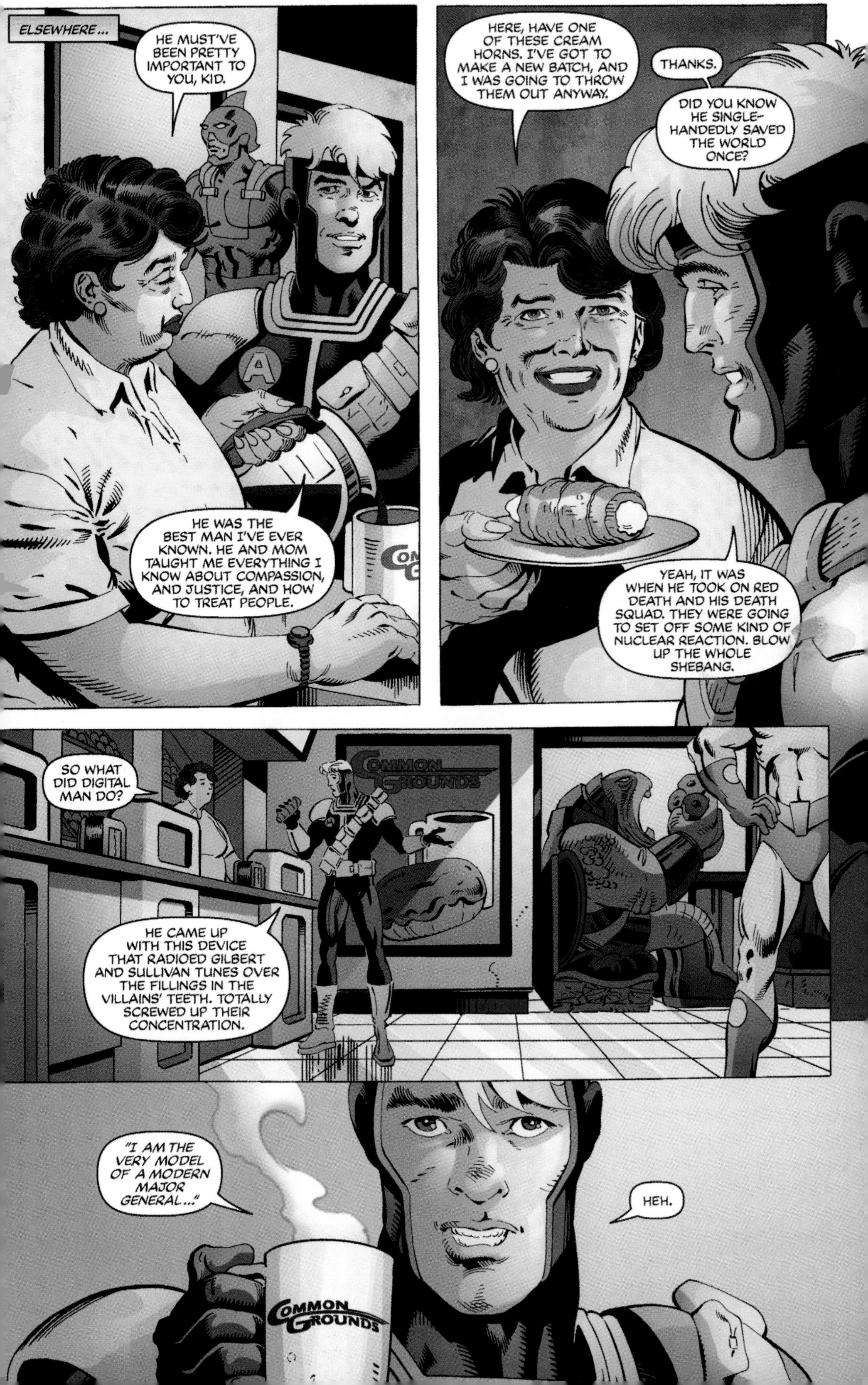
ELSEWHERE...
HE MUST'VE BEEN PRETTY IMPORTANT TO YOU, KID.
HE WAS THE BEST MAN I'VE EVER KNOWN. HE AND MOM TAUGHT ME EVERYTHING I KNOW ABOUT COMPASSION, AND JUSTICE, AND HOW TO TREAT PEOPLE.
HERE, HAVE ONE OF THESE CREAM HORNS. I'VE GOT TO MAKE A NEW BATCH, AND I WAS GOING TO THROW THEM OUT ANYWAY.
THANKS.
DID YOU KNOW HE SINGLE-HANDEDLY SAVED THE WORLD ONCE?
YEAH, IT WAS WHEN HE TOOK ON RED DEATH AND HIS DEATH SQUAD. THEY WERE GOING TO SET OFF SOME KIND OF NUCLEAR REACTION. BLOW UP THE WHOLE SHEBANG.
SO WHAT DID DIGITAL MAN DO?
COMMON GROUNDS
HE CAME UP WITH THIS DEVICE THAT RADIOED GILBERT AND SULLIVAN TUNES OVER THE FILLINGS IN THE VILLAINS' TEETH. TOTALLY SCREWED UP THEIR CONCENTRATION.
"I AM THE VERY MODEL OF A MODERN MAJOR GENERAL..."
HEH.
COMMON GROUNDS

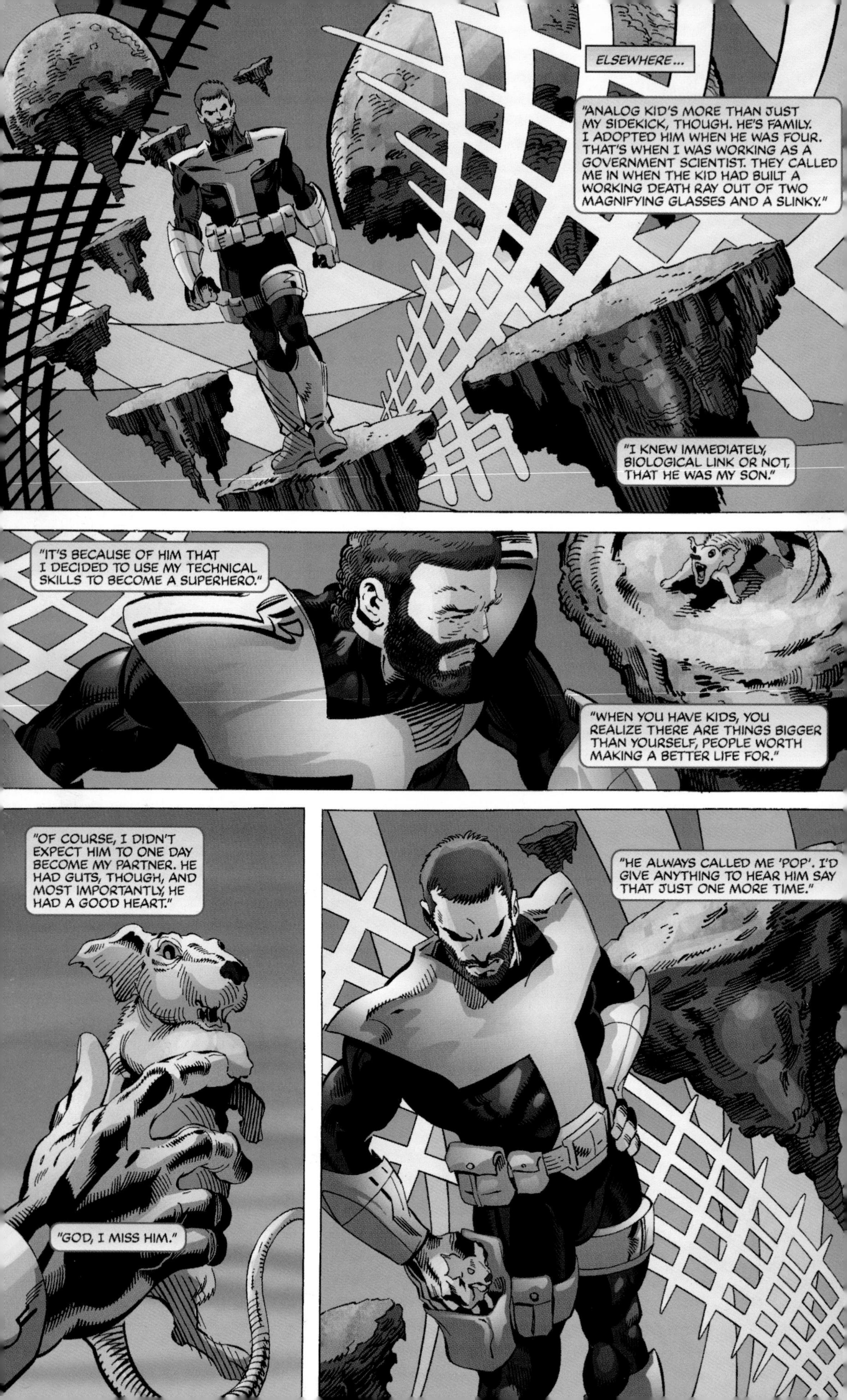
ELSEWHERE...
"ANALOG KID'S MORE THAN JUST MY SIDEKICK, THOUGH. HE'S FAMILY. I ADOPTED HIM WHEN HE WAS FOUR. THAT'S WHEN I WAS WORKING AS A GOVERNMENT SCIENTIST. THEY CALLED ME IN WHEN THE KID HAD BUILT A WORKING DEATH RAY OUT OF TWO MAGNIFYING GLASSES AND A SLINKY."
"I KNEW IMMEDIATELY, BIOLOGICAL LINK OR NOT, THAT HE WAS MY SON."
"IT'S BECAUSE OF HIM THAT I DECIDED TO USE MY TECHNICAL SKILLS TO BECOME A SUPERHERO."
"WHEN YOU HAVE KIDS, YOU REALIZE THERE ARE THINGS BIGGER THAN YOURSELF, PEOPLE WORTH MAKING A BETTER LIFE FOR."
"OF COURSE, I DIDN'T EXPECT HIM TO ONE DAY BECOME MY PARTNER. HE HAD GUTS, THOUGH, AND MOST IMPORTANTLY, HE HAD A GOOD HEART."
"GOD, I MISS HIM."
"HE ALWAYS CALLED ME 'POP'. I'D GIVE ANYTHING TO HEAR HIM SAY THAT JUST ONE MORE TIME."

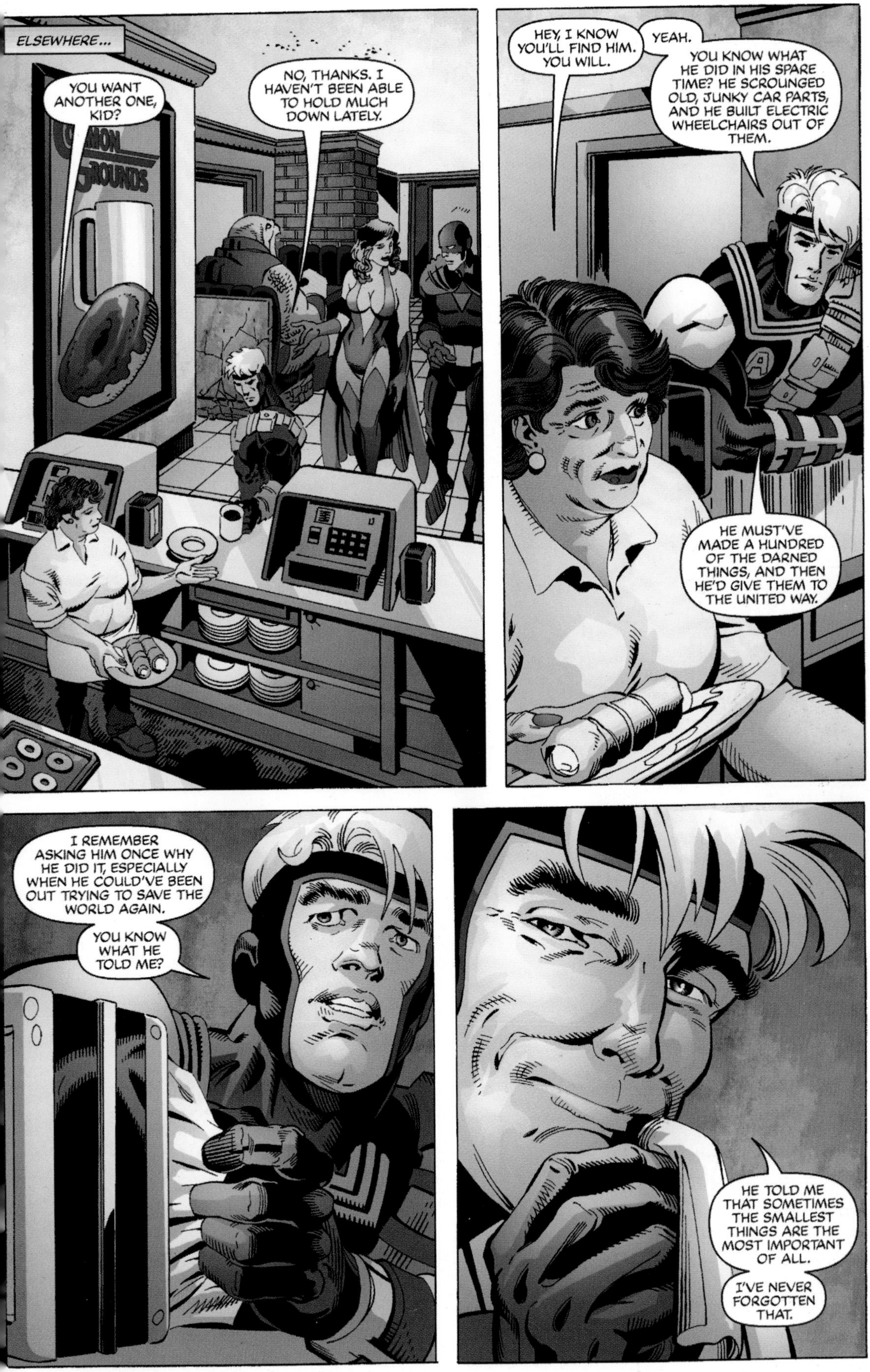
ELSEWHERE...
YOU WANT ANOTHER ONE, KID?
NO, THANKS. I HAVEN'T BEEN ABLE TO HOLD MUCH DOWN LATELY.
HEY, I KNOW YOU'LL FIND HIM. YOU WILL.
YEAH.
YOU KNOW WHAT HE DID IN HIS SPARE TIME? HE SCROUNGED OLD, JUNKY CAR PARTS, AND HE BUILT ELECTRIC WHEELCHAIRS OUT OF THEM.
HE MUST'VE MADE A HUNDRED OF THE DARNED THINGS, AND THEN HE'D GIVE THEM TO THE UNITED WAY.
I REMEMBER ASKING HIM ONCE WHY HE DID IT, ESPECIALLY WHEN HE COULD'VE BEEN OUT TRYING TO SAVE THE WORLD AGAIN.
YOU KNOW WHAT HE TOLD ME?
HE TOLD ME THAT SOMETIMES THE SMALLEST THINGS ARE THE MOST IMPORTANT OF ALL.
I'VE NEVER FORGOTTEN THAT.

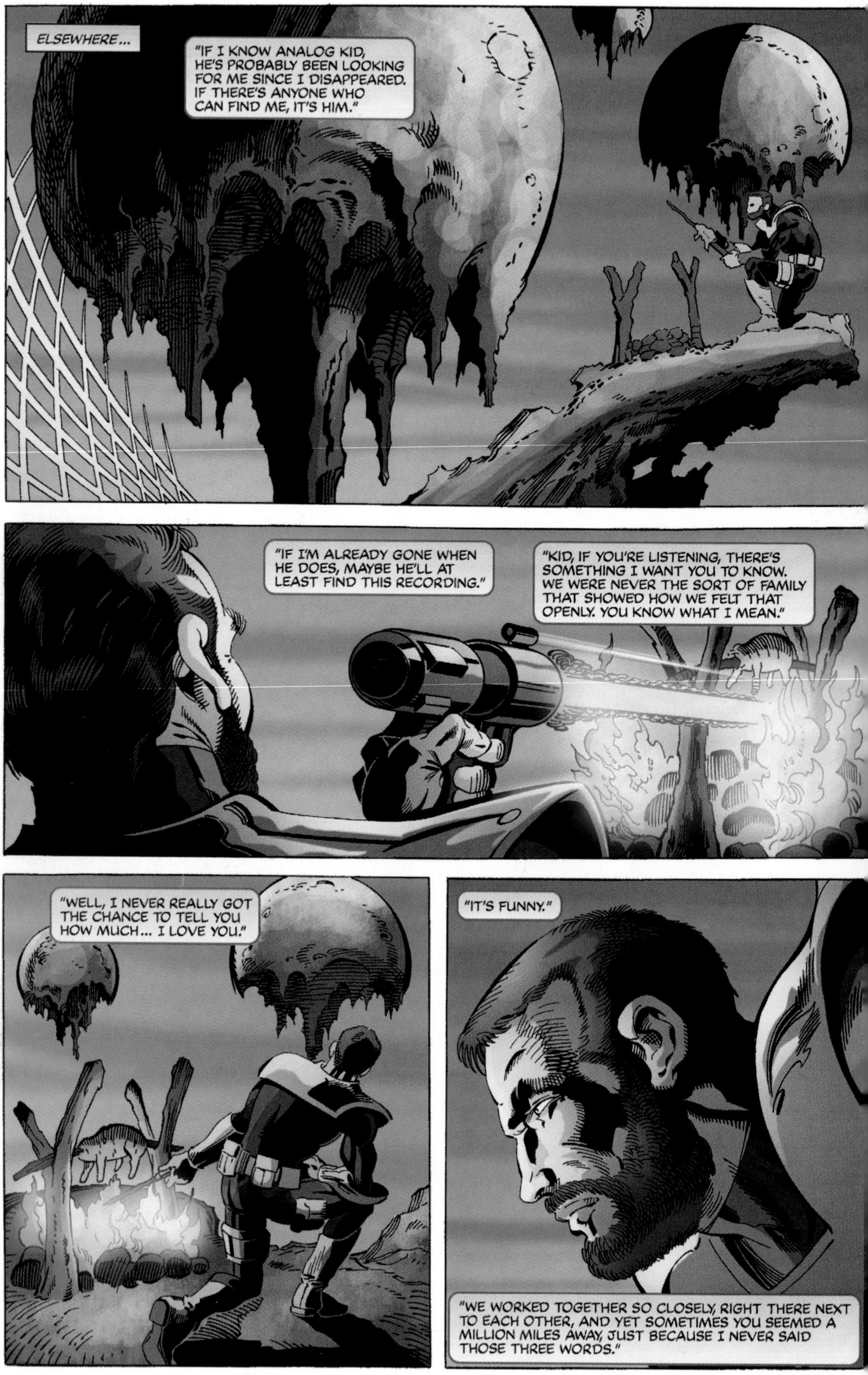
ELSEWHERE...
"IF I KNOW ANALOG KID, HE'S PROBABLY BEEN LOOKING FOR ME SINCE I DISAPPEARED. IF THERE'S ANYONE WHO CAN FIND ME, IT'S HIM."
"IF I'M ALREADY GONE WHEN HE DOES, MAYBE HE'LL AT LEAST FIND THIS RECORDING."
"KID, IF YOU'RE LISTENING, THERE'S SOMETHING I WANT YOU TO KNOW. WE WERE NEVER THE SORT OF FAMILY THAT SHOWED HOW WE FELT THAT OPENLY. YOU KNOW WHAT I MEAN."
"WELL, I NEVER REALLY GOT THE CHANCE TO TELL YOU HOW MUCH... I LOVE YOU."
"IT'S FUNNY."
"WE WORKED TOGETHER SO CLOSELY, RIGHT THERE NEXT TO EACH OTHER, AND YET SOMETIMES YOU SEEMED A MILLION MILES AWAY, JUST BECAUSE I NEVER SAID THOSE THREE WORDS."

ELSEWHERE...

WHAT COULD HAVE HAPPENED? WHERE COULD YOU HAVE GONE? I KNOW I CAN FIGURE IT OUT IF I JUST KEEP THINKING. YOU TAUGHT ME TO ALWAYS KEEP THINKING.

I WILL FIND YOU.

I'LL NEVER GIVE UP ON YOU, POP.

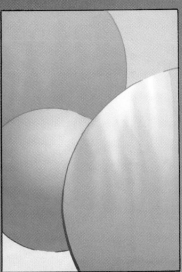

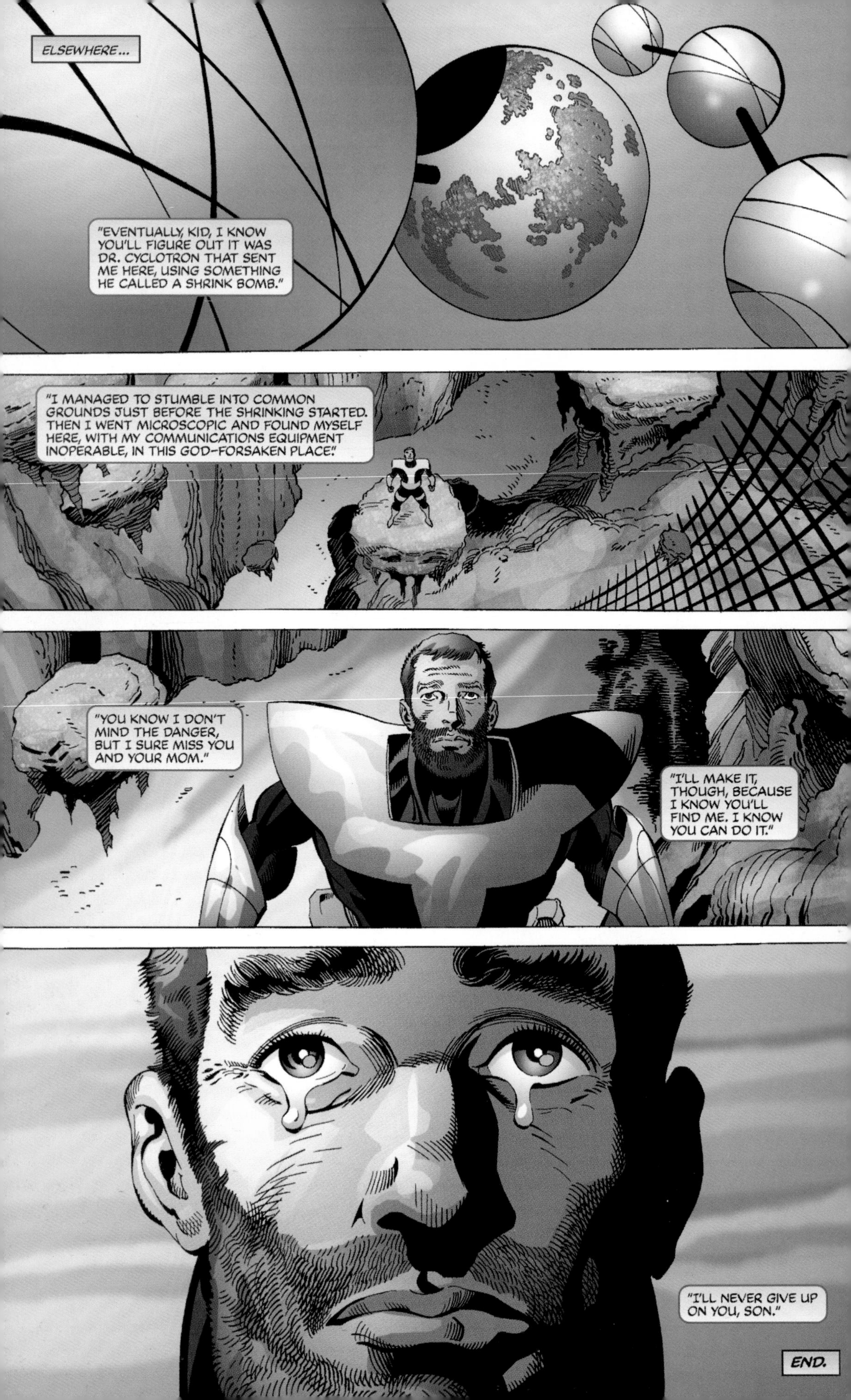
ELSEWHERE...
"EVENTUALLY, KID, I KNOW YOU'LL FIGURE OUT IT WAS DR. CYCLOTRON THAT SENT ME HERE, USING SOMETHING HE CALLED A SHRINK BOMB."
"I MANAGED TO STUMBLE INTO COMMON GROUNDS JUST BEFORE THE SHRINKING STARTED. THEN I WENT MICROSCOPIC AND FOUND MYSELF HERE, WITH MY COMMUNICATIONS EQUIPMENT INOPERABLE, IN THIS GOD-FORSAKEN PLACE."
"YOU KNOW I DON'T MIND THE DANGER, BUT I SURE MISS YOU AND YOUR MOM."
"I'LL MAKE IT, THOUGH, BECAUSE I KNOW YOU'LL FIND ME. I KNOW YOU CAN DO IT."
"I'LL NEVER GIVE UP ON YOU, SON."
END.

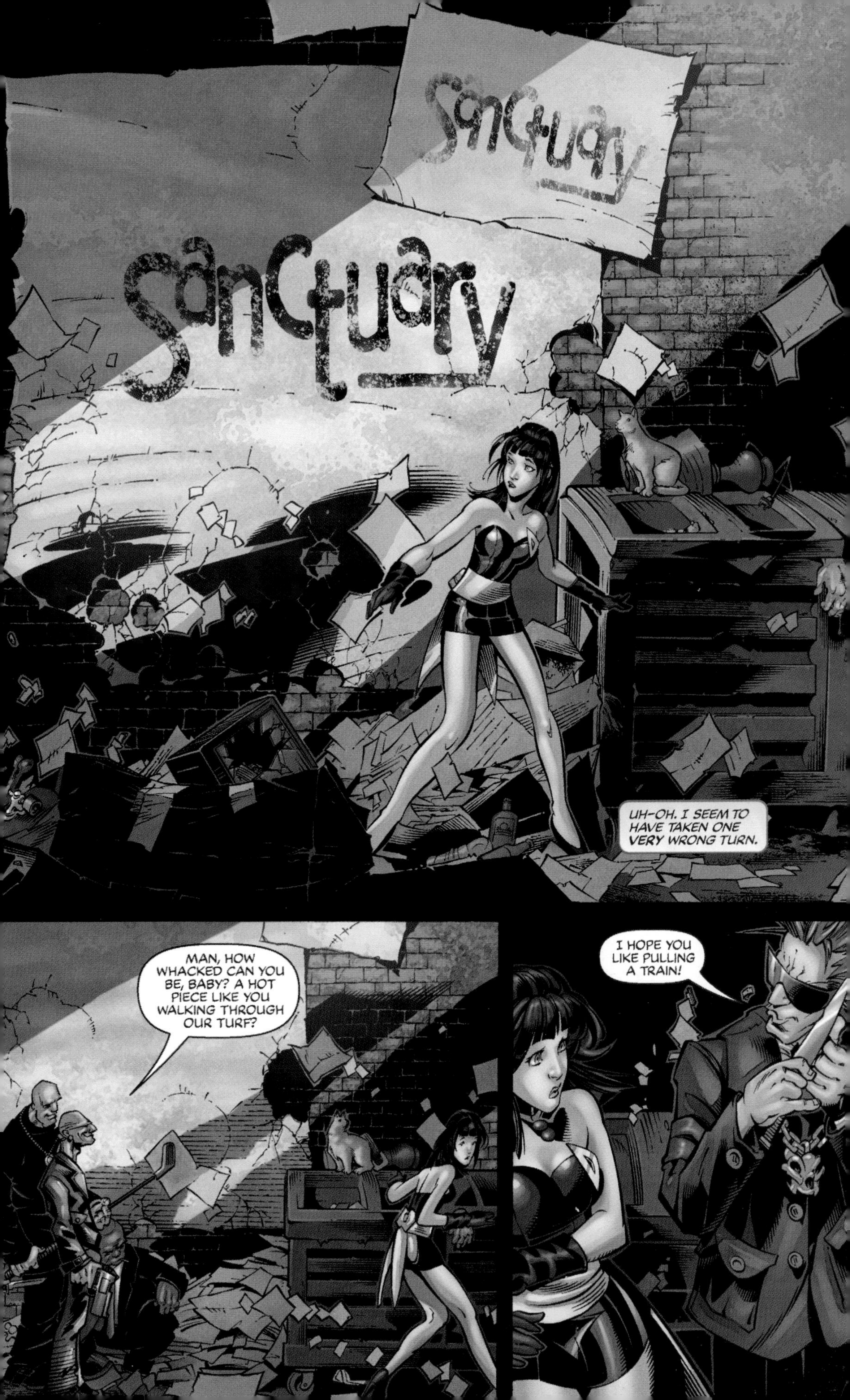
Sanctuary
Sanctuary
UH-OH. I SEEM TO HAVE TAKEN ONE VERY WRONG TURN.
MAN, HOW WHACKED CAN YOU BE, BABY? A HOT PIECE LIKE YOU WALKING THROUGH OUR TURF?
I HOPE YOU LIKE PULLING A TRAIN!

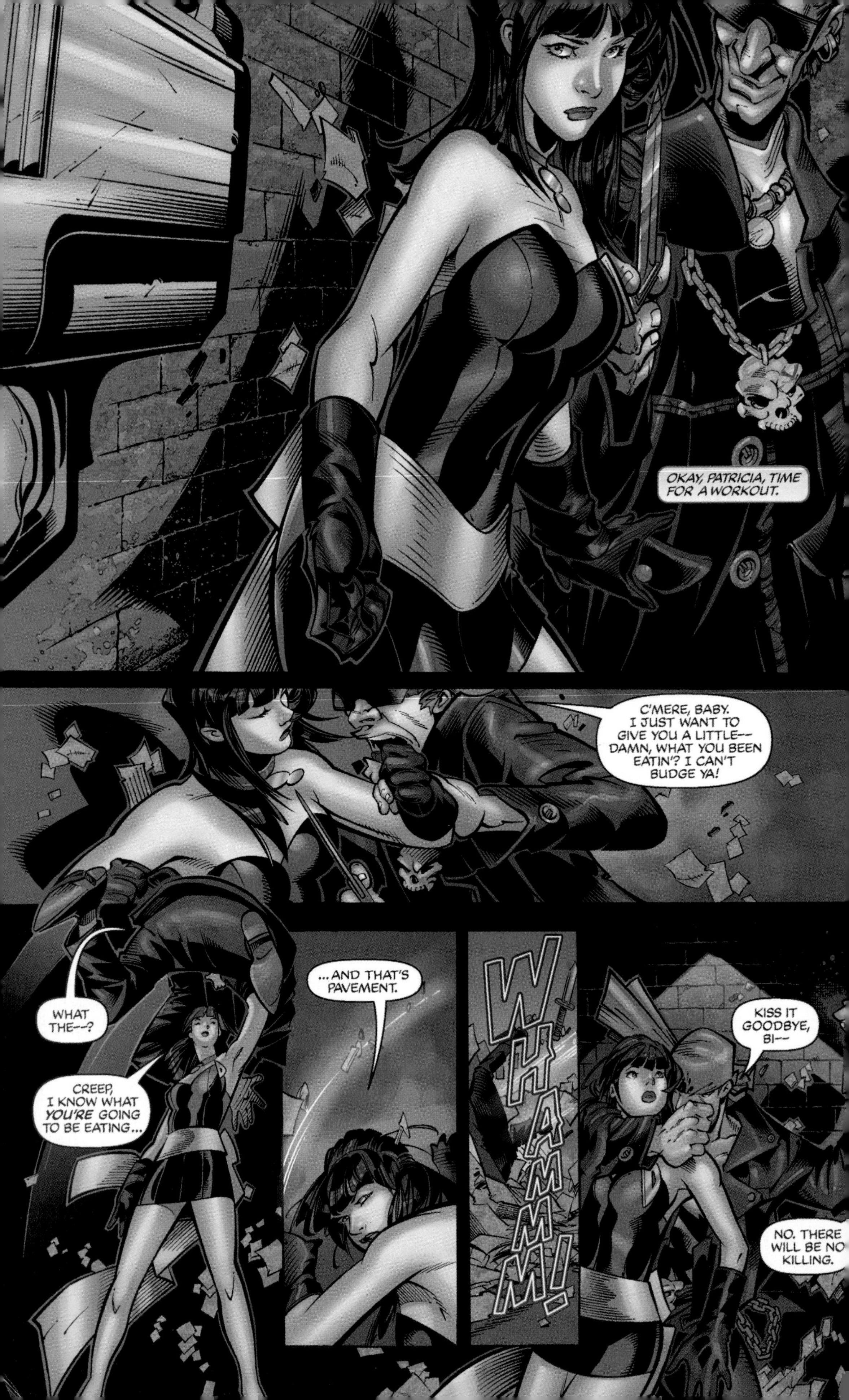
OKAY, PATRICIA, TIME FOR A WORKOUT.
C'MERE, BABY. I JUST WANT TO GIVE YOU A LITTLE-- DAMN, WHAT YOU BEEN EATIN'? I CAN'T BUDGE YA!
WHAT THE--?
CREEP, I KNOW WHAT *YOU'RE* GOING TO BE EATING...
...AND THAT'S PAVEMENT.
WHAMMM!
KISS IT GOODBYE, BI--
NO. THERE WILL BE NO KILLING.

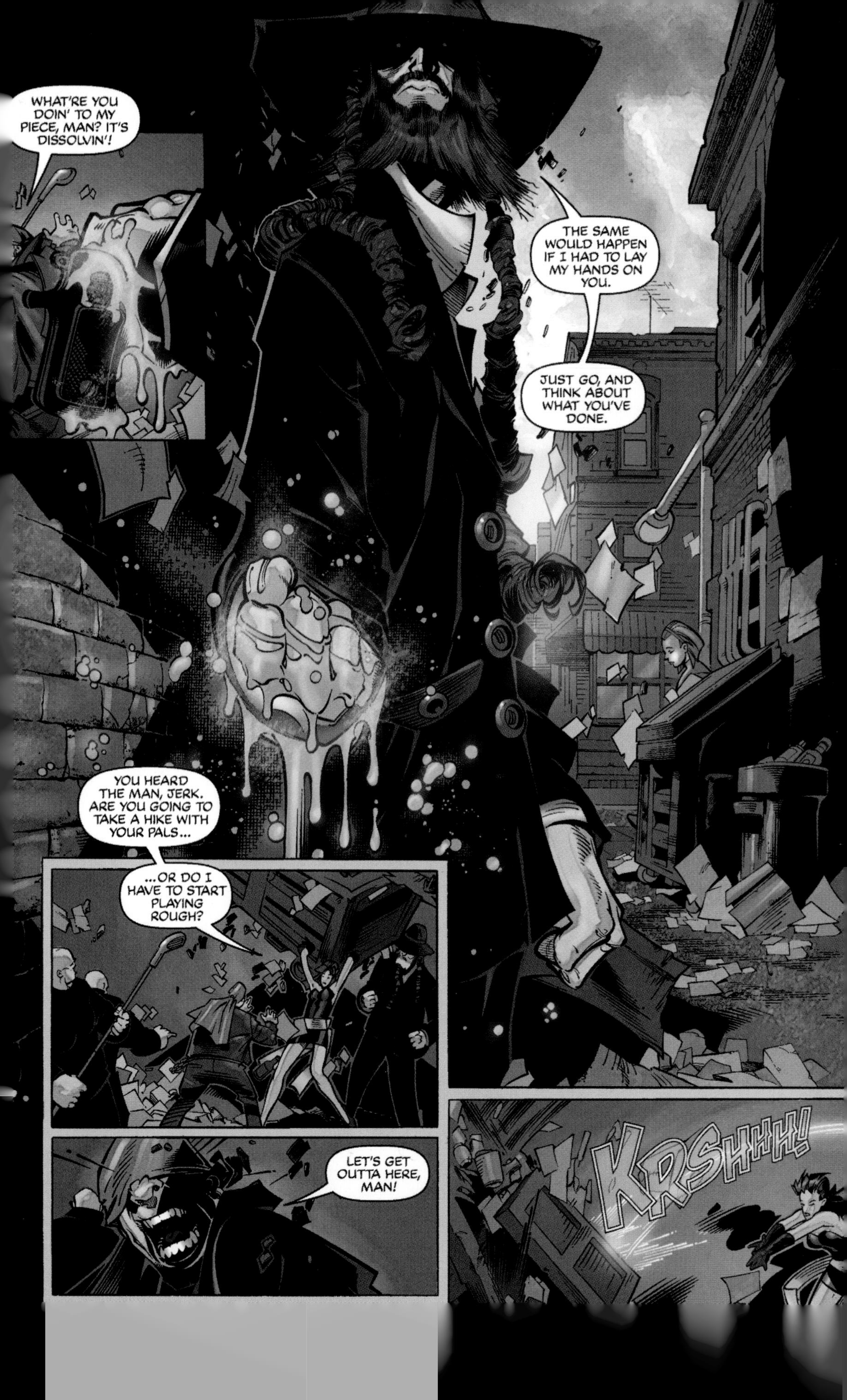
WHAT'RE YOU DOIN' TO MY PIECE, MAN? IT'S DISSOLVIN'!
THE SAME WOULD HAPPEN IF I HAD TO LAY MY HANDS ON YOU.
JUST GO, AND THINK ABOUT WHAT YOU'VE DONE.
YOU HEARD THE MAN, JERK. ARE YOU GOING TO TAKE A HIKE WITH YOUR PALS...
...OR DO I HAVE TO START PLAYING ROUGH?
LET'S GET OUTTA HERE, MAN!
KRSHHH!

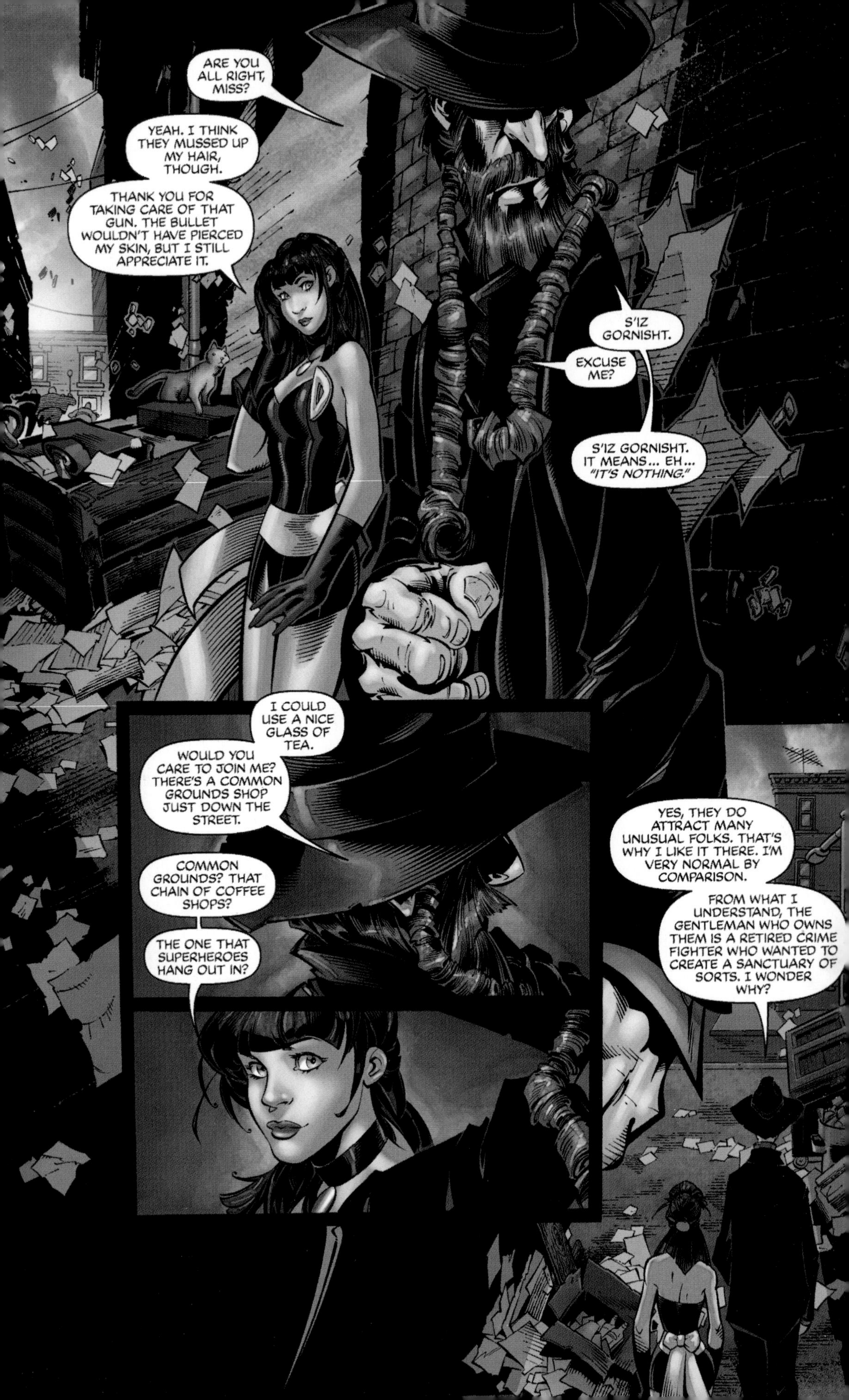
ARE YOU ALL RIGHT, MISS?
YEAH. I THINK THEY MUSSED UP MY HAIR, THOUGH.
THANK YOU FOR TAKING CARE OF THAT GUN. THE BULLET WOULDN'T HAVE PIERCED MY SKIN, BUT I STILL APPRECIATE IT.
S'IZ GORNISHT.
EXCUSE ME?
S'IZ GORNISHT. IT MEANS... EH... *"IT'S NOTHING."*
I COULD USE A NICE GLASS OF TEA.
WOULD YOU CARE TO JOIN ME? THERE'S A COMMON GROUNDS SHOP JUST DOWN THE STREET.
COMMON GROUNDS? THAT CHAIN OF COFFEE SHOPS?
THE ONE THAT SUPERHEROES HANG OUT IN?
YES, THEY DO ATTRACT MANY UNUSUAL FOLKS. THAT'S WHY I LIKE IT THERE. I'M VERY NORMAL BY COMPARISON.
FROM WHAT I UNDERSTAND, THE GENTLEMAN WHO OWNS THEM IS A RETIRED CRIME FIGHTER WHO WANTED TO CREATE A SANCTUARY OF SORTS. I WONDER WHY?

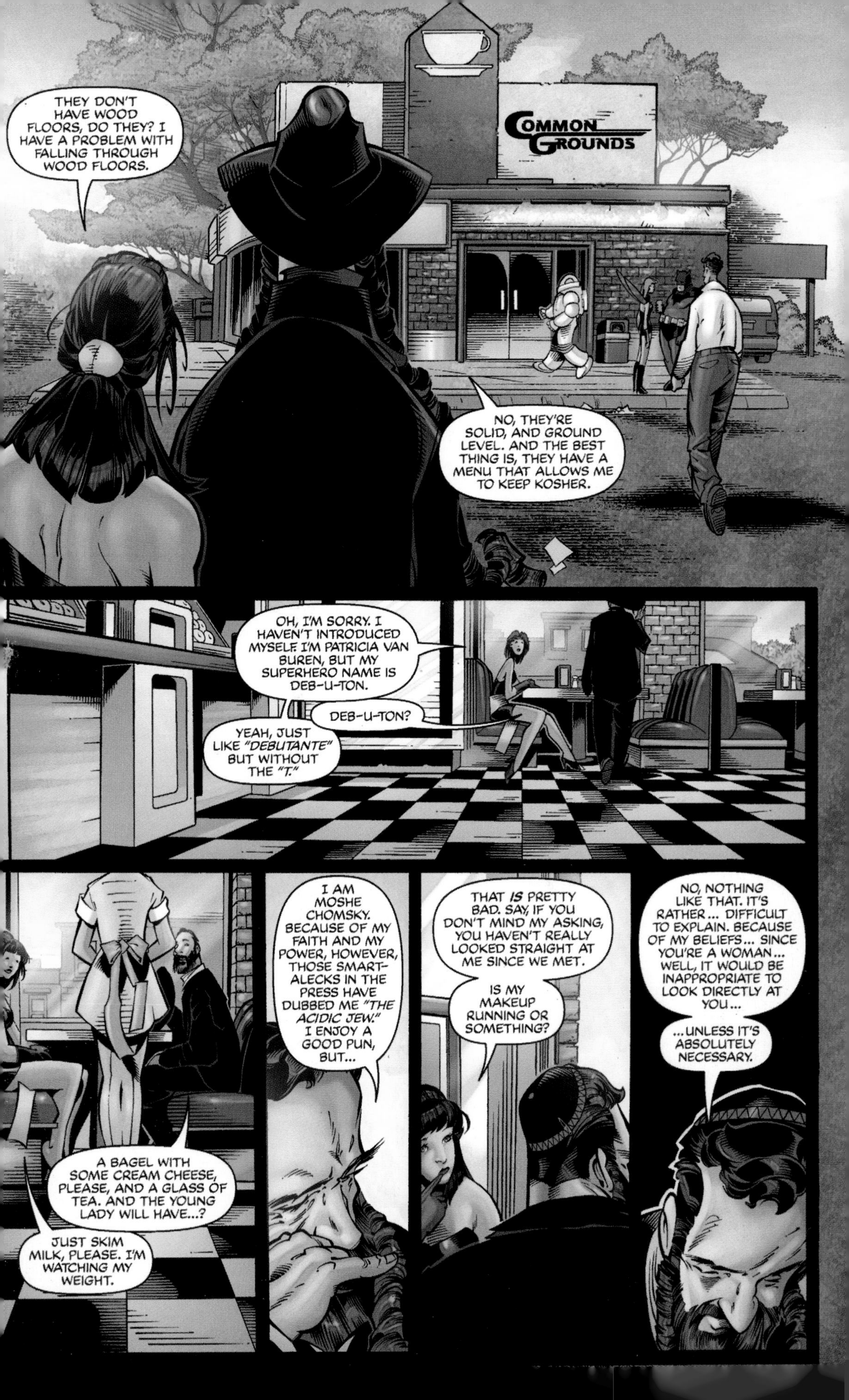
COMMON GROUNDS
THEY DON'T HAVE WOOD FLOORS, DO THEY? I HAVE A PROBLEM WITH FALLING THROUGH WOOD FLOORS.
NO, THEY'RE SOLID, AND GROUND LEVEL. AND THE BEST THING IS, THEY HAVE A MENU THAT ALLOWS ME TO KEEP KOSHER.
OH, I'M SORRY. I HAVEN'T INTRODUCED MYSELF. I'M PATRICIA VAN BUREN, BUT MY SUPERHERO NAME IS DEB-U-TON.
DEB-U-TON?
YEAH, JUST LIKE "DEBUTANTE" BUT WITHOUT THE "T."
A BAGEL WITH SOME CREAM CHEESE, PLEASE, AND A GLASS OF TEA. AND THE YOUNG LADY WILL HAVE...?
JUST SKIM MILK, PLEASE. I'M WATCHING MY WEIGHT.
I AM MOSHE CHOMSKY. BECAUSE OF MY FAITH AND MY POWER, HOWEVER, THOSE SMART-ALECKS IN THE PRESS HAVE DUBBED ME "THE ACIDIC JEW." I ENJOY A GOOD PUN, BUT...
THAT IS PRETTY BAD. SAY, IF YOU DON'T MIND MY ASKING, YOU HAVEN'T REALLY LOOKED STRAIGHT AT ME SINCE WE MET.
IS MY MAKEUP RUNNING OR SOMETHING?
NO, NOTHING LIKE THAT. IT'S RATHER... DIFFICULT TO EXPLAIN. BECAUSE OF MY BELIEFS... SINCE YOU'RE A WOMAN... WELL, IT WOULD BE INAPPROPRIATE TO LOOK DIRECTLY AT YOU...
...UNLESS IT'S ABSOLUTELY NECESSARY.

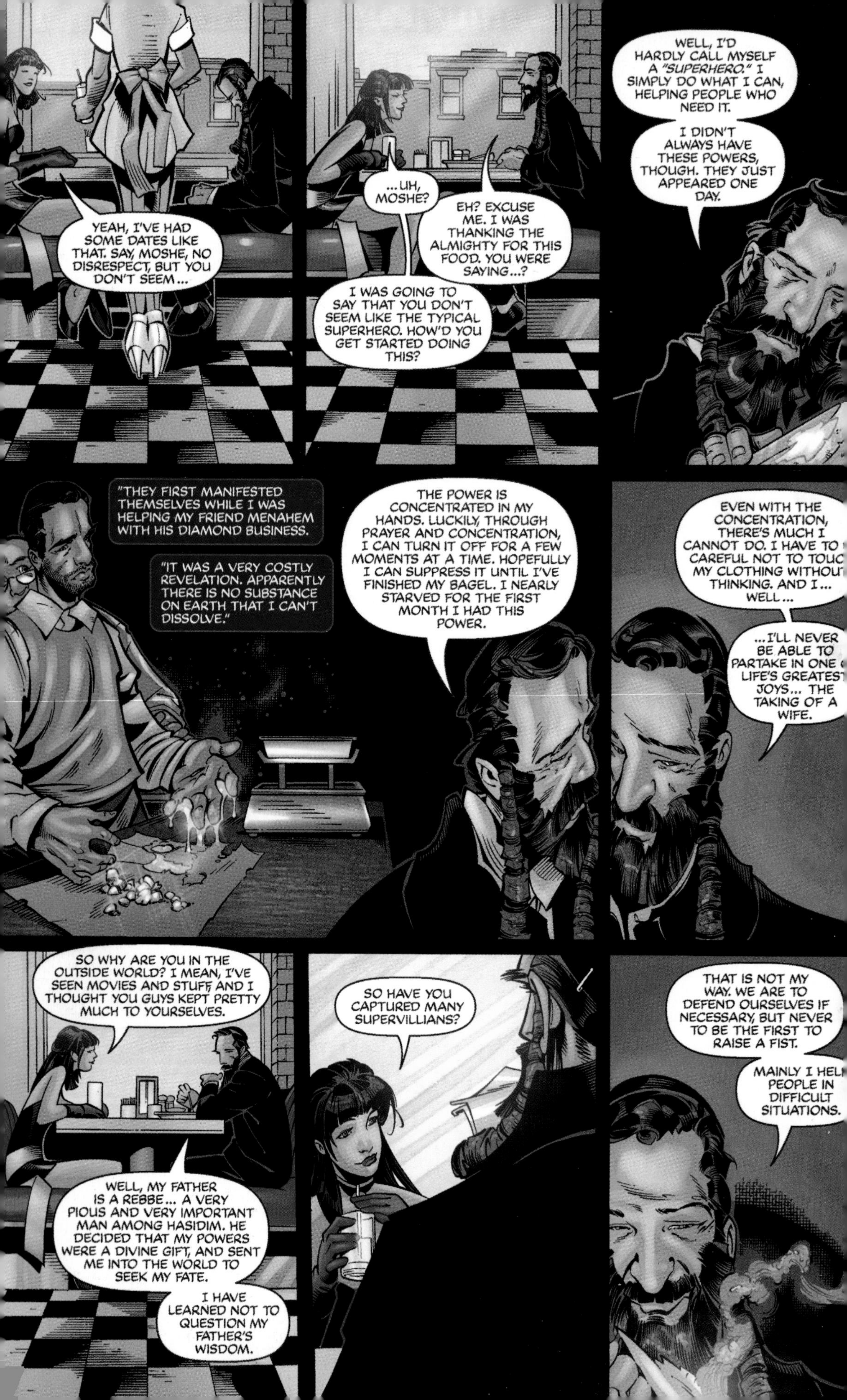
YEAH, I'VE HAD SOME DATES LIKE THAT. SAY, MOSHE, NO DISRESPECT, BUT YOU DON'T SEEM...
...UH, MOSHE?
EH? EXCUSE ME. I WAS THANKING THE ALMIGHTY FOR THIS FOOD. YOU WERE SAYING...?
I WAS GOING TO SAY THAT YOU DON'T SEEM LIKE THE TYPICAL SUPERHERO. HOW'D YOU GET STARTED DOING THIS?
WELL, I'D HARDLY CALL MYSELF A "SUPERHERO." I SIMPLY DO WHAT I CAN, HELPING PEOPLE WHO NEED IT.
I DIDN'T ALWAYS HAVE THESE POWERS, THOUGH. THEY JUST APPEARED ONE DAY.
"THEY FIRST MANIFESTED THEMSELVES WHILE I WAS HELPING MY FRIEND MENAHEM WITH HIS DIAMOND BUSINESS.
"IT WAS A VERY COSTLY REVELATION. APPARENTLY THERE IS NO SUBSTANCE ON EARTH THAT I CAN'T DISSOLVE."
THE POWER IS CONCENTRATED IN MY HANDS. LUCKILY, THROUGH PRAYER AND CONCENTRATION, I CAN TURN IT OFF FOR A FEW MOMENTS AT A TIME. HOPEFULLY I CAN SUPPRESS IT UNTIL I'VE FINISHED MY BAGEL. I NEARLY STARVED FOR THE FIRST MONTH I HAD THIS POWER.
EVEN WITH THE CONCENTRATION, THERE'S MUCH I CANNOT DO. I HAVE TO CAREFUL NOT TO TOUC MY CLOTHING WITHOUT THINKING. AND I... WELL...
...I'LL NEVER BE ABLE TO PARTAKE IN ONE LIFE'S GREATEST JOYS... THE TAKING OF A WIFE.
SO WHY ARE YOU IN THE OUTSIDE WORLD? I MEAN, I'VE SEEN MOVIES AND STUFF, AND I THOUGHT YOU GUYS KEPT PRETTY MUCH TO YOURSELVES.
WELL, MY FATHER IS A REBBE... A VERY PIOUS AND VERY IMPORTANT MAN AMONG HASIDIM. HE DECIDED THAT MY POWERS WERE A DIVINE GIFT, AND SENT ME INTO THE WORLD TO SEEK MY FATE.
I HAVE LEARNED NOT TO QUESTION MY FATHER'S WISDOM.
SO HAVE YOU CAPTURED MANY SUPERVILLIANS?
THAT IS NOT MY WAY. WE ARE TO DEFEND OURSELVES IF NECESSARY, BUT NEVER TO BE THE FIRST TO RAISE A FIST.
MAINLY I HEL PEOPLE IN DIFFICULT SITUATIONS.

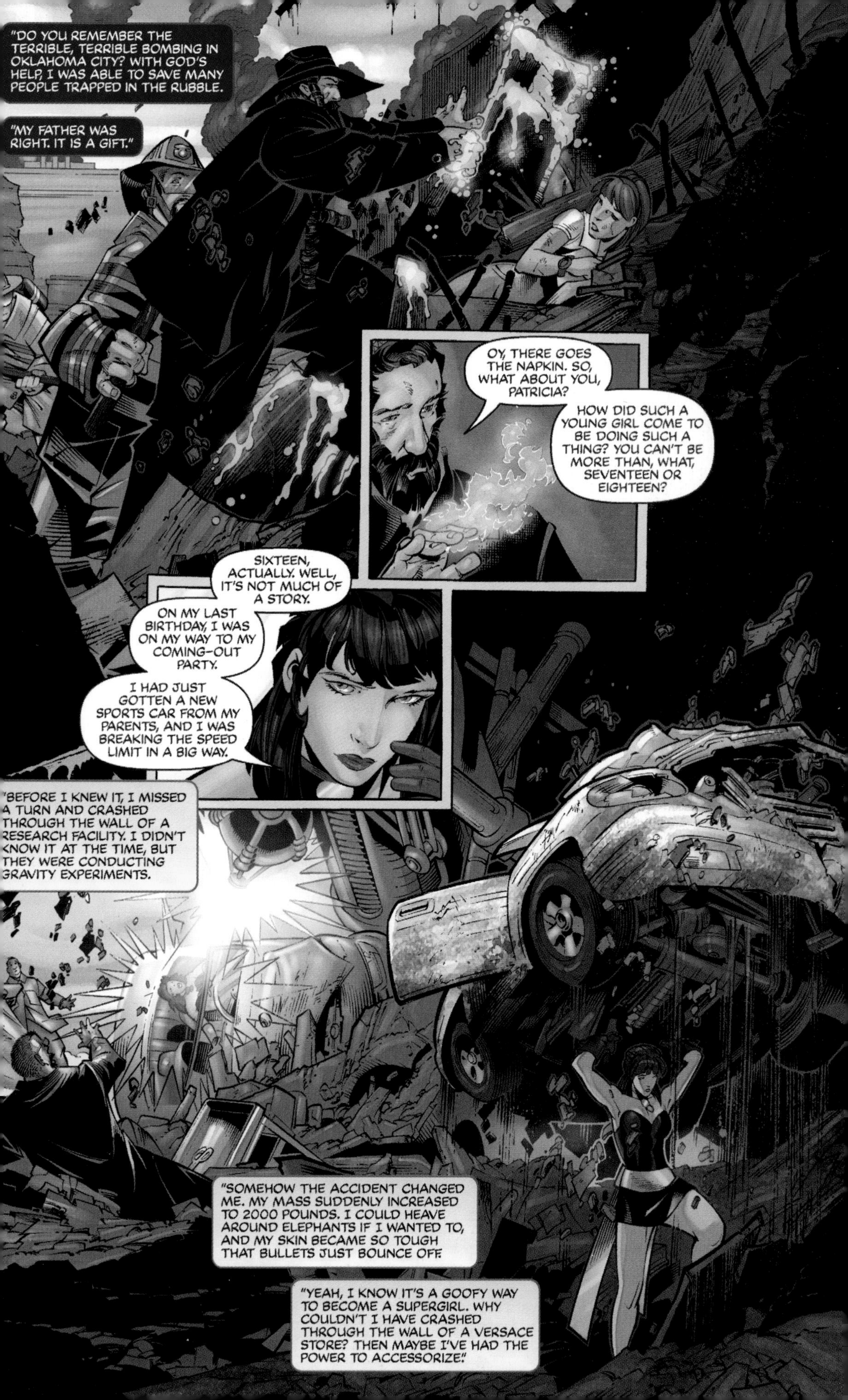
"DO YOU REMEMBER THE TERRIBLE, TERRIBLE BOMBING IN OKLAHOMA CITY? WITH GOD'S HELP, I WAS ABLE TO SAVE MANY PEOPLE TRAPPED IN THE RUBBLE.
"MY FATHER WAS RIGHT. IT IS A GIFT."
OY, THERE GOES THE NAPKIN. SO, WHAT ABOUT YOU, PATRICIA?
HOW DID SUCH A YOUNG GIRL COME TO BE DOING SUCH A THING? YOU CAN'T BE MORE THAN, WHAT, SEVENTEEN OR EIGHTEEN?
SIXTEEN, ACTUALLY. WELL, IT'S NOT MUCH OF A STORY.
ON MY LAST BIRTHDAY, I WAS ON MY WAY TO MY COMING-OUT PARTY.
I HAD JUST GOTTEN A NEW SPORTS CAR FROM MY PARENTS, AND I WAS BREAKING THE SPEED LIMIT IN A BIG WAY.
"BEFORE I KNEW IT, I MISSED A TURN AND CRASHED THROUGH THE WALL OF A RESEARCH FACILITY. I DIDN'T KNOW IT AT THE TIME, BUT THEY WERE CONDUCTING GRAVITY EXPERIMENTS.
"SOMEHOW THE ACCIDENT CHANGED ME. MY MASS SUDDENLY INCREASED TO 2000 POUNDS. I COULD HEAVE AROUND ELEPHANTS IF I WANTED TO, AND MY SKIN BECAME SO TOUGH THAT BULLETS JUST BOUNCE OFF.
"YEAH, I KNOW IT'S A GOOFY WAY TO BECOME A SUPERGIRL. WHY COULDN'T I HAVE CRASHED THROUGH THE WALL OF A VERSACE STORE? THEN MAYBE I'VE HAD THE POWER TO ACCESSORIZE."

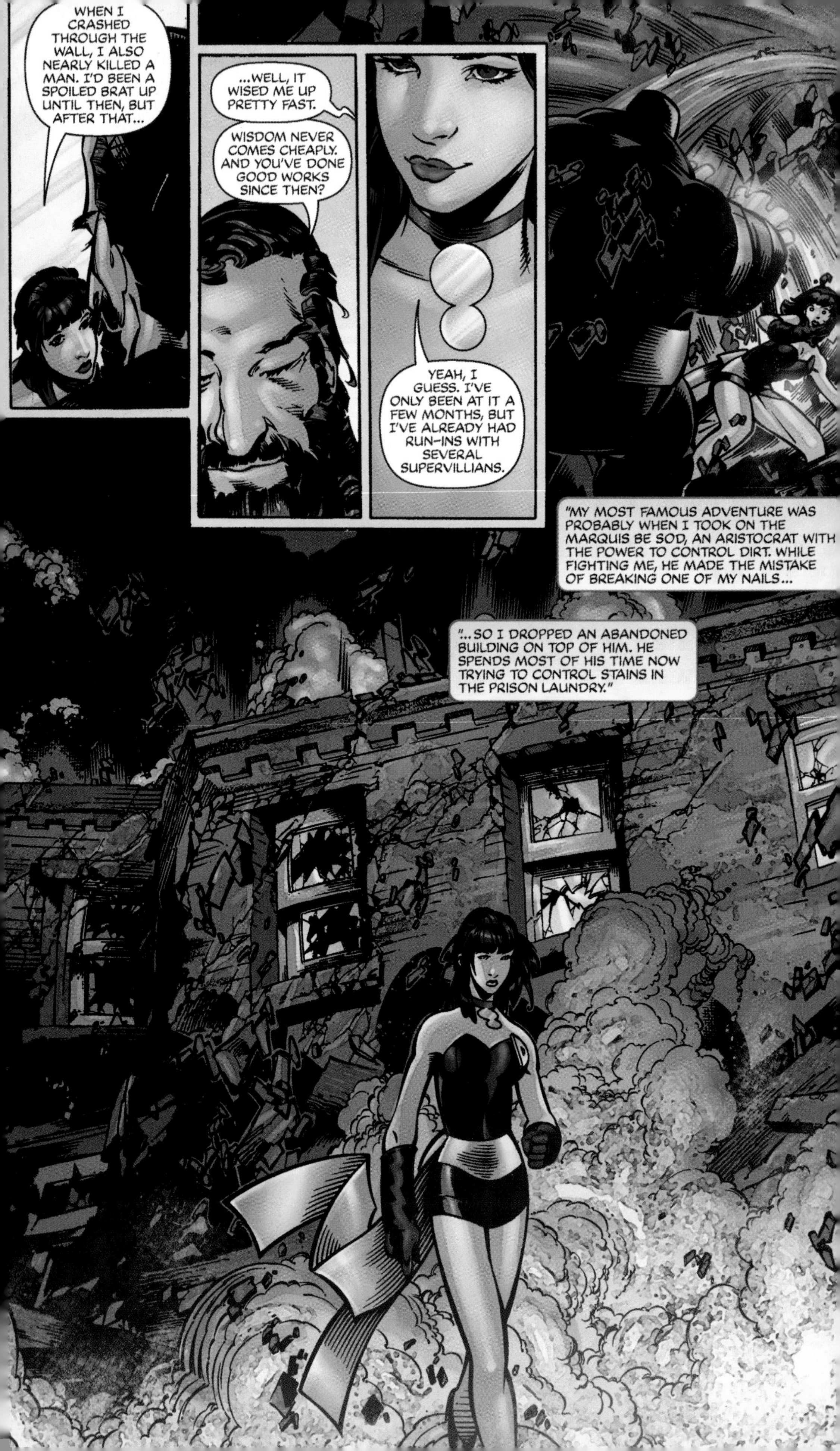
WHEN I CRASHED THROUGH THE WALL, I ALSO NEARLY KILLED A MAN. I'D BEEN A SPOILED BRAT UP UNTIL THEN, BUT AFTER THAT...
...WELL, IT WISED ME UP PRETTY FAST.
WISDOM NEVER COMES CHEAPLY. AND YOU'VE DONE GOOD WORKS SINCE THEN?
YEAH, I GUESS. I'VE ONLY BEEN AT IT A FEW MONTHS, BUT I'VE ALREADY HAD RUN-INS WITH SEVERAL SUPERVILLIANS.
"MY MOST FAMOUS ADVENTURE WAS PROBABLY WHEN I TOOK ON THE MARQUIS BE SOD, AN ARISTOCRAT WITH THE POWER TO CONTROL DIRT. WHILE FIGHTING ME, HE MADE THE MISTAKE OF BREAKING ONE OF MY NAILS...
"...SO I DROPPED AN ABANDONED BUILDING ON TOP OF HIM. HE SPENDS MOST OF HIS TIME NOW TRYING TO CONTROL STAINS IN THE PRISON LAUNDRY."

LATELY, THOUGH, I'VE BEEN THINKING ABOUT GIVING IT UP. WITH ALL THE CRIME OUT THERE, I'M JUST A LITTLE FISH IN A BIG, MUDDY POND.

UM, WAITRESS, COULD I GET A DOUBLE CHOCOLATE ECLAIR, PLEASE? SCREW IT, SO I'LL WEIGH 2001 POUNDS.

ANYWAY, I'M STARTING TO THINK MAYBE THIS ISN'T THE WAY FOR ME. I MEAN, EVEN WITH ALL THESE POWERS, ANYTHING I DO IS A DROP IN THE BUCKET. MAYBE I SHOULD JUST GO BACK TO BEING A NORMAL TEENAGER, Y'KNOW?

IT IS NOT FOR ME TO TELL YOU WHAT TO DO. I WILL SAY, THOUGH, THAT YOU, LIKE ALL OF GOD'S CHILDREN, HAVE A RESPONSIBILITY TO THE PIECE OF THE WORLD ENTRUSTED TO YOU.

THAT IS YOUR GREATNESS.

I'M NOT SURE I UNDERSTAND.

OUR WORTH IS BASED NOT ON WHO WE ARE, BUT ON WHAT WE'VE DONE TO MAKE EARTH INTO HEAVEN. WE EACH DO WHAT WE CAN, AND IT CANNOT BE COMPARED TO WHAT OTHERS DO.

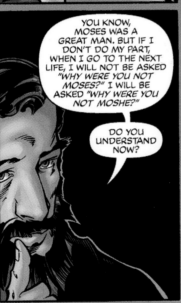

YOU KNOW, MOSES WAS A GREAT MAN. BUT IF I DON'T DO MY PART, WHEN I GO TO THE NEXT LIFE, I WILL NOT BE ASKED "WHY WERE YOU NOT MOSES?" I WILL BE ASKED "WHY WERE YOU NOT MOSHE?"

DO YOU UNDERSTAND NOW?

HMMM... I THINK SO. Y'KNOW, I'M NOT SURE WHAT I'LL DO, BUT YOU'VE GIVEN ME A LOT TO THINK ABOUT, MOSHE.

THANK YOU. THANK YOU VERY MUCH.

S'IZ GORNISHT.

The End.

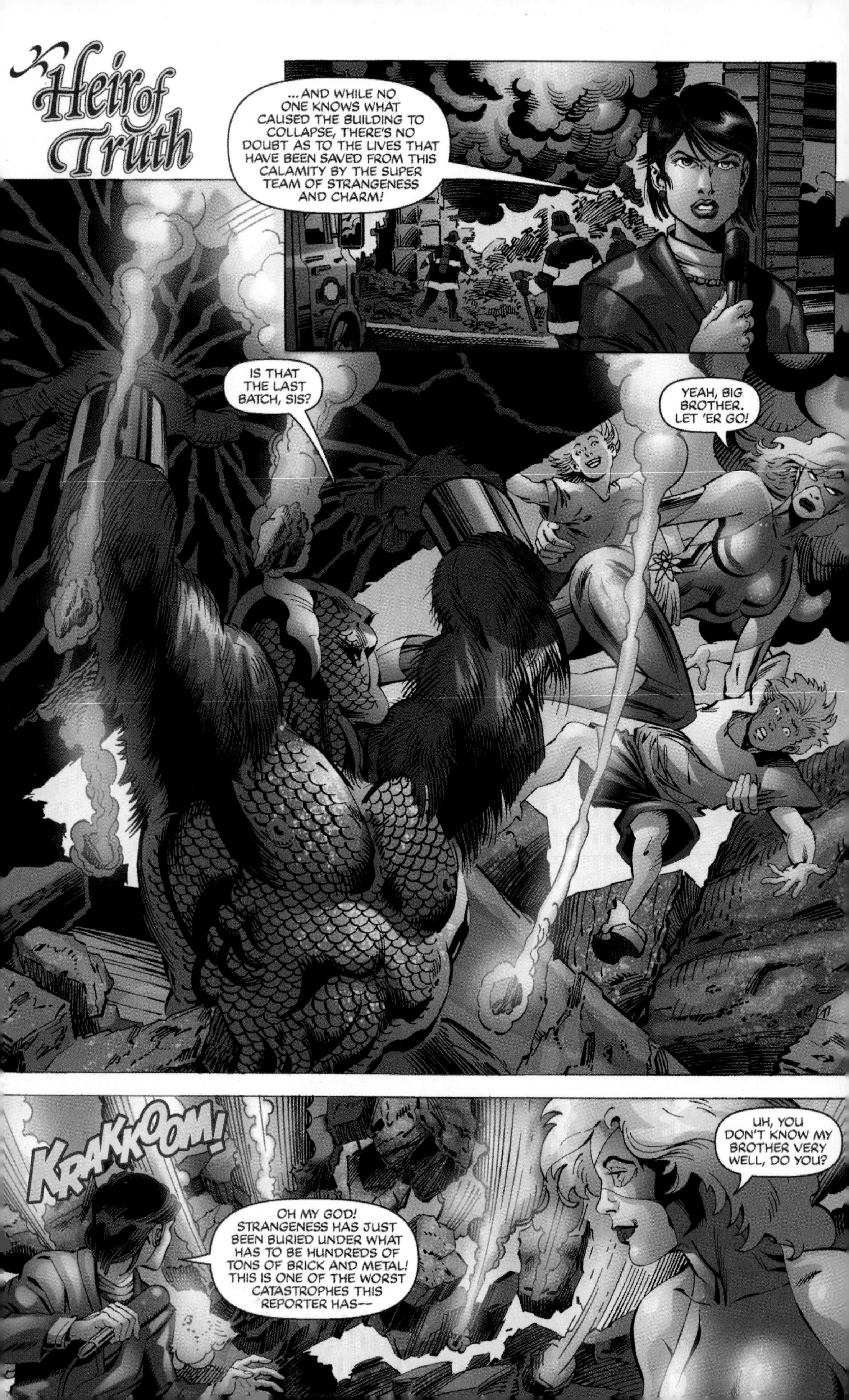
Heir of Truth
...AND WHILE NO ONE KNOWS WHAT CAUSED THE BUILDING TO COLLAPSE, THERE'S NO DOUBT AS TO THE LIVES THAT HAVE BEEN SAVED FROM THIS CALAMITY BY THE SUPER TEAM OF STRANGENESS AND CHARM!
IS THAT THE LAST BATCH, SIS?
YEAH, BIG BROTHER. LET 'ER GO!
KRAKKOOM!
UH, YOU DON'T KNOW MY BROTHER VERY WELL, DO YOU?
OH MY GOD! STRANGENESS HAS JUST BEEN BURIED UNDER WHAT HAS TO BE HUNDREDS OF TONS OF BRICK AND METAL! THIS IS ONE OF THE WORST CATASTROPHES THIS REPORTER HAS--

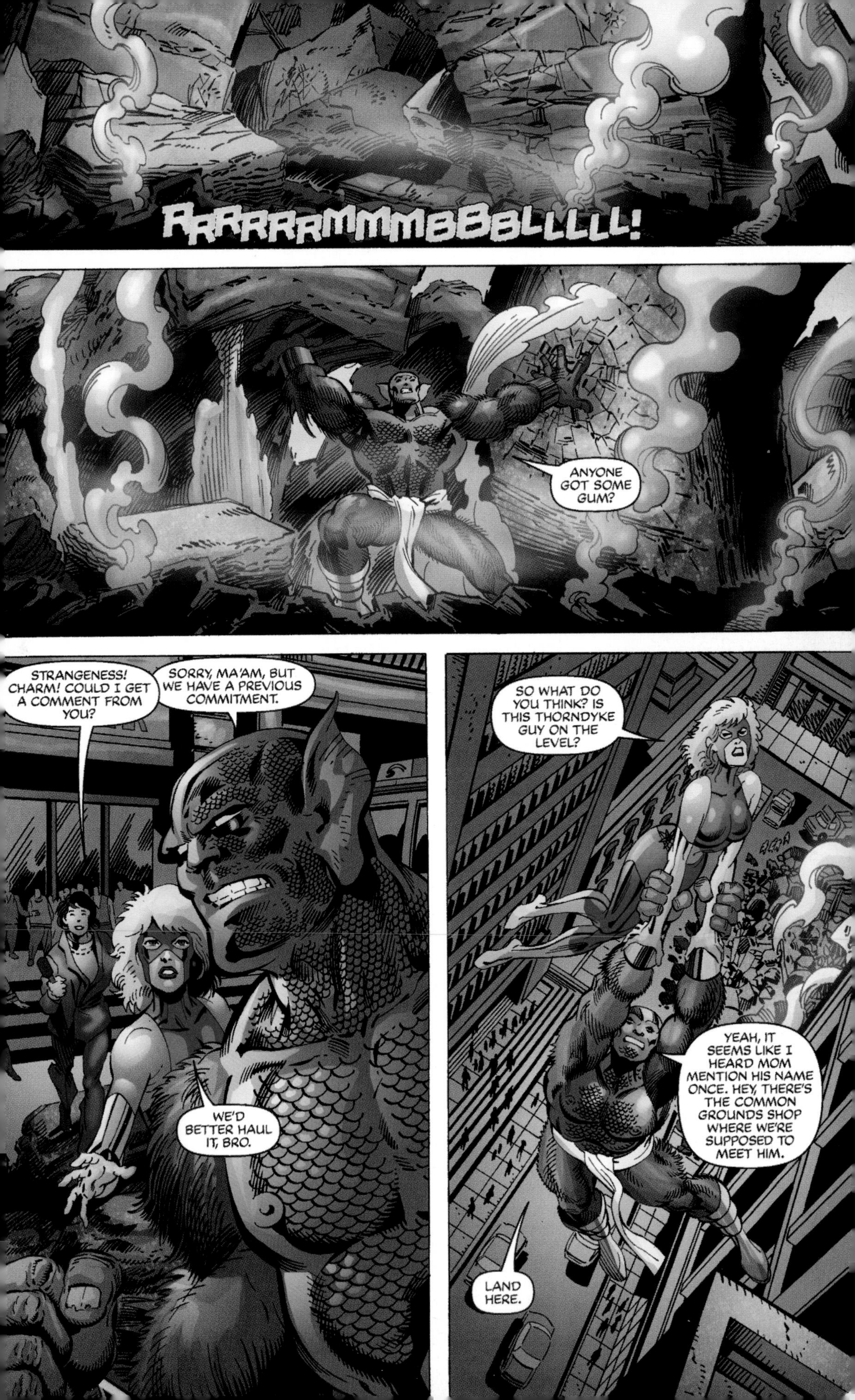
RRRRRRMMMMBBBLLLLL!
ANYONE GOT SOME GUM?
STRANGENESS! CHARM! COULD I GET A COMMENT FROM YOU?
SORRY, MA'AM, BUT WE HAVE A PREVIOUS COMMITMENT.
WE'D BETTER HAUL IT, BRO.
SO WHAT DO YOU THINK? IS THIS THORNDYKE GUY ON THE LEVEL?
YEAH, IT SEEMS LIKE I HEARD MOM MENTION HIS NAME ONCE. HEY, THERE'S THE COMMON GROUNDS SHOP WHERE WE'RE SUPPOSED TO MEET HIM.
LAND HERE.

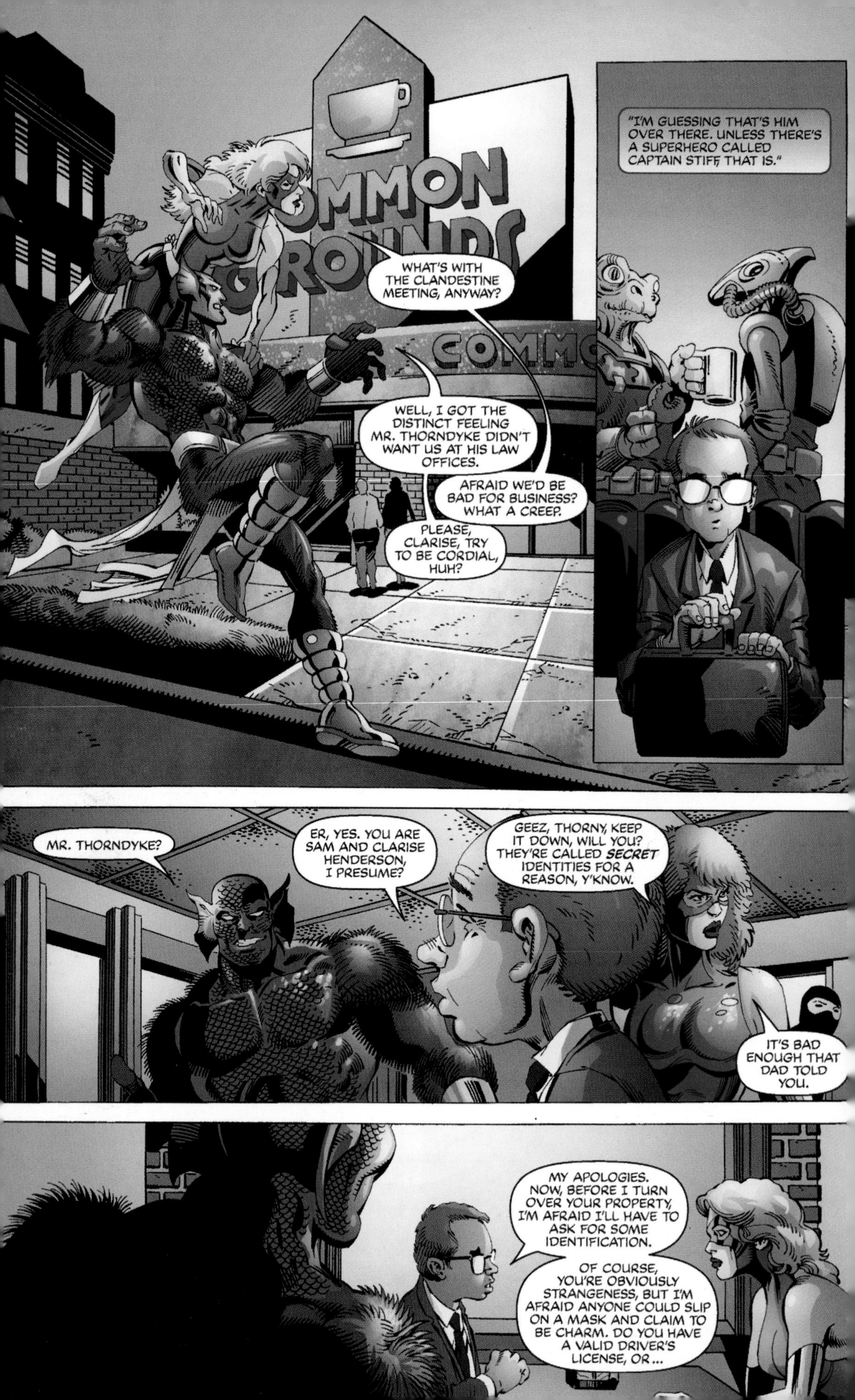

COMMON GROUNDS
WHAT'S WITH THE CLANDESTINE MEETING, ANYWAY?
WELL, I GOT THE DISTINCT FEELING MR. THORNDYKE DIDN'T WANT US AT HIS LAW OFFICES.
AFRAID WE'D BE BAD FOR BUSINESS? WHAT A CREEP.
PLEASE, CLARISE, TRY TO BE CORDIAL, HUH?
"I'M GUESSING THAT'S HIM OVER THERE. UNLESS THERE'S A SUPERHERO CALLED CAPTAIN STIFF, THAT IS."
MR. THORNDYKE?
ER, YES. YOU ARE SAM AND CLARISE HENDERSON, I PRESUME?
GEEZ, THORNY, KEEP IT DOWN, WILL YOU? THEY'RE CALLED *SECRET* IDENTITIES FOR A REASON, Y'KNOW.
IT'S BAD ENOUGH THAT DAD TOLD YOU.
MY APOLOGIES. NOW, BEFORE I TURN OVER YOUR PROPERTY, I'M AFRAID I'LL HAVE TO ASK FOR SOME IDENTIFICATION.
OF COURSE, YOU'RE OBVIOUSLY STRANGENESS, BUT I'M AFRAID ANYONE COULD SLIP ON A MASK AND CLAIM TO BE CHARM. DO YOU HAVE A VALID DRIVER'S LICENSE, OR...

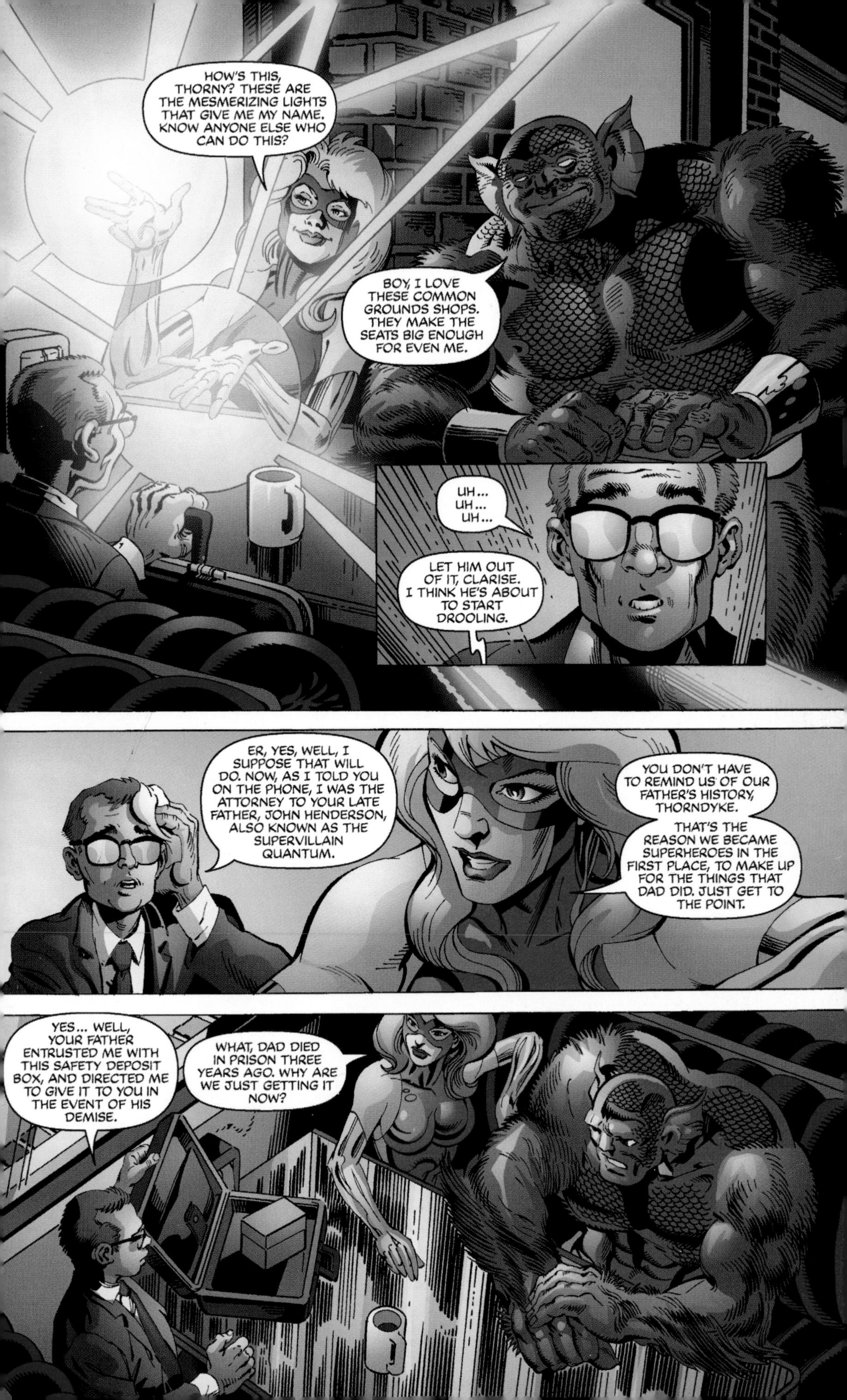
HOW'S THIS, THORNY? THESE ARE THE MESMERIZING LIGHTS THAT GIVE ME MY NAME. KNOW ANYONE ELSE WHO CAN DO THIS?
BOY, I LOVE THESE COMMON GROUNDS SHOPS. THEY MAKE THE SEATS BIG ENOUGH FOR EVEN ME.
UH... UH... UH...
LET HIM OUT OF IT, CLARISE. I THINK HE'S ABOUT TO START DROOLING.
ER, YES, WELL, I SUPPOSE THAT WILL DO. NOW, AS I TOLD YOU ON THE PHONE, I WAS THE ATTORNEY TO YOUR LATE FATHER, JOHN HENDERSON, ALSO KNOWN AS THE SUPERVILLAIN QUANTUM.
YOU DON'T HAVE TO REMIND US OF OUR FATHER'S HISTORY, THORNDYKE.
THAT'S THE REASON WE BECAME SUPERHEROES IN THE FIRST PLACE, TO MAKE UP FOR THE THINGS THAT DAD DID. JUST GET TO THE POINT.
YES... WELL, YOUR FATHER ENTRUSTED ME WITH THIS SAFETY DEPOSIT BOX, AND DIRECTED ME TO GIVE IT TO YOU IN THE EVENT OF HIS DEMISE.
WHAT, DAD DIED IN PRISON THREE YEARS AGO. WHY ARE WE JUST GETTING IT NOW?

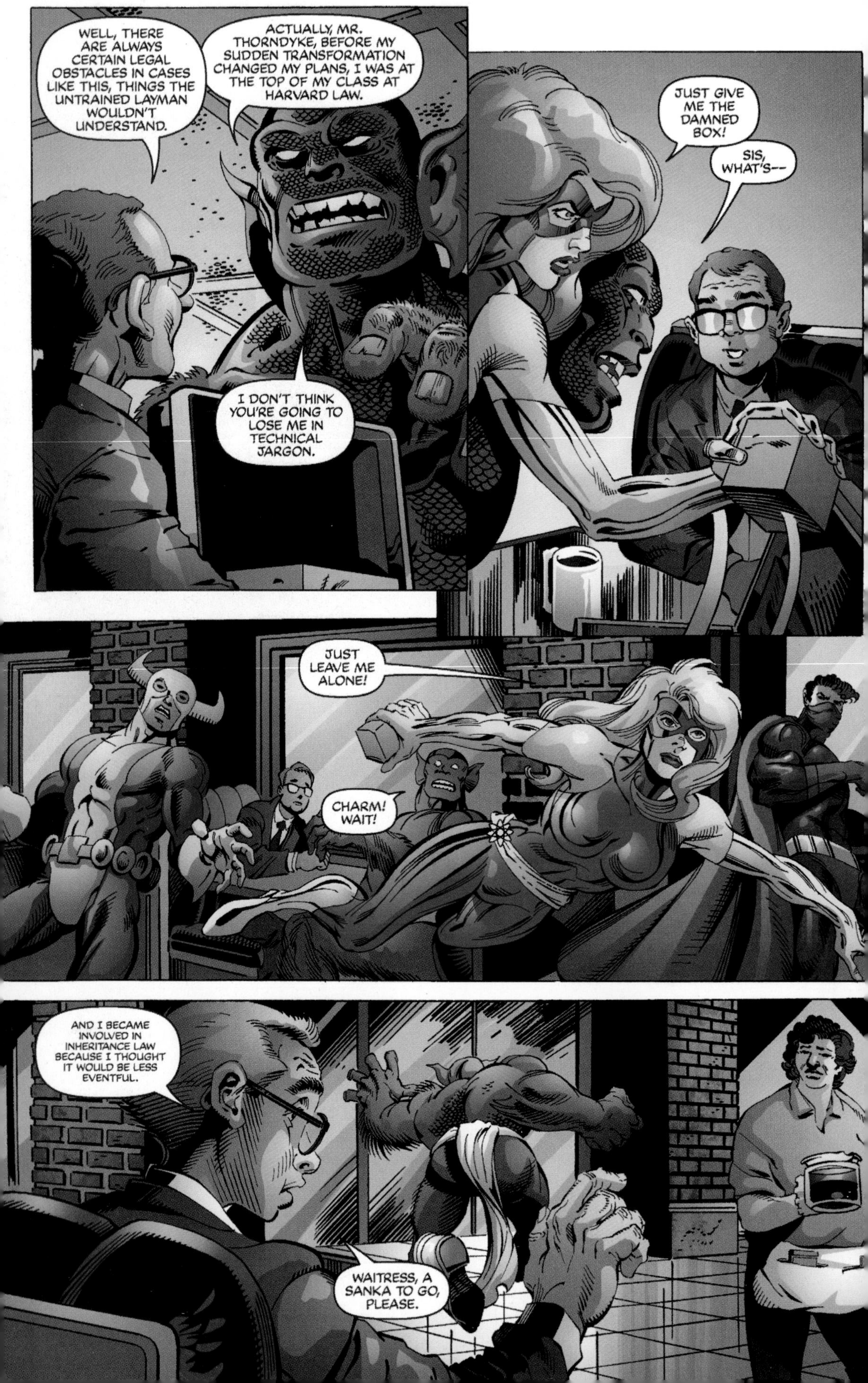
WELL, THERE ARE ALWAYS CERTAIN LEGAL OBSTACLES IN CASES LIKE THIS, THINGS THE UNTRAINED LAYMAN WOULDN'T UNDERSTAND.
ACTUALLY, MR. THORNDYKE, BEFORE MY SUDDEN TRANSFORMATION CHANGED MY PLANS, I WAS AT THE TOP OF MY CLASS AT HARVARD LAW.
I DON'T THINK YOU'RE GOING TO LOSE ME IN TECHNICAL JARGON.
JUST GIVE ME THE DAMNED BOX!
SIS, WHAT'S--
JUST LEAVE ME ALONE!
CHARM! WAIT!
AND I BECAME INVOLVED IN INHERITANCE LAW BECAUSE I THOUGHT IT WOULD BE LESS EVENTFUL.
WAITRESS, A SANKA TO GO, PLEASE.

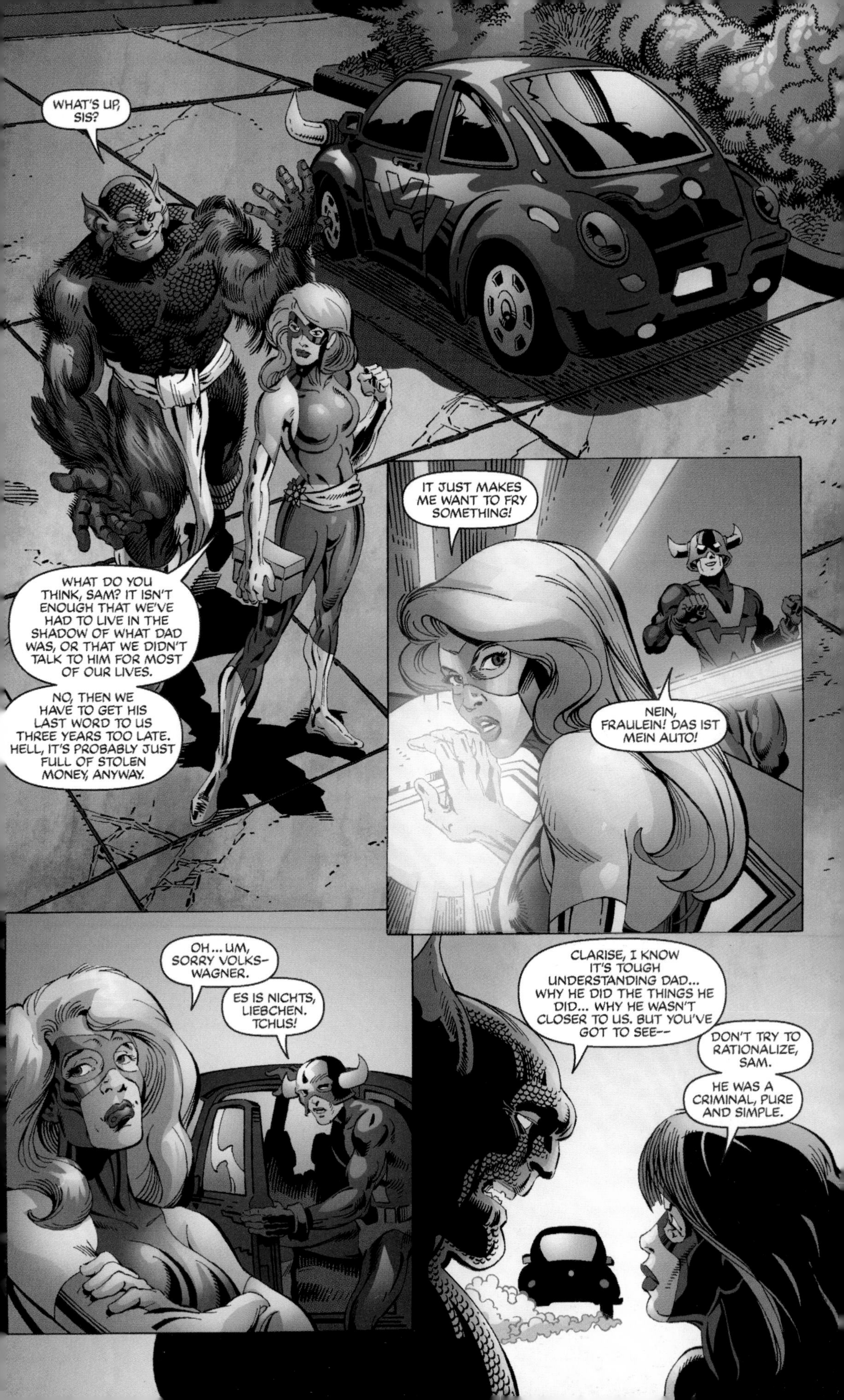
WHAT'S UP, SIS?
WHAT DO YOU THINK, SAM? IT ISN'T ENOUGH THAT WE'VE HAD TO LIVE IN THE SHADOW OF WHAT DAD WAS, OR THAT WE DIDN'T TALK TO HIM FOR MOST OF OUR LIVES.
NO, THEN WE HAVE TO GET HIS LAST WORD TO US THREE YEARS TOO LATE. HELL, IT'S PROBABLY JUST FULL OF STOLEN MONEY, ANYWAY.
IT JUST MAKES ME WANT TO FRY SOMETHING!
NEIN, FRAULEIN! DAS IST MEIN AUTO!
OH...UM, SORRY VOLKS-WAGNER.
ES IS NICHTS, LIEBCHEN. TCHUS!
CLARISE, I KNOW IT'S TOUGH UNDERSTANDING DAD... WHY HE DID THE THINGS HE DID... WHY HE WASN'T CLOSER TO US. BUT YOU'VE GOT TO SEE--
DON'T TRY TO RATIONALIZE, SAM.
HE WAS A CRIMINAL, PURE AND SIMPLE.

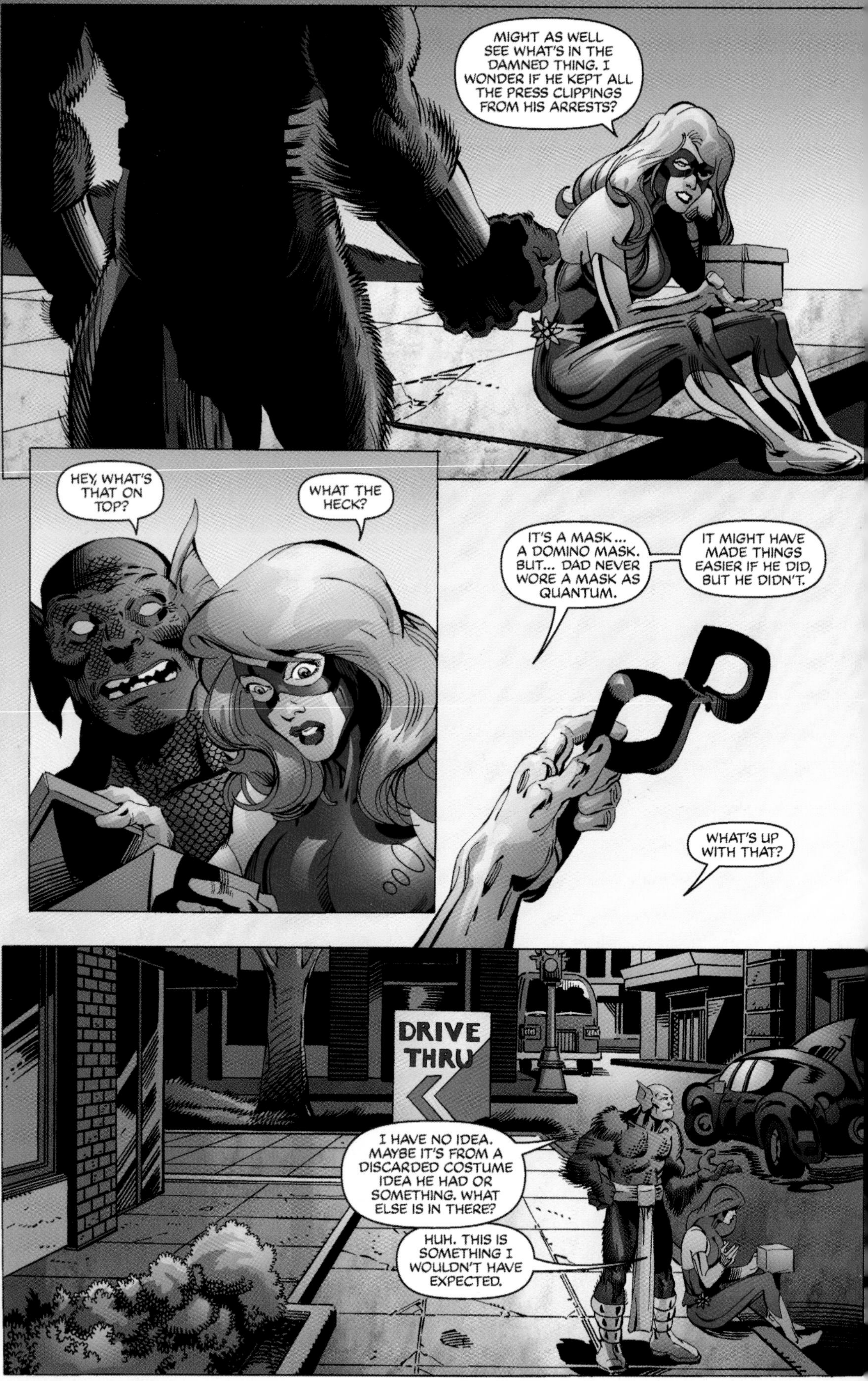
MIGHT AS WELL SEE WHAT'S IN THE DAMNED THING. I WONDER IF HE KEPT ALL THE PRESS CLIPPINGS FROM HIS ARRESTS?
HEY, WHAT'S THAT ON TOP?
WHAT THE HECK?
IT'S A MASK... A DOMINO MASK. BUT... DAD NEVER WORE A MASK AS QUANTUM.
IT MIGHT HAVE MADE THINGS EASIER IF HE DID, BUT HE DIDN'T.
WHAT'S UP WITH THAT?
DRIVE THRU
I HAVE NO IDEA. MAYBE IT'S FROM A DISCARDED COSTUME IDEA HE HAD OR SOMETHING. WHAT ELSE IS IN THERE?
HUH. THIS IS SOMETHING I WOULDN'T HAVE EXPECTED.

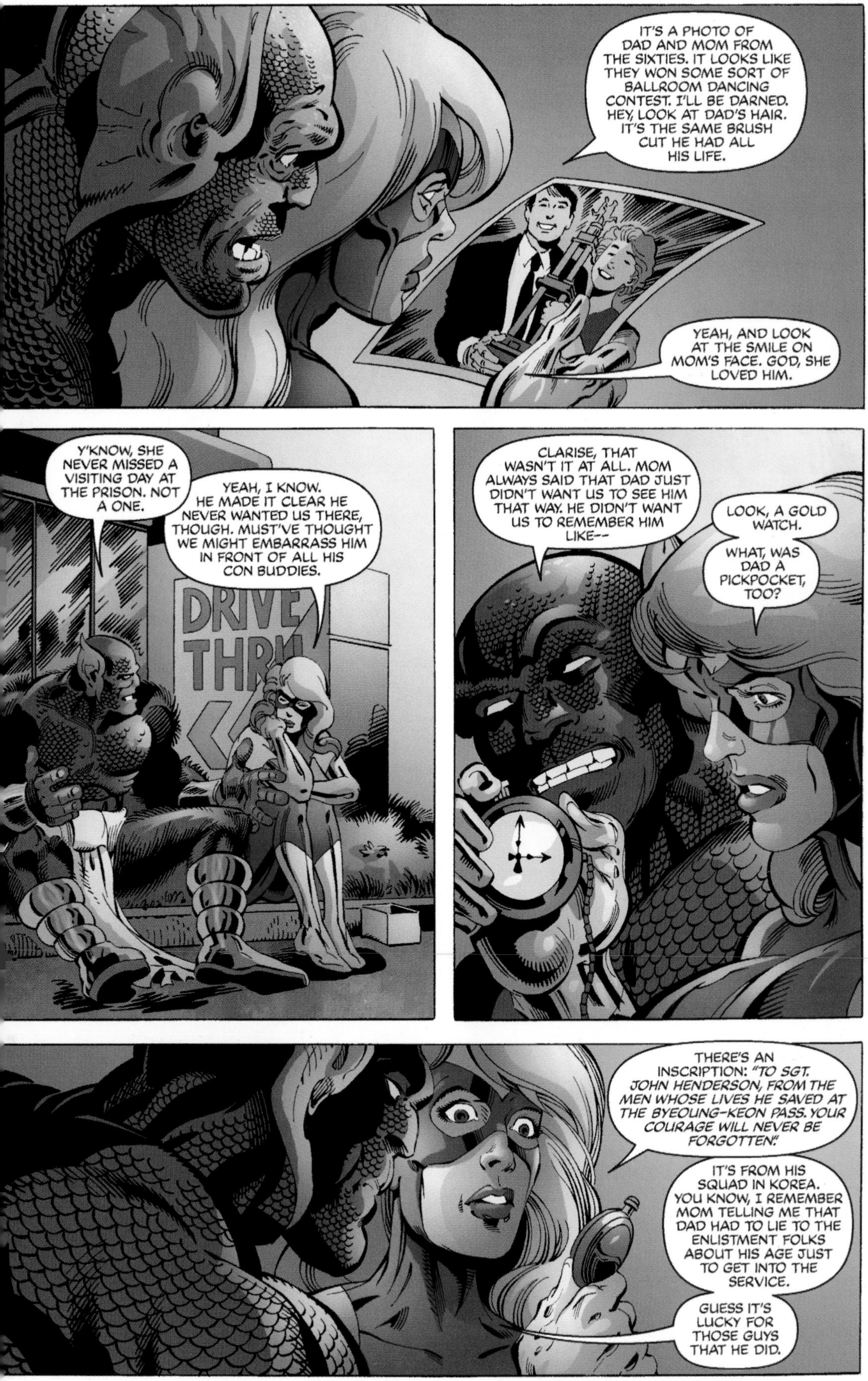
IT'S A PHOTO OF DAD AND MOM FROM THE SIXTIES. IT LOOKS LIKE THEY WON SOME SORT OF BALLROOM DANCING CONTEST. I'LL BE DARNED. HEY, LOOK AT DAD'S HAIR. IT'S THE SAME BRUSH CUT HE HAD ALL HIS LIFE.
YEAH, AND LOOK AT THE SMILE ON MOM'S FACE. GOD, SHE LOVED HIM.
Y'KNOW, SHE NEVER MISSED A VISITING DAY AT THE PRISON. NOT A ONE.
YEAH, I KNOW. HE MADE IT CLEAR HE NEVER WANTED US THERE, THOUGH. MUST'VE THOUGHT WE MIGHT EMBARRASS HIM IN FRONT OF ALL HIS CON BUDDIES.
DRIVE
CLARISE, THAT WASN'T IT AT ALL. MOM ALWAYS SAID THAT DAD JUST DIDN'T WANT US TO SEE HIM THAT WAY. HE DIDN'T WANT US TO REMEMBER HIM LIKE--
LOOK, A GOLD WATCH.
WHAT, WAS DAD A PICKPOCKET, TOO?
THERE'S AN INSCRIPTION: "TO SGT. JOHN HENDERSON, FROM THE MEN WHOSE LIVES HE SAVED AT THE BYEOUNG-KEON PASS. YOUR COURAGE WILL NEVER BE FORGOTTEN."
IT'S FROM HIS SQUAD IN KOREA. YOU KNOW, I REMEMBER MOM TELLING ME THAT DAD HAD TO LIE TO THE ENLISTMENT FOLKS ABOUT HIS AGE JUST TO GET INTO THE SERVICE.
GUESS IT'S LUCKY FOR THOSE GUYS THAT HE DID.

YEAH, BUT IT WAS JUST AFTER THE WAR THAT THEY STATIONED HIM NEAR THE ATOMIC TESTING GROUNDS. IF IT WASN'T FOR THAT, HE'D NEVER HAVE BECOME QUANTUM, AND WE--

AND WE'D NEVER HAVE INHERITED HIS MUTATED GENES.

NOBODY COULD HAVE KNOWN THAT THOUGH, SIS.

YOU GOT THAT RIGHT. AN HOUR AFTER MY FIRST COLLEGE DANCE, AND I FOUND MYSELF FLOATING OVER THE STUDENT UNION.

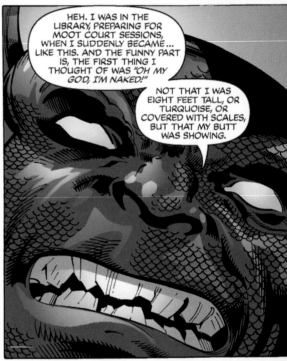

HEH. I WAS IN THE LIBRARY, PREPARING FOR MOOT COURT SESSIONS, WHEN I SUDDENLY BECAME... LIKE THIS. AND THE FUNNY PART IS, THE FIRST THING I THOUGHT OF WAS "OH MY GOD, I'M NAKED!"

NOT THAT I WAS EIGHT FEET TALL, OR TURQUOISE, OR COVERED WITH SCALES, BUT THAT MY BUTT WAS SHOWING.

AND THEN I HAD TO BREAK MY ENGAGEMENT WITH ANGELA. BUT YOU SEE, THAT'S WHAT I WAS SAYING ABOUT--

WOW, CHECK THIS OUT.

IT LOOKS LIKE A DIARY OR SOMETHING.

I CAN'T IMAGINE DAD KEEPING SOMETHING LIKE THIS. IT'S GOT A LITTLE PADLOCK ON IT, THOUGH. YOU WANT TO DO THE HONORS?

MY PLEASURE.

KKRUNCH!

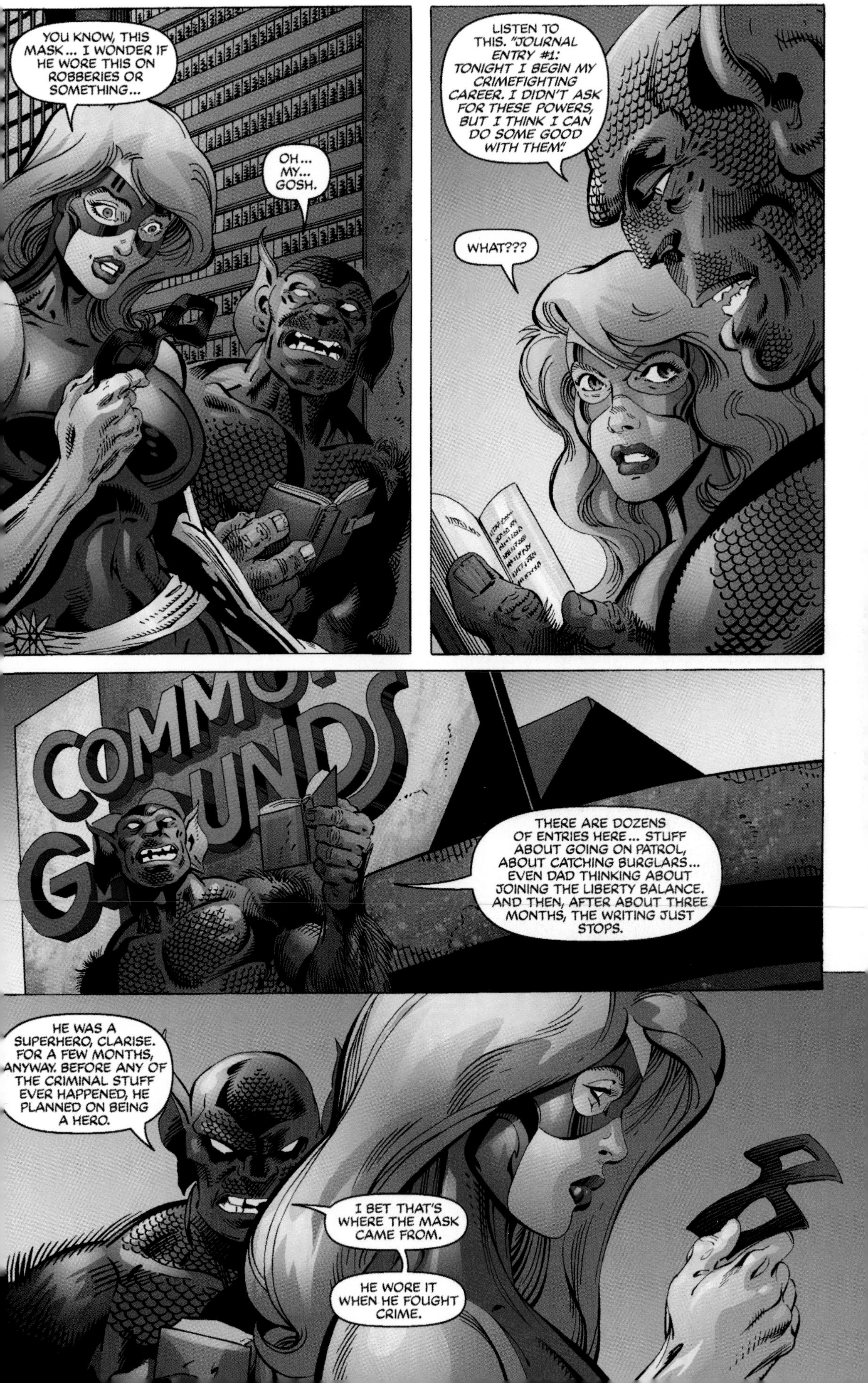

YOU KNOW, THIS MASK... I WONDER IF HE WORE THIS ON ROBBERIES OR SOMETHING...
OH... MY... GOSH.
LISTEN TO THIS. "JOURNAL ENTRY #1: TONIGHT I BEGIN MY CRIMEFIGHTING CAREER. I DIDN'T ASK FOR THESE POWERS, BUT I THINK I CAN DO SOME GOOD WITH THEM."
WHAT???
THERE ARE DOZENS OF ENTRIES HERE... STUFF ABOUT GOING ON PATROL, ABOUT CATCHING BURGLARS... EVEN DAD THINKING ABOUT JOINING THE LIBERTY BALANCE. AND THEN, AFTER ABOUT THREE MONTHS, THE WRITING JUST STOPS.
HE WAS A SUPERHERO, CLARISE. FOR A FEW MONTHS, ANYWAY. BEFORE ANY OF THE CRIMINAL STUFF EVER HAPPENED, HE PLANNED ON BEING A HERO.
I BET THAT'S WHERE THE MASK CAME FROM.
HE WORE IT WHEN HE FOUGHT CRIME.

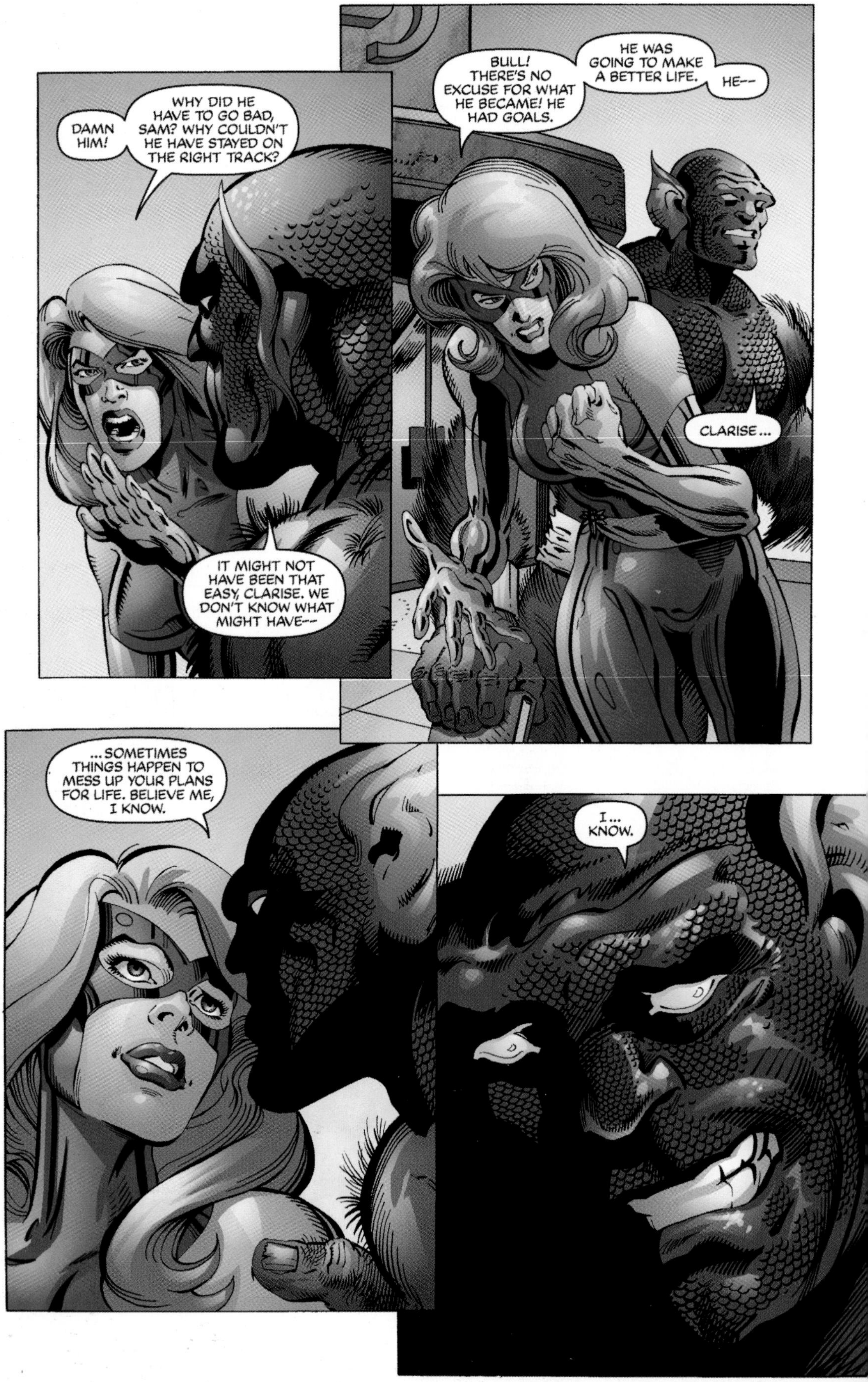
DAMN HIM!
WHY DID HE HAVE TO GO BAD, SAM? WHY COULDN'T HE HAVE STAYED ON THE RIGHT TRACK?
IT MIGHT NOT HAVE BEEN THAT EASY, CLARISE. WE DON'T KNOW WHAT MIGHT HAVE--
BULL! THERE'S NO EXCUSE FOR WHAT HE BECAME! HE HAD GOALS.
HE WAS GOING TO MAKE A BETTER LIFE.
HE--
CLARISE...
...SOMETIMES THINGS HAPPEN TO MESS UP YOUR PLANS FOR LIFE. BELIEVE ME, I KNOW.
I... KNOW.

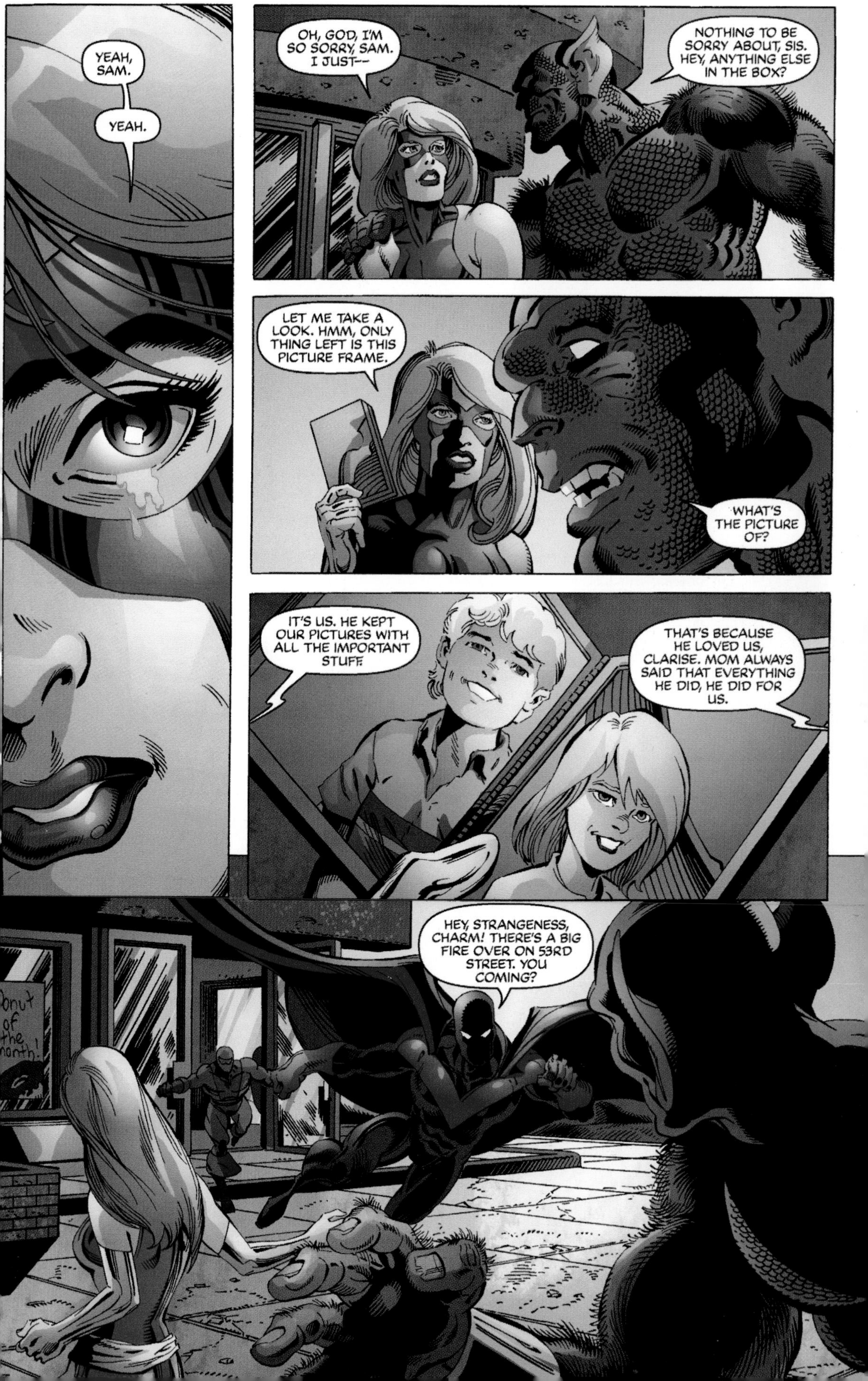
YEAH, SAM.
YEAH.
OH, GOD, I'M SO SORRY, SAM. I JUST--
NOTHING TO BE SORRY ABOUT, SIS. HEY, ANYTHING ELSE IN THE BOX?
LET ME TAKE A LOOK. HMM, ONLY THING LEFT IS THIS PICTURE FRAME.
WHAT'S THE PICTURE OF?
IT'S US. HE KEPT OUR PICTURES WITH ALL THE IMPORTANT STUFF.
THAT'S BECAUSE HE LOVED US, CLARISE. MOM ALWAYS SAID THAT EVERYTHING HE DID, HE DID FOR US.
HEY, STRANGENESS, CHARM! THERE'S A BIG FIRE OVER ON 53RD STREET. YOU COMING?

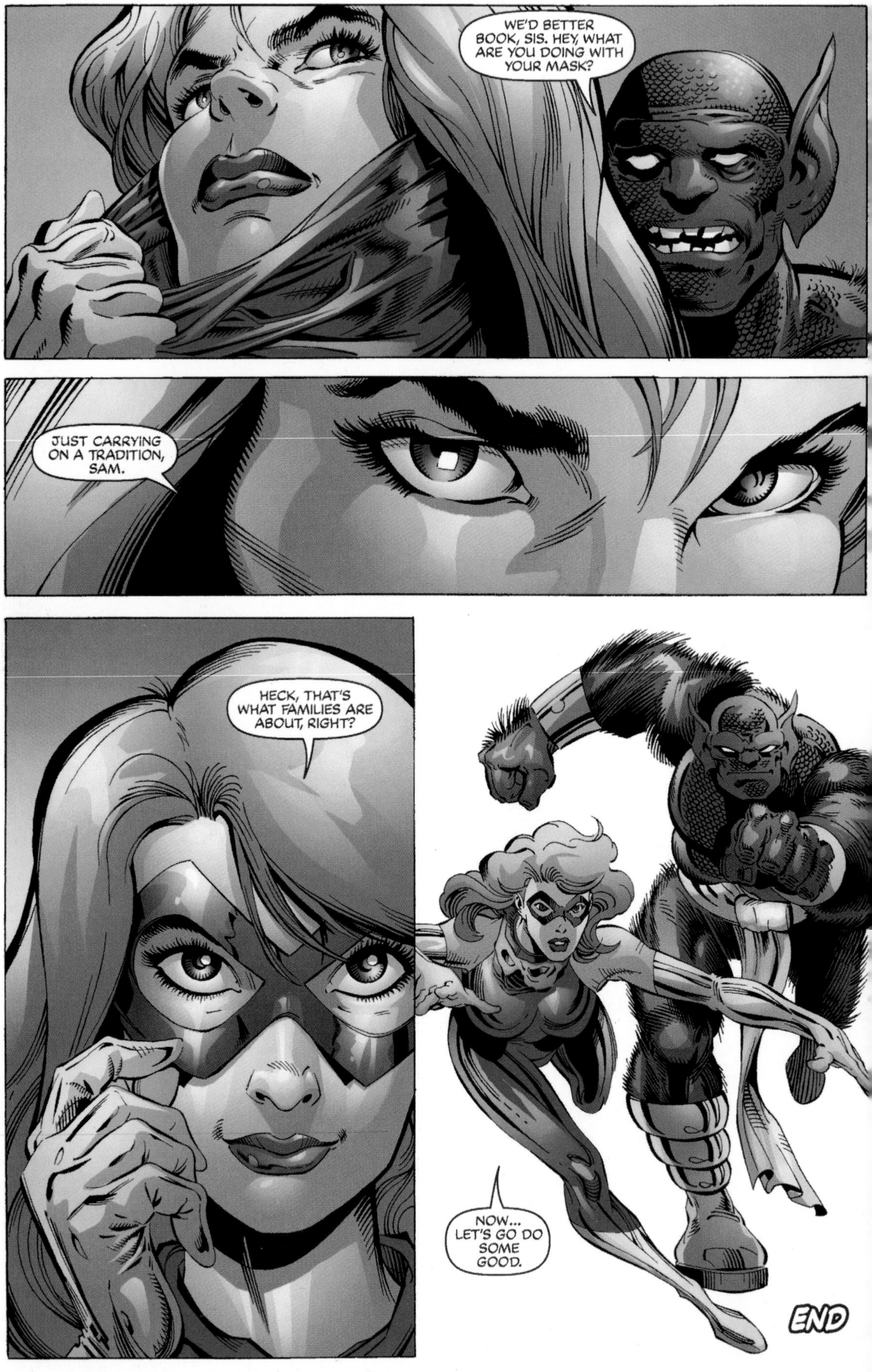
WE'D BETTER BOOK, SIS. HEY, WHAT ARE YOU DOING WITH YOUR MASK?
JUST CARRYING ON A TRADITION, SAM.
HECK, THAT'S WHAT FAMILIES ARE ABOUT, RIGHT?
NOW... LET'S GO DO SOME GOOD.
END

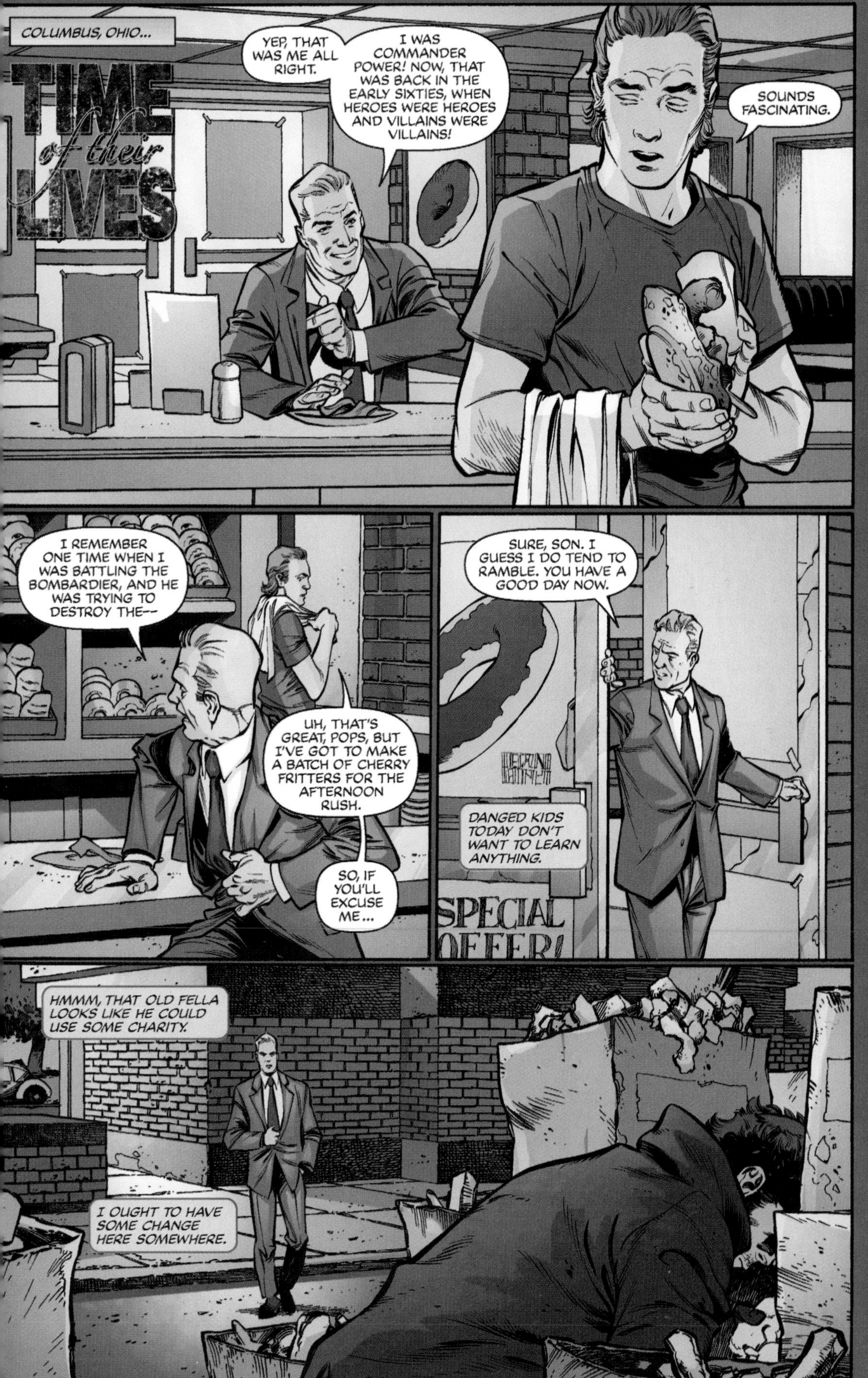
COLUMBUS, OHIO...
TIME of their LIVES
YEP, THAT WAS ME ALL RIGHT.
I WAS COMMANDER POWER! NOW, THAT WAS BACK IN THE EARLY SIXTIES, WHEN HEROES WERE HEROES AND VILLAINS WERE VILLAINS!
SOUNDS FASCINATING.
I REMEMBER ONE TIME WHEN I WAS BATTLING THE BOMBARDIER, AND HE WAS TRYING TO DESTROY THE--
UH, THAT'S GREAT, POPS, BUT I'VE GOT TO MAKE A BATCH OF CHERRY FRITTERS FOR THE AFTERNOON RUSH.
SO, IF YOU'LL EXCUSE ME...
SURE, SON. I GUESS I DO TEND TO RAMBLE. YOU HAVE A GOOD DAY NOW.
DANGED KIDS TODAY DON'T WANT TO LEARN ANYTHING.
SPECIAL OFFER!
HMMM, THAT OLD FELLA LOOKS LIKE HE COULD USE SOME CHARITY.
I OUGHT TO HAVE SOME CHANGE HERE SOMEWHERE.

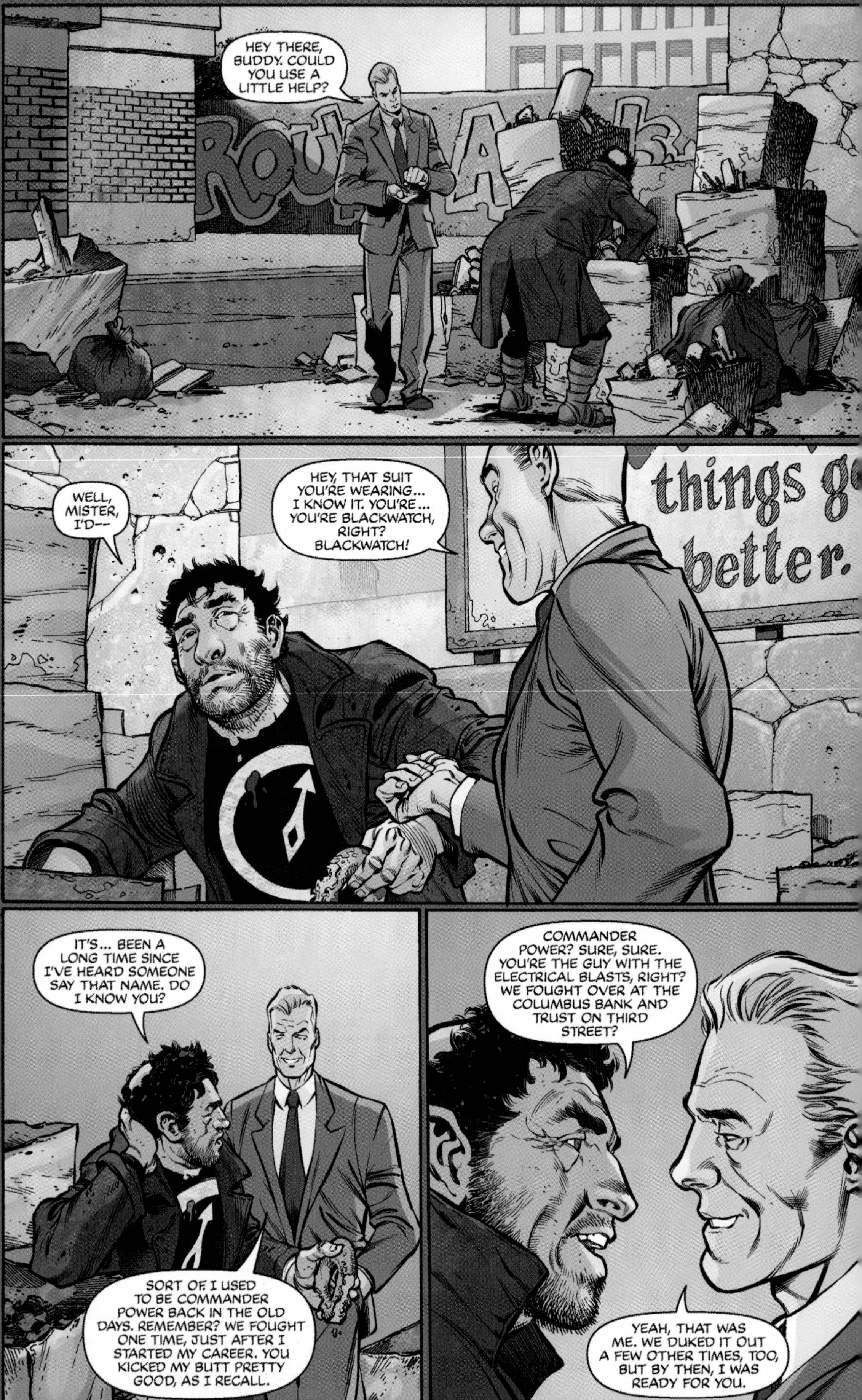
HEY THERE, BUDDY. COULD YOU USE A LITTLE HELP?
WELL, MISTER, I'D--
HEY, THAT SUIT YOU'RE WEARING... I KNOW IT. YOU'RE... YOU'RE BLACKWATCH, RIGHT? BLACKWATCH!
things g
better.
IT'S... BEEN A LONG TIME SINCE I'VE HEARD SOMEONE SAY THAT NAME. DO I KNOW YOU?
SORT OF. I USED TO BE COMMANDER POWER BACK IN THE OLD DAYS. REMEMBER? WE FOUGHT ONE TIME, JUST AFTER I STARTED MY CAREER. YOU KICKED MY BUTT PRETTY GOOD, AS I RECALL.
COMMANDER POWER? SURE, SURE. YOU'RE THE GUY WITH THE ELECTRICAL BLASTS, RIGHT? WE FOUGHT OVER AT THE COLUMBUS BANK AND TRUST ON THIRD STREET?
YEAH, THAT WAS ME. WE DUKED IT OUT A FEW OTHER TIMES, TOO, BUT BY THEN, I WAS READY FOR YOU.

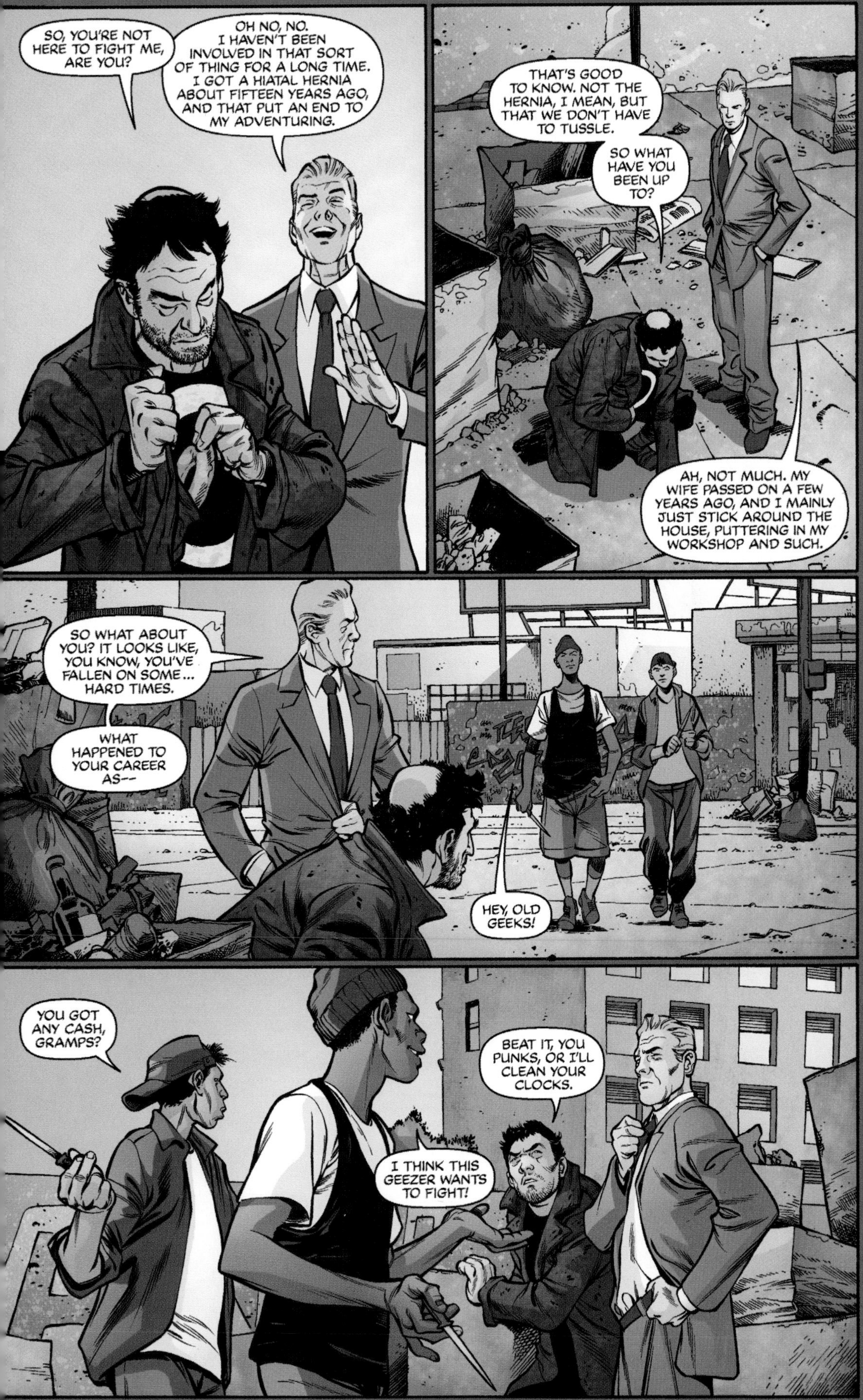
SO, YOU'RE NOT HERE TO FIGHT ME, ARE YOU?
OH NO, NO. I HAVEN'T BEEN INVOLVED IN THAT SORT OF THING FOR A LONG TIME. I GOT A HIATAL HERNIA ABOUT FIFTEEN YEARS AGO, AND THAT PUT AN END TO MY ADVENTURING.
THAT'S GOOD TO KNOW. NOT THE HERNIA, I MEAN, BUT THAT WE DON'T HAVE TO TUSSLE.
SO WHAT HAVE YOU BEEN UP TO?
AH, NOT MUCH. MY WIFE PASSED ON A FEW YEARS AGO, AND I MAINLY JUST STICK AROUND THE HOUSE, PUTTERING IN MY WORKSHOP AND SUCH.
SO WHAT ABOUT YOU? IT LOOKS LIKE, YOU KNOW, YOU'VE FALLEN ON SOME... HARD TIMES.
WHAT HAPPENED TO YOUR CAREER AS--
HEY, OLD GEEKS!
YOU GOT ANY CASH, GRAMPS?
BEAT IT, YOU PUNKS, OR I'LL CLEAN YOUR CLOCKS.
I THINK THIS GEEZER WANTS TO FIGHT!

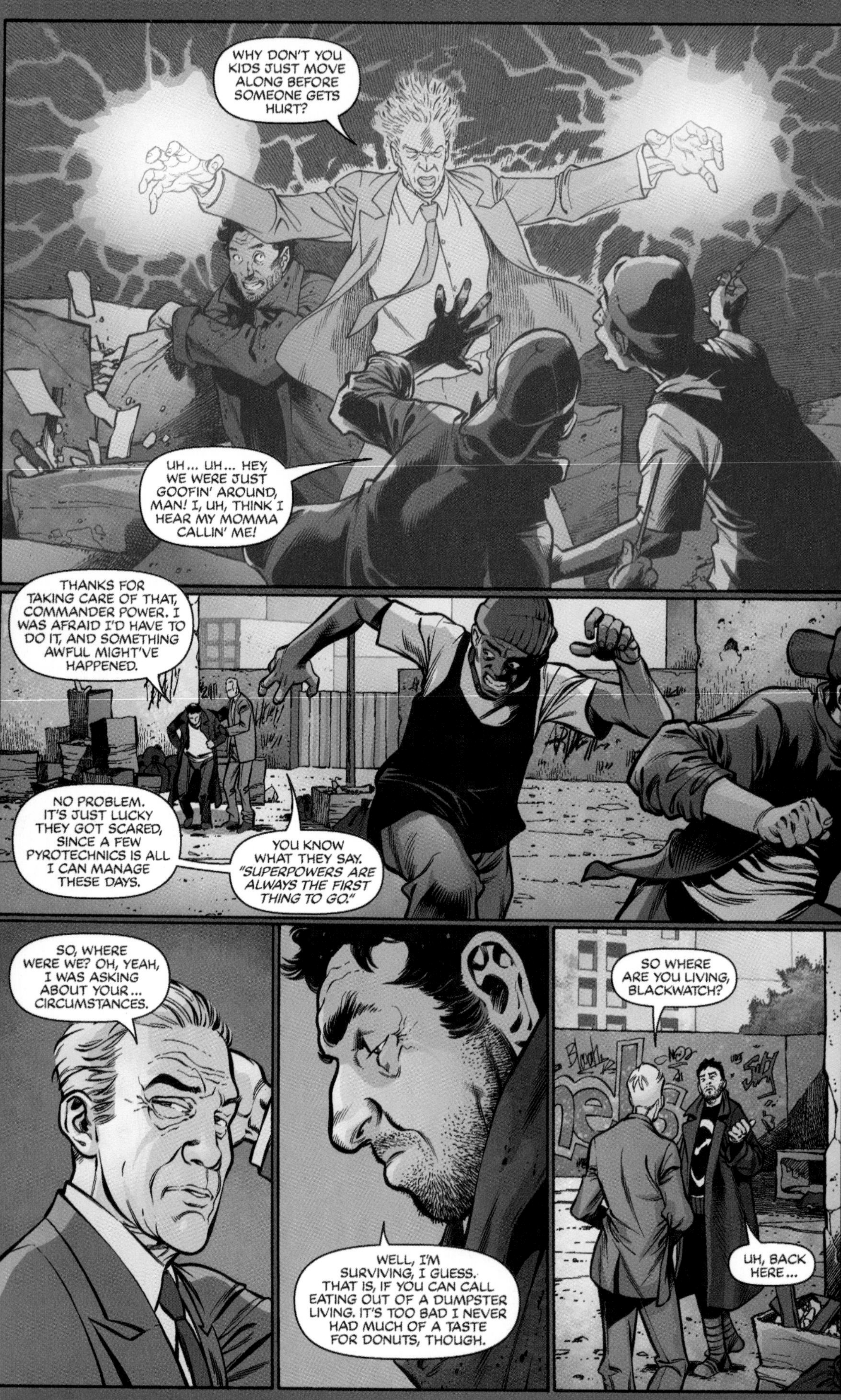
WHY DON'T YOU KIDS JUST MOVE ALONG BEFORE SOMEONE GETS HURT?
UH... UH... HEY, WE WERE JUST GOOFIN' AROUND, MAN! I, UH, THINK I HEAR MY MOMMA CALLIN' ME!
THANKS FOR TAKING CARE OF THAT, COMMANDER POWER. I WAS AFRAID I'D HAVE TO DO IT, AND SOMETHING AWFUL MIGHT'VE HAPPENED.
NO PROBLEM. IT'S JUST LUCKY THEY GOT SCARED, SINCE A FEW PYROTECHNICS IS ALL I CAN MANAGE THESE DAYS.
YOU KNOW WHAT THEY SAY. "SUPERPOWERS ARE ALWAYS THE FIRST THING TO GO."
SO, WHERE WERE WE? OH, YEAH, I WAS ASKING ABOUT YOUR... CIRCUMSTANCES.
WELL, I'M SURVIVING, I GUESS. THAT IS, IF YOU CAN CALL EATING OUT OF A DUMPSTER LIVING. IT'S TOO BAD I NEVER HAD MUCH OF A TASTE FOR DONUTS, THOUGH.
SO WHERE ARE YOU LIVING, BLACKWATCH?
UH, BACK HERE...

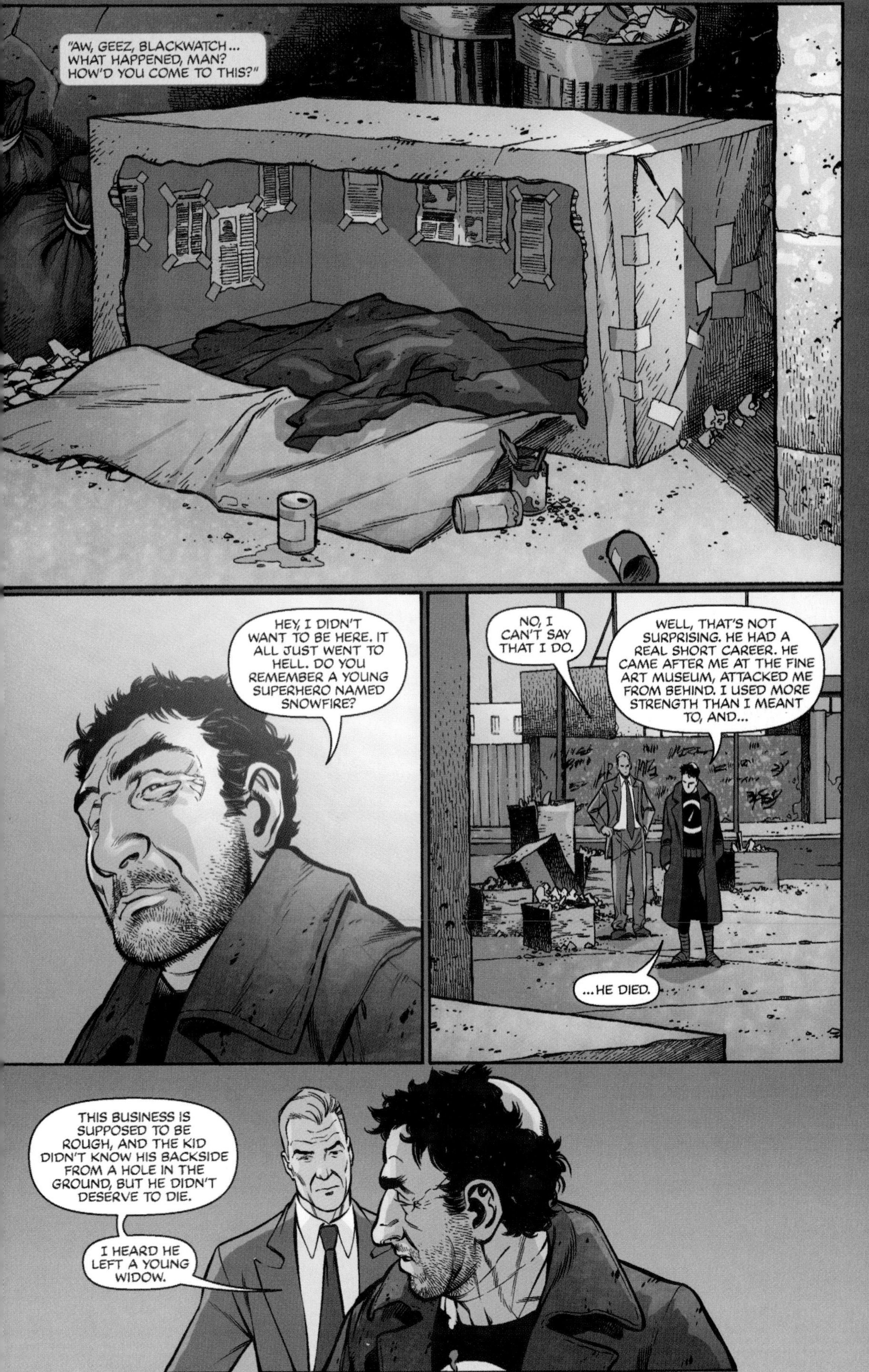
"AW, GEEZ, BLACKWATCH... WHAT HAPPENED, MAN? HOW'D YOU COME TO THIS?"
HEY, I DIDN'T WANT TO BE HERE. IT ALL JUST WENT TO HELL. DO YOU REMEMBER A YOUNG SUPERHERO NAMED SNOWFIRE?
NO, I CAN'T SAY THAT I DO.
WELL, THAT'S NOT SURPRISING. HE HAD A REAL SHORT CAREER. HE CAME AFTER ME AT THE FINE ART MUSEUM, ATTACKED ME FROM BEHIND. I USED MORE STRENGTH THAN I MEANT TO, AND...
...HE DIED.
THIS BUSINESS IS SUPPOSED TO BE ROUGH, AND THE KID DIDN'T KNOW HIS BACKSIDE FROM A HOLE IN THE GROUND, BUT HE DIDN'T DESERVE TO DIE.
I HEARD HE LEFT A YOUNG WIDOW.

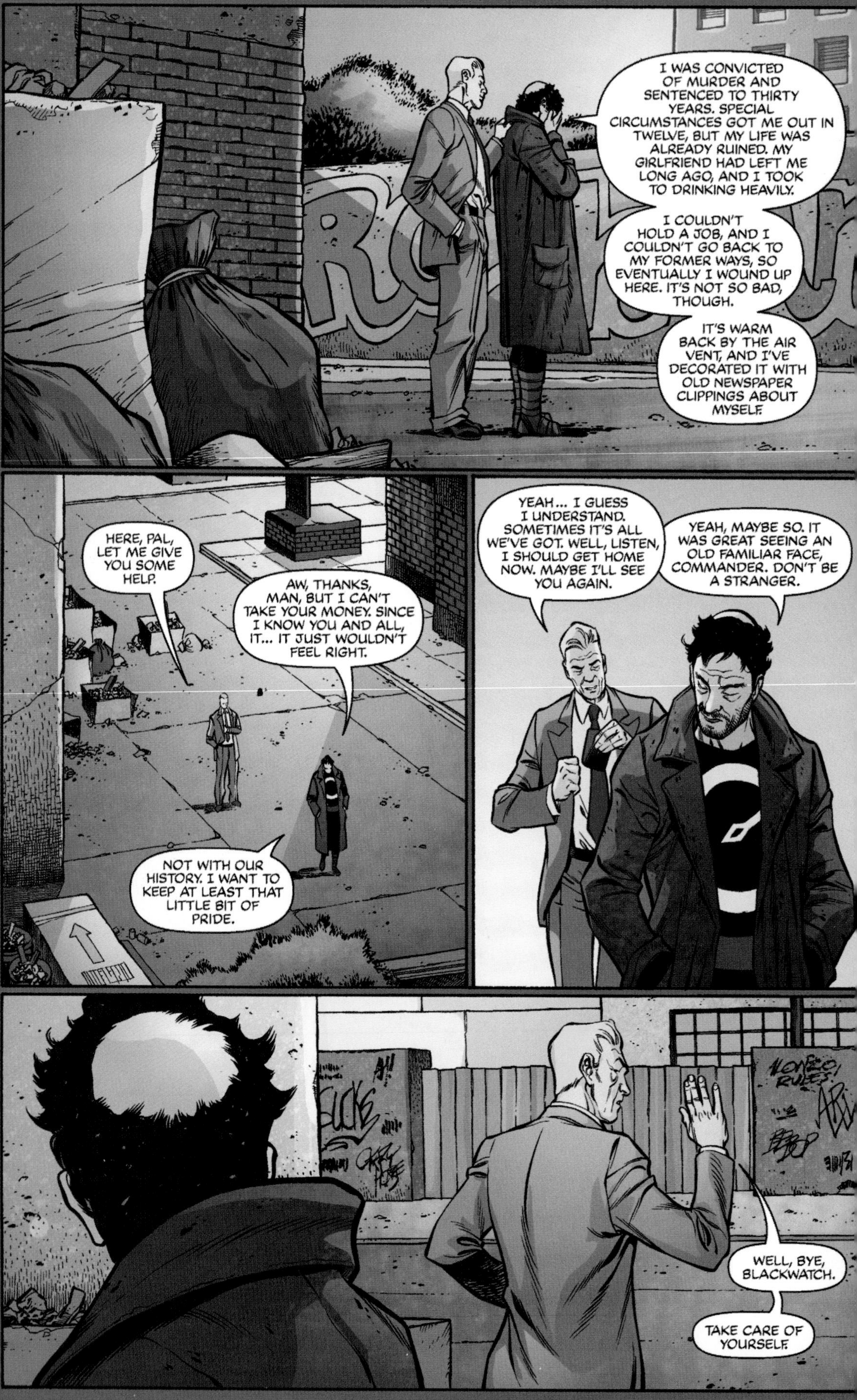
I WAS CONVICTED OF MURDER AND SENTENCED TO THIRTY YEARS. SPECIAL CIRCUMSTANCES GOT ME OUT IN TWELVE, BUT MY LIFE WAS ALREADY RUINED. MY GIRLFRIEND HAD LEFT ME LONG AGO, AND I TOOK TO DRINKING HEAVILY.
I COULDN'T HOLD A JOB, AND I COULDN'T GO BACK TO MY FORMER WAYS, SO EVENTUALLY I WOUND UP HERE. IT'S NOT SO BAD, THOUGH.
IT'S WARM BACK BY THE AIR VENT, AND I'VE DECORATED IT WITH OLD NEWSPAPER CLIPPINGS ABOUT MYSELF.
HERE, PAL, LET ME GIVE YOU SOME HELP.
AW, THANKS, MAN, BUT I CAN'T TAKE YOUR MONEY. SINCE I KNOW YOU AND ALL, IT... IT JUST WOULDN'T FEEL RIGHT.
NOT WITH OUR HISTORY. I WANT TO KEEP AT LEAST THAT LITTLE BIT OF PRIDE.
YEAH... I GUESS I UNDERSTAND. SOMETIMES IT'S ALL WE'VE GOT. WELL, LISTEN, I SHOULD GET HOME NOW. MAYBE I'LL SEE YOU AGAIN.
YEAH, MAYBE SO. IT WAS GREAT SEEING AN OLD FAMILIAR FACE, COMMANDER. DON'T BE A STRANGER.
WELL, BYE, BLACKWATCH.
TAKE CARE OF YOURSELF.

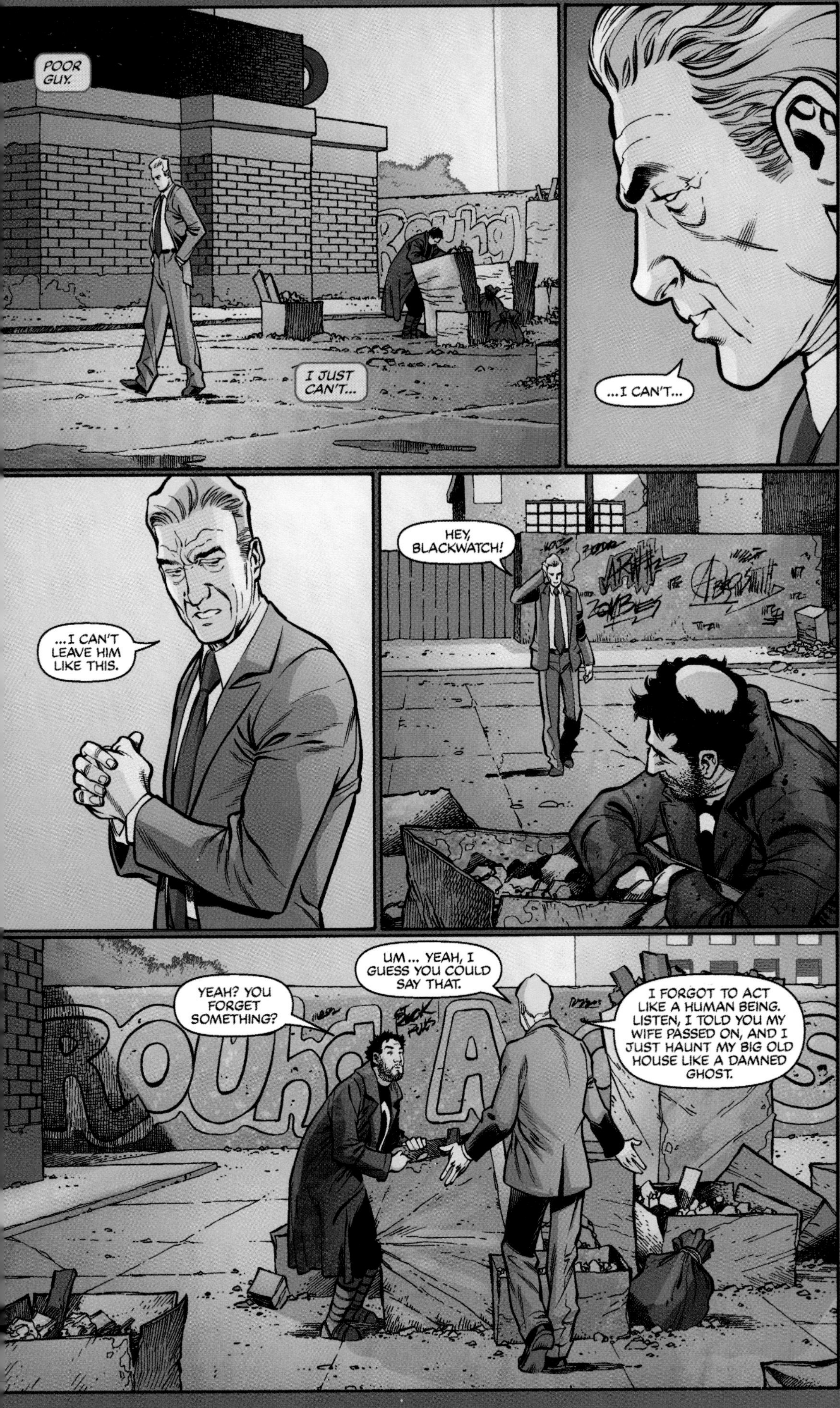
POOR GUY.
I JUST CAN'T...
...I CAN'T...
...I CAN'T LEAVE HIM LIKE THIS.
HEY, BLACKWATCH!
YEAH? YOU FORGET SOMETHING?
UM... YEAH, I GUESS YOU COULD SAY THAT.
I FORGOT TO ACT LIKE A HUMAN BEING. LISTEN, I TOLD YOU MY WIFE PASSED ON, AND I JUST HAUNT MY BIG OLD HOUSE LIKE A DAMNED GHOST.

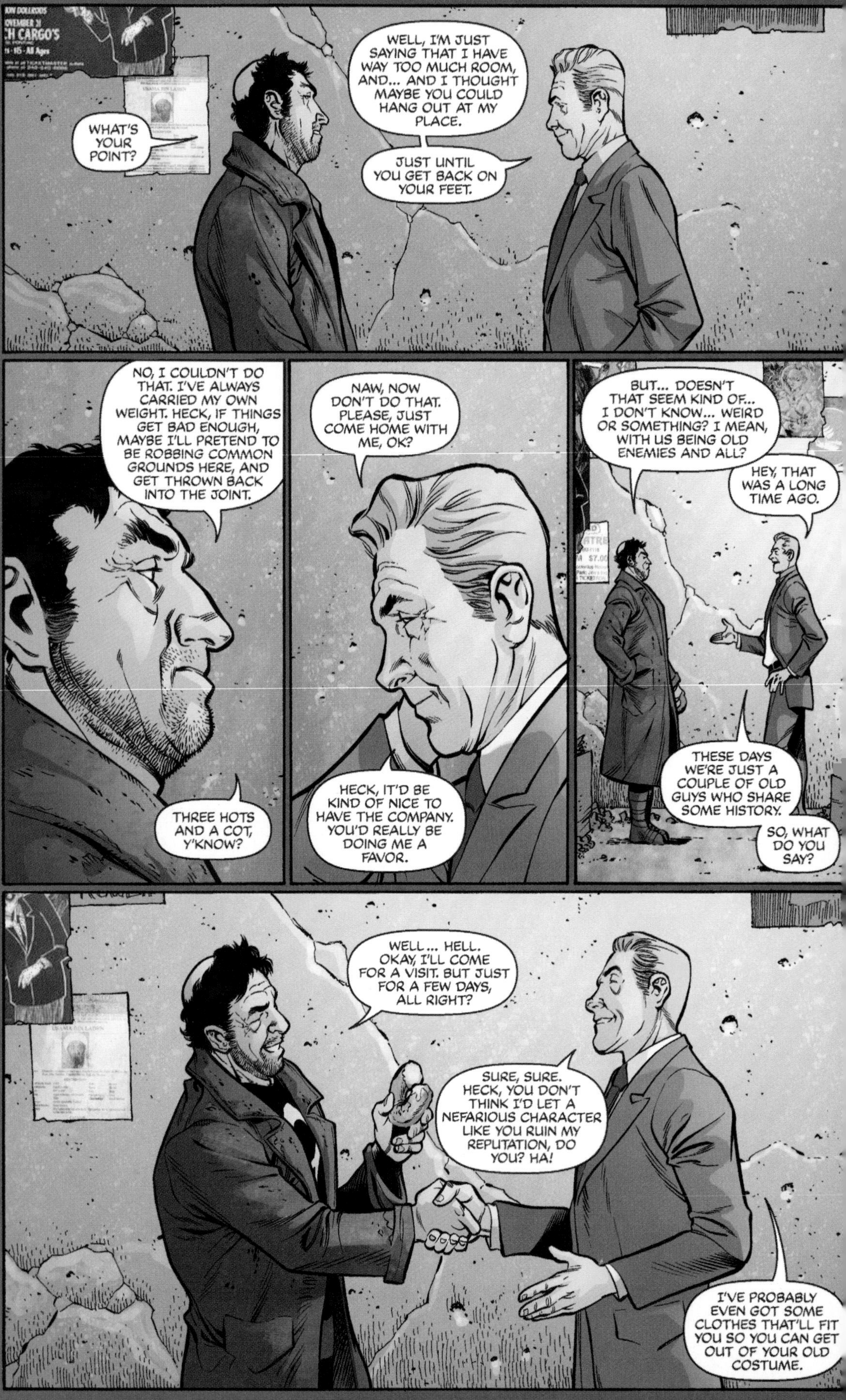
WHAT'S YOUR POINT?
WELL, I'M JUST SAYING THAT I HAVE WAY TOO MUCH ROOM, AND... AND I THOUGHT MAYBE YOU COULD HANG OUT AT MY PLACE.
JUST UNTIL YOU GET BACK ON YOUR FEET.
NO, I COULDN'T DO THAT. I'VE ALWAYS CARRIED MY OWN WEIGHT. HECK, IF THINGS GET BAD ENOUGH, MAYBE I'LL PRETEND TO BE ROBBING COMMON GROUNDS HERE, AND GET THROWN BACK INTO THE JOINT.
THREE HOTS AND A COT, Y'KNOW?
NAW, NOW DON'T DO THAT. PLEASE, JUST COME HOME WITH ME, OK?
HECK, IT'D BE KIND OF NICE TO HAVE THE COMPANY. YOU'D REALLY BE DOING ME A FAVOR.
BUT... DOESN'T THAT SEEM KIND OF... I DON'T KNOW... WEIRD OR SOMETHING? I MEAN, WITH US BEING OLD ENEMIES AND ALL?
HEY, THAT WAS A LONG TIME AGO.
THESE DAYS WE'RE JUST A COUPLE OF OLD GUYS WHO SHARE SOME HISTORY.
SO, WHAT DO YOU SAY?
WELL... HELL. OKAY, I'LL COME FOR A VISIT. BUT JUST FOR A FEW DAYS, ALL RIGHT?
SURE, SURE. HECK, YOU DON'T THINK I'D LET A NEFARIOUS CHARACTER LIKE YOU RUIN MY REPUTATION, DO YOU? HA!
I'VE PROBABLY EVEN GOT SOME CLOTHES THAT'LL FIT YOU SO YOU CAN GET OUT OF YOUR OLD COSTUME.

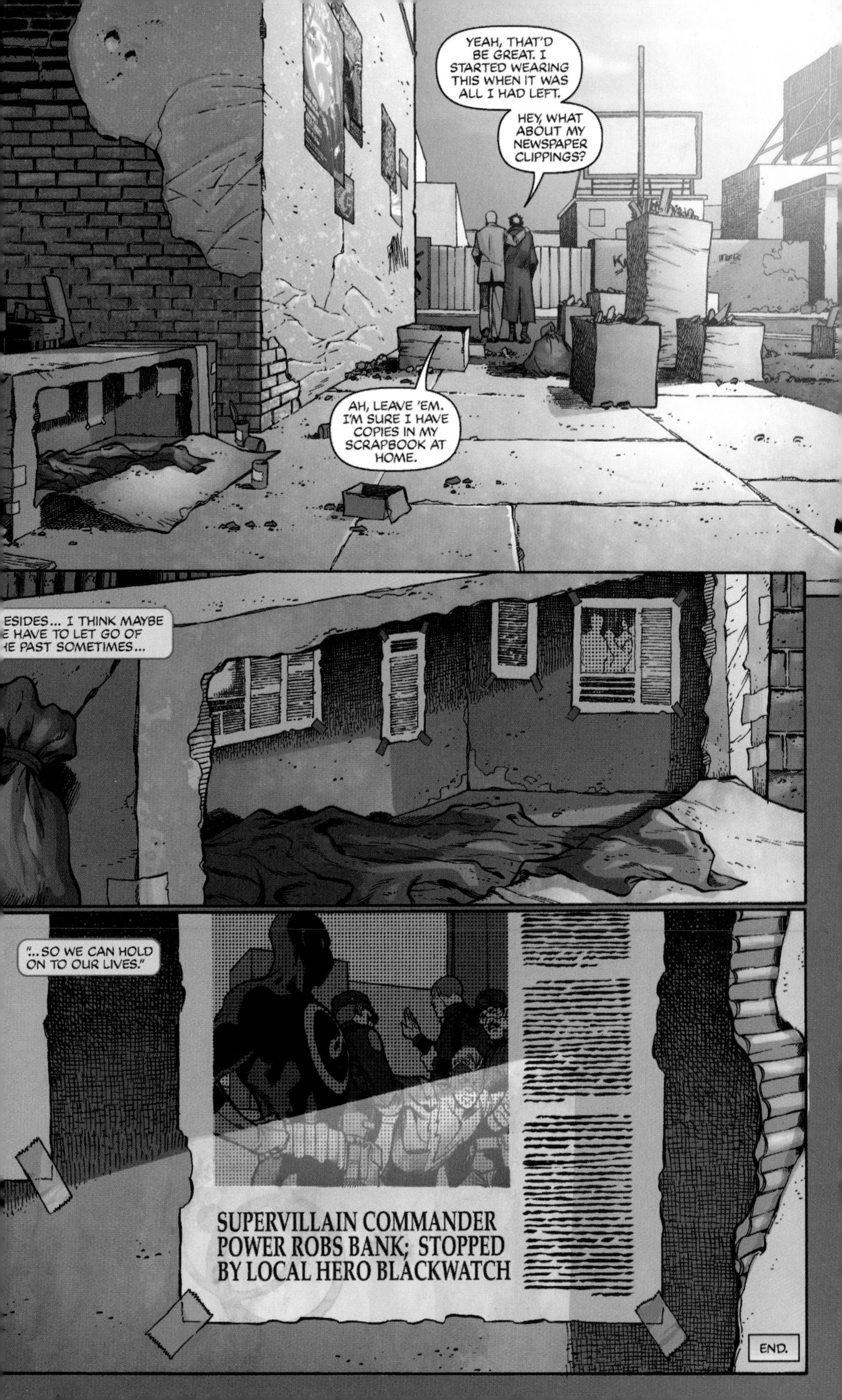

YEAH, THAT'D BE GREAT. I STARTED WEARING THIS WHEN IT WAS ALL I HAD LEFT.
HEY, WHAT ABOUT MY NEWSPAPER CLIPPINGS?
AH, LEAVE 'EM. I'M SURE I HAVE COPIES IN MY SCRAPBOOK AT HOME.
ESIDES... I THINK MAYBE E HAVE TO LET GO OF HE PAST SOMETIMES...
"...SO WE CAN HOLD ON TO OUR LIVES."
SUPERVILLAIN COMMANDER POWER ROBS BANK; STOPPED BY LOCAL HERO BLACKWATCH
END.

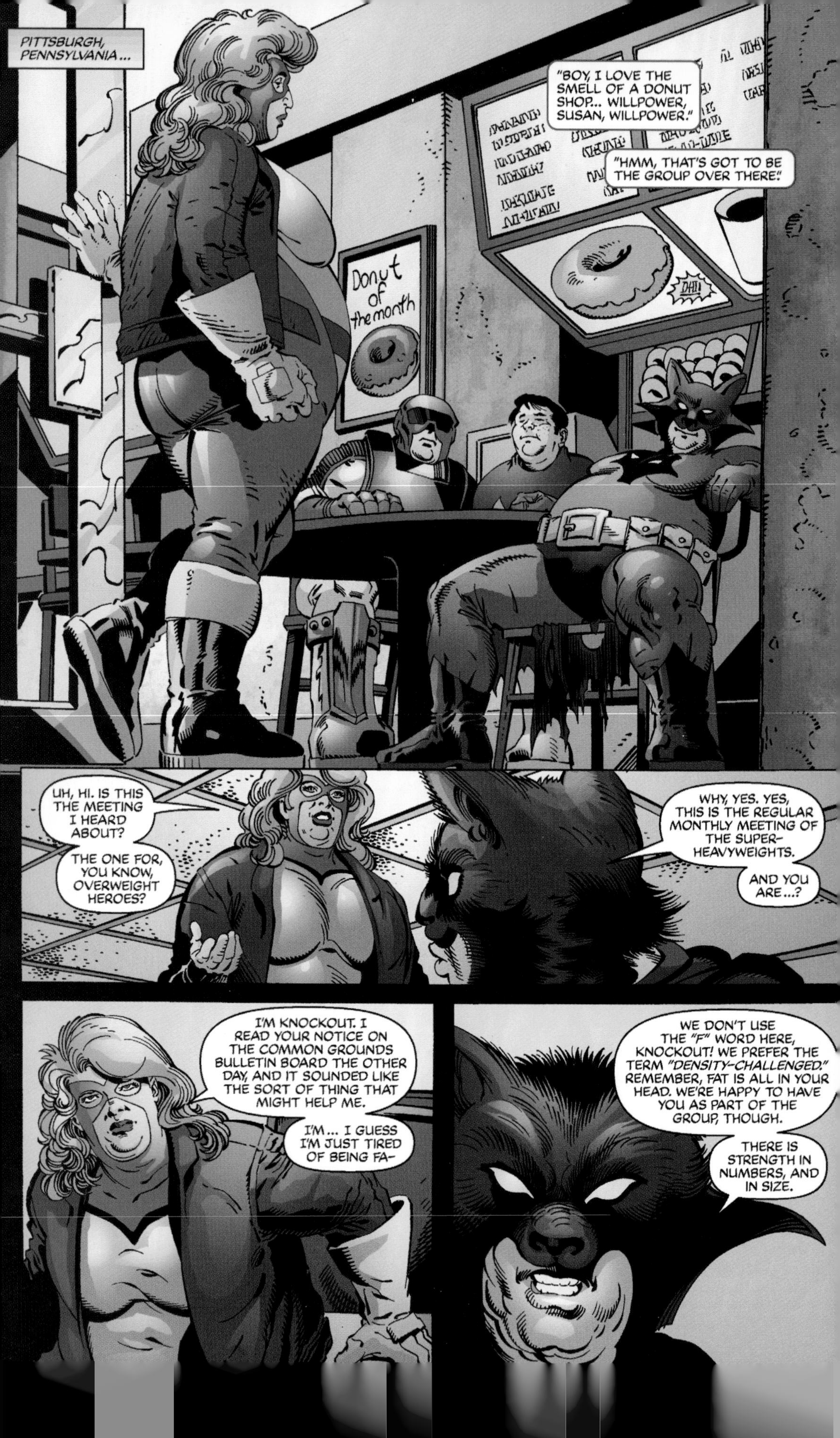
PITTSBURGH, PENNSYLVANIA...
"BOY, I LOVE THE SMELL OF A DONUT SHOP... WILLPOWER, SUSAN, WILLPOWER."
"HMM, THAT'S GOT TO BE THE GROUP OVER THERE."
Donut of the month
UH, HI. IS THIS THE MEETING I HEARD ABOUT?
THE ONE FOR, YOU KNOW, OVERWEIGHT HEROES?
WHY, YES. YES, THIS IS THE REGULAR MONTHLY MEETING OF THE SUPER-HEAVYWEIGHTS.
AND YOU ARE...?
I'M KNOCKOUT. I READ YOUR NOTICE ON THE COMMON GROUNDS BULLETIN BOARD THE OTHER DAY, AND IT SOUNDED LIKE THE SORT OF THING THAT MIGHT HELP ME.
I'M... I GUESS I'M JUST TIRED OF BEING FA-
WE DON'T USE THE "F" WORD HERE, KNOCKOUT! WE PREFER THE TERM "DENSITY-CHALLENGED." REMEMBER, FAT IS ALL IN YOUR HEAD. WE'RE HAPPY TO HAVE YOU AS PART OF THE GROUP, THOUGH.
THERE IS STRENGTH IN NUMBERS, AND IN SIZE.

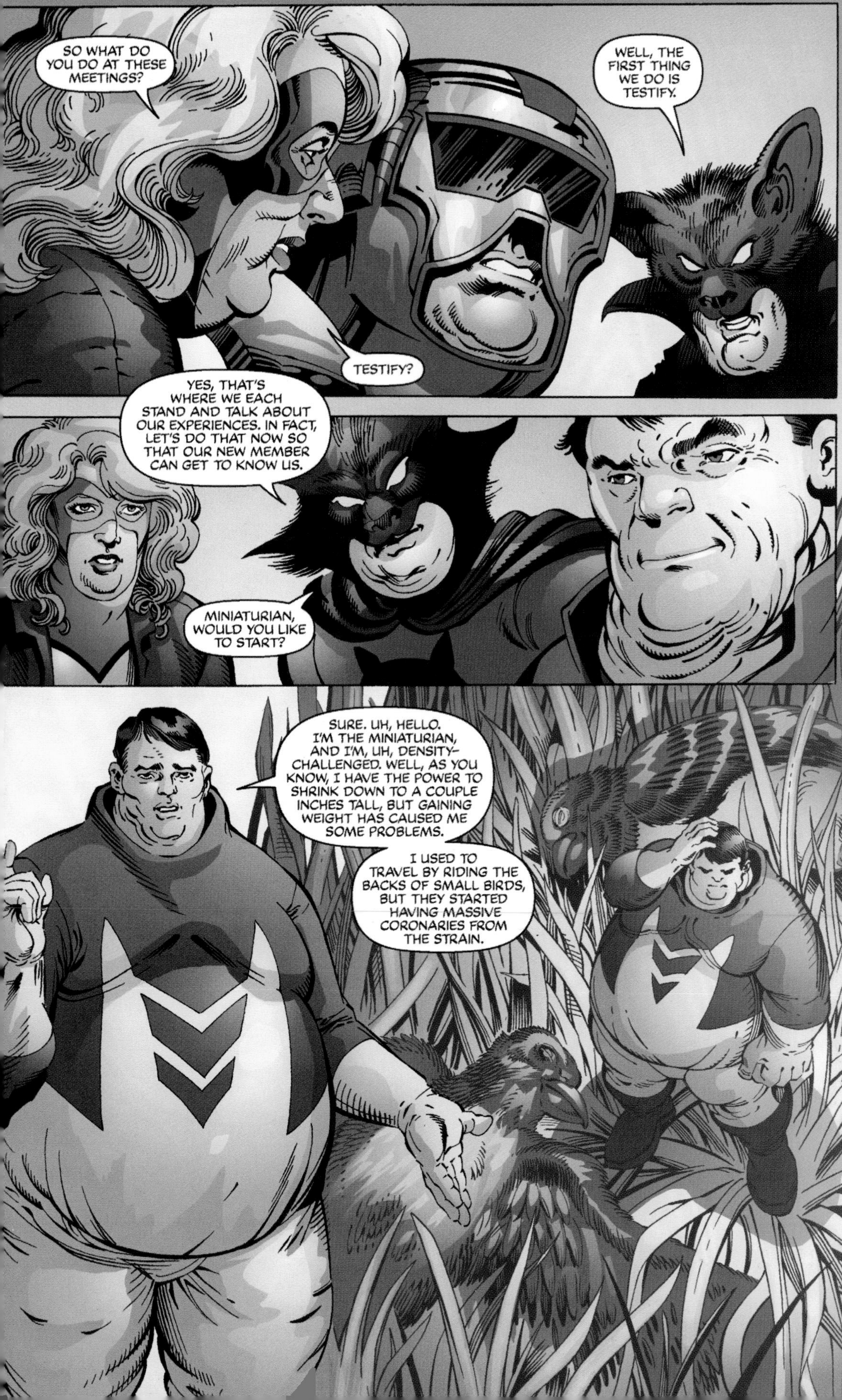
SO WHAT DO YOU DO AT THESE MEETINGS?
WELL, THE FIRST THING WE DO IS TESTIFY.
TESTIFY?
YES, THAT'S WHERE WE EACH STAND AND TALK ABOUT OUR EXPERIENCES. IN FACT, LET'S DO THAT NOW SO THAT OUR NEW MEMBER CAN GET TO KNOW US.
MINIATURIAN, WOULD YOU LIKE TO START?
SURE. UH, HELLO. I'M THE MINIATURIAN, AND I'M, UH, DENSITY-CHALLENGED. WELL, AS YOU KNOW, I HAVE THE POWER TO SHRINK DOWN TO A COUPLE INCHES TALL, BUT GAINING WEIGHT HAS CAUSED ME SOME PROBLEMS.
I USED TO TRAVEL BY RIDING THE BACKS OF SMALL BIRDS, BUT THEY STARTED HAVING MASSIVE CORONARIES FROM THE STRAIN.

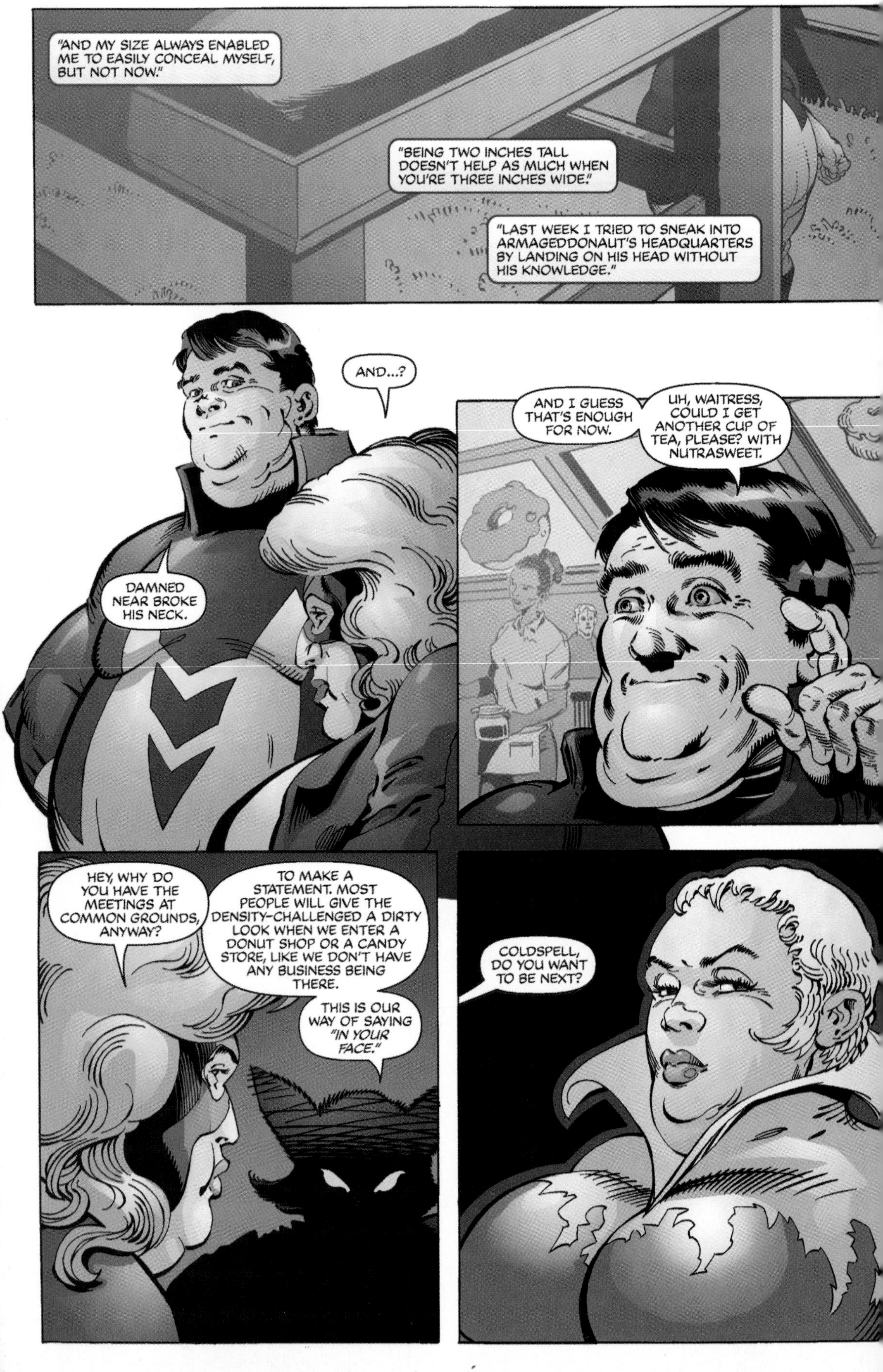
"AND MY SIZE ALWAYS ENABLED ME TO EASILY CONCEAL MYSELF, BUT NOT NOW."
"BEING TWO INCHES TALL DOESN'T HELP AS MUCH WHEN YOU'RE THREE INCHES WIDE."
"LAST WEEK I TRIED TO SNEAK INTO ARMAGEDDONAUT'S HEADQUARTERS BY LANDING ON HIS HEAD WITHOUT HIS KNOWLEDGE."
AND...?
DAMNED NEAR BROKE HIS NECK.
AND I GUESS THAT'S ENOUGH FOR NOW.
UH, WAITRESS, COULD I GET ANOTHER CUP OF TEA, PLEASE? WITH NUTRASWEET.
HEY, WHY DO YOU HAVE THE MEETINGS AT COMMON GROUNDS, ANYWAY?
TO MAKE A STATEMENT. MOST PEOPLE WILL GIVE THE DENSITY-CHALLENGED A DIRTY LOOK WHEN WE ENTER A DONUT SHOP OR A CANDY STORE, LIKE WE DON'T HAVE ANY BUSINESS BEING THERE.
THIS IS OUR WAY OF SAYING *"IN YOUR FACE."*
COLDSPELL, DO YOU WANT TO BE NEXT?

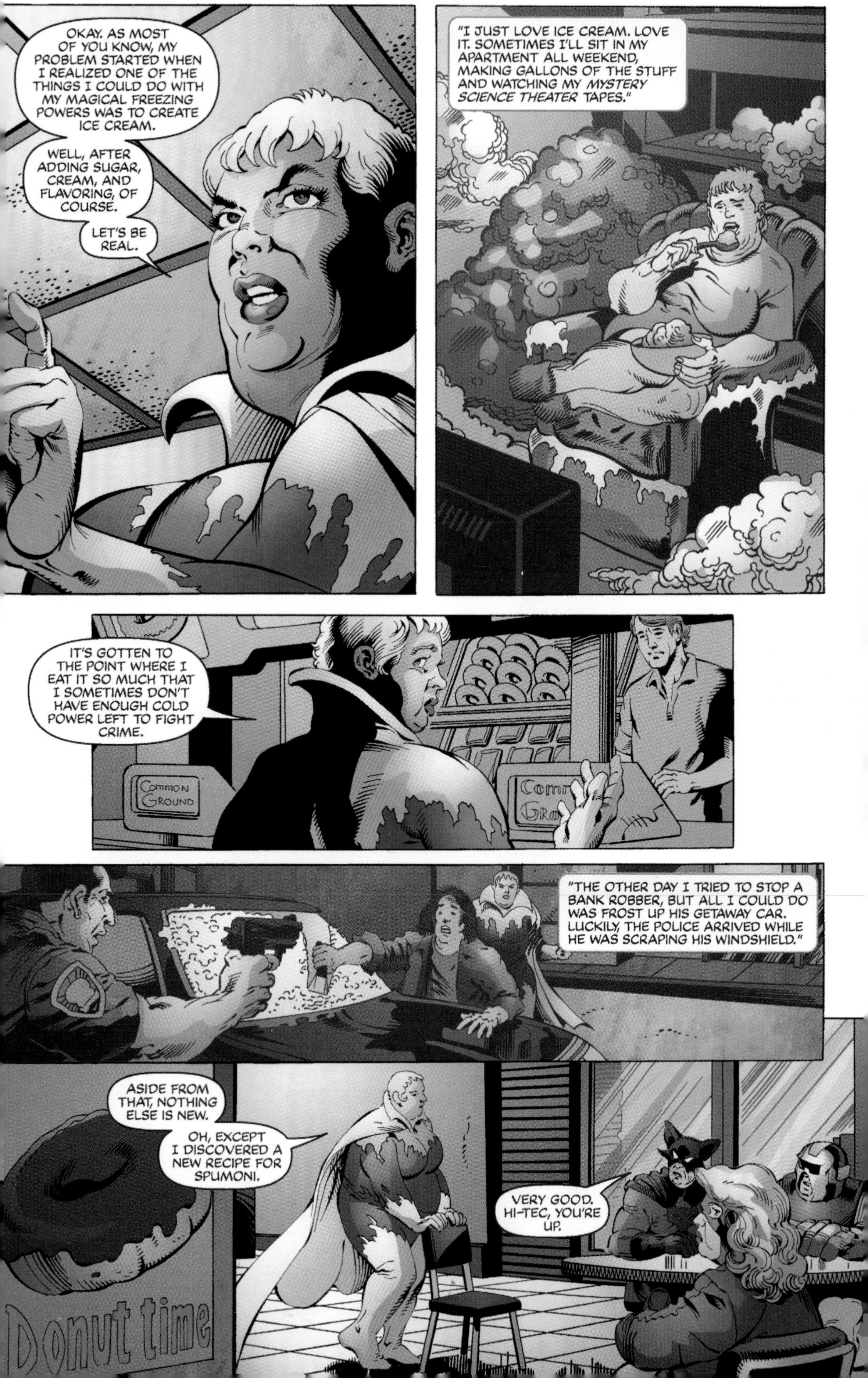

OKAY. AS MOST OF YOU KNOW, MY PROBLEM STARTED WHEN I REALIZED ONE OF THE THINGS I COULD DO WITH MY MAGICAL FREEZING POWERS WAS TO CREATE ICE CREAM.
WELL, AFTER ADDING SUGAR, CREAM, AND FLAVORING, OF COURSE.
LET'S BE REAL.
"I JUST LOVE ICE CREAM. LOVE IT. SOMETIMES I'LL SIT IN MY APARTMENT ALL WEEKEND, MAKING GALLONS OF THE STUFF AND WATCHING MY *MYSTERY SCIENCE THEATER* TAPES."
IT'S GOTTEN TO THE POINT WHERE I EAT IT SO MUCH THAT I SOMETIMES DON'T HAVE ENOUGH COLD POWER LEFT TO FIGHT CRIME.
Common Ground
"THE OTHER DAY I TRIED TO STOP A BANK ROBBER, BUT ALL I COULD DO WAS FROST UP HIS GETAWAY CAR. LUCKILY, THE POLICE ARRIVED WHILE HE WAS SCRAPING HIS WINDSHIELD."
ASIDE FROM THAT, NOTHING ELSE IS NEW.
OH, EXCEPT I DISCOVERED A NEW RECIPE FOR SPUMONI.
VERY GOOD. HI-TEC, YOU'RE UP.
Donut time

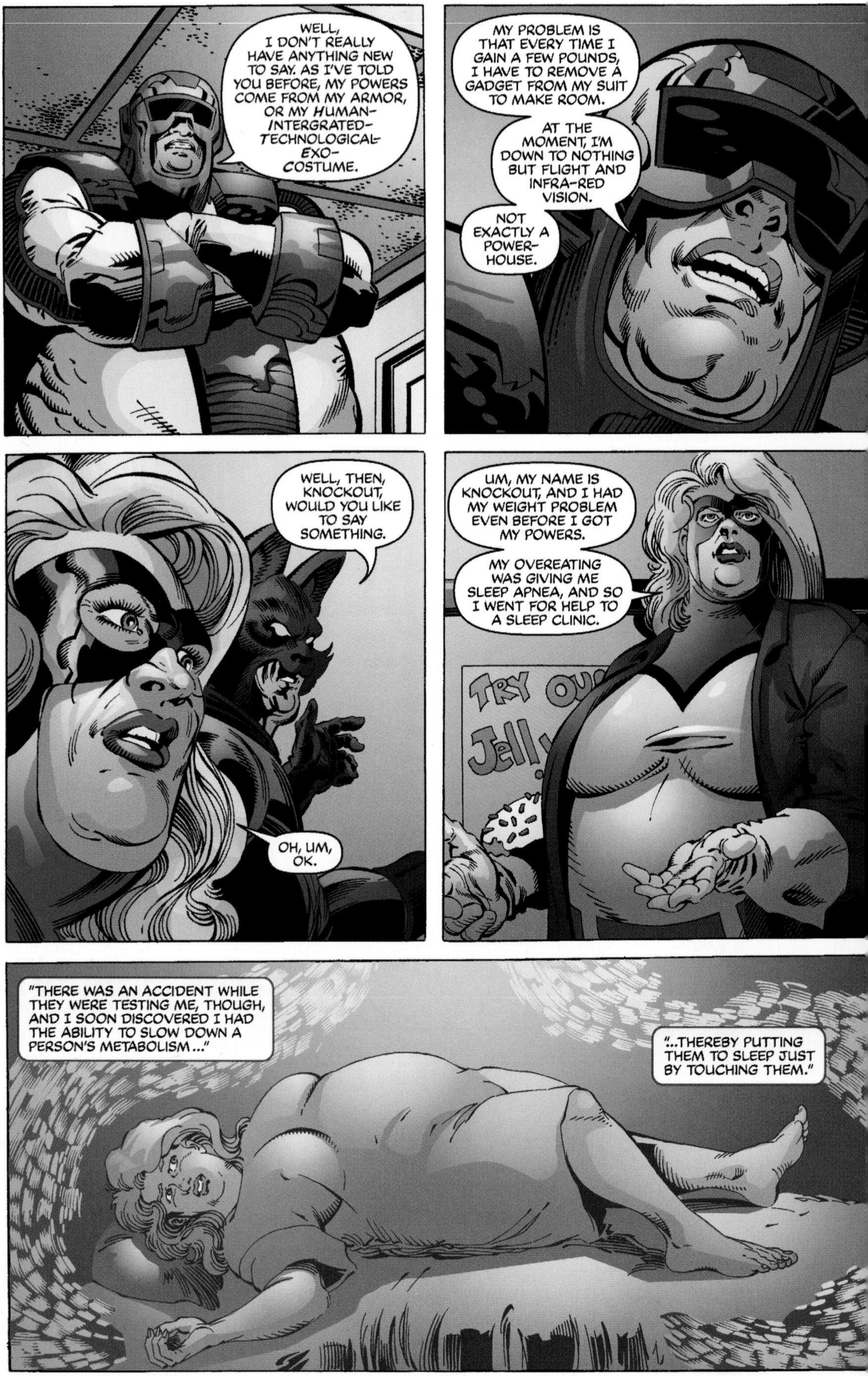
WELL, I DON'T REALLY HAVE ANYTHING NEW TO SAY. AS I'VE TOLD YOU BEFORE, MY POWERS COME FROM MY ARMOR, OR MY HUMAN-INTERGRATED-TECHNOLOGICAL-EXO-COSTUME.
MY PROBLEM IS THAT EVERY TIME I GAIN A FEW POUNDS, I HAVE TO REMOVE A GADGET FROM MY SUIT TO MAKE ROOM.
AT THE MOMENT, I'M DOWN TO NOTHING BUT FLIGHT AND INFRA-RED VISION.
NOT EXACTLY A POWER-HOUSE.
WELL, THEN, KNOCKOUT, WOULD YOU LIKE TO SAY SOMETHING.
OH, UM, OK.
UM, MY NAME IS KNOCKOUT, AND I HAD MY WEIGHT PROBLEM EVEN BEFORE I GOT MY POWERS.
MY OVEREATING WAS GIVING ME SLEEP APNEA, AND SO I WENT FOR HELP TO A SLEEP CLINIC.
"THERE WAS AN ACCIDENT WHILE THEY WERE TESTING ME, THOUGH, AND I SOON DISCOVERED I HAD THE ABILITY TO SLOW DOWN A PERSON'S METABOLISM..."
"..THEREBY PUTTING THEM TO SLEEP JUST BY TOUCHING THEM."

"Glory Days"

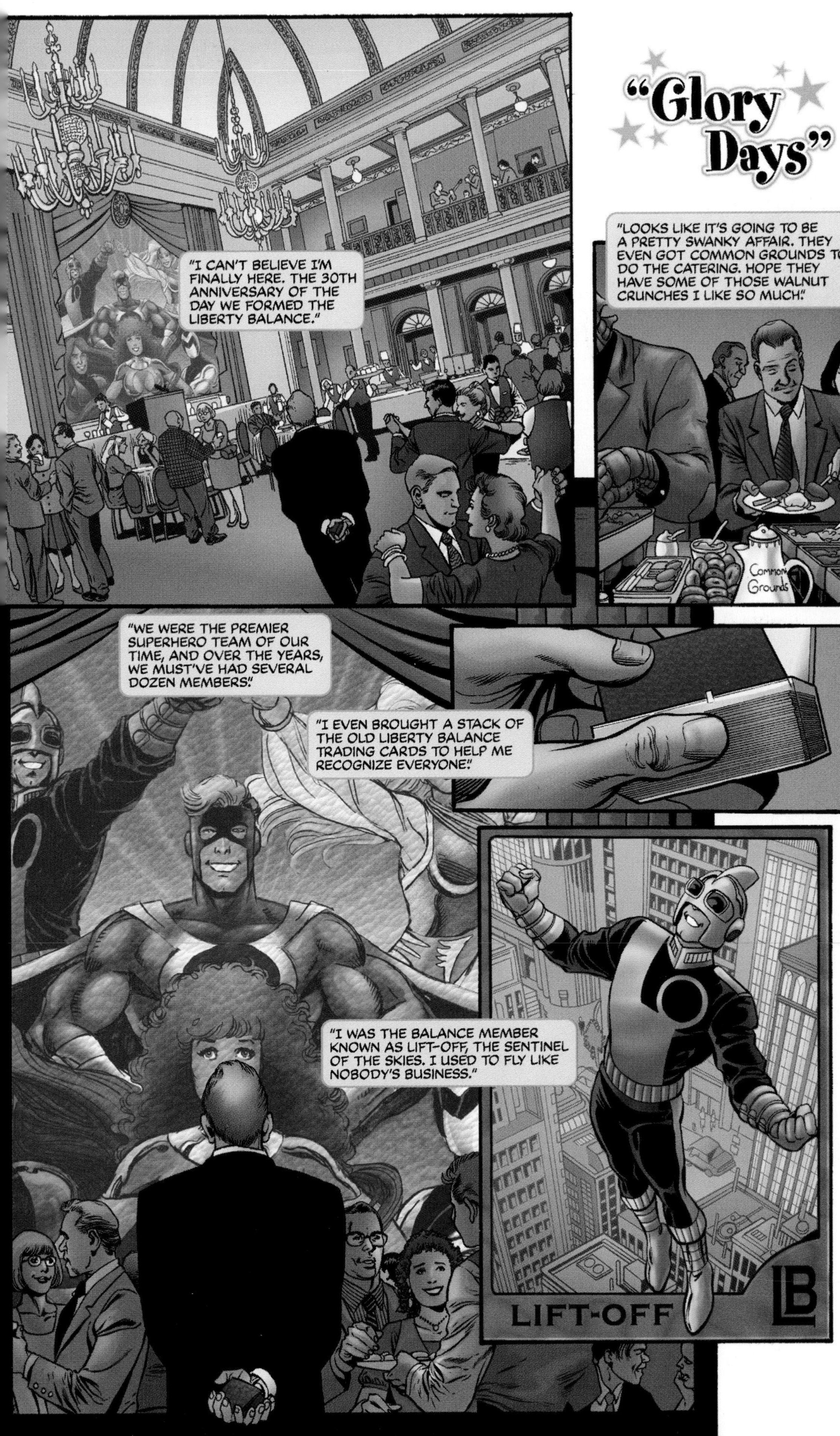
"I CAN'T BELIEVE I'M FINALLY HERE. THE 30TH ANNIVERSARY OF THE DAY WE FORMED THE LIBERTY BALANCE."
"LOOKS LIKE IT'S GOING TO BE A PRETTY SWANKY AFFAIR. THEY EVEN GOT COMMON GROUNDS TO DO THE CATERING. HOPE THEY HAVE SOME OF THOSE WALNUT CRUNCHES I LIKE SO MUCH."
Common Grounds
"WE WERE THE PREMIER SUPERHERO TEAM OF OUR TIME, AND OVER THE YEARS, WE MUST'VE HAD SEVERAL DOZEN MEMBERS."
"I EVEN BROUGHT A STACK OF THE OLD LIBERTY BALANCE TRADING CARDS TO HELP ME RECOGNIZE EVERYONE."
"I WAS THE BALANCE MEMBER KNOWN AS LIFT-OFF, THE SENTINEL OF THE SKIES. I USED TO FLY LIKE NOBODY'S BUSINESS."
LIFT-OFF
LB

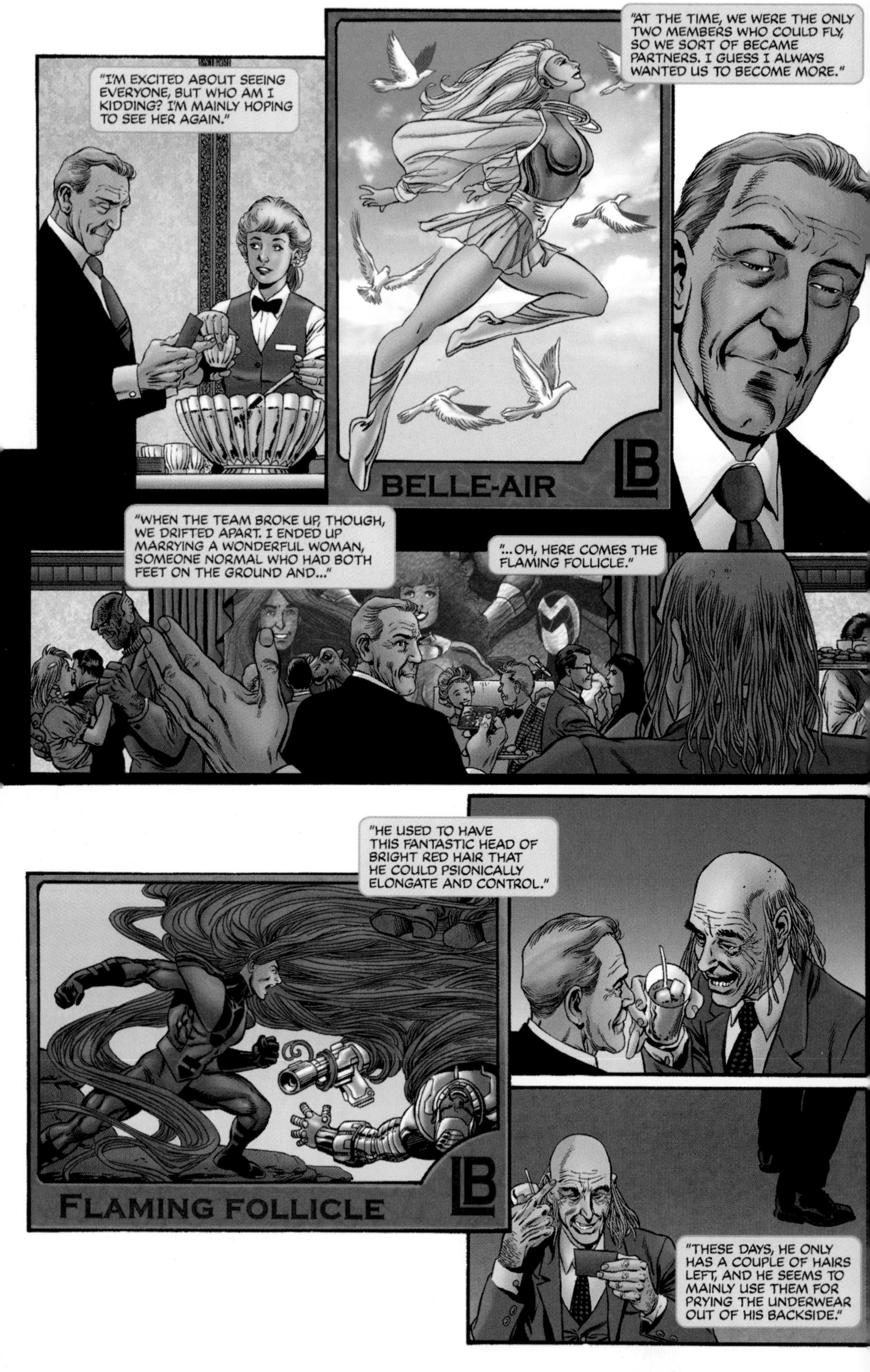
"I'M EXCITED ABOUT SEEING EVERYONE, BUT WHO AM I KIDDING? I'M MAINLY HOPING TO SEE HER AGAIN."
"AT THE TIME, WE WERE THE ONLY TWO MEMBERS WHO COULD FLY, SO WE SORT OF BECAME PARTNERS. I GUESS I ALWAYS WANTED US TO BECOME MORE."
BELLE-AIR
LB
"WHEN THE TEAM BROKE UP, THOUGH, WE DRIFTED APART. I ENDED UP MARRYING A WONDERFUL WOMAN, SOMEONE NORMAL WHO HAD BOTH FEET ON THE GROUND AND..."
"...OH, HERE COMES THE FLAMING FOLLICLE."
"HE USED TO HAVE THIS FANTASTIC HEAD OF BRIGHT RED HAIR THAT HE COULD PSIONICALLY ELONGATE AND CONTROL."
FLAMING FOLLICLE
LB
"THESE DAYS, HE ONLY HAS A COUPLE OF HAIRS LEFT, AND HE SEEMS TO MAINLY USE THEM FOR PRYING THE UNDERWEAR OUT OF HIS BACKSIDE."

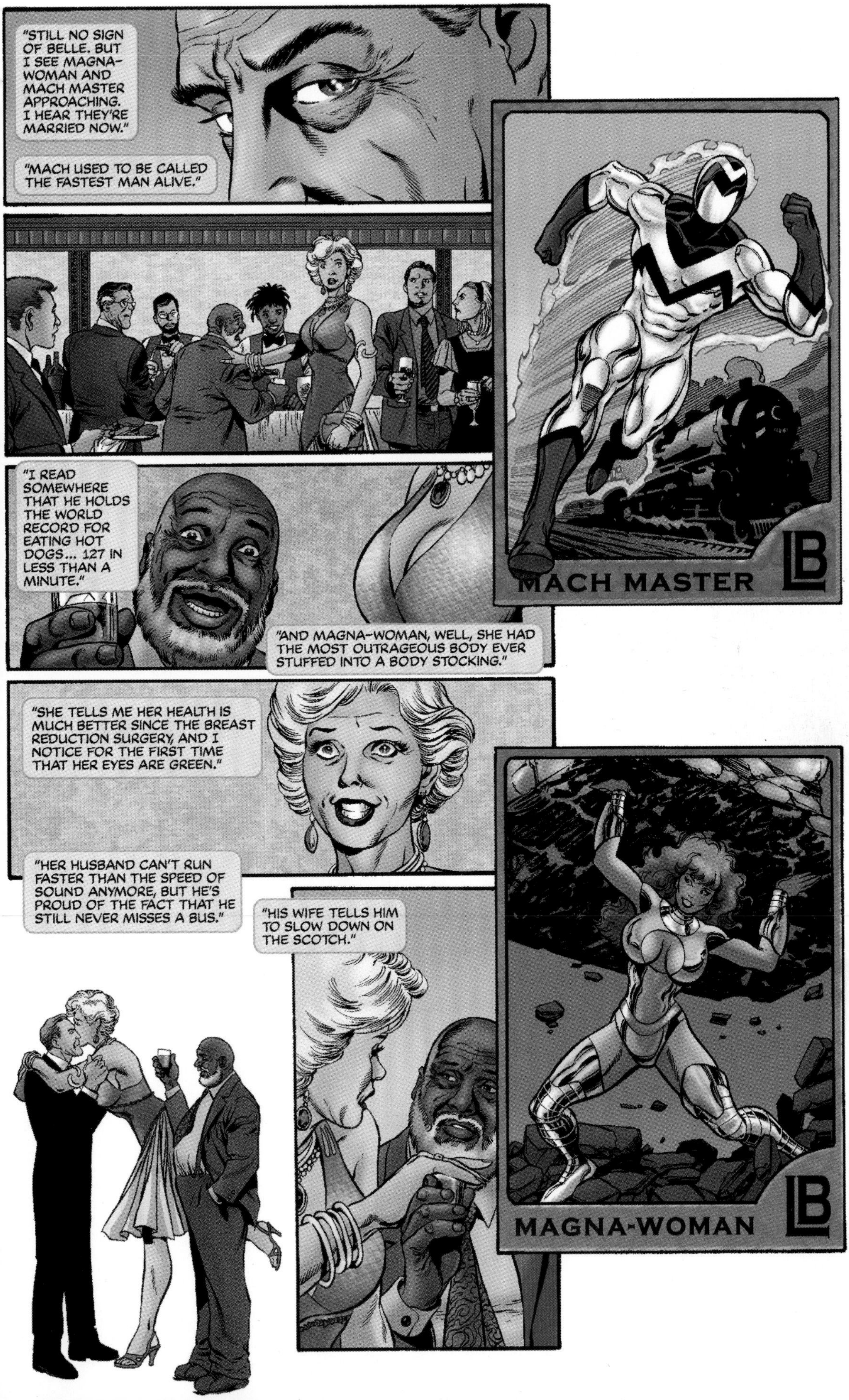
"STILL NO SIGN OF BELLE. BUT I SEE MAGNA-WOMAN AND MACH MASTER APPROACHING. I HEAR THEY'RE MARRIED NOW."
"MACH USED TO BE CALLED THE FASTEST MAN ALIVE."
MACH MASTER
"I READ SOMEWHERE THAT HE HOLDS THE WORLD RECORD FOR EATING HOT DOGS... 127 IN LESS THAN A MINUTE."
"AND MAGNA-WOMAN, WELL, SHE HAD THE MOST OUTRAGEOUS BODY EVER STUFFED INTO A BODY STOCKING."
"SHE TELLS ME HER HEALTH IS MUCH BETTER SINCE THE BREAST REDUCTION SURGERY, AND I NOTICE FOR THE FIRST TIME THAT HER EYES ARE GREEN."
MAGNA-WOMAN
"HER HUSBAND CAN'T RUN FASTER THAN THE SPEED OF SOUND ANYMORE, BUT HE'S PROUD OF THE FACT THAT HE STILL NEVER MISSES A BUS."
"HIS WIFE TELLS HIM TO SLOW DOWN ON THE SCOTCH."

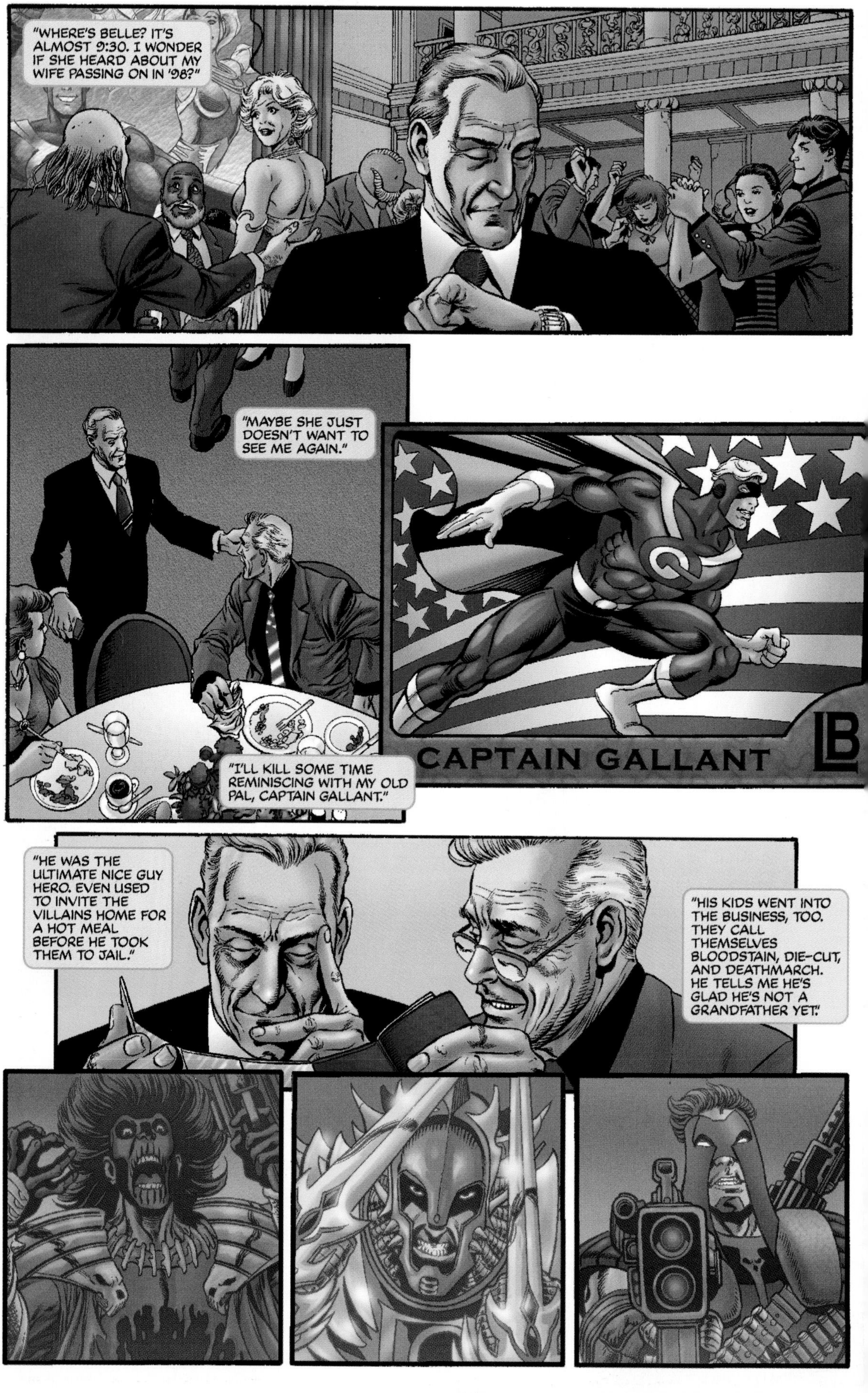
"WHERE'S BELLE? IT'S ALMOST 9:30. I WONDER IF SHE HEARD ABOUT MY WIFE PASSING ON IN '98?"
"MAYBE SHE JUST DOESN'T WANT TO SEE ME AGAIN."
"I'LL KILL SOME TIME REMINISCING WITH MY OLD PAL, CAPTAIN GALLANT."
CAPTAIN GALLANT
"HE WAS THE ULTIMATE NICE GUY HERO. EVEN USED TO INVITE THE VILLAINS HOME FOR A HOT MEAL BEFORE HE TOOK THEM TO JAIL."
"HIS KIDS WENT INTO THE BUSINESS, TOO. THEY CALL THEMSELVES BLOODSTAIN, DIE-CUT, AND DEATHMARCH. HE TELLS ME HE'S GLAD HE'S NOT A GRANDFATHER YET."

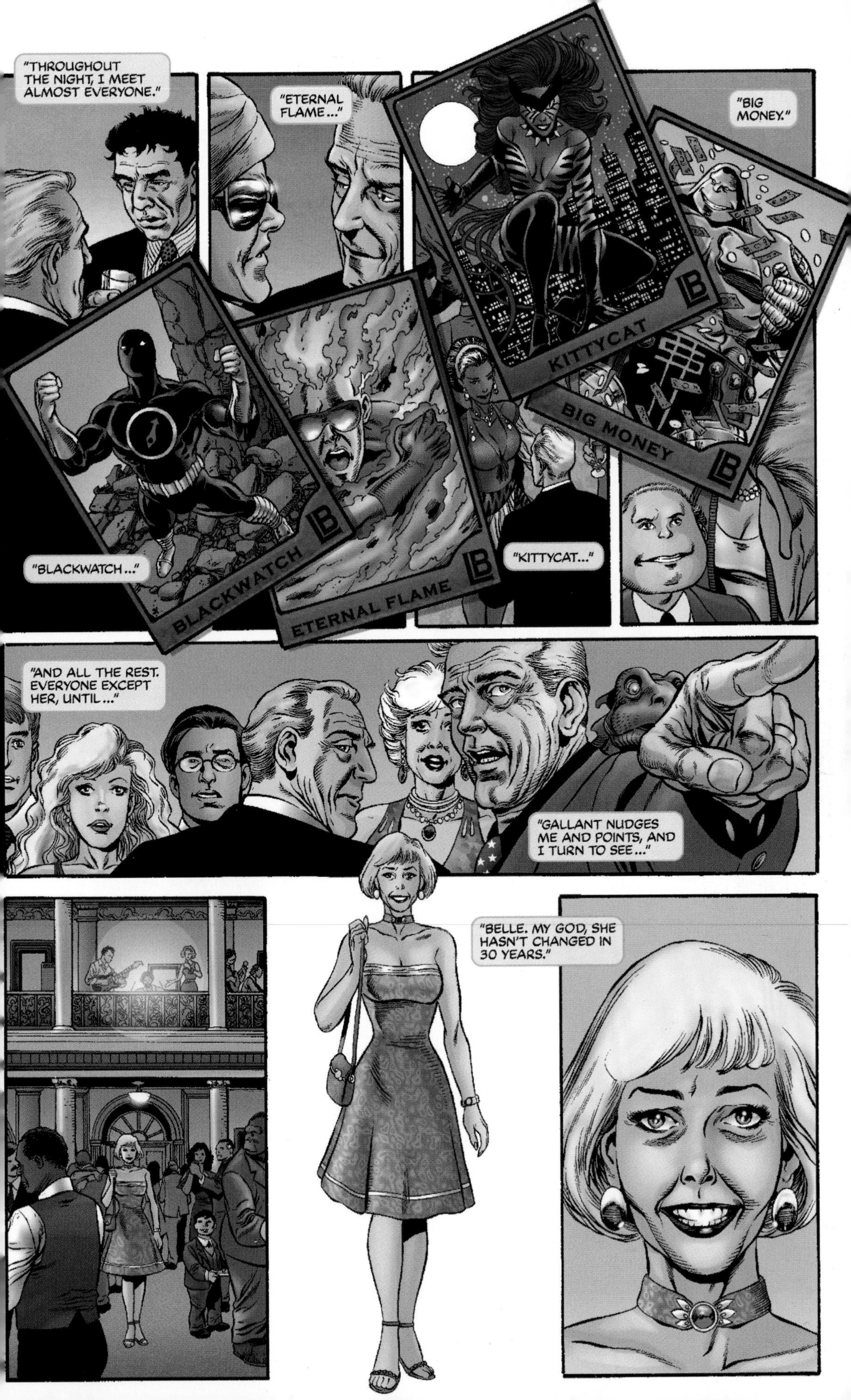
"THROUGHOUT THE NIGHT, I MEET ALMOST EVERYONE."
"ETERNAL FLAME..."
"BIG MONEY."
KITTYCAT
BIG MONEY
BLACKWATCH
ETERNAL FLAME
"BLACKWATCH..."
"KITTYCAT..."
"AND ALL THE REST. EVERYONE EXCEPT HER, UNTIL..."
"GALLANT NUDGES ME AND POINTS, AND I TURN TO SEE..."
"BELLE. MY GOD, SHE HASN'T CHANGED IN 30 YEARS."

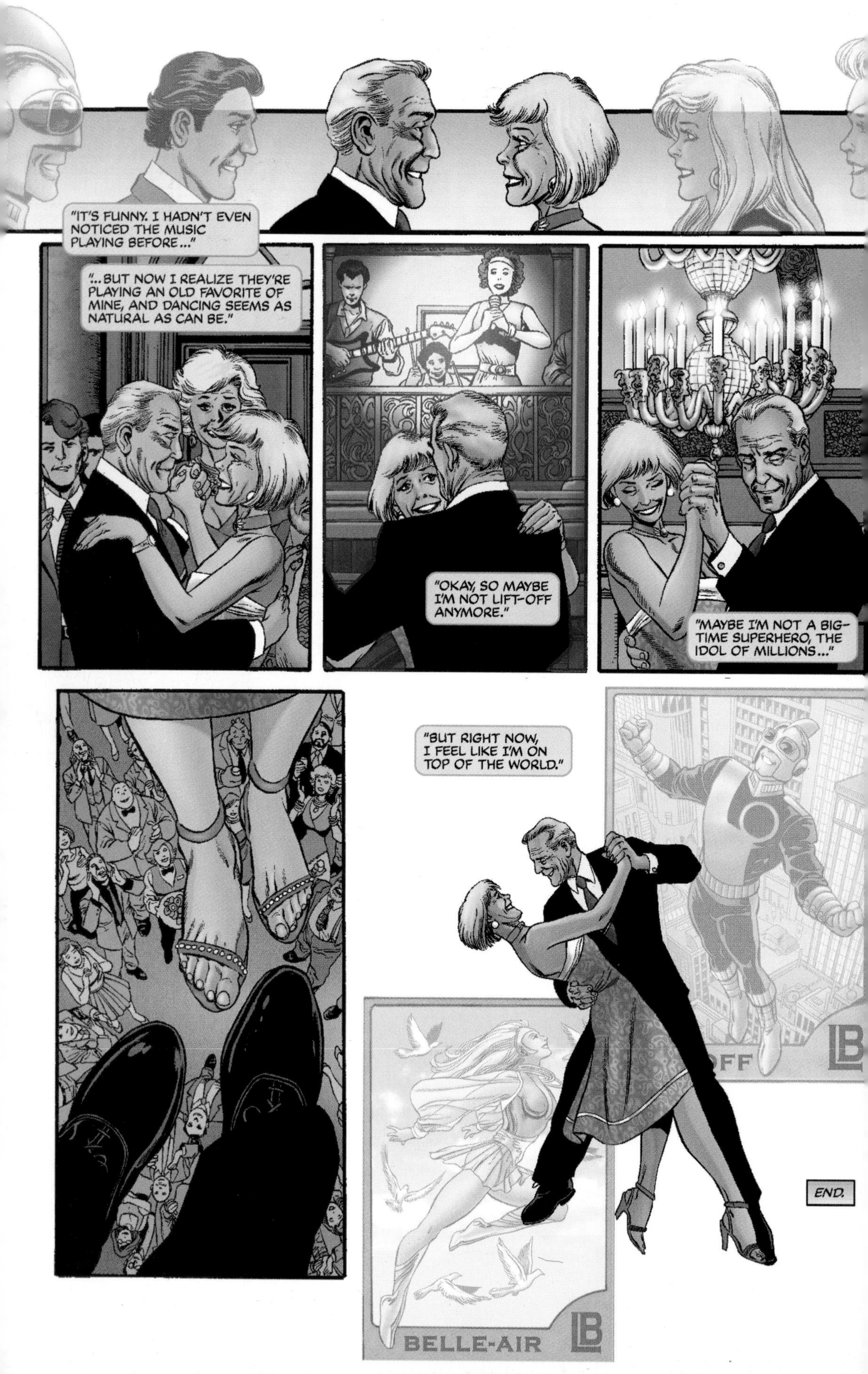
"IT'S FUNNY. I HADN'T EVEN NOTICED THE MUSIC PLAYING BEFORE..."
"...BUT NOW I REALIZE THEY'RE PLAYING AN OLD FAVORITE OF MINE, AND DANCING SEEMS AS NATURAL AS CAN BE."
"OKAY, SO MAYBE I'M NOT LIFT-OFF ANYMORE."
"MAYBE I'M NOT A BIG-TIME SUPERHERO, THE IDOL OF MILLIONS..."
"BUT RIGHT NOW, I FEEL LIKE I'M ON TOP OF THE WORLD."
OFF
BELLE-AIR
END.

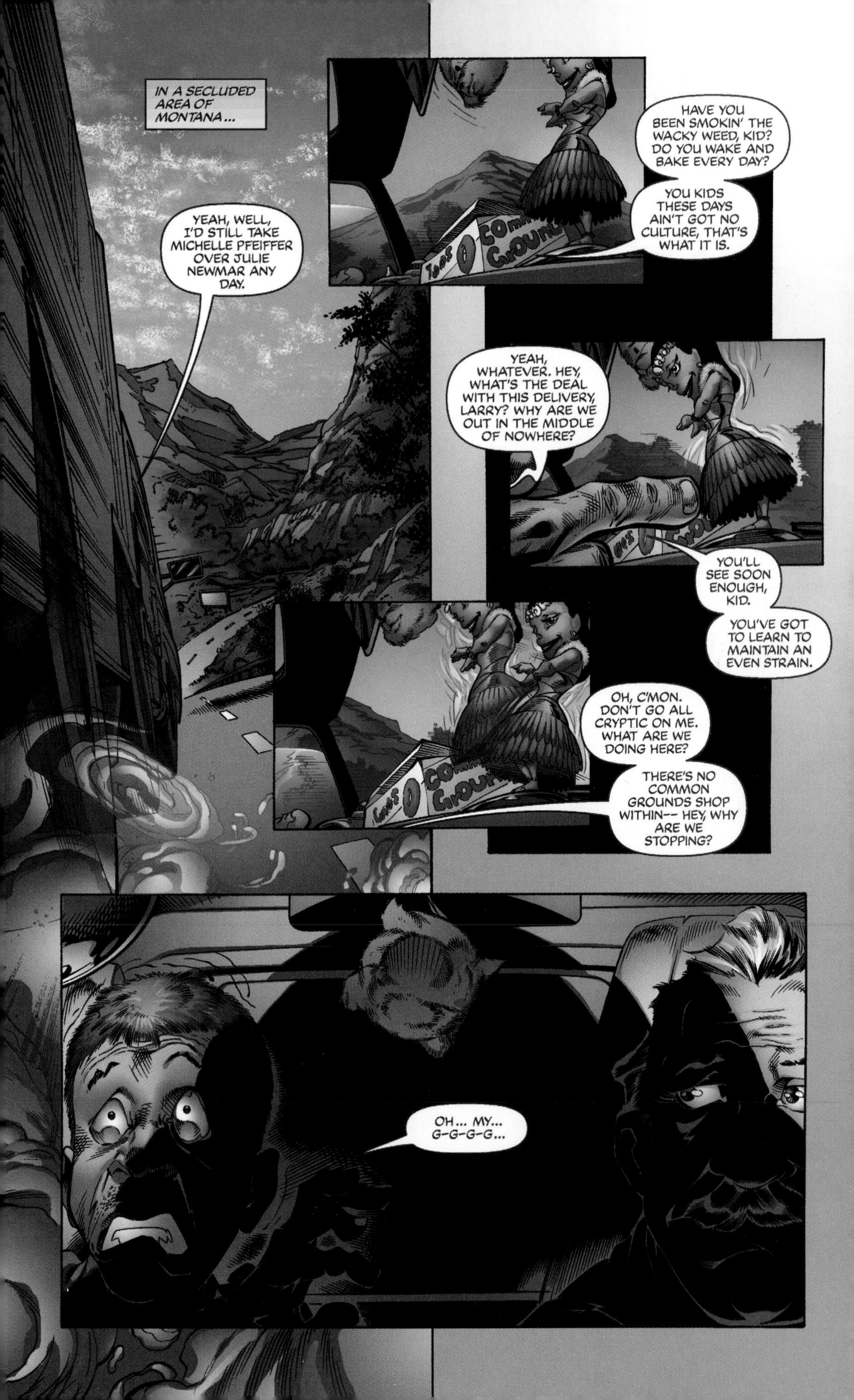
IN A SECLUDED AREA OF MONTANA...
YEAH, WELL, I'D STILL TAKE MICHELLE PFEIFFER OVER JULIE NEWMAR ANY DAY.
HAVE YOU BEEN SMOKIN' THE WACKY WEED, KID? DO YOU WAKE AND BAKE EVERY DAY?
YOU KIDS THESE DAYS AIN'T GOT NO CULTURE, THAT'S WHAT IT IS.
YEAH, WHATEVER. HEY, WHAT'S THE DEAL WITH THIS DELIVERY, LARRY? WHY ARE WE OUT IN THE MIDDLE OF NOWHERE?
YOU'LL SEE SOON ENOUGH, KID.
YOU'VE GOT TO LEARN TO MAINTAIN AN EVEN STRAIN.
OH, C'MON. DON'T GO ALL CRYPTIC ON ME. WHAT ARE WE DOING HERE?
THERE'S NO COMMON GROUNDS SHOP WITHIN-- HEY, WHY ARE WE STOPPING?
OH... MY... G-G-G-G...

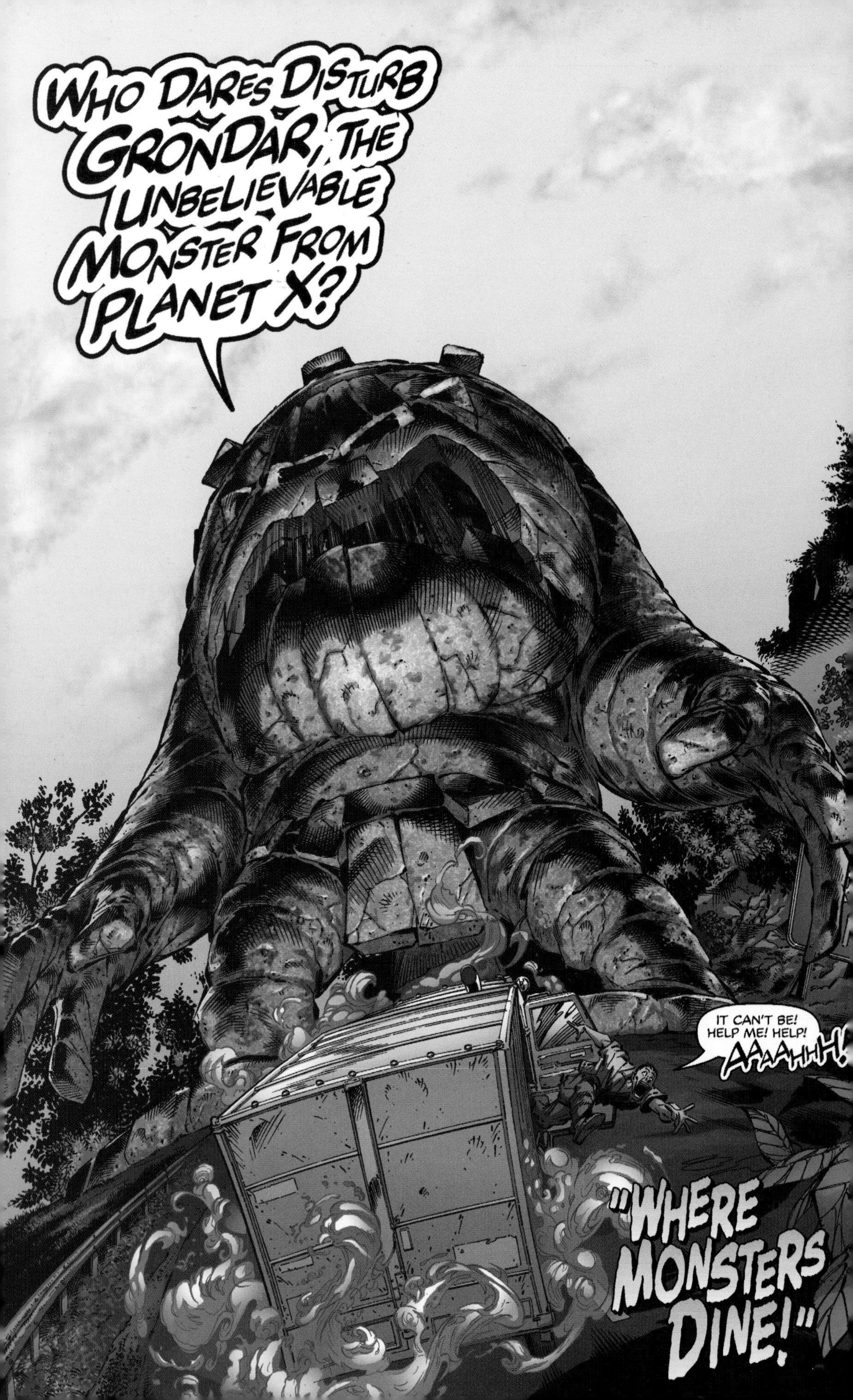
WHO DARES DISTURB GRONDAR, THE UNBELIEVABLE MONSTER FROM PLANET X?
IT CAN'T BE! HELP ME! HELP! AAAHHH!
"WHERE MONSTERS DINE!"

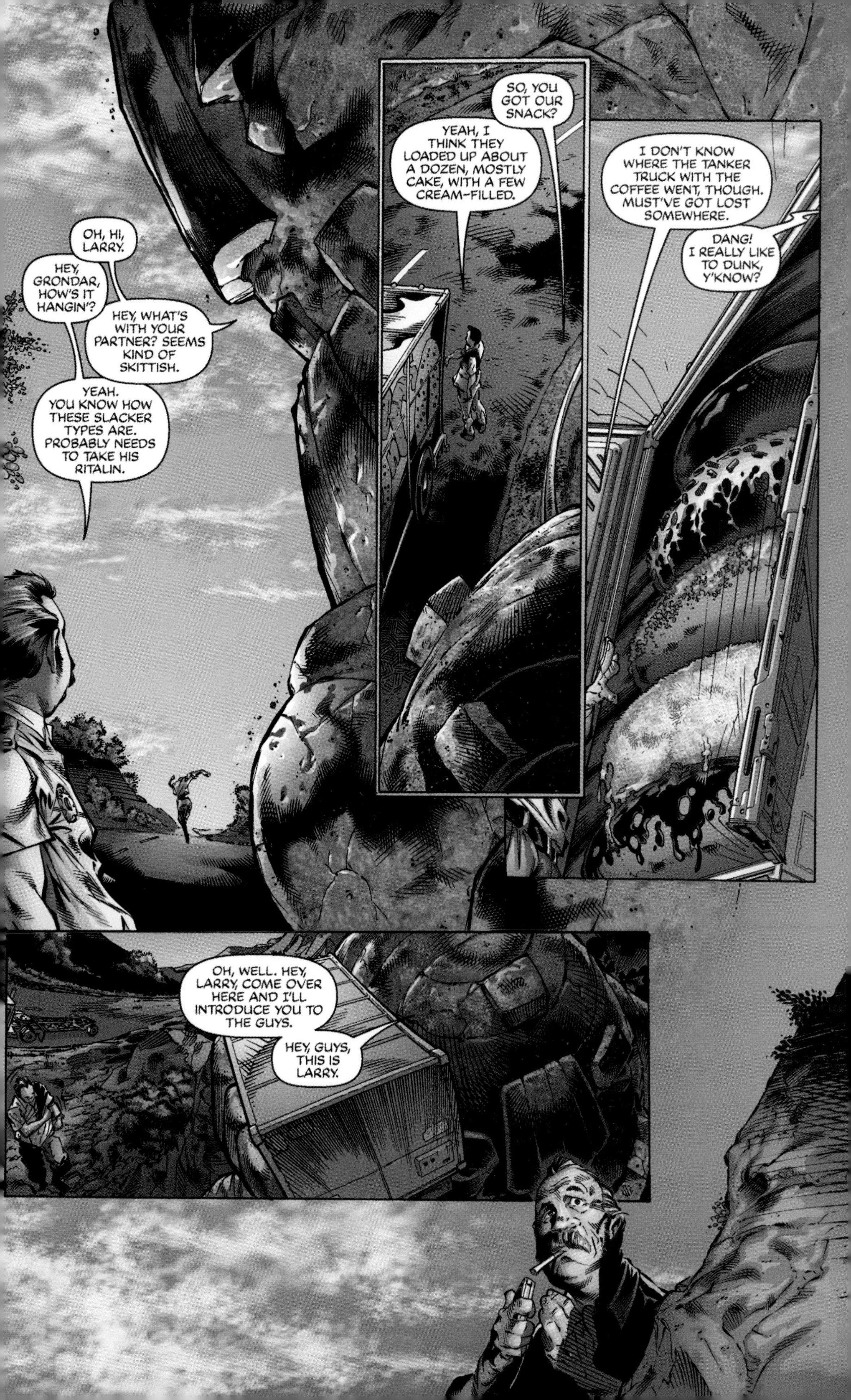
OH, HI, LARRY.
HEY, GRONDAR, HOW'S IT HANGIN'?
HEY, WHAT'S WITH YOUR PARTNER? SEEMS KIND OF SKITTISH.
YEAH. YOU KNOW HOW THESE SLACKER TYPES ARE. PROBABLY NEEDS TO TAKE HIS RITALIN.
SO, YOU GOT OUR SNACK?
YEAH, I THINK THEY LOADED UP ABOUT A DOZEN, MOSTLY CAKE, WITH A FEW CREAM-FILLED.
I DON'T KNOW WHERE THE TANKER TRUCK WITH THE COFFEE WENT, THOUGH. MUST'VE GOT LOST SOMEWHERE.
DANG! I REALLY LIKE TO DUNK, Y'KNOW?
OH, WELL. HEY, LARRY, COME OVER HERE AND I'LL INTRODUCE YOU TO THE GUYS.
HEY, GUYS, THIS IS LARRY.

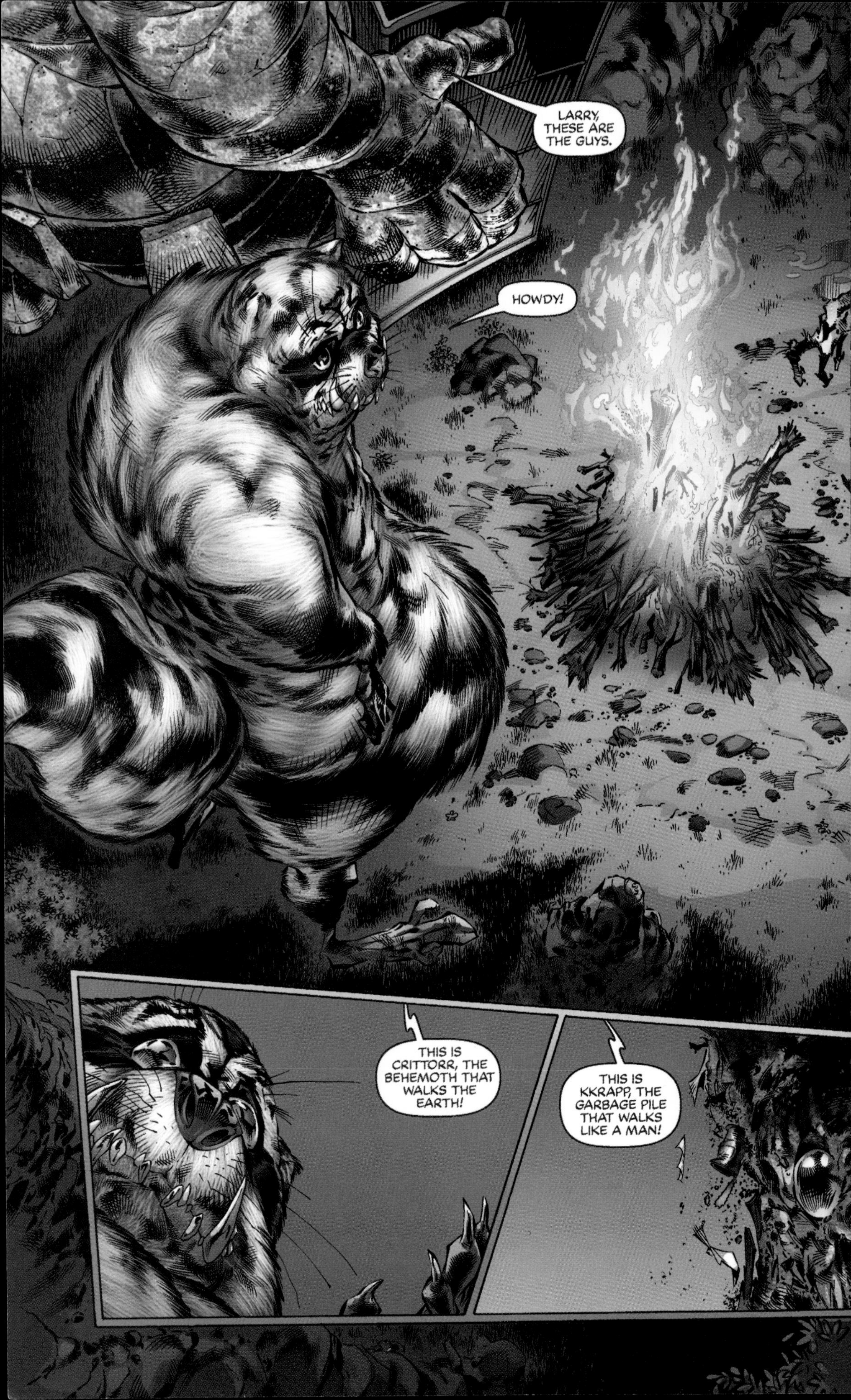
LARRY, THESE ARE THE GUYS.
HOWDY!
THIS IS CRITTORR, THE BEHEMOTH THAT WALKS THE EARTH!
THIS IS KKRAPP, THE GARBAGE PILE THAT WALKS LIKE A MAN!

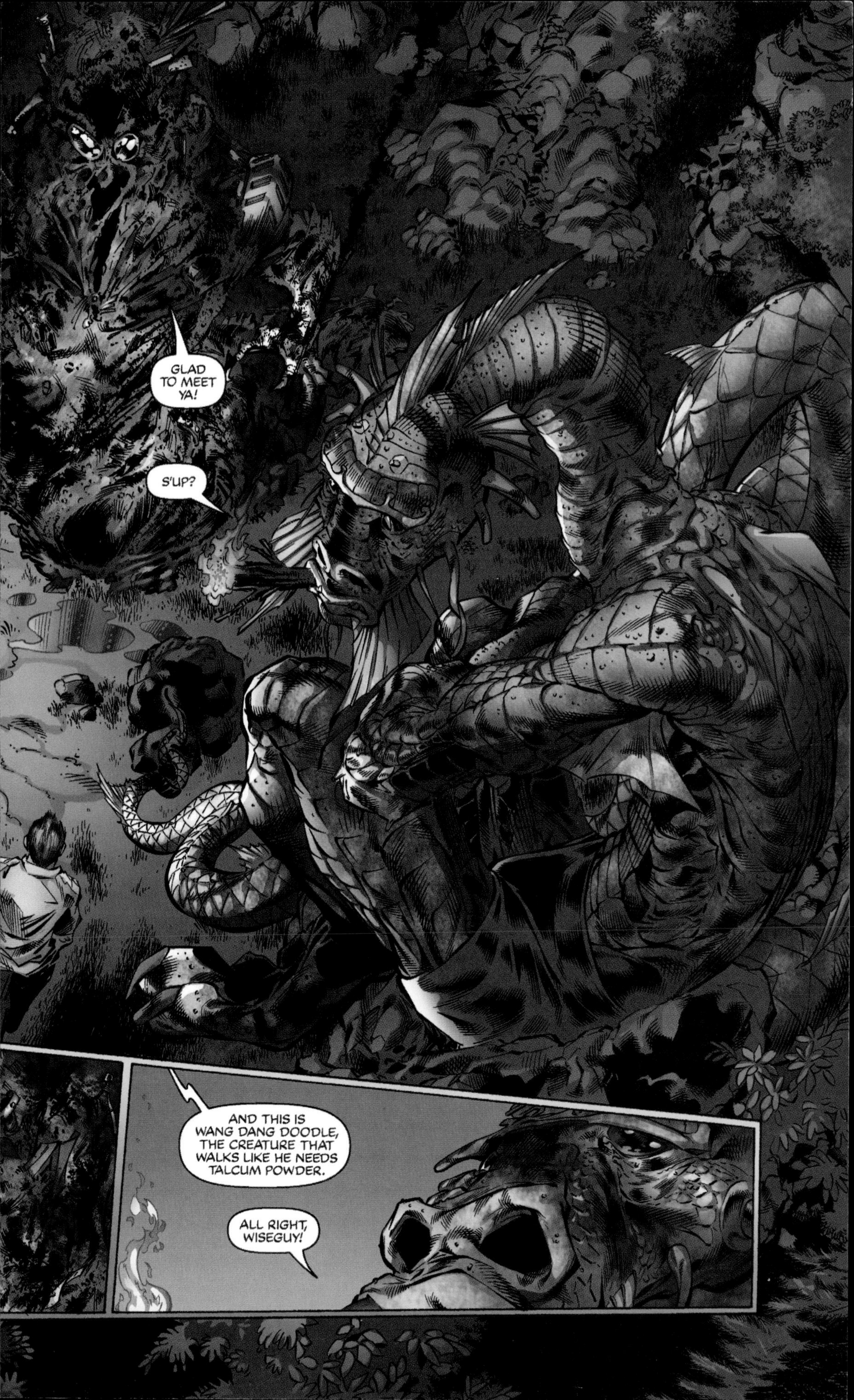
GLAD TO MEET YA!
S'UP?
AND THIS IS WANG DANG DOODLE, THE CREATURE THAT WALKS LIKE HE NEEDS TALCUM POWDER.
ALL RIGHT, WISEGUY!

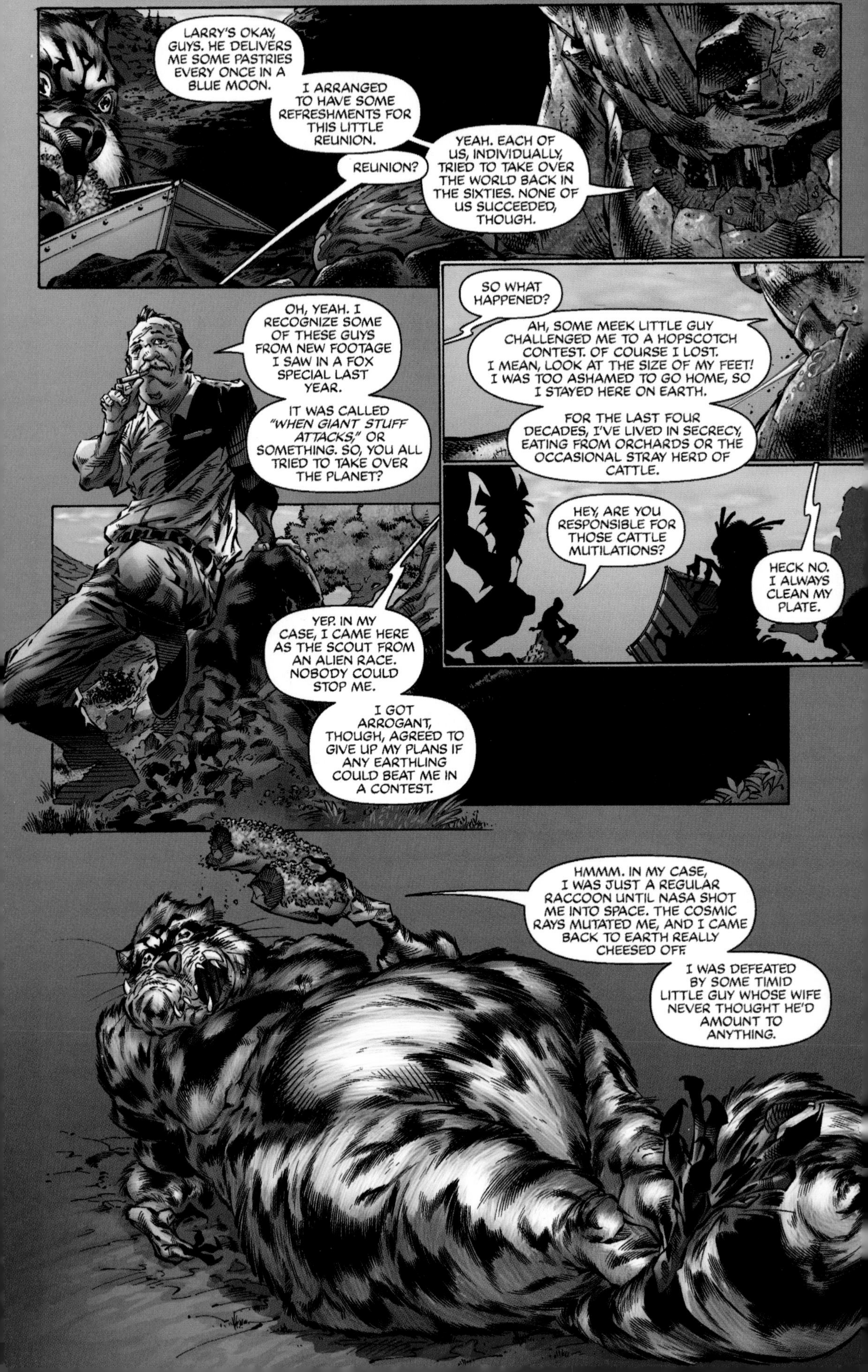

LARRY'S OKAY, GUYS. HE DELIVERS ME SOME PASTRIES EVERY ONCE IN A BLUE MOON.
I ARRANGED TO HAVE SOME REFRESHMENTS FOR THIS LITTLE REUNION.
REUNION?
YEAH. EACH OF US, INDIVIDUALLY, TRIED TO TAKE OVER THE WORLD BACK IN THE SIXTIES. NONE OF US SUCCEEDED, THOUGH.
OH, YEAH. I RECOGNIZE SOME OF THESE GUYS FROM NEW FOOTAGE I SAW IN A FOX SPECIAL LAST YEAR.
IT WAS CALLED *"WHEN GIANT STUFF ATTACKS,"* OR SOMETHING. SO, YOU ALL TRIED TO TAKE OVER THE PLANET?
YEP. IN MY CASE, I CAME HERE AS THE SCOUT FROM AN ALIEN RACE. NOBODY COULD STOP ME.
I GOT ARROGANT, THOUGH, AGREED TO GIVE UP MY PLANS IF ANY EARTHLING COULD BEAT ME IN A CONTEST.
SO WHAT HAPPENED?
AH, SOME MEEK LITTLE GUY CHALLENGED ME TO A HOPSCOTCH CONTEST. OF COURSE I LOST. I MEAN, LOOK AT THE SIZE OF MY FEET! I WAS TOO ASHAMED TO GO HOME, SO I STAYED HERE ON EARTH.
FOR THE LAST FOUR DECADES, I'VE LIVED IN SECRECY, EATING FROM ORCHARDS OR THE OCCASIONAL STRAY HERD OF CATTLE.
HEY, ARE YOU RESPONSIBLE FOR THOSE CATTLE MUTILATIONS?
HECK NO. I ALWAYS CLEAN MY PLATE.
HMMM. IN MY CASE, I WAS JUST A REGULAR RACCOON UNTIL NASA SHOT ME INTO SPACE. THE COSMIC RAYS MUTATED ME, AND I CAME BACK TO EARTH REALLY CHEESED OFF.
I WAS DEFEATED BY SOME TIMID LITTLE GUY WHOSE WIFE NEVER THOUGHT HE'D AMOUNT TO ANYTHING.

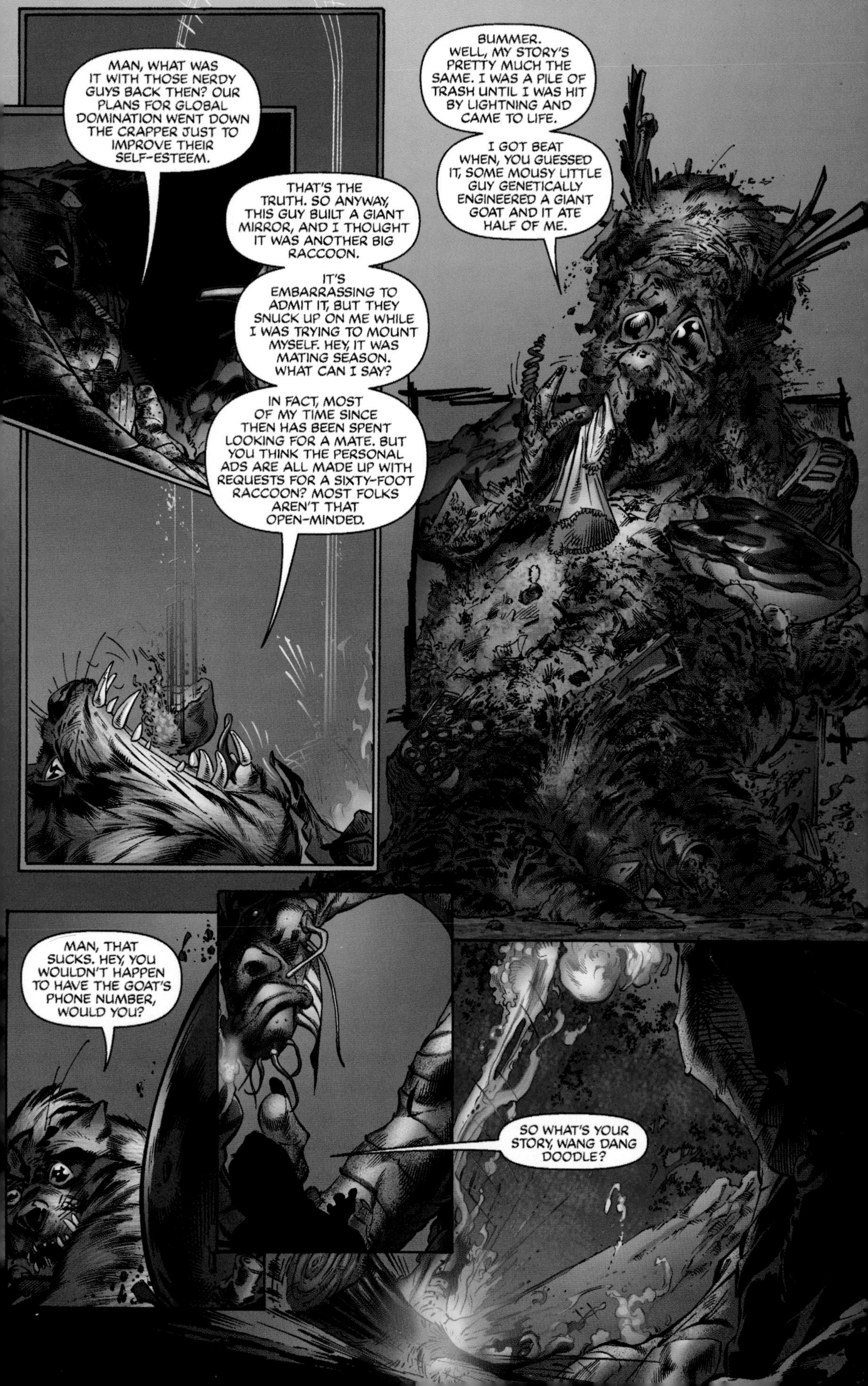

MAN, WHAT WAS IT WITH THOSE NERDY GUYS BACK THEN? OUR PLANS FOR GLOBAL DOMINATION WENT DOWN THE CRAPPER JUST TO IMPROVE THEIR SELF-ESTEEM.
THAT'S THE TRUTH. SO ANYWAY, THIS GUY BUILT A GIANT MIRROR, AND I THOUGHT IT WAS ANOTHER BIG RACCOON.
IT'S EMBARRASSING TO ADMIT IT, BUT THEY SNUCK UP ON ME WHILE I WAS TRYING TO MOUNT MYSELF. HEY, IT WAS MATING SEASON. WHAT CAN I SAY?
IN FACT, MOST OF MY TIME SINCE THEN HAS BEEN SPENT LOOKING FOR A MATE. BUT YOU THINK THE PERSONAL ADS ARE ALL MADE UP WITH REQUESTS FOR A SIXTY-FOOT RACCOON? MOST FOLKS AREN'T THAT OPEN-MINDED.
BUMMER. WELL, MY STORY'S PRETTY MUCH THE SAME. I WAS A PILE OF TRASH UNTIL I WAS HIT BY LIGHTNING AND CAME TO LIFE.
I GOT BEAT WHEN, YOU GUESSED IT, SOME MOUSY LITTLE GUY GENETICALLY ENGINEERED A GIANT GOAT AND IT ATE HALF OF ME.
MAN, THAT SUCKS. HEY, YOU WOULDN'T HAPPEN TO HAVE THE GOAT'S PHONE NUMBER, WOULD YOU?
SO WHAT'S YOUR STORY, WANG DANG DOODLE?

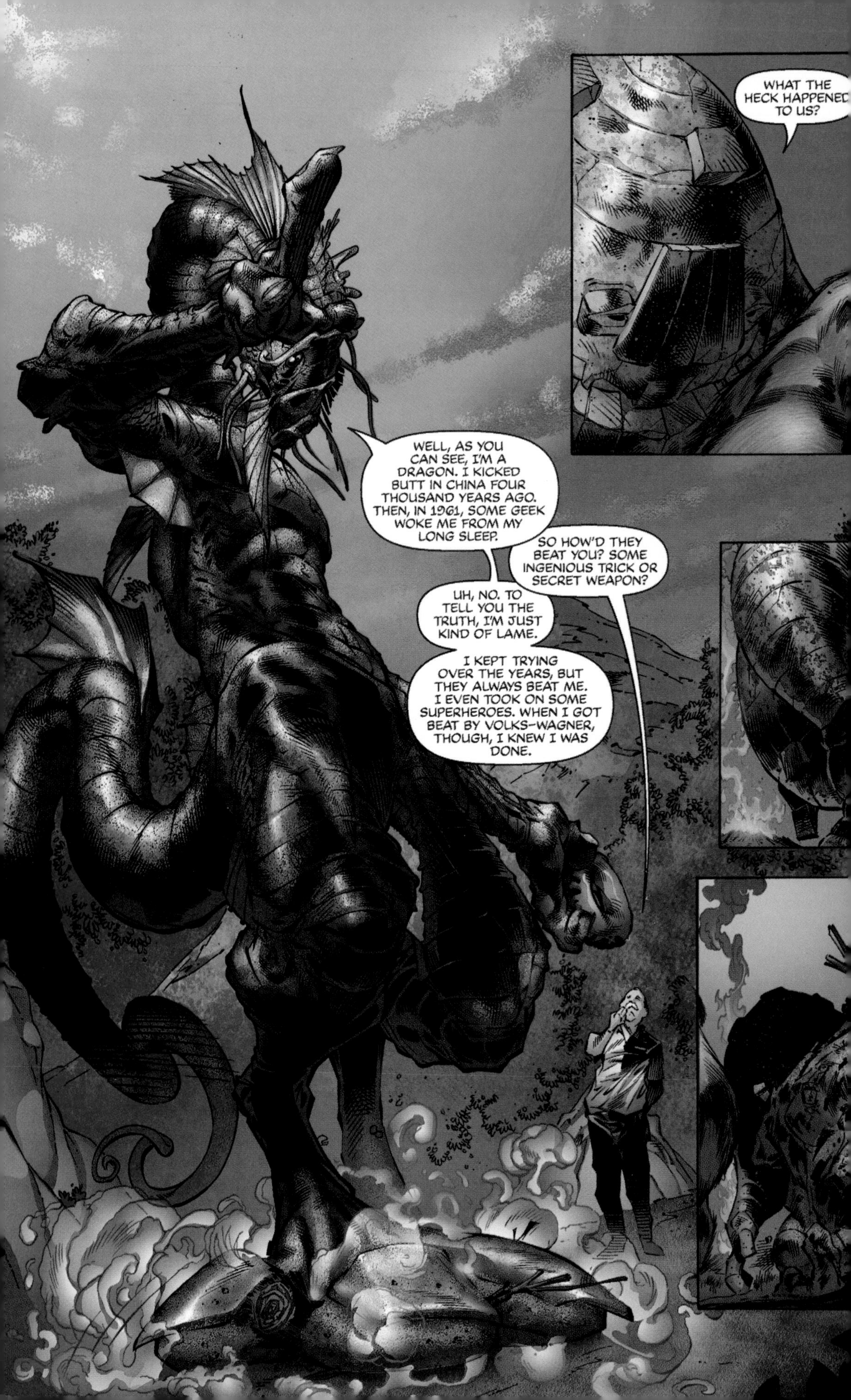
WHAT THE HECK HAPPENED TO US?
WELL, AS YOU CAN SEE, I'M A DRAGON. I KICKED BUTT IN CHINA FOUR THOUSAND YEARS AGO. THEN, IN 1961, SOME GEEK WOKE ME FROM MY LONG SLEEP.
SO HOW'D THEY BEAT YOU? SOME INGENIOUS TRICK OR SECRET WEAPON?
UH, NO. TO TELL YOU THE TRUTH, I'M JUST KIND OF LAME.
I KEPT TRYING OVER THE YEARS, BUT THEY ALWAYS BEAT ME. I EVEN TOOK ON SOME SUPERHEROES. WHEN I GOT BEAT BY VOLKS-WAGNER, THOUGH, I KNEW I WAS DONE.

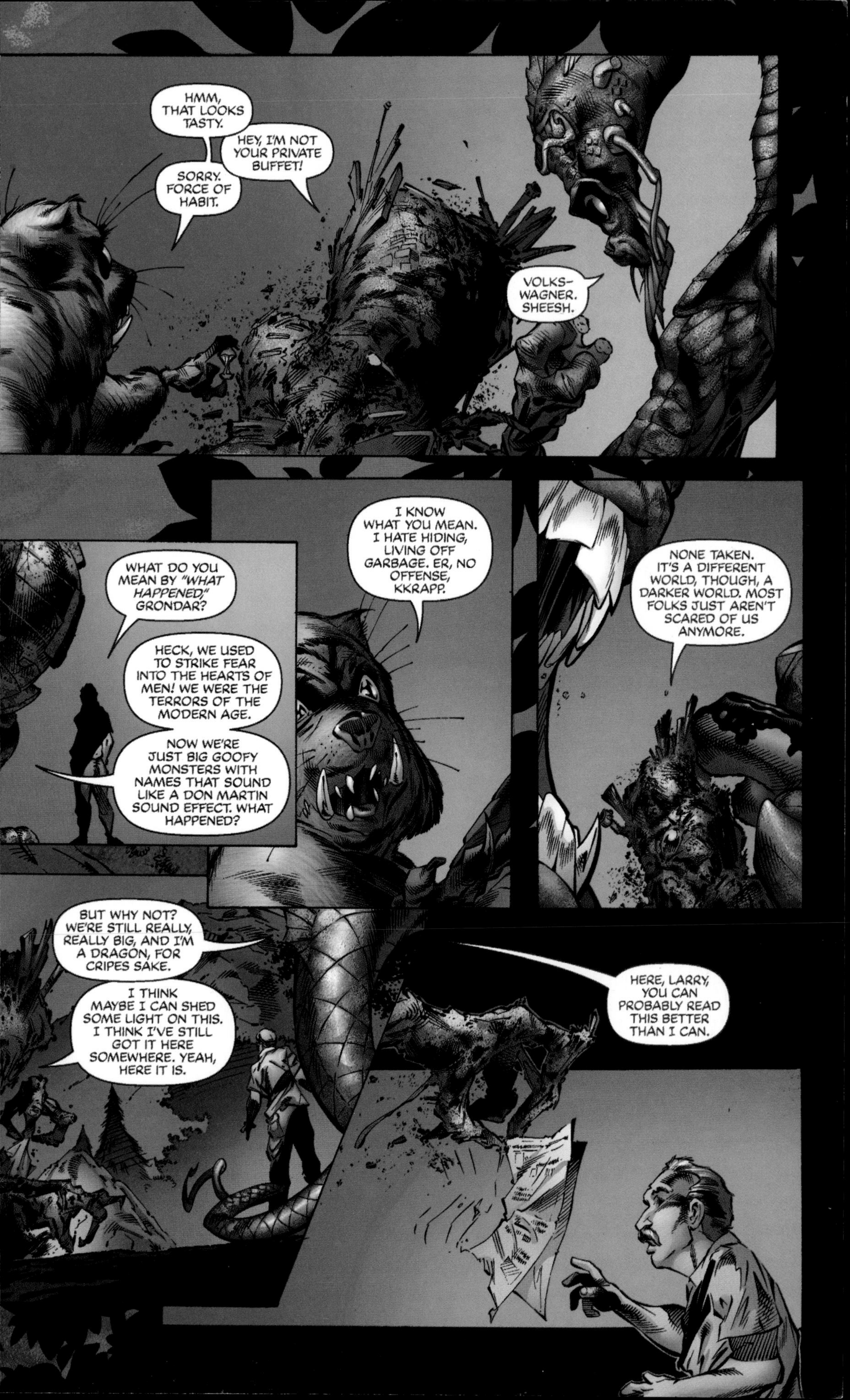
HMM, THAT LOOKS TASTY.
HEY, I'M NOT YOUR PRIVATE BUFFET!
SORRY. FORCE OF HABIT.
VOLKS-WAGNER. SHEESH.
WHAT DO YOU MEAN BY "WHAT HAPPENED," GRONDAR?
HECK, WE USED TO STRIKE FEAR INTO THE HEARTS OF MEN! WE WERE THE TERRORS OF THE MODERN AGE.
NOW WE'RE JUST BIG GOOFY MONSTERS WITH NAMES THAT SOUND LIKE A DON MARTIN SOUND EFFECT. WHAT HAPPENED?
I KNOW WHAT YOU MEAN. I HATE HIDING, LIVING OFF GARBAGE. ER, NO OFFENSE, KKRAPP.
NONE TAKEN. IT'S A DIFFERENT WORLD, THOUGH, A DARKER WORLD. MOST FOLKS JUST AREN'T SCARED OF US ANYMORE.
BUT WHY NOT? WE'RE STILL REALLY, REALLY BIG, AND I'M A DRAGON, FOR CRIPES SAKE.
I THINK MAYBE I CAN SHED SOME LIGHT ON THIS. I THINK I'VE STILL GOT IT HERE SOMEWHERE. YEAH, HERE IT IS.
HERE, LARRY, YOU CAN PROBABLY READ THIS BETTER THAN I CAN.

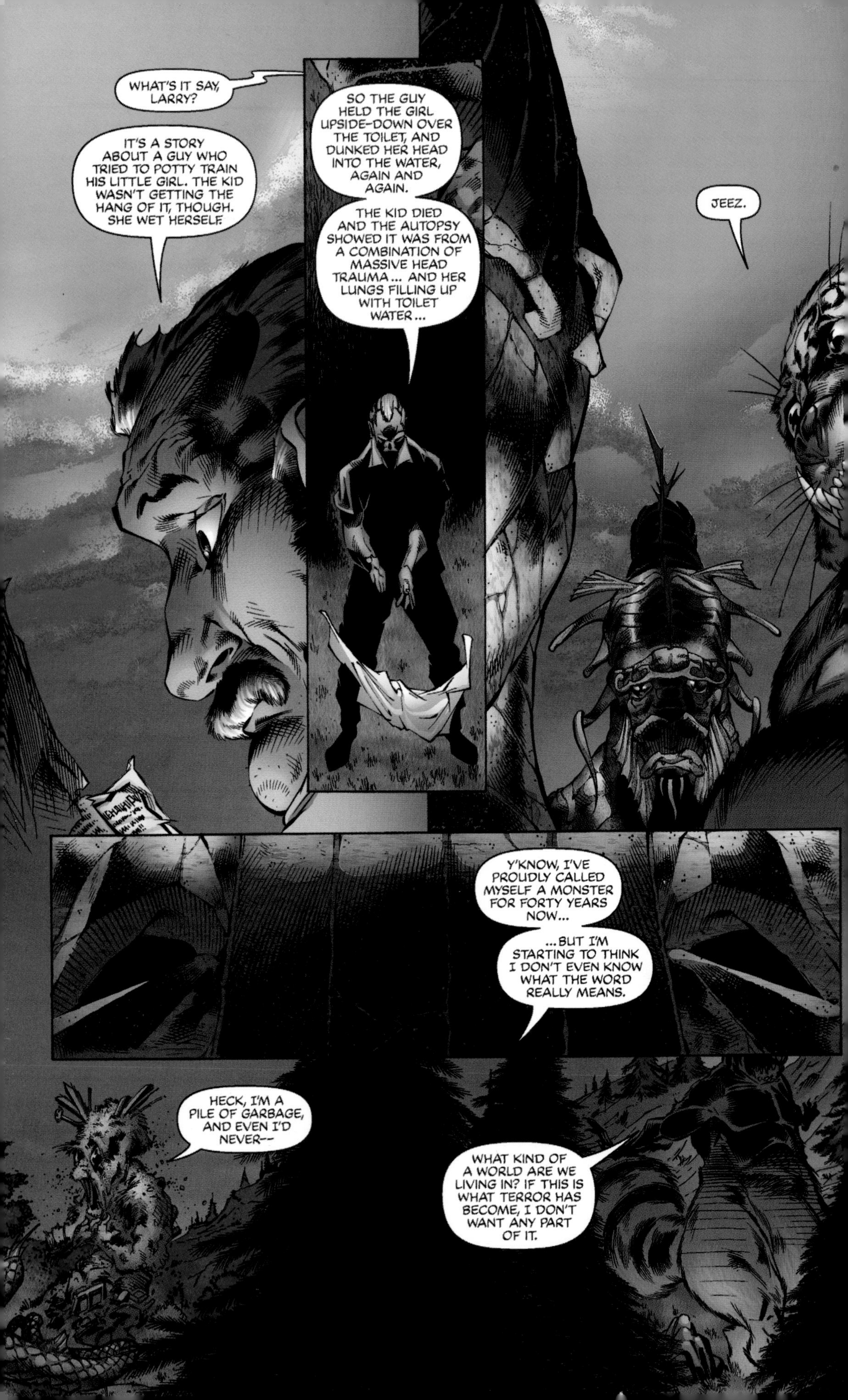
WHAT'S IT SAY, LARRY?
IT'S A STORY ABOUT A GUY WHO TRIED TO POTTY TRAIN HIS LITTLE GIRL. THE KID WASN'T GETTING THE HANG OF IT, THOUGH. SHE WET HERSELF.
SO THE GUY HELD THE GIRL UPSIDE-DOWN OVER THE TOILET, AND DUNKED HER HEAD INTO THE WATER, AGAIN AND AGAIN.
THE KID DIED AND THE AUTOPSY SHOWED IT WAS FROM A COMBINATION OF MASSIVE HEAD TRAUMA... AND HER LUNGS FILLING UP WITH TOILET WATER...
JEEZ.
Y'KNOW, I'VE PROUDLY CALLED MYSELF A MONSTER FOR FORTY YEARS NOW...
...BUT I'M STARTING TO THINK I DON'T EVEN KNOW WHAT THE WORD REALLY MEANS.
HECK, I'M A PILE OF GARBAGE, AND EVEN I'D NEVER--
WHAT KIND OF A WORLD ARE WE LIVING IN? IF THIS IS WHAT TERROR HAS BECOME, I DON'T WANT ANY PART OF IT.

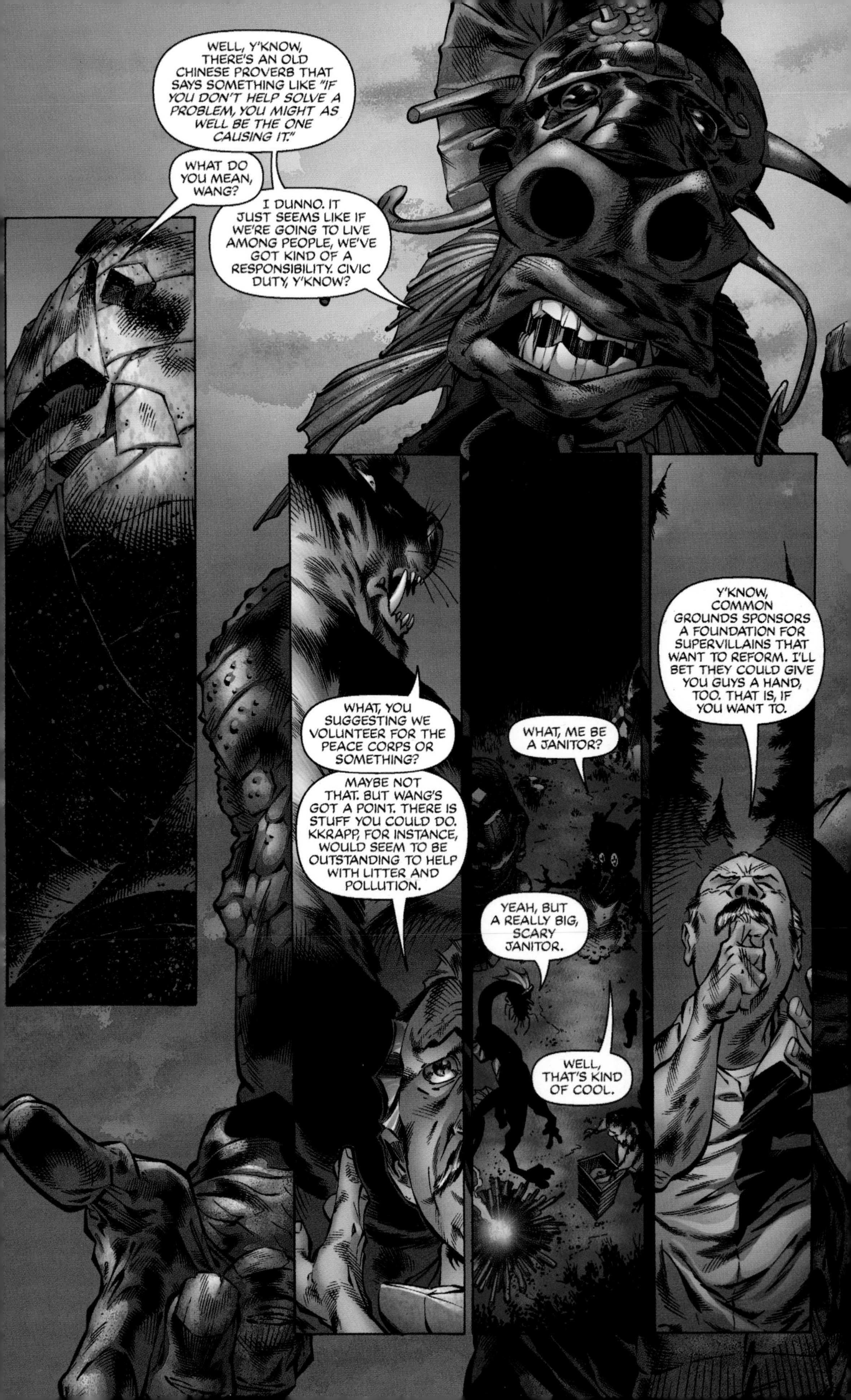
WELL, Y'KNOW, THERE'S AN OLD CHINESE PROVERB THAT SAYS SOMETHING LIKE "IF YOU DON'T HELP SOLVE A PROBLEM, YOU MIGHT AS WELL BE THE ONE CAUSING IT."
WHAT DO YOU MEAN, WANG?
I DUNNO. IT JUST SEEMS LIKE IF WE'RE GOING TO LIVE AMONG PEOPLE, WE'VE GOT KIND OF A RESPONSIBILITY. CIVIC DUTY, Y'KNOW?
WHAT, YOU SUGGESTING WE VOLUNTEER FOR THE PEACE CORPS OR SOMETHING?
MAYBE NOT THAT. BUT WANG'S GOT A POINT. THERE IS STUFF YOU COULD DO. KKRAPP, FOR INSTANCE, WOULD SEEM TO BE OUTSTANDING TO HELP WITH LITTER AND POLLUTION.
WHAT, ME BE A JANITOR?
YEAH, BUT A REALLY BIG, SCARY JANITOR.
WELL, THAT'S KIND OF COOL.
Y'KNOW, COMMON GROUNDS SPONSORS A FOUNDATION FOR SUPERVILLAINS THAT WANT TO REFORM. I'LL BET THEY COULD GIVE YOU GUYS A HAND, TOO. THAT IS, IF YOU WANT TO.

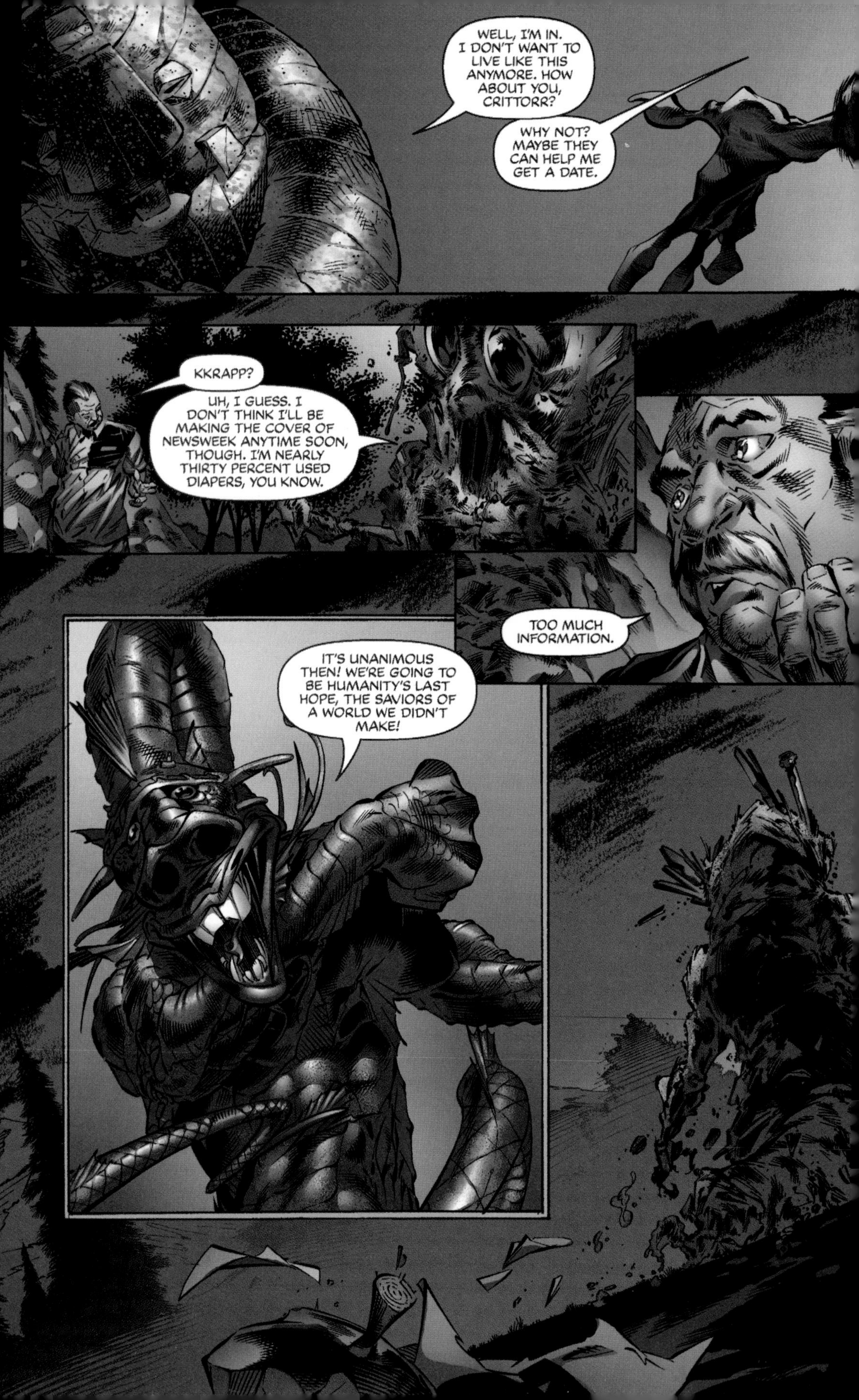
WELL, I'M IN. I DON'T WANT TO LIVE LIKE THIS ANYMORE. HOW ABOUT YOU, CRITTORR?
WHY NOT? MAYBE THEY CAN HELP ME GET A DATE.
KKRAPP?
UH, I GUESS. I DON'T THINK I'LL BE MAKING THE COVER OF NEWSWEEK ANYTIME SOON, THOUGH. I'M NEARLY THIRTY PERCENT USED DIAPERS, YOU KNOW.
TOO MUCH INFORMATION.
IT'S UNANIMOUS THEN! WE'RE GOING TO BE HUMANITY'S LAST HOPE, THE SAVIORS OF A WORLD WE DIDN'T MAKE!

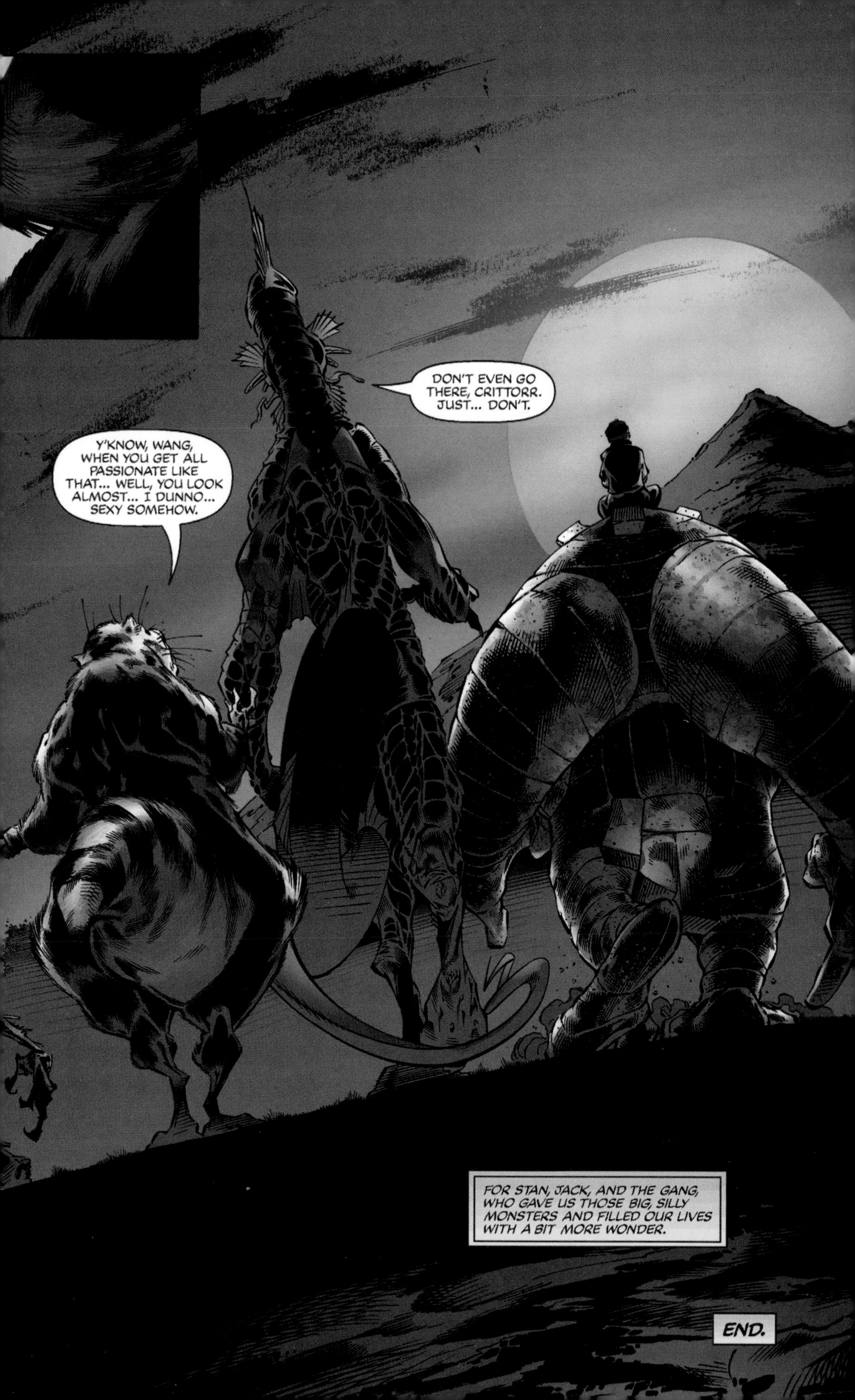
Y'KNOW, WANG, WHEN YOU GET ALL PASSIONATE LIKE THAT... WELL, YOU LOOK ALMOST... I DUNNO... SEXY SOMEHOW.
DON'T EVEN GO THERE, CRITTORR. JUST... DON'T.
FOR STAN, JACK, AND THE GANG, WHO GAVE US THOSE BIG, SILLY MONSTERS AND FILLED OUR LIVES WITH A BIT MORE WONDER.
END.

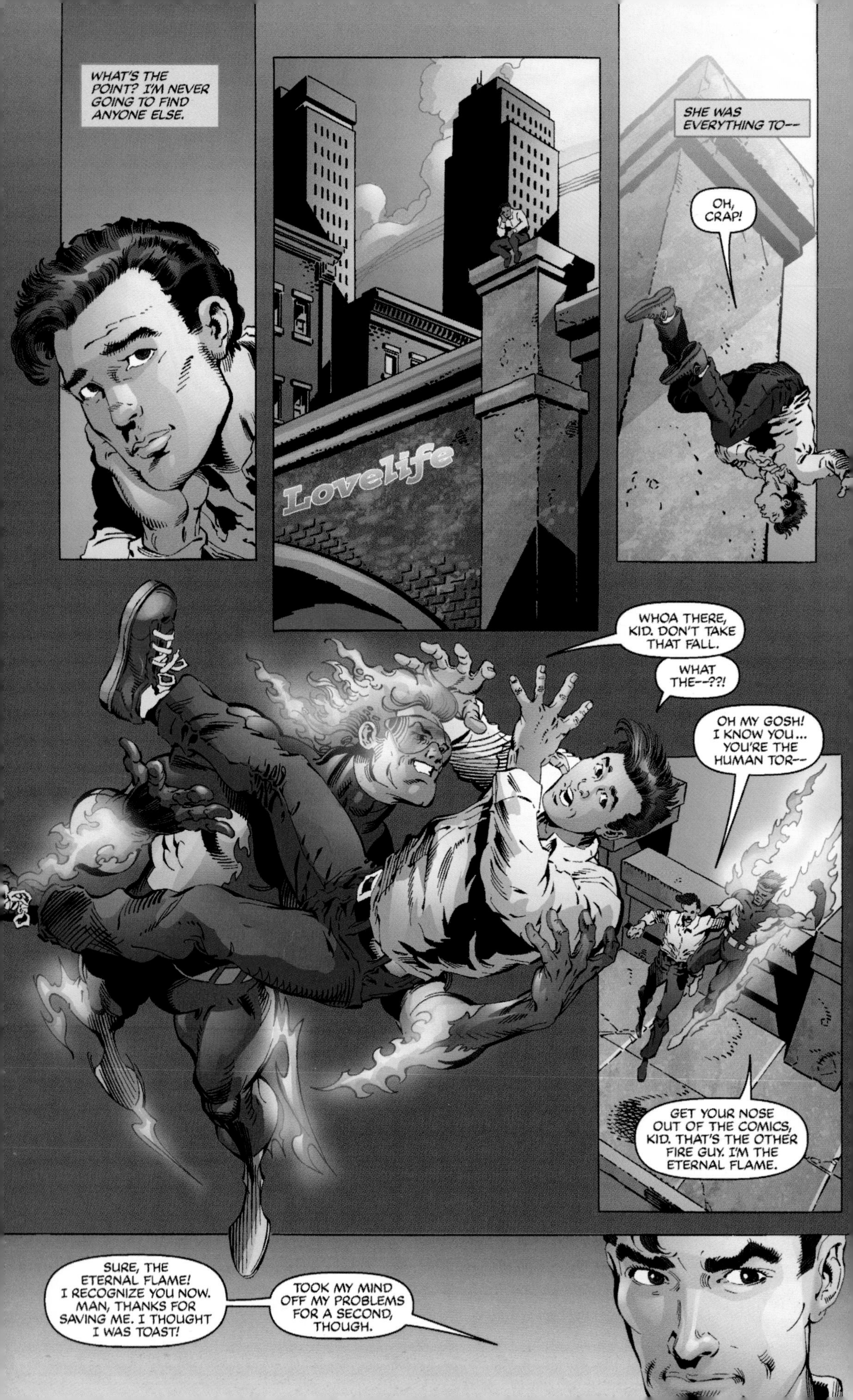
WHAT'S THE POINT? I'M NEVER GOING TO FIND ANYONE ELSE.
Lovelife
SHE WAS EVERYTHING TO--
OH, CRAP!
WHOA THERE, KID. DON'T TAKE THAT FALL.
WHAT THE--??!
OH MY GOSH! I KNOW YOU... YOU'RE THE HUMAN TOR--
GET YOUR NOSE OUT OF THE COMICS, KID. THAT'S THE OTHER FIRE GUY. I'M THE ETERNAL FLAME.
SURE, THE ETERNAL FLAME! I RECOGNIZE YOU NOW. MAN, THANKS FOR SAVING ME. I THOUGHT I WAS TOAST!
TOOK MY MIND OFF MY PROBLEMS FOR A SECOND, THOUGH.

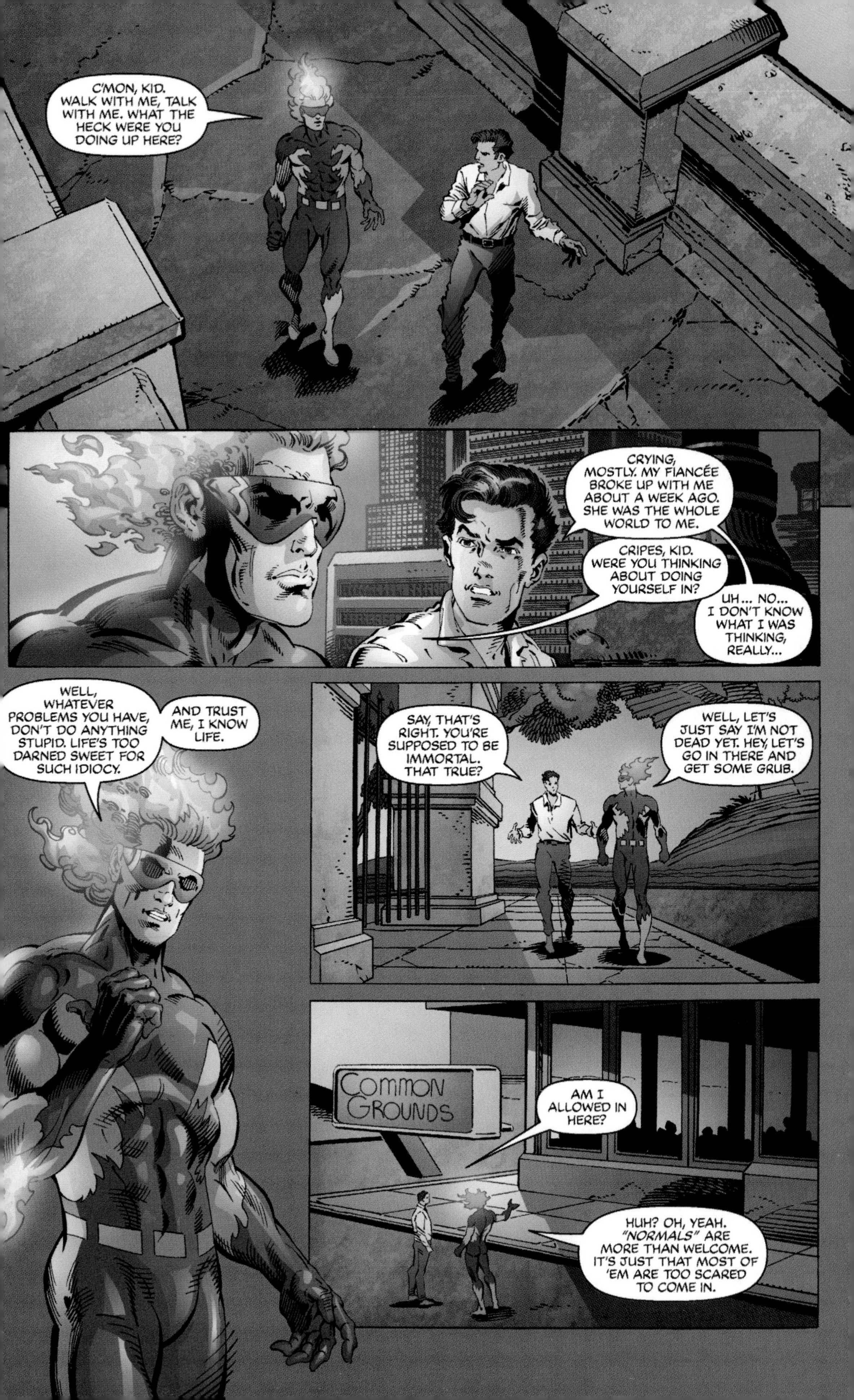
C'MON, KID. WALK WITH ME, TALK WITH ME. WHAT THE HECK WERE YOU DOING UP HERE?
CRYING, MOSTLY. MY FIANCÉE BROKE UP WITH ME ABOUT A WEEK AGO. SHE WAS THE WHOLE WORLD TO ME.
CRIPES, KID. WERE YOU THINKING ABOUT DOING YOURSELF IN?
UH... NO... I DON'T KNOW WHAT I WAS THINKING, REALLY...
WELL, WHATEVER PROBLEMS YOU HAVE, DON'T DO ANYTHING STUPID. LIFE'S TOO DARNED SWEET FOR SUCH IDIOCY.
AND TRUST ME, I KNOW LIFE.
SAY, THAT'S RIGHT. YOU'RE SUPPOSED TO BE IMMORTAL. THAT TRUE?
WELL, LET'S JUST SAY I'M NOT DEAD YET. HEY, LET'S GO IN THERE AND GET SOME GRUB.
COMMON GROUNDS
AM I ALLOWED IN HERE?
HUH? OH, YEAH. *"NORMALS"* ARE MORE THAN WELCOME. IT'S JUST THAT MOST OF 'EM ARE TOO SCARED TO COME IN.

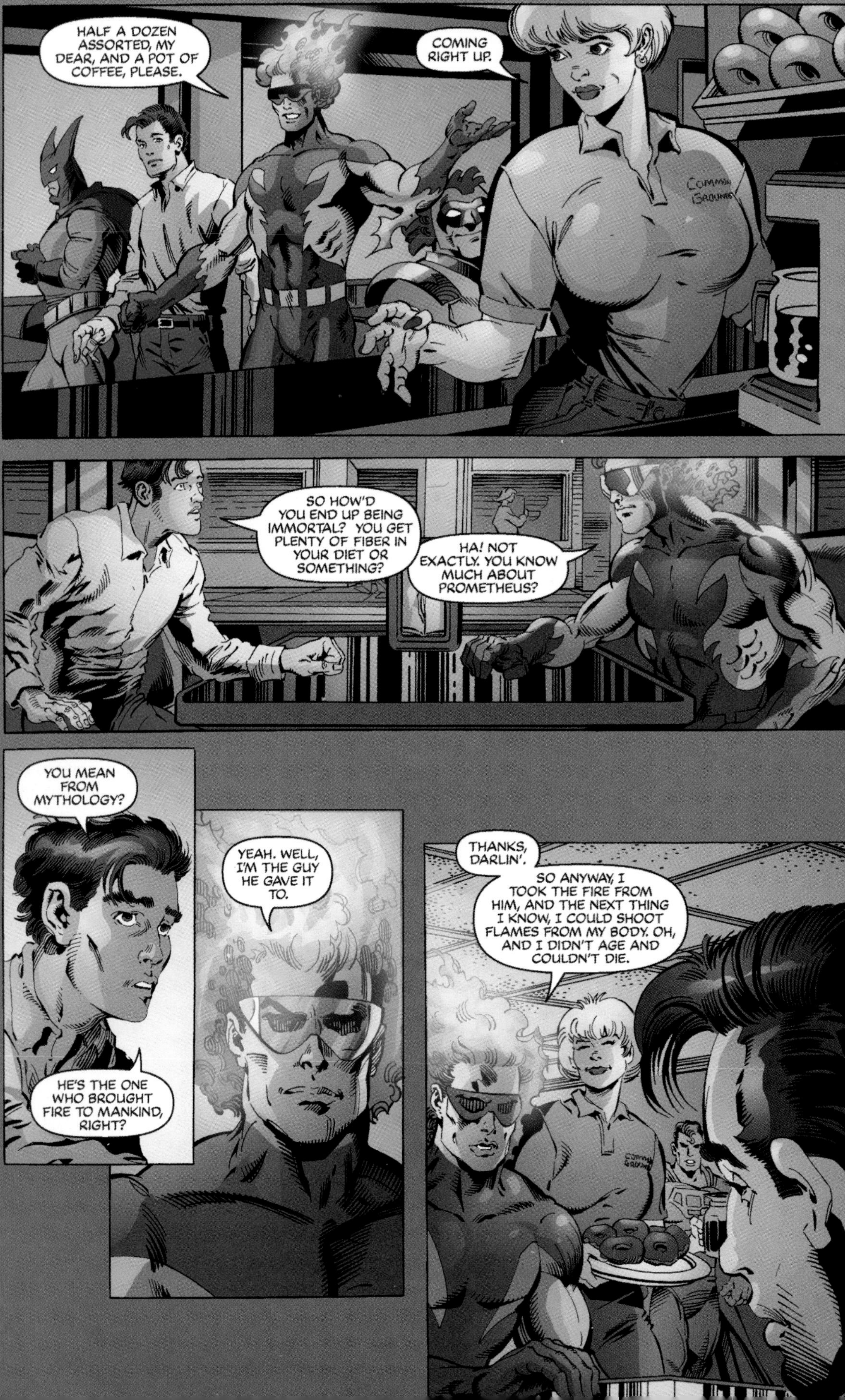
HALF A DOZEN ASSORTED, MY DEAR, AND A POT OF COFFEE, PLEASE.
COMING RIGHT UP.
SO HOW'D YOU END UP BEING IMMORTAL? YOU GET PLENTY OF FIBER IN YOUR DIET OR SOMETHING?
HA! NOT EXACTLY. YOU KNOW MUCH ABOUT PROMETHEUS?
YOU MEAN FROM MYTHOLOGY?
HE'S THE ONE WHO BROUGHT FIRE TO MANKIND, RIGHT?
YEAH. WELL, I'M THE GUY HE GAVE IT TO.
THANKS, DARLIN'.
SO ANYWAY, I TOOK THE FIRE FROM HIM, AND THE NEXT THING I KNOW, I COULD SHOOT FLAMES FROM MY BODY. OH, AND I DIDN'T AGE AND COULDN'T DIE.

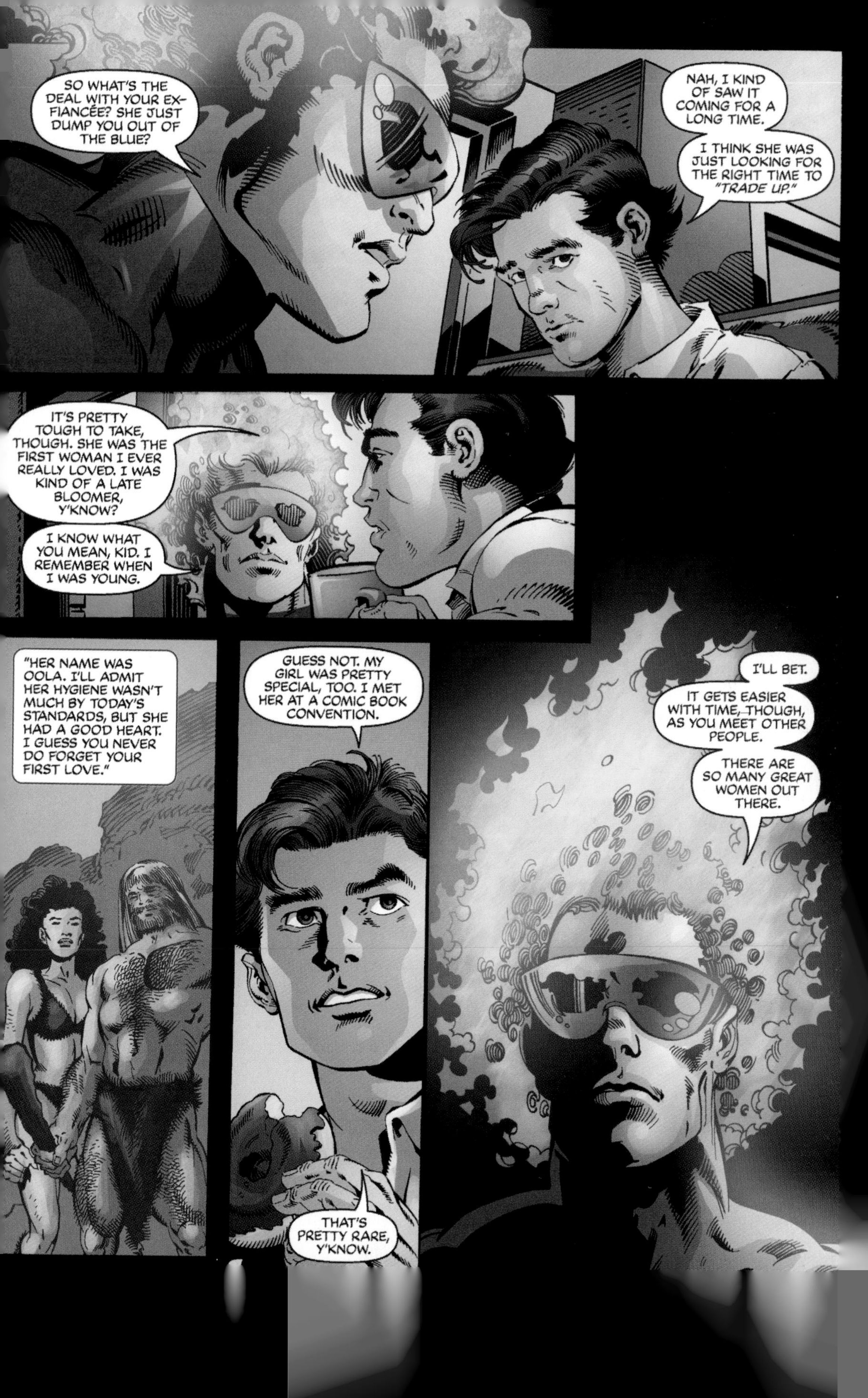
SO WHAT'S THE DEAL WITH YOUR EX-FIANCÉE? SHE JUST DUMP YOU OUT OF THE BLUE?
NAH, I KIND OF SAW IT COMING FOR A LONG TIME.
I THINK SHE WAS JUST LOOKING FOR THE RIGHT TIME TO "TRADE UP."
IT'S PRETTY TOUGH TO TAKE, THOUGH. SHE WAS THE FIRST WOMAN I EVER REALLY LOVED. I WAS KIND OF A LATE BLOOMER, Y'KNOW?
I KNOW WHAT YOU MEAN, KID. I REMEMBER WHEN I WAS YOUNG.
"HER NAME WAS OOLA. I'LL ADMIT HER HYGIENE WASN'T MUCH BY TODAY'S STANDARDS, BUT SHE HAD A GOOD HEART. I GUESS YOU NEVER DO FORGET YOUR FIRST LOVE."
GUESS NOT. MY GIRL WAS PRETTY SPECIAL, TOO. I MET HER AT A COMIC BOOK CONVENTION.
THAT'S PRETTY RARE, Y'KNOW.
I'LL BET.
IT GETS EASIER WITH TIME, THOUGH, AS YOU MEET OTHER PEOPLE.
THERE ARE SO MANY GREAT WOMEN OUT THERE.

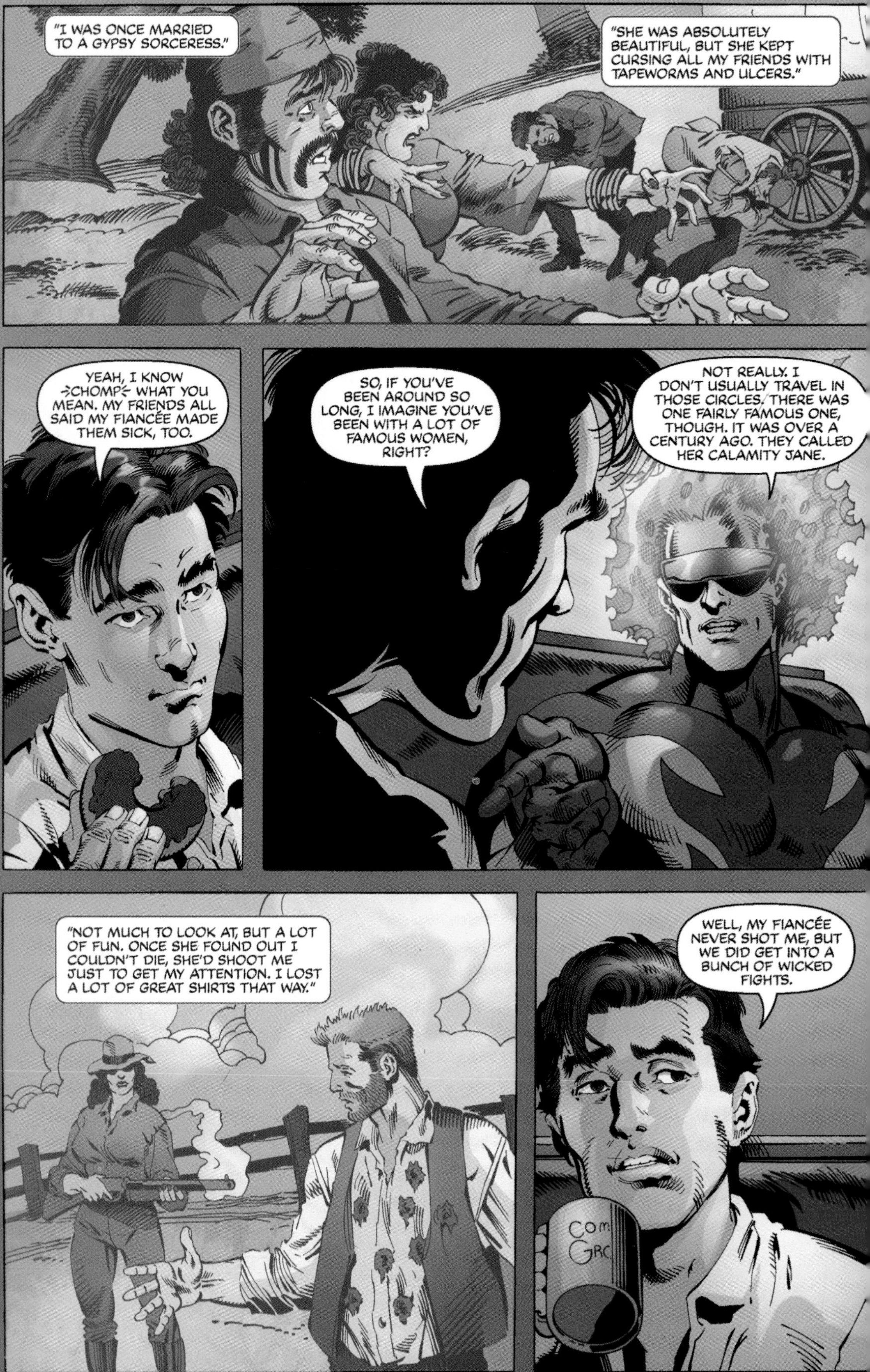
"I WAS ONCE MARRIED TO A GYPSY SORCERESS."
"SHE WAS ABSOLUTELY BEAUTIFUL, BUT SHE KEPT CURSING ALL MY FRIENDS WITH TAPEWORMS AND ULCERS."
YEAH, I KNOW →CHOMP← WHAT YOU MEAN. MY FRIENDS ALL SAID MY FIANCÉE MADE THEM SICK, TOO.
SO, IF YOU'VE BEEN AROUND SO LONG, I IMAGINE YOU'VE BEEN WITH A LOT OF FAMOUS WOMEN, RIGHT?
NOT REALLY. I DON'T USUALLY TRAVEL IN THOSE CIRCLES. THERE WAS ONE FAIRLY FAMOUS ONE, THOUGH. IT WAS OVER A CENTURY AGO. THEY CALLED HER CALAMITY JANE.
"NOT MUCH TO LOOK AT, BUT A LOT OF FUN. ONCE SHE FOUND OUT I COULDN'T DIE, SHE'D SHOOT ME JUST TO GET MY ATTENTION. I LOST A LOT OF GREAT SHIRTS THAT WAY."
WELL, MY FIANCÉE NEVER SHOT ME, BUT WE DID GET INTO A BUNCH OF WICKED FIGHTS.

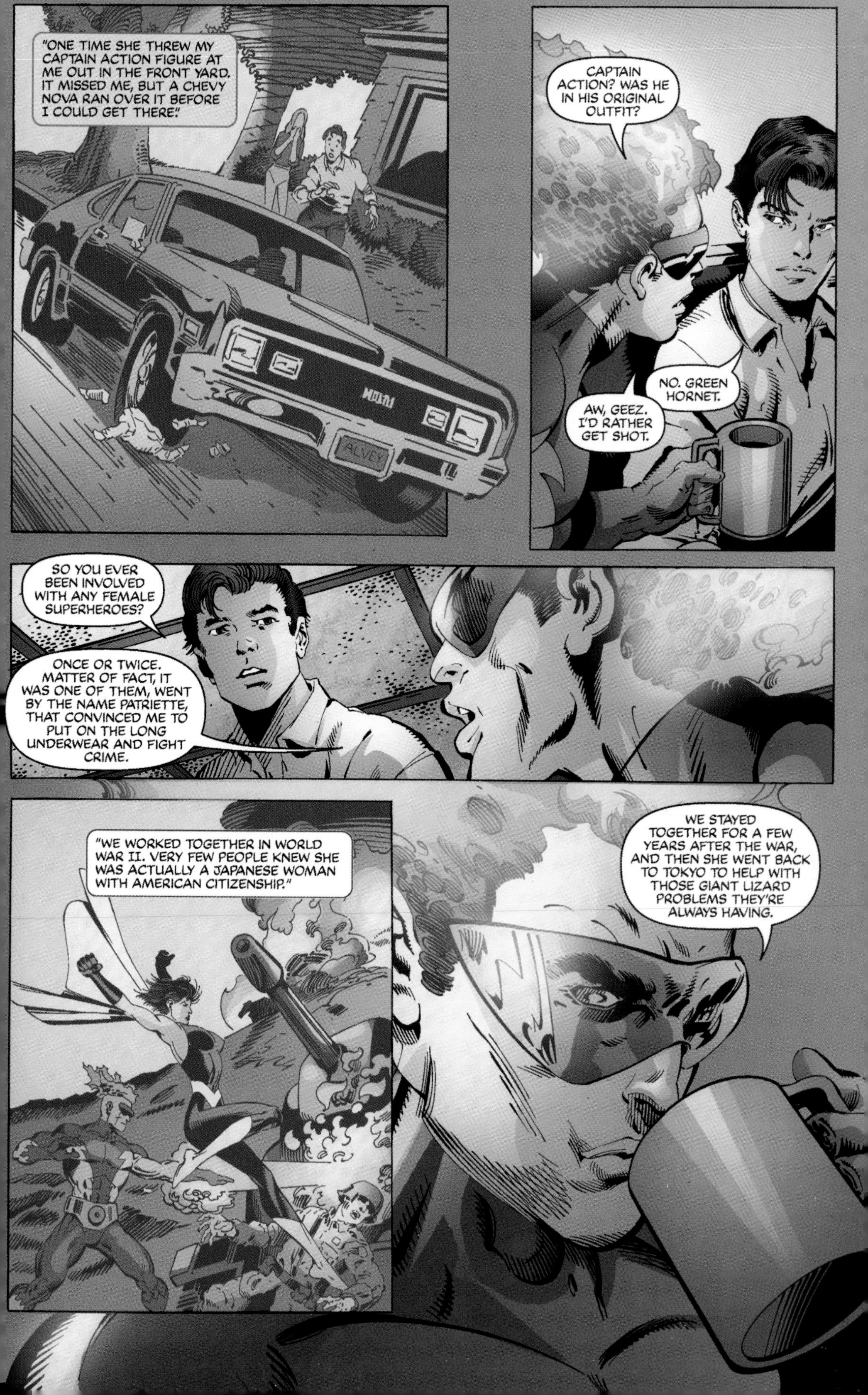
"ONE TIME SHE THREW MY CAPTAIN ACTION FIGURE AT ME OUT IN THE FRONT YARD. IT MISSED ME, BUT A CHEVY NOVA RAN OVER IT BEFORE I COULD GET THERE."
ALVEY
CAPTAIN ACTION? WAS HE IN HIS ORIGINAL OUTFIT?
NO. GREEN HORNET.
AW, GEEZ. I'D RATHER GET SHOT.
SO YOU EVER BEEN INVOLVED WITH ANY FEMALE SUPERHEROES?
ONCE OR TWICE. MATTER OF FACT, IT WAS ONE OF THEM, WENT BY THE NAME PATRIETTE, THAT CONVINCED ME TO PUT ON THE LONG UNDERWEAR AND FIGHT CRIME.
"WE WORKED TOGETHER IN WORLD WAR II. VERY FEW PEOPLE KNEW SHE WAS ACTUALLY A JAPANESE WOMAN WITH AMERICAN CITIZENSHIP."
WE STAYED TOGETHER FOR A FEW YEARS AFTER THE WAR, AND THEN SHE WENT BACK TO TOKYO TO HELP WITH THOSE GIANT LIZARD PROBLEMS THEY'RE ALWAYS HAVING.

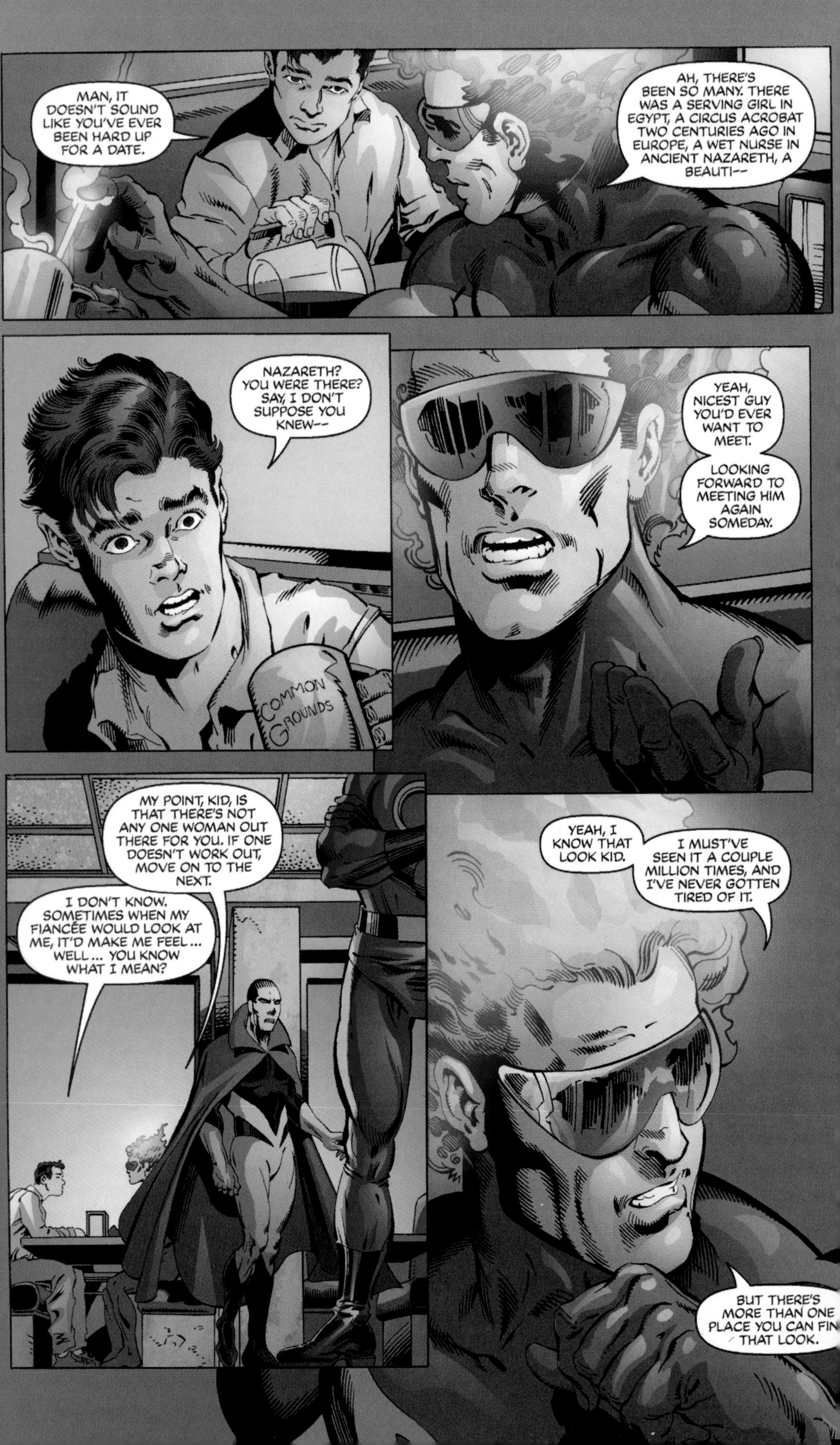
MAN, IT DOESN'T SOUND LIKE YOU'VE EVER BEEN HARD UP FOR A DATE.
AH, THERE'S BEEN SO MANY. THERE WAS A SERVING GIRL IN EGYPT, A CIRCUS ACROBAT TWO CENTURIES AGO IN EUROPE, A WET NURSE IN ANCIENT NAZARETH, A BEAUTI--
NAZARETH? YOU WERE THERE? SAY, I DON'T SUPPOSE YOU KNEW--
COMMON GROUNDS
YEAH, NICEST GUY YOU'D EVER WANT TO MEET.
LOOKING FORWARD TO MEETING HIM AGAIN SOMEDAY.
MY POINT, KID, IS THAT THERE'S NOT ANY ONE WOMAN OUT THERE FOR YOU. IF ONE DOESN'T WORK OUT, MOVE ON TO THE NEXT.
I DON'T KNOW. SOMETIMES WHEN MY FIANCÉE WOULD LOOK AT ME, IT'D MAKE ME FEEL... WELL... YOU KNOW WHAT I MEAN?
YEAH, I KNOW THAT LOOK KID.
I MUST'VE SEEN IT A COUPLE MILLION TIMES, AND I'VE NEVER GOTTEN TIRED OF IT.
BUT THERE'S MORE THAN ONE PLACE YOU CAN FIN THAT LOOK.

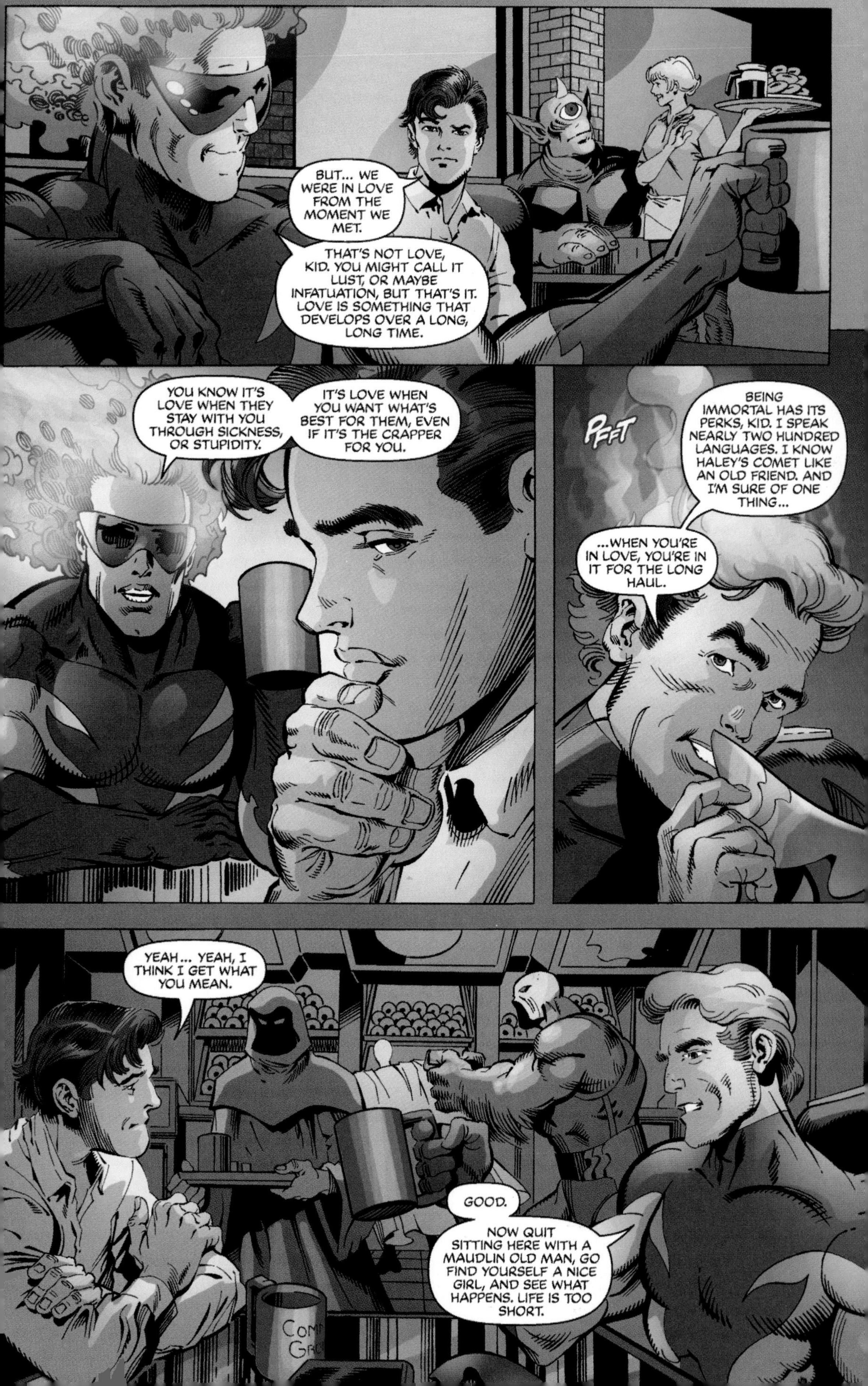

BUT... WE WERE IN LOVE FROM THE MOMENT WE MET.
THAT'S NOT LOVE, KID. YOU MIGHT CALL IT LUST, OR MAYBE INFATUATION, BUT THAT'S IT. LOVE IS SOMETHING THAT DEVELOPS OVER A LONG, LONG TIME.
YOU KNOW IT'S LOVE WHEN THEY STAY WITH YOU THROUGH SICKNESS, OR STUPIDITY.
IT'S LOVE WHEN YOU WANT WHAT'S BEST FOR THEM, EVEN IF IT'S THE CRAPPER FOR YOU.
PFFT
BEING IMMORTAL HAS ITS PERKS, KID. I SPEAK NEARLY TWO HUNDRED LANGUAGES. I KNOW HALEY'S COMET LIKE AN OLD FRIEND. AND I'M SURE OF ONE THING...
...WHEN YOU'RE IN LOVE, YOU'RE IN IT FOR THE LONG HAUL.
YEAH... YEAH, I THINK I GET WHAT YOU MEAN.
GOOD.
NOW QUIT SITTING HERE WITH A MAUDLIN OLD MAN, GO FIND YOURSELF A NICE GIRL, AND SEE WHAT HAPPENS. LIFE IS TOO SHORT.

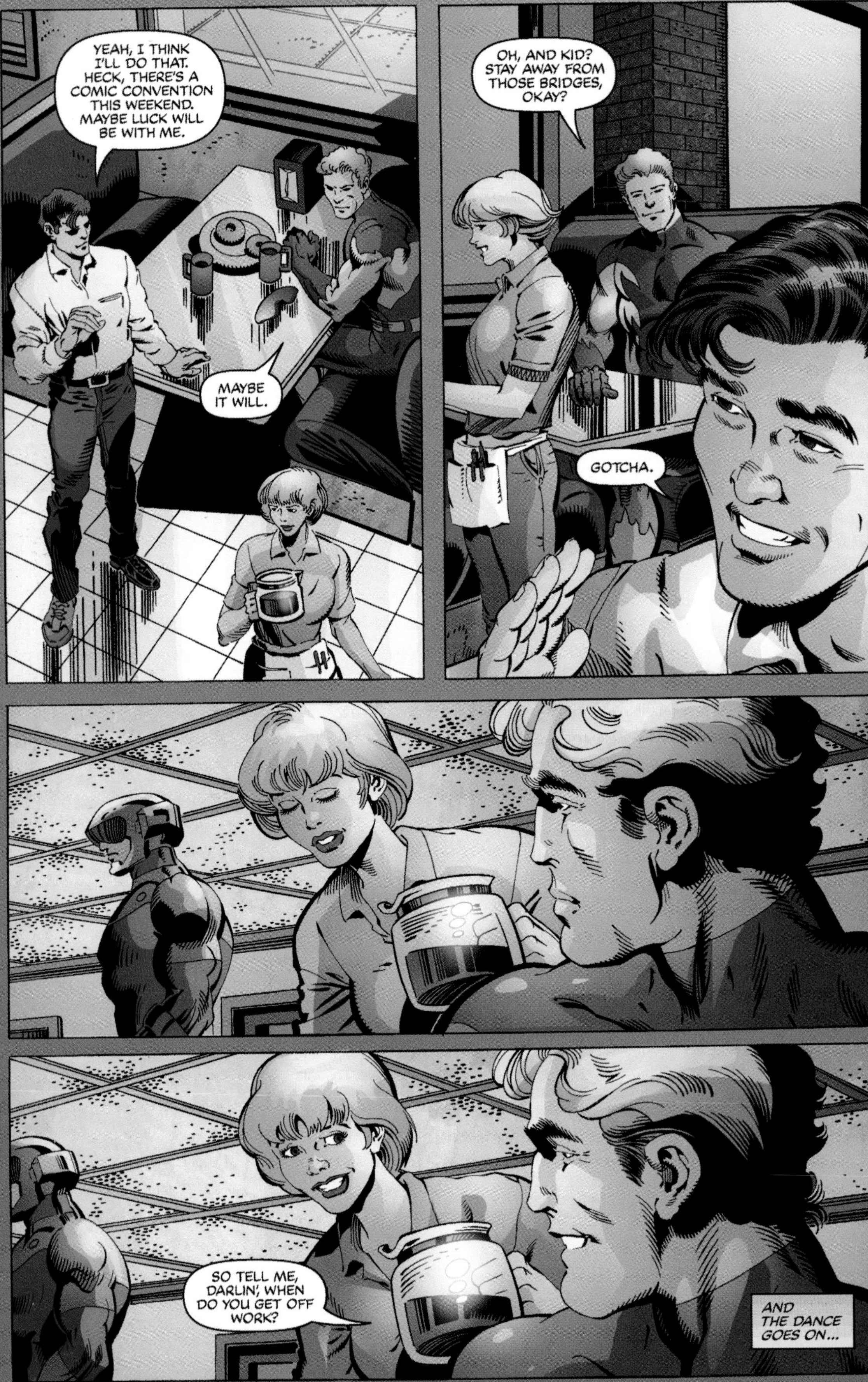
YEAH, I THINK I'LL DO THAT. HECK, THERE'S A COMIC CONVENTION THIS WEEKEND. MAYBE LUCK WILL BE WITH ME.
MAYBE IT WILL.
OH, AND KID? STAY AWAY FROM THOSE BRIDGES, OKAY?
GOTCHA.
SO TELL ME, DARLIN', WHEN DO YOU GET OFF WORK?
AND THE DANCE GOES ON...

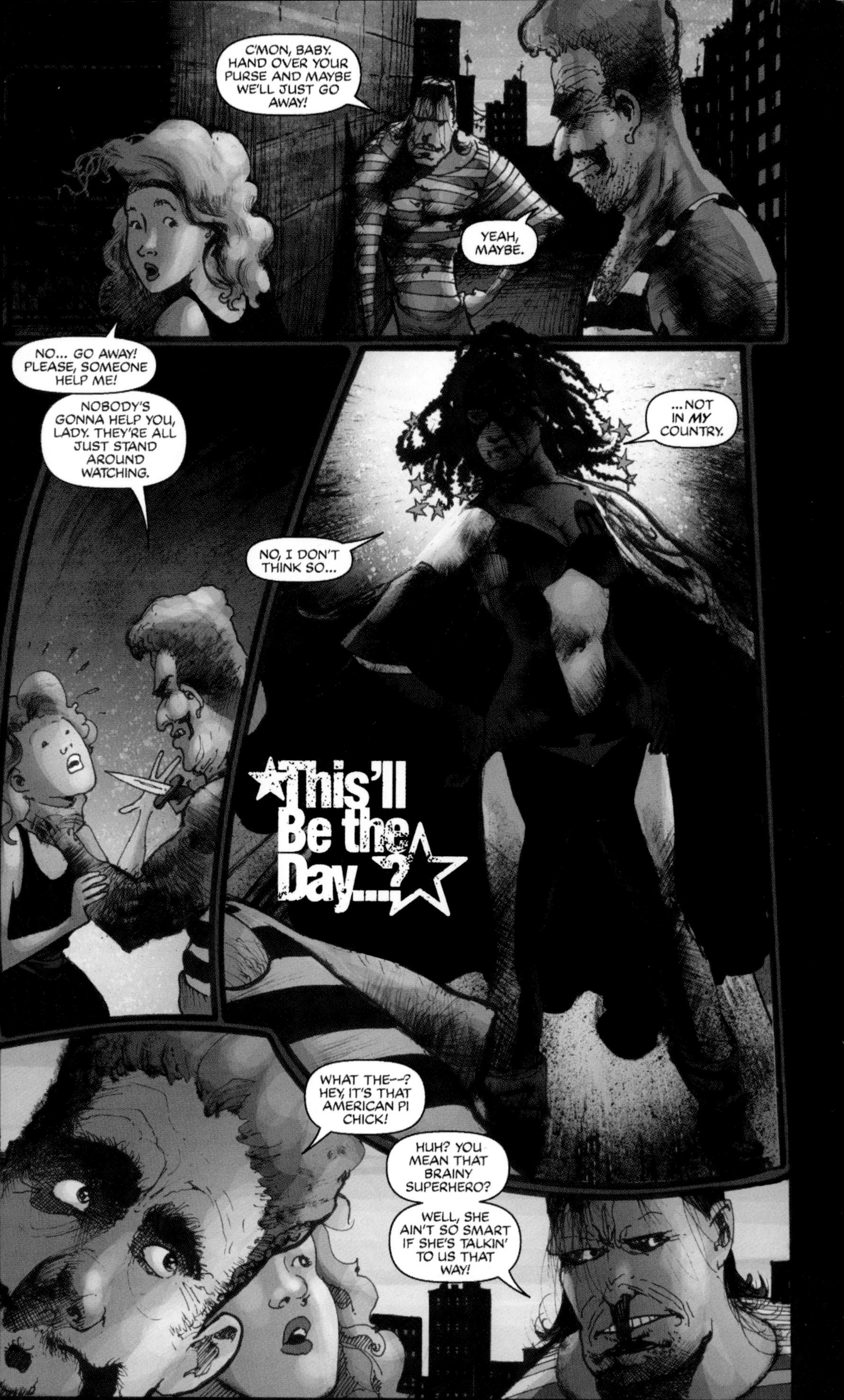
C'MON, BABY. HAND OVER YOUR PURSE AND MAYBE WE'LL JUST GO AWAY!
YEAH, MAYBE.
NO... GO AWAY! PLEASE, SOMEONE HELP ME!
NOBODY'S GONNA HELP YOU, LADY. THEY'RE ALL JUST STAND AROUND WATCHING.
NO, I DON'T THINK SO...
...NOT IN *MY* COUNTRY.
This'll Be the Day...?
WHAT THE--? HEY, IT'S THAT AMERICAN PI CHICK!
HUH? YOU MEAN THAT BRAINY SUPERHERO?
WELL, SHE AIN'T SO SMART IF SHE'S TALKIN' TO US THAT WAY!

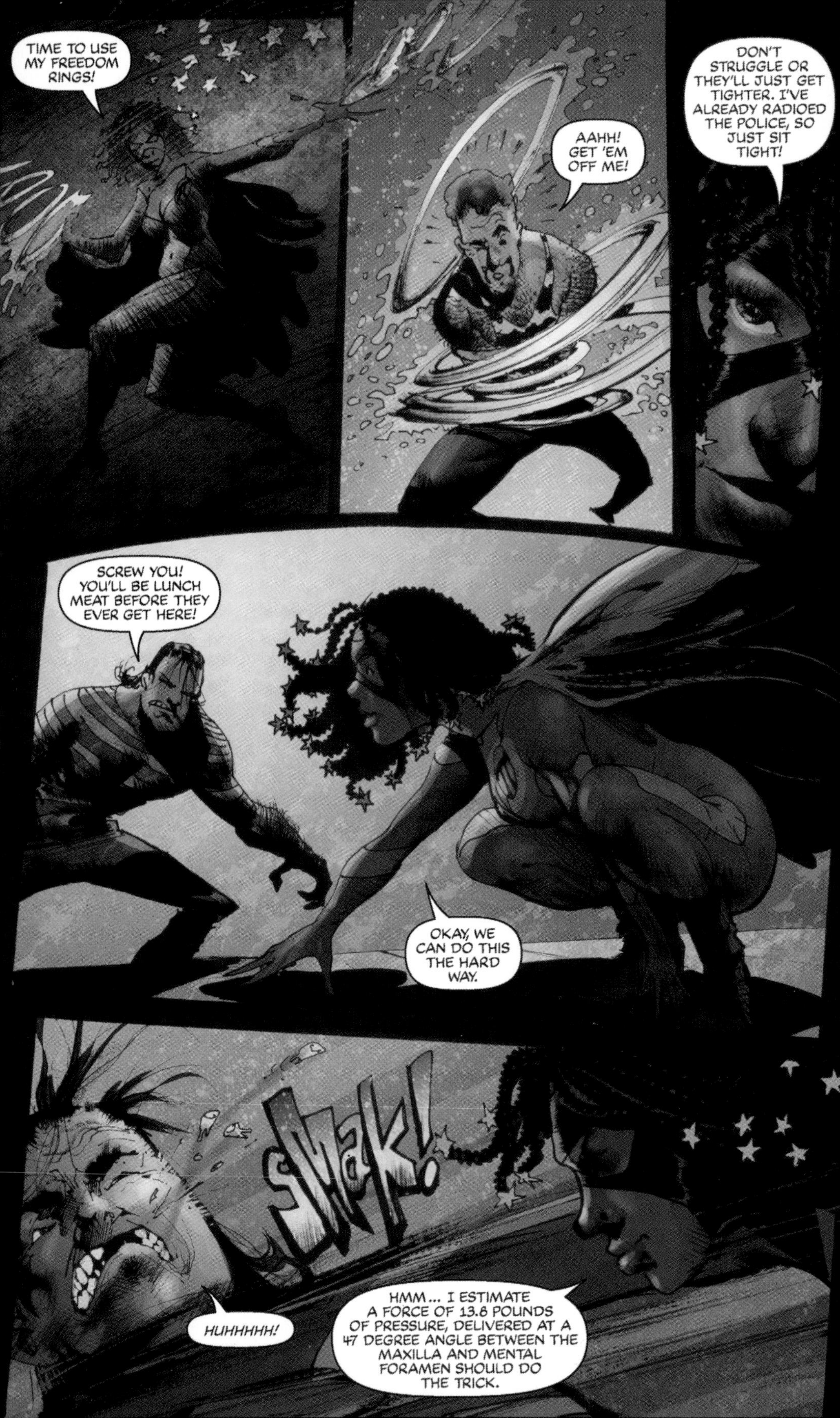
TIME TO USE MY FREEDOM RINGS!
AAHH! GET 'EM OFF ME!
DON'T STRUGGLE OR THEY'LL JUST GET TIGHTER. I'VE ALREADY RADIOED THE POLICE, SO JUST SIT TIGHT!
SCREW YOU! YOU'LL BE LUNCH MEAT BEFORE THEY EVER GET HERE!
OKAY, WE CAN DO THIS THE HARD WAY.
SMAK!
HUHHHHH!
HMM... I ESTIMATE A FORCE OF 13.8 POUNDS OF PRESSURE, DELIVERED AT A 47 DEGREE ANGLE BETWEEN THE MAXILLA AND MENTAL FORAMEN SHOULD DO THE TRICK.

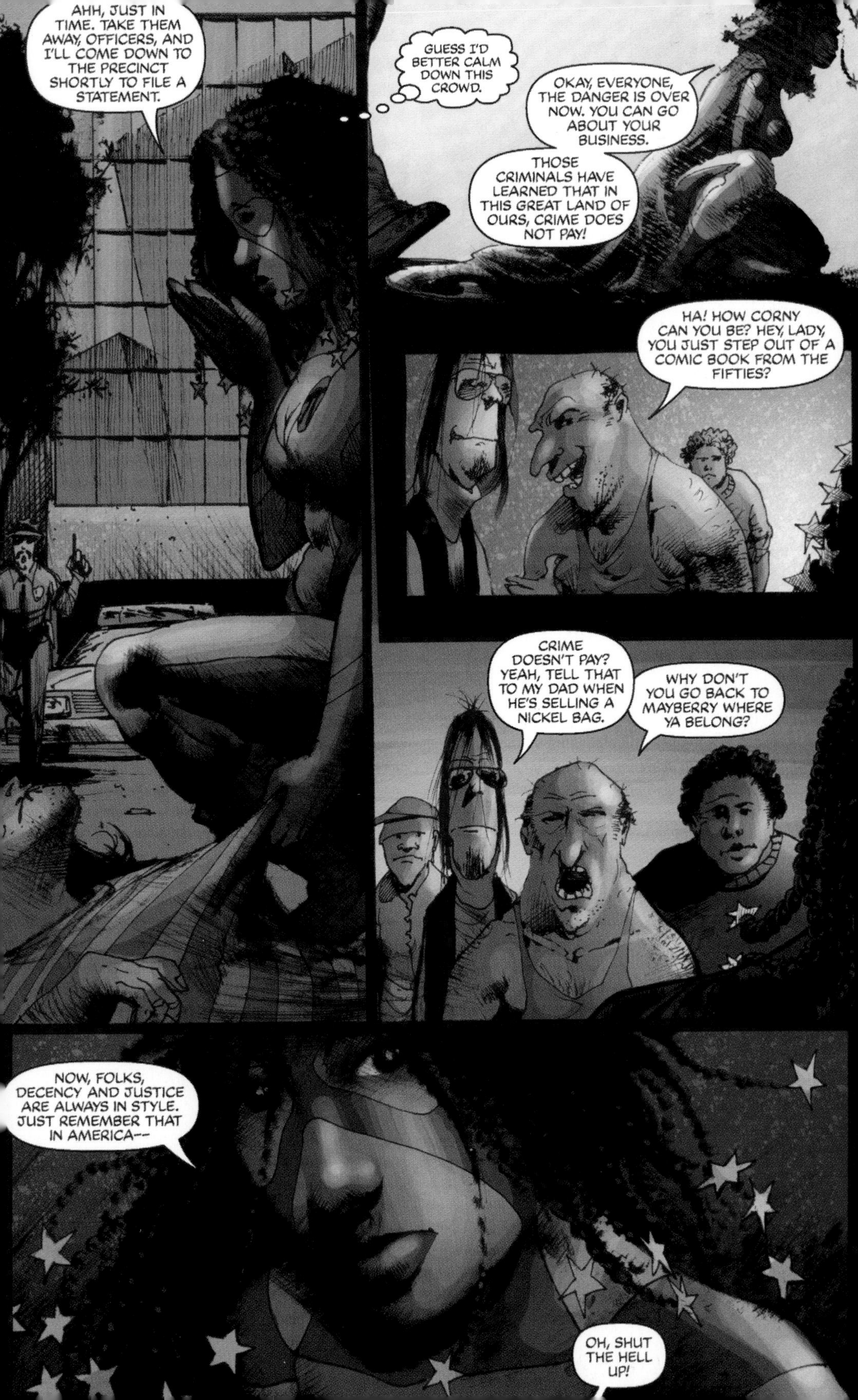
AHH, JUST IN TIME. TAKE THEM AWAY, OFFICERS, AND I'LL COME DOWN TO THE PRECINCT SHORTLY TO FILE A STATEMENT.
GUESS I'D BETTER CALM DOWN THIS CROWD.
OKAY, EVERYONE, THE DANGER IS OVER NOW. YOU CAN GO ABOUT YOUR BUSINESS.
THOSE CRIMINALS HAVE LEARNED THAT IN THIS GREAT LAND OF OURS, CRIME DOES NOT PAY!
HA! HOW CORNY CAN YOU BE? HEY, LADY, YOU JUST STEP OUT OF A COMIC BOOK FROM THE FIFTIES?
CRIME DOESN'T PAY? YEAH, TELL THAT TO MY DAD WHEN HE'S SELLING A NICKEL BAG.
WHY DON'T YOU GO BACK TO MAYBERRY WHERE YA BELONG?
NOW, FOLKS, DECENCY AND JUSTICE ARE ALWAYS IN STYLE. JUST REMEMBER THAT IN AMERICA--
OH, SHUT THE HELL UP!

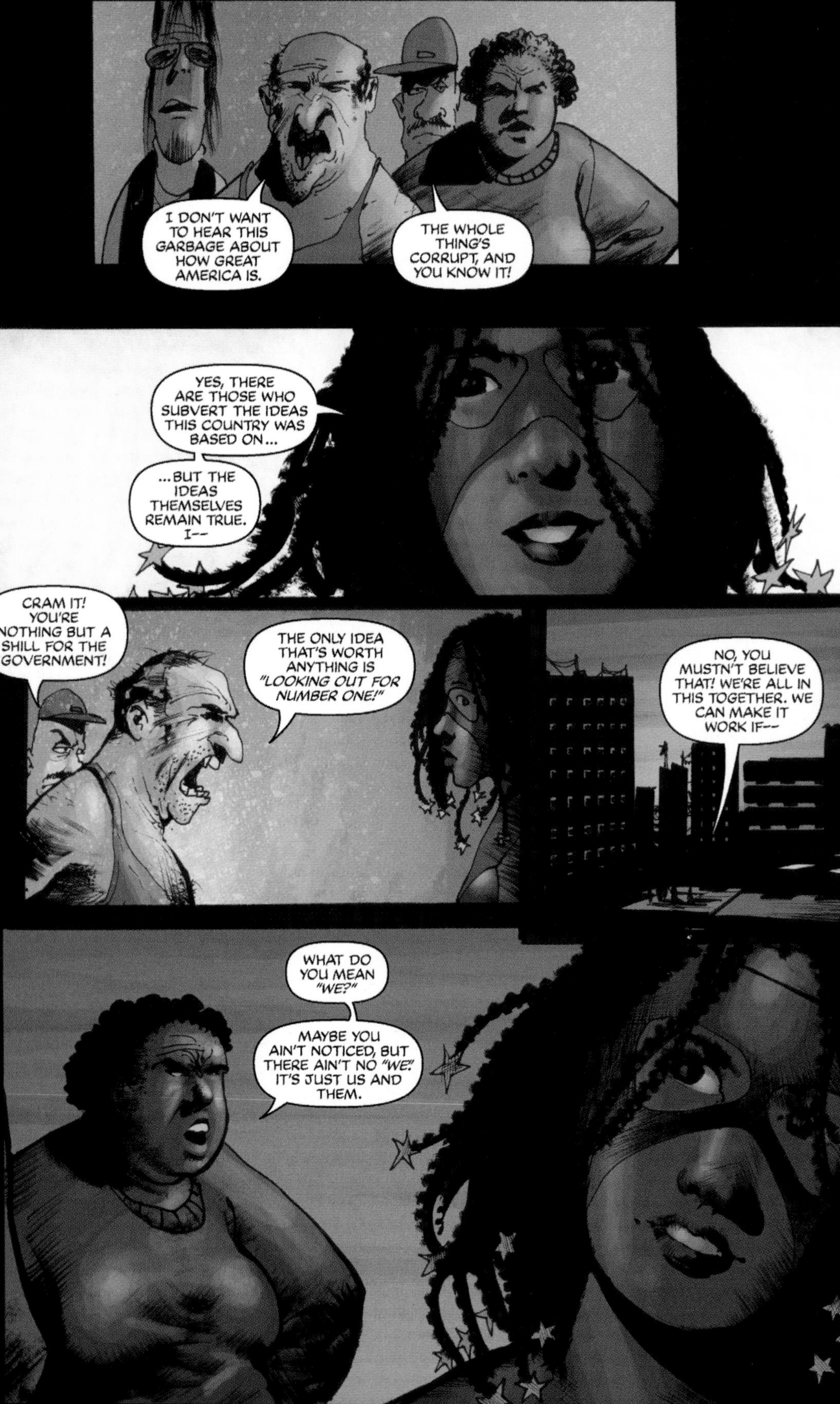
I DON'T WANT TO HEAR THIS GARBAGE ABOUT HOW GREAT AMERICA IS.
THE WHOLE THING'S CORRUPT, AND YOU KNOW IT!
YES, THERE ARE THOSE WHO SUBVERT THE IDEAS THIS COUNTRY WAS BASED ON...
...BUT THE IDEAS THEMSELVES REMAIN TRUE. I--
CRAM IT! YOU'RE NOTHING BUT A SHILL FOR THE GOVERNMENT!
THE ONLY IDEA THAT'S WORTH ANYTHING IS "LOOKING OUT FOR NUMBER ONE!"
NO, YOU MUSTN'T BELIEVE THAT! WE'RE ALL IN THIS TOGETHER. WE CAN MAKE IT WORK IF--
WHAT DO YOU MEAN "WE?"
MAYBE YOU AIN'T NOTICED, BUT THERE AIN'T NO "WE." IT'S JUST US AND THEM.

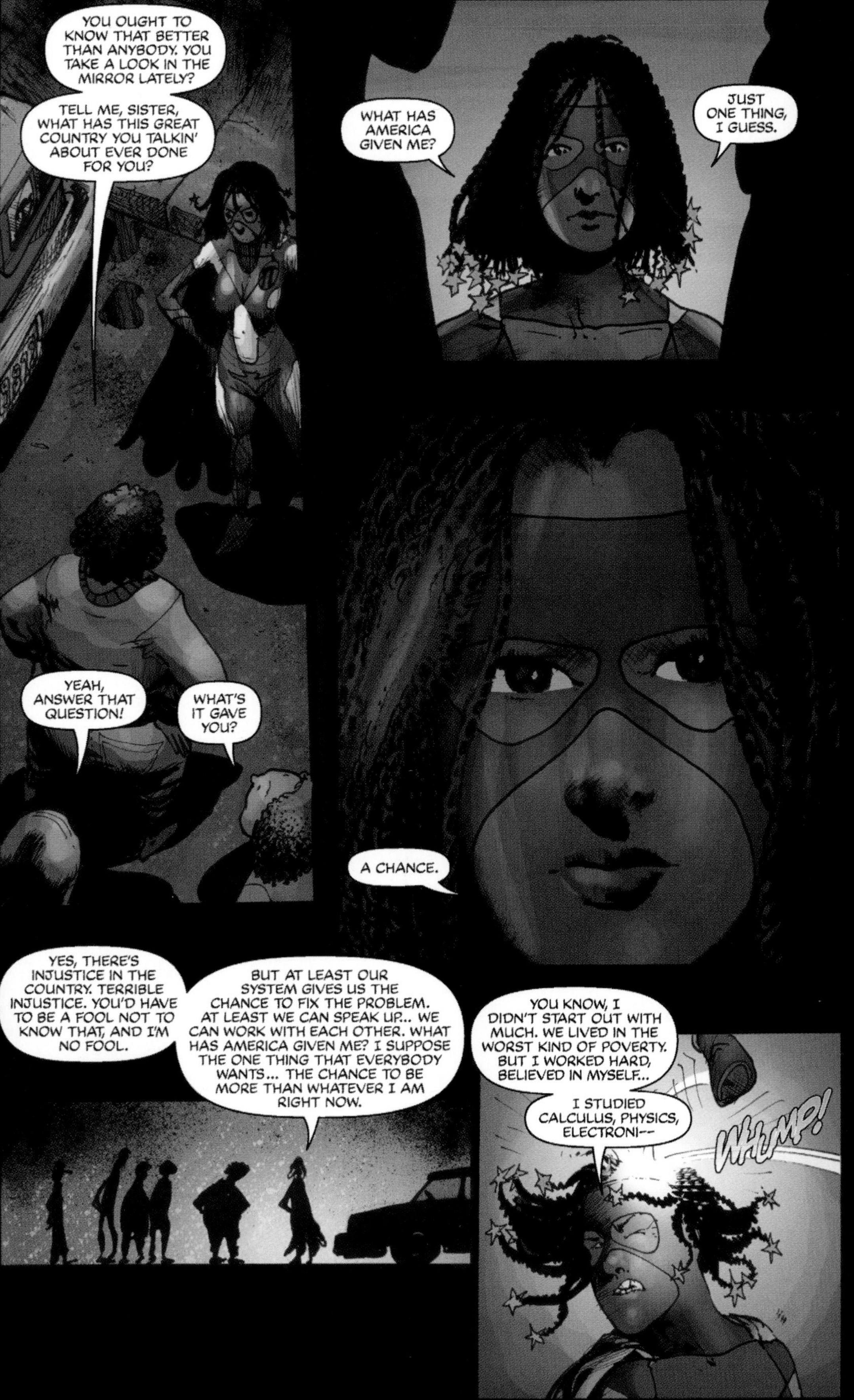

YOU OUGHT TO KNOW THAT BETTER THAN ANYBODY. YOU TAKE A LOOK IN THE MIRROR LATELY?
TELL ME, SISTER, WHAT HAS THIS GREAT COUNTRY YOU TALKIN' ABOUT EVER DONE FOR YOU?
YEAH, ANSWER THAT QUESTION!
WHAT'S IT GAVE YOU?
WHAT HAS AMERICA GIVEN ME?
JUST ONE THING, I GUESS.
A CHANCE.
YES, THERE'S INJUSTICE IN THE COUNTRY. TERRIBLE INJUSTICE. YOU'D HAVE TO BE A FOOL NOT TO KNOW THAT, AND I'M NO FOOL.
BUT AT LEAST OUR SYSTEM GIVES US THE CHANCE TO FIX THE PROBLEM. AT LEAST WE CAN SPEAK UP... WE CAN WORK WITH EACH OTHER. WHAT HAS AMERICA GIVEN ME? I SUPPOSE THE ONE THING THAT EVERYBODY WANTS... THE CHANCE TO BE MORE THAN WHATEVER I AM RIGHT NOW.
YOU KNOW, I DIDN'T START OUT WITH MUCH. WE LIVED IN THE WORST KIND OF POVERTY. BUT I WORKED HARD, BELIEVED IN MYSELF...
I STUDIED CALCULUS, PHYSICS, ELECTRONI--
WHUMP!

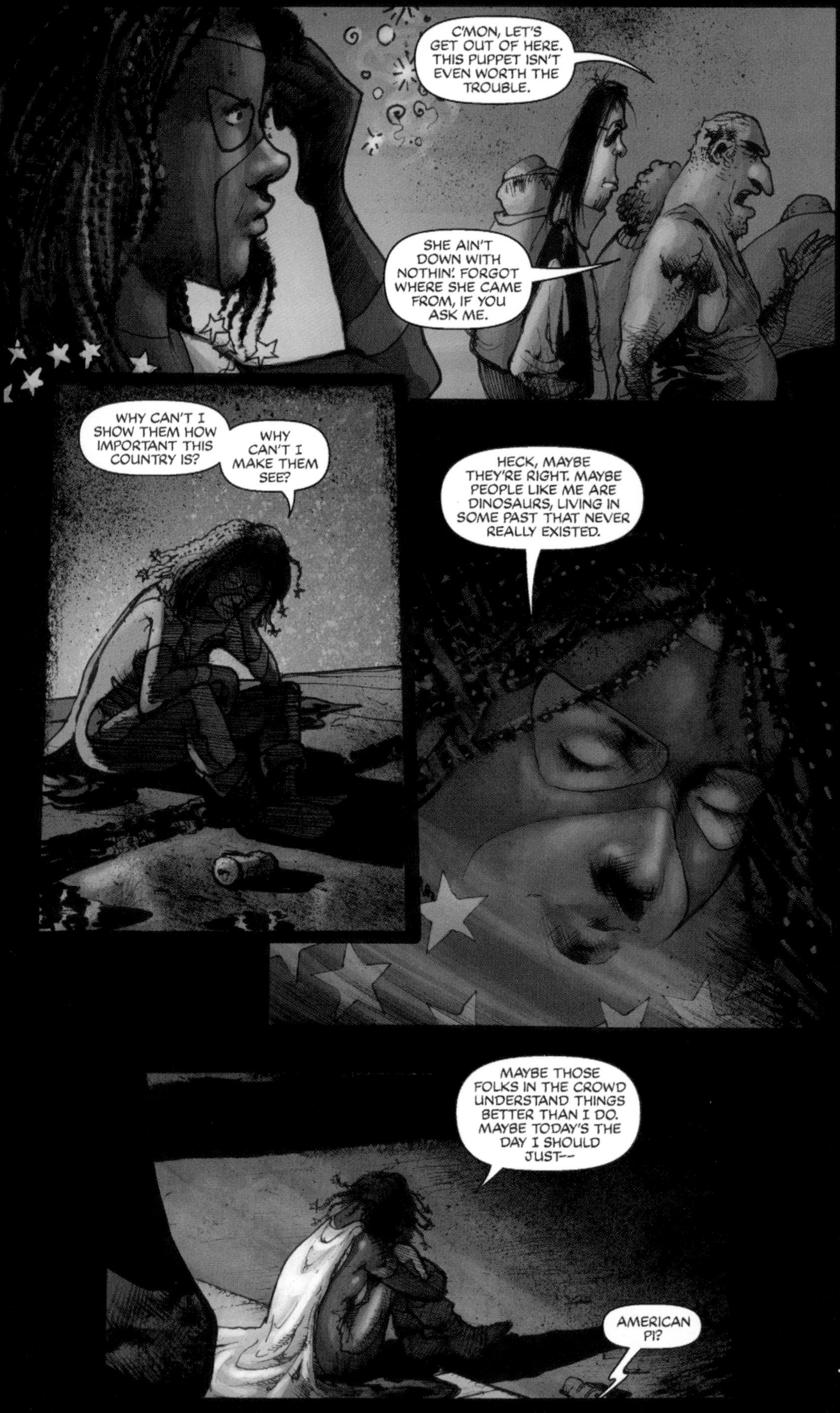
C'MON, LET'S GET OUT OF HERE. THIS PUPPET ISN'T EVEN WORTH THE TROUBLE.
SHE AIN'T DOWN WITH NOTHIN'. FORGOT WHERE SHE CAME FROM, IF YOU ASK ME.
WHY CAN'T I SHOW THEM HOW IMPORTANT THIS COUNTRY IS?
WHY CAN'T I MAKE THEM SEE?
HECK, MAYBE THEY'RE RIGHT. MAYBE PEOPLE LIKE ME ARE DINOSAURS, LIVING IN SOME PAST THAT NEVER REALLY EXISTED.
MAYBE THOSE FOLKS IN THE CROWD UNDERSTAND THINGS BETTER THAN I DO. MAYBE TODAY'S THE DAY I SHOULD JUST--
AMERICAN PI?

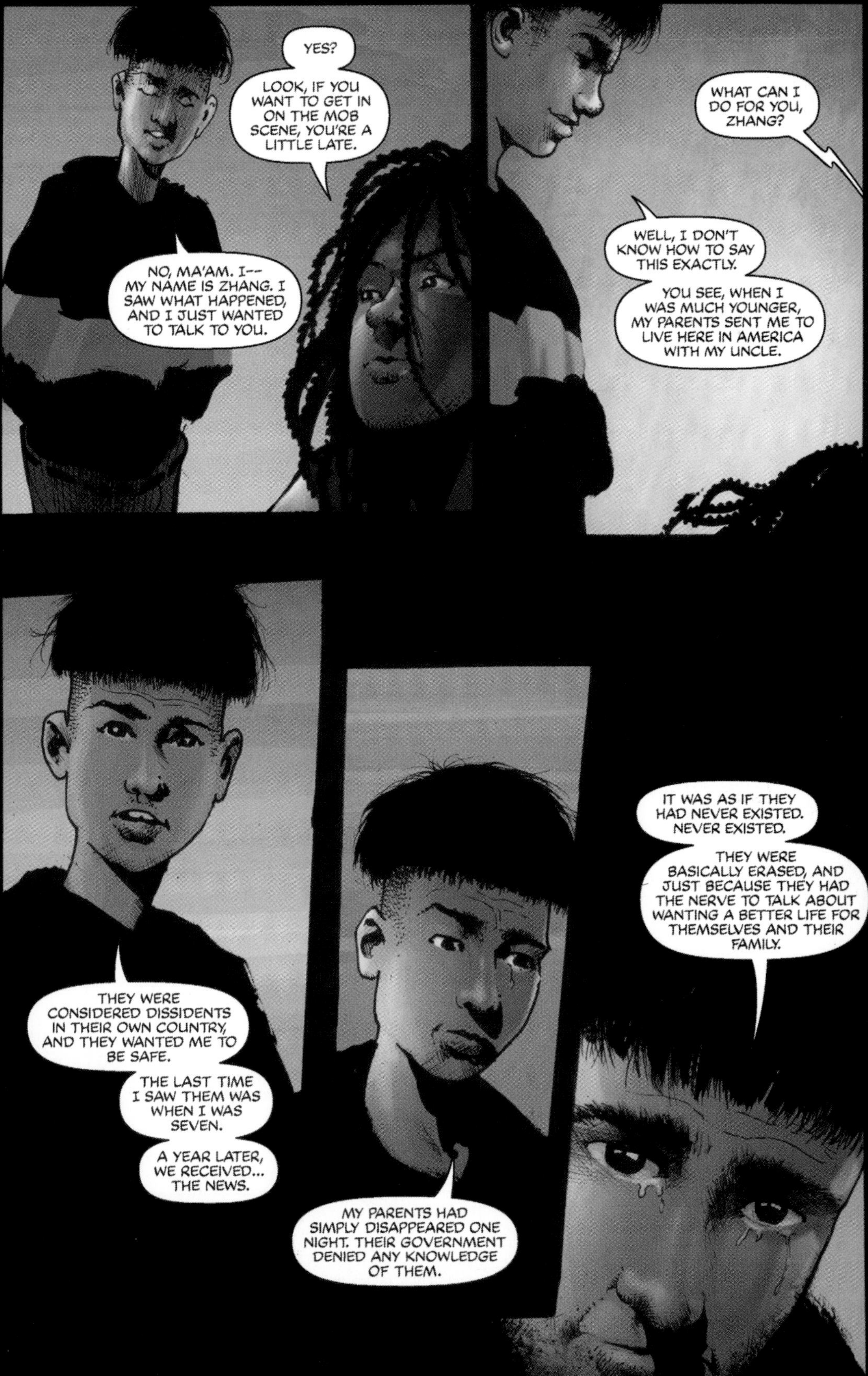
YES?
LOOK, IF YOU WANT TO GET IN ON THE MOB SCENE, YOU'RE A LITTLE LATE.
NO, MA'AM. I-- MY NAME IS ZHANG. I SAW WHAT HAPPENED, AND I JUST WANTED TO TALK TO YOU.
WHAT CAN I DO FOR YOU, ZHANG?
WELL, I DON'T KNOW HOW TO SAY THIS EXACTLY.
YOU SEE, WHEN I WAS MUCH YOUNGER, MY PARENTS SENT ME TO LIVE HERE IN AMERICA WITH MY UNCLE.
THEY WERE CONSIDERED DISSIDENTS IN THEIR OWN COUNTRY, AND THEY WANTED ME TO BE SAFE.
THE LAST TIME I SAW THEM WAS WHEN I WAS SEVEN.
A YEAR LATER, WE RECEIVED... THE NEWS.
MY PARENTS HAD SIMPLY DISAPPEARED ONE NIGHT. THEIR GOVERNMENT DENIED ANY KNOWLEDGE OF THEM.
IT WAS AS IF THEY HAD NEVER EXISTED. NEVER EXISTED.
THEY WERE BASICALLY ERASED, AND JUST BECAUSE THEY HAD THE NERVE TO TALK ABOUT WANTING A BETTER LIFE FOR THEMSELVES AND THEIR FAMILY.

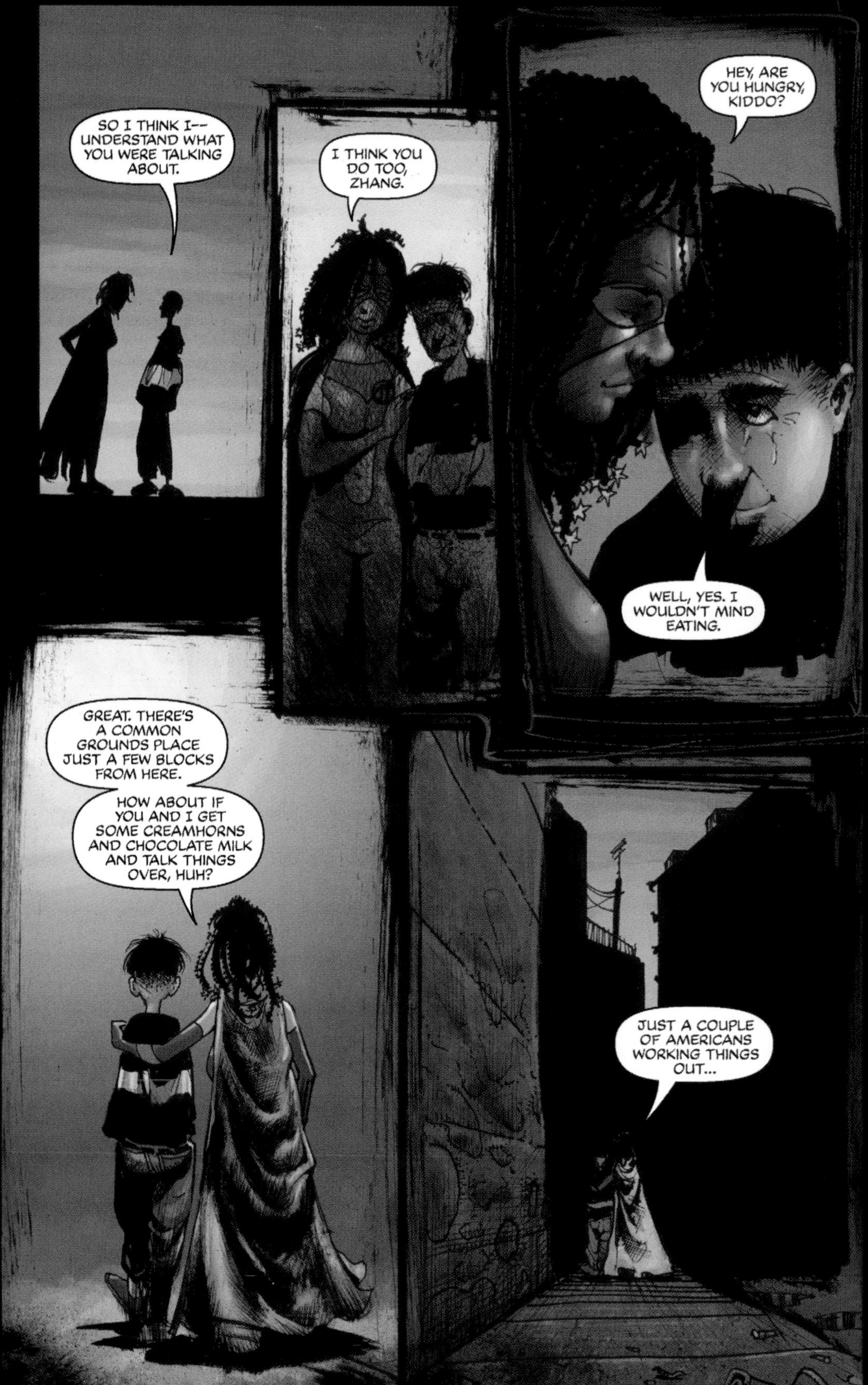
SO I THINK I-- UNDERSTAND WHAT YOU WERE TALKING ABOUT.
I THINK YOU DO TOO, ZHANG.
HEY, ARE YOU HUNGRY, KIDDO?
WELL, YES. I WOULDN'T MIND EATING.
GREAT. THERE'S A COMMON GROUNDS PLACE JUST A FEW BLOCKS FROM HERE.
HOW ABOUT IF YOU AND I GET SOME CREAMHORNS AND CHOCOLATE MILK AND TALK THINGS OVER, HUH?
JUST A COUPLE OF AMERICANS WORKING THINGS OUT...

END

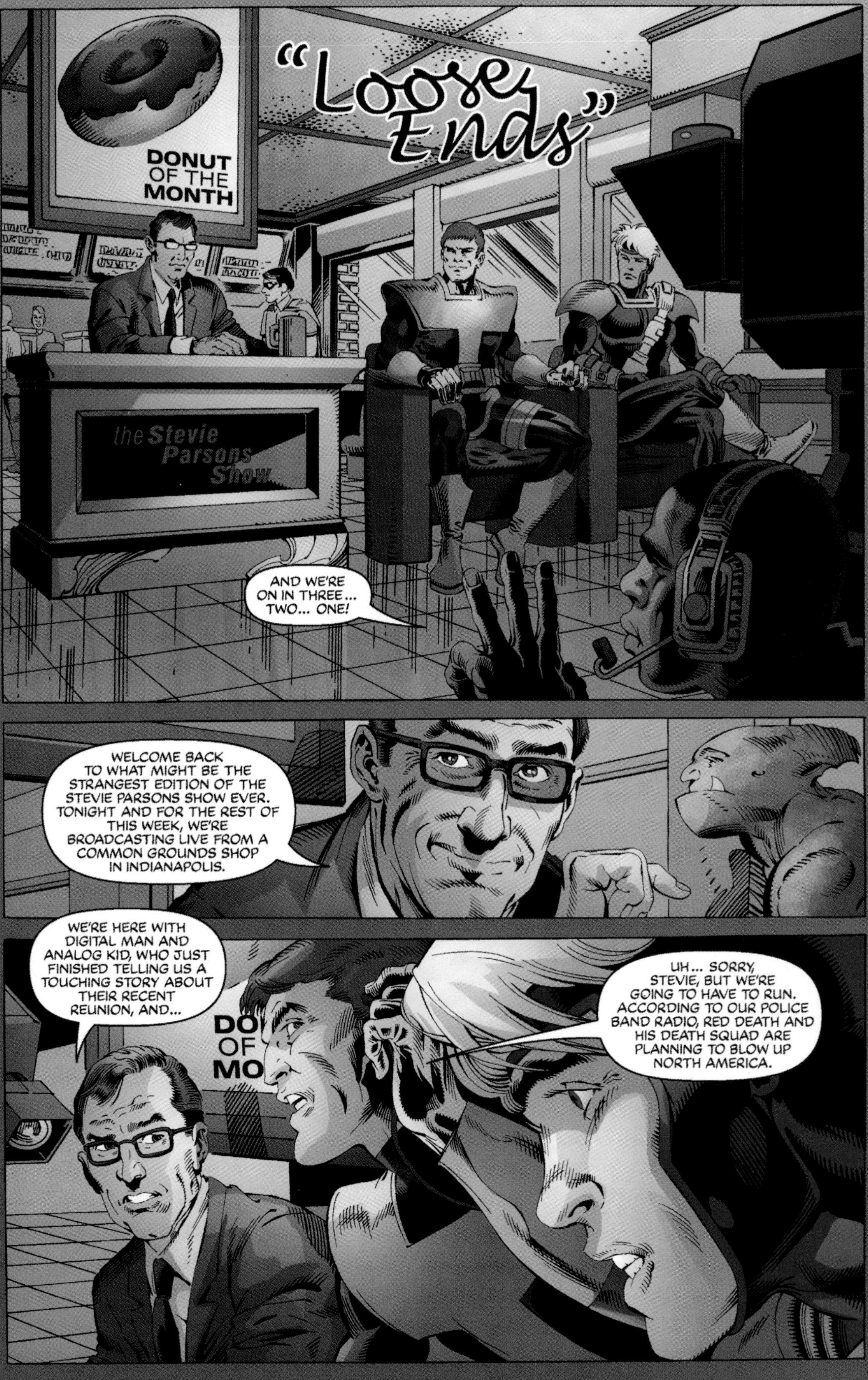
DONUT OF THE MONTH
"Loose Ends"
the Stevie Parsons Show
AND WE'RE ON IN THREE... TWO... ONE!
WELCOME BACK TO WHAT MIGHT BE THE STRANGEST EDITION OF THE STEVIE PARSONS SHOW EVER. TONIGHT AND FOR THE REST OF THIS WEEK, WE'RE BROADCASTING LIVE FROM A COMMON GROUNDS SHOP IN INDIANAPOLIS.
WE'RE HERE WITH DIGITAL MAN AND ANALOG KID, WHO JUST FINISHED TELLING US A TOUCHING STORY ABOUT THEIR RECENT REUNION, AND...
UH... SORRY, STEVIE, BUT WE'RE GOING TO HAVE TO RUN. ACCORDING TO OUR POLICE BAND RADIO, RED DEATH AND HIS DEATH SQUAD ARE PLANNING TO BLOW UP NORTH AMERICA.

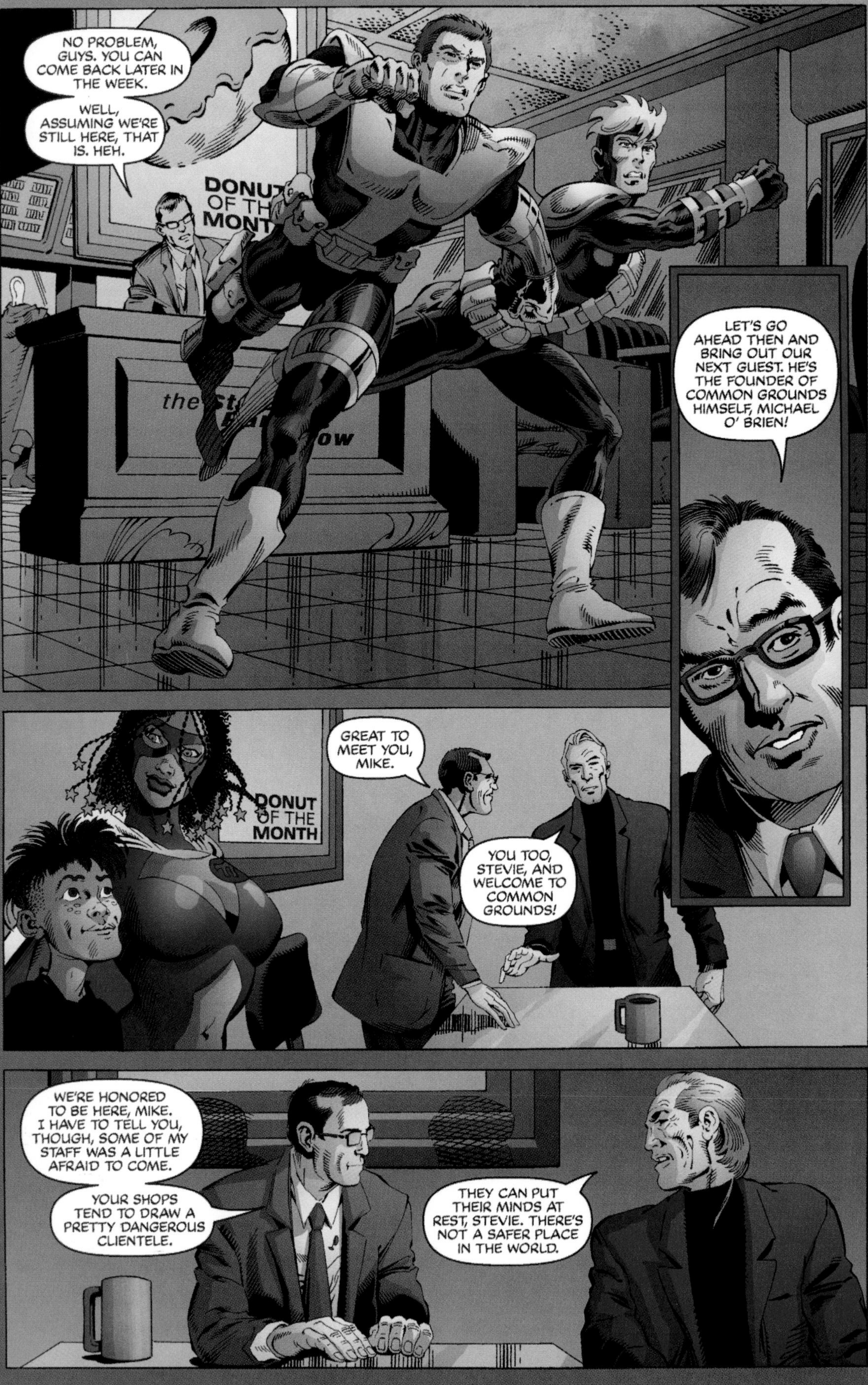

NO PROBLEM, GUYS. YOU CAN COME BACK LATER IN THE WEEK.
WELL, ASSUMING WE'RE STILL HERE, THAT IS. HEH.
DONUT OF THE MONTH
LET'S GO AHEAD THEN AND BRING OUT OUR NEXT GUEST. HE'S THE FOUNDER OF COMMON GROUNDS HIMSELF, MICHAEL O' BRIEN!
GREAT TO MEET YOU, MIKE.
DONUT OF THE MONTH
YOU TOO, STEVIE, AND WELCOME TO COMMON GROUNDS!
WE'RE HONORED TO BE HERE, MIKE. I HAVE TO TELL YOU, THOUGH, SOME OF MY STAFF WAS A LITTLE AFRAID TO COME.
YOUR SHOPS TEND TO DRAW A PRETTY DANGEROUS CLIENTELE.
THEY CAN PUT THEIR MINDS AT REST, STEVIE. THERE'S NOT A SAFER PLACE IN THE WORLD.

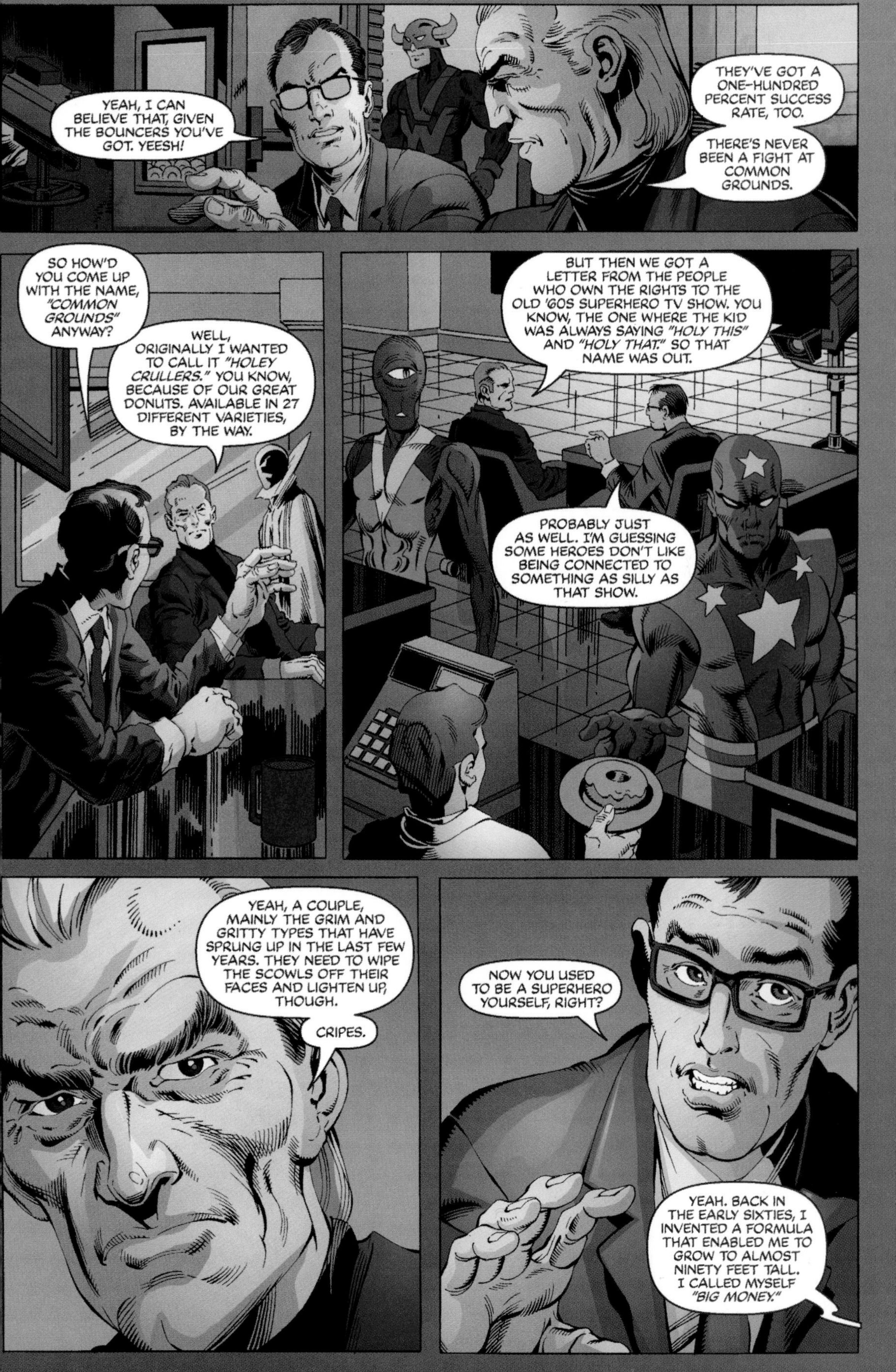

YEAH, I CAN BELIEVE THAT, GIVEN THE BOUNCERS YOU'VE GOT. YEESH!
THEY'VE GOT A ONE-HUNDRED PERCENT SUCCESS RATE, TOO.
THERE'S NEVER BEEN A FIGHT AT COMMON GROUNDS.
SO HOW'D YOU COME UP WITH THE NAME, *"COMMON GROUNDS"* ANYWAY?
WELL, ORIGINALLY I WANTED TO CALL IT *"HOLEY CRULLERS."* YOU KNOW, BECAUSE OF OUR GREAT DONUTS. AVAILABLE IN 27 DIFFERENT VARIETIES, BY THE WAY.
BUT THEN WE GOT A LETTER FROM THE PEOPLE WHO OWN THE RIGHTS TO THE OLD '60S SUPERHERO TV SHOW. YOU KNOW, THE ONE WHERE THE KID WAS ALWAYS SAYING *"HOLY THIS"* AND *"HOLY THAT."* SO THAT NAME WAS OUT.
PROBABLY JUST AS WELL. I'M GUESSING SOME HEROES DON'T LIKE BEING CONNECTED TO SOMETHING AS SILLY AS THAT SHOW.
YEAH, A COUPLE, MAINLY THE GRIM AND GRITTY TYPES THAT HAVE SPRUNG UP IN THE LAST FEW YEARS. THEY NEED TO WIPE THE SCOWLS OFF THEIR FACES AND LIGHTEN UP, THOUGH.
CRIPES.
NOW YOU USED TO BE A SUPERHERO YOURSELF, RIGHT?
YEAH. BACK IN THE EARLY SIXTIES, I INVENTED A FORMULA THAT ENABLED ME TO GROW TO ALMOST NINETY FEET TALL. I CALLED MYSELF *"BIG MONEY."*

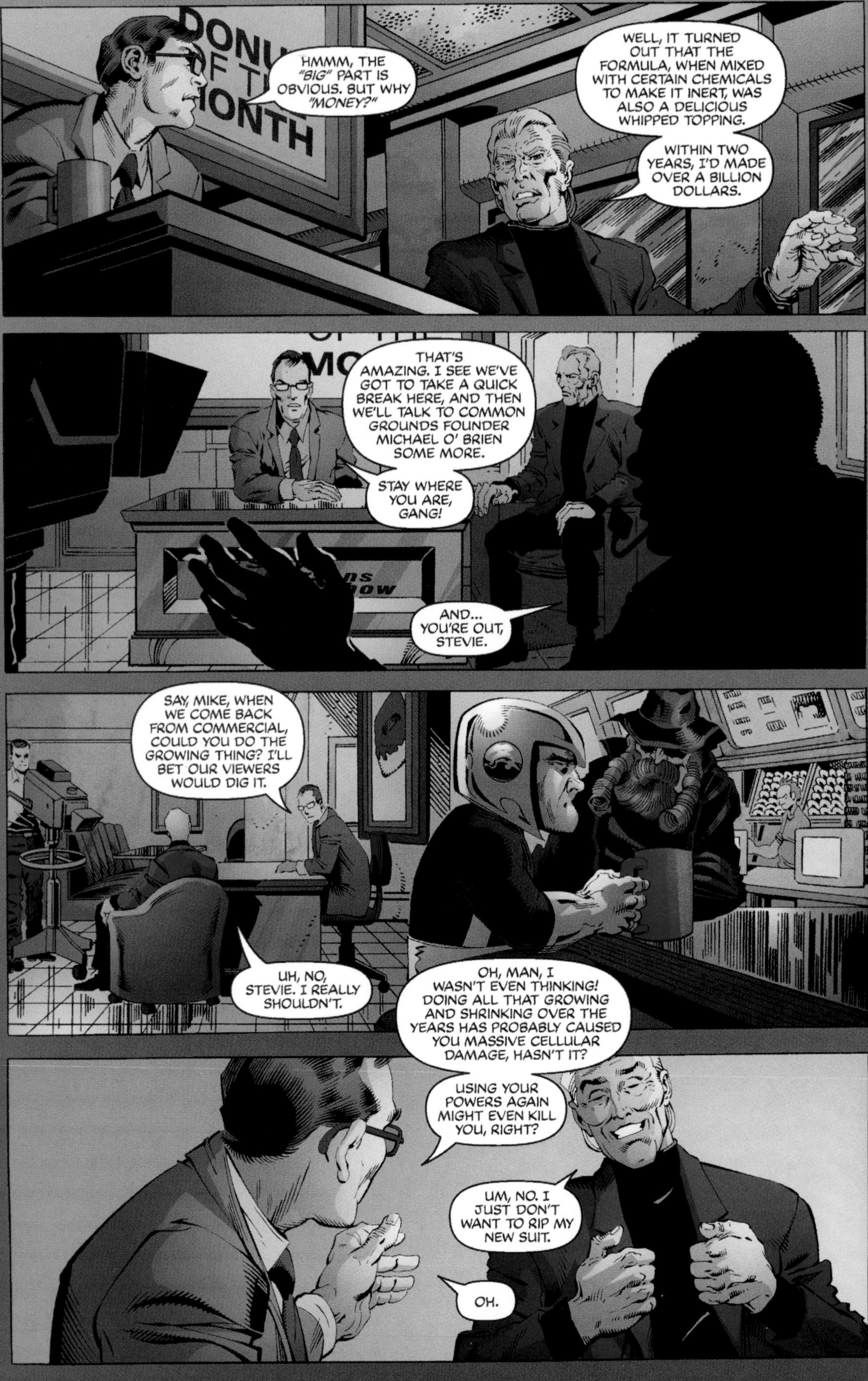
DONUT OF THE MONTH
HMMM, THE "BIG" PART IS OBVIOUS. BUT WHY "MONEY?"
WELL, IT TURNED OUT THAT THE FORMULA, WHEN MIXED WITH CERTAIN CHEMICALS TO MAKE IT INERT, WAS ALSO A DELICIOUS WHIPPED TOPPING.
WITHIN TWO YEARS, I'D MADE OVER A BILLION DOLLARS.
THAT'S AMAZING. I SEE WE'VE GOT TO TAKE A QUICK BREAK HERE, AND THEN WE'LL TALK TO COMMON GROUNDS FOUNDER MICHAEL O' BRIEN SOME MORE.
STAY WHERE YOU ARE, GANG!
AND... YOU'RE OUT, STEVIE.
SAY, MIKE, WHEN WE COME BACK FROM COMMERCIAL, COULD YOU DO THE GROWING THING? I'LL BET OUR VIEWERS WOULD DIG IT.
UH, NO, STEVIE. I REALLY SHOULDN'T.
OH, MAN, I WASN'T EVEN THINKING! DOING ALL THAT GROWING AND SHRINKING OVER THE YEARS HAS PROBABLY CAUSED YOU MASSIVE CELLULAR DAMAGE, HASN'T IT?
USING YOUR POWERS AGAIN MIGHT EVEN KILL YOU, RIGHT?
UM, NO. I JUST DON'T WANT TO RIP MY NEW SUIT.
OH.

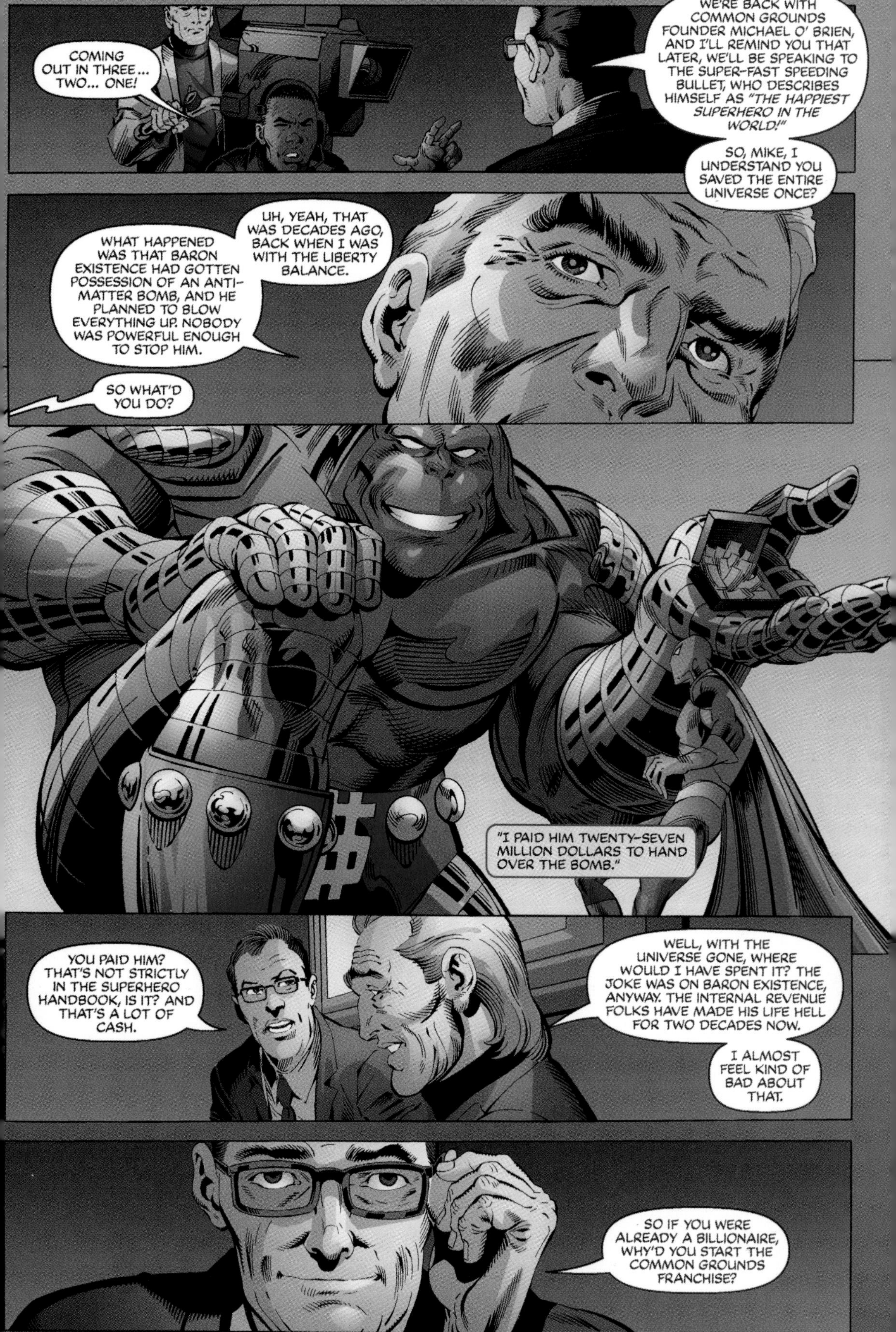
COMING OUT IN THREE... TWO... ONE!
WE'RE BACK WITH COMMON GROUNDS FOUNDER MICHAEL O' BRIEN, AND I'LL REMIND YOU THAT LATER, WE'LL BE SPEAKING TO THE SUPER-FAST SPEEDING BULLET, WHO DESCRIBES HIMSELF AS *"THE HAPPIEST SUPERHERO IN THE WORLD!"*
SO, MIKE, I UNDERSTAND YOU SAVED THE ENTIRE UNIVERSE ONCE?
UH, YEAH, THAT WAS DECADES AGO, BACK WHEN I WAS WITH THE LIBERTY BALANCE.
WHAT HAPPENED WAS THAT BARON EXISTENCE HAD GOTTEN POSSESSION OF AN ANTI-MATTER BOMB, AND HE PLANNED TO BLOW EVERYTHING UP. NOBODY WAS POWERFUL ENOUGH TO STOP HIM.
SO WHAT'D YOU DO?
"I PAID HIM TWENTY-SEVEN MILLION DOLLARS TO HAND OVER THE BOMB."
YOU PAID HIM? THAT'S NOT STRICTLY IN THE SUPERHERO HANDBOOK, IS IT? AND THAT'S A LOT OF CASH.
WELL, WITH THE UNIVERSE GONE, WHERE WOULD I HAVE SPENT IT? THE JOKE WAS ON BARON EXISTENCE, ANYWAY. THE INTERNAL REVENUE FOLKS HAVE MADE HIS LIFE HELL FOR TWO DECADES NOW.
I ALMOST FEEL KIND OF BAD ABOUT THAT.
SO IF YOU WERE ALREADY A BILLIONAIRE, WHY'D YOU START THE COMMON GROUNDS FRANCHISE?

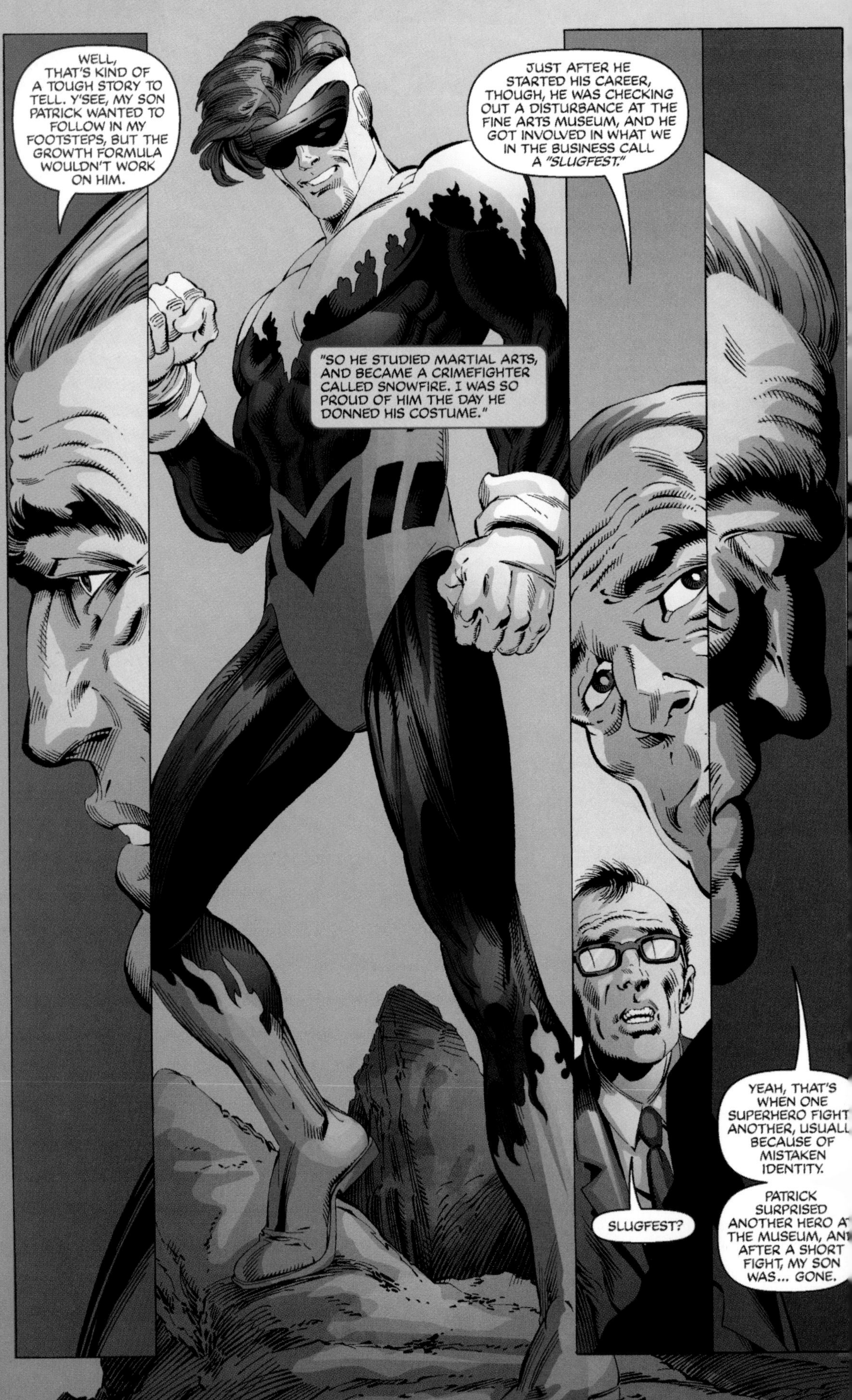
WELL, THAT'S KIND OF A TOUGH STORY TO TELL. Y'SEE, MY SON PATRICK WANTED TO FOLLOW IN MY FOOTSTEPS, BUT THE GROWTH FORMULA WOULDN'T WORK ON HIM.
"SO HE STUDIED MARTIAL ARTS, AND BECAME A CRIMEFIGHTER CALLED SNOWFIRE. I WAS SO PROUD OF HIM THE DAY HE DONNED HIS COSTUME."
JUST AFTER HE STARTED HIS CAREER, THOUGH, HE WAS CHECKING OUT A DISTURBANCE AT THE FINE ARTS MUSEUM, AND HE GOT INVOLVED IN WHAT WE IN THE BUSINESS CALL A "SLUGFEST."
SLUGFEST?
YEAH, THAT'S WHEN ONE SUPERHERO FIGHT ANOTHER, USUALL BECAUSE OF MISTAKEN IDENTITY.
PATRICK SURPRISED ANOTHER HERO A THE MUSEUM, AN AFTER A SHORT FIGHT, MY SON WAS... GONE.

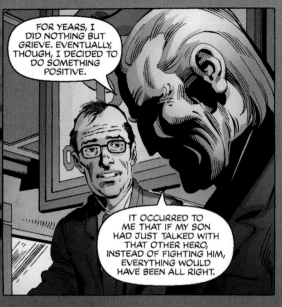

FOR YEARS, I DID NOTHING BUT GRIEVE. EVENTUALLY, THOUGH, I DECIDED TO DO SOMETHING POSITIVE.

IT OCCURRED TO ME THAT IF MY SON HAD JUST TALKED WITH THAT OTHER HERO, INSTEAD OF FIGHTING HIM, EVERYTHING WOULD HAVE BEEN ALL RIGHT.

AH, I SEE.

SO, YOU DECIDED TO CREATE A PLACE WHERE HEROES COULD TALK TO EACH OTHER WITHOUT ALL THE FIGHTING?

NOT JUST HEROES, BUT VILLAINS, TOO. AS LONG AS ANYBODY NEEDS SOMEONE TO TALK TO, I WANT THERE TO BE A COMMON GROUNDS.

FASCINATING STUFF. I'M SO SORRY ABOUT YOUR SON, THOUGH.

HEY, IT'S OKAY. HE'LL BE BACK.

UH, WHAT DO YOU MEAN?

HECK, IF THERE'S ONE THING I KNOW ABOUT THE SUPERHERO BUSINESS, IT'S THAT EVERYONE COMES BACK.

EVERY VILLAIN, EVERY SIDEKICK, NO MATTER HOW MINOR, ALWAYS MAKES A MIRACULOUS RETURN.

SO CERTAINLY A HERO LIKE MY SON IS GOING TO RETURN, RIGHT? IT'LL ALL BE A HOAX, OR A DREAM, OR MAYBE JUST SOME IMAGINARY STORY SOMEONE MADE UP, RIGHT?

RIGHT?

YEAH.

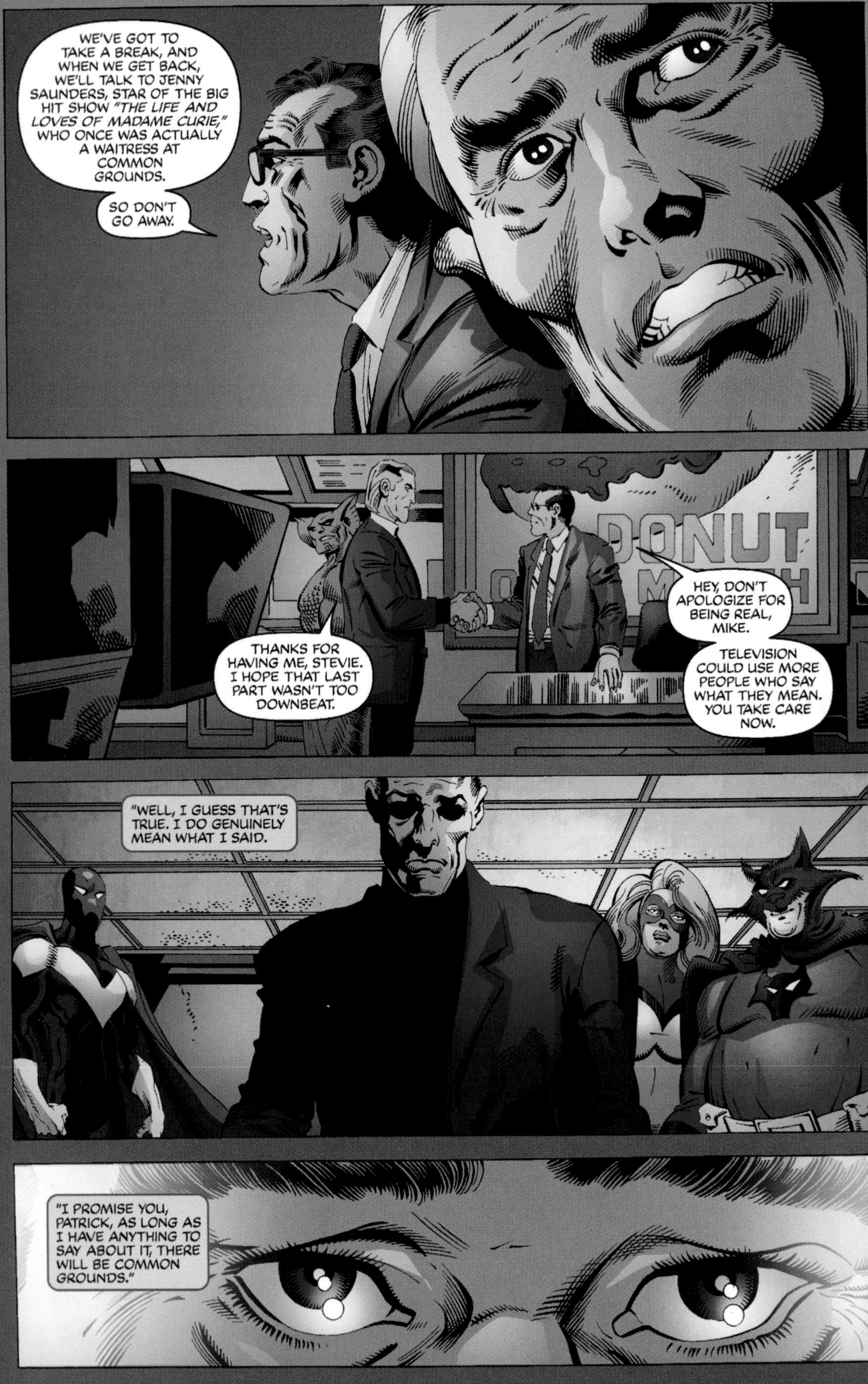
WE'VE GOT TO TAKE A BREAK, AND WHEN WE GET BACK, WE'LL TALK TO JENNY SAUNDERS, STAR OF THE BIG HIT SHOW *"THE LIFE AND LOVES OF MADAME CURIE,"* WHO ONCE WAS ACTUALLY A WAITRESS AT COMMON GROUNDS.
SO DON'T GO AWAY.
DONUT
THANKS FOR HAVING ME, STEVIE. I HOPE THAT LAST PART WASN'T TOO DOWNBEAT.
HEY, DON'T APOLOGIZE FOR BEING REAL, MIKE.
TELEVISION COULD USE MORE PEOPLE WHO SAY WHAT THEY MEAN. YOU TAKE CARE NOW.
"WELL, I GUESS THAT'S TRUE. I DO GENUINELY MEAN WHAT I SAID.
"I PROMISE YOU, PATRICK, AS LONG AS I HAVE ANYTHING TO SAY ABOUT IT, THERE WILL BE COMMON GROUNDS."

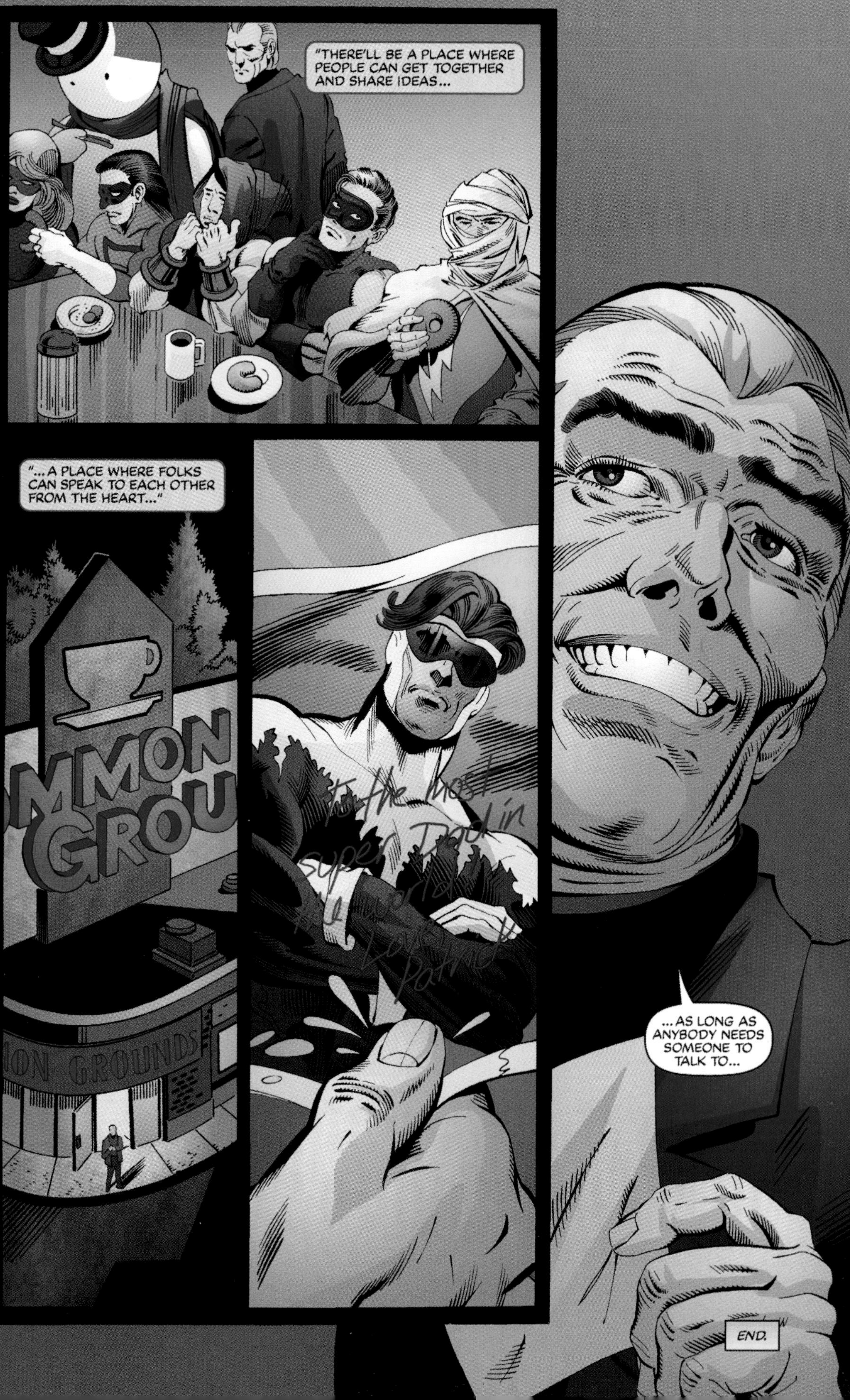
"THERE'LL BE A PLACE WHERE PEOPLE CAN GET TOGETHER AND SHARE IDEAS...
"...A PLACE WHERE FOLKS CAN SPEAK TO EACH OTHER FROM THE HEART..."
MMON GROU
ION GROUNDS
to the most super Dad in the world Love Patrick
...AS LONG AS ANYBODY NEEDS SOMEONE TO TALK TO...
END.

ONE MORE THING about stories: they never really end. At most they merely pause while the storyteller takes his next breath. Though the lights may dim inside our friendly little coffee shop, we can rest assured that as long as there are donuts to be dunked, as long as there are tales to tell, as long as there is a spark in the heroic spirit and a fire in the human heart, there will be Common Grounds. As always, we'll save you a seat at the counter…

Troy Hickman 2004

COVER GALLERY

Issue #1 Cover A by: **J. Scott Campbell and Matt Milla**— Pg. 132

Issue #1 Cover B and Issues #2 through #6 by: **Rodolfo Migliari, The Pride of Argentina**— Pg. 133-138

Issue #4 Cover by: **Rodolfo Migliari inspired by Edward Hopper's painting "Nighthawks."**— Pg. 136

Common Grounds Pinup by: **James Raiz, Roland Paris and Sonia Oback**— Pg. 139

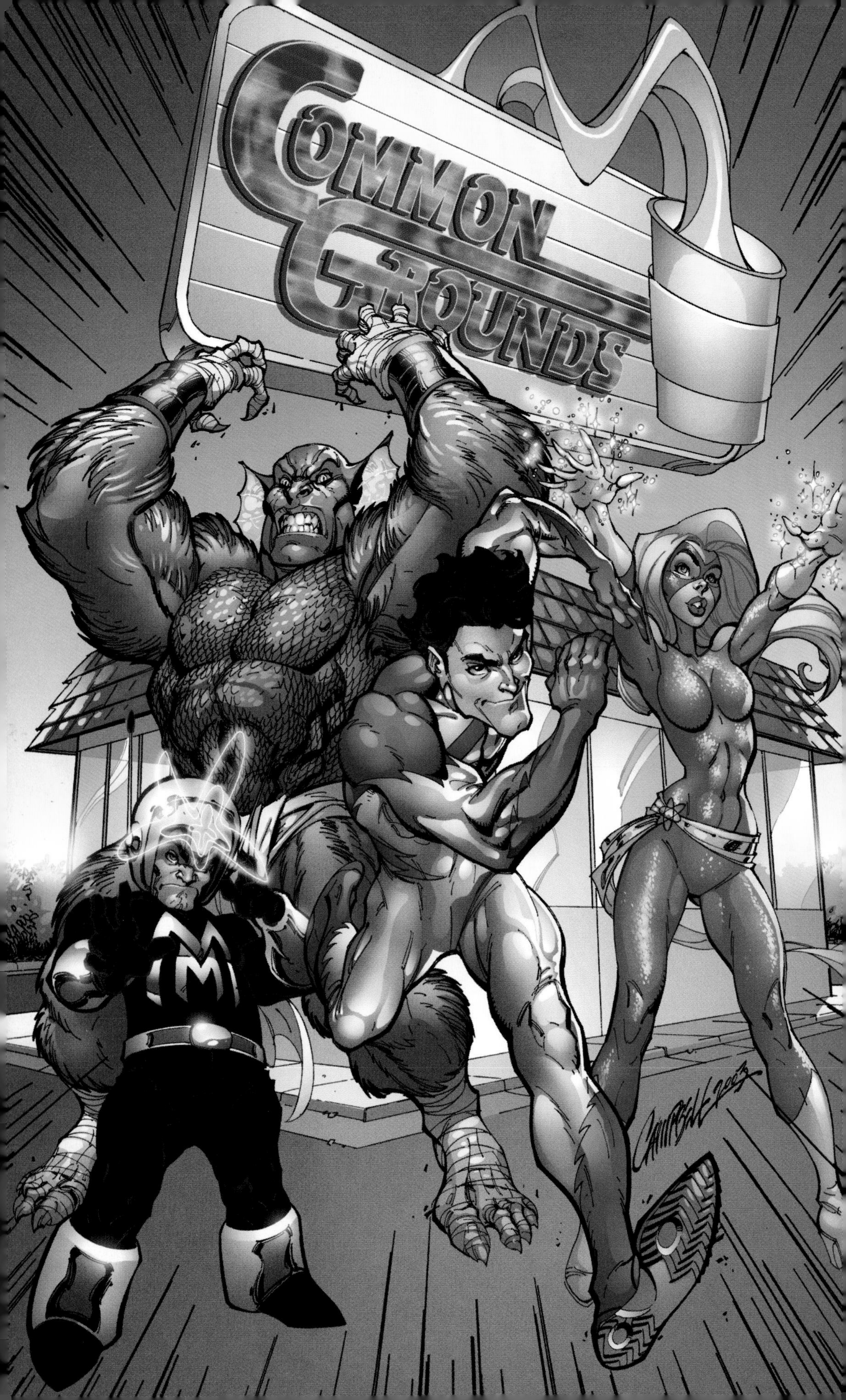
COMMON GROUNDS

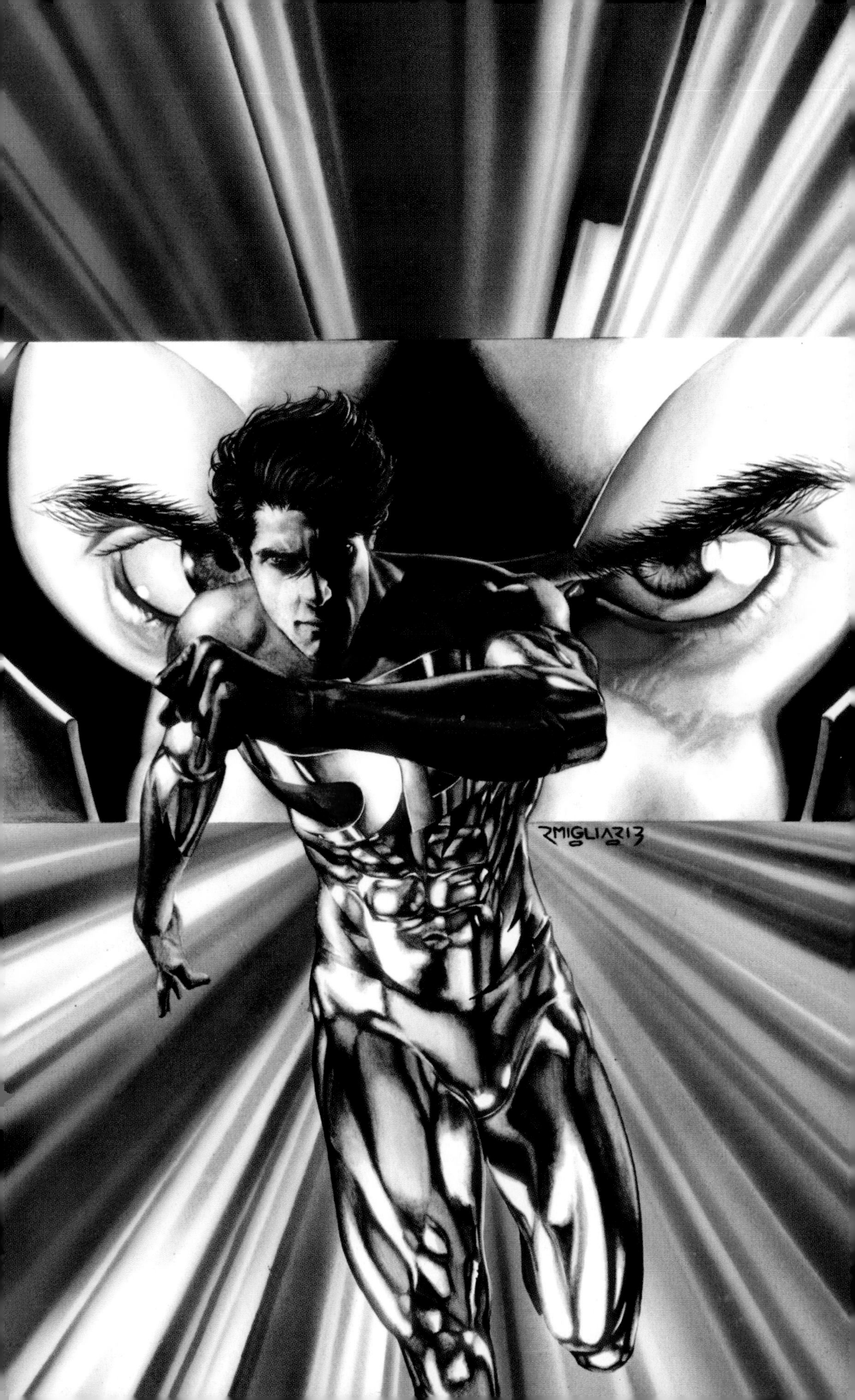

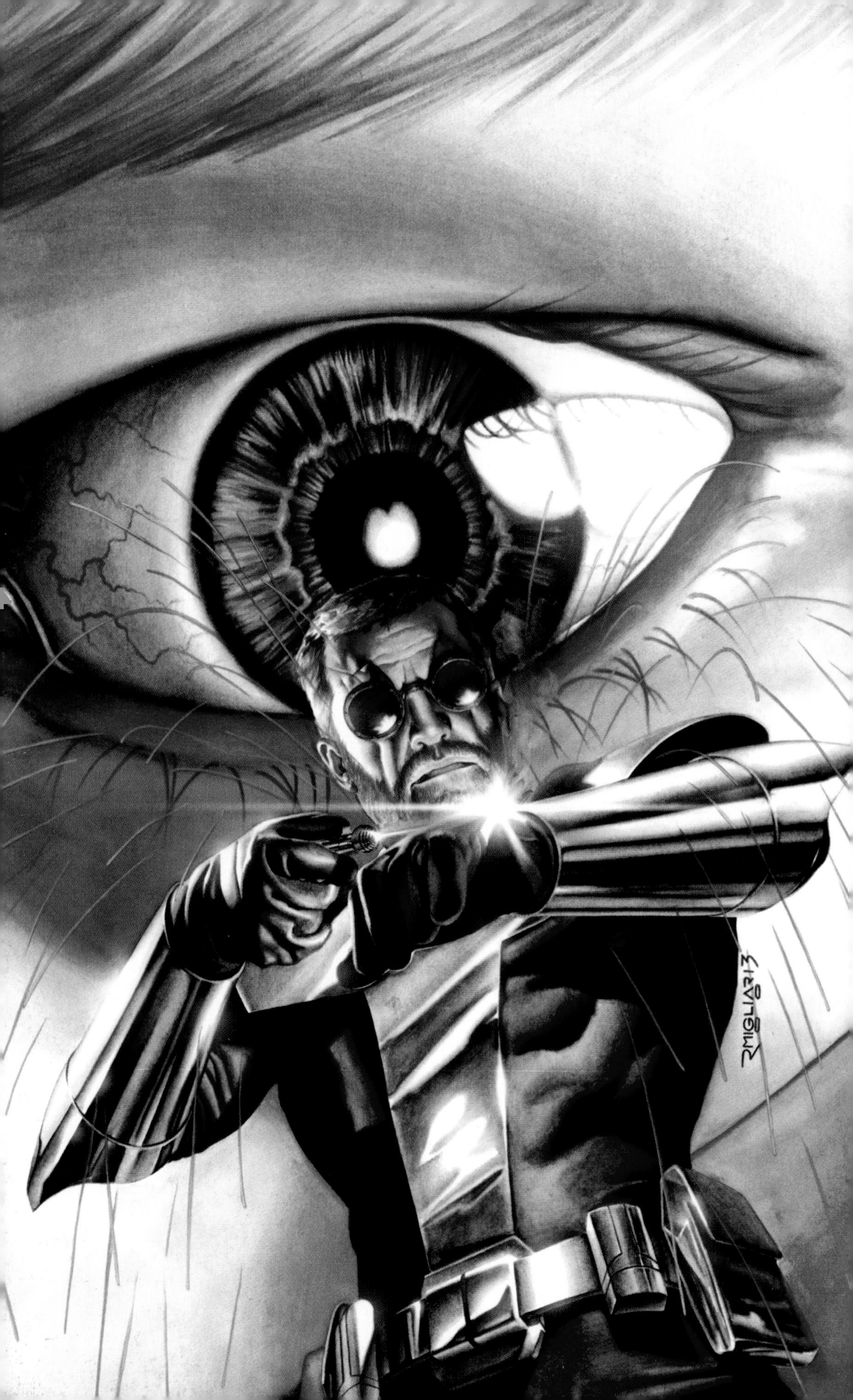

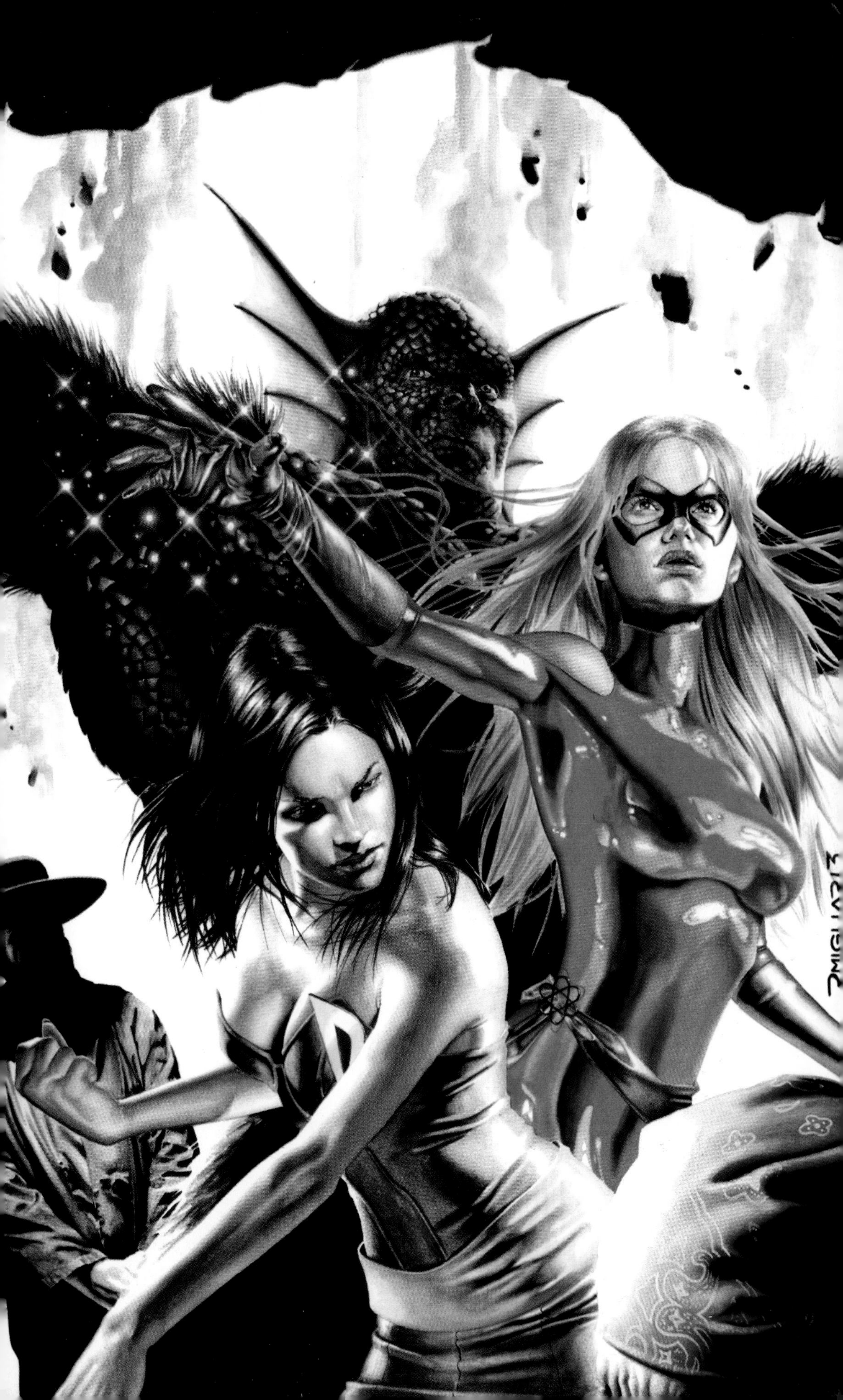

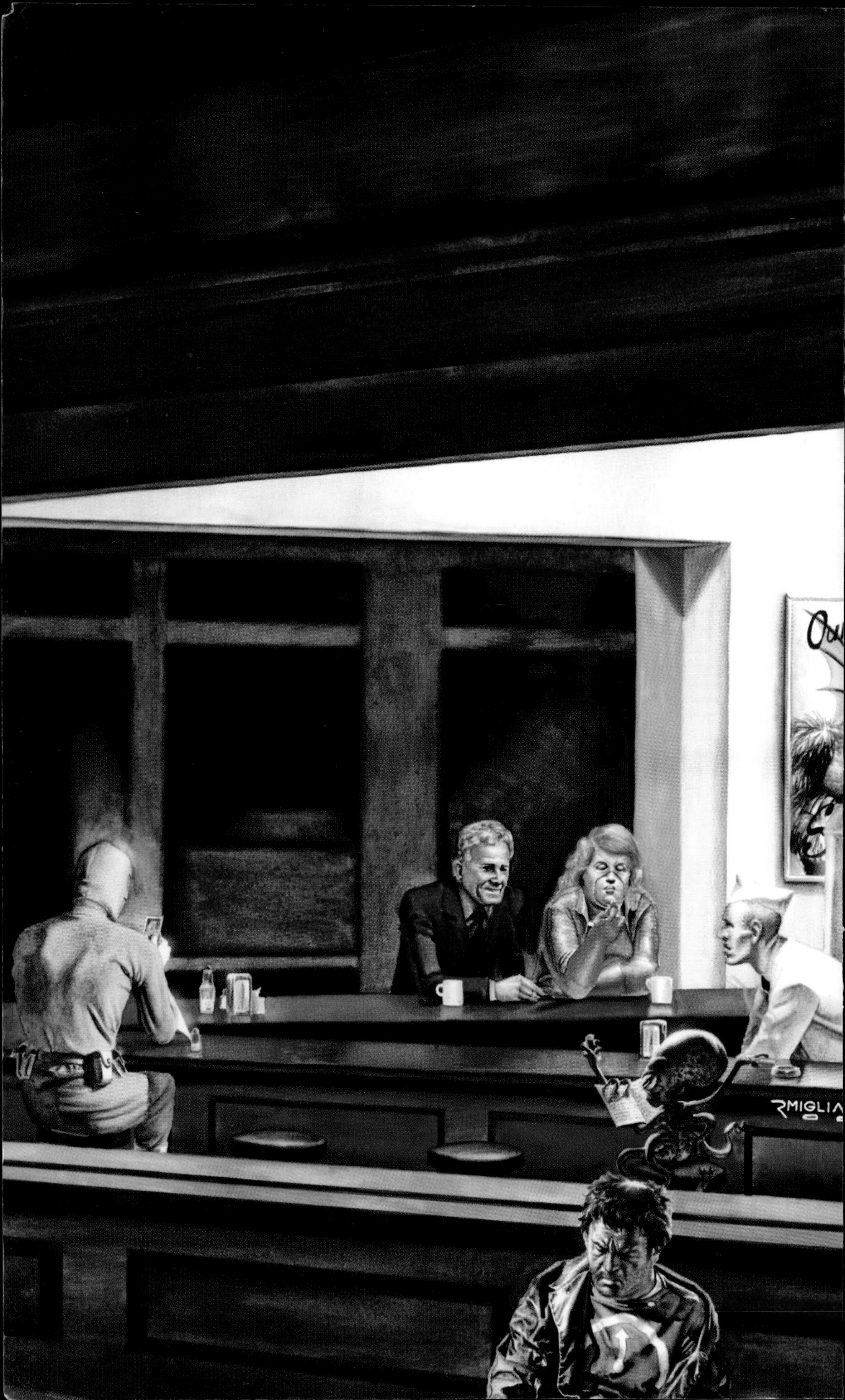

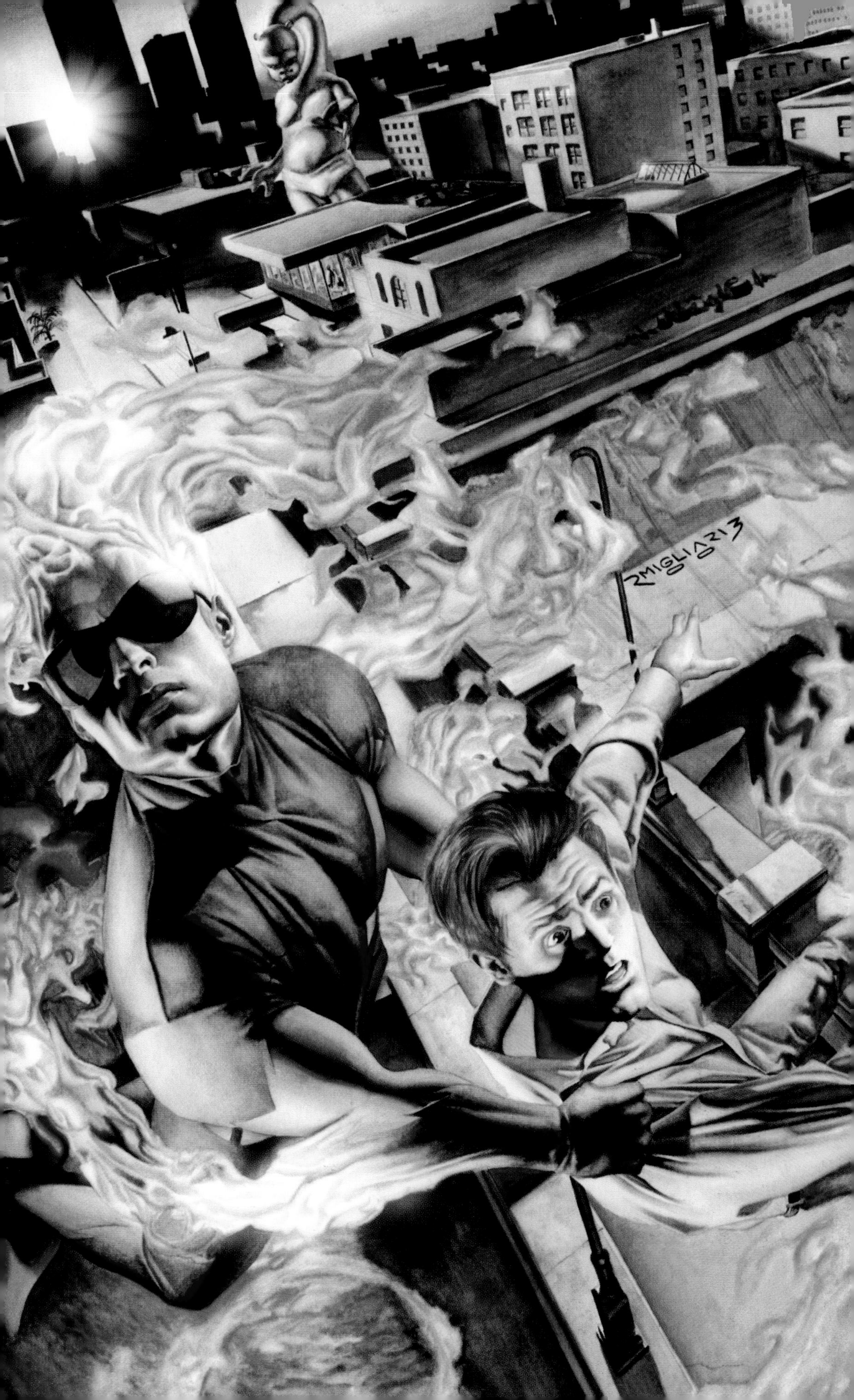

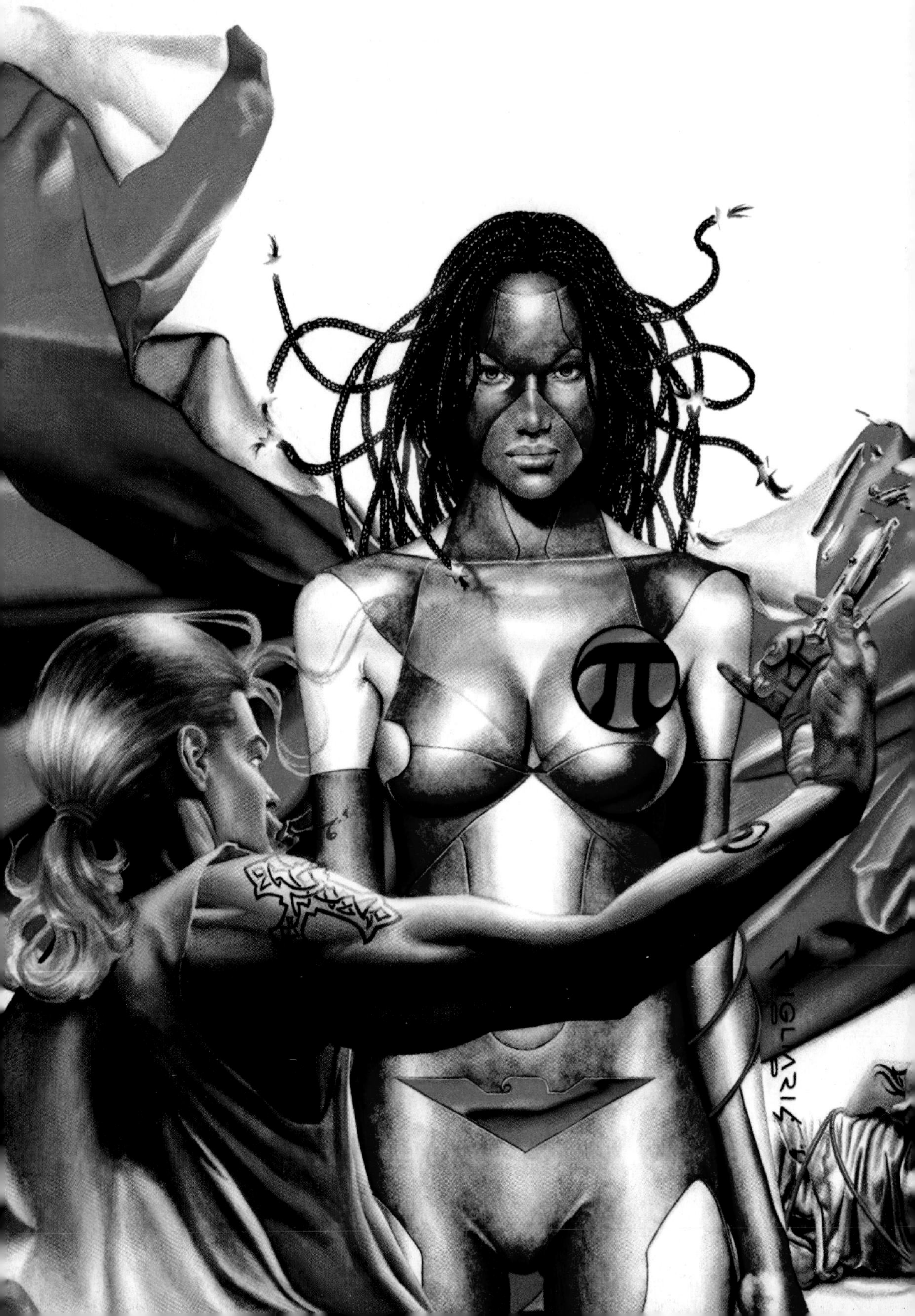

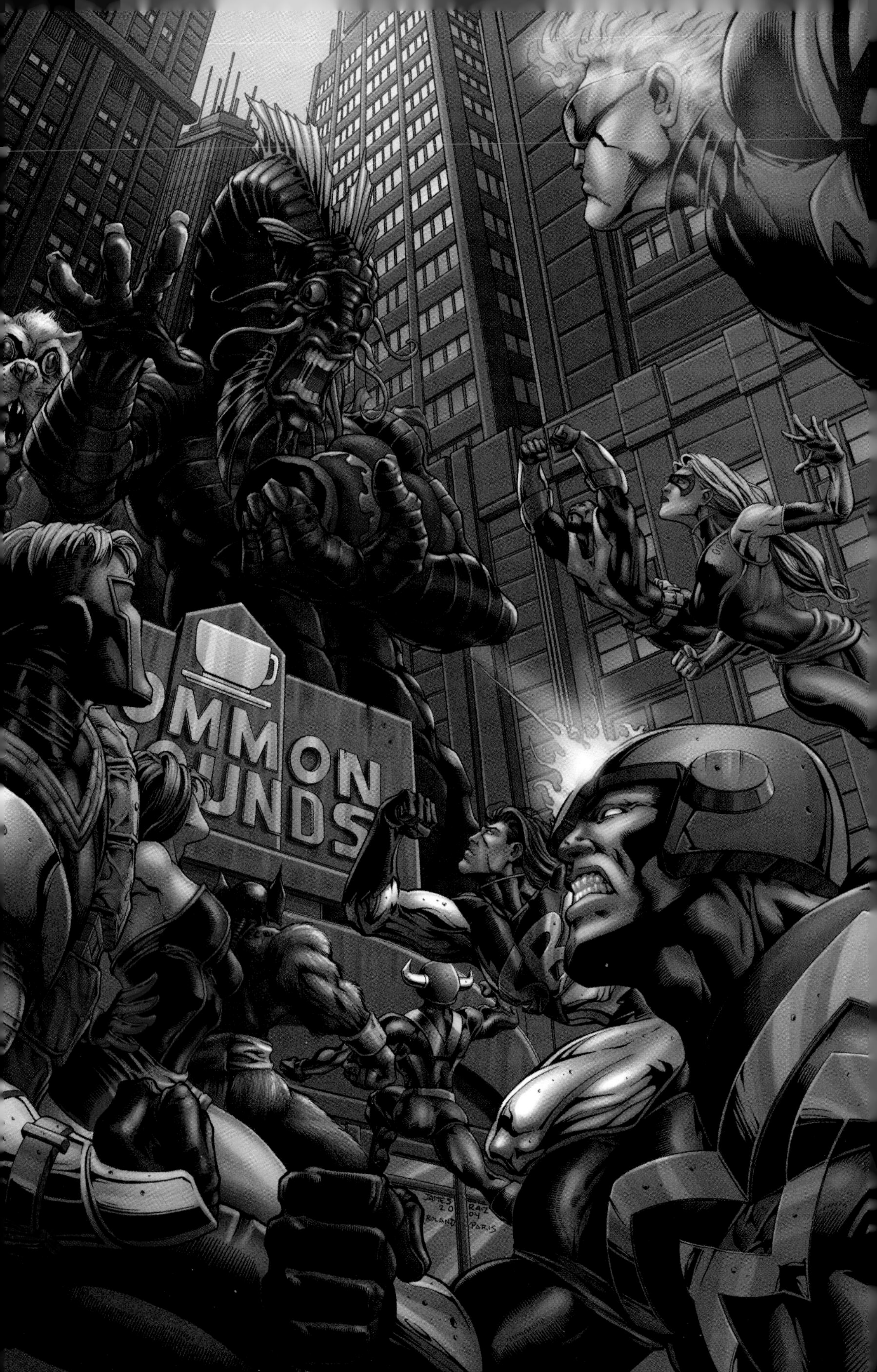
OMMON
UNDS
JAMES 20 RAIZ 04
ROLAND PARIS

TIMELINE

100,000 B.C.?— Prometheus gives fire to the man who will become the Eternal Flame.

2112 B.C.— Wang Dang Doodle terrorizes China, but is defeated soundly and in a very humiliating manner.

June, 1941— Eternal Flame begins his superheroic career.

March, 1942— The Free Association forms (charter mem include Capt. Liberty, Eternal Fla Patriette, and the original Red F

February, 1961— Raccoon grows to gigantic proportions, becomes Crittorr, easily bested by humans.

August, 1961— Wang Dang Doodle wakes from 4000 year sleep, tries to conquer the world, fails pathetically.

September, 1969— Michael O'Brien develops growth formula, becomes Big Money.

April, 1974— Liberty Balance is formed (charter members include Lift-Off, Belle Air, Flaming Follicle, Capt. Gallant, Mach Master, and Magna Woman).

June, 1974— John Henderson becomes Quantum.

June, 1977— James McLain becomes Blackwatch.

September, 1978— Sam a Clarise Henderson are born.

November, 1985— Liberty Balance disbands (members at the time include Blackwatch, Eternal Flame, Kittycat, Big Money II, Lift-Off, and Belle Air).

February, 1989— Gabe Alexander becomes Mental Midget.

June, 1989— Commander Power retires.

October, 1992— Moshe Chomsky's acidic powers appear.

July, 1993— Heinrich von Kartoffelsalat builds a super-car, becomes the costumed Volks-Wagner.

March, 1994— Wang Dang Doodle defeated by Volks-Wagner...never fully recovers.

June, 1994— Michael O'Brie opens the first Common Grounds restaurant.

February, 1999— Chris and Tim Lesley become Digital Man & Analog Kid.

September, 2000— New Liberty Balance forms (members include Eternal Flame, Strangeness & Charm, Mental Midget, American Pi, and Coldspell).

December, 2000— Red Death forms his Death Squad (the Marquis De Sod, Bloodwart, and Armageddonaut).

July, 2001— The supervi Quantum dies in prison.

March, 2004— Strangeness and Charm learn the truth about their villainous father, Quantum, from reading his diary.

April, 2004— Commander Power and Blackwatch become housemates.

June, 2004— Reunion of the Liberty Balance.